DATA STRUCTURES AND ALGORITHMS IN C++

The PWS Series in Computer Science

ABERNETHY AND ALLEN, *Experiments in Computing: Laboratories for Introductory Computer Science in Think Pascal*

ABERNETHY AND ALLEN, *Experiments in Computing: Laboratories for Introductory Computer Science in Turbo Pascal*

ABERNETHY AND ALLEN, *Exploring the Science of Computing*

BAILEY AND LUNDGAARD, *Program Design with Pseudocode, Third Edition*

BENT AND SETHARES, *BASIC: An Introduction to Computer Programming, Fourth Edition*

BENT AND SETHARES, *Microsoft BASIC: Programming the IBM PC, Third Edition*

BENT AND SETHARES, *QBASIC*

BENT AND SETHARES, *QuickBASIC: An Introduction to Computer Science Programming with the IBM PC*

CLEMENTS, *68000 Family Assembly Language*

CLEMENTS, *Principles of Computer Hardware, Second Edition*

COBURN, *Visual BASIC Made Easy*

COSNARD AND TRYSTRAM, *Parallel Algorithms and Architecture*

DECKER AND HIRSHFIELD, *Pascal's Triangle: Reading, Writing, and Reasoning About Programs*

DECKER AND HIRSHFIELD, *The Analytical Engine: An Introduction to Computer Science Using HyperCard 2.1, Second Edition*

DECKER AND HIRSHFIELD, *The Analytical Engine: An Introduction to Computer Science Using ToolBook*

DECKER AND HIRSHFIELD, *The Object Concept: An Introduction to Computer Programming Using C++*

DECKER AND HIRSHFIELD, *Working Classes: Data Structures and Algorithms Using C++*

DERSHEM AND JIPPING, *Programming Languages: Structures and Models, Second Edition*

DROZDEK, *Data Structures and Algorithms in C++*

DROZDEK AND SIMON, *Data Structures in C*

EGGEN AND EGGEN, *An Introduction to Computer Science Using C*

FIREBAUGH, *Artificial Intelligence: A Knowledge-Based Approach, Second Edition*

FLYNN AND MCHOES, *Understanding Operating Systems*

GIARRATANO AND RILEY, *Expert Systems: Principles and Programming, Second Edition*

HENNEFELD, *Using Turbo Pascal 6.0–7.0, Third Edition*

HOCHBAUM, *Approximation Algorithms for NP-hard Problems*

HOUSE, *Beginning with C*

JAMISON, RUSSELL, AND SNOVER, *Laboratories for a Second Course in Computer Science: ANSI Pascal*

JAMISON, RUSSELL, AND SNOVER, *Laboratories for a Second Course in Computer Science: Turbo Pascal*

LIEBERHERR, *Adaptive Object-Oriented Programming: The Demeter Method with Propagation Patterns*

LOUDEN, *Programming Languages: Principles and Practice*

PAVLIDIS, *Interactive Computer Graphics in X*

POPKIN, *Comprehensive Structured COBOL, Fourth Edition*

ROOD, *Logic and Structured Design for Computer Programmers, Second Edition*

RUNNION, *Structured Programming in Assembly Language for the IBM PC and PS/2, Second Edition*

SAAD, *Iterative Methods for Sparse Linear Systems*

SHAY, *Understanding Data Communications and Networks*

SIPSER, *Introduction to the Theory of Computation, Preliminary Edition*

STUBBS AND WEBRE, *Data Structures with Abstract Data Types and Ada*

STUBBS AND WEBRE, *Data Structures with Abstract Data Types and Pascal, Second Edition*

SUHY, *CICS using COBOL: A Structured Approach*

WANG, *An Introduction to ANSI C on UNIX*

WANG, *An Introduction to Berkeley UNIX*

WANG, *C++ with Object-Oriented Programming*

WHALE, *Data Structures and Abstraction Using C*

ZIRKEL AND BERLINGER, *Understanding FORTRAN 77 & 90*

DATA STRUCTURES AND ALGORITHMS IN C++

Adam Drozdek
Duquesne University

PWS Publishing Company

IⓉ**P**   An International Thomson Publishing Company

Boston • Albany • Bonn • Cincinnati • Detroit • London • Madrid • Melbourne • Mexico City
New York • Paris • San Francisco • Singapore • Tokyo • Toronto • Washington

PWS PUBLISHING COMPANY
20 Park Plaza, Boston, MA 02116-4324

Copyright © 1996 by PWS Publishing Company, a division of International Thomson Publishing Inc.

I(T)P ™

International Thomson Publishing
The trademark ITP is used under license

For more information, contact:

PWS Publishing Company
20 Park Plaza
Boston, MA 02116

International Thomson Publishing Europe
Berkshire House I68–I73
High Holborn
London WC1V 7AA
England

Thomas Nelson Australia
102 Dodds Street
South Melbourne, 3205
Victoria, Australia

Nelson Canada
1120 Birchmount Road
Scarborough, Ontario
Canada M1K 5G4

International Thomson Publishing GmbH
Königswinterer Strasse 418
53227 Bonn, Germany

International Thomson Publishing Japan
Hirakawacho Kyowa Building, 31
2-2-1 Hirakawacho
Chiyoda-ku, Tokyo 102
Japan

International Thomson Publishing Asia
221 Henderson Road
#05–10 Henderson Building
Singapore 0315

International Thomson Editores
Campos Eliseos 385, Piso 7
Col. Polanco
11560 Mexico D.F., Mexico

Sponsoring Editor: Michael J. Sugarman
Developmental Editor: Mary Thomas Stone
Editorial Assistant: Tanja Brull
Production Editor: Abigail M. Heim
Interior Designer: Patricia Adams
Interior Illustrator: Lotus Art
Cover Designer: Elise S. Kaiser
Cover Photo: David Bishop/San Francisco
Market Development Manager: Nathan Wilbur
Manufacturing Coordinator: Wendy Kilborn
Compositor: Integre Technical Publishing Co., Inc.
Cover Printer: Henry N. Sawyer Company, Inc.
Text Printer and Binder: R.R. Donnelley & Sons/Crawfordsville

Library of Congress Cataloging-in-Publication Data
Drozdek, Adam.
  Data structures and algorithms in C++ / Adam Drozdek.
    p. cm.
  Includes bibliographical references and index.
  ISBN 0-534-94974-6
  1. C++ (Computer program language)   2. Data structures (Computer science)   3. Computer algorithms.   I. Title.
QA76.73.C153D76   1996
005.13'3 — dc20   95-38032
                                                        CIP

Printed and bound in the United States of America.
95 96 97 98 99 — 10 9 8 7 6 5 4 3 2 1

 This book is printed on recycled, acid-free paper.

To my daughters, Justyna and Kasia

CONTENTS

PREFACE

The study of data structures, a fundamental component of a computer science education, serves as the foundation upon which many other computer science fields are built. Some knowledge of data structures is a must for students who wish to do work in design, implementation, testing, or maintenance of virtually any software system. The scope and presentation of material in *Data Structures and Algorithms in C++* provides students with the necessary knowledge to perform such work.

This book highlights three important aspects of data structures. First, a very strong emphasis is placed on the connection between data structures and their algorithms, including analyzing algorithms' complexity. Second, data structures are presented in the object-oriented setting, in accordance with the current design and implementation paradigm. In particular the information-hiding principle, to advance encapsulation and decomposition, is stressed. Finally, an important component of the book is data structure implementation, which leads to the choice of C++ as the programming language.

The language C++, an object-oriented descendant of C, is gaining momentum in industry and academia as an excellent programming language, and is also useful and natural for introducing data structures. Traditionally, Pascal has been used to teach data structures, although Modula-2 and Ada have also been used. However, because of the wide use of C++ in application programming and the object-oriented characteristics of the language, using C++ to teach a data structures and algorithms course, even on the introductory level, is well justified.

This book provides the material for a course that includes the topics listed under CS2 and CS7 of the old ACM curriculum. It also meets the requirements for most of the courses $C_{\mathcal{A}}$ 202, $C_{\mathcal{D}}$ 202, and $C_{\mathcal{F}}$ 204 of the new ACM curriculum.

Most chapters include a case study that illustrates a complete context in which certain algorithms and data structures can be used. These case studies were chosen from different areas of computer science such as graphics, interpreters, symbolic computation, and file processing, to indicate the wide range of applications to which topics under discussion may apply.

Brief examples of C++ code are included throughout the book to illustrate the practical importance of data structures. However, theoretical analysis is equally important so presentations of algorithms are integrated with analyses of efficiency.

Great care is taken in the presentation of recursion, since even advanced students have problems with it. Our experience has shown that recursion can be explained best if the run-time stack is taken into consideration. Changes to the stack are shown when tracing a recursive function not only in the chapter on recursion, but in other chapters as well. For example, a surprisingly short procedure for tree traversal may remain a mystery if work done by the system on the run-time stack is not included in the explanation. Standing aloof from the system and retaining only a purely theoretical perspective when discussing data structures and algorithms is not necessarily helpful.

Another feature of this book is the inclusion of an extended example using graphics, a fractal known as the von Koch snowflake. To my knowledge no current C++ data structure book discusses graphics examples. This book also includes comprehensive chapters on data compression and memory management.

The thrust of this book is data structures and other topics are treated here only as much as necessary to ensure a proper understanding of this subject. Algorithms are discussed from the perspective of data structures, so that the reader will not find a comprehensive discussion of different kinds of algorithms and all the facets that a full presentation of algorithms requires. However, as mentioned, recursion is covered in depth. Also, complexity analysis of algorithms will be presented in some detail. However, although I recognize the validity of the well-known equation given by Niklaus Wirth, *algorithms + data structures = programs*, the second element of this equation, data structures, is the topic of this book and the first element, algorithms, is treated only instrumentally.

Chapters 1–8 present a number of different data structures and the algorithms that operate on them. The efficiency of each algorithm is analyzed and improvements to the algorithm are suggested.

- Chapter 1 presents the basic principles of object-oriented programming.
- Chapter 2 describes the notation used to assess the efficiency of algorithms.
- An introduction to dynamic memory allocation and the use of pointers and linked lists is contained in Chapter 3.
- Chapter 4 presents stacks and queues and their applications.
- Chapter 5 contains a detailed discussion of recursion. Different types of recursion are discussed and a recursive call is dissected.
- Chapter 6 discusses binary trees, including implementation, traversal, and search. Balanced trees are also included in this chapter.
- Chapter 7 details more generalized trees such as tries, 2–4 trees, and B-trees.
- Graphs are presented in Chapter 8.

Chapters 9–12 show different applications of data structures introduced in the previous chapters. They emphasize the data structure aspects of each topic under consideration.

- Chapter 9 analyzes sorting in detail, and several elementary and nonelementary methods are presented.
- Chapter 10 discusses hashing, one of the most important areas in searching. Various techniques are presented with an emphasis on the utilization of data structures.
- Data compression algorithms and data structures are discussed in Chapter 11.
- Chapter 12 presents various techniques and data structures for memory management.
- Big-O notation, introduced in Chapter 2, is discussed in greater detail in Appendix A.

Each chapter contains a discussion of the material illustrated with appropriate diagrams and tables. Most of the chapters include a case study, which is an extended example using the features discussed in that chapter. All case studies have been tested using the g++ compiler on a Sun IPX workstation except the von Koch snowflake, which runs on a PC under Turbo C++. Following the text of the chapter is a set of exercises of varying degrees of difficulty. Most chapters also include programming assignments. An up-to-date list of references to relevant literature completes each chapter.

Chapters 1–6 (excluding Sections 4.3, 6.4.3, and 6.8) contain the core material that forms the basis of any data structures course. These chapters should be studied in sequence. The remaining six chapters can be taken in any order. A one-semester course could include Chapters 1–6 and any three of the remaining chapters. If students are not familiar with the C++ language, then the entire book could be a part of a two-semester sequence that includes studying the language.

The source code for the text example programs is available via the gopher site gopher.mathcs.duq.edu. Choose DATA STRUCTURES AND ALGORITHMS IN C++ from the menu. A list of files available for copying will be displayed.

I would like to thank the following reviewers, whose comments and advice helped me to improve this book:

Owen Astrachan
Duke University

Ronald Gould
Emory University

Thomas Hain
University of South Alabama

Ali R. Salehnia
South Dakota State University

David B. Teague
Western Carolina University

Edward B. Wright
Western Oregon State College

I would also like to thank my colleagues at Duquesne University whose understanding and help created an atmosphere conducive to writing this book. Moreover, I wish to extend my gratitude to Abby Heim, Sarah Lemaire, Mary Thomas Stone, and Michael Sugarman, whose inestimable help and assistance enabled me to bring the book to its present form. However, the ultimate content is my responsibility, and I would appreciate hearing from readers about any shortcomings or strengths (my email address is drozdek@mathcs.duq.edu).

Adam Drozdek

1

OBJECT-ORIENTED PROGRAMMING USING C++

■ 1.1 ABSTRACT DATA TYPES

Before a program is written, we should have a fairly good idea how to accomplish the task being implemented by this program. Hence, an outline of the program containing its requirements should precede the coding process. The larger and more complex the project, the more detailed the outline phase should be. The implementation details should be delayed to the later stages of the project. In particular, the details of the particular data structures to be used in the implementation should not be specified at the beginning.

From the start, it is important to specify each task in terms of input and output. At the beginning stages, we should be more concerned with what the program should do, not how it should or could be done. Behavior of the program is more important than the gears of the mechanism accomplishing it. For example, if an item is needed to accomplish some tasks, the item is specified in terms of operations performed on it rather than in terms of its inner structure. These operations may act upon this item, for example modifying it, searching for some details in it, or storing something in it. After these operations are precisely specified, the implementation of the program may start. The implementation decides which data structure should be used to make execution most efficient in terms of time and space. An item specified in terms of operations is called an *abstract data type*. An abstract data type is not a part of a program, since a program written in a programming language requires the definition of a data structure, not just the operations on the data structure. However, an object-oriented language (OOL) such as C++ has a direct link to abstract data types by implementing them as a class.

1

■ 1.2 ENCAPSULATION

Object-oriented programming (OOP) revolves around the concept of an object. An *object* is a piece of software that includes data specification and functions operating on these data. Combining the data and related operations is called data *encapsulation*. Functions used in objects are called *methods, member functions*, or *function members*. However, in contradistinction to functions in languages that are not object-oriented, objects make the connection between data and member functions much tighter and more meaningful. In languages that are not object-oriented, declarations of data and definitions of functions can be interspersed through the entire program and only the program documentation indicates that there is a connection between them. In OOLs, a connection is established right at the outset; in fact, the program is based on this connection. An object is defined by related data and operations, and because there may be many objects used in the same program, the objects communicate by exchanging messages which reveal to each other as little detail about their internal structure as necessary for an adequate communication. Structuring programs in terms of objects allows us to accomplish several goals.

First, this strong coupling of data and operations can be used much better in modeling a fragment of the world, which is emphasized especially by software engineering. Not surprisingly, OOP has its roots in simulation, that is, in modeling real world events. The first OOL was called Simula and it was developed in the 1960s in Norway.

Second, objects allow for easier error finding, since operations are localized to the confines of their objects. Even if side effects occur, they are easier to trace.

Third, objects allow us to conceal certain details of their operations from other objects, so that these operations may not be adversely affected by other objects. This is known as the *information hiding* principle. In languages that are not object-oriented, this principle can be found to some extent in the case of local variables, or, as in Pascal, local functions or procedures, which can only be used and accessed by the function defining them. This is, however, a very tight hiding or no hiding at all. Sometimes we may need to use (again, as in Pascal) a function $f2$ defined in $f1$ outside of $f1$, but we cannot. Sometimes we may need to access some data local to $f1$ without exactly knowing the structure of these data, but we cannot. Hence, some modification is needed, and it is accomplished in OOLs.

An object in OOL is like a watch. As users, we are interested in what the hands show, but not in the inner working of the watch. We are aware that there are gears and springs inside the watch. But because we usually know very little about why all these parts are in a particular configuration, we should not have access to this mechanism so that we do not damage it, inadvertently or on purpose. This mechanism is hidden from us, we have no immediate access to it, and the watch is protected and will work better than when its mechanism is open to everyone.

An object is like a black box whose behavior is very well defined and we use the object because we know what it does, not because we have an insight in how it does it. This opacity of objects is extremely useful for maintaining them independently of each other. If communication channels between the objects are well defined, then changes made inside an object can affect other objects only as much as these changes affect the communication channels. Knowing the kind of information sent out and received by an object, the object can be replaced easier by another object more suitable in a particular situation: a new object can perform the same task differently but quicker in a certain hardware environment. An object discloses only as much as is needed for the user to utilize it. It has a public part which can be accessed by any user when the user sends a message matching any of the member function names revealed by the object. In this public part, the object displays to the user buttons which can be pushed to invoke the object's operations. The user knows only the names of these operations and the expected behavior.

Information hiding tends to blur the division line between data and operations. In Pascal-like languages, the distinction between data and functions or procedures is clear and rigid. They are defined differently and their roles are very distinct. OOLs put data and methods together, and, to the user of the object, this distinction is much less noticeable. To some extent, this incorporates the features of functional languages. Lisp, one of the earliest programming languages, allows the user to treat data and functions similarly, since the structure of both is the same. The more rigid distinction of data and functions is enforced by von Neumann architecture and OOP attempts to overcome this great divide.

So far we have not made a distinction between particular objects and object types. We write functions to be used with different variables, and by analogy, we do not like to be forced to write as many object declarations as the number of objects required by the program. Certain objects are of the same type and we would like only to use a reference to a general object specification. For single variables, we make a distinction between type declaration and variable declaration. In the case of objects, we have a class declaration and object instantiation. For instance, in the following class declaration, **Country** is a class and particular countries are objects.

```
class Country {
public:
     Country() { }
     Country(char *s) { name = new char[strlen(s+1)]; strcpy(name,s); }
     void internationalLoan(double l = 0.0, char *s = "unknown")
         { loan = l; sender = new char[strlen(s+1)]; strcpy(name,s);}
     void printInfo() {
         cout.precision(2);
         cout << name << ": area = " << area <<
                 ", population = " << population <<
                 ", density = " << Density();
     }
     . . . . . . . . . . . . . . . .
protected:
     long population;
     double loan, area;
     char *name, *sender;
     . . . . . . . . . . . . . . . .
     double Density()
         { return area / population; }
     . . . . . . . . . . . . . . . .
};
```

```
. . . . . . . . . . . . . . . . .
Country Poland("Poland"), SierraLeone("Sierra Leone"),
        USA("The United States");
```

Message passing is equivalent to a function call in traditional languages. However, to stress the fact that in OOLs, the member functions are relative to objects, this new term is used. For example, the call to public member function `printInfo()` with respect to the object `Poland`,

```
Poland.printInfo();
```

is seen as message `printInfo()` sent to the object `Poland`. Upon receiving the message, the object invokes its member function and displays all relevant information. Messages can include parameters, so that

```
Poland.internationalLoan(1000000000.0);
```

is the message `internationalLoan()` with parameter one billion received by `Poland`.

The lines containing these messages are either in the main program, in a function, or in a member function of another object. Therefore, the sender of the message is identifiable, but not necessarily the receiver. If `Poland` receives the message `printInfo()`, it does not know where the message originated. It only responds to it by displaying the information `printInfo()` encapsulates. The same goes for `internationalLoan()`. In the latter case, this can be detrimental to the sender, since the receiver does not know to whom to repay the loan. Therefore, the sender may prefer sending a message including also its identification, as follows:

```
Poland.internationalLoan(1000000000.0,"Germany");
```

■ 1.3 INHERITANCE

OOLs allow programmers to create a hierarchy of classes so that objects do not have to be instantiations of a single base class. For example, before instantiating country objects, it may be desirable to categorize countries by grouping them according to the continent they are in, military or economic alliances they have, official languages, etc. To achieve this, we have the following declarations:

```
class EuropeanCountry: public virtual Country {
. . . . . . . . . . . . . . . . .
};

class AfricanCountry : public virtual Country {
. . . . . . . . . . . . . . . . .
};
```

but also

```
class NATOcountry : public virtual Country {
.  .  .  .  .  .  .  .  .  .  .  .  .  .  .  .  .
};


class neutralCountry : public virtual Country {
.  .  .  .  .  .  .  .  .  .  .  .  .  .  .  .  .
};
```

The class **Country** is a *base class*. Other classes are derived from it in that they can all use the member functions which are specified by **Country** as protected and public. They inherit all these member functions from its base class so that they do not have to repeat the same definitions. However, a derived class can modify the definition of a member function by introducing its own definition. In this way, both the base class and the derived class have some measure of control over their member functions. The base class can decide which member functions can be revealed to the derived class so that the principle of information hiding holds not only with respect to the user of the base class, but also to the derived classes. In addition, the derived class can decide which parts of the public and protected member functions to retain and use and which to modify. Moreover, it can add some new member functions of its own. Such a class can become a base class for other classes that can be derived from it so that the inheritance hierarchy can be deliberately extended.

A derived class does not have to be limited to one base class only. It can be derived from more than one base class. For example, we can declare

```
class MediterraneanCountry : public EuropeanCountry, public AfricanCountry,
                    public AsianCountry {
.  .  .  .  .  .  .  .  .  .  .  .  .  .  .  .  .  .
};
```

where **MediterraneanCountry** class inherits all the member functions of the three classes listed after the colon. However, it also inherits the same member functions from the base class, **Country**, three times since all three classes used in the declaration of **MediterraneanCountry** are derived from **Country**. To prevent this redundancy, which could lead to ambiguity, the declarations of these three classes included the modifier **virtual** which means that **MediterraneanCountry** contains only one copy of each member function from **Country**.

■ 1.4 POLYMORPHISM

Polymorphism refers to many forms acquired by a programming language constructs. These constructs can manifest themselves in a variety of forms depending on the context in which they are used. A certain construct is declared once, but it is defined in a general enough form so that it can be used under different disguises and adapted to different situations.

An important aspect of polymorphism in OOP is that programmers can declare generic classes by using type parameters in the class declaration. For example, if we need to declare a class that uses an array for storing some items, then we may declare this class as

```
class intClass {
    int storage[50];
    ................
};
```

However, in this way we limit the usability of this class to integers only; if we need a class that performs the same operations as **intClass** except that it operates on float numbers, then a new declaration is needed, such as

```
class floatClass {
    float storage[50];
    ................
};
```

If **storage** is to hold structures, or pointers to characters, then two more classes must be declared. It is much better to declare a generic class and decide to what type of items the object is referring only when defining the object. Fortunately, C++ allows us to declare a class in this way, and the declaration for the example is

```
template<class genType>
class genClass {
    genType storage[50];
    ................
};
```

Later we will make the decision about how to initialize **genType**:

```
genClass<int> intObject;
genClass<float> floatObject;
```

This generic class manifests itself in different forms depending on the specific declaration. One generic declaration suffices for enabling such different forms.

We can go even further than that by not committing ourselves to 50 cells in **storage** and by delaying that decision until the object definition stage. But just in case, we may leave a default value, so that the class declaration is now

```
template<class genType, int size = 50>
class genClass {
    genType storage[size];
    ................
};
```

The object definition is now

```
genClass<int> intObject1; // use the default size;
genClass<int,100> intObject2;
genClass<float,123> floatObject;
```

This method of using generic types is not limited to classes only; we can use them in member function declarations as well. For example, the standard operation for swapping two values can be defined by the function

```
template<class genType>
inline void
Swap(genType& el1, genType& el2)
{
    genType tmp = el1; el1 = el2; el2 = tmp;
}
```

This example also indicates the need for adapting built-in operators to specific situations. If `genType` is a number, a character, or a structure, then the assignment operator, `=`, performs its function properly. But if `genType` is an array, then we can expect a problem in `Swap()`. The problem can be resolved by overloading the assignment operator by adding to it the functionality required by a specific data type.

After a generic function has been declared, a proper function can be generated at the compilation time. For example, if the compiler sees two calls,

```
Swap(n,m); // swap two integers;
Swap(x,y); // swap two floats;
```

it generates two swap functions to be used during execution of the program. This way of resolving the type problem is called *static binding*. However, polymorphism in OOLs also has another feature: the type of a function to be executed can be delayed until the run time. This is called *dynamic binding*. For example, suppose that `genClass` and the derived class declarations are now

```
template<class genType, int size = 50>
class genClass {
    genType storage[size];
    . . . . . . . . . . . . . . . . .
    void Process();
};


class intClass : public genClass<int> {
    . . . . . . . . . . . . . . . .
    void Process();
};
```

If the definition of `Process()` given in `intClass` is different than in `genClass`, then we may execute the wrong member function unintentionally. For example, after the declarations,

```
intClass intObject;
genClass<int> *intObjectPtr = &intObject;
```

the call

```
intObjectPtr->Process()
```

invokes `Process()` belonging to `genClass`, since this is required by the type of `intObjectPtr`, notwithstanding the assignment `intObjectPtr = &intObject` made in declaration of this pointer, which suggests that we want `Process()` belonging to `intClass` to be executed. In order to make it possible and invoke the member function according to the type of object for which it is called (and according to the type of pointer through which this object is being referred), we should use **virtual** functions, as in

```
template<class genType, int size = 50>
class genClass {
    genType storage[size];
    . . . . . . . . . . . . . . . . .
    virtual void Process();
};
```

The qualifier **virtual** is the signal that the decision about which member function to use should be made during the execution of the program, not during its compilation.

The use of virtual functions is a powerful tool in OOP. It is enough to send a standard message to many different objects without specifying how the message will be followed. There is no need to know of what type the objects are. The receiver is responsible for interpreting the message and following it. The sender does not have to modify the message depending on the type of the receiver. No need for switch or if-else statements. Also, new units can be added to a complex program without needing to recompile the entire program.

■ 1.5 C++ AND OBJECT-ORIENTED PROGRAMMING

The previous discussion presumed that C++ is an OOL, and all the features of OOLs that we discussed have been illustrated with C++ code. However, C++ is not a pure OOL. C++ is more object-oriented than C or Pascal which have no OO features or Ada which supports classes (packages) and instances. C++ is less object-oriented than pure OOLs such as Smalltalk or Eiffel.

C++ does not enforce the OO approach. We can program in C++ without knowing that such features are a part of the language. The reason for this is the popularity of C. C++ is a superset of C, so a C programmer can easily switch to C++, adapting only to its more friendly features such as I/O, call-by-reference mechanism, default values for function parameters, operator overloading, inline functions, and the like. Using an OOL such as C++ does not guarantee that we are doing OOP. On the other hand, invoking the entire machinery of classes and member functions may not always be necessary, especially in small programs, so not enforcing OOP is not necessarily a disadvantage. Also, C++ is easier to integrate with existing C code than other OOLs.

C++ has an excellent encapsulation facility which allows for well-controlled information hiding. There is, however, a relaxation to this rule in the use of so-called friend functions. The problem is that private information of a certain class cannot be accessed by anyone, and the public information is accessible to every user. But sometimes we would like to allow only some users to have access to the private pool of information. This can be accomplished if the class lists the user functions as its friends. For example, if the definition is

```
class abc {
      int n;
      friend int f();
} pqr;
```

function **f()** has direct access to variable **n** belonging to the class **abc**, as in

```
int f ()
{    return 10 * pqr.n;  }
```

This could be considered a violation of the information hiding principle; however, the class **abc** itself grants the right to make public to some users what is private and inaccessible to others. Thus, since the class has control over whom to consider a friend function, the friend function mechanism can be considered an extension of the information hiding principle. This mechanism, admittedly, is used to facilitate programming and speed up execution, since rewriting code without using friend functions can be a major problem. Such a relaxation of some rules is, by the way, not uncommon in computer science and we can mention the existence of loops in functional languages, such as Lisp, or storing some information at the beginning of data files in violation of the relational database model, as in dBaseIII+.

Although polymorphism is very powerful in C++, variables cannot be used in a truly polymorphic fashion. C++ is a typed language: if a variable is declared to be of a particular type, it is primarily used with values of that type. Although typing in C++ is not as strong as in, say, Pascal, even if casting is applied, certain limitations imposed by variable declarations cannot be overcome, such as the case where an assignment from an integer variable to a character variable can result in a loss or distortion of information.

■ 1.6 DATA STRUCTURES AND OBJECT-ORIENTED PROGRAMMING

Although the computer operates on bits, we do not usually think in these terms; in fact, we would not like to. Although an integer is a sequence of, say, 16 bits, we prefer seeing an integer as an entity with its own individuality which is reflected in operations that can be performed on integers but not on variables of other types. And as an integer uses bits as its building blocks, other objects can use integers as their atomic elements. Some data types are already built into a particular language, but some data types can and need to be defined by the user. New data types have a distinctive structure, a new configuration of their elements, and this structure determines the behavior of objects of these new types. The task given to the data structures domain is to explore such new structures and investigate their behavior in terms of time and space requirements. Unlike the object-oriented approach, where we start with behavior and then try to find the most suitable data type which allows for an efficient performance of desirable operations, we now start with a data type specification of some data structure and then look at what it can do, how it does it, and how efficiently. The data structures field is designed for building tools to be incorporated in and used by application programs, and for finding data structures that can perform certain operations speedily and without imposing too much burden on the computer memory. This field is interested in building classes by concentrating on the mechanics of these classes, on their gears and cogs, which in most cases are not visible to the user of the classes. The data structures field investigates the operability of these classes and its improvement by modifying the data structures found inside the classes, since it has a direct access to them. It sharpens tools and advises the user to what purposes they can be applied. Because of inheritance, the user can add some more operations to these classes and try to squeeze from them more than the class designer did, but because the data structures are hidden from the user, these new operations can be tested by running and not by having access to the insides of the class, unless the user has access to the source code.

The data structures field performs best if done in the object-oriented fashion. In this way, it can build tools without the danger that these tools will be inadvertently misused in the application. By encapsulating the data structures into a class and making public only what is necessary for proper usage of the class, the data structures field can develop tools whose functions are not compromised by unnecessary tampering.

■ 1.7 EXERCISES

1. Early versions of C++ did not support templates, but generic classes could be introduced using parametrized macros. In what respect is the use of templates better than the use of such macros?

2. Since the standard for the way templates should be processed is still in flux, different compilers treat certain aspects of template processing differently. Write simple tests to check whether your compiler

   (a) is able to create a generic subclass using a generic base class;

   (b) lets you use constant parameters in generic functions;

   (c) requires template class declarations to be put with member function implementations in the same file.

3. What is the meaning of **private, protected**, and **public** parts of classes?

4. What should be the type of constructors and destructors defined in classes?

5. Assume the following class declaration:

```
template<class genType>
class genClass {
    ...
    char aFunction(...);
    ... };
```

What is wrong with this function definition:

```
char genClass::aFunction(...) { ... };
```

6. Overloading is a powerful tool in C++, but there are some exceptions. What operators must not be overloaded?

7. If **classA** includes a **private** variable **n**, a **protected** variable **m**, and a **public** variable **k**, and **classB** is derived from **classA**, which of these variables can be in **classA**? Can n become in **classB private**? **protected**? **public**? How about variables **m** and **k**? Does it make a difference whether the derivation of **classB** was **private**, **protected**, or **public**?

8. Transform the declaration

```
template<class genType, int size = 50>
class genClass {
    genType storage[size];
    .................
    void memberFun() {
        ............
        if (someVar < size) { ...... }
        ............
    }
};
```

which uses an integer variable **size** as a parameter to **template** to a declaration of **genClass** which does not include **size** as a parameter to **template** and yet it allows for flexibility of the value of **size**. Consider a declaration of **genClass**'s constructor. Is there any advantage of one version over another?

9. What is the difference between function members which are **virtual** and those which are not?

10. What happens if the declaration of **genClass**:

```
class genClass {
    .................
    virtual void Process1(char);
    virtual void Process2(char);
};
```

is followed by the following declaration of **derivedClass**:

```
class derivedClass : public genClass {
    .................
    void Process1(int);
    int Process2(char);
};
```

Which member functions are invoked if the declaration of two pointers

```
genClass *objectPtr1 = &derivedClass, *objectPtr2 = &derivedClass;
```

is followed by the following statements:

```
objectPtr1->Process1(1000);
objectPtr2->Process2('A');
```

■ 1.8 PROGRAMMING ASSIGNMENTS

1. Write a **fractionClass** which defines adding, subtracting, multiplying, and dividing fractions by overloading standard operators for these operations. Write a function method for reducing factors and overload I/O operators to input and output fractions.

2. Write a class **quaternion** which defines the four basic operations of quaternions and the two I/O operations. Quaternions, as defined in 1843 by William Hamilton, and published in his *Lectures on Quaternions* in 1853, are an extension of complex numbers. Quaternions are quadruples of real numbers, $(a, b, c, d) = a + bi + cj + dk$, where $1 = (1, 0, 0, 0)$, $i = (0, 1, 0, 0)$, $j = (0, 0, 1, 0)$, and $k = (0, 0, 0, 1)$ and the following equations hold:

$$i^2 = j^2 = k^2 = -1$$

$$ij = k, \ jk = i, \ ki = j, \ ji = -k, \ kj = -i, \ ik = -j$$

$$(a + bi + cj + dk) + (p + qi + rj + sk)$$

$$= (a + p) + (b + q)i + (c + r)j + (d + s)k$$

$$(a + bi + cj + dk) * (p + qi + rj + sk)$$

$$= (ap - bq - cr - ds) + (aq + bp + cs - dr)i$$

$$+ (ar + cp + dq - bs)j + (as + dp + br - cq)k.$$

Use these equations in implementing a quaternion class.

3. Write a generic class **set** which defines function methods for set union, intersection, and difference. Include a function method for creating a power set which is a set of all subsets of a certain set. For example,

$$powerSet(\{A\ B\ C\}) = \{\varnothing, \{A\}, \{B\}, \{C\}, \{A\ B\}, \{A\ C\}, \{B\ C\}, \{A\ B\ C\}\}.$$

Implement each set as a file. For simplicity, assume that each element is on a separate line in a file so that an element of a power set is identified by the content of one line. Also assume that power sets of power sets are not created.

BIBLIOGRAPHY

Object-Oriented Programming

[1] Cardelli, Luca and Wegner, Peter, "On Understanding Types, Data Abstraction, and Polymorphism," *Computing Surveys* 17 (1985), 471–522.

[2] Ege, Raimund K., *Programming in an Object-Oriented Environment*, San Diego: Academic Press, 1992.

[3] *Journal of Object-Oriented Programming*, a magazine published since 1988.

[4] Khoshafian, Setrag and Razmik, Abnous, *Object Orientation: Concepts, Languages, Databases, User Interfaces*, New York: Wiley, 1990.

[5] Meyer, Bertrand, *Object-Oriented Software Construction*, New York: Prentice-Hall, 1988.

C++

[6] *C/C++ Users Journal*, a magazine published since 1983 (a successor of *C Users' Group Newsletter* and *The C Journal*).

[7] *C++ Report*, a magazine published since 1990.

[8] Fleming, Bryan, *Practical Data Structures in C++*, New York: Wiley, 1993.

[9] Johnsonbaugh, Richard and Kalin, Martin, *Object-Oriented Programming in C++*, Englewood Cliffs: Prentice-Hall, 1995.

[10] Lippman, Stanley B., *C++ Primer*, Reading: Addison-Wesley, 1989.

[11] Stroustrup, Bjarne, *The C++ Programming Language*, Reading: Addison-Wesley, 1986.

[12] Wang, Paul S., *C++ with Object-Oriented Programming*, Boston: PWS, 1994.

2

COMPLEXITY ANALYSIS

■ 2.1 COMPUTATIONAL AND ASYMPTOTIC COMPLEXITY

The same problem can frequently be solved with different algorithms which differ in efficiency. The differences between the algorithms may be immaterial for processing a small number of data items, but these differences grow proportionally with the amount of data. To compare the efficiency of algorithms, a measure of the degree of difficulty of an algorithm called *computational complexity* was developed by Juris Hartmanis and Richard E. Stearns.

Computational complexity indicates how much effort is needed to apply an algorithm or how costly it is. This cost can be measured in a variety of ways and the particular context determines its meaning. This book concerns itself with the two efficiency criteria: time and space. The factor of time is more important than that of space so efficiency considerations usually focus on the amount of time elapsed when processing data. However, the most inefficient algorithm run on a Cray computer can execute much faster than the most efficient algorithm run on a PC so run time is always system-dependent. For example, to compare a hundred algorithms, all of them would have to be run on the same machine. Furthermore, the results of run-time tests depend on the language in which a given algorithm is written even if the tests are performed on the same machine. If programs are compiled, they execute much faster than when they are interpreted. A program written in C or Pascal may be 20 times faster than the same program encoded in BASIC or Lisp.

To evaluate an algorithm's efficiency, real-time units such as microseconds and nanoseconds should not be used. Rather, logical units that express a relationship between the size n of a file or an array and the amount of time t required to process the data should be used. If there is a linear relationship between the size n and time t, that is, $t_1 = cn_1$, then an increase of data by a factor of 5 results in the increase of the execution time by the same factor; if $n_2 = 5n_1$, then $t_2 = 5t_1$. Similarly, if $t_1 = \log_2 n$, then doubling n increases t by only one unit of time. Therefore, if $t_2 = \log_2(2n)$, then $t_2 = t_1 + 1$.

A function expressing the relationship between n and t is usually much more complex, and calculating such a function is important only in regard to large bodies of data; any terms which do not substantially change the function's magnitude should be eliminated from the function. The resulting function gives only an approximate measure of efficiency of the original function. However, this approximation is sufficiently close to the original, especially for a function which processes large quantities of data. This measure of efficiency is called *asymptotic complexity* and is used when disregarding certain terms of a function to express the efficiency of an algorithm, or when calculating a function is difficult or impossible and only approximations can be found. To illustrate the first case, consider the following example:

$$f(n) = n^2 + 100n + \log_{10} n + 1000. \tag{2.1}$$

For small values of n, the last term, 1000, is the largest. When n equals 10, the second($100n$) and last (1000) terms are on equal footing with the other terms making a small contribution to the function value. When n reaches the value of 100, the first and the second terms make the same contribution to the result. But when n becomes larger than 100, the contribution of the second term becomes less significant. Hence, for large values of n, due to the quadratic growth of the first term (n^2), the value of the function f depends mainly on the value of this first term, as Figure 2.1 demonstrates. Other terms can be disregarded in the long run.

■ 2.2 BIG-O NOTATION

The most commonly used notation for specifying asymptotic complexity, that is, for estimating the rate of function growth, is the big-O notation introduced in 1894 by Paul Bachmann. Given two positive-valued functions f and g, consider the following definition:

Definition 1: $f(n)$ is $O(g(n))$ if there exist positive numbers c and N such that $f(n) \leq cg(n)$ for all $n \geq N$.

This definition reads: f is big-O of g if there is a positive number c such that f is not larger than cg for sufficiently large ns, that is, for all ns larger than some number N. The

n	$f(n)$	n^2		$100n$		$\log_{10} n$		1,000	
	value	value	%	value	%	value	%	value	%
1	1,101	1	0.1	100	9.1	0	0.0	1000	90.82
10	2,101	100	4.76	1,000	47.6	1	0.05	1000	47.62
100	21,002	10,000	47.6	10,000	47.6	2	0.001	1000	4.76
1,000	1,101,003	1,000,000	90.8	100,000	9.1	3	0.0003	1000	0.09
10,000	101,001,004	100,000,000	99.0	1,000,000	0.99	4	0.0	1000	0.001
100,000	10,010,001,005	10,000,000,000	99.9	10,000,000	0.099	5	0.0	1000	0.00

Figure 2.1: **The growth rate of all terms of function $f(n) = n^2 + 100n + \log_{10} n + 1000$.**

relationship between f and g can be expressed by stating either that $g(n)$ is an upper bound on the value of $f(n)$, or that in the long run, f grows at most as fast as g.

The problem with this definition is that, first, it states only that there must exist certain c and N, but it does not give any hint how to calculate these constants. Second, it does not put any restrictions on these values and gives little guidance in situations when there are many candidates. In fact, there are usually infinitely many pairs of cs and Ns that can be given for the same pair of functions f and g. For example, for

$$f(n) = 2n^2 + 3n + 1 = O(n^2) \qquad \textbf{(2.2)}$$

where $g(n) = n^2$, candidate values for c and N are shown in Figure 2.2.

We obtain these values by solving the inequality:

$$2n^2 + 3n + 1 \le cn^2$$

or, equivalently

$$2 + \frac{3}{n} + \frac{1}{n^2} \le c$$

for different ns. The first inequality results in substituting the quadratic function from Equation 2.2 for $f(n)$ in the definition of the big-O notation and n^2 for $g(n)$. Since it is one inequality with two unknowns, different pairs of constants c and N for the same function $g(= n^2)$ can be determined. In order to choose the best c and N, it should be determined for which N a certain term in f becomes the largest and stays the largest. In Equation 2.2, the only candidates for the largest term are $2n^2$ and $3n$; these terms can be compared using the inequality $2n^2 > 3n$ that holds for $n > 1$. Thus, $N = 2$ and $c \ge 3\frac{3}{4}$, as Figure 2.2 indicates.

What is the practical significance of the pairs of constants just listed? All of them are related to the same function $g(n) = n^2$ and to the same $f(n)$. For a fixed g, an infinite number of pairs of cs and Ns can be identified. The point is that f and g grow at the same rate. The definition states, however, that g is almost always greater than or equal to f if it is multiplied by a constant c. "Almost always" means for all ns not less than a constant N. The crux of the matter is that the value of c depends on which N is chosen and vice versa. For example, if 1 is chosen as the value of N, i.e., if g is multiplied by c so that $cg(n)$ will not be less than f right away, then c has to be equal to 6 or greater. If $cg(n)$ is greater than or equal to $f(n)$ starting from $n = 2$, then it is enough that c is equal to 3.75. The constant c has to be at least $3\frac{1}{9}$ if $cg(n)$ is not less than $f(n)$ starting from $n = 3$. Figure 2.3 shows the graphs of the functions f and g. The function g is plotted with different coefficients c. Also, N is always a point where the functions $cg(n)$ and f intersect each other.

c	≥ 6	$\ge 3\frac{3}{4}$	$\ge 3\frac{1}{9}$	$\ge 2\frac{13}{16}$	$\ge 2\frac{16}{25}$	$\cdots$	$\longrightarrow$	2
N	1	2	3	4	5	$\cdots$	$\longrightarrow$	∞

Figure 2.2: **Different values of c and N for function $f(n) = 2n^2 + 3n + 1 = O(n^2)$ calculated according to the definition of big-O.**

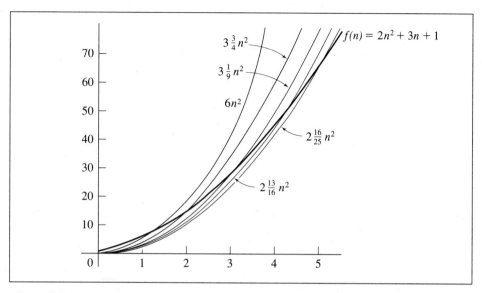

Figure 2.3: **Comparison of functions for different values of c and N from Figure 2.2.**

The inherent imprecision of the big-O notation goes even further, since there can be infinitely many functions g for a given function f. For example, the f from Equation 2.2 is big-O not only of n^2, but also of $n^3, n^4, \ldots, n^k, \ldots$ for any positive k. In order to avoid this embarrassment of riches, the smallest function g is chosen, n^2 in this case.

The approximation of function f can be refined using big-O notation only for the part of the equation suppressing irrelevant information. For example, in Equation 2.1, the contribution of the third and last terms to the value of the function can be omitted (see Equation 2.3).

$$f(n) = n^2 + 100n + O(\log_{10} n) \qquad \textbf{(2.3)}$$

Similarly, the function f in Equation 2.2 can be approximated as

$$f(n) = 2n^2 + O(n). \qquad \textbf{(2.4)}$$

Eventually, both of the functions Equations 2.1 and 2.2 can be approximated by $O(n^2)$, where any distinction between them disappears. The approximations in Equations 2.3 and 2.4 reflect the fact that the functions are different even after omitting the terms that have little impact on the final result.

■ 2.3 PROPERTIES OF BIG-O NOTATION

Big-O notation has some useful properties that can be taken advantage of when estimating the efficiency of algorithms.

Fact 1. (transitivity) If $f(n)$ is $O(g(n))$ and $g(n)$ is $O(h(n))$, then $f(n)$ if $O(h(n))$. (This can be rephrased as $O(O(g(n)))$ is $O(g(n))$.)

Proof: According to the definition, $f(n)$ is $O(g(n))$ if there exist positive numbers c_1 and N_1 such that $f(n) \leq c_1 g(n)$ for all $n \geq N_1$, and $g(n)$ is $O(h(n))$ if there exist positive numbers c_2 and N_2 such that $g(n) \leq c_2 h(n)$ for all $n \geq N_2$.

Hence $c_1 g(n) \leq c_1 c_2 h(n)$ for $n \geq N$ where N is the larger of N_1 and N_2. If we take $c = c_1 c_2$, then $f(n) \leq ch(n)$ for $n \geq N$, which means that f is big-O of h. ∎

Fact 2. If $f(n)$ is $O(h(n))$ and $g(n)$ is $O(h(n))$ then $f(n) + g(n)$ is $O(h(n))$.

Proof: After setting c equal to $c_1 + c_2$, $f(n) + g(n) \leq ch(n)$. ∎

Fact 3. The function an^k is $O(n^k)$.

Proof: In order for the inequality $an^k \leq cn^k$ to hold, $c \geq a$ is necessary. ∎

Fact 4. The function n^k is $O(n^{k+j})$ for any positive j.

Proof: The statement holds if $c = N = 1$. ∎

It follows from all these facts that every polynomial is big-O of n raised to the largest power, or

$$f(n) = a_k n^k + a_{k-1} n^{k-1} + \cdots + a_1 n + a_0 \text{ is } O(n^k).$$

It is also obvious that in the case of polynomials, $f(n)$ is $O(n^{k+j})$ for any positive j.

One of the most important functions in the evaluation of the efficiency of algorithms is the logarithmic function. In fact, if it can be stated that the complexity of an algorithm is on the order of the logarithmic function, the algorithm can be regarded as very good. There are an infinite number of functions that can be considered better than the logarithmic function, among which only a few, such as $O(\lg \lg n)$ or $O(1)$, have practical bearing. Before we show an important fact about logarithmic functions, let us state without proof:

Fact 5. If $f(n) = cg(n)$ then $f(n)$ is $O(g(n))$.

Fact 6. The function $\log_a n$ is $O(\log_b n)$ for any numbers a and b greater than 1.

This correspondence holds between logarithmic functions. Fact 6 states that regardless of their bases, logarithmic functions are big-O of each other, that all these functions have the same rate of growth.

Letting $\log_a n = x$ and $\log_b n = y$, we have, by the definition of logarithm, $a^x = n$ and $b^y = n$.

Taking ln of both sides results in

$$x \ln a = \ln n \qquad \text{and} \qquad y \ln b = \ln n.$$

Thus,

$$x \ln a = y \ln b,$$

$$\ln a \, \log_a n = \ln b \, \log_b n,$$

$$\log_a n = \frac{\ln b}{\ln a} \log_b n = c \log_b n$$

which proves that $\log_a n$ and $\log_b n$ are multiples of each other. By Fact 5, $\log_a n$ is $O(\log_b n)$.

Because the base of the logarithm is irrelevant in the context of big-O notation, it can be dropped and Fact 6 can be written as

Fact 7. $\log_a n$ is $O(\lg n)$ for any positive a, where $\lg n = \log_2 n$.

■ 2.4 Ω AND Θ NOTATIONS

Big-O notation refers to the upper bounds of functions. There is a symmetrical definition for a lower bound in the definition of big-Ω:

Definition 2: The function $f(n)$ is $\Omega(g(n))$ if there exist positive numbers c and N such that $f(n) \geq cg(n)$ for all $n \geq N$.

This definition reads: f is Ω (big-omega) of g if there is a positive number c such that f is at least equal to cg for almost all ns. In other words, $cg(n)$ is a lower bound on the size of $f(n)$, or that in the long run, f grows at least at the rate of g.

The only difference between this definition and the definition of big-O notation is the direction of the inequality; one definition can be turned into the other by replacing "$\geq$" by "$\leq$." There is an interconnection between these two notations expressed by the equivalence

$$f(n) \text{ is } \Omega\big(g(n)\big) \text{ iff } g(n) \text{ is } O\big(f(n)\big).$$

Ω notation suffers from the same profusion problem as does big-O notation: there is an unlimited number of choices for the constants c and N. For Equation 2.2, the same Figure 2.2 of candidate values can be used except that all the $\geq$ symbols must be replaced with $\leq$ symbols. Also, if g is an Ω of f and $h \geq g$ then h is an Ω of f; if for f, we can find one g being an Ω of f, then we can find infinitely many. For example, n^2 is an Ω of function 2.2 and so are $n, n^{\frac{1}{2}}, n^{\frac{1}{3}}, n^{\frac{1}{4}}, \ldots$, but also $\lg n, \lg \lg n, \ldots$ and many other functions. For practical purposes, only the closest Ωs are the most interesting, the largest lower bounds. This restriction is made implicitly each time we choose an Ω of a function f.

There are an infinite number of possible lower bounds for the function f; there is an infinite set of gs such that $f(n)$ is $\Omega(g(n))$ as well as an unbounded number of possible upper bounds of f. This may be somewhat disquieting, so we restrict our attention to the smallest upper bounds and the largest lower bounds. Note that there is a common ground for big-O and Ω notations indicated by the equalities in the definitions of these notations: big-O is defined in terms of "$\leq$," Ω in terms of "$\geq$"; "$=$" is included in both inequalities. This suggests a way of restricting the sets of possible lower and upper bounds. This restriction can be accomplished by the following definition of Θ (theta) notation:

Definition 3: $f(n)$ is $\Theta(g(n))$ if there exist positive numbers c_1, c_2, and N such that $c_1 g(n) \leq f(n) \leq c_2 g(n)$ for all $n \geq N$.

This definition reads: f has an order of magnitude g, f is on the order of g, or both functions grow at the same rate in the long run. We see that $f(n)$ is $\Theta(g(n))$ iff $f(n)$ is $O(g(n))$ and $f(n)$ is $\Omega(g(n))$.

The only function listed above being both big-O and Ω of the function 2.2 is n^2. However, it is not the only choice and there are still an infinite number of choices, since the functions $2n^2, 3n^2, 4n^2, \ldots$, are also Θ of function 2.2. But it is rather obvious that the simplest, n^2, will be chosen.

When applying any of these notations (big-O, Ω, and Θ), do not forget that they are approximations that hide some detail which in many cases may be considered important.

■ 2.5 POSSIBLE PROBLEMS

All the notations serve the purpose of comparing the efficiency of various algorithms designed for solving the same problem. However, if only big-Os are used to represent the efficiency of algorithms, then some of them may be rejected prematurely. The problem is that in the definition of big-O notation, f is considered big-O of g if the inequality $f(n) \leq cg(n)$ holds in the long run for all natural numbers with a few exceptions. The number of ns violating this inequality is always finite. It is enough to meet the condition of the definition. As Figure 2.2 indicates, this number of exceptions can be reduced by choosing a sufficiently large c. However, in practice, this may be of little practical significance if the constant c in $f(n) \leq cg(n)$ is prohibitively large, say 10^8, although the function g taken by itself seems to be promising.

Consider that there are two algorithms to solve a certain problem and suppose that the number of operations required by these algorithms is $10^8 n$ and $10n^2$. The first function is big-O of n and the second is big-O of n^2. Using just the big-O information, the second algorithm is rejected, since it grows too fast. It is true but, again, in the long run, since for $n \leq 10^7$, which is ten million, the second algorithm performs fewer operations than the first. Although ten million elements is not an unheard-of number of elements to be processed by an algorithm, in most cases the number is much lower, and in these cases the second algorithm is preferable.

For these reasons it may be desirable to use one more notation that includes constants which are very large for practical reasons. Udi Manber proposes a double-O (OO) notation to indicate such functions: f is $OO(g(n))$ if it is big-O of $g(n)$ and the constant c is too large to have a practical significance. Thus, $10^8 n$ is $OO(n)$. However, the definition of "too large" depends on the particular application.

■ 2.6 EXAMPLES OF COMPLEXITIES

Algorithms can be classified by their time or space complexities, and in this respect, several classes of such algorithms can be distinguished, as Figure 2.4 illustrates. Their growth is also displayed in Figure 2.5. For example, an algorithm is called *constant* if its execution time remains the same for any number of elements; it is called *quadratic* if its execution time is $O(n^2)$. For each of these classes, a number of operations are shown along with the real time needed for executing them on a machine able to perform a million operations per second, or one operation per microsecond (μsec). The table in Figure 2.4 indicates that some ill-designed algorithms, or algorithms whose complexity cannot be improved, have no practical application on available computers. In order to process a million items with a

class	complexity	number of operations and execution time (1 instr/μsec)					
n:		10		10^2		10^3	
constant	$O(1)$	1	1 μsec	1	1 μsec	1	1 μsec
logarithmic	$O(\lg n)$	3.32	3 μsec	6.64	7 μsec	9.97	10 μsec
linear	$O(n)$	10	10 μsec	10^2	100 μsec	10^3	1 msec
$O(n\lg n)$	$O(n\lg n)$	33.2	33 μsec	664	664 μsec	9970	10 msec
quadratic	$O(n^2)$	10^2	100 μsec	10^4	10 msec	10^6	1 sec
cubic	$O(n^3)$	10^3	1 msec	10^6	1 sec	10^9	16.7 min
exponential	$O(2^n)$	1024	10 msec	10^{30}	$3.17 * 10^{16}$ yrs	10^{301}	
n:		10^4		10^5		10^6	
constant	$O(1)$	1	1 μsec	1	1 μsec	1	1 μsec
logarithmic	$O(\lg n)$	13.3	13 μsec	16.6	17 μsec	19.93	20 μsec
linear	$O(n)$	10^4	10 msec	10^5	.1 sec	10^6	1 sec
$O(n\lg n)$	$O(n\lg n)$	$133 * 10^3$	133 msec	$166 * 10^4$	1.6 sec	$199.3 * 10^5$	20 sec
quadratic	$O(n^2)$	10^8	1.7 min	10^{10}	16.7 min	10^{12}	11.6 days
cubic	$O(n^3)$	10^{12}	11.6 days	10^{15}	31.7 yrs	10^{18}	27,397 yrs
exponential	$O(2^n)$	10^{3010}		10^{30103}		10^{301030}	

Figure 2.4: **Classes of algorithms and their execution times on a computer executing a million operations per second (1 second = 10^6 μsec = 10^3 ms).**

quadratic algorithm, over eleven days are needed, and for a cubic algorithm, thousands of years. Even if a computer can perform one operation per nanosecond (one billion operations per second) the quadratic algorithm finishes in only 16.7 seconds, but the cubic algorithm requires over 27 years. Even a thousand-fold improvement in execution speed has very little practical bearing for this algorithm. Analyzing the complexity of algorithms is of extreme importance and cannot be abandoned on account of the argument that we have entered an era when, at relatively little cost, a computer on our desktop can execute millions of operations per second. The importance of analyzing the complexity of algorithms, in any context but

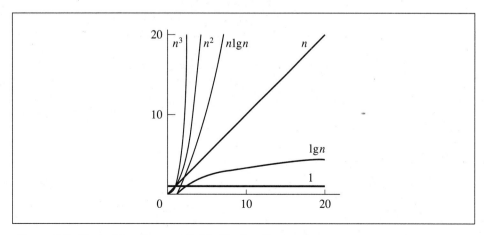

Figure 2.5: **Typical functions applied in big-O estimates.**

in the context of data structures in particular, cannot be overstressed. The impressive speed of computers is of limited use if the programs that run on them use inefficient algorithms.

■ 2.7 FINDING ASYMPTOTIC COMPLEXITY: EXAMPLES

Asymptotic bounds are used to estimate the efficiency of algorithms by assessing the amount of time and memory needed to accomplish the task for which the algorithms were designed. This section illustrates how this complexity can be determined.

In most cases, we are interested in time complexity, which usually measures the number of assignments and comparisons performed during the execution of a program. Chapter 9, which deals with sorting algorithms, considers both types of operations; this chapter considers only the number of assignment statements.

Begin with a simple loop to calculate the sum of numbers in an array:

```
for(i = sum = 0; i < n; i++)
    sum += a[i];
```

This **for** loop iterates n times and during each iteration it executes two assignments, one of which updates **sum** and the other updates **i**. Thus, there are $2n$ assignments for the complete run of this **for** loop; its asymptotic complexity is $O(n)$.

Complexity usually grows if nested loops are used, as in the following code which outputs the sums of all the subarrays which begin with position 0:

```
for(i = 0; i < n; i++) {
    for(j = 1, sum = a[0]; j <= i; j++)
        sum += a[j];
    cout<<"sum for subarray 0 through "<< i <<" is "<<sum<<endl;
}
```

Before the loops start, **i** is initialized. The outer loop is performed n times, executing in each iteration an inner **for** loop, print statement, and assignment statements for **i**, **j**, and **sum**. The inner loop is executed i times for each $i \in \{1, \ldots, n - 1\}$ with two assignments in each iteration: one for **sum** and one for **j**. Therefore, there are $1 + 3n + \sum_{i=1}^{n-1} 2i = 1 + 3n + 2(1 + 2 + \cdots + n - 1) = 1 + 3n + n(n - 1) = O(n) + O(n^2) = O(n^2)$ assignments executed before the program is completed.

For nested loops, complexity usually grows in comparison with one loop, but it does not have to grow at all. For example, we may request printing sums of numbers in the last five cells of the subarrays starting in position 0. We adopt the code above and transform it to

```
for(i = 4; i < n; i++) {
    for(j = i-3, sum = a[i-4]; j <= i; j++)
        sum += a[j];
    cout<<"sum for subarray "<<i-4<<" through "<< i <<" is "<<sum<<endl;
}
```

For each i, the inner loop is executed only five times; for each iteration of the outer loop there are eight assignments. This number does not depend on the size of the array. The program makes $1 + 8*4 + 8*5 + \cdots + 8*(n-1) + n - 4 = O(n)$ assignments, although the use of nested loops suggests something else.

Analysis of these two examples is relatively uncomplicated since the number of times the loops executed did not depend on the ordering of the arrays. Computation of asymptotic complexity is more involved if the number of iterations is not always the same. This point can be illustrated with a loop used to determine the longest subarray with the numbers in increasing order. For example, in [1 8 1 2 5 0 11 12], this subarray is [1 2 5]. The code is

```
for(i = 0, length = 1; i < n-1; i++) {
    for(i1 = i2 = k = i; k < n-1 && a[k] < a[k+1]; k++,i2++);
    if(length < i2 - i1 + 1)
        length = i2 - i1 + 1;
}
```

Notice that if all numbers in the array are in decreasing order, the outer loop is executed $n - 1$ times, but in each iteration the inner loop executes just one time. Thus, the algorithm is $O(n)$. The algorithm is least efficient if the numbers are in increasing order. In this case, the outer **for** loop is executed $n - 1$ times and the inner loop is executed i times for each $i \in \{1, \ldots, n - 1\}$. Thus, the algorithm is $O(n^2)$. In most cases, the arrangement of data is less orderly and measuring the efficiency in these cases is of great importance. However, it is far from trivial to determine the efficiency in the average cases. The efficiency of a random ordering for our example will not be analyzed here; Chapter 9 deals with the analysis of random ordering in more detail.

A fifth example used to determine the computational complexity is the *binary search algorithm* which is used to locate an element in an ordered array. If it is an array of numbers and we try to locate number k, then the algorithm accesses the middle element of the array first. If that element is equal to k, then the algorithm returns its position; if not, the algorithm continues. In the second trial, only half of the original array is considered: the first half, if k is smaller than the middle element, and the second otherwise. Now, the middle element of the chosen subarray is accessed and compared to k. If it is the same, the algorithm completes successfully. Otherwise the subarray is divided into two halves and if k is larger than this middle element, the first half is discarded; otherwise the first half is retained. This process of halving and comparing continues until k is found or the array can no longer be divided into two subarrays. This relatively simple algorithm can be coded as follows:

```
template<class genType>  // overloaded operator < is used;
int
BinarySearch(const genType arr[], const int arrSize, const genType& key)
{   int lo = 0, mid, hi = arrSize-1;

    while (lo <= hi) {
        mid = (lo + hi)/2;
```

```
    if (key < arr[mid])
        hi = mid - 1;
    else if (arr[mid] < key)
        lo = mid + 1;
    else return mid;    // success: return the index of
}                       //   the cell occupied by key;
    return -1;          // failure: key is not in the array;
}
```

If **key** is in the middle of the array, the loop executes only one time. How many times does the loop execute in the case where **key** is not in the array? First the algorithm looks at the entire array of size n, then at one of its halves of size $\frac{n}{2}$, then at one of the halves of this half, of size $\frac{n}{2^2}$, and so on, until the array is of size 1. Hence we have the sequence $n, \frac{n}{2}, \frac{n}{2^2}, \dots, \frac{n}{2^m}$, and we want to know the value of m. But the last term of this sequence $\frac{n}{2^m}$ equals 1, from which we have $m = \lg n$. So the fact that k is not in the array can be determined after $\lg n$ iterations of the loop.

These examples indicate the need for distinguishing at least three cases for which the efficiency of algorithms has to be determined. The *worst case* is when an algorithm requires a maximum number of steps, the *best case* is when the number of steps is the smallest, and the *average case* is a case falling between these extremes. Identifying these cases is not always an easy task and they have to be determined for each algorithm. Also, finding the complexity for these cases may be a challenging enterprise. Usually the complexity of average cases is the most difficult to compute. If the computation is very complex, approximations are used, and that is where we find the big-O, Ω, and Θ notations most useful.

■ 2.8 EXERCISES

1. Assuming that $f_1(n)$ is $O(g_1(n))$ and $f_2(n)$ is $O(g_2(n))$, prove the following statements:

   (a) $f_1(n) + f_2(n)$ is $O(\max(g_1(n), g_2(n)))$.

   (b) If a number k can be determined such that for all $n > k$, $g_1(n) \leq g_2(n)$, then $O(g_1(n)) + O(g_2(n))$ is $O(g_2(n))$.

   (c) $f_1(n) * f_2(n)$ is $O(g_1(n) * g_2(n))$ (rule of product).

   (d) $O(cg(n))$ is $O(g(n))$.

   (e) c is $O(1)$.

2. Prove the following statements:

   (a) $\sum_{i=1}^{n} i^2$ is $O(n^3)$ and more generally, $\sum_{i=1}^{n} i^k$ is $O(n^{k+1})$.

   (b) $an^k / \lg n$ is $O(n^k)$ but $an^k / \lg n$ is not $\Theta(n^k)$.

   (c) $n^{1.1} + n \lg n$ is $\Theta(n^{1.1})$.

   (d) 2^n is $O(n!)$ and $n!$ is not $O(2^n)$.

3. Make the same assumptions as in Exercise 2 and by finding counterexamples, refute the following statements:

(a) $f_1(n) - f_2(n)$ is $O(g_1(n) - g_2(n))$.

(b) $f_1(n)/f_2(n)$ is $O(g_1(n)/g_2(n))$.

4. Find functions f_1 and f_2 such that both $f_1(n)$ and $f_2(n)$ are both $O(g(n))$, but that $f_1(n)$ is not $O(f_2)$.

5. The algorithm presented in this chapter for finding the longest subarray with the numbers in increasing order is inefficient, since there is no need to continue to search for another array if the length of the array already found is greater than the length of the subarray to be located. Thus, if the entire array is already in order, we can discontinue the search right away, converting the worst case into the best. The change needed is in the outer loop which now has one more test:

```
for(i = 0, length = 1; i < n-1 && length < n-i; i++)
```

What is the worst case now? Is the efficiency in the worst case still $O(n^2)$?

6. Determine the complexity of the following implementations of the algorithms for adding, multiplying, and transposing $n \times n$ matrices:

```
for(i = 0; i < n; i++)
    for(j = 0; j < n; j++)
        a[i,j] = b[i,j] + c[i,j];

for(i = 0; i < n; i++)
    for(j = a[i,j] = 0; j < n; j++)
        for(k = 0; k < n; k++)
            a[i,j] += b[i,k] * c[k,j];

for(i = 0; i < n - 1; i++)
    for(j = i+1; j < n; j++) {
        tmp = a[i,j];
        a[i,j] = a[j,i];
        a[j,i] = tmp;
    }
```

BIBLIOGRAPHY

Computational Complexity

[1] Hartmanis, Juris and Hopcroft, John E., "An Overview of the Theory of Computational Complexity," *Journal of the ACM* 18 (1971), 444–475.

[2] Hartmanis, Juris and Stearns, Richard E., "On the Computational Complexity of Algorithms," *Transactions of the American Mathematical Society* 117 (1965), 285–306.

[3] Preparata, Franco P., "Computational Complexity," in Pollack, S. V. (ed.), *Studies in Computer Science*, The Mathematical Association of America, 1982, 196–228.

Big-O, Ω, and Θ Notations

[4] Brassard, G., "Crusade for a Better Notation," *SIGACT News* 17 (1985), 60–64.

[5] Knuth, Donald, "Big Omicron and Big Omega and Big Theta," *SIGACT News*, April-June, 8 (1976), 18–24.

[6] Knuth, Donald, *The Art of Computer Programming, Vol. 1: Seminumerical Algorithms*, Reading, MA: Addison-Wesley, 1973.

[7] Vitanyi, P.M.B. and Meertens, L., "Big Omega versus the Wild Functions," *SIGACT News* 16 (1985), 56–59.

OO Notation

[8] Manber, Udi, *Introduction to Algorithms: A Creative Approach*, Reading, MA: Addison-Wesley, 1989.

3

LINKED LISTS

An array is a very useful data structure provided in programming languages. However, it has at least two limitations: 1) its size has to be known at the compilation time, and 2) the data in the array are separated in computer memory by the same distance, which means that inserting an item inside the array requires shifting other data in this array. This limitation can be overcome by using *linked structures*. A linked structure is a collection of nodes storing data and links to other nodes. In this way, nodes can be located anywhere in the memory, and passing from one node of the list to another is accomplished by storing the addresses of other nodes on the list. Although linked structures can be implemented in a variety of ways, the most flexible implementation is by using pointers.

■ 3.1 POINTERS

Variables used in a program can be considered as boxes which are never empty; they are filled with some content either by the programmer or, if uninitialized, by the operating system. Such a variable has at least two attributes: the content or value and the location of the box or variable in computer memory. This content can be a number, character, or a compound item such as a structure or union. However, this content can also be the location of another variable, and variables with such contents are called *pointers*. Pointers are usually auxiliary variables which allow us to access the values of other variables indirectly. A pointer is analogous to a road sign which leads us to a certain location or to a slip of paper on which an address has been jotted down. They are variables leading to variables, humble auxiliaries which point to some other variables as the focus of attention.

For example, in the declaration

```
int i = 15, j, *p, *q;
```

i and j are numerical variables and p and q are pointers to numbers where the star in front of p and q indicates their function. Assuming that the addresses of the variables i, j, p, and q are 1080, 1082, 1084, and 1086, then after assigning 15 to i in the declaration, the positions and values of the variables in computer memory are as in Figure 3.1a.

Now, we could make the assignment p = i (or p = (int*) i if the compiler does not accept it), but the variable p was created to store the address of an integer variable, not its value. Therefore, the proper assignment is p = &i where the ampersand in front of i means that the address of i is meant and not its content. Figure 3.1b illustrates this situation. In Figure 3.1c, the arrow from p to i indicates that p is a pointer that holds the address of i.

We have to be able to distinguish the value of p, which is an address, from the value of the location whose address the pointer holds. For example, to assign the number 20 to the variable pointed to by p, the assignment statement is

```
*p = 20;
```

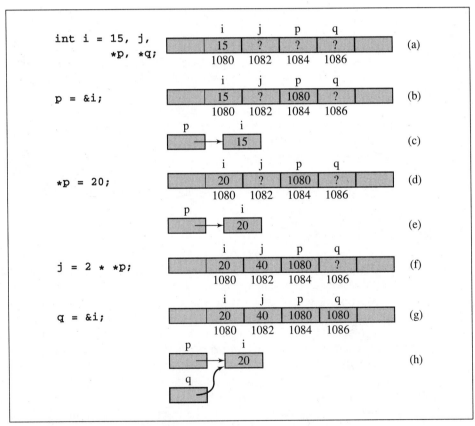

Figure 3.1: **Changes of values after assignments are made using pointer**   **continued**
variables. Note that (b) and (c) show the same situation and so
do (d) and (e), (g) and (h), (i) and (j), (k) and (l), and (m) and
(n).

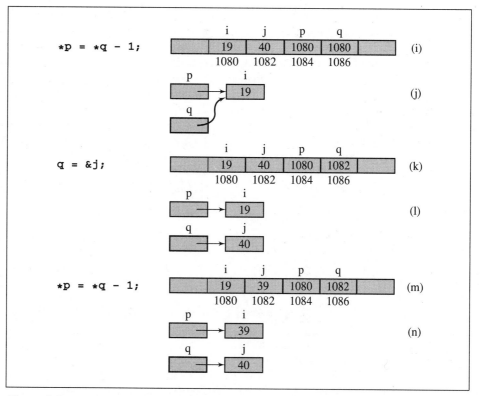

Figure 3.1: **Changes of values after assignments are made using pointer variables. Note that (b) and (c) show the same situation and so do (d) and (e), (g) and (h), (i) and (j), (k) and (l), and (m) and (n).**

The star * here is an indirection operator which forces the system to first retrieve the contents of **p**, then access the location whose address has just been retrieved from **p**, and only afterwards, assign the number 20 to this location (Figure 3.1d). Figures 3.1e through 3.1n give more examples of assignment statements and how the values are stored in computer memory.

In fact, pointers—like all variables—also have two attributes: a content and a location. This location can be stored in another variable, which would then be a pointer to a pointer.

In the examples in Figure 3.1, the pointer **p** referred to a specific variable which existed before its address was stored in **p**. A more interesting situation is when a pointer refers to a structure which is created and modified dynamically. This is a situation we would like to have in order to overcome the aforementioned restrictions imposed by arrays. Arrays in C++ and in most programming languages have to be declared in advance; therefore, their size is known before the program starts. This means that the programmer has to have a fair knowledge of the problem being programmed to choose the right size for the array. If the size is too big, then the array unnecessarily occupies memory space which is wasted. If the size is too small, the array can overflow with data and the program will abort. Sometimes the size of the array simply cannot be predicted. Therefore, we need a structure which can allocate only as much memory as currently needed by the program. If more memory is needed, then the program requests it; if currently used memory is not needed any more, the program returns it to the operating system. This is where pointers come in very handy. Pointers point to data structures whose size can change while always allowing the structure to be completely scanned and monitored.

To dynamically allocate and deallocate memory, two functions are used. One function, **new**, takes from memory as much space as needed to store an object whose type follows **new**. For example, having the declarations

```
struct Node {
        char name[20];
        int age;
} *nodePtr;
char *s;
```

we can issue two requests, as in

```
nodePtr = new Node;
s = new char[20];
```

After these two assignments, 22 bytes (assuming that one **int** occupies 2 bytes) are pointed to by **nodePtr**, with the address of the first byte stored in this pointer variable. The pointer **s** points to a string of 20 cells, with the address of the first cell stored in **s**. If these structures are no longer needed, they can be returned to the pool of free memory locations managed by the operating system by issuing the following two statements:

```
delete nodePtr;
delete [] s;
```

However, after executing these statements, the addresses of these structures are still in **nodePtr** and in **s**, although the structures, as far as the program is concerned, do not exist any more. It is like treating an address of a house which has been demolished as the address of the existing location. If we use this address to find someone, the result is easily foreseen. Similarly, if after issuing the **delete** statement we do not erase the address from the pointer variable participating in deletion, the program will crash when trying to access nonexisting locations. This is the *dangling reference problem*. To avoid this problem, an address must be assigned to a pointer; if it cannot be the address of any location, it should be a null address, which is simply 0, as in **nodePtr = 0** and **s = 0**.

■ 3.2   SINGLY LINKED LISTS

However we still may not be convinced as to the usefulness of pointers if we only look at the example of declaring the pointer variable **nodePtr**. Do we gain anything by it? Why not use a regular variable, as in

```
struct Node {
       char name[20];
       int age;
} someVar;
```

The advantage of using pointer variables in such situations is obvious when the structure also has a pointer field which stores an address of another structure which also has a pointer field containing the address of still another structure, and so on. In this way, many structures can be strung together using only one pointer variable to access the entire sequence of nodes. Such a sequence of nodes is the most frequently used implementation of a *linked list* which is a data structure composed of nodes, each node holding some information and a pointer to another node in the list. Also, because a node has a link only to its successor in this sequence, the list is called a *singly linked list*. Figure 3.2 contains an example of such a list. Notice that only one variable name is used, **p**, which is the name of the pointer variable used to access the list. Although the list consists of four nodes, no node has an explicit name allowing for *direct* access so that each node has to be accessed *indirectly* through the pointer **p**. The last node on the list is the null pointer field.

First, let us declare a node:

```
struct Node {
       int info;
       Node *next;
       Node() { next = 0; }    // default constructor;
       Node(int el, Node *ptr = 0) { info = el; next = ptr; }
} *p;
```

Note that **Node** is defined in terms of itself, since one field, **next**, is a pointer to a node of the same type which is just being defined. This circularity is allowed in C++.

Now, let us create the linked list in Figure 3.2.

```
p = new Node(10);
p->next = new Node(8);
p->next->next = new Node(50);
p->next->next->next = new Node(22);
```

The constructor **Node()** makes initializing of fields easier, since no extra assignments are needed to initialize the **info** and **next** fields. The first field is initialized to the value supplied as a parameter to **Node()**; the second is initialized by default to null.

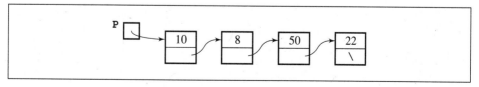

Figure 3.2: **A singly linked list.**

Notice that the fields of nodes pointed to by **p** are accessed using the arrow notation, which is clearer than using a dot notation, as in **(*p).next**.

Our linked list example illustrates a certain inconvenience in using pointers: the longer the linked list, the longer the chain of **next** fields to access the nodes at the end of the list. In this example, **p->next->next->next** allows us to access the **next** field of the third node on the list. But what if it were the hundred and third node or, worse, the thousand and third node on the list? Typing one thousand and three **next** fields as in **p->next->...->next** would be a daunting task. If we miss one **next** in this chain, then an incorrect assignment is made and the flexibility of using linked lists is diminished. Therefore, other ways of accessing nodes in linked lists are needed. One way is to maintain two pointers to the linked list, one to the first node, one to the last. Using this approach, we can implement some basic operations on linked lists, this time using not only **struct** but also a **class**, as shown in Figure 3.3.

```
//*********************  intSLLst.h  *************************
//          singly-linked list class to store integers

#ifndef INT_LINKED_LIST
#define INT_LINKED_LIST

class intSLList {
public:
    intSLList()      { head = tail = 0;  }
    void AddToHead(int);
    void AddToTail(int);
    int  RemoveFromHead(); // remove the head and return its info;
    int  RemoveFromTail(); // remove the tail and return its info;
protected:
    struct Node {
        int info;
        Node *next;
        Node(int el, Node *ptr = 0)
                { info = el; next = ptr; }
    } *head, *tail, *tmp;
    int el;
};

#endif
```

Figure 3.3: **An implementation of a singly linked list.**   **continued**

```cpp
//*********************    intSLLst.cpp    *************************

#include "intSLLst.h"

void
intSLList::AddToHead(int el)
{
    head = new Node(el,head);
    if (!tail)
       tail = head;
}

void
intSLList::AddToTail(int el)
{
    if (tail) {                    // if list not empty;
        tail->next = new Node(el);
        tail = tail->next;
    }
    else head = tail = new Node(el);
}

int
intSLList::RemoveFromHead()
{
    if (head) {                    // if non-empty list;
        el = head->info;
        tmp = head;
        if (head == tail)   // if only one record on the list;
             head = tail = 0;
        else head = head->next;
        delete tmp;
        return el;
    }
    else return 0;
}

int
intSLList::RemoveFromTail()
```

Figure 3.3: **An implementation of a singly linked list.**   **continued**

```
{
    if (tail) {                        // if non-empty list;
        el = tail->info;
        if (head == tail) { // if only one record on the list;
            delete head;
            head = tail = 0;
        }
        else {                         // if more than one record in the list,
                                       // find the predecessor of tail;
            for (tmp = head; tmp->next != tail; tmp = tmp->next);
            delete tail;
            tail = tmp;     // the predecessor of tail becomes tail;
            tail->next = 0;
        }
        return el;
    }
    else return 0;
}
```

Figure 3.3: **An implementation of a singly linked list.**

To add one node at the beginning of the list, some assignments have to be made. First, a new node has to be created, then its fields have to be initialized: its **info** field is initialized with the number being included in the list, and the **next** field is initialized with the address of the first node on the list. The new node becomes the first node on the list, but this fact has to be reflected in the value of **head**, hence the updated value of **head** is the address of the new node (see Figure 3.4). In our implementation, the initialization of both fields of the new node is done by the constructor **Node()**, and creating the node and assigning its

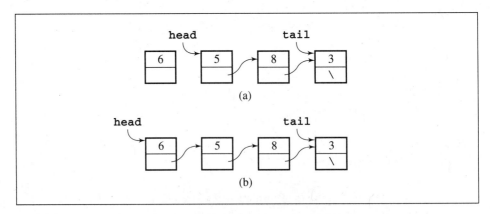

Figure 3.4: **Adding a new node at the beginning of a singly linked list.**

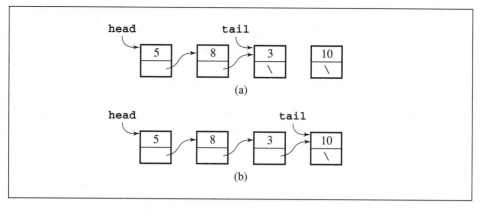

Figure 3.5: **Adding a new node at the end of a singly linked list.**

address to **head** is the task performed in the body of the method **AddToHead()**. This method singles out one special case, namely inserting a new node to an empty linked list. In an empty linked list, both the **head** and **tail** are null. Therefore, both these pointers have to be set to the address of the only node of the new list. In other cases, only **head** needs to be updated.

If a node is added to the end of the list, then the **next** field of the node pointed to by **tail** is set to the address of a new node and the fields of the new node are initialized to the number being included in the list and to the null pointer. Afterwards, **tail** also has to be updated so that it always points to the last node of the list (Figure 3.5). A special case, as before, is when the first node is added to the list. In this case, **head** also has to be initialized to the address of this single node.

Another pair of operations are the opposites of the ones just discussed. The first is deleting a node at the beginning of the list and returning the value stored in it. This operation is implemented by the method **RemoveFromHead()**. In this operation, the information from the first node is retrieved, the node itself is deleted, and **head** now points to what was the second node (Figure 3.6). It is critical to execute these operations in a proper order:

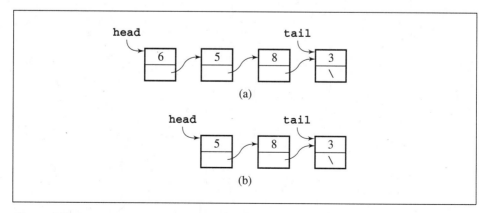

Figure 3.6: **Deleting a node at the beginning of a singly linked list.**

since **delete** has to be executed before **return**, temporary variables are used so as not to lose access to the node being deleted and to the information retrieved from it. If we take a shortcut and execute **delete head**, then access to the rest of the list is lost. If we execute **delete tmp** without retaining the number stored in it, the number is not returned.

Unlike before, there are two special cases to consider. One case is when we attempt to delete a node from an empty linked list. In this implementation, 0 is returned. This may not be a satisfactory solution if 0 can be stored on the list as a value. How do we know that the 0 returned is the sign of failure and not a 0 retrieved from the list? To avoid confusion, the method **IsEmpty()** is later added to the **SinglyLinkedList** class (see the Chapter 3 case study) and is used as follows:

```
if (!list.IsEmpty())
    n = list.RemoveFromHead();
else do not delete;
```

The second special case in **RemoveFromHead()** is when the list has only one node to be deleted. In this case, the list becomes empty, which requires setting **tail** to null.

Deleting a node from the end of the list is the most complex operation discussed so far. The problem is that after deleting the node, **tail** should point to the new tail of the list; that is, **tail** has to be moved backward by one node. But moving backward is impossible, since there is no direct link from the last node to its predecessor. Hence, this predecessor has to be found by searching from the beginning of the list and stopping right before **tail**. This is accomplished by using a temporary pointer that scans the list within the **for** loop (Figure 3.7a,b). After the predecessor is reached, appropriate changes are made to the list (Figure 3.7c). Note that the **next** field of the predecessor, which is becoming the last node in the list, has to be set to null to indicate the end of the list. If it is not done, a dangling reference problem occurs leading inevitably, although not immediately, to a program crash.

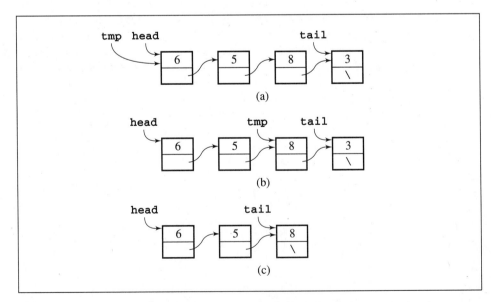

Figure 3.7: **Deleting a node from the end of a singly linked list.**

In deleting the last node there are also two special cases. If the list is empty, then nothing can be deleted and 0 is returned. The second case is when a single-node list becomes empty after deletion, which requires setting **head** to null.

The foregoing discussion emphasized the operations on pointers. However, a linked list is built for the sake of storing and processing information, not for the sake of itself. Therefore, the approach used in this section is limited in that the list can only store integers. If we want a linked list for, say, float numbers or arrays of numbers, then a new class must be declared with a new set of methods, all of them resembling the ones discussed here. It is more advantageous to declare such a class only once without deciding in advance what type of data will be stored in it.

This leads us to the use of templates in declaring a generic class for linked lists. In declaring such a class, all the methods are generalized in that the user has to instantiate such a class by supplying the type of information stored in the **info** field. An example of such generalization is stored in the header file **genSLLst.h**. For the contents of this file, see the case study at the end of this chapter. Note that not all methods from **intSLLst.h** (Figure 3.3) have their counterparts in **genSLLst.h** and that the linked list implemented there does not use a pointer **tail**. Also note that in generalizing our methods, the equality operator, **==**, and the output operator, **<<**, have to be generalized as well. However, this simply cannot be done, since these operators can only be overloaded if we know exactly the types of operands used with these operators. In creating generic functions this is exactly the type of information we do not possess and we do not want to include; after all, we are generalizing. Therefore, the user of this header file must define the new meanings of these two operators by overloading them.

■ 3.3 DOUBLY LINKED LISTS

The method **RemoveFromTail()** indicates a problem inherent to singly linked lists. The nodes in such lists contain only pointers to the successors; therefore, there is no immediate access to the predecessors. For this reason, **RemoveFromTail()** was implemented with a loop which allowed us to find the predecessor of **tail**. Although this predecessor is, so to say, within sight, it is out of reach. We have to scan the entire list to stop right in front of **tail** to delete it. For long lists and for frequent executions of **RemoveFromTail()**, this may be an impediment to swift list processing. To avoid this problem, the linked list is redefined so that each node in the list has two pointer fields, one to the successor and one to the predecessor. A list of this type is called a *doubly linked list* and is illustrated in Figure 3.8. Figure 3.9 contains a declaration for a generic **DoublyLinkedList** class.

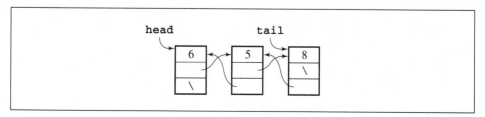

Figure 3.8: **A doubly linked list.**

```
//*************************  genDLLst.h  **************************
//                   generic doubly linked list class

#ifndef DOUBLY_LINKED_LIST
#define DOUBLY_LINKED_LIST

#include <iostream.h>

template<class genClass>
class DoublyLinkedList {
public:
    DoublyLinkedList()  { head = tail = 0;  }
    int IsEmpty() const { return head == 0; }
    void SetToNull()    { head = tail = 0;  }
    void AddToDLListHead(const genClass&);
    void AddToDLListTail(const genClass&);
    genClass* RemoveFromDLListHead();
    genClass* RemoveFromDLListTail();
    void PrintAll(ostream& out) const;
    genClass* Find(const genClass&) const;
protected:
    struct ElNode {
        genClass info;
        ElNode *next, *prev;
        ElNode(genClass el, ElNode *n = 0, ElNode *p = 0)
            { info = el; next = n; prev = p; }
    } *head, *tail, *tmp;
    genClass el;
};

template<class genClass>
void
DoublyLinkedList<genClass>::AddToDLListHead(const genClass& el)
{
    if (head) {
        head = new ElNode(el,head,0);
        head->next->prev = head;
    }
    else head = tail = new ElNode(el);
}
```

Figure 3.9: **An implementation of a doubly linked list.**   **continued**

```
template<class genClass>
void
DoublyLinkedList<genClass>::AddToDLListTail(const genClass& el)
{
    if (tail) {
        tail = new ElNode(el,0,tail);
        tail->prev->next = tail;
    }
    else head = tail = new ElNode(el);
}


template<class genClass>
genClass*
DoublyLinkedList<genClass>::RemoveFromDLListHead()
{
    if (head) {                 // if nonempty list;
        el = head->info;
        if (head == tail) { // if only one record on the list;
            delete head;
            head = tail = 0;
        }
        else {                  // if more than one record in the list;
            head = head->next;
            delete head->prev;
            head->prev = 0;
        }
        return &el;
    }
    else return 0;
}


template<class genClass>
genClass*
DoublyLinkedList<genClass>::RemoveFromDLListTail()
{
    if (tail) {                 // if nonempty list;
        el = tail->info;
        if (head == tail) { // if only one record on the list;
            delete head;
            head = tail = 0;
        }
```

Figure 3.9: **An implementation of a doubly linked list.**   **continued**

```
            else {                    // if more than one record in the list;
                  tail = tail->prev;
                  delete tail->next;
                  tail->next = 0;
            }
            return &el;
      }
      else return 0;
}


template<class genClass>
void
DoublyLinkedList<genClass>::PrintAll(ostream& out) const
{   ElNode *tmp;

      for (tmp = head; tmp; tmp = tmp->next)
          out << tmp->info << ' ';
}


template<class genClass>
genClass*
DoublyLinkedList<genClass>::Find(const genClass& el) const
{   ElNode *tmp;

      for (tmp = head; tmp && !(tmp->info == el);   // overloaded ==
                      tmp = tmp->next);
      if (!tmp)
            return 0;
      else return &tmp->info;
}

#endif
```

Figure 3.9: **An implementation of a doubly linked list.**

Methods for processing doubly linked lists are slightly more complicated than for singly linked lists, since there is one more pointer field to be maintained. There are two major methods for processing a doubly linked list. The code to insert a node at the end of a doubly linked list and to delete a node at the end are in Figure 3.9 and illustrated in Figures 3.10 and 3.11. Note that now, no loop is needed to make such a deletion. Methods for operating at the beginning of the doubly linked list are easily obtained from these two by changing **head** to **tail** and vice versa, changing **next** to **predecessor** and vice versa, and exchanging the order of parameters when executing **new**.

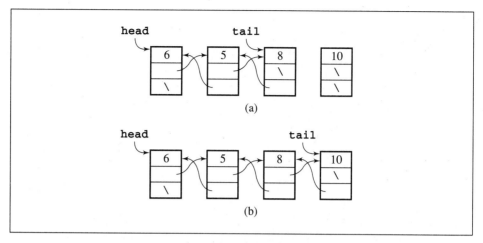

Figure 3.10: **Adding a new node at the end of a doubly linked list.**

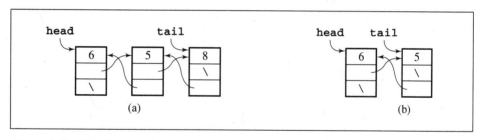

Figure 3.11: **Deleting a node from the end of a doubly linked list.**

■ 3.4 CIRCULAR LISTS

In some situations a *circular list* is needed in which nodes form a ring: the list is finite and each node has a successor. An example of such a situation is when several processes are using the same resource for the same amount of time, and we have to assure that no process accesses the resource before all other processes did. Therefore, all processes—let their numbers be 6, 5, 8, and 10 as in Figure 3.12d—are put on a circular list accessible through the pointer **current**. After one node of the list is accessed and the process number is retrieved from the node to activate this process, **current** moves to the next node so that the next time, the next process can be activated.

Implementing a circular list depends strongly on the purpose for which it is designated. In the example of a list of processes, the main operation is to advance **current** after each node access. Nodes are inserted once and then the list remains the same. Therefore, we may use a singly linked circular list. However, if the order of incoming data must be preserved on the list, as illustrated in Figure 3.12a–d, then the insertion method uses a loop to access the predecessor of **current**. But if the order of the data in the list does not matter, as in Figure 3.13, insertion can be implemented without a loop.

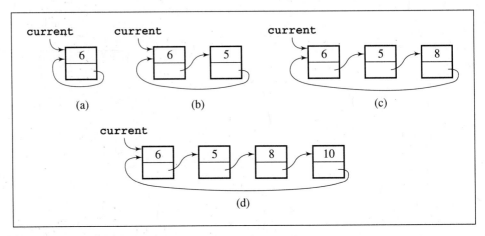

Figure 3.12: **Including nodes in a circular singly linked list.**

If the order of data needs to be preserved and the list is used for frequent insertion and deletion, then using a loop in implementation should be avoided. In this case, use a doubly linked circular list (Figure 3.14).

■ 3.5 SKIP LISTS

Linked lists have one serious drawback: they require sequential scanning to locate an element searched for. The search starts from the beginning of the list and stops when either an element searched for is found or the end of the list is reached without finding this element. Ordering elements on the list can speed up searching, but sequential search is still required. Therefore, we may think about lists which would allow for skipping certain nodes

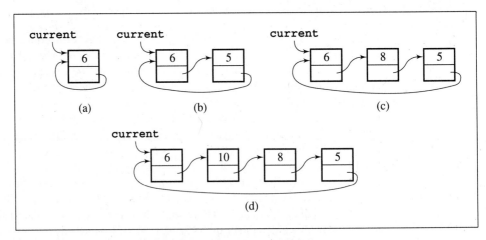

Figure 3.13: **Another way of including nodes in a circular list.**

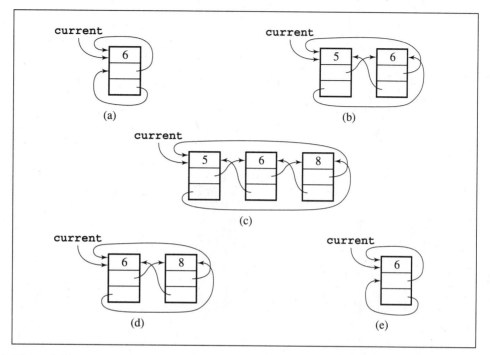

Figure 3.14: **Including (a–c) and deleting (d–e) nodes in a circular doubly-
linked list.**

to avoid sequential processing. A *skip list* is an interesting variant of the ordered linked list
which makes such a non-sequential search possible (Pugh 1990).

In a skip list of n nodes, for each k and i such that $1 \leq k \leq \lfloor \lg n \rfloor$ and $1 \leq i \leq \lfloor \frac{n}{k} \rfloor - 1$,
the node in position $k \cdot i$ points to the node in position $k \cdot (i + 1)$. This means that every
second node points to the node two positions ahead, every fourth node points to the node four
positions ahead, etc., as shown in Figure 3.15a. This is accomplished by having different
numbers of pointer fields in nodes on the list: half of the nodes have just one pointer field,
one-fourth of the nodes have two pointer fields, one-eighth of the nodes have three pointer
fields, and so on. The number of pointer fields indicates the *level* of each node and the
number of levels is $MaxLevel = \lfloor \lg n \rfloor + 1$.

Searching for an element consists of following the pointers in descending order and
then trying the links of the lower order after passing over the element searched for. For
example, to look for number 16 in the list in Figure 3.15a, we try the level four first, which
is unsuccessful, since the first node on this level has number 22. Next we try the third level
list starting from the root: it first leads to number 10, then again to number 22. Then we
try the second level list starting from the node holding number 10: it leads to number 17.
The last try starts at the first level list which begins in node 10: the first node of this list
has number 12 and the next node has number 17. Since there is no lower level, the search
is pronounced unsuccessful. Figure 3.16 contains the code for this search procedure.

Searching appears to be efficient, which would be more convincing for large lists.
However, the design of skip lists can lead to very inefficient insertion and deletion

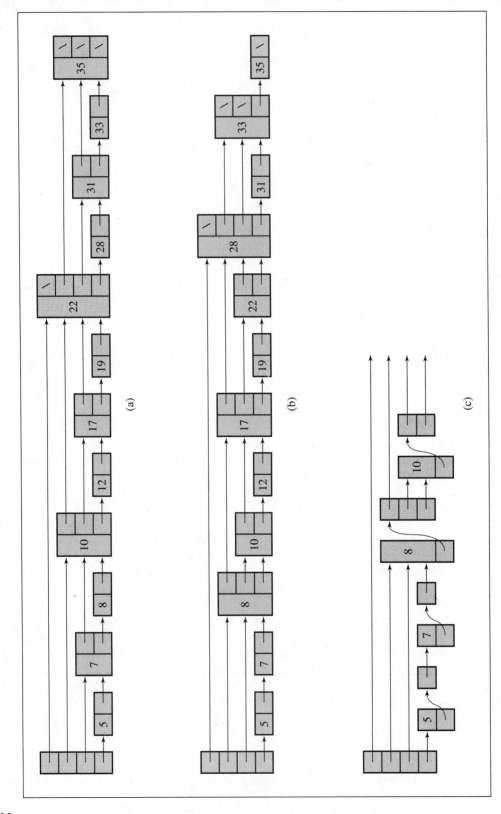

Figure 3.15: A skip list with (a) evenly and (b) unevenly spaced nodes of different levels; (c) the skip list with pointer nodes clearly shown.

```
//************************  genSkipL.h  **************************
//                    generic skip list class

const int maxLevel = 4;

template<class genElem>
class SkipList {
public:
      SkipList();
      void ChoosePowers();
      int  ChooseLevel();
      nodePtr SkipListSearch(genElem);
      void SkipListInsert(genElem);
private:
      struct Node {
            genElem key;
            Node **next;
      };
      typedef struct Node *nodePtr;
      nodePtr root[maxLevel];
      int powers[maxLevel], i;
};

SkipList<genElem>::SkipList()
{
    for (i = 0; i < maxLevel; i++)
        root[i] = 0;
}


void
SkipList<genElem>::ChoosePowers()
{  int i, j;

   powers[maxLevel-1] = maxLevel * maxLevel - 1;
   for (i = maxLevel - 2, j = 1; i >= 0; i--, j++)
       powers[i] = powers[i+1] - j * j;
}
```

Figure 3.16: **An implementation of a skip list.**   **continued**

```
int
SkipList<genElem>::ChooseLevel()
{   int i, r = rand() % powers[maxLevel-1] + 1;


    for (i = 1; i < maxLevel; i++)
        if (r < powers[i])
                return i-1; // return a level < the highest level;
    return i-1;             // return the highest level;
}


SkipList<genElem>::nodePtr
SkipList<genElem>::SkipListSearch (genElem key)
{   nodePtr prev, curr;
    int lvl;
                                              // find the highest non-null
    for (lvl = maxLevel-1; !root[lvl] && lvl >= 0; lvl--);    // level;
    for (prev = curr = root[lvl]; curr && lvl >= 0; ) {
        if (key == curr->key)                     // success if equal;
            return curr;
        else if (key < curr->key) {               // if smaller, go down
            if (curr == root[lvl])                // by one level
                curr = root[--lvl];               // starting from the
            else curr = *(prev->next + --lvl); // predecessor which
        }                                         // can be the root;
        else {                                    // if greater,
            prev = curr;                          // go to the next
            if (*(curr->next + lvl) != 0)         // nonnull node
                curr = *(curr->next + lvl);       // on the same level
            else curr = *(curr->next + --lvl); // or to the list on
        }                                         // lower level;
    }
    return 0;
}


void
SkipList<genElem>::SkipListInsert (genElem key)
{   nodePtr curr[maxLevel], prev[maxLevel];
    nodePtr newNode = new Node;
    int lvl, i;
```

Figure 3.16: **An implementation of a skip list.**   **continued**

```
curr[maxLevel-1] = root[maxLevel-1];
prev[maxLevel-1] = 0;
for (lvl = maxLevel - 1; lvl >= 0; lvl--) {
    while (curr[lvl] && curr[lvl]->key < key) { // go to the next
        prev[lvl] = curr[lvl];                  // if smaller;
        curr[lvl] = *(curr[lvl]->next + lvl);
    }
    if (lvl > 0)                            // go one level down
        if (prev[lvl] == 0) {               // if not the lowest
            curr[lvl-1] = root[lvl-1];      // level, using a link
            prev[lvl-1] = 0;                // either from the root
        }
        else {                              // or from the predecessor;
            curr[lvl-1] = *(prev[lvl]->next + lvl-1);
            prev[lvl-1] = prev[lvl];
        }
}
lvl = ChooseLevel();        // generate randomly level for newNode;
newNode->next = new nodePtr[sizeof(nodePtr) * (lvl+1)];
newNode->key  = key;
for (i = 0; i <= lvl; i++) {        // initialize next fields of
    *(newNode->next + i) = curr[i]; // newNode and reset to newNode
    if (prev[i] == 0)               // either fields of the root
        root[i] = newNode;          // or next fields of newNode's
    else *(prev[i]->next + i) = newNode; // predecessors;
}
}
```

Figure 3.16: **An implementation of a skip list.**

procedures. To insert a new element, all nodes following the node just inserted have to be restructured; the number of pointer fields and the value of pointers have to be changed. In order to retain some of the advantages which skip lists offer with respect to searching and avoid problems with restructuring the lists when inserting and deleting nodes, the requirement on the positions of nodes of different levels is now abandoned and only the requirement on the number of nodes of different levels is kept. For example, the list in Figure 3.15a becomes the list in Figure 3.15b: both lists have six nodes in level one, three nodes in level two, two nodes in level three and one node in level four. The new list is searched exactly the same way as the original list. Inserting does not require a list restructuring, and nodes are generated so that the distribution of the nodes on different levels is kept adequate. How can this be accomplished?

Assume that *MaxLevel* = 4. For fifteen elements, the required number of nodes on level one is 8, on level two is 4, on level three is 2, and in level one is 1. Each time a node is inserted, a random number r between 1 and 15 is generated, and if $r < 9$, then a node of level one is inserted. If $r < 13$, a second-level node is inserted, if $r < 15$, it is a third-level node, and if $r = 15$, the node of level four is generated and inserted. If *MaxLevel* = 5, then for 31 elements the correspondence between the value of r and the level of node is as follows:

r	Level of node to be inserted
31	5
29 – 30	4
25 – 28	3
17 – 24	2
1 – 16	1

To determine such a correspondence between r and the level of node for any *MaxLevel*, the function **ChoosePowers()** initializes the array **powers[]** by putting lower bounds for each range. For example, for *MaxLevel* = 4, the array is [1 9 13 15] and for *MaxLevel* = 5 it is [1 17 25 29 31]. **ChooseLevel()** uses **powers[]** to determine the level of the node about to be inserted. Figure 3.16 contains the code for **ChoosePowers()** and **ChooseLevel()**. Note that the levels range between 0 and *MaxLevel*−1 (and not between 1 and *MaxLevel*) so that the array indexes can be used as levels. For example, the first level is level zero.

But we also have to address the question of implementing a node. The easiest way is to make each node have *MaxLevel* pointer fields, but this is wasteful. We need only as many pointer fields per one node as the level of the node requires. To accomplish this, the **next** field of each node is not a pointer to the next node, but to an array of pointer(s) to the next node(s). The size of this array is determined by the level of the node. The **Node** and a **SkipList** class encompassing it are declared as in Figure 3.16. In this way, the list in Figure 3.15b is really a list whose first four nodes are shown in Figure 3.15c.

Only now can an inserting procedure be implemented, as in Figure 3.16.

How efficient are skip lists? In the ideal situation, which is exemplified by the list in Figure 3.15a, the search time is $O(\lg n)$. In the worst situation, when all lists are on the same level, the skip list turns into a regular singly linked list, and the search time is $O(n)$. However, the latter situation is unlikely to occur; in the random skip list the search time is of the same order, as in the best case, that is, $O(\lg n)$. This is an improvement over the efficiency of search in regular linked lists. It also turns out that skip lists fare extremely well in comparison with more sophisticated data structures, such as self-adjusting trees or AVL trees (cf. Sections 6.7.3, 6.8), and therefore they are a viable alternative to these data structures (see also the table in Figure 3.19, p. 51).

■ 3.6 SELF-ORGANIZING LISTS

The introduction of skip lists was motivated by the need to speed up the searching process. Although singly and doubly linked lists require sequential search to locate an element or to see that it is not in the list, we can improve the efficiency of the search by dynamically organizing the list in a certain manner. This organization depends on the configuration of data; the stream of data requires reorganizing the nodes already on the list. There are many different ways to organize the lists, and this section describes four of them.

1. *Move-to-front method.* After the desired element is located, put it at the beginning of the list.
2. *Transpose method.* After the desired element is located, swap it with its predecessor unless it is at the head of the list.
3. *Count method.* Order the list by the number of times elements are being accessed.
4. *Ordering method.* Order the list using certain criteria natural for information under scrutiny.

In the first three methods, new information is stored in a node added to the end of the list; in the fourth method, new information is stored in a node inserted somewhere in the list to maintain the order of the list. An example of searching for elements in a list organized by these different methods is shown in Figure 3.17.

With the first three methods, we try to locate the elements most likely to be looked for near the beginning of the list, most explicitly with the move-to-front method, and most cautiously with the transpose method. The ordering method already uses some properties inherent to the information stored in the list. For example, if we are storing nodes pertaining to people, then the list can be organized alphabetically by the name of the person or the city, or in an ascending or descending order using, say, birthday or salary. This is particularly advantageous when searching for information which is not in the list, since the search can terminate without scanning the entire list. Searching all the nodes of the list, however, is necessary in such cases using the other three methods. The count method can be subsumed in the category of the ordering methods if frequency is part of the information. In many cases, however, the count itself is an additional piece of information required solely to maintain the list; hence it may not be considered "natural" to the information at hand.

Analyses of the efficiency of these methods customarily compare their efficiency to that of *optimal static ordering*. With this ordering, all the data are already ordered by the frequency of their occurrence in the body of data, so that the list is used only for searching, not for inserting new items. Therefore, this approach requires two passes through the body of data, one to build the list and another to use the list for search alone.

To measure the efficiency of these methods, the number of all actual comparisons was compared to the maximum number of possible comparisons. The latter number is calculated by adding the lengths of the list at the moment of processing each element. For example, in the table in Figure 3.18, the body of data contains fourteen letters, five of them being different, which means that fourteen letters were processed. The length of the list before processing each letter is recorded, and the result, $0 + 1 + 2 + 3 + 3 + 4 + 4 + 4 + 4 + 4 + 4 + 4 + 4 + 5 = 46$, is used to compare the number of all made comparisons to this combined length. In this way we know what percentage of the list was scanned during the entire process. For all the list organizing methods except for optimal ordering, this combined length is the same; only the number of comparisons can change. For example, when using the move-to-front technique for the data in the table in Figure 3.18, 33 comparisons were made, which is 71.7% when compared to 46. This is the worst possible case, the combined length of intermediate lists every time all the nodes in the list are looked at. Plain search, with no reorganization, required only 30 comparisons, which is 65.2%.

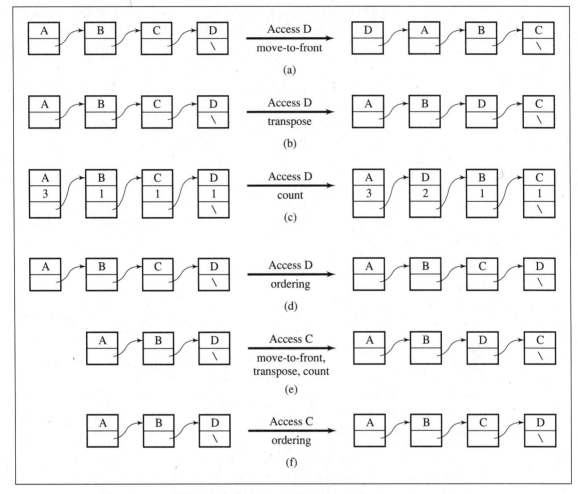

Figure 3.17: **Accessing an element on a linked list and changes on the list depicting on the self-organization technique applied: (a) move-to-front method, (b) transpose method, (c) count method, and (d) ordering method, in particular, alphabetical ordering which leads to no change. In the case when the desired element is not in the list, (e) the first three methods add a new node with this element at the end of the list and (f) the ordering method maintains an order on the list.**

These samples are in agreement with theoretical analyses which indicate that count and move-to-front methods are in the long run at most twice as costly as the optimal static ordering; the transpose method approaches, in the long run, the cost of the move-to-front method. However, it is difficult to establish more precise relations, since the efficiency of these methods depends on the distribution of data, in what order and with what frequency they arrive.

Element searched for	Plain	Move-to-front	Transpose	Count	Ordering
A:	A	A	A	A	A
C:	A C	A C	A C	A C	A C
B:	A C B	A C B	A C B	A C B	A B C
C:	A C B	C A B	C A B	C A B	A B C
D:	A C B D	C A B D	C A B D	C A B D	A B C D
A:	A C B D	C A B D	C A B D	C A B D	A B C D
D:	A C B D	D A C B	A C D B	D C A B	A B C D
A:	A C B D	A D C B	A C D B	A D C B	A B C D
C:	A C B D	C A D B	C A D B	C A D B	A B C D
A:	A C B D	A C D B	A C D B	A C D B	A B C D
C:	A C B D	C A D B	C A D B	A C D B	A B C D
C:	A C B D	C A D B	C A D B	C A D B	A B C D
E:	A C B D E	C A D B E	C A D B E	C A D B E	A B C D E
E:	A C B D E	E C A D B	C A D E B	C A E D B	A B C D E

Figure 3.18: **Processing the stream of data, A C B C D A D A C A C C E E, by different methods of organizing linked lists. Linked lists are presented in an abbreviated form, for example, the transformation shown in Figure 3.17a is abbreviated as transforming list A B C D into list D A B C.**

Figure 3.19 contains sample runs of the self-organizing lists. The first two columns of numbers refer to files containing programs and the remaining columns refer to files containing English text. Except for alphabetical ordering, all methods improve their efficiency with the size of the file. The move-to-front and count methods are almost the same in their efficiency and both of them outperform the transpose, plain, and ordering methods. The poor performance for smaller files is due to the fact that all of the methods are busy including new words to the lists, which requires an exhaustive search of the lists. Later, the methods concentrate on organizing the lists to reduce the number of searches. The table in Figure 3.19 includes also data for a skip list. There is an overwhelming difference between the skip list's efficiency compared to the other methods. However, keep in mind that in the table in Figure 3.19, only comparisons of data are included with no indication of the other operations needed for execution of the analyzed methods. In particular, there is no indication of how many pointers are used and relinked, which, when included, may make the difference between various methods less dramatic.

Different words/All words	149/423	550/2847	156/347	609/1510	1163/5866	2013/23065
optimal	26.4	17.6	28.5	24.5	16.2	10.0
plain	71.2	56.3	70.3	67.1	51.7	35.4
move to front	49.5	31.3	61.3	54.5	30.5	18.4
transpose	69.5	53.3	68.8	66.1	49.4	32.9
count	51.6	34.0	61.2	54.7	32.0	19.8
alphabetical order	45.6	55.7	50.9	48.0	50.4	50.0
skip list	12.3	5.5	15.1	6.6	4.8	3.8

Figure 3.19: **Comparison of run times (given in milliseconds) of different methods to organize linked lists.**

These sample runs show that for lists of modest size, the linked list would suffice. With the increase in the amount of data and in the frequency with which they have to be accessed, more sophisticated methods and data structures need to be used.

■ 3.7 SPARSE TABLES

In many applications, the choice of a table seems to be the most natural one, but space considerations may preclude this choice. This is particularly true if only a small fraction of the table is actually used. A table of this type is called a *sparse table* since the table is populated sparsely by data and most of its cells are empty. In this case, the table can be replaced by a system of linked lists.

As an example, consider the problem of storing grades for all students in a university for a certain semester. Assume that there are 8,000 students and 300 classes. A natural implementation is a two-dimensional array *grades* where student numbers are indexes of the columns and class numbers the indexes of the rows (see Figure 3.20). An association of student names and numbers is represented by the one-dimensional array *students* and an association of class names and numbers by the array *classes*. The names do not have to be ordered. If order is required, then another array can be used where each array element is occupied by a record with two fields, name and number,[1] or the original array can be sorted each time an order is required. This, however, would lead to the constant reorganization of *grades*, and is not recommended.

Each cell of *grades* stores a grade obtained by each student after finishing a class. If signed grades such as A−, B+, or C+ are used, then two bytes are required to store each grade. To reduce the table size by one-half, the array *GradeCodes* in Figure 3.20c associates each grade with a letter which requires only one byte of storage.

The entire table (Figure 3.20d) occupies 8,000 students · 300 students · 1 byte = 2.4 million bytes. This table is very large but is sparsely populated by grades. Assuming that, on the average, students take four classes a semester, each column of the table has only four cells occupied by grades, and the rest of the cells, 296 cells or 98.7%, are unoccupied and wasted.

A better solution is to use two 2-dimensional arrays. *ClassesTaken* represents all the classes taken by every student and *StudentsInClasses* represents all students participating in each class (see Figure 3.21). A cell of each table is a record with two fields: student or class number and a grade. We assume that a student can take at most eight classes and that there can be at most 250 students signed up for a class. We need two arrays, since with only one array it would be very time-consuming to produce lists. For example, if only *ClassesTaken* is used, then printing a list of all students taking a particular class requires an exhaustive search of *ClassesTaken*.

Assume that the computer on which this program is being implemented requires two bytes to store an integer. With this new structure, three bytes are needed for each cell. Therefore, *ClassesTaken* occupies 8,000 students · 8 classes · 3 bytes = 192,000 bytes, *StudentsInClasses* occupies 300 classes · 250 students · 3 bytes = 225,000 bytes, and both ta-

---

[1]This is called an *index-inverted table*.

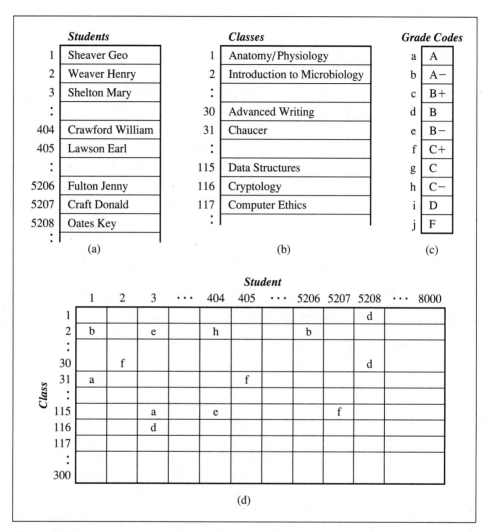

Figure 3.20: **Arrays and sparse table used for storing student grades.**

bles require a total of 417,000 bytes, less than one-fifth of the number of bytes required for the sparse table in Figure 3.20.

Although this is a much better implementation than before, it still suffers from a wasteful use of space; seldom if ever will both arrays be full since most classes have less than 250 students and most students take less than eight classes. This structure is also inflexible: if a class can be taken by more than 250 students, a problem occurs which has to be circumvented in an artificial way. One way is to create a nonexistent class which holds students from the overflowing class. Another way is to recompile the program with a new table size, which may not be practical at a future time. Another, more flexible, solution is needed that uses space frugally.

Classes Taken

	1	2	3	...	404	405	...	5206	5207	5208	...	8000
1	2 b	30 f	2 e		2 h	31 f		2 b	115 f	1 d		
2	31 a		115 a		115 e	64 f		33 b	121 a	30 d		
3	124 g		116 d		218 b	120 a		86 c	146 b	208 a		
4	136 g				221 b			121 d	156 b	211 b		
5					285 h			203 a		234 d		
6					292 b							
7												
8												

(a)

Students in Classes

	1	2	...	30	31	...	115	116	...	300
1	5208 d	1 b		2 f	1 a		3 a	3 d		
2		3 e		5208 d	405 f		404 e			
3		404 h					5207 f			
4		5206 b								
:										
250										

(b)

Figure 3.21: **Two-dimensional arrays for storing student grades.**

Two one-dimensional arrays of linked lists can be used as in Figure 3.22. Each cell of the array *class* is a pointer to a linked list of students taking a class, and each cell of the array *student* indicates a linked list of classes taken by a student. The linked lists contain records of five fields: student number, class number, grade, a pointer to the next student, and a pointer to the next class. Assuming that each pointer requires only two bytes, one record occupies nine bytes, and the entire structure can be stored in 8,000 students $*$ 4 classes (on the average) $*$ 9 bytes $= 288,000$ bytes, which is approximately 10% of the space required for the first implementation and about 70% of the space of the second. No space is used unnecessarily, there is no restriction imposed on the number of students per class, and the lists of students taking a class can be printed immediately.

3.8 CONCLUDING REMARKS

Linked lists have been introduced to overcome limitations of arrays by allowing dynamic allocation of necessary amounts of memory. Also, linked lists allow easy insertion and deletion of new information, since such operations have a local impact on the list. To insert a new element at the beginning of an array, all elements in the array have to be shifted to

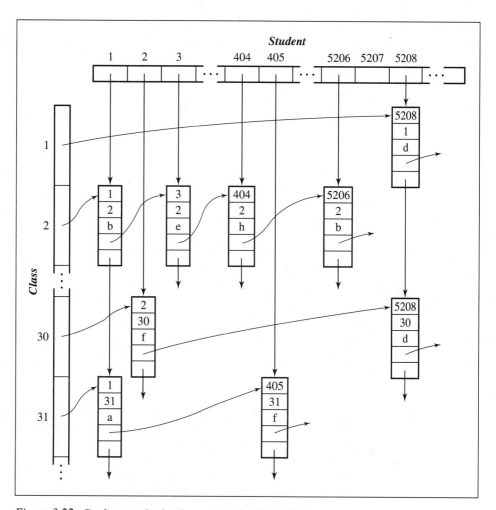

Figure 3.22: **Student grades implemented using linked lists.**

make room for the new item; hence insertion has a global impact on the array. Deletion is the same. So should we always use linked lists instead of arrays?

Arrays have some advantages over linked lists, namely that they allow random accessing. To access the tenth node in a linked list, all nine preceding nodes have to be passed. In the array, we can go to the tenth cell immediately. Therefore, if an immediate access of any element is necessary, then an array is a better choice. This was the case with binary search and it will be the case with most sorting algorithms (see Chapter 9). But if we are constantly accessing only some elements—the first, the second, the last, and the like—and if changing the structure is the core of an algorithm, then using a linked list is a better option. A good example is a queue which is discussed in the next chapter.

Another advantage in the use of arrays is space. To hold items in arrays, the cells have to be of the size of the items. In linked lists, we store one item per node and the node also includes at least one pointer field; in doubly linked lists, the node contains two pointer fields. For large linked lists, a significant amount of memory is needed to store the pointers. Therefore, if a problem does not require many shifts of data, then having an oversized array may not be wasteful at all if its size is compared to the amount of space needed for the linked structure storing the same data as the array.

■ 3.9 CASE STUDY: A LIBRARY

This case study is a program that can be used in a small library to include new books in the library, to check out books to people, and to return them.

As this program is a practice in the use of linked lists, almost everything is implemented in terms of such lists. But in order to make the program more interesting, it uses linked lists of linked lists that also contain cross references (see Figure 3.23).

First, there could be a list including all authors of all books in the library. However, searching through such a list can be time-consuming, so the search can be sped up by choosing at least one of the two following strategies:

- The list can be ordered alphabetically, and the search can be interrupted if we find the name, if we encounter an author's name greater than the one we are searching for, or we reach the end of list.
- We can use an array of pointers to the author structures and indexed with letters; each slot of the array points to the linked list of authors whose names start with the same letter.

The best strategy is to combine both approaches. However, in this case study only the second approach is used, and the reader is urged to amplify the program by adding the first approach.

Because we can have several books by the same author, one field of the author structure is a pointer to the list of books of this author that can be found in the library.

Second, we have a linked list **people** of persons who have used the library at least once. Since each person can check out several books, the person structure contains a field pointing to the list of books currently checked out by this person. This fact is indicated by setting the **PersonNode** field of the book being checked out to point to the structure of person who is taking the book out.

Third, books can be returned, and that fact is indicated by deleting the appropriate **CheckedOutBookNode** from the list of the checked out books of the person who returns them. The pointer of the **PersonNode** field in the structure of the book that is being returned has to be reset to null.

Four types of structures are defined: **AuthorNode**, **BookNode**, **PersonNode**, and **CheckedOutBookNode**. To avoid writing a separate set of functions for four different types of linked lists, the header file **genSLLst.h** includes a generic linked list class. The program defines four classes corresponding with the four structures: **Author**, **Book**, **Person**, and **CheckedOutBook**. Since member functions in this file rely on overloading the operators == and <<, four pairs of definitions also have to be included in this program. The rest is rather simple and the simplicity of the program is reflected in its size.

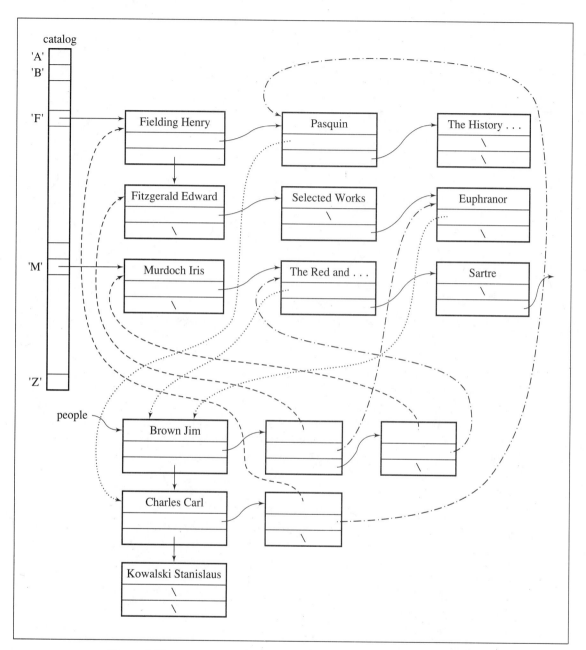

Figure 3.23: **Linked lists indicating the library status.**

A menu is printed at the beginning and the user can choose one of the following five operations: including a book, checking a book out, returning it, showing the current status of the library, and exiting the program. The status for the example shown in Figure 3.23 results in the following output:

```
      Library has the following books:

      Fielding Henry
            * Pasquin - checked out to Charles Carl
            * The History of Tom Jones
      Fitzgerald Edward
            * Selected Works
            * Euphranor - checked out to Brown Jim
      Murdoch Iris
            * The Red and the Green - checked out to Brown Jim
            * Sartre
            * The Bell


      The following people are using the library:

      Brown Jim has the following books
            * Fitzgerald Edward, Euphranor
            * Murdoch Iris, The Red and the Green
      Charles Carl has the following books
            * Fielding Henry, Pasquin
      Kowalski Stanislaus has no books
```

Note that the diagram in Figure 3.23 is somewhat simplified, since strings are not stored directly in structures, only pointers to strings. Hence, technically, each name and title should be shown outside structures with links leading to them. Figure 3.24 contains the code for the library program.

```
//*********************  genSLLst.h  ****************************
//        generic singly linked list class with head only

#ifndef SINGLY_LINKED_LIST
#define SINGLY_LINKED_LIST

template<class genType>
class SinglyLinkedList {
    struct Node {
        genType info;
        Node *next;
        Node() { }
        Node(genType el, Node *ptr = 0)
```

Figure 3.24: **The library program.**   **continued**

```
                        { info = el; next = ptr; }
        } *head, *tmp;
        genType el;
public:
        SinglyLinkedList()  { head = 0; }
        ~SinglyLinkedList() { Clear();  }
        void Clear();
        void SetToNull()      { head = 0; }
        void PrintAll(ostream& out) const;
        genType* Find(const genType&) const;
        void Add(const genType& el) { head = new Node(el,head); }
        genType* Remove();            // remove the head and return its info;
        void Remove(genType&);        // find a node and remove it;
        int IsEmpty() const           { return head == 0;    }
        genType* First()              { return &head->info; }
        Node* Head()                  { return head;        }
};



template<class genType>
void
SinglyLinkedList<genType>::Clear()
{
    while (head) {
        tmp = head;
        head = head->next;
        delete tmp;
    }
}


template<class genType>
genType*
SinglyLinkedList<genType>::Remove()
{
    if (head) {                    // if nonempty list;
        el = head->info;
        tmp = head;
        head = head->next;
        delete tmp;
```

Figure 3.24: **The library program.**   **continued**

```
            return &el;
        }
        else return 0;
    }


    template<class genType>
    void
    SinglyLinkedList<genType>::PrintAll(ostream& out) const
    {   Node *tmp;

        for (tmp = head; tmp; tmp = tmp->next)
            out << tmp->info << " ";                    // overloaded <<
    }


    template<class genType>
    genType*
    SinglyLinkedList<genType>::Find(const genType& el) const
    {   Node *tmp;

        for (tmp = head; tmp && !(tmp->info == el);  // overloaded ==
                            tmp = tmp->next);
        if (!tmp)
            return 0;
        else return &(tmp->info);
    }


    template<class genType>
    void
    SinglyLinkedList<genType>::Remove(genType& el)
    {
        if (head)                    // if nonempty list;
            if (el == head->info) { // if head needs to be removed;
                Node *pred = head;
                head = head->next;
                delete pred;
            }
            else {
                Node *pred;
                for (pred = head, tmp = head->next; // non-head
```

Figure 3.24: **The library program.**   **continued**

```
                              tmp && !(tmp->info == el);      // is deleted;
                              pred = pred->next, tmp = tmp->next);
                    if (tmp) {  // if found
                              pred->next = tmp->next;
                              delete tmp;
                    }
              }
      }

      #endif


      //************************* library.cpp *************************

      #include <iostream.h>
      #include <string.h>
      #include <ctype.h>
      #include "genSLLst.h"

      struct PersonNode;                // forward declarations;
      struct AuthorNode;
      struct BookNode;

      struct CheckedOutBookNode {
              AuthorNode *author;
              BookNode   *book;
      };

      class CheckedOutBook : public SinglyLinkedList<CheckedOutBookNode> {
      public:
            ~CheckedOutBook() { SetToNull(); }
      };

      struct BookNode {
              char *title;
              PersonNode *person;
              BookNode() { person = 0; }
              int operator== (const BookNode& bk)
                      { return strcmp(title,bk.title) == 0; }
      };
```

Figure 3.24: **The library program.**   **continued**

```
class Book : public SinglyLinkedList<BookNode> {
public:
        ~Book() { SetToNull(); }
};


struct AuthorNode {
        char *name;
        Book books;
        int operator== (const AuthorNode& ar)
                  { return strcmp(name,ar.name) == 0; }
};


class Author : public SinglyLinkedList<AuthorNode> { } catalog['Z'+1];


struct PersonNode {
        char *name;
        CheckedOutBook books;
        int operator== (const PersonNode& pn)
                  { return strcmp(name,pn.name) == 0; }
};


class Person : public SinglyLinkedList<PersonNode> {
public:
        friend void CheckOutBook();
} people;




ostream&
operator<< (ostream& out, const BookNode& bk)
{
    out << "    * " << bk.title;
    if (bk.person)
        out << " - checked out to " << bk.person->name;
    out << endl;
    return out;
}
```

Figure 3.24: **The library program.**   **continued**

```cpp
ostream&
operator<< (ostream& out, const AuthorNode& ar)
{
    out << ar.name << endl << ' ';
    ar.books.PrintAll(out);
    return out;
}


int
operator== (CheckedOutBookNode& bk1, const CheckedOutBookNode& bk2)
{
    return strcmp(bk1.book->title, bk2.book->title)  == 0 &&
           strcmp(bk1.author->name,bk2.author->name) == 0;
}


ostream&
operator<< (ostream& out, const CheckedOutBookNode& bk)
{
    out << "    * " << bk.author->name << ", "
                 << bk.book->title << endl;
    return out;
}


ostream&
operator<< (ostream& out, const PersonNode& pr)
{
    out << pr.name;
    if (!(pr.books.IsEmpty())) {
        out << " has the following books:\n ";
        pr.books.PrintAll(out);
    }
    else out << " has no books\n";
    return out;
}



char*
GetString(char *msg)
{   char s[82], i, *destin;
```

Figure 3.24: **The library program.**

continued

```
    cout << msg;
    cin.get(s,80);
    while (cin.get(s[81]) && s[81] != '\n');   // discard overflowing
    destin = new char[strlen(s)+1];            // characters;
    for (i = 0; destin[i] = toupper(s[i]); i++);
    return destin;
}


void
Status()
{   register int i;

    cout << "Library has the following books:\n\n ";
    for (i = 'A'; i <= 'Z'; i++)
        if (!catalog[i].IsEmpty())
            catalog[i].PrintAll(cout);
    cout << "\nThe following people are using the library:\n\n ";
    people.PrintAll(cout);
}


void
IncludeBook()
{   AuthorNode newAuthor, *oldAuthor;
    BookNode newBook;

    newAuthor.name = GetString("Enter author's name: ");
    newBook.title  = GetString("Enter the title of the book: ");
    oldAuthor = catalog[newAuthor.name[0]].Find(newAuthor);
    if (oldAuthor == 0) {
        newAuthor.books.Add(newBook);
        catalog[newAuthor.name[0]].Add(newAuthor);
    }
    else oldAuthor->books.Add(newBook);
}


void
CheckOutBook()
{   PersonNode person, *personRef;
    AuthorNode author, *authorRef = 0;
```

Figure 3.24: **The library program.**   **continued**

```
        BookNode    book, *bookRef = 0;
        CheckedOutBookNode bookToCheckOut;

        person.name = GetString("Enter person's name: ");
        while (!authorRef) {
            author.name = GetString("Enter author's name: ");
            if (!(authorRef = catalog[author.name[0]].Find(author)))
                cout << "Misspelled author's name\n";
        }
        while (!bookRef) {
            book.title = GetString("Enter the title of the book: ");
            if (!(bookRef = authorRef->books.Find(book)))
                cout << "Misspelled title\n";
        }
        bookToCheckOut.author = authorRef;
        bookToCheckOut.book   = bookRef;
        personRef = people.Find(person);
        if (!personRef) {          // a new person in the library;
            person.books.Add(bookToCheckOut);
            people.Add(person);
            bookRef->person = &people.head->info;
        }
        else {
            personRef->books.Add(bookToCheckOut);
            bookRef->person = personRef;
        }
    }

void
ReturnBook()
{   PersonNode person, *personRef = 0;
    CheckedOutBookNode checkedOutBook;
    BookNode book, *bookRef = 0;
    AuthorNode author, *authorRef = 0;

    while (!personRef) {
        person.name = GetString("Enter person's name: ");
        if (!(personRef = people.Find(person)))
```

Figure 3.24: **The library program.**   **continued**

```
                        cout << "Person's name misspelled\n";
    }
    while (!authorRef) {
        author.name = GetString("Enter author's name: ");
        if (!(authorRef = catalog[author.name[0]].Find(author)))
            cout << "Misspelled author's name\n";
    }
    while (!bookRef) {
        book.title = GetString("Enter the title of the book: ");
        if (!(bookRef = authorRef->books.Find(book)))
            cout << "Misspelled title\n";
    }
    checkedOutBook.author = authorRef;
    checkedOutBook.book   = bookRef;
    bookRef->person = 0;
    personRef->books.Remove(checkedOutBook);
}


Menu()
{   int option;

    cout << "\nEnter one of the following options:\n"
         << "1. Include a book in the catalog\n2. Check out a book\n"
         << "3. Return a book\n4. Status\n5. Exit\n"
         << "Your option? ";
    cin  >> option;
    cin.get();            // discard eoln;
    return option;
}


main()
{
    while (1)
        switch (Menu()) {
            case 1: IncludeBook();  break;
            case 2: CheckOutBook(); break;
            case 3: ReturnBook();   break;
            case 4: Status();       break;
            case 5: return 0;
            otherwise: cout << "Wrong option, try again: ";
        }
}
```

Figure 3.24: **The library program.**

■ 3.10 EXERCISES

1. Providing that the declarations

```
int intArray[] = {1, 2, 3}, p = intArray;
```

have been made, what will be the content of **intArray** and **p** after executing

(a) `*p++;`

(b) `(*p)++;`

(c) `*p++; (*p)++;`

2. Using only pointers (no array indexing), write

(a) A function to add all numbers in an integer array,

(b) A function to remove all odd numbers from an ordered array; the array should remain ordered. Would it be easier to write this function if the array were unordered?

3. Using pointers only, implement the following string functions:

(a) `strlen()`

(b) `strcmp()`

(c) `strcat()`

(d) `strchr()`.

4. What is the difference between `if (p == q) { ... }` and `if (*p == *q) { ... }`?

5. Assume that a circular doubly linked list has been created, as in Figure 3.25. After each of the following assignments indicate changes made in the list by showing which links have been modified.

```
list->next->next->next = list->prev;
list->prev->prev->prev = list->next->next->next->prev;
list->next->next->next->prev = list->prev->prev->prev;
list->next = list->next->next;
list->next->prev->next = list->next->next->next;
```

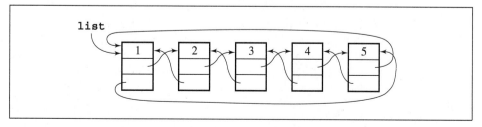

Figure 3.25: **A circular doubly linked list.**

6. How many nodes does the shortest linked list have? The longest linked list?

7. Merge two ordered singly linked lists of integers into one ordered list.

8. Delete an ith node on a linked list. Be sure that such a node exists.

9. Delete from list L_1 nodes whose positions are to be found in an ordered list L_2. For instance, if $L_1 =$ (A B C D E) and $L_2 =$ (2 4 8), then the second and the fourth nodes are to be deleted from list L_1 (the eighth node does not exist), and after deletion, $L_1 =$ (A C E).

10. Delete from list L_1 nodes occupying positions indicated in ordered lists L_2 and L_3. For instance, if $L_1 =$ (A B C D E), $L_2 =$ (2 4 8), and $L_3 =$ (2 5), then after deletion, $L_1 =$ (A C).

11. Delete from an ordered list L nodes occupying positions indicated in list L itself. For instance, if $L =$ (1 3 5 7 8), then after deletion, $L =$ (1 7).

12. A linked list does not have to be implemented with pointers. Suggest other implementations of linked lists.

13. Write a member function to check whether two singly linked lists have the same contents.

14. Write a member function to reverse a singly linked list using only one pass through the list.

15. Insert a new node into a singly linked list (a), before and (b), after a node pointed by **p** in this list (possibly the first or the last). Do not use a loop in either operation.

16. Attach a singly linked list to the end of another singly linked list.

17. Put numbers in a singly linked list in ascending order. Use this operation to find the median in the list of numbers.

18. How can a singly linked list be implemented so that insertion requires no test for whether **head** is null?

19. Write four methods for maintaining a doubly linked circular list: **AddAtCurrent()** (see Figure 3.14a,b), **AddBeforeCurrent()** (Figure 3.14b,c), **DeleteAtCurrent()** (Figure 3.14c,d), and **DeleteBeforeCurrent()** (Figure 3.14d,e).

20. How likely is the worst case for searching a skip list to occur?

21. Consider the move-to-front, transpose, count, and ordering methods.

    (a) In what case will a list maintained by these methods not be changed?

    (b) In what case would these methods require an exhaustive search of lists for each search, assuming that only elements in the list are searched for?

22. In the discussion of self-organizing lists only the number of comparisons was considered as the measure of different methods' efficiency. This measure can, however, be greatly affected by a particular implementation of the list. Discuss how the efficiency of the move-to-front, transpose, count, and ordering methods will be affected in the case when the list is implemented as

    (a) an array;

    (b) a singly linked list;

    (c) a doubly linked list.

23. For doubly linked lists, there are two variants of the move-to-front and transpose methods (Valiveti, Oommen 1993). A *move-to-end* method moves a node being accessed to the end opposite from which the search started. For instance, if the doubly linked list is a list of items *A B C D*, and the search starts from the left end to access node *C*, then the reorganized list would be *A B D C*. If the search for *C* started from the right end, the resulting list would be *C A B D*.

　　The *swapping* technique transposes a node with its predecessor, also with respect to the end from which the search started. Assuming that only elements of the list are in the data, what is the worst case for a move-to-end doubly linked list when the search is made alternately from the left and from the right? For a swapping list?

24. What is the maximum number of comparisons for optimal search for the fourteen letters shown in Figure 3.18?

25. Adapt the binary search to linked lists. How efficient can this search be?

■ 3.11 PROGRAMMING ASSIGNMENTS

1. Farey fractions of level one are defined as sequence $\left(\frac{0}{1}, \frac{1}{1}\right)$. This sequence is extended in level two to form a sequence $\left(\frac{0}{1}, \frac{1}{2}, \frac{1}{1}\right)$, sequence $\left(\frac{0}{1}, \frac{1}{3}, \frac{1}{2}, \frac{2}{3}, \frac{1}{1}\right)$ at level three, sequence $\left(\frac{0}{1}, \frac{1}{4}, \frac{1}{3}, \frac{1}{2}, \frac{2}{3}, \frac{3}{4}, \frac{1}{1}\right)$ at level four, so that at each level n, a new fraction $\frac{a+b}{c+d}$ is inserted between two neighbor fractions $\frac{a}{c}$ and $\frac{b}{d}$ only if $c + d \leq n$. Write a program which for a number n entered by the user creates—by constantly extending it—a linked list of fractions at level n and then displays them.

2. Write a program to simulate managing files on disk. Define the disk as a one dimensional array **disk** of size **numOfSectors*sizeOfSector**, where **sizeOfSector** indicates the number of characters stored in one sector. (For the sake of debugging make it a very small number.) A pool of available sectors is kept in a linked list **sectors** of three-field structures: two fields to indicate ranges of available sectors, and one **next** field. Files are kept in a linked list **files** of four-field structures: file name, the number of characters in the file, a pointer to a linked list of sectors where the contents of the file can be found, and the **next** field.

(a) In the first part, implement functions to save and delete files. Saving files requires claiming a sufficient number of sectors from **pool**, if available. The sectors may not be contiguous, so the linked list assigned to the file may contain several nodes. Then the contents of the file have to be written to the sectors assigned to the file. Deletion of a file only requires removing the nodes corresponding with this file (one from **files** and the rest from its own linked list of sectors) and transferring the sectors assigned to this file back to **pool**. No changes are made in **disk**.

(b) File fragmentation slows down file retrieval. In the ideal situation, one cluster of sectors is assigned to one file. However, after many operations with files, it may not be possible. Extend the program to include a function **Together()** to transfer files to contiguous sectors, that is, to create a situation illustrated in Figure 3.26. Fragmented files **file1** and **file2** occupy only one cluster of sectors after **Together()** is

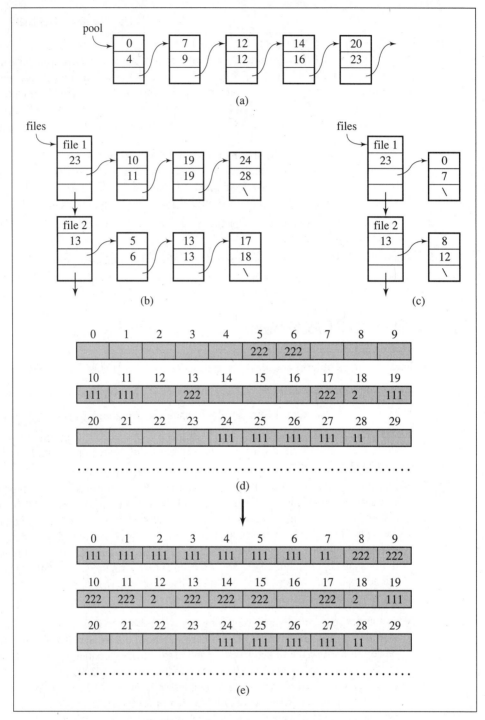

Figure 3.26: Linked lists used to allocate disk sectors for files: (a) a pool of available sectors; two files (b) before and (c) after putting them in contiguous sectors; the situation in sectors of the disk before (d) and (e) after this operation.

finished. However, particular care should be taken not to overwrite sectors occupied by other files. For example, `file1` requires eight sectors; five sectors are free at the beginning of `pool`, but sectors 5 and 6 are occupied by `file2`. Therefore, a file f occupying such sectors has to be located first by scanning `files`. The contents of these sectors must be transferred to unoccupied positions, which requires updating the sectors belonging to f in the linked list; only then can the released sectors be utilized. In the example in Figure 3.26, the first available sector is used to temporarily move sectors of f, hence contents of sectors 5 and 6 were moved to sectors 14 and 15.

3. Write a simple line editor. Keep the entire text on a linked list, one line in a separate node. Start the program with entering **EDIT file**, after which a prompt appears along with the line number. If the letter **I** is entered with a number n following it, then insert the text to be followed before line n. If **I** is not followed by a number then insert the text before the current line. If **D** is entered with two numbers n and m, one n, or no number following it, then delete lines n through m, or line n, or the current line. Similarly with the command **L** which stands for listing lines. If **A** is entered, then append the text to the existing lines. Entry **E** signifies exit and saving the text in a file. Here is an example:

```
EDIT testfile
1> The first line
2>
3> And another line
2> I 3
3> The second line
4> One more line
5> L
1> The first line
2>
3> The second line
4> One more line
5> And another line   // This is now line 5, not 3;
5> D 2                // line 5, since L was issued from line 5;
4> L                  // line 4, since one line was deleted;
1> The first line
2> The second line    // this and the following lines
3> One more line      // now have new numbers;
4> And another line
4> E
```

4. Certain languages, for example, Algol-68 or APL, allow for arrays whose size can be changed at any time when the program is running. Such arrays, called *flexible arrays*, are not readily available in C++. One way to simulate them is to declare a linked list of arrays, each array being relatively short. For example, if each node of such a list holds an array of 10 cells and then a 77-cell array is needed, a linked list of eight nodes can

represent such an array. Write all the necessary functions for such an implementation of flexible arrays and test it on the following problem.

The problem is to reconstruct a text from a concordance of words. This was a real problem of reconstructing some unpublished texts of the Dead Sea Scrolls using concordances. For example, here is William Wordsworth's poem, *Nature and the Poet*, and a concordance of words corresponding with the poem.

> So pure the sky, so quiet was the air!
>
> So like, so very like, was day to day!
>
> Whene'er I look'd, thy image still was there;
>
> It trembled, but it never pass'd away.

The 33 word concordance is as follows:

> 1:1 so quiet was the *air!
>
> 1:4 but it never pass'd *away.
>
> 1:4 It trembled, *but it never
>
> 1:2 was *day to day!
>
> 1:2 was day to *day!
>
> 1:3 thy *image still was there;
>
> ....
>
> 1:2 so very like, *was day
>
> 1:3 thy image still *was there;
>
> 1:3 *Whene'er I look'd,

In this concordance, each word is shown in context of up to five words and the word referred to on each line is preceded with a star. For larger concordances, two numbers have to be included, a number corresponding with a poem and a number of the line where the words can be found. For example, assuming that 1 is the number of *Nature and the Poet*, line "1:4 but it never pass'd *away." means that the word "away" is found in this poem in line 4. Note that punctuation marks are included in the context.

Write a program that loads a concordance from a file and creates a flexible array where each cell is associated with one line of the concordance. Then, using a binary search, reconstruct the text.

5. A more challenging task is to implement two-dimensional flexible arrays. Implement such an array with a linked list of linked lists where each node has a small two-dimensional array. Write all necessary functions and use them to solve the word search puzzle.

The word search puzzle consists of finding positions of words from a predetermined list of words in a rectangle of letters. Create a file containing such a rectangle and a list of words to be located in the rectangle. Use only small letters in the rectangle and the program should capitalize all found words. Figure 3.27 contains an example of such a file, an initialized linked structure, and the structure after processing. The rectangle is separated by a blank line from the list of words which follows it. In the linked structure, the arrays have 6 × 6 cells. To avoid constant checking of bounds of the array, use tilde, ~, as a frame.

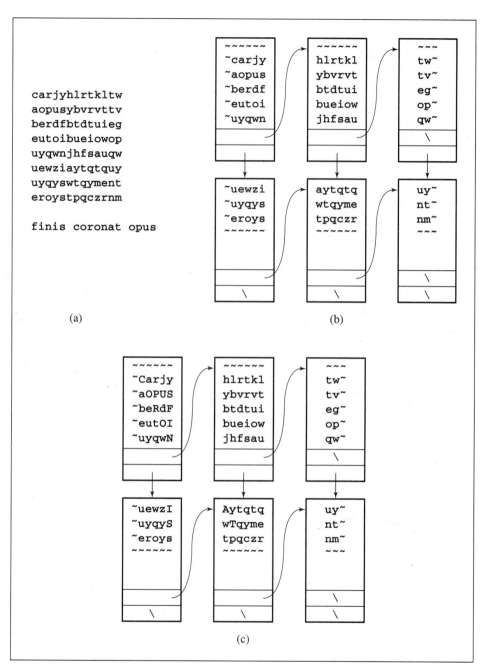

Figure 3.27: **Word search puzzle implemented with a two-dimensional dynamic array: (a) the content of an input file; (b) the array containing the word puzzled before and (c) after finding the words,** *finis ornat opus.*

6. Extend the case study program in this chapter to have it store all the information in the file **Library** at exit and initialize all the linked lists using this information at the invocation of the program. Also, extend it by adding more error checking, such as not allowing the same book to be checked out at the same time to more than one person or not including the same person more than once in the library.

7. Test the efficiency of skip lists. In addition to the functions given in this chapter, implement **SkipListDelete()** and then compare the number of node accesses in searching, deleting, and inserting for large numbers of elements. Compare this efficiency with the efficiency of linked lists and ordered linked lists. Test your program on a randomly generated order of operations to be executed on the elements. These elements should be processed in random order. Then try your program on nonrandom samples.

8. Write a rudimentary lint program to check whether all variables have been initialized and whether local variables have the same names as global variables. Create a linked list of global variables, and, for each function, create a linked list of local variables. In both lists, store information on the first initialization of each variable and check if any initialization has been made before a variable is used for the first time. Also, compare both lists to detect possible matches and issue a warning if a match is found. The list of local variables is removed after the processing of one function is finished and created anew when a new function is encountered. Consider the possibility of maintaining an alphabetical order on both lists.

BIBLIOGRAPHY

[1] Bentley, Jon L. and McGeoch, Catherine C., "Amortized Analyses of Self-organizing Sequential Search Heuristics," *Communications of the ACM* 28 (1985), 404–411.

[2] Foster, John M., *List Processing*, London: MacDonald, 1967.

[3] Hansen, Wilfred J.,"A Predecessor Algorithm for Ordered Lists," *Information Processing Letters* 7 (1978), 137–138.

[4] Hester, James H. and Hirschberg, Daniel S., "Self-organizing Linear Search," *Computing Surveys* 17 (1985), 295–311.

[5] Pugh, William, "Skip Lists: A Probabilistic Alternative to Balanced Trees," *Communications of the ACM* 33 (1990), 668–676.

[6] Rivest, Ronald, "On Self-organizing Sequential Search Heuristics," *Communications of the ACM* 19 (1976), No. 2, 63–67.

[7] Sleator, Daniel D. and Tarjan, Robert E., "Amortized Efficiency of List Update and Paging Rules," *Communications of the ACM* 28 (1985), 202–208.

[8] Valiveti, R.S. and Oommen, B.J., "Self-organizing Doubly Linked Lists," *Journal of Algorithms* 14 (1993), 88–114.

[9] Wilkes, Maurice V., "Lists and Why They Are Useful," *Computer Journal* 7 (1965), 278–281.

STACKS AND QUEUES

As the first chapter explained, abstract data types allow us to delay the specific implementation of a data type until it is well understood what operations are required to operate on the data. In fact, these operations determine which implementation of the data type is most efficient in a particular situation. This situation is illustrated by two data types, stacks and queues, which are described by a list of operations. Only after the list of the required operations is determined shall we present some possible implementations and compare them.

■ 4.1 STACKS

A *stack* is a linear data structure which can be accessed only at one of its ends for storing and retrieving data. Such a stack resembles a stack of trays in a cafeteria: new trays are put on the top of the stack and taken off the top. The last tray put on the stack is the first tray removed from the stack. For this reason, a stack is called a *LIFO* structure: last in, first out.

A tray can be taken only if there are trays on the stack, and a tray can be added to the stack only if there is enough room, that is, if the stack is not too high. Therefore, a stack is defined in terms of operations which change its status and operations which check this status. The operations are as follows:

- *Clear()* — Clear the stack.
- *IsEmpty()* — Check to see if the stack is empty.
- *IsFull()* — Check to see if the stack is full.
- *Push(el)* — Put the element *el* on the top of the stack.
- *Pop()* — Take the topmost element from the stack.

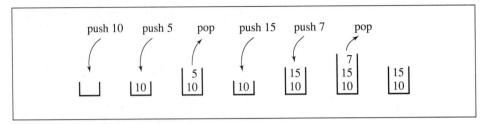

Figure 4.1: **A series of operations executed on a stack.**

A series of *Push()* and *Pop()* operations is shown in Figure 4.1. This example suggests that an array can be used to represent a stack. However, what does it mean for such an array to be empty? There are always certain values in the array, whether put there by the user or by the operating system. An array is never truly empty. Hence, a special value can be used to mark unused cells of the array such as zero. But can we distinguish zeros marking empty cells from zeros stored in the stack? The array can consist of structures with two fields, a data field and a marker field. But such an implementation is unnecessarily complicated and requires searching for the topmost position. A simpler solution uses an external variable indicating the topmost free position (see Figure 4.2a). This variable is initially set to zero, and it is incremented when a new element is added to the stack and decremented if an element is popped off the stack.

Figure 4.3 contains a generic stack class definition.

This implementation is not without a flaw. It uses an array, limiting the number of elements that can be stored on the stack. If **size** is declared too small, stack overflow may prematurely occur, and if **size** is too large, a certain amount of memory is unnecessarily blocked. A previous chapter suggests another method, using a linked list for stack implementation, as in Figure 4.2b. Figure 4.4 shows the implementation.

As an example, consider adding very large numbers. The largest magnitude of integers is limited, so we would not be able to add 18,274,364,583,929,273,748,459,595,684,373 and 8,129,498,165,026,350,236, since integer variables cannot hold such large values, let alone the sum of them. The problem can be solved if we treat these numbers as strings of numerals, store the numbers corresponding to these numerals on two stacks, and then perform addition by popping numbers from the stacks. The pseudocode for this algorithm is as follows:

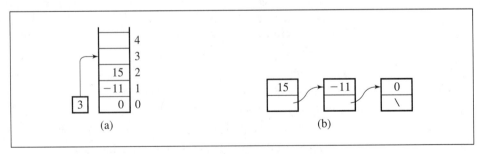

Figure 4.2: **Five implementations of a stack holding the numbers 0, −11, and 15.**

```
// ********************  genStack.h  **************************
//      generic class for array implementation of stack

#ifndef STACK
#define STACK

template<class elType, int size = 50>
class Stack {
public:
    Stack()       { top = 0; }
    void Clear() { top = 0; }
    int  IsEmpty() const { return top == 0;    }
    int  IsFull()  const { return top == size; }
    elType TopEl() const { return pool[top-1]; }
    void Push(const elType& el) { pool[top++] = el; }
    elType Pop()             { return pool[--top]; }
private:
    elType pool[size];
    int top;
};

#endif
```

Figure 4.3: **Array implementation of a stack.**

*read the numerals of the first number and store the numbers corresponding to
them on one stack;*
*read the numerals of the second number and store the numbers corresponding
to them on another stack;*
result = 0;
while *at least one stack is not empty*
    pop a number from each nonempty stack and add them;
    push the unit part on the result stack;
    store carry in **result;**
push carry on the result stack if it is not zero;
pop numbers from the result stack and display them;

Figure 4.5 contains the implementation of this algorithm.

■ 4.2 QUEUES

A *queue* is simply a waiting line, which grows by adding elements to its end and shrinks by taking elements from its front. Unlike a stack, a queue is a structure in which both ends are used: one for adding new elements,and one for removing them. Therefore, the last element

```
//********************    genLstSt.h    *******************

#ifndef SLL_STACK
#define SLL_STACK

#include "genSLLst.h"

template<class genClass>
class SLLStack {
public:
    SLLStack() { }
    void Push(const genClass& el) { list.Add(el);            }
    genClass Pop()                { return *list.Remove();   }
    int IsEmpty() const           { return list.IsEmpty();   }
    void PrintAll(ostream& out) const { list.PrintAll(out);  }
    void Clear()                  { list.Clear();            }
private:
    SinglyLinkedList<genClass> list;
};
#endif
```

Figure 4.4: **Implementing a stack as a linked list.**

has to wait until all elements preceding it on the queue are removed. A queue is a FIFO structure: first in, first out.

Queue operations are similar to stack operations. The following operations are needed to properly manage a queue:

- *Clear()* — Clear the queue.
- *IsEmpty()* — Check to see if the queue is empty.
- *IsFull()* — Check to see if the queue is full.
- *Enqueue(el)* — Put the element *el* at the end of the queue.
- *Dequeue()* — Take the first element from the queue.

A series of *Enqueue()* and *Dequeue()* operations is shown in Figure 4.6. This time — unlike for stacks — the changes have to be monitored both at the beginning of the queue and at the end.

One possible queue implementation is an array, although this may not be the best choice. Elements are added to the end of the queue, but they may be removed from its beginning, thereby releasing array cells. These cells should not be wasted. Therefore, they are utilized to enqueue new elements, whereby the end of the queue may occur at the beginning of the array. This situation is better pictured as a circular array as Figure 4.7c illustrates. The queue is full if the first element immediately precedes in the counterclockwise direction

```
#include <iostream.h>
#include <ctype.h>
#include "genStack.h"

main()
{   Stack<int> operandStack1, operandStack2, resultStack;
    int resultNum = 0;
    char ch;

    cout << "Enter two numbers to be added: ";
    cin >> ch;
    while (isdigit(ch) && !operandStack1.IsFull()) {
        operandStack1.Push(ch-'0');
        cin.get(ch);
    }
    cin >> ch;
    while (isdigit(ch) && !operandStack2.IsFull()) {
        operandStack2.Push(ch-'0');
        cin.get(ch);
    }
    while (!operandStack1.IsEmpty() || !operandStack2.IsEmpty()) {
        if (!operandStack1.IsEmpty())
            resultNum += operandStack1.Pop();
        if (!operandStack2.IsEmpty())
            resultNum += operandStack2.Pop();
        if (resultNum > 9 && !resultStack.IsFull()) {
            resultStack.Push(resultNum - 10);
            resultNum = 1;
        }
        else if (!resultStack.IsFull()) {
            resultStack.Push(resultNum);
            resultNum = 0;
        }
    }
    if (resultNum > 0 && !resultStack.IsFull())
        resultStack.Push(resultNum);
    while (!resultStack.IsEmpty())
        cout << resultStack.Pop();
    return 0;
}
```

Figure 4.5: **Program to add large integers using two stacks.**

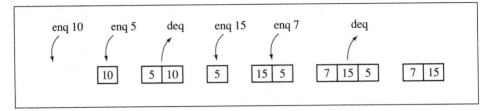

Figure 4.6: **A series of operations executed on a queue.**

the last element. However, because a circular array is implemented with a "normal" array, the queue is full if either the first element is in the first cell and the last element in the last cell (Figure 4.7a), or the first element is right after the last (Figure 4.7b). Similarly, *Enqueue()* and *Dequeue()* have to consider the possibility of wrapping around the array when adding or removing elements. For example, *Enqueue()* can be viewed as operating

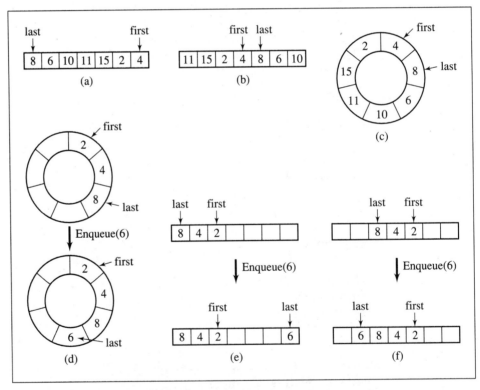

Figure 4.7: **(a–b) Two possible configurations in an array implementation of a queue when the queue is full. (c) The same queue viewed as a circular array. (d) Enqueuing number 6 to a queue storing numbers 2, 4, and 8. (e–f) The same queue seen as a one-dimensional array with the last element at the end of the array (e) and in the middle (f).**

on a circular array (Figure 4.7c), but in reality, it is operating on a one-dimensional array. Therefore, if the last element is in the last cell and if any cells are available at the beginning of the array, a new element is placed there (Figure 4.7e). If the last element is in any other position, then the new element is put after the last, space permitting (Figure 4.7f). These two situations must be distinguished when implementing a queue viewed as circular array (Figure 4.7d).

Figure 4.8 contains possible implementations of member functions which operate on queues.

A more natural queue implementation is a linked list. Functions that operate on linked lists can be used: a function to add a new element to the end of a queue and a function for removing an element from its beginning. Implementing other linked list functions is left as an exercise.

Queues are frequently used in simulation to the extent that a well-developed and mathematically sophisticated theory of queues exists, called queueing theory, in which various scenarios are analyzed and models are built which use queues. In queuing processes, there are a number of customers coming to servers to receive service. The throughput of the server may be limited. Therefore, customers have to wait in queues before they are served and they spend some amount of time while they are being served. By customers, we mean not only people, but also objects. For example, parts on an assembly line in the process of being assembled into a machine, trucks waiting for service at a weighing station on an interstate, or barges waiting for a sluice to be opened so they can pass through a channel also wait in queues. The most familiar examples are lines in stores, post offices, or banks. The type of problems posed in simulations are: How many servers are needed to avoid long queues? How large must the waiting space be to put the entire queue in it? Is it cheaper to increase this space or to open one more server?

```
template<class genType, int size = 100>
class AQueue {
public:
    AQueue() { first = last = -1; }
    void Enqueue(genType);
    genType Dequeue();
    int IsFull()  { return first == 0 && last == size-1 ||
                           first == last + 1; }
    int IsEmpty() { first == -1; }
private:
    int first, last;
    genType storage[size];
};
```

Figure 4.8: **Array implementation of a queue.** **continued**

```
template<class genType, int size>
void
AQueue<genType,size>::Enqueue(genType el)
{
    if (!IsFull())
        if (last == size-1 || last == -1) {
            storage[0] = el;
            last = 0;
            if (first == -1)
                first = 0;
        }
        else storage[++last] = el;
    else cout << "Full queue.\n";
}


template<class genType, int size>
genType
AQueue<genType,size>::Dequeue()
{   genType tmp;

    if (!IsEmpty()) {
        tmp = storage[first];
        if (first == last)
            last = first = -1;
        else if (first == size-1)
            first = 0;
        else first++;
        return tmp;
    }
    else cout << "Empty queue.\n";
}
```

Figure 4.8: **Array implementation of a queue.**

As an example, consider the city's Bank One which, over a period of three months, recorded the number of customers coming to the bank and the amount of time needed to serve them. The table in Figure 4.9a shows the number of customers who arrived during one-minute intervals throughout the day. For 15% of such intervals, no customer arrived, for 20%, only one arrived, etc. Currently, six clerks are employed, no lines are ever observed, and the bank management wants to know whether six clerks is too many. Would five suffice? Four? Maybe even three? Can lines be expected at any time? To answer these questions, a simulation program is written which applies the recorded data and checks different scenarios.

The Amount of Time Needed for Service in Seconds	Percent of Customers	Range
0	0	—
10	0	—
20	0	—
30	10	1–10
40	5	11–15
50	10	16–25
60	10	26–35
70	0	—
80	15	36–50
90	25	51–75
100	10	76–85
110	15	86–100

(b)

Number of Customers per Minute	Percent of One-minute Intervals	Range
0	15	1–15
1	20	16–35
2	25	36–60
3	10	61–70
4	30	71–100

(a)

Figure 4.9: **Bank One example: (a) Data for number of arrived customers per one-minute interval and (b) transaction time in seconds per customer.**

The number of customers depends on the value of a randomly generated number between 1 and 100. The table in Figure 4.9a identifies five ranges of numbers from 1 to 100, based on the percentages of one-minute intervals which had 0, 1, 2, 3, or 4 customers. If the random number is 21, then the number of customers is 1; if the random number is 90, then the number of customers is 4. This method simulates the rate of customers arriving at Bank One.

In addition, analysis of the recorded observations indicates that no customer required 10-second or 20-second transactions, 10% required 30 seconds, etc., as indicated in Figure 4.9b. The table in 4.9b includes ranges for random numbers to generate the length of a transaction in seconds.

Figure 4.10 contains the code simulating customer arrival and transaction time at Bank One. The program uses three arrays. `arrivals[]` records the percentages of one-minute intervals depending on the number of the arrived customers. The array `service[]` is used to store the distribution of time needed for service. The amount of time is obtained by multiplying the index of a given array cell by 10. For example, `service[3]` is equal to 10, which means that 10% of the time a customer required 3 * 10 seconds for service. The array `clerks[]` records the length of transaction time in seconds.

For each minute (represented by the variable `t`), the number of arriving customers is randomly chosen, and for each customer, the transaction time is also randomly determined. The function `Option()` generates a random number, finds the range into which it falls, and then outputs the position, which is either the number of customers or the number of seconds multiplied by ten.

Executions of this program indicate that six and five clerks are too many. With four clerks, service is performed smoothly; 25% of the time there is a short line of waiting customers. However, three clerks are always busy and there is always a long line of customers waiting. Bank management would certainly decide to employ four clerks.

```
#include <iostream.h>
#include <stdlib.h>
#include "genQueue.h"


int
Option(int percents[])
{    register int i = 0, choice = rand()%100+1, perc;

     for (perc = percents[0]; perc < choice; perc += percents[i+1], i++);
     return i;

}


main()
{    int arrivals[] = {15,20,25,10,30};
     int service[] = {0,0,0,10,5,10,10,0,15,25,10,15};
     int clerks[] = {0,0,0,0,0}, clerksSize = sizeof(clerks)/sizeof(int);
     int customers, t, i, thereIsLine = 0, numOfMinutes = 100, x;
     float maxWait = 0.0, currWait = 0.0;
     Queue<int> simulQ;

     cout.precision(2);
     for (t = 1; t <= numOfMinutes; t++) {
         cout << " t = " << t;
         for (i = 0; i < clerksSize; i++)// after each minute subtract
             if (clerks[i] < 60)          // at most 60 seconds from time
                 clerks[i] = 0;           // left to service the current
             else clerks[i] -= 60;        // customer by clerk i;
         customers = Option(arrivals);
         for (i = 0; i < customers; i++) { // enqueue all new customers
             x = Option(service)*10;       // (or rather service time
             simulQ.Enqueue(x);            // they require);
             currWait += x;
         }
         // dequeue customers when clerks are available:
         for (i = 0; i < clerksSize && !simulQ.IsEmpty(); )
             if (clerks[i] < 60) {
                     x = simulQ.Dequeue(); // assign more than one customer
                     clerks[i] += x;       // to a clerk if service time
                     currWait  -= x;       // is still below 60 sec;
             }
```

Figure 4.10: Bank One example: implementation code.   **continued**

```
          else i++;
      if (!simulQ.IsEmpty()) {
          thereIsLine++;
          cout << " wait = " << currWait/60.0;
          if (maxWait < currWait)
              maxWait = currWait;
      }
      else cout << " wait = 0;";
   }
   cout << "For " << clerksSize << " clerks, there was a line "
        << float(thereIsLine)/numOfMinutes*100.0 << "% of the time;\n"
        << "maximum wait time was " << maxWait/60.0 << " min.";
   return 0;
}
```

Figure 4.10: **Bank One example: implementation code.**

■ 4.3 PRIORITY QUEUES

In many situations simple queues are inadequate, since first in, first out scheduling has to be overruled using some priority criteria. In a post office example, a handicapped person may have a priority over others. Therefore, when a clerk is available, a handicapped person is served instead of someone from the front of the queue. On roads with toll booths, some vehicles may be put through immediately, even without paying (police cars, ambulances, fire engines, etc.). In a sequence of processes, process P_2 may need to be executed before process P_1 for the proper functioning of a system, even though P_1 was put on the queue of waiting processes before P_2. In situations like these, a modified queue, or *priority queue*, is needed. In priority queues, elements are dequeued according to their priority and to their current queue position.

The problem with a priority queue is in finding an efficient implementation which allows relatively fast enqueuing and dequeuing. Since elements may arrive randomly to the queue, there is no guarantee that the front elements will be the most likely to be dequeued, and the elements put at the end will be the last candidates for dequeuing. The situation is complicated because a wide spectrum of possible priority criteria can be used in different cases such as frequency of use, birthday, salary, position, status, and others. It can also be the time of scheduled execution on the queue of processes, which explains the convention used in priority queue discussions in which higher priorities are associated with lower numbers indicating priority.

Priority queues can be represented by two variations of linked lists. In one type of linked list, all elements are entry ordered and in another, order is maintained by putting a new element in its proper position according to its priority. In both cases the total operational times are $O(n)$, since, for an unordered list, adding an element is immediate but searching is $O(n)$, and in a sorted list, taking an element is immediate but adding an element is $O(n)$.

Another queue representation uses a short ordered list and an unordered list, and a threshold priority is determined (Blackstone et al. 1981). The number of elements in the sorted list depends on a threshold priority. This means that in some cases this list can be empty and the threshold may change dynamically to have some elements in this list. Another way is to have always the same number of elements in the sorted list; the number $\sqrt{n}$ is a good candidate. Enqueuing takes on the average $O(\sqrt{n})$ time and dequeuing is immediate.

Another implementation of queues was proposed by J.O. Hendriksen (1977, 1983). It uses a simple linked list with an additional array of pointers to this list to find a range of elements in the list in which a newly arrived element should be included.

Experiments by Douglas W. Jones (1986) indicate that a linked list implementation, in spite of its $O(n)$ efficiency, is best for ten elements or less. The efficiency of the two-list version depends greatly on the distribution of priorities, and it may be excellent or as poor as that of the simple list implementation for large numbers of elements. Hendriksen's implementation, with its $O(\sqrt{n})$ complexity, operates consistently well with queues of any size.

■ 4.4 CASE STUDY: VON KOCH SNOWFLAKE

A stack is a useful data structure when certain decisions have to be deferred and made later in a particular order. To illustrate this, the construction of the von Koch snowflake is presented.

Figure 4.11 contains examples of von Koch snowflakes. The snowflake is a combination of three identical curves drawn in different angles and joined together. One such curve is drawn in the following fashion:

1. Divide an interval *side* into three even parts.
2. Go one third of *side* in the direction specified by *angle*.
3. Turn to the left 60° (i.e., turn −60°) and go forward one third of *side*.

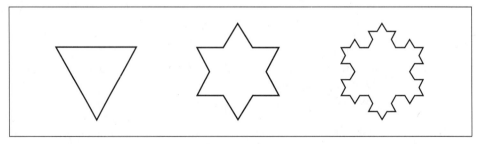

Figure 4.11: **Examples of von Koch snowflakes.**

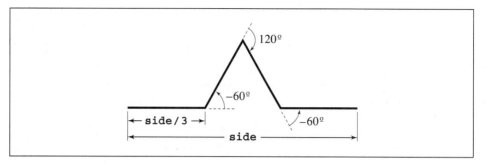

Figure 4.12: **The process of drawing four sides of one segment of the von Koch snowflake.**

4. Turn to the right 120° and proceed forward by one third of *side*.

5. Turn left 60° and again draw a line one third of *side* long.

Figure 4.12 illustrates these five steps.

This curve, however, becomes more jagged if each of the four intervals became a miniature of the whole curve, that is, if the process of drawing four lines were made for each of these *side/3* long intervals. As a result, 16 intervals *side/9* long are drawn. The process may continue indefinitely — at least in theory. Computer graphics resolution prevents us from going too far since if the lines are smaller than the diameter of a pixel, we see just one dot on the screen.

At any level of the division process we have to retain information about the divisions which have been made, so that when drawing a line, we know how much to turn and in what direction to draw the next interval. The only information that needs to be stored is the angles indicating these turns, since the interval drawn is always of the same length, *side/3^{level}*, where *level* indicates the number of times the intervals should be divided into subintervals, subintervals into sub-subintervals, etc.

The detailed procedure is presented in Figure 4.13. First, the angles −60°, 120°, and −60° are stored on a **stack** for the intervals of size **side/3** (Figure 4.13a). Next, the same three angles are pushed on **tmpStack**, sandwiched between the values popped from **stack** (Figures 4.13b,c). Finally, the content of **tmpStack** is transferred onto **stack** (whereby **tmpStack** is freed for the next iteration) so that the proper order for drawing is restored (Figure 4.13d). But why should this be done? Comparing Figures 4.13c and 4.13d indicates that the stacks have the same content, so this transfer seems to be redundant. And this is true for this case, and cases like these. There is a symmetry at the very beginning which is perpetuated throughout the execution of this algorithm: each time, three angles are pushed on the stack, −60°, 120°, and −60°, and it does not matter whether the first −60° is the angle by which to turn after drawing line AB in Figure 4.13a, or the angle to be considered before drawing line DE. But if these were, for example, the angles −70°, 120°, and −30°, then the order of storing these angles would be crucial for the proper outcome. For the sake of generalization, the step from Figure 4.13c to 4.13d is included in the algorithm.

Figure 4.14 contains the complete code for these algorithms.

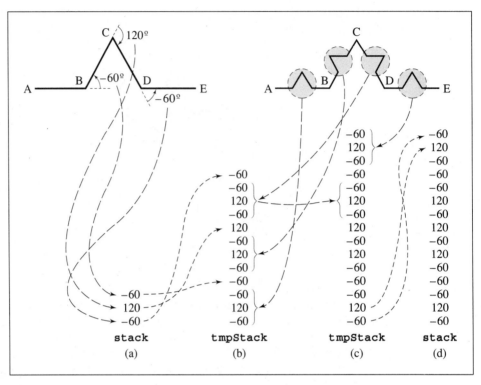

Figure 4.13: **Drawing four sides of one segment of the von Koch snowflake utilizing two stacks.**

```
******************** Turbo C++ program ********************
#include <iostream.h>
#include <graphics.h>
#include <stdlib.h>
#include <math.h>
#include "genStack.h"


class Curve {
public:
    Curve() { angle = 0.0; }
    void ReadInitValues();
    void Snowflake();
private:
    Stack<double,1500> stack, tmpStack;
```

Figure 4.14: **Code for von Koch snowflake algorithms.**   **continued**

```
        int level;
        double side, angle;

        void Push1(double x)
             { !stack.IsFull()    ? stack.Push(x)    : exit(1); }
        void Push2(double x)
             { !tmpStack.IsFull() ? tmpStack.Push(x) : exit(1); }
        double Pop1()  { return stack.Pop();       }
        double Pop2()  { return tmpStack.Pop();  }
        int IsEmpty1() { return stack.IsEmpty();     }
        int IsEmpty2() { return tmpStack.IsEmpty(); }
        void Turn(double x) { angle += x; }
        void Forward(double);
        void ThreePushes1() { Push1(-60.0); Push1(120.0); Push1(-60.0); }
        void ThreePushes2() { Push2(-60.0); Push2(120.0); Push2(-60.0); }
        void DrawOneSide(double side);
};

void
Curve::ReadInitValues()
{
    setcolor(WHITE);
    setbkcolor(BLUE);
    moveto (200,150);
    cout << "Enter side and level: ";
    cin  >> side >> level;
}

void
inline Curve::Forward(double distance)    // arguments to sin() and
{                                         // cos() are angles specified
    linerel(cos(angle*M_PI/180)*distance, // in radians, i.e.,
            sin(angle*M_PI/180)*distance); // the coefficient
}                                         // 3.14/180 is necessary;

void
Curve::DrawOneSide(double side)
{    int i;
```

Figure 4.14: Code for von Koch snowflake algorithms.   **continued**

```
    ThreePushes1();                 // see Figure 4.13a
    tmpStack.Clear();
    for (i = 2; i <= level; i++) {
        side /= 3;
        while (!IsEmpty1()) {    // see Figure 4.13b
            ThreePushes2();
            Push2(Pop1());
        }
        ThreePushes2();             // see Figure 4.13c
        while (!IsEmpty2())         // see Figure 4.13d
            Push1(Pop2());
    }
    Forward(side);
    while (!IsEmpty1()) {
        Turn(Pop1());
        Forward(side);
    }
}


void
Curve::Snowflake()
{   int i;
    double stash;

    for (i = 1, stash = side; level > 0 && i <= 3; i++) {
        stack.Clear();
        DrawOneSide(stash);
        Turn(120);
    }
}


int
main()
{   int grBoard = DETECT, grMode, grResult, grError;
    Curve curve;

    initgraph(&grBoard,&grMode,"c:\\tc\\bgi");
    grError = graphresult();
```

Figure 4.14: **Code for von Koch snowflake algorithms.**   **continued**

```
    if (grError != grOk) {
        cerr << "error: " << grapherrormsg(grError) << endl;
        return 1;
    }
    curve.ReadInitValues();
    curve.Snowflake();
    return 0;
}
```

Figure 4.14: **Code for von Koch snowflake algorithms.**

■ 4.5 EXERCISES

1. Reverse the contents of stack S

   (a) using two additional stacks

   (b) using one additional queue

   (c) using one additional stack and some additional variables

2. Put the elements on the stack S in ascending order using one additional stack and some additional variables.

3. Transfer elements from stack S_1 to stack S_2 so that the elements from S_2 will be in the same order as on S_1

   (a) using one additional stack

   (b) using no additional stack but only some additional variables

4. Suggest an implementation of a stack to hold elements of two different types, such as structures and float numbers.

5. Using additional variables, order all elements on a queue using also

   (a) two additional queues

   (b) one additional queue

6. Write an outline of a program which checks whether the parentheses, square brackets, and curly brackets are properly balanced in a C++ program.

7. Write functions implementing a two-list version of a priority queue. There may be at least two variations, one using two separate lists, ordered and unordered, and one using just one list with the proper pointers.

8. What changes would have to be made in the program presented in the von Koch snowflake case study to draw a line as in Figure 4.15? Try it, and experiment with other possibilities to generate other curves.

9. In this chapter, two different implementations were developed for a stack, class **Stack** and class **SLLStack**. The names of member functions in both classes suggest that the

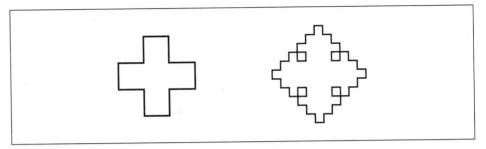

Figure 4.15: **Lines to be drawn with modified program in Figure 4.14.**

same data structure is meant; however, a tighter connection between these two classes can be established. Define an abstract base class for a stack and derive from it both class **Stack** and class **SLLStack**.

10. In array implementations of a stack in this chapter, no test is made in **Push()** for stack overflow. The test should be made by the user to avoid abnormal program termination. Similarly, no test for stack underflow is made in **Pop()** and in **TopEl()**. The tests can be incorporated in all these member functions in variety of ways. Here are some examples.

    (a) `void Push(const elType& el, int& full) { ... }`
       In this definition, **full** is set by **Push()** to, say, 0 if stack is full and to 1 if **el** can be pushed onto the stack. The variable **full** is tested by the user after **Push()** is finished.

    (b) `int Push(const elType& el) { ... }`
       In this version, the return value plays the same role as **full** in the previous version. **Push()** returns 1 if **el** was pushed successfully, 0 otherwise.

    (c) `void Push(const elType& el) { if (IsFull()) exit(0);`
    `else ... }`
       Interrupt the program when an attempt is made to push an element onto a full stack, possibly printing an error message, and push the element on the stack otherwise.

    (d) `elType* TopEl() { ... }`
       Member function **TopEl()** returns null if the stack is empty, and the pointer to the topmost element otherwise.

    What are the disadvantages of these definitions?

■ 4.6 PROGRAMMING ASSIGNMENTS

1. Write a program that determines whether or not an input string is a palindrome, that is, whether or not it can be read the same way forward and backward. At each point you can read only one character of the input string; do not use an array to first store this string and then analyze it (except, possibly, in a stack implementation). Consider using multiple stacks.

2. Write a program to convert a number from decimal notation to a number expressed in a number system whose base (or radix) is a number between 2 and 9. The conversion is performed by repetitious division by the base to which a number is being converted and then taking the remainders of division in the reverse order. For example, number 6 requires three such divisions: 6/2 = 3 remainder 0, 3/2 = 1 remainder 1, and, finally, 1/2 = 0 remainder 1. The remainders 0, 1, and 1 are put in the reverse order, so that the binary equivalent of 6 is equal to 110.

Modify your program so that it can perform a conversion in the case when the base is a number between 11 and 27. Number systems with bases greater than 10 require more symbols. Therefore, use capital letters. For example, a hexadecimal system requires sixteen digits: 0, 1, ..., 9, A, B, C, D, E, F. In this system, decimal number 26 is equal to 1A in hexadecimal notation, since 26/16 = 1 remainder 10 (that is, A), and 1/16 = 0 remainder 1.

3. Write a program to perform the four basic arithmetic operations, $+, -, *,$ and $/$, on very large integers; the result of division should also be an integer. Apply these operations to compute 123^{45}, or the hundredth number in the sequence $1 * 2 + 3, 2 * 3^2 + 4, 3 * 4^3 + 5, \ldots$. Also, apply them to compute the Gödel numbers of arithmetical expressions.

The Gödel numbering function GN first establishes a correspondence between basic elements of language and numbers:

Symbol	Gödel Number GN
=	1
+	2
*	3
-	4
/	5
(	6
)	7
^	8
0	9
S	10
x_i	$11 + 2 * i$
X_i	$12 + 2 * i$

where S is the successor function. Then, for any formula $F = s_1 s_2 \ldots s_n$:

$$GN('s_1 s_2 \ldots s'_n) = 2^{GN(s_1)} * 3^{GN(s_2)} * \cdots * p_n^{GN(s_n)},$$

where p_n is the nth prime. For example,

$$GN(1) = GN(S0) = 2^{10} * 3^9$$

and

$$GN('x_1 + x_3 = x'_4) = 2^{11+2} * 3^2 * 5^{11+6} * 7^1 * 11^{11+8}.$$

In this way, every arithmetical expression can be assigned a unique number. This method has been used by Gödel to prove theorems, known as Gödel's theorems, which are of extreme importance for the foundations of mathematics.

4. Write a program for adding very large floating-point numbers. Extend this program to other arithmetic operations.

BIBLIOGRAPHY

Queues

[1]   Sloyer, Clifford, Copes, Wayne, Sacco, William, and Starck, Robert, *Queues: Will This Wait Never End!*, Providence, RI: Janson, 1987.

Priority Queues

[2]   Blackstone, John H., Hogg, Gary L., and Phillips, Don T., "A Two-List Synchronization Procedure for Discrete Event Simulation," *Communications of the ACM* 24 (1981), 825–829.

[3]   Hendriksen, James O., "An Improved Events List Algorithm," *Proceedings of the 1977 Winter Simulation Conference*, Piscataway, NJ: IEEE, 1977, 547–557.

[4]   Hendriksen, James O., "Event List Management — A Tutorial," *Proceedings of the 1983 Winter Simulation Conference*, Piscataway, NJ: IEEE, 1983, 543–551.

[5]   Jones, Douglas W., "An Empirical Comparison of Priority-Queue and Event-Set Implementations," *Communications of the ACM* 29 (1986), 300–311.

5

RECURSION

■ 5.1 RECURSIVE DEFINITIONS

One of the basic rules for defining new objects or concepts is that the definition should contain only such terms that have already been defined or that are obvious. Therefore, an object which is defined in terms of itself is a serious violation of this rule — a vicious circle. On the other hand, there are many programming concepts that define themselves. As it turns out, formal restrictions imposed on definitions such as existence and uniqueness are satisfied and no violation of the rules takes place. Such definitions are called *recursive definitions* and are used primarily to define infinite sets. When defining such a set, giving a complete list of elements is impossible, and for large finite sets, it is inefficient. Thus, a more efficient way has to be devised to determine if an object belongs to a set.

A recursive definition consists of two parts. In the first part, called the *anchor* or the *ground case*, the basic elements that are the building blocks of all other elements of the set are listed. In the second part, rules are given that allow for the construction of new objects out of basic elements or objects that have already been constructed. These rules are applied again and again to generate new objects. For example, to construct the set of natural numbers, one basic element, 0, is singled out and the operation of incrementing by one is given as:

1. $0 \in \mathbf{N}$;
2. if $n \in \mathbf{N}$, then $(n + 1) \in \mathbf{N}$;
3. there are no other objects in the set $\mathbf{N}$.

(More axioms are needed to ensure that only the set that we know as the natural numbers can be constructed by these rules.)

According to these rules, the set of natural numbers **N** consists of the following items: $0, 0 + 1, 0 + 1 + 1, 0 + 1 + 1 + 1$, etc. Although the set **N** contains objects (and only such objects) that we call natural numbers, the definition results in a somewhat unwieldy list of elements. Can you imagine doing arithmetic on large numbers using such a specification? Therefore, it is more convenient to use the following definition which encompasses the whole range of Arabic numeric heritage:

1. $0, 1, 2, 3, 4, 5, 6, 7, 8, 9 \in$ **N**;
2. if $n \in$ **N**, then $n0, n1, n2, n3, n4, n5, n6, n7, n8, n9 \in$ **N**;
3. these are the only natural numbers.

Then the set **N** includes all possible combinations of the basic building blocks 0 through 9.

Recursive definitions serve two purposes: *generating* new elements, as already indicated, and *testing* whether or not an element belongs to a set. In the case of testing, the problem is solved by reducing it to a simpler problem, and if the simpler problem is still too complex, it is reduced to an even simpler problem, and so on, until it is reduced to a problem indicated in the anchor. For instance, is 123 a natural number? According to the second condition of the definition introducing the set **N**, $123 \in$ **N** if $12 \in$ **N** and the first condition already says that $3 \in$ **N**; but $12 \in$ **N** if $1 \in$ **N** and $2 \in$ **N**, and they both belong to **N**.

The ability to decompose a problem into simpler subproblems of the same kind is sometimes a real blessing, as we shall see in the discussion of quicksort in a later chapter, or a curse, as we shall see shortly in this chapter.

Recursive definitions are frequently used to define functions and sequences of numbers. For instance, the factorial function, !, can be defined in the following manner:

$$n! = \begin{cases} 1 & \text{if } n = 0 \text{ (anchor)}, \\ n * (n - 1)! & \text{if } n > 0 \text{ (inductive step)} \end{cases}$$

Using this definition we can generate the sequence of numbers

$$1, 1, 2, 6, 24, 120, 720, 5040, 40320, 362880, 3628800, \ldots$$

which includes the factorials of the numbers $0, 1, 2, \ldots, 10, \ldots$.

Another example is the definition

$$f(n) = \begin{cases} 1 & \text{if } n = 0, \\ f(n - 1) + \dfrac{1}{f(n - 1)} & \text{if } n > 0 \end{cases}$$

which generates the sequence of rational numbers

$$1, 2, \frac{5}{2}, \frac{29}{10}, \frac{941}{290}, \frac{969581}{272890}, \ldots$$

Recursive definitions of sequences have one undesirable feature: to determine the value of an element s_n of a sequence, we first have to compute the values of some or all of the previous elements, $s_1, \ldots, s_{n-1}$. For example, calculating the value of 3! requires us to first compute the values of 0!, 1!, and 2!. Computationally, this is undesirable since it forces us to make calculations in a roundabout way. Therefore, we want to find an equivalent definition or formula that makes no references to other elements of the sequence. Generally, finding such a formula is a difficult problem which cannot always be solved. But the formula is preferable to a recursive definition because it simplifies the computational process and allows us to find the answer for an integer n without computing the values for integers $0, 1, \ldots, n - 1$. For example, a definition of the sequence g,

$$g(n) = \begin{cases} 1 & \text{if } n = 0, \\ 2 * g(n - 1) & \text{if } n > 0 \end{cases}$$

can be converted into the simple formula

$$g(n) = 2^n.$$

In the foregoing discussion, recursive definitions have been dealt with only theoretically, as a definition used in mathematics. Naturally, our interest is in computer science. One area where recursive definitions are used extensively is in the specification of the grammars of programming languages. Every programming language manual contains — either as an appendix or throughout the text — a specification of all valid language elements. Grammar is specified either in terms of block diagrams or in terms of the Backus-Naur form (BNF). For example, the syntactic definition of a statement in the C++ language can be presented in the block diagram form:

or in BNF:

```
<statement> ::= while (<expression>) <statement> |
                if (<expression>) <statement> |
                if (<expression>) <statement> else <statement> |
                . . .
```

The language element <statement> is defined recursively, in terms of itself. Such definitions naturally express the possibility of creating such syntactic constructs as nested statements or expressions.

Recursive definitions are also used in programming. The good news is that virtually no effort is needed to make the transition from a recursive definition of a function to its implementation in C++. We simply make a translation from the formal definition into C++ syntax. Hence, for example, a C++ equivalent of factorial would be the function

```
int
Factorial (int n)
{
  if (n == 0)
      return 1;
```

```
    else return n * Factorial (n - 1);
}
```

The problem now seems to be more critical since it is far from clear how a function calling itself can possibly work, let alone return the correct result. This chapter will show that it is possible for such a function to work properly. Recursive definitions on most computers are eventually implemented using a run-time stack, although the whole work of implementing recursion is done by the operating system, and the source code includes no indication of how it is performed. E. W. Dijkstra introduced the idea of using a stack to implement recursion. To better understand recursion and to see how it works, it is necessary to discuss the processing of function calls and to look at operations carried out by the system at function invocation and function exit.

■ 5.2 FUNCTION CALLS AND RECURSION IMPLEMENTATION

What happens when a function is called? If the function has formal parameters, they have to be initialized to the values passed as actual parameters. In addition, the system has to know where to resume execution of the program after the function has finished. The function can be called by other functions or by the main program (the function `main()`). The information indicating where it has been called from has to be remembered by the system. This could be done by storing the return address in main memory in a place set aside for return addresses, but we do not know in advance how much space might be needed, and allocating too much space for that purpose alone is not efficient.

For a function call, more information has to be stored than just a return address. Therefore, dynamic allocation using the run-time stack is a much better solution. But what information should be preserved when a function is called? First, automatic (local) variables must be stored. If function `f1()` which contains a declaration of an automatic variable `x` calls function `f2()` which locally declares the variable `x`, the system has to make a distinction between these two variables `x`. If `f2()` uses a variable `x`, then its own `x` is meant; if `f2()` assigns a value to `x`, then `x` belonging to `f1()` should be left unchanged. When `f2()` is finished, `f1()` can use the value assigned to its private `x` before `f2()` was called. This is especially important in the context of the present chapter, when `f1() = f2()`, when a function calls itself recursively. How does the system make a distinction between these two variables `x`?

The state of each function, including `main()`, is characterized by the contents of all automatic variables, by the values of the function's parameters, and by the return address indicating where to restart its caller. The data area containing all this information is called an *activation record* or *stack frame* and is allocated on the run-time stack. An activation record exists for as long as a function owning it is executing. This record is a private pool of information for the function, a repository that stores all information necessary for its proper execution and how to return to where it was called from. Activation records usually have a short lifespan because they are dynamically allocated at function entry and deallocated upon exiting. Only the activation record of `main()` outlives every other activation record.

An activation record usually contains the following information:

- Values for all parameters to the function; location of the first cell, if an array is passed or a variable is passed by reference, and copies of all other data items.

- Local (automatic) variables which can be stored elsewhere, in which case, the activation record contains only their descriptors and pointers to the locations where they are stored.

- The return address to resume control by the caller, the address of the caller's instruction immediately following the call.

- A dynamic link, which is a pointer to the caller's activation record.

- The returned value for a function not declared as **void**. Since the size of the activation record may vary from one call to another, the returned value is placed right above the activation record of the caller.

As mentioned above, if a function is called either by **main()** or by another function then its activation record is created on the run-time stack. The run-time stack always reflects the current state of the function. For example, suppose that **main()** calls function **f1()**, **f1()** calls **f2()**, and **f2()** in turn calls **f3()**. If **f3()** is being executed, then the state of the run-time stack is as shown in Figure 5.1. By the nature of the stack, if the activation record for **f3()** is popped by moving the stack pointer right below the return value of **f3()**, then **f2()** resumes execution and now has free access to the private pool of information necessary for reactivation of its execution. On the other hand, if **f3()**

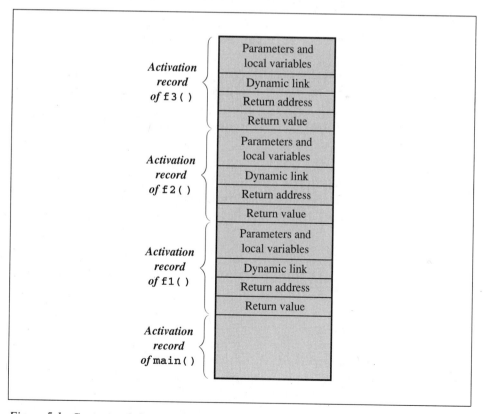

Figure 5.1: **Contents of the run-time stack when main() calls function f1(), f1() calls f2(), and f2() calls f3().**

happens to call another function **f4()**, then the run-time stack increases its height since the activation record for **f4()** is created on the stack and the activity of **f3()** is suspended.

Creating an activation record whenever a procedure is called allows the system to handle recursion properly. Recursion is calling a procedure that happens to have the same name as the caller. Therefore, a recursive call is not literally a function calling itself, but rather an instantiation of a function calling another instantiation of the same original. These invocations are represented internally by different activation records and are thus differentiated by the system.

■ 5.3 ANATOMY OF A RECURSIVE CALL

The function that defines raising any number x to a nonnegative integer power n is a good example of a recursive function. The most natural definition of this function is given by:

$$x^n = \begin{cases} 1 & \text{if } n = 0, \\ x * x^{n-1} & \text{if } n > 0 \end{cases}$$

A C++ function for computing x^n can be written directly from the definition of a power:

```
/* 102 */   float Power (float x, int n)
            {
/* 103 */     if (!n)      // if (n == 0)
/* 104 */       return 1.0;
            // else
/* 105 */     return x * Power(x,n-1);
            }
```

What if we called the function with a negative n? To avoid this problem, we can add another test in the function, such as **if (n < 0)**, and return a special value, say, -1, or print an error message, or we can make sure before **Power()** is called that $n \geq 0$.

Using this definition, the value of x^4 can be computed in the following way:

$$x^4 = x * x^3 = x * (x * x^2) = x * (x * (x * x^1)) = x * (x * (x * (x * x^0)))$$

$$= x * (x * (x * (x * 1))) = x * (x * (x * (x))) = x * (x * (x * x))$$

$$= x * (x * x * x) = x * x * x * x.$$

The repetitive application of the inductive step eventually leads to the anchor which is the last step in the chain of recursive calls. The anchor produces 1 as a result of raising x to the power of zero; the result is passed back to the previous recursive call. Now, that call, whose execution has been pending, returns its result, $x * 1 = x$. The third call, which has been waiting for this result, computes its own result, namely $x * x$, and returns it. Next, this number $x * x$ is received by the second call which multiplies it by x and returns the result, $x * x * x$, to the first invocation of **Power()**. This call receives $x * x * x$, multiplies it by

x, and returns the final result. In this way, each new call increases the level of recursion, as shown below:

call 1	$x^4 = x * x^3$	$= x * x * x * x$
call 2	$x * x^2$	$= x * x * x$
call 3	$x * x^1$	$= x * x$
call 4	$x * x^0 = x * 1 = x$	
call 5	1	

or, alternatively, as

```
call 1        Power(x,4)
call 2          Power(x,3)
call 3            Power(x,2)
call 4              Power(x,1)
call 5                Power(x,0)
call 5                1
call 4              x
call 3            x * x
call 2          x * x * x
call 1        x * x * x * x
```

What does the system do as the function is being executed? As we already know, the system keeps track of all calls on its run-time stack. Each line of code is assigned a number by the system[1] and if a line is a function call, then its number is a return address. The address is used by the system to remember where to resume execution after the function has completed. For this example, assume that the lines in the function **Power()** are assigned the numbers 102 through 105, and that it is called in **main()** from the statement

```
          main()
          { ...
/* 136 */   y = Power(5.6,2);
            ...
          }
```

A trace of the recursive calls is relatively simple, as indicated by this diagram

```
call 1        Power(5.6,2)
call 2          Power(5.6,1)
call 3            Power(5.6,0)
call 3            1
call 2          5.6
call 1        31.36
```

since most of the operations are performed on the run-time stack.

---

[1]This is not quite precise since the system uses assembly code rather than source code to execute programs. This means that one line of source program is usually implemented by several lines of assembly statements.

When the function is invoked for the first time, four items are pushed onto the run-time stack: the return address 136, the actual parameters 5.6 and 2, and one location reserved for the value returned by **Power()**. Figure 5.2a represents this situation. (In this and subsequent diagrams, SP is a stack pointer, AR is an activation record, and question marks stand for locations reserved for the returned values. To distinguish values from addresses, the latter are parenthesized, although addresses are numbers exactly like function arguments.)

Now, the function **Power()** is executed. First, the value of the second argument, 2, is checked, and **Power()** tries to return the value of 5.6* **Power(5.6,1)**, because that argument is not 0. This cannot be done immediately since the system does not know the value of **Power(5.6,1)**; it must be computed first. Therefore, **Power()** is called again with the arguments 5.6 and 1. But before this call is executed, the run-time stack receives new items, and its contents are shown in Figure 5.2b.

Again, the second argument is checked to see if it is 0. Since it is equal to 1, **Power()** is called for the third time with the arguments 5.6 and 0. Before the function is executed, the system remembers the arguments and the return address by putting them on the stack, not forgetting to allocate one cell for the result. Figure 5.2c contains the new contents of the stack.

Again, the question arises: is the second argument equal to zero? Because it finally is, a concrete value — namely 1.0 — can be returned and placed on the stack, and the function is finished without making any additional calls. At this point there are two pending calls

	(a)	(b)	(c)	(d)	(e)	(f)	(g)	(h)
Third call to Power()				0 ← SP 5.6 (105) ?	0 ← SP 5.6 (105) 1.0	0 5.6 (105) 1.0		
Second call to Power()		1 ← SP 5.6 (105) ?	1 5.6 (105) ?	1 5.6 (105) ?	1 ← SP 5.6 (105) ?	1 ← SP 5.6 (105) 5.6	1 5.6 (105) 5.6	
First call to Power()	2 ← SP 5.6 (136) ?	2 5.6 (136) ?	2 5.6 (136) ?	2 5.6 (136) ?	2 5.6 (136) ?	2 5.6 (136) ?	2 ← SP 5.6 (136) ?	2 ← SP 5.6 (136) 31.36
AR for main()	⋮ y ⋮	⋮ y ⋮	⋮ y ⋮	⋮ y ⋮	⋮ y ⋮	⋮ y ⋮	⋮ y ⋮	⋮ y ⋮

Key: SP Stack pointer
AR Activation record
? Location reserved for returned value

Figure 5.2: **Changes to the run-time stack during execution of** **Power(5.6,2).**

on the run-time stack — the calls to **Power()** — that have to be completed. How is this done? The system first eliminates the activation record of **Power()** that has just finished. This is performed logically by popping all its fields (the result, two arguments, and the return address) off the stack. We say "logically" since physically all these fields remain on the stack and only the SP is decremented appropriately. This is important since we do not want the result to be destroyed since it has not been used yet. Before and after completion of the last call of **Power()**, the stack looks the same, but the SP's value is changed (see Figure 5.2d and 5.2e).

Now the second call to **Power()** can complete since it waited for the result of the call **Power(5.6,0)**. This result, 1.0, is multiplied by 5.6 and stored in the field allocated for the result. After that, the system can pop the current activation record off the stack by decrementing the SP and can finish the execution of the first call to **Power()** that needed the result from the second call. Figure 5.2f shows the contents of the stack before changing the SP's value, and Figure 5.2g shows the contents of the stack after this change. At this moment, **Power()** can finish its first call by multiplying the result of its second call, 5.6, by its first argument, also 5.6. The system now returns to the function that invoked **Power()**, and the final value, 31.36, is assigned to **y**. Right before the assignment is executed, the content of the stack looks like Figure 5.2h.

The function **Power()** can be implemented differently, without using any recursion, as in the following loop:

```
float
NonRecPower(float x, int n)
{float result = 1;

  if (n > 0)
    for (result = x ; n > 1; --n)
        result *= x;
  return result;
}
```

Do we gain anything by using recursion instead of a loop? The recursive version seems to be more intuitive since it is similar to the original definition of the power function. The definition is simply expressed in C++ without losing the original structure of the definition. The recursive version increases program readability, improves self-documentation, and simplifies coding. In our example, the code of the nonrecursive version is not substantially larger than in the recursive version, but for most recursive implementations the code is shorter than it is in the nonrecursive implementations.

■ 5.4 TAIL RECURSION

All recursive definitions contain a reference to a set or function being defined. There are, however, a variety of ways such a reference can be implemented. This reference can be done in a straightforward manner or in an intricate fashion, just once or many times. There may be many possible levels of recursion, or different levels of complexity. In the following sections, some of these types are discussed, starting with the simplest case, *tail recursion*.

Tail recursion is characterized by the use of only one recursive call at the very end of a function implementation. In other words, when the call is made, there are no statements left to be executed by the function; the recursive call is not only the last statement, but there are no earlier recursive calls, direct or indirect. For example, the function **Tail()** defined as

```
void
Tail (int i)
{
 if (i > 0) {
    cout << i << ' ';
    Tail(i-1);
 }
}
```

is an example of a function with tail recursion, whereas the function **NoTail()**, defined as

```
void
NoTail (int i)
{
 if (i > 0) {
    NoTail(i-1);
    cout << i << ' ';
    NoTail(i-1);
 }
}
```

is not. Tail recursion is simply a glorified loop and can be easily replaced by such. In this example, it is replaced by substituting a loop for the **if** statement, and incrementing or decrementing the variable in accordance with recursive call. In this way **Tail()** can be expressed by an iterative function:

```
void
IterativeEquivalentOfTail (int i)
{
 for ( ; i > 0; i--)
    cout << i << ' ';
}
```

Is there any advantage in using tail recursion over iteration? For languages such as C++ there may be no compelling advantage, but in a language such as Prolog, which has no explicit loop construct (loops are simulated by recursion), tail recursion acquires a much greater weight. In languages endowed with a loop or its equivalents, such as **if** statement combined with a **goto** statement, tail recursion is not a recommended feature.

■ 5.5 NONTAIL RECURSION

Another problem that can be implemented in recursion is printing an input line in reverse order. Here is a simple recursive implementation:

```
            void
/* 200 */ Reverse()
          {   char ch;
/* 201 */     cin.get(ch);
/* 202 */     if (ch != '\n') {
/* 203 */         Reverse();
/* 204 */         cout.put(ch);
              }
          }
```

Where is the trick? It does not seem possible that the function does anything. But, it turns out that, by the power of recursion, it does exactly what it was designed for. **main()** calls **Reverse()** and the input is the string: "ABC." First, an activation record is created with cells for the variable **ch** and the return address. There is no need to reserve a cell for a result, since no value is returned, which is indicated by using **void** in front of the function's name. The function **get()** reads in the first character, "A". Figure 5.3a shows the contents of the run-time stack right before **Reverse()** calls itself recursively for the first time.

The second character is read in and checked to see if it is the end-of-line character, and if not, **Reverse()** is called again. But in either case, the value of **ch** is pushed onto the run-time stack along with the return address. Before **Reverse()** is called for a third time (the second time recursively), there are two more items on the stack (see Figure 5.3b).

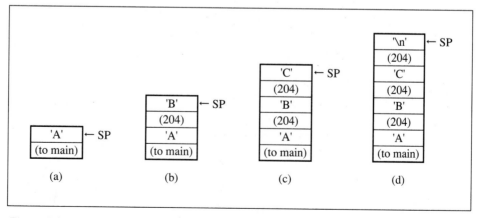

Figure 5.3: **Changes on the run-time stack during the execution of**
            Reverse().

Note that the function is called as many times as the number of characters contained in the input string, including the end-of-line character. In our example, **Reverse()** is called four times, and the run-time stack during the last call is shown in Figure 5.3d.

On the fourth call, **get()** finds the end-of-line character and **Reverse()** executes no other statement. The system retrieves the return address from the activation record and discards this record by decrementing SP by the proper number of bytes. Execution resumes from line 204, which is a print statement. Because the activation record of the third call is now active, the value of **ch**, the letter "C," is output as the first character. Next, the activation record of the third call to **Reverse()** is discarded and now SP points to where the letter "B" is stored. The second call is about to be finished but first "B" is assigned to **ch** and then the statement on line 204 is executed, which results in printing "B" on the screen right after "C". Finally, the activation record of the first call to **Reverse()** is reached. The letter "A" is then printed, and what can be seen on the screen is the string "CBA." The first call is finally finished and the program continues execution in **main()**.

Compare the recursive implementation with a nonrecursive version of the same function:

```
void
SimpleIterativeReverse()
{char stack[80];
 register int top;

 cin.getline(stack,80);
 for (top = strlen(stack) - 1; top >= 0; cout.put(stack[top--]));
}
```

The function is quite short and, perhaps a bit more cryptic than its recursive counter-part. What is the difference then? Keep in mind that the brevity and relative simplicity of the second version are due mainly to the fact that we want to reverse a string or array of characters. This means that functions like **strlen()** and **getline()** from the standard C++ library can be used. If we are not supplied with such functions, then our iterative function has to be implemented differently:

```
void
IterativeReverse()
{char stack[80];
 register int top = 0;

 cin.get(stack[top]);
 while(stack[top]!='\n')
   cin.get(stack[++top]);
 for (top -= 2; top >= 0; cout.put(stack[top--]));
}
```

The **while** loop replaces **getline()** and the autoincrement of variable **top** replaces **strlen()**. The **for** loop is about the same as before. This discussion is not purely theoretical because reversing an input line consisting of integers uses the same implementation as `IterativeReverse()` after changing the data type of **stack** from **char** to **int** and modifying the **while** loop.

Note that the variable name **stack** used for the array is not accidental. We are just making explicit what is done implicitly by the system. Our stack takes over the run-time stack's duty. Its use is necessary here since one simple loop does not suffice, as in the case of tail recursion. In addition, the statement **put()** from the recursive version has to be accounted for. Note also that the variable **stack** was local to the function `IterativeReverse()`. However, if it were a requirement to have a global stack object **st**, then this implementation can be written as

```
void
NonRecursiveReverse()
{   int ch;

    st.Clear();
    cin.get(ch);
    while (ch != '\n') {
        st.Push(ch);
        cin.get(ch);
    }
    while (!st.IsEmpty())
        cout.put(st.Pop());
}
```

It is assumed that a class **stack** and its member functions have already been defined. This means that the code is much larger than in our original recursive version and more things must be taken care of.

After comparing `IterativeReverse()` to `NonRecursiveReverse()`, we can conclude that the first version is better because it is faster, because no procedure calls are made and the function is self-sufficient, whereas `NonRecursiveReverse()` calls at least one function during each loop iteration, slowing down execution. We can define **Push()**, **Pop()**, etc. as inline functions. This means that the compiler embeds these functions in the source code. Execution is then faster at the cost of a slightly longer compile time. This is a more satisfying solution for cases more complex than the function **Reverse()**.

One way or the other, the transformation of recursion into iteration usually involves the explicit handling of a stack. Furthermore, when converting a function from a recursive into an iterative version, program clarity can be diminished and the brevity of program formulation lost. Iterative versions of recursive C++ functions are not as verbose as in other programming languages so program brevity may not be an issue.

An excellent example of a program that can be greatly simplified by the use of recursion is the Chapter 4 case study, drawing a curve resembling a snowflake. As already explained, on a given level, first a line is drawn, then the next line is drawn after making a 60° left turn, the next after a 120° right turn, and finally, after having made a 60° left turn, the last line is drawn. These four lines and three turns form one cycle only. Each of these four lines can also be compound lines drawn by the use of the described cycle. This is a situation in which recursion is well suited, which is reflected by the following pseudocode:

```
DrawFourLines (level)
    if (level = 0)
        draw a line;
    else
        DrawFourLines(level-1);
        turn left 60°;
        DrawFourLines(level-1);
        turn left 120°;
        DrawFourLines(level-1);
        turn left 60°;
        DrawFourLines(level-1);
```

This pseudocode can be rendered almost without change into C++ code. However, remember that a line drawn must not be of deliberate length, because the snowflake drawn will not be a closed line. Therefore, the original line is divided in three parts, each of which is divided in three parts also, `level-1` times. Figure 5.4 contains the C++ code for this example.

■ 5.6 INDIRECT RECURSION

The preceding sections discussed only direct recursion, where a function `f()` called itself. However, `f()` can call itself indirectly via a chain of other calls. For example, `f()` can call `g()`, and `g()` can call `f()`. This is the simplest case of indirect recursion.

The chain of intermediate calls can be of an arbitrary length, as in:

```
f() -> f1() -> f2() -> ... -> fn() -> f()
```

There is also the situation when `f()` can call itself indirectly through different chains. Thus, in addition to the chain just given, another chain might also be possible. For instance

```
f() -> g1() -> g2() -> ... -> gm() -> f()
```

This situation can be exemplified by three functions used for decoding information. `receive()` stores the incoming information in a buffer, `decode()` converts it into legible form, and `store()` stores it in a file. `receive()` fills the buffer and calls `decode()`, which, in turn, after finishing its job, submits the buffer with decoded information to `store()`. After `store()` accomplishes its task, it calls `receive()` to intercept more encoded information using the same buffer. Therefore we have the chain of calls

```
receive() -> decode() -> store() -> receive() -> decode() -> ...
```

which is finished when no new information arrives. These three functions work in the following manner:

```
//                              Turbo C++ program
class RecursiveCurve {
public:
     RecursiveCurve() { angle = 0.0; }
     void ReadInitValues();
     void Snowflake();
private:
     double side, angle;
     int level;
     void Right(double x) { angle += x; }
     void Left (double x) { angle -= x; }
     void DrawFourLines(double side, int level);
};


void
RecursiveCurve::DrawFourLines(double side, int level)
{                                         // arguments to sin()
   if (level == 0)                        // and cos() are angles
       linerel((cos(angle*3.14/180)*side),  // specified in radians,
               (sin(angle*3.14/180)*side));  // i.e., the coefficient
   else {                                 // 3.14/180 is necessary;
       DrawFourLines(side/3.0,level-1);
       Left (60);
       DrawFourLines(side/3.0,level-1);
       Right(120);
       DrawFourLines(side/3.0,level-1);
       Left (60);
       DrawFourLines(side/3.0,level-1);
   }
}


void
RecursiveCurve::Snowflake()
{   int i;

   for (i = 1; i <= 3; i++) {
       DrawFourLines(side,level);
       Right(120);
   }
}
```

Figure 5.4: **Recursive implementation of the von Koch snowflake.**

```
receive(buffer)
    while buffer is not filled up
        if information is still incoming
            get a character and store it in buffer;
        else exit();
        decode(buffer);

decode(buffer)
    decode information in buffer;
    store(buffer);

store(buffer)
    transfer information from buffer to file;
    receive(buffer);
```

A more mathematically oriented example concerns formulas calculating the trigonometric functions sine, cosine, and tangent:

$$\sin(x) = \sin\left(\frac{x}{3}\right) * \frac{\left(3 - \tan^2\left(\frac{x}{3}\right)\right)}{\left(1 + \tan^2\left(\frac{x}{3}\right)\right)}$$

$$\tan(x) = \frac{\sin(x)}{\cos(x)}$$

$$\cos(x) = 1 - \sin\left(\frac{x}{2}\right)$$

As usual in the case of recursion, there has to be an anchor in order to avoid falling into an infinite loop of recursive calls. In the case of sine, we can use the following approximation:

$$\sin(x) \approx x - \frac{x^3}{6}$$

where small values of x give a better approximation. In order to compute the sine of a number x such that its absolute value is greater than an assumed tolerance, we have to compute $\sin\left(\frac{x}{3}\right)$ directly, $\sin\left(\frac{x}{3}\right)$ indirectly through tangent, and, also indirectly, $\sin\left(\frac{x}{6}\right)$ through tangent and cosine. If the absolute value of $\frac{x}{3}$ is sufficiently small, which would not require other recursive calls, we can represent all the calls as a tree, as in Figure 5.5.

■ 5.7 NESTED RECURSION

A more complicated case of recursion is found in definitions in which a function is not only defined in terms of itself but it is also used as one of the parameters. The following definition is an example of such a nesting:

$$h(n) = \begin{cases} 0 & \text{if } n = 0, \\ n & \text{if } n > 4, \\ h(2 + h(2n)) & \text{if } n \le 4. \end{cases}$$

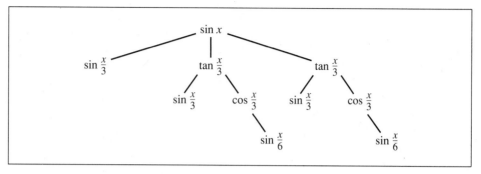

Figure 5.5: **A tree of recursive calls for sin (x).**

Function *h* has a solution for all $n \geq 0$. This fact is obvious for all $n > 4$, but it has to be proven for $n = 1, 2, 3$, and 4. Thus, $h(2) = h(2 + h(4)) = h(2 + h(2 + h(8))) = 12$. (What are the values of $h(n)$ for $n = 1, 3$, and 4?)

Another example of nested recursion is a very important function originally suggested by Wilhelm Ackermann in 1928 and later modified by Rozsa Peter:

$$A(n, m) = \begin{cases} m + 1 & \text{if } n = 0, \\ A(n - 1, m) & \text{if } n > 0, m = 0, \\ A(n - 1, A(n, m - 1)) & \text{otherwise.} \end{cases}$$

This function is interesting because of its remarkably rapid growth. It grows so fast that it is guaranteed not to have a representation by a formula that uses arithmetical operations such as addition, multiplication, and exponentiation. To illustrate the rate of growth of the Ackermann function, we need only show that

$$A(3, m) = 2^{m+3} - 3$$

$$A(4, m) = 2^{2^{2^{.^{.^{2^{16}}}}}} - 3$$

with a stack of *m* 2s in the exponent; $A(4, 1) = 2^{2^{16}} - 3 = 2^{65536} - 3$, which exceeds even the number of atoms in the universe (which is 10^{80} according to current theories).

The definition translates very nicely into C++, while the task of expressing it in a nonrecursive form would be truly troublesome.

■ 5.8 EXCESSIVE RECURSION

Logical simplicity and readability are used as an argument supporting the use of recursion. The price for using recursion is slowing down execution time and storing on the run-time stack more things than required in a nonrecursive approach. If recursion is too deep (for example, computing $5.6^{100,000}$), then we can run out of space on the stack and our program crashes. But usually the number of recursive calls is much smaller than 100,000 so the danger of overflowing the stack may not be imminent.[2] However, if some recursive function repeats the computations for some parameters, the run time can be prohibitively long even for very simple cases.

Consider Fibonacci numbers. A sequence of Fibonacci numbers is defined as follows:

$$\text{Fib}(n) = \begin{cases} n & \text{if } n < 2, \\ \text{Fib}(n-2) + \text{Fib}(n-1) & \text{otherwise.} \end{cases}$$

The definition states that if the first two numbers are 0 and 1, then any number in the sequence is the sum of its two predecessors. But these predecessors are in turn sums of their predecessors, and so on, to the beginning of the sequence. The sequence produced by the definition is

$$0, 1, 1, 2, 3, 5, 8, 13, 21, 34, 55, 89, \ldots$$

How can this definition be implemented in C++? It takes almost term-by-term translation to have a recursive version, which is

```
int
Fib (int n)
{
  if (n < 2)
    return n;
  // else
    return Fib(n-2) + Fib(n-1);
}
```

The function is simple and easy to understand but extremely inefficient. To see it, compute **Fib(6)**, the seventh number of the sequence, which is 8. Based on the definition, the computation runs as follows:

```
Fib(6) =                        Fib(4)                        + Fib(5)
       =      Fib(2)         +          Fib(3)                + Fib(5)
       =   Fib(0)+Fib(1)     +          Fib(3)                + Fib(5)
       =    0  +   1         +          Fib(3)                + Fib(5)
       =        1            + Fib(1)+     Fib(2)             + Fib(5)
       =        1            + Fib(1)+Fib(0)+Fib(1)  + Fib(5)
```

etc.

This is just the beginning of our calculation process, and even here there are certain shortcuts. All these calculations can be expressed more concisely in the form of the tree shown in Figure 5.6. Tremendous inefficiency results because the **Fib()** is called 25 times in order to determine the seventh element of the Fibonacci sequence. The source of this

---

[2]Even if we try to compute the value of $5.6^{100,000}$ using an iterative algorithm, we are not completely free from a troublesome situation since the number is much too large to fit even a variable of double length. Thus, although the program would not crash, the computed value would be incorrect (why?) which may be even more dangerous than a program crash.

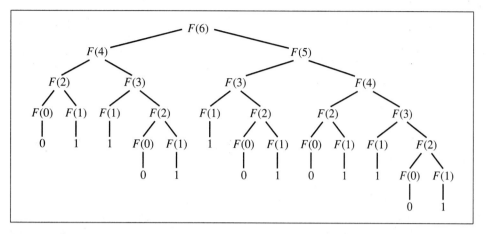

Figure 5.6: **The tree of calls for `Fib(6)`.**

inefficiency is the repetition of the same calculations since the system forgets what has already been calculated. For example, **`Fib()`** is called eight times with parameter **n**= 1 to decide that 1 can be returned. For each number of the sequence, the function computes all its predecessors without taking into account that it would suffice to do this only once. To find **`Fib(6)`** = 8, it computes **`Fib(5)`**, **`Fib(4)`**, **`Fib(3)`**, **`Fib(2)`**, **`Fib(1)`**, and **`Fib(0)`** first. To determine these values, **`Fib(4)`**, . . . , **`Fib(0)`** have to be computed to know the value of **`Fib(5)`**. Independently of this, the chain of computations **`Fib(3)`**, . . . , **`Fib(0)`** is executed to find **`Fib(4)`**. Why must this happen if **`Fib(4)`** has already been computed?

We can prove that the number of additions required to find **`Fib(n)`** using a recursive definition is equal to Fib$(n + 1) - 1$. Counting two calls per one addition plus the very first call means that **`Fib()`** is called $2 * \text{Fib}(n + 1) - 1$ times in order to compute **`Fib(n)`**. This number can be exceedingly large for fairly small ns, as the table in Figure 5.7 indicates.

It takes almost a quarter of a million calls in order to find the twenty-fifth Fibonacci number, and nearly three million calls to determine the thirtieth! This is too heavy a price for the simplicity of the recursive algorithm. As the number of calls and the run time grow exponentially with n, the algorithm has to be abandoned except for very small numbers.

n	Fib(n+1)	Number of Additions	Number of Calls
6	13	12	25
10	89	88	177
15	987	986	1973
20	10946	10945	21891
25	121393	121392	242785
30	1346269	1346268	2692537

Figure 5.7: **Number of addition operations and number of recursive calls to calculate Fibonacci numbers.**

An iterative algorithm may be produced rather easily as follows:

```
int
IterativeFib (int n)
{
    if (n < 2)
        return n;
    else {
        register int i = 2, tmp, current = 1, last = 0;
        for ( ; i <= n; ++i) {
            tmp = current;
            current += last;
            last = tmp;
        }
        return current;
    }
}
```

For each $n > 2$, the function loops $n-2$ times making three assignments per iteration and only one addition, disregarding the autoincrement of i (see Figure 5.8).

However, there is another, numerical method for computing Fib(n), using a formula discovered by A. de Moivre:

$$\text{Fib}(n) = \frac{\phi^n - \hat{\phi}^n}{\sqrt{5}}$$

where $\phi = \frac{1}{2}(1 + \sqrt{5})$ and $\hat{\phi} = 1 - \phi = \frac{1}{2}(1 - \sqrt{5}) \approx -0.618034$. Because $-1 < \hat{\phi} < 0$, $\hat{\phi}^n$ becomes very small when n grows. Therefore, it can be omitted from the formula and

$$\text{Fib}(n) = \frac{\phi^n}{\sqrt{5}}$$

		Assignments	
n	Number of Additions	Iterative Algorithm	Recursive Algorithm
6	5	15	25
10	9	27	177
15	14	42	1973
20	19	57	21891
25	24	72	242785
30	29	87	2692537

Figure 5.8: **Comparison of iterative and recursive algorithms for calculating Fibonacci numbers.**

approximated to the nearest integer. This leads us to the third implementation for computing a Fibonacci number. To round the result to the nearest integer, we use the function `ceil` (for ceiling):

```
int
deMoivreFib (int n)
{
  return ceil(exp(n*log(1.6180339897) - log(2.2360679775)) - .5);
}
```

Try to justify this implementation using the definition of logarithm.

■ 5.9 BACKTRACKING

In solving some problems, a situation arises where there are different ways leading from a given position, none of them known to lead to a solution. After trying one path unsuccessfully, we return to this crossroads and try to find a solution using another path. However, we must ascertain that such a return is possible and that all paths can be tried. This technique is called *backtracking* and it allows us to systematically try all available avenues from a certain point after some of them lead to nowhere. Using backtracking, we can always return to a position which offers other possibilities for successfully solving the problem. This technique is used in artificial intelligence, and one of the problems in which backtracking is very useful is the eight queens problem.

The eight queens problem attempts to place eight queens on a chessboard in such a way that no queen is attacking any other. The rules of chess say that a queen can take another piece if it lies on the same row, on the same column, or on the same diagonal as the queen (see Figure 5.9). To solve this problem, we try to put the first queen on the board,

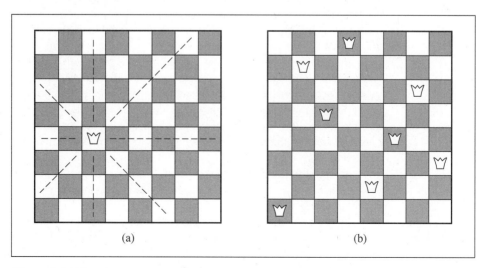

(a)   (b)

Figure 5.9: **The eight queens problem.**

then the second, so that it cannot take the first, then the third, so that it is not in conflict with the two already placed, and so on, until all of the queens are placed. What happens if, for instance, the sixth queen cannot be placed in a nonconflicting position? We choose another position for the fifth queen and try again with the sixth. If this does not work, the fifth queen is moved again. If all the possible positions for the fifth queen have been tried, the fourth queen is moved and then the process restarts. This process requires a great deal of effort, most of which is spent backtracking to the first crossroads offering some untried avenues. In terms of code, however, the process is rather simple due to the power of recursion which is a natural implementation of backtracking. Pseudocode for this backtracking algorithm is as follows (the last line pertains to backtracking):

```
PutQueen(row)
    for every position col on the same row
        if position col is available
            place the next queen in position col;
            if (row < 8)
                PutQueen(row+1);
            else success ;
            remove the queen from position col;
```

This algorithm finds all possible solutions without regard to the fact that some of them are symmetrical.

The most natural approach for implementing this algorithm is to declare an 8×8 array **board** of 1s and 0s representing a chessboard. The array is initialized to 1s and each time a queen is put in a position (r, c), **board[r,c]** is set to 0. Also, a function must set to 0, as not available, all positions on row r, in column c, and on both diagonals that cross each other in position (r, c). When backtracking, the same positions, that is, positions on corresponding row, column and diagonals have to be set back to 1, as again available. Since we can expect hundreds of attempts to find available positions for queens, the setting and resetting process is the most time-consuming part of the implementation; for each queen, between 22 and 28 positions would have to be set and then reset, 15 for row and column, and between 7 and 13 for diagonals.

In this approach, the board is viewed from the perspective of the player who sees the entire board along with all the pieces at the same time. However, if we focus solely on the queens, we can consider the chessboard from their perspective. For the queens, the board is not divided into squares, but into rows, columns, and diagonals. If a queen is placed on a single square, it resides not only on this field square, but on the entire row, column, and diagonal, treating them as its own temporary property. A different data structure can be utilized to represent this.

To simplify the problem for the first solution, we use a 4×4 chessboard instead of the regular 8×8 board. Later, we can make the rather obvious changes in the program to accommodate it to the regular board.

Figure 5.10 contains the 4×4 chessboard. Notice that indexes in all fields in the indicated left diagonal all add up to three, $r + c = 3$; this number is associated with this diagonal. There are seven left diagonals, 0 through 6. Indexes in the fields of the indicated right diagonal all have the same difference, $r - c = -1$, and this number is unique among all right diagonals. Therefore, right diagonals are assigned numbers -3 through 3. The

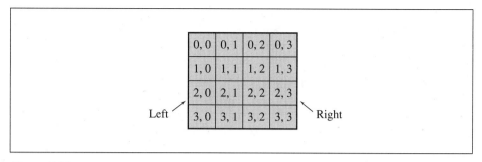

Figure 5.10: **A 4 × 4 chessboard.**

data structure used for all left diagonals is simply an array indexed by numbers 0–6. For right diagonals it is also an array, but it cannot be indexed by negative numbers. Therefore, it is an array of seven cells, but in order to account for negative values obtained from the formula $r - c$, the same number is always added to it in order not to cross the bounds of this array.

An analogous array is also needed for columns, but not for rows, since a queen i is moved along row i and all queens $< i$ have already been placed in rows $< i$. Figure 5.11 contains the code to implement these arrays. The program is short due to recursion, which hides some of the goings-on from the user's sight.

```
const int available = 1, squares = 4, norm = squares-1;

class ChessBoard {
public:
      ChessBoard();
      void FindSolutions()    { PutQueen(0); }
      void NumberOfSolutions() { cout << howMany << " solutions found.\n"; }
private:
      void PutQueen(const int);
      int column[squares], positionInRow[squares], howMany,
          leftDiagonal[squares*2 - 1], rightDiagonal[squares*2 - 1];
      void PrintBoard(ostream& out);
}

ChessBoard::ChessBoard()
{   register int i;

    for (i = 0; i < squares; i++)
        positionInRow[i] = -1;
```

Figure 5.11: **Eight queens problem implementation.**   **continued**

```
    for (i = 0; i < squares; i++)
        column[i] = available;
    for (i = 0; i <= squares*2 - 1; i++)
        leftDiagonal[i] = rightDiagonal[i] = available;
    howMany = 0;
};


void
ChessBoard::PutQueen(const int row)
{   int col;

    for (col = 0; col < squares; col++)
        if (column[col] == available &&
            leftDiagonal [row+col] == available &&
            rightDiagonal[row-col+norm] == available) {
            positionInRow[row] = col;
            column[col] = !available;
            leftDiagonal[row+col] = !available;
            rightDiagonal[row-col+norm] = !available;
            if (row < squares-1)
                 PutQueen(row+1);
            else PrintBoard(cout);
            column[col] = available;
            leftDiagonal[row+col] = available;
            rightDiagonal[row-col+norm] = available;
        }
}
```

Figure 5.11: **Eight queens problem implementation.**

Move	Queen	row	col	
{1}	1	0	0	
{2}	2	1	2	failure
{3}	2	1	3	
{4}	3	2	1	failure
{5}	1	0	1	
{6}	2	1	3	
{7}	3	2	0	
{8}	4	3	2	

Figure 5.12: **Steps leading to the first successful configuration of four queens as found by the function** PutQueen().

PositionInRow	Column	LeftDiagonal	RightDiagonal	row
$(0, 2, ,)$ $\{1\}\{2\}$	$(!a, a, !a, a)$ $\{1\}$ $\{2\}$	$(!a, a, a, !a, a, a, a)$ $\{1\}$ $\{2\}$	$(a, a, !a, !a, a, a, a)$ $\{2\}\{1\}$	$0, 1$ $\{1\}\{2\}$
$(0, 3, 1,)$ $\{1\}\{3\}\{4\}$	$(!a, !a, a, !a)$ $\{1\}$ $\{4\}$ $\{3\}$	$(!a, a, a, !a, !a, a, a)$ $\{1\}$ $\{4\}\{3\}$	$(a, !a, a, !a, !a, a, a)$ $\{3\}$ $\{1\}\{4\}$	$1, 2$ $\{3\}\{4\}$
$(1, 3, 0, 2)$ $\{5\}\{6\}\{7\}\{8\}$	$(!a, !a, !a, !a)$ $\{7\}\{5\}\{8\}\{6\}$	$(a, !a, !a, a, !a, !a, a)$ $\{5\}\{7\}$ $\{6\}\{8\}$	$(a, !a, !a, a, !a, !a, a)$ $\{6\}\{5\}$ $\{8\}\{7\}$	$0, 1, 2, 3$ $\{5\}\{6\}\{7\}\{8\}$

Figure 5.13: **Changes in the four arrays used by function PutQueen().**

Figure 5.12 through 5.15 document the steps taken by **PutQueen()** to place four queens on the chessboard. Figure 5.12 contains the move number, queen number, and row and column number for each attempt to place a queen. Figure 5.13 contains the changes to the arrays **PositionInRow**, **Column**, **LeftDiagonal**, and **RightDiagonal**. Figure 5.14 shows the changes to the run-time stack during the eight steps. All changes to the run-time stack are depicted by an activation record for each iteration of the **for** loop, which mostly lead to a new invocation of **PutQueen()**. Each activation record stores a return address and the values of **row** and **col**. Figure 5.15 illustrates the changes to the chessboard.

The detailed description of each step follows.

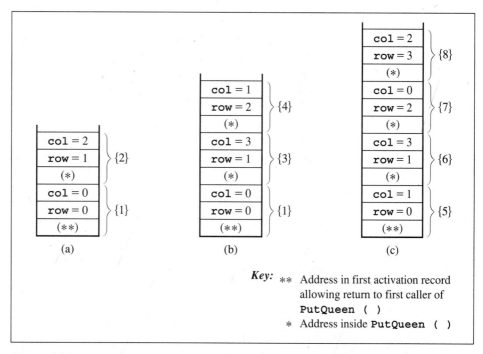

Figure 5.14: **Changes on the run-time stack for the first successful completion of PutQueen().**

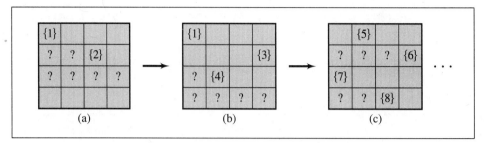

Figure 5.15: **Changes to the chessboard leading to the first successful configuration.**

{1} We start by trying to put the first queen in the upper left corner $(0, 0)$. Since it is the very first move, the condition in the **if** statement is met, and the queen is placed in this square. After the queen is placed, the column 0, the main right diagonal, and the leftmost diagonal are marked as unavailable. In Figure 5.13, {1} is put underneath cells reset to **!available** in this step.

{2} Since **row<3**, **PutQueen()** calls itself with **row+1**, but before its execution, an activation record is created on the run-time stack (see Figure 5.14a). Now, we check the availability of a field on the second row (i.e., **row==1**). For **col==0**, column 0 is guarded, for **col==1**, main right diagonal is checked, and for **col==2**, all three parts of the **if** statement condition are true. Therefore, the second queen is placed in position $(1, 2)$ and this fact is immediately reflected in the proper cells of all three arrays. Again, **row<3**. **PutQueen()** is called trying to locate the third queen in row 2. After all the positions in this row, 0 through 3, are tested, no available position is found and the **for** loop is exited without executing the body of the **if** statement, and this call to **PutQueen()** is complete. But this call was executed by **PutQueen()** dealing with the second row, to which control is now returned.

{3} Values of **col** and **row** are restored and the execution of the second call of **PutQueen()** continues by resetting some fields in all arrays back to **available**, and since **col==2**, the **for** loop can continue iteration. The test in the **if** statement allows the second queen to be placed on the board, this time in position $(1, 3)$.

{4} Afterwards, **PutQueen()** is called again with **row==2**, and the third queen is put in $(2, 1)$, and after the next call to **PutQueen()**, an attempt to place the fourth queen is unsuccessful (see Figure 5.15b). No calls are made, the call from step 3 is resumed, and the third queen is once again moved, but no position can be found for it. At the same time, **col** becomes 3, and the **for** loop is finished.

{5} As a result, the first call of **PutQueen()** resumes execution by placing the first queen in position $(0, 1)$.

{6–8} This time execution continues smoothly and we obtain a complete solution.

Figure 5.16 contains a trace of all calls leading to the first successful placement of four queens on a 4×4 chessboard.

```
PutQueen(0);
  col = 0;
  PutQueen(1);
    col = 0;
    col = 1;
    col = 2;
    PutQueen(2);
      col = 0;
      col = 1;
      col = 2;
      col = 3;
    col = 3;
    PutQueen(2);
      col = 0;
      col = 1;
      PutQueen(3);
        col = 0;
        col = 1;
        col = 2;
        col = 3;
      col = 2;
      col = 3;
  col = 1;
  PutQueen(1);
    col = 0;
    col = 1;
    col = 2;
    col = 3;
    PutQueen(2)
      col = 0;
      PutQueen(3)
        col = 0;
        col = 1;
        col = 2;
        success;
```

Figure 5.16: **Trace of calls to** PutQueen() **to place four queens.**

■ 5.10 CONCLUDING REMARKS

After looking at all these examples (and one more to follow), what can be said about recursion as a programming tool? Like any other topic in data structures, it should be used with good judgment. There are no general rules prescribing when to use it and when to refrain from using it. Each particular problem decides. Recursion is usually less efficient than its iterative equivalent. But if a recursive program takes 100 milliseconds (ms) for execution, for example, and the iterative version only 10 ms, then although the latter is ten times faster than the former, the difference is hardly perceivable. If there is an advantage in the clarity, readability, and simplicity of the code, the difference in the execution time between these two versions can be disregarded. Recursion is often simpler than the iterative solution and more consistent with the logic of the original algorithm. The factorial and power functions are such examples, and we will see more interesting cases in chapters to follow.

Although every recursive procedure can be converted into an iterative version, the conversion is not always a trivial task. In particular, it may involve explicitly manipulating a stack. That is where the time-space tradeoff comes into play: using iteration often necessitates the introduction of a new data structure to implement a stack, whereas recursion relieves the programmer of this task by handing it over to the system. One way or the other, if nontail recursion is involved, very often a stack has to be maintained by the programmer or by the system. But it is the programmer who decides who carries the load.

Two situations can be presented in which a nonrecursive implementation is preferable even if a recursion is a more natural solution. First, iteration should be used in programs where an immediate response is vital for proper functioning of the program. For example, in military environments, in the space shuttle, or in certain types of scientific experiments, it may matter whether the response time is 10 ms or 100 ms. Second, the programmer is encouraged to avoid recursion in programs that are executed hundreds of times. The best example of this kind of program is a compiler.

But these remarks should not be treated too stringently, because sometimes a recursive version is faster than a nonrecursive implementation. Hardware can be the reason since it may have built-in stack operations that considerably speed up functions operating on the run-time stack, such as recursive functions. Running a simple routine implemented recursively and iteratively and comparing the two run times can help to decide if recursion is advisable — in fact, recursion can execute faster than iteration. Such a test is especially important if tail recursion comes into play. However, when a stack cannot be eliminated from the iterative version, the use of recursion is usually recommended, since the execution time for both versions does not differ substantially — certainly not by a factor of ten.

Recursion should be eliminated if some part of work is unnecessarily repeated to compute the answer. The Fibonacci series computation is a good example of such a situation. It shows that the ease of using recursion can sometimes be deceptive and this is where iteration can grapple effectively with run-time limitations and inefficiencies. Whether a recursive implementation leads to unnecessary repetitions may not be immediately apparent, therefore drawing a tree of calls similar to Figure 5.6 can be very helpful. This tree shows that **Fib(n)** is called many times with the same argument **n**. A tree drawn for power or factorial functions is reduced to a linked list with no repetitions in it. If such a tree is very deep, that is, it has many levels, then the program can endanger the run-time stack with an overflow. If the tree is shallow and bushy, with many nodes on the same level, then recursion seems to be a good approach — only if the number of repetitions is very moderate.

■ 5.11   CASE STUDY: A RECURSIVE DESCENT INTERPRETER

All programs written in any programming language have to be translated into a representation that the computer system can work on. However, this is not a simple process. Depending on the system and programming language, the process may consist of translating one executable statement at a time and immediately executing it, which is called *interpretation*, or translating the entire program first and then executing it, which is called *compilation*. Whichever strategy is used, the program should not contain sentences or formulas that violate the formal specification of the programming language in which the program is written. For example, if we want to assign a value to a variable, we must put the variable first, then the equal sign, and then a value after it. However, the same sentence has to have the symbol `:=` instead of `=` if this sentence is a part of a Pascal program. If the programmer uses `:=` in place of `=` in a C++ program, the compiler rejects this obvious typographical error and refuses to do anything with the sentence containing it until the colon is deleted.

There are some more exotic conventions for assignment. In Lisp, an operator is put before its operands. In Forth, assignment follows the only given operand and the second operand (a value to be assigned) is popped off the run-time stack.

Writing an interpreter is by no means a trivial task. As an example, this case study is a sample interpreter for a limited programming language. Our language consists only of assignment statements; it contains no declarations, `if-else` statements, loops, procedures, etc. For this limited language, we would like to write a program that accepts any input and

- determines if it contains valid assignment statements (this process is known as parsing); and simultaneously,
- evaluates all expressions.

Our program is an interpreter in that it not only checks the syntactically correct assignment statements, but also executes the assignments.

The program is to work in the following way. If we enter the assignment statements

```
var1 = 5;
var2 = var1;
var3 = 44/2.0 * (var2 + var1);
```

then the system can be prompted for the value of each variable separately. For instance, after entering

```
print var3
```

the system should respond by printing

```
var3 = 220.00
```

Evaluation of all variables stored so far may be requested by entering

```
status
```

and the following values should be printed in our example:

```
var3 = 220.00
var2 = 5.00
var1 = 5.00
```

All current values are to be stored on `idList` and updated if necessary. Thus, if

```
var2 = var2 * 5;
```

is entered, then

```
print var2
```

should return

```
var2 = 25.00
```

The interpreter prints a message if any undefined identifier is used and if statements and expressions do not conform to common grammatical rules such as unmatched parentheses, two identifiers in a row, etc.

The program can be written in a variety of ways, but to illustrate recursion, we choose a method known as *recursive descent*. This consists of several mutually recursive procedures according to the diagrams in Figure 5.17.

These diagrams serve to define a statement and its parts. For example, a term is a factor or a factor followed by either the multiplication symbol "`*`" or the division symbol "`/`" and then another factor. A factor, in turn, is either an identifier, a number, an expression enclosed in a pair of matching parentheses, or a negated factor. In this method, a statement is looked at in more and more detail. It is broken down into its components and if the components are compound, they are separated into their constituent parts until the simplest language elements are found: numbers, variable names, operators, and parentheses. Thus, the program recursively descends from a global overview of the statement to more detailed elements.

The diagrams in Figure 5.17 indicate that recursive descent is a combination of direct and indirect recursion. For example, a factor can be a factor preceded by a minus, an expression can be a term, a term can be a factor, a factor can be an expression that, in turn, can be a term, until the level of identifiers or numbers is found. Thus, an expression can be composed of expressions, a term of terms, and a factor of factors.

How can the recursive descent interpreter be implemented? The simplest approach is to treat every word in the diagrams as a function name. For instance, `Term()` is a function returning a float number. This function always calls `Factor()` first, and if the nonblank character currently being looked at is either "`*`" or "`/`", then `Term()` calls `Factor()` again. The diagrams indicate that a function `TermTail()` should be implemented and called after "`*`" or "`/`" is found, but it is more efficient to incorporate

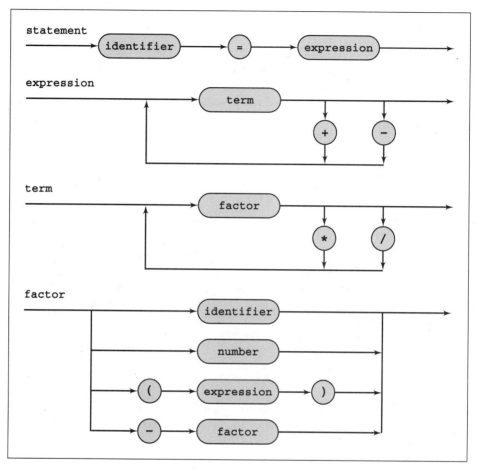

Figure 5.17: **Diagrams of procedures used by the recursive descent interpreter.**

it in **Term()** as a loop whose body contains a call to **Factor()** if one of the operators "*****" or "**/**" is reached. Each time, the value already accumulated by **Term()** is either multiplied or divided by the value returned by the subsequent call of **Term()** to **Factor()**. Every call of **Term()** can invoke another call to **Term()** indirectly through the chain **Term() -> Factor() -> Expression() -> Term()**. Pseudocode for the function **Term()** looks like the following:

```
Term()
    f1 = Factor();
    check current character ch;
    while ch is either / or *
        f2 = Factor();
        f1 = f1 * f2 or f1 / f2;
    return f1;
```

The function `Expression()` has exactly the same structure, and the pseudocode for `Factor()` is:

```
Factor()
    process all +s and -s preceding a factor;
    if current character ch is a letter
        store in id all consecutive letters and/or digits starting with ch;
        return value assigned to id;
    else if ch is a digit
        store in id all consecutive digits starting from ch;
        return number represented by string id;
    else if ch is (
        e = Expression();
        if ch is )
            return e;
```

We have tacitly assumed that `ch` is a global variable which is used for scanning an input character by character.

However, in the pseudocode we assumed that only valid statements are entered for evaluation. What happens if a mistake is made, such as entering two equal signs, mistyping a variable name, or forgetting an operator? In the interpreter, parsing is simply discontinued after printing an error message.

Figure 5.18 contains the complete code for our interpreter.

```cpp
//************************ statemnt.h ********************
#ifndef STATEMENT
#define STATEMENT

#include <iostream.h>
#include <stdlib.h>     // exit();
#include <string.h>
#include "genSLLst.h" // see Chapter 3

const int idLen = 20;

struct IdNode {
    char id[idLen];
    float value;
    int operator== (const IdNode& node)
          { return strcmp(id,node.id) == 0; }
};
```

Figure 5.18: **Implementation of a simple language interpreter.**   **continued**

```cpp
class IdList : public SinglyLinkedList<IdNode> {
public:
    IdList() { }
    void  IssueError(char *s) { cerr << s << endl; exit(1); }
    float FindValue(char*);
    void  ProcessNode(char*, float);
private:
    IdNode tmpNode, *p;
};

class Statement {
public:
    Statement() { }
    void GetStatement();
private:
    IdList idList;
    char   ch;
    float Factor();
    float Term();
    float Expression();
    void  ReadId(char *id);
    void  ProcessNode(char* el, float f) { idList.ProcessNode(el,f);    }
    float FindValue(char* id)            { return idList.FindValue(id); }
    void  PrintAll(ostream& out)         { idList.PrintAll(out);        }
    void  IssueError(char* s)            { idList.IssueError(s);        }
};
#endif
//*********************** statemnt.cpp  **********************

#include <iostream.h>
#include <ctype.h>
#include <string.h>
#include <stdlib.h>
#include "statemnt.h"

float
IdList::FindValue(char *id)
{
    strcpy(tmpNode.id,id);
    if (p = Find(tmpNode))
```

Figure 5.18: **Implementation of a simple language interpreter.**   **continued**

```
        return p->value;
    else IssueError("Unknown variable");
}


void
IdList::ProcessNode(char* id ,float e)
{
    strcpy(tmpNode.id,id);
    tmpNode.value = e;
    if (p = Find(tmpNode))
        p->value = e;
    else Add(tmpNode);
}


ostream&
operator<< (ostream& out, const IdNode& r)
{
    out << r.id << " = " << r.value << endl;
    return out;
}


// ReadId() reads strings of letters and digits that start with
// a letter, and stores them in array passed to it as an actual
// parameter. Identifier can have at most idLen-1 characters.
// Examples of identifiers are: var1, x, pqr123xyz, aName, etc.


void
Statement::ReadId(char *id)
{   int i = 0;

    if (isspace(ch))
        cin >> ch;          // skip blanks;
    if (isalpha(ch)) {
        while (isalnum(ch)) {
            if (i < idLen-1)
                id[i++] = ch;
            cin.get(ch); // don't skip blanks;
        }
```

Figure 5.18: **Implementation of a simple language interpreter.**   **continued**

```
            id[i] = '\0';
        }
    else IssueError("Identifier expected");
}


float
Statement::Factor()
{   float var, minus = 1.0;
    char id[idLen];

    cin >> ch;
    while (ch == '+' || ch == '-') {        // take all '+'s and '-'s.
        if (ch == '-')
            minus *= -1.0;
        cin >> ch;
    }
    if (isdigit(ch) || ch == '.') {        // Factor can be a number
        cin.putback(ch);
        cin >> var >> ch;
    }
    else if (ch == '(') {                  // or a parenthesized expression,
        var = Expression();
        if (ch == ')')
            cin >> ch;
        else IssueError("Right paren left out");
    }
    else {
        ReadId(id);                        // or an identifier.
        if (isspace(ch))
            cin >> ch;
        var = FindValue(id);
    }
    return minus * var;
}


float
Statement::Term()
{   float f;
```

Figure 5.18: **Implementation of a simple language interpreter.**   **continued**

```
        f = Factor();
        while (1) {
            switch (ch) {
                case '*' : f *= Factor(); break;
                case '/' : f /= Factor(); break;
                default  : return f;
            }
        }
}


float
Statement::Expression()
{   float t;

    t = Term();
    while (1) {
        switch (ch) {
            case '+' : t += Term(); break;
            case '-' : t -= Term(); break;
            default  : return t;
        }
    }
}


void
Statement::GetStatement()
{   char id[idLen], command[idLen];
    float e;

    cout << "Enter a statement: ";
    cin  >> ch;
    ReadId(id);
    strupr(strcpy(command,id));
    if (!strcmp(command,"STATUS"))
        PrintAll(cout);
    else if (!strcmp(command,"PRINT")) {
        ReadId(id);
        cout << id << " = " << FindValue(id) << endl;
    }
```

Figure 5.18: **Implementation of a simple language interpreter.**   **continued**

```
        else if (!strcmp(command,"END"))
            exit(0);
        else {
            if (isspace(ch))
                cin >> ch;
            if (ch == '=') {
                e = Expression();
                if (ch != ';')
                    IssueError("There are some extras in the statement");
                else ProcessNode(id,e);
            }
            else IssueError("'=' is missing");
        }
}


//*********************** interpreter.cpp  **********************

#include <iostream.h>
#include "statemnt.h"

main()
{   Statement statement;

    cout << "The program processes statements of the following format:\n"
         << "\t<id> = <expr>;\n\tprint <id>\n\tstatus\n\tend\n\n";
    while (1)                      // This infinite loop is broken by exit(1)
        statement.GetStatement(); // in Statement() or upon finding an error.
}
```

Figure 5.18: **Implementation of a simple language interpreter.**

■ 5.12 EXERCISES

1. The set of natural numbers **N** defined at the beginning of this chapter includes the numbers $10, 11, \ldots, 20, 21, \ldots$, but also the numbers $00, 000, 01, 001, \ldots$. Modify this definition to allow only numbers with no leading zeros.

2. Write a recursive function that calculates and returns the length of a linked list.

3. What is the output for the following version of **Reverse()**:

```
        void
        Reverse()
```

```
{   int ch;

    cin.pet(ch);
    if (ch  != '\n')
        Reverse();
    cout.put(ch);

}
```

4. What is the output of the same function if **ch** is declared as

   `static char ch;`

5. An early application of recursion can be found in the sixteenth century, in John Napier's method of finding logarithms. The method was as follows:

   > start with two numbers **n, m** and their logarithms **logn, logm** if they are known;
   > **while** not done
   >> for a geometric mean of two earlier numbers find a logarithm which is an arithmetic mean of two earlier logarithms, that is, **logk** = (**logn+logm**) /2 for **k** = $\sqrt{nm}$;
   >> proceed recursively for pairs (**n**,$\sqrt{nm}$) and ($\sqrt{nm}$,**m**);

   For example, the ten-based logarithms of 100 and 1000 are numbers 2 and 3, the geometric mean of 100 and 1000 is 316.23 and the arithmetic mean of their logarithms, 2 and 3, is 2.5. Thus, the logarithm of 316.23 equals 2.5. The process can be continued: the geometric mean of 100 and 316.23 is 177.83 whose logarithm is equal to $(2 + 2.5)/2 = 2.25$.

   (a) Write a recursive function **Logarithm()** that outputs logarithms until the difference between adjacent logarithms is smaller than a certain small number.

   (b) Modify this function so that a new function **LogarithmOf()** finds a logarithm of a specific number x between 100 and 1000. Stop processing if you reach a number y such that $y - x < \epsilon$ for some ϵ.

   (c) Add a function which calls **LogarithmOf()** after determining between what powers of ten a number x falls, so that is does not have to be a number between 100 and 1000.

6. The algorithms for both versions of the power function given in this chapter are rather simple-minded. Is it really necessary to make eight multiplications in order to compute x^8? It can be observed that $x^8 = (x^4)^2$, $x^4 = (x^2)^2$, and $x^2 = x * x$; that is, only three multiplications are needed to find the value of x^8. Using this observation, improve both algorithms for computing x^n. Hint: a special case is needed for odd exponents.

7. Execute by hand the functions **Tail()** and **NoTail()** for the parameter values of 0, 2, and 4. Definitions of these functions are given in Section 5.4.

8. Write a function that recursively converts a string of numerals into an integer. For instance, **Convert("1234")** would return the integer 1234.

9. Write a recursive function to compute the binomial coefficient according to the definition

$$\binom{n}{k} = \begin{cases} 1 & \text{if } k = 0 \text{ or } k = n, \\ \binom{n-1}{k-1} + \binom{n-1}{k} & \text{otherwise} \end{cases}$$

10. Write a recursive function to add the first n terms of the series

$$1 + \frac{1}{2} - \frac{1}{3} + \frac{1}{4} - \frac{1}{5} \cdots$$

11. Write a recursive function GCD(n,m) that returns the greatest common denominator of two integers **n** and **m** according to the following definition:

$$GCD(n,m) = \begin{cases} m & \text{if } m \le n \text{ and } n \bmod m = 0, \\ GCD(m,n) & \text{if } n < m, \\ GCD(m, n \bmod m) & \text{otherwise} \end{cases}$$

12. Give a recursive version of the following function:

```
void
cubes int(n)
{register int i;
  for (i = 1; i <= n; i++)
      cout << i*i*i<<'';
}
```

13. Check recursively if the following objects are palindromes:

    (a) a word

    (b) a sentence (ignoring blanks, lower and upper case differences, and punctuation marks so that "Madam, I'm Adam" is accepted as a palindrome)

14. For a given character recursively, without using **strchr()** or **strrchr()**,

    (a) Check if it is in a string.

    (b) Count all its occurrences in a string.

    (c) Remove all its occurrences from a string.

15. Write equivalents of the last three functions for substrings (do not use **strstr()**).

16. Create a tree of calls for sin(x) assuming that only $\frac{x}{18}$ (and smaller values) do not trigger other calls.

17. Write recursive and nonrecursive functions to print out a nonnegative integer in binary. The functions should not use bit-wise operations.

18. The nonrecursive version of the function for computing Fibonacci numbers uses information accumulated during computation, whereas the recursive version does not. However, it does not mean that no recursive implementation can be given which can

collect the same information as the nonrecursive counterpart. In fact, such an implementation can be obtained directly from the nonrecursive version. What would it be? Consider using two functions instead of one; one would do all the work, the other would only invoke it with the proper parameters.

19. Execute the following program by hand from the case study, using these two entries:

    (a) `v = x + y*w - z`
    (b) `v = x * (y - w) --z`

    Indicate clearly which procedures are called at which stage of parsing these sentences.

20. The function `PutQueen()` does not recognize that certain configurations are symmetric. Adapt function `PutQueen()` for a full 8 × 8 chessboard, write the function `PrintBoard()`, and run a program for solving the eight queens problem so that it does not print symmetric solutions.

21. Extend our interpreter so that it can also process exponentiation, `^`. Remember that exponentiation has precedence over all other operations, so that `2 - 3^4 * 5` is the same as `2 - ((3^4) * 5)`. Notice also that `2^3^4` is the same as `2^(3^4)` and not `(2^3)^4`.

22. In C++, the division operator, `/`, returns an integer result when it is applied to two integers; for instance, `11/5` equals 2. However, in our interpreter the result is `2.2`. Modify this interpreter so that division works the same way as in C++.

23. Our interpreter is unforgiving when a mistake is made by the user, since it finishes execution if a problem is detected. For example, when the name of a variable is mistyped when requesting its value, the program notifies the user and exits and destroys the list of identifiers. Modify the program so that it continues execution after finding an error.

■ 5.13 PROGRAMMING ASSIGNMENTS

1. Compute the standard deviation σ for n values x_k stored in an array **data** and for the equal probabilities $\frac{1}{n}$ associated with them. The standard deviation is defined as

$$\sigma = \sqrt{V},$$

where the variance, V, is defined by

$$V = \frac{1}{n-1}\Sigma_k(x_k - \bar{x})^2$$

and the mean, $\bar{x}$, by

$$\bar{x} = \frac{1}{n}\Sigma_k x_k.$$

Write recursive and iterative versions of both V and $\bar{x}$, and compute the standard deviation using both versions of the mean and variance. Run your program for $n = 500$, 1000, 1500, and 2000 and compare the run times.

2. Write a program to do symbolic differentiation. Use the following formulas:

$$\text{Rule 1:} \quad (fg)' = fg' + f'g$$

$$\text{Rule 2:} \quad (f + g)' = f' + g'$$

$$\text{Rule 3:} \quad \left(\frac{f}{g}\right)' = \frac{f'g - fg'}{g^2}$$

$$\text{Rule 4:} \quad (ax^n)' = nax^{n-1}$$

An example of application of these rules is given below:

$$\left(5x^3 + \frac{6x}{y} - 10x^2y + 100\right)'$$

$$= (5x^3)' + \left(\frac{6x}{y}\right)' + (-10x^2y)' + (100)' \quad \text{by Rule 2}$$

$$= 15x^2 + \left(\frac{6x}{y}\right)' + (-10x^2y)' \quad\quad\quad \text{by Rule 4}$$

$$= 15x^2 + \frac{(6x)'y - (6x)y'}{y^2} + (-10x^2y)' \quad \text{by Rule 3}$$

$$= 15x^2 + \frac{6y}{y^2} + (-10x^2y)' \quad\quad\quad\quad \text{by Rule 4}$$

$$= 15x^2 + \frac{6y}{y^2} + (-10x^2)y' + (-10x^2)'y \quad \text{by Rule 1}$$

$$= 15x^2 + \frac{6}{y} - 20xy \quad\quad\quad\quad\quad \text{by Rule 4.}$$

First run your program for polynomials only, and then add formulas for derivatives of trigonometric functions, logarithms, etc. that extend the range of functions handled by your program.

3. An $n \times n$ square consists of black and white cells arranged in a certain way. The problem is to determine the number of white areas and the number of white cells in each area. For example, a regular 8×8 chessboard has 32 one-cell white areas; the square in Figure 5.19a consists of ten areas, two of them of ten cells, and eight of two cells; the square in Figure 5.19b has five white areas of 1, 3, 21, 10, and 2 cells.

Write a program that, for a given $n \times n$ square, outputs the number of white areas and their sizes. Use an $(n + 2) \times (n + 2)$ array with properly marked cells. Two additional rows and columns constitute a frame of black cells surrounding the entered square, to simplify your implementation. For instance, the square in Figure 5.19b is stored as the square in Figure 5.19c.

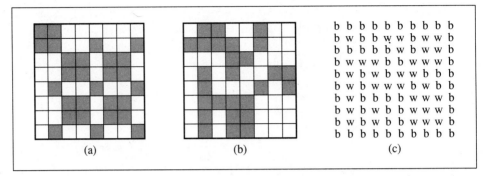

Figure 5.19: **(a)–(b) Two $n \times n$ squares of black and white cells and (c) an $(n + 2) \times (n + 2)$ array implementing square (b).**

Traverse the square row by row and for the first unvisited cell encountered, invoke a function that processes one area. The secret is in using four recursive calls in this function for each unvisited white cell and marking it with a special symbol as visited (counted).

4. Write a program for *pretty printing* C++ programs, that is, for printing programs with consistent use of indentation, the number of spaces between tokens such as key words, parentheses, brackets, operators, etc., the number of blank lines between blocks of code (classes, functions, etc.), aligning braces with key words, aligning **else** statements with the corresponding **if** statements, and so on. The program takes as input a C++ file and prints code in this file according to the rules incorporated in the pretty printing program. For example, the code

```
  if (n == 1) { n = 2 * m;
if (m < 10)
classA.memberFunA(n,m-1); else classA.memberFunA(n,m-2); } else n = 3 * m;
```

should be transformed into

```
      if (n == 1) {
          n = 2 * m;
          if (m < 10)
              classA.memberFunA(n,m-1);
          else classA.memberFunA(n,m-2);
      }
      else n = 3 * m;
```

BIBLIOGRAPHY

Recursion and Applications of Recursion

[1] Barron, David W., *Recursive Techniques in Programming*, New York: Elsevier, 1968.

[2] Berlioux, Pierre, and Bizard, Philippe, *Algorithms: The Construction, Proof, and Analysis of Programs*, New York: Wiley, 1986, Chs. 4–6.

[3]   Bird, Richard S., *Programs and Machines*, New York: Wiley, 1976.

[4]   Burge, William H., *Recursive Programming Techniques*, Reading, MA: Addison-Wesley, 1975.

[5]   Lorentz, Richard, *Recursive Algorithms*, Norwood: Ablex, 1994.

[6]   Roberts, Eric, *Thinking Recursively*, New York: Wiley, 1986.

[7]   Rohl, Jeffrey S., *Recursion via Pascal*, Cambridge: Cambridge University Press, 1984.

Transformations between Recursion and Iteration

[8]   Auslander, M.A., and Strong, H.R., "Systematic Recursion Removal," *Communications of the ACM* 21 (1978), 127–134.

[9]   Bird, R.S., "Notes on Recursion Elimination," *Communications of the ACM* 20 (1977), 434–439.

[10] Dijkstra, Edsger W., "Recursive Programming," *Numerische Mathematik* 2 (1960), 312–318.

Algorithm to Solve the Eight Queens Problem

[11] Wirth, Niklaus, *Algorithms and Data Structures*, Englewood Cliffs, NJ: Prentice-Hall, 1986.

BINARY TREES

■ 6.1 TREES, BINARY TREES, AND BINARY SEARCH TREES

Linked lists usually provide greater flexibility than arrays, but they are linear structures and it is difficult to use them to organize a hierarchical representation of objects. Although stacks and queues reflect some hierarchy, they are limited to only one dimension. To overcome this limitation, we create a new data type called a *tree* that consists of *nodes* and *arcs*. Unlike natural trees, these trees are depicted upside down with the *root* at the top and the *leaves* at the bottom. The root is a node that has no parent; it can have only child nodes. Leaves, on the other hand, have no children. A tree can be defined recursively as the following:

1. An empty structure is an empty tree.

2. If $t_1, \ldots, t_k$ are disjoint trees, then the structure whose root has as its children the roots of $t_1, \ldots, t_k$, is also a tree.

3. Only structures generated by rules 1 and 2 are trees.

Figure 6.1 contains examples of trees. Each node has to be reachable from the root through a unique sequence of arcs, called a *path*. The number of arcs in a path is called the *length* of the path. The *level* of a node is the length of the path from the root to the node plus one, which is the number of nodes in the path. The *height* of a nonempty tree is the maximum level of a node in the tree. The empty tree is a legitimate tree of height 0 (by definition), and a single node is a tree of height 1. This is the only case in which a node is both the root and a leaf. The depth of a node must be between one (the level of the root) and the height of the tree, which in the extreme case is the level of the only leaf in a degenerate tree resembling a linked list.

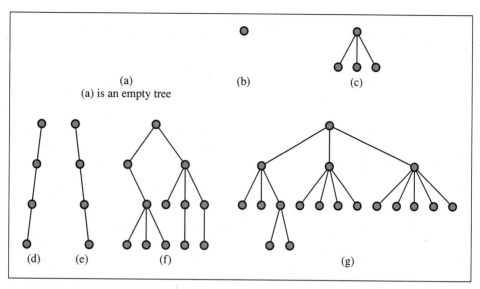

Figure 6.1: **Examples of trees.**

Figure 6.2 contains an example of a tree that reflects the hierarchy of a university. Other examples of trees are genealogical trees, trees reflecting the grammatical structure of sentences, and trees showing taxonomic structure of organisms, plants, or characters. Virtually all areas of science make use of trees to represent hierarchical structures.

The definition of a tree does not impose any condition on the number of children of a given node. This number can vary from 0 to any integer. In hierarchical trees this is a welcome property. For example, the university has only two branches, but each campus can have a different number of departments. Such trees are used in database management systems, especially in the hierarchical model. But, representing hierarchies is not the only reason for using trees. In fact, in the discussion to follow, that aspect of trees is treated rather lightly, mainly in the discussion of expression trees. This chapter focuses on tree operations that allow us to accelerate the search process.

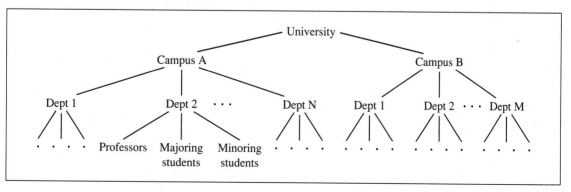

Figure 6.2: **Hierarchical structure of a university shown as a tree.**

Consider a linked list of n elements. To locate an element, the search has to start from the beginning of the list and the list must be scanned until the element is found or the end of list is reached. Even if the list is ordered, the search of the list always has to start from the first record. Thus if the list has 10,000 records and the information in the last record is to be accessed, then all 9,999 of its predecessors have to be traversed, an obvious inconvenience. If all the elements are stored in an *orderly tree*, a tree where all elements are stored according to some predetermined criterion of ordering, the number of tests can be reduced substantially even when the element to be located is the one farthest away. For example, the linked list in Figure 6.3a can be transformed into the tree in Figure 6.3b.

Was a reasonable criterion of ordering applied to construct this tree? To test whether the number 31 is in the linked list, eight tests have to be performed. Can this number be reduced further if the same elements are ordered from top to bottom and from left to right in the tree? What would an algorithm be like that forces us to make three tests only: one for the root, 2, one for its middle child, 12, and one for the only child of this child, 31? The number 31 could be located on the same level as 12, or it could be a child of 10. With this ordering of the tree nothing really interesting is achieved in the context of searching. (The heap discussed later in this chapter uses this approach.) Consequently, a better criterion must be chosen.

Again, note that each node can have any number of children. In fact, there are algorithms developed for trees with a deliberate number of children (see the next chapter), but this chapter discusses only binary trees. A *binary tree* is a tree whose nodes have children (possibly empty) and each child is designated as either a left child or a right child. For example, the trees in Figure 6.4 are binary trees, whereas the university tree in Figure 6.2 is not. An important characteristic of binary trees, which will be used later in assessing an expected efficiency of sorting algorithms, is the number of leaves.

The *level* of a node is the number of arcs traversed from the root to the node plus one. According to this definition, the root is at level 1, its immediate children are at level 2, and so on. If all the nodes at all levels except the last had two children, then there would be $1 = 2^0$ node at level 1, $2 = 2^1$ nodes at level 2, $4 = 2^2$ nodes at level 3, and, generally, 2^i

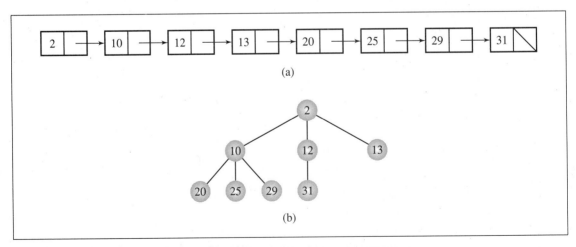

(a)

(b)

Figure 6.3: **Transforming a linked list (a) into a tree (b).**

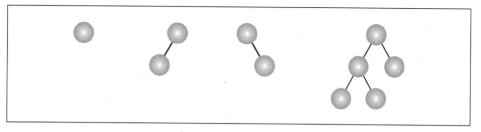

Figure 6.4: **Examples of binary trees.**

nodes at level $i + 1$. A tree satisfying this condition is referred to as a *complete binary tree*. In this tree, all nonterminal nodes have both their children, and all leaves are at the same level. Consequently, in all binary trees there are at most 2^i nodes at level $i + 1$. In Chapter 9, we will calculate the number of leaves in a *decision tree*, which is a binary tree in which all nodes have either zero or two nonempty children. Because leaves can be interspersed throughout a decision tree and appear at each level except level 1, no generally applicable formula can be given to calculate the number of nodes because it may vary from tree to tree. But, the formula can be approximated by noting first that

> *For all nonempty binary trees whose nonterminal nodes have exactly two nonempty children, the number of leaves m is greater than the number of nonterminal nodes k and* $m = k + 1$.

If a tree has only a root, this observation holds trivially. If it holds for a certain tree, then after attaching two leaves to one of the already existing leaves, this leaf turns into a nonterminal node, whereby m is decremented by 1 and k is incremented by 1. However, because two new leaves have been grafted onto the tree, m is incremented by 2. After these two increments and one decrement, the equation $(m - 1) + 2 = (k + 1) + 1$ is obtained and $m = k + 1$, which is exactly the result aimed at (see Figure 6.5). It implies that an $i + 1$-

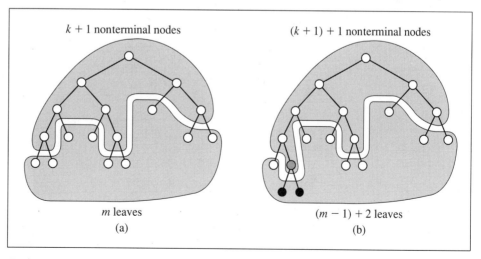

Figure 6.5: **Adding a leaf to tree (a), preserving the relation of the number of leaves to the number of nonterminal nodes.**

level complete decision tree has 2^i leaves, and, on account of the preceding observation, it also has $2^i - 1$ nonterminal nodes which makes $2^i + 2^i - 1 = 2^{i+1} - 1$ nodes in total.

In this chapter, the *binary search trees*, also called *ordered binary trees*, are of particular interest. A binary search tree has the following property: if a node *n* of the tree contains the value *v*, then all values stored in its left subtree (the tree whose root is the left child) are less than *v*, and all values stored in the right subtree are greater than *v*. For reasons that will be discussed later, storing multiple copies of the same value in the same tree is avoided. An attempt to do so can be treated as an error. The meanings of "less than" or "greater than" depend on the type of the values stored in the tree. Usually, the notations "<" and ">" are used if the numbers are the values to be stored in the tree. Alphabetical order is also used in the case of strings. The trees in Figure 6.6 are binary search trees.

Note that Figure 6.6c contains a tree with the same data as the linked list whose searching was to be optimized. An algorithm for locating an element in this tree is quite straightforward. For every node, compare the key to be located with the value stored in the node currently pointed at. If the key is less than the value, go to the left subtree and try again. If it is greater than that value, try the right subtree. If it is the same, obviously the search can be discontinued. The search is also aborted if there is no way to go, indicating that the key is not in the tree. For example, to locate the number 31, only three tests are performed. First, the tree is checked to see if the number is in the root node. Next, because 31 is greater than 13, the root's right child containing the value 25 is tried. Finally, since 31 is again greater than the value of the currently tested node, the right child is tried again, and the value 31 is found.

The worst case for this binary tree is when it is searched for the numbers 26, 27, 28, or 30, because those searches each require four tests (why?). In the case of all other integers, the number of tests is less than four. It can now be seen why an element should only occur in a tree once. If it occurs more than once, then two approaches are possible. One approach locates the first occurrence of an element and disregards the others. In this case, the tree contains redundant nodes that are never used for their own sake; they are accessed only for testing. In the second approach, all occurrences of an element may have to be located. Such a search always has to finish with a leaf. For example, to locate all instances of the number 13 in the tree, the root node 13 has to be tested, then its right child 25, and finally the node 20. The search proceeds along the worst case scenario: when the leaf level has

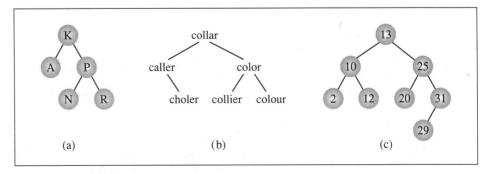

Figure 6.6: **Examples of binary search trees.**

Index	Info	Left	Right
0	13	4	2
1	31	6	−1
2	25	7	1
3	12	−1	−1
4	10	5	3
5	2	−1	−1
6	29	−1	−1
7	20	−1	−1

Figure 6.7: **Array representation of the tree in Figure 6.6c.**

to be reached in hope (or fear) that some more occurrences of the desired element can be encountered.

Before implementing the algorithm to scan a binary search tree containing no repeated values, we must choose a way to implement binary trees.

■ 6.2 IMPLEMENTING BINARY TREES

Binary trees can be implemented in at least two ways: as arrays and as linked structures. To implement a tree as an array, a node is declared as a structure with an information field and two "pointer" fields. These "pointer" fields contain the indexes of the array cells in which the left and right children are stored, if there are any. For example, the tree from Figure 6.6c can be represented as the array in Figure 6.7. The root is always located in the first cell, cell 0, and −1 indicates a null child. In this representation, the two children of node 13 are located in positions 4 and 2, and the right child of node 31 is null.

However, this implementation may be inconvenient, particularly with static allocation, since the size of the array has to become a part of the program and must be known in advance. It is a problem because the data may overflow the array if too little space is allocated, or memory space may be wasted if too much space is allocated. This is important because trees often change and it may be hard to predict how many nodes will be created during a program execution. However, sometimes an array implementation of a tree is convenient and desirable. It will be used when discussing the heap sort, although an array of data rather than an array of structures will be used there. But usually, a dynamic data structure is a more efficient way to represent a tree. This chapter's examples will use dynamic data structures.

Each node is a structure composed of an information field and two pointer fields, but this time the pointers are real pointers, not indexes to other array elements. This structure is used and operated on by member functions embedded in the following class:

```
template<class genType>
struct TreeNode {
        genType key;
        TreeNode *left, *right;
        TreeNode() { left = right = 0; }
        TreeNode(genType& el, TreeNode *l = 0, TreeNode *r = 0)
```

```
                                { key = el; left = l; right = r; }
                   };


                   template<class genType>
                   class BinarySearchTree {
                   public:
                        BinarySearchTree()   { root = 0;              }
                        Clear()              { Clear(root); root = 0; }
                        ~BinarySearchTree() { Clear();               }
                        int IsEmpty()        { return root == 0; }
                        void Insert(genType&);
                        void Preorder()      { Preorder(root);     }
                        . . . . . . . . . . . . . . . . . . . . .
                   protected:
                        TreeNode<genType>* root;
                        void Clear(TreeNode<genType>*);
                        void Preorder(TreeNode<genType>*);
                        . . . . . . . . . . . . . . . . . . . .
                   };
```

■ 6.3 SEARCHING A BINARY SEARCH TREE

Binary search trees, as the name indicates, have been introduced primarily with the purpose of accelerating the search process. Using the pointer representation, a procedure for searching a binary tree can be given the following form:

```
template<class genType>
TreeNode<genType>*
BinarySearchTree<genType>::Search(TreeNode<genType>* p, genType& el)
{
    while (p)
        if (el == p->key)
            return p;
        else if (el < p->key)
            p = p->left;
        else p = p->right;
    return 0;
}
```

The complexity of searching is measured by the number of comparisons performed during the searching process. This number depends on the number of nodes encountered on the unique path leading from the root to the node being searched for. Therefore, the complexity is the length of the path leading to this node plus 1. Complexity depends on the shape of the tree and the position of the node in the tree.

The *internal path length* (IPL) is the sum of all path lengths of all nodes, which is calculated by summing $\sum(i-1)l_i$ over all levels i, where l_i is the number of nodes on level i. A position of a node in the tree is determined by the path length. An average position, called an *average path length*, is given by the formula IPL/n, which depends on the shape of the tree. In the worst case, when the tree turns into a linked list, $path_{worst} = \frac{1}{n}\sum_{i=1}^{n}(i-1) = \frac{n-1}{2} = O(n)$, and an unsuccessful search takes always n time units.

The best case occurs when all leaves in the tree of height h are in at most two levels and only nodes in the next to the last level can have one child. To simplify the computation, we approximate the average path length for such a tree, $path_{best}$, by the average path of a complete binary tree of the same height.

By looking at simple examples we can determine that for the complete binary tree of height h, IPL $= \sum_{i=1}^{h-1} i2^i$. From this and from the fact that $\sum_{i=1}^{h-1} 2^i = 2^h - 2$ we have

$$\text{IPL} = 2\text{IPL} - \text{IPL} = (h-1)2^h - \sum_{i=1}^{h-1} 2^i = (h-2)2^h + 2.$$

As has already been established, the number of nodes in the complete binary tree $n = 2^h - 1$, so

$$path_{best} = \text{IPL}/n = \left((h-2)2^h + 2\right)/(2^h - 1) \approx h - 2,$$

which is in accordance with the fact that in this tree one-half of the nodes are in the leaf level with path length $h-1$. Also, in this tree, the height $h = \lg(n+1)$, so $path_{best} = \lg(n+1) - 2$; the average path length in a perfectly balanced tree is $\lceil \lg(n+1) \rceil = O(\lg n)$ where $\lceil x \rceil$ is the closest integer greater than x.

The average case in an average tree is somewhere between $\frac{n-1}{2}$ and $\lg(n+1) - 2$. Is a search for a node in an average position in a tree of average shape closer to $O(n)$ or $O(\lg n)$? First, the average shape of the tree has to be represented computationally.

The root of a binary tree can have an empty left subtree and a right subtree with all $n-1$ nodes. It also can have one node in the left subtree and $n-2$ nodes in the right, and so on. Finally, it can have an empty right subtree with all remaining nodes in the left. The same reasoning can be applied to both subtrees of the root, to the subtrees of these subtrees, down to the leaves. The average internal path length would be the average of all these $n!$ differently shaped trees.

Assume that the tree contains nodes 1 through n. If i is the root, then its left subtree has $i-1$ nodes, and its right subtree has $n-i$ nodes. If $path_{i-1}$ and $path_{n-i}$ are average paths in these subtrees, then the average path of this tree is

$$path_n(i) = ((i-1)(path_{i-1} + 1) + (n-i)(path_{n-i} + 1))/n.$$

Assuming that elements are coming randomly to the tree, the root of the tree can be any number i, $1 \le i \le n$. Therefore, the average path of an average tree is obtained by averaging all values of $path_n(i)$ over all values of i. This gives the formula

$$path_n = \frac{1}{n}\sum_{i=1}^{n} path_n(i) = \frac{1}{n^2}\sum_{i=1}^{n}((i-1)(path_{i-1}+1)+(n-i)(path_{n-i}+1))$$

$$= \frac{2}{n^2}\sum_{i=1}^{n-1} i(path_i+1),$$

from which, and from $path_1 = 0$, we obtain $2\ln n = 2\ln 2\lg n = 1.386\lg n$ as an approximation for $path_n$ (see Appendix A4). This is an approximation for the average number of comparisons in an average tree. This number is $O(\lg n)$, which is closer to the best case than to the worst case. This number also indicates that there is little room for improvement, since $path_{best}/path_n \approx .7215$ and the average path length in the best case is different by only 27.85% from the expected path length in the average case. Searching in a binary tree is, therefore, in most cases very efficient, even without balancing the tree. However, this is true only for randomly created trees, since in highly unbalanced and elongated trees whose shapes resemble linked lists, search time is $O(n)$, which is unacceptable considering that $O(\lg n)$ efficiency can be achieved.

■ 6.4 TREE TRAVERSAL

Tree traversal is the process of visiting each node in the tree exactly one time. Traversal may be interpreted as putting all nodes on one line or linearizing a tree.

The definition of traversal specifies only one condition — visiting each node only one time — but it does not specify the order in which the nodes are visited. Hence, there are as many tree traversals as there are permutations of nodes; for a tree with n nodes, there are $n!$ different traversals. Most of them, however, are rather chaotic and do not indicate much regularity, so that implementing such traversals lacks generality: for each n, a separate set of traversal procedures must be implemented and only a few of them can be used for a different number of data. For example, two possible traversals of the tree in Figure 6.6c that may be of some use are the sequence 2, 10, 12, 20, 13, 25, 29, 31 and the sequence 29, 31, 20, 12, 2, 25, 10, 13. The first sequence lists even numbers and then odd numbers in ascending order. The second sequence lists all nodes from level to level right to left, starting from the lowest level up to the root. The sequence: 13, 31, 12, 2, 10, 29, 20, 25 does not indicate any regularity in the order of numbers nor in the order of the traversed nodes. It is just a random jumping from node to node that in all likelihood is of no use. Nevertheless, all these sequences are the results of three legitimate traversals out of 8! = 40,320. In the face of such an abundance of traversals and the apparent uselessness of most of these traversals we would like to restrict our attention to two classes only, namely breadth-first and depth-first traversals.

6.4.1 Breadth-First Traversal

Breadth-first traversal is visiting each node starting from the root and moving down level by level, visiting nodes on each level from left to right. When the tree in Figure 6.6c is traversed in the breadth-first fashion the result will be the sequence 13, 10, 25, 2, 12, 20, 31, 29.

Implementation of this kind of traversal is straightforward when a queue is used. After a node is visited, its children, if any, are placed at the end of the queue, and the node at the beginning of the queue is visited. Considering that for a node on level n, its children are on level $n + 1$, by placing these children at the end of the queue, they are visited after all nodes from level n are visited. Thus, the restriction that all nodes on level $n + 1$ must be visited before visiting any nodes on level n is accomplished.

An implementation of the corresponding member function is shown in Figure 6.8. This example assumes that the object **queue** has been declared in

```
Queue<TreeNode<genType>*> queue
```

6.4.2   Depth-First Traversal

Depth-first traversal proceeds as far as possible to the left (or right), then backs up until the first crossroad, goes one step to the right (or left), and again as far as possible to the left (or right). We repeat this process until all nodes are visited. This definition, however, does not clearly specify exactly when nodes are visited: before proceeding down the tree or after backing up? There are some variations of the depth-first traversal.

There are three tasks of interest in this type of traversal:

V — visiting a node

L — traversing the left subtree

R — traversing the right subtree

```
template<class genType>
void
BinarySearchTree<genType>::BreadthFirst()
{    TreeNode<genType> *p = root;

    if (p) {
        queue.Enqueue(p);
        while (!queue.IsEmpty()) {
            p = queue.Dequeue();
            Visit(p);
            if (p->left)
                queue.Enqueue(p->left);
            if (p->right)
                queue.Enqueue(p->right);
        }
    }
}
```

Figure 6.8: **Breadth-first traversal implementation.**

An orderly traversal takes place if these tasks are performed in the same order for each node. The three tasks can themselves be ordered in 3! = 6 ways, so there are six possible traversals:

$$
\begin{array}{ll}
\text{VLR} & \text{VRL} \\
\text{LVR} & \text{RVL} \\
\text{LRV} & \text{RLV}
\end{array}
$$

If the number of different orders still seems like a lot, it can be reduced to three traversals where the move is always from left to right and attention is focused on the first column. The three traversals are given these standard names:

VLR — preorder tree traversal

LVR — inorder tree traversal

LRV — postorder tree traversal

Short and elegant procedures can be implemented directly from the symbolic descriptions of these three traversals, as shown in Figure 6.9.

These functions may seem too simplistic, but their real power lies in recursion, in fact, double recursion. The real job is done by the system on the run-time stack. This simplifies coding but lays a heavy burden upon the system. To better understand this process, inorder tree traversal is discussed in some detail.

In inorder traversal, the left subtree of the current node is visited first, then the node itself, and finally the right subtree. All of this, obviously, holds if the tree is not empty. Before drawing aside the run-time curtain by analyzing the run-time stack, the output given by the inorder traversal is determined by referring to Figure 6.10. The following steps correspond with the letters in that figure:

(a) Node 15 is the root on which `Inorder()` is called for the first time. The function calls itself for node 15's left child, node 4.

(b) Node 4 is not null so `Inorder()` is called on node 1. Because node 1 is a leaf, that is, both its subtrees are empty, invocations of `Inorder()` on the subtrees do not result in other recursive calls of `Inorder()`, as the condition in the `if` statement is not met. Node 1 is visited, then node 4. Node 4 has no right subtree so `Inorder()` is called only to check that, and immediately afterwards, node 15 is visited.

(c) Node 15 has a right subtree so `Inorder()` is called for node 20.

(d) `Inorder()` is called again on node 16. The node is visited and afterwards node 20 is also visited.

(e) `Inorder()` is called on node 25, then on its empty left subtree, then node 25 is visited, and finally `Inorder()` is called on node 25's empty right subtree.

If the visit includes printing the value stored in a node, then the output will be

`1 4 15 16 20 25.`

The key to the traversal is that the three tasks, L, V, and R, are performed for each node separately. This means that the traversal of the right subtree of a node is held pending

```
template<class genType>
void
BinarySearchTree<genType>::Inorder(TreeNode<genType> *p)
{
     if (p) {
          Visit(p);
          Inorder(p->left);
          Inorder(p->right);
     }
}


template<class genType>
void
BinarySearchTree<genType>::Preorder(TreeNode<genType> *p)
{
     if (p) {
          Visit(p);
          Preorder(p->left);
          Preorder(p->right);
     }
}


template<class genType>
void
BinarySearchTree<genType>::Postorder(TreeNode<genType>* p)
{
     if (p) {
          Postorder(p->left);
          Postorder(p->right);
          Visit(p);
     }
}
```

Figure 6.9: **Depth-first traversal implementation.**

until the first two tasks, L and V, are accomplished. If the latter two are finished, they sink into oblivion and can be crossed out as in Figure 6.11.

In order to present the way **Inorder()** works, the behavior of the run-time stack is observed. The numbers in parentheses indicate return addresses shown on the left-hand side of the code for **Inorder()**.

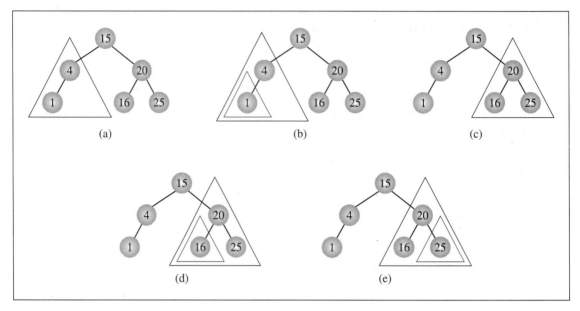

Figure 6.10: **Inorder tree traversal.**

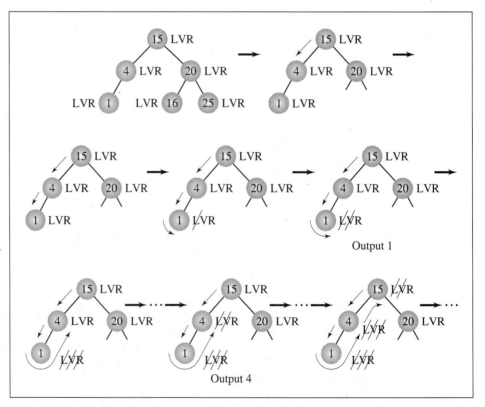

Figure 6.11: **Details of several of the first steps of inorder traversal.**

```
           template<class genType>
           void
           BinarySearchTree<genType>::Inorder(TreeNode<genType>*node)
           {
            if (node) {
/* 1 */          Inorder (node->left);
/* 2 */          Visit (node);
/* 3 */          Inorder (node->right);
/* 4 */          }
           }
```

A rectangle with an up arrow and a number indicates the current value of **node** pushed onto the stack. For example, ↑4 means that **node** points to the node of the tree whose value is the number 4. Figure 6.12 shows the changes of the run-time stack when **Inorder()** is executed for the tree in Figure 6.10.

(a) Initially, the run-time stack is empty (or rather it is assumed that the stack is empty by disregarding what has been stored on it before the first call to **Inorder()**).

(b) Upon the first call, the return address of **Inorder()** and the value of **node**, ↑15, are pushed onto the run-time stack. The tree, pointed to by **node**, is not empty, the condition in the **if** statement is satisfied, and **Inorder()** is called again with node 4.

(c) Before it is executed, the return address, (2), and current value of **node**, ↑4, are pushed onto the stack. Since **node** is not null, **Inorder()** is about to be invoked for **node**'s left child, ↑1.

(d) First the return address, (2), and the **node**'s value are stored. The **node** points to node 1, and this pointer and the address (2) are saved on the stack.

(e) **Inorder()** is called with node 1's left child. The address (2) and the current value of parameter **node**, null, are stored on the stack. Since **node** is null, **Inorder()** is exited immediately; upon exit, the activation record is removed from the stack.

(f) The system goes now to its run-time stack, restores the value of the **node**, ↑1, executes the statement under (2), and prints the number 1. Since **node** is not completely processed, the value of **node** and address (2) are still on the stack.

(g) With the right child of **node** ↑1, the statement under (3) is executed which is the next call to **Inorder()**. First, however, the address (4) and **node**'s current value, null, are pushed onto the stack. Because **node** is null, **Inorder()** is exited; upon exit, the stack is cleaned up.

(h) The system now restores the old value of the **node**, ↑1, and executes statement (4).

(i) Since this is **Inorder()**'s exit, the system refers again to the stack, restores the **node**'s value, ↑4, and resumes execution from statement (2). This prints the number 4, and then calls **Inorder()** for the right child of **node**, which is null.

The above steps are just the beginning. All of the steps are shown in Figure 6.12.

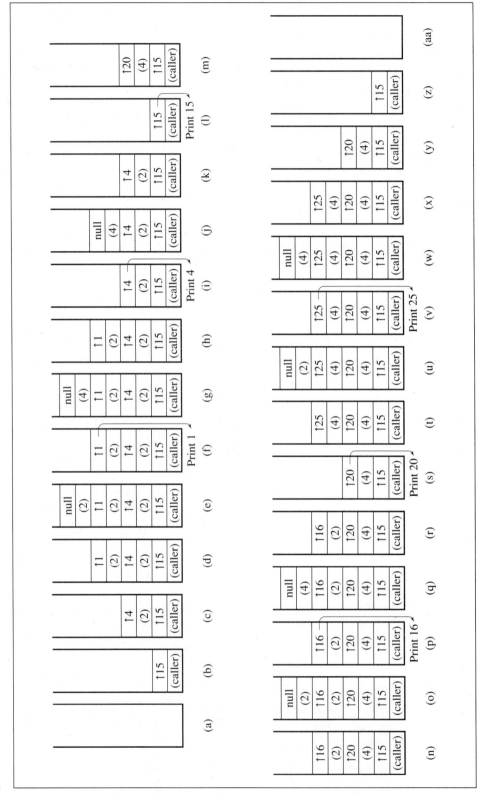

Figure 6.12: **Changes in the run time stack during inorder traversal.**

At this point consider the problem of a nonrecursive implementation of the three traversal algorithms. As indicated in Chapter 5, a recursive implementation has a tendency to be less efficient than a nonrecursive counterpart. If two recursive calls are used in a function, then the problem of possible inefficiency doubles. Can recursion be eliminated from the implementation? The answer has to be positive, since if it is not eliminated in the source code, the system does it for us anyway. So the question should be rephrased: Is it expedient to do so?

Look first at a nonrecursive version of the preorder tree traversal:

```
template<class genType>
void
BinarySearchTree<genType>::IterativePreorder()
{    TreeNode<genType> *p = root;

    if (p) {
        travStack.Push(p);
        while (!travStack.IsEmpty()) {
            p = travStack.Pop();
            Visit(p);
            if (p->right)
                travStack.Push(p->right);
            if (p->left)                    // left child pushed after right
                travStack.Push(p->left); // to be on the top of the stack;
        }
    }
}
```

The procedure `IterativePreorder()` is twice as large as `Preorder()`, but it is still short and legible. However, it uses a stack heavily. Therefore, supporting functions are necessary to process the stack, and the overall implementation is not so short. Although two recursive calls are omitted, there are now up to four calls per iteration of `while` loop: up to two calls of `Push()`, one call of `Pop()`, and one call of `Visit()`. This can hardly be considered an improvement in efficiency. But if inline functions are used, then efficiency can be improved.

In the recursive implementations of the three traversals, note that the only difference is in the order of the lines of code. For example, in `Preorder()`, first a node is visited, and then there are calls for the left and right subtrees. On the other hand, in `Postorder()`, visiting a node succeeds both calls. Can we so easily transform the nonrecursive version of preorder traversal into a nonrecursive postorder traversal? Unfortunately, no. In `IterativePreorder()`, visiting occurs before both children are pushed onto the stack. But this order does not really matter. If the children are pushed first and then the node is visited; that is, if `Visit(p)` is placed after both calls to `Push()`, the resulting implementation is still a preorder traversal. What matters here is that `Visit()` has to follow `Pop()` and the latter has to precede both calls of `Push()`. Therefore, nonrecursive implementations of inorder and postorder traversals have to be developed independently.

A nonrecursive version of postorder traversal can be obtained rather easily if we observe that the sequence generated by a left-to-right postorder traversal (a LRV order) is the same as the reversed sequence generated by right-to-left preorder traversal (a VRL order). In this case, the implementation of **IterativePreorder()** can be adopted to create **IterativePostorder()**. (How exactly can it be done?)

A nonrecursive inorder tree traversal is a more complicated matter. One possible implementation is given below:

```
template<class genType>
void
BinarySearchTree<genType>::IterativeInorder()
{    TreeNode<genType> *p = root;

     while (p) {
         while(p) {                        // stack the right child (if any)
             if (p->right)                 // and the node itself when going
                 travStack.Push(p->right); // to the left;
             travStack.Push(p);
             p = p->left;
         }
         p = travStack.Pop();              // pop a node with no left child
         while (!travStack.IsEmpty() && !(p->right)) { // visit it and all
             Visit(p);                     // nodes with no right child;
             p = travStack.Pop();
         }
         Visit(p);                         // visit also the first node with
         if (!travStack.IsEmpty())         // a right child (if any);
             p = travStack.Pop();
         else p = 0;
     }
}
```

In this case we can clearly see the power of recursion: **IterativeInorder()** is almost unreadable and without thorough explanation, it is not easy to determine the purpose of this procedure. On the other hand, recursive **Inorder()** immediately demonstrates a purpose and logic. Therefore, **IterativeInorder()** can be defended in one case only: if it is shown that there is a substantial gain in execution time and that the procedure is called often in a program. Otherwise, **Inorder()** is preferable to its iterative counterpart.

6.4.3   Stackless Depth-First Traversal

Threaded Trees

The traversal procedures analyzed in the preceding section were either recursive or non-recursive, but both kinds used a stack either implicitly or explicitly, to store information about nodes whose processing has not been finished. In the case of recursive procedures, the run-time stack was utilized. In the case of nonrecursive variants, an explicitly defined and user-maintained stack was used. The concern is that some additional time has to be spent to maintain the stack, and some more space has to be set aside for the stack itself. In the worst case, when the tree is unfavorably skewed, the stack may hold information about almost every node of the tree, a serious concern for very large trees.

It is more efficient to incorporate the stack as a part of the tree. This is done by incorporating *threads* in a given node. Threads are pointers to the predecessor and successor of the node according to a certain sequence, and trees whose nodes use threads are called *threaded trees*. Four pointer fields are needed for each node in the tree, which again takes up valuable space.

The problem can be solved by overloading existing pointer fields. In trees, left or right pointers are pointers to children, but they can also be used as pointers to predecessors and successors, thereby being overloaded with meaning. How do we distinguish these meanings? For an overloaded operator, context is always a disambiguating factor. In trees, however, a new field has to be used to indicate the current meaning of the pointers.

Because a pointer can point to one node at a time, the left pointer is either a pointer to the left child or to the predecessor. Analogously, the right pointer points either to the right subtree or to the successor. The meaning of predecessor and successor differs depending on the sequence under scrutiny. Since we are interested primarily in sequences created by preorder, inorder, and postorder tree traversals, Figure 6.13 gives examples of threaded trees created according to these three sequences.

Figure 6.13 suggests that both pointers to predecessors and to successors have to be maintained, which is not always the case. It may be sufficient to use only one thread as shown in the following implementation of the inorder traversal of a threaded tree, which requires only pointers to successors (Figure 6.14).

The procedure is relatively simple. The dashed line in Figure 6.15 indicates the order in which **p** accesses nodes in the tree. Note that only one variable, **p**, is needed to traverse the tree. No stack is needed, therefore space is saved. But is it really? As indicated, nodes have to have a field indicating how the right pointer is being used. In the implementation of `ThreadedInorder()`, the field `successor` plays this role. This field can have only two values, "yes" or "no." The best choice is to implement it as a bit field, as in the following declaration:

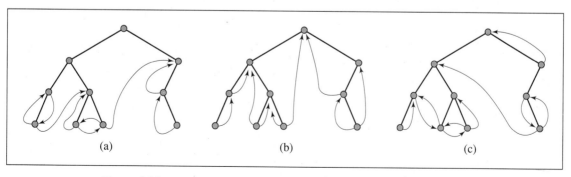

(a)   (b)   (c)

Figure 6.13: **Threaded trees to be used for (a) preorder, (b) inorder, and (c)
               postorder traversals.**

```
template<class genClass>
void
ThreadedTree<genType>::ThreadedInorder(ThTreeNode<genType>*p)
{
  ThTreeNode<genType> *prev;

  if (p) {                  // process only nonempty trees;
    while (p->left)         // go to the leftmost node;
      p = p->left;
    while (p) {
      visit(p);
      prev = p;
      p = p->right;         // go to the right node and only
      if (p && prev->successor == 0) // if it is a child
        while (p->left) // go to the leftmost node,
          p = p->left;  // otherwise visit the successor;
    }
  }
}
```

Figure 6.14: **Implementation of the inorder traversal of a threaded tree.**

```
template<class genType>
struct ThTreeNode {
      genType key;
      unsigned successor : 1;
      ThTreeNode *left, *right;
      ThTreeNode() { left = right = 0; }
      ThTreeNode(genType& el, ThTreeNode *l = 0, ThTreeNode *r = 0)
              { key = el; left = l; right = r; successor = 0; }
};
```

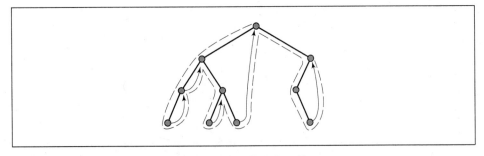

Figure 6.15: **Inorder traversal's path in threaded tree.**

```
template<class genType>
class ThreadedTree {
public:
    ThreadedTree()   { root = 0;                 }
    void Clear()     { Clear(root); root = 0;    }
    int Empty()      { return root == 0;         }
    ~ThreadedTree()  { Clear();                  }
    void ThreadedInorder()        { ThreadedInorder(root);    }
    ..................................................
protected:
    ThTreeNode<genType>* root;
    void Clear(ThTreeNode<genType>*);
    void ThreadedInorder(ThTreeNode<genType>*);
    ..................................................
};
```

Using this declaration, **successor** requires only one bit of computer memory, insignificant in comparison with other fields. However, the exact details are highly dependent on the implementation. The operating system almost certainly pads a bit structure with a hole for proper alignment of machine words. If so, our **successor** field needs at least one byte, if not an entire word, defeating the argument about saving space by using threaded trees. As indicated, the traversal algorithm uses a stack, but only in extreme cases is the stack large (assuming that it is implemented as a linked list, not as an array). In most cases it is insignificantly small in comparison with the size of a large tree. And time? Sample runs show that **ThreadedInorder()** is faster than **IterativeInorder()** by 5–15%. Therefore an argument of speed does not rule out **IterativeInorder()** as a reasonable choice.

Traversal through Tree Transformation

The first set of traversal algorithms analyzed earlier in this chapter needed a stack to retain some information necessary for successful processing. Threaded trees incorporated a stack as a part of the tree at the cost of extending the nodes by one field to make a distinction between the interpretation of the right pointer as a pointer to the child or to the successor. Two such tag fields are needed if both successor and predecessor are considered. However, it is possible to traverse a tree without using any stack or threads. There are many such algorithms, all of them made possible by making temporary changes in the tree during traversal. These changes consist of reassigning new values to some pointer fields. However, the tree may temporarily lose its tree structure which needs to be restored before traversal is finished. The technique is illustrated by an elegant algorithm devised by Joseph M. Morris applied to inorder traversal.

First, it is easy to notice that inorder traversal is very simple for degenerate trees, in which no node has a left child (see Figure 6.1e). No left subtree has to be considered for any node. Therefore, the usual three steps, LVR (visit left subtree, visit node, visit right subtree), for each node in inorder traversal turn into two steps, VR. No information needs to be retained about the current status of the node being processed before traversing its left child, simply because there is no left child. Morris' algorithm takes into account this observation by temporarily transforming the tree so that the node being processed has no left child; hence, this node can be visited and its right subtree processed. The algorithm can be summarized as follows:

> **while** *not finished*
>> **if** *node has no left descendant*
>>> *visit it;*
>>> *go to the right;*
>> **else** *make this node right child of the rightmost node in its left descendant;*
>>> *go to this left descendant;*

This algorithm successfully traverses the tree but only once, since it destroys its original structure. Therefore, some information has to be retained to allow the tree to restore its original form. This is achieved by retaining the left pointer of the node moved down its right child, as indicated in Figure 6.16.

```
template<class genType>
void
  BinarySearchTree<genType>::MorrisInorder()
{ TreeNode<gentype> *p = root, *tmp;

  while (p)
    if (p->left == 0) {
        Visit(p);
        p = p->right;
    }
    else {
        tmp = p->left;
        while (tmp->right &&        // go to the rightmost node of
               tmp->right != p)     // the left subtree or
            tmp = tmp->right;       // to the temporary parent of p;
        if (tmp->right == 0)   {    // if 'true' rightmost node was
            tmp->right = p;         // reached, make it a temporary
            p = p->left;            // parent of the current root,
        }
        else {                      // else a temporary parent has been
            Visit(p);               // found; visit node p and then cut
            tmp->right = 0;         // the right pointer of the current
            p = p->right;           // parent, whereby it ceases to be
        }                           // a parent;
    }
}
```

Figure 6.16: **Implementation of the Morris algorithm for inorder traversal.**

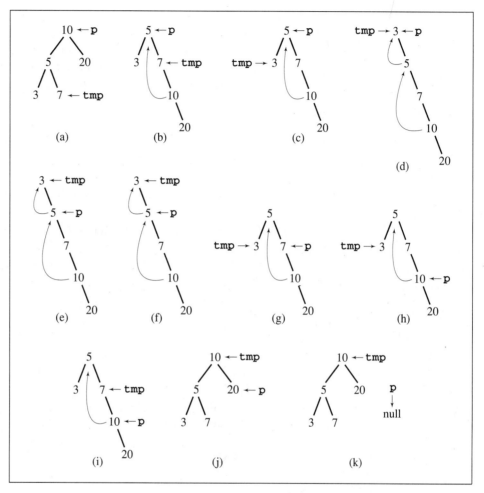

Figure 6.17: **Tree traversal with the Morris method.**

Details of the execution are illustrated in Figure 6.17. The following description is divided into actions performed in consecutive iterations of the outer **while** loop:

1. Initially, **p** points to the root, which has a left child. As a result, the inner **while** loop takes **tmp** to node 7, which is the rightmost node of the left child of node 10, pointed to by **p** (Figure 6.17a). Since no transformation has been done, **tmp** has no right child, and in the inner **if** statement, the root, node 10, is made the right child of **tmp**. Node 10 retains its left pointer to node 5, its original left child. Now, the tree is not a tree any more, since there are two paths from the root to itself (Figure 6.17b). This completes the first iteration.

2. Pointer **p** points to node 5, which also has a left child. First, **tmp** reaches the largest node in this subtree, which is 3 (Figure 6.17c), and then the current root, node 5, becomes the right child of node 3 while retaining contact with node 3 through its left pointer (Figure 6.17d).

3. Because node 3, pointed to by **p**, has no left child, in the third iteration, this node is visited, and **p** is reassigned to its right child, node 5 (Figure 6.17e).

4. Node 5 has a nonempty left pointer, so **tmp** finds a temporary parent of node 5, which is the same node currently pointed to by **tmp** (Figure 6.17f). Next, node 5 is visited, and configuration of the tree in Figure 6.17b is re-established by setting the right pointer of node 3 to null (Figure 6.17g).

5. Node 7, pointed to now by **p**, is visited, and **p** moves down to its right child (6.17h).

6. **tmp** is updated to point to the temporary parent of node 10 (Figure 6.17i). Next, node 10 is visited, and then re-established to its status of root by nullifying the right pointer of node 7 (Figure 6.17j).

7. Finally, node 20 is visited without further ado, since it has no left child, nor has its position been altered.

This completes the execution of Morris' algorithm. Notice that there are seven iterations of the outer **while** loop for only five nodes in the tree in Figure 6.17. This is due to the fact that there are two left children in the tree so the number of extra iterations depends on the number of left children in the entire tree. The algorithm performs worse for trees with a large number of such children.

■ 6.5 INSERTION

Searching a binary tree does not modify the tree. It scans the tree in a predetermined way to access some or all of the keys in the tree, but the tree itself remains undisturbed after such an operation. Tree traversals can change the tree but they may also leave it in the same condition. Whether or not the tree is modified depends on the actions prescribed by **Visit()**. There are certain operations which always make some systematic changes in the tree, such as adding nodes, deleting them, modifying elements, merging trees, and balancing trees to reduce their height. This section deals only with inserting a node into a binary search tree.

To insert a new node, called *n_node*, a tree node, called *t_node*, with a dead end has to be reached, and the new node has to be attached to it. A *t_node* is found using the same technique that tree searching used; the key of the *n_node* to be inserted is compared to the value of a node, denoted as *c_node*, currently being examined during a tree scan. If it is less than that value, the left child (if any) is tried, otherwise the right child is tested. If the child of the *c_node* to be tested is empty, the scanning is discontinued and the *n_node* becomes this child. The procedure is illustrated in Figure 6.18.

Figure 6.19 contains the algorithm to insert a node.

In analyzing the problem of traversing binary trees, three approaches have been presented: traversing with the help of a stack, traversing with the aid of threads, and traversing through tree transformation. The first approach does not change the tree during the process. The third approach changes it, but restores it to the same condition as before it started. Only the second approach needs some preparatory operations on the tree in order to become feasible: it requires threads. These threads may be created each time before the traversal procedure starts its task and removed each time it is finished. If the traversal is performed infrequently, this becomes a viable option. A fourth approach is to

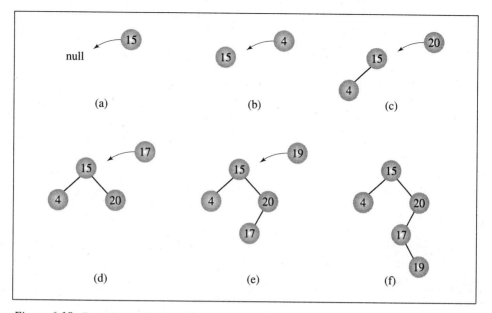

Figure 6.18: **Inserting nodes into binary search trees.**

```
template<class genType>
void
BinarySearchTree<genType>::Insert(genType& el)
{   TreeNode<genType> *p = root, *prev = 0;

    while (p) {          // find a place for inserting new node;
        prev = p;
        if (p->key < el)
            p = p->right;
        else p = p->left;
    }
    if (root == 0)     // tree is empty;
        root = new TreeNode<genType>(el);
    else if (prev->key < el)
        prev->right = new TreeNode<genType>(el);
    else prev->left  = new TreeNode<genType>(el);
}
```

Figure 6.19: **Implementation of the insertion algorithm.**

maintain the threads in all operations on the tree when inserting a new element in the binary search tree.

The procedure for inserting a node in a threaded tree is a simple extension of `Insert()` for regular binary search trees to adjust threads whenever applicable. This procedure is for inorder tree traversal and it only takes care of successors, not predecessors.

A node with a right child has a successor some place in its right subtree. Therefore it does not need a successor thread. Such threads are needed to allow climbing the tree, not

```
template<class genType>
void
ThreadedTree<genType>::ThreadedInsert(genType& el)
{    ThTreeNode<genType> *p, *prev = 0, *newNode;

     newNode = new ThTreeNode<genType>(el);
     if (!root) {                     // tree is empty
         root = newNode;
         return;
     }
     p = root;              // find a place for inserting newNode;
     while (p) {
         prev = p;
         if (p->key > el)
              p = p->left;
         else if (p->successor == 0)    // go to the right only if it is
              p = p->right;             // a descendant, not a successor;
         else break;                    // don't follow successor link;
     }
     if (prev->key > el) {              // if newNode is left child of
         prev->left  = newNode;        // its parent, the parent becomes
         newNode->successor = 1;       // also its successor;
         newNode->right = prev;
     }
     else if (prev->successor == 1) {  // if parent of the newNode
         newNode->successor = 1;       // is not the rightmost node,
         prev->successor = 0;          // make parent's successor
         newNode->right = prev->right; // newNode's successor,
         prev->right = newNode;
     }
     else prev->right = newNode;       // otherwise has no successor;
}
```

Figure 6.20: **Implementation of the algorithm to insert node into a threaded tree.**

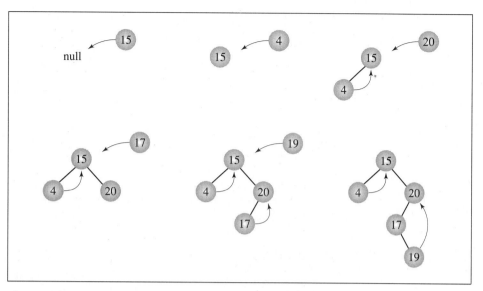

Figure 6.21: **Inserting nodes into a threaded tree.**

going down it. A node with no right child has its successor somewhere above it. Except for one node, all nodes with no right children will have threads to their successors. If a node becomes the right child of another node, it inherits the successor from its new parent. If a node becomes a left child of another node, this parent becomes its successor. Figure 6.20 contains the implementation of this algorithm, `ThreadedInsert()`. The first few insertions are shown in Figure 6.21.

■ 6.6 DELETION

Deleting a node is another operation necessary to maintain a binary search tree. The level of complexity in performing the operation depends on the position of the node to be deleted in the tree. It is by far more difficult to delete a node having two subtrees than to delete a leaf; the complexity of the deletion algorithm is proportional to the number of children the node has. There are three cases of deleting a node from the binary search tree:

1. The node is a leaf, it has no children. This is the easiest case to deal with. The appropriate pointer of its parent is set to null and the node is disposed of by `Delete()` as in Figure 6.22.

2. The node has one child. This case is not complicated. The parent's pointer to the node is reset to point to the node's child. In this way, the node's children are lifted up by one level and all great-great-...grandchildren lose one "great" from their kinship designations. For example, the node containing 20 (see Figure 6.23) is deleted by setting the right pointer of its parent containing 15 to point to 20's only child which is 16.

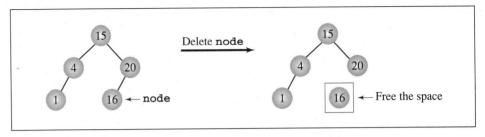

Figure 6.22: **Deleting a leaf.**

3. The node has two children. In this case, no one-step operation can be performed since the parent's right or left pointer cannot point to both node's children at the same time. This section discusses two different solutions to this problem.

6.6.1 First Solution

This solution makes one tree out of the two subtrees of the node and then attaches it to the node's parent. This technique is called *deleting by merging.* But how can we merge these subtrees? By the nature of binary search trees, every value of the right subtree is greater than every value of the left subtree so the best thing to do is to find in the left subtree the node with the greatest value and make it a parent of the right subtree. Symmetrically, the node with the lowest value can be found in the right subtree and made a parent of the left subtree.

The desired node is the rightmost node of the left subtree. It can be located by moving along this subtree and taking right pointers until null is encountered. This means that this node will not have a right child, and there is no danger of violating the property of binary search trees in the original tree by setting that rightmost node's right pointer to the right subtree. The same could be done by setting the left pointer of the leftmost node of the right subtree to the left subtree. Figure 6.24 depicts this operation. Figure 6.25 contains the implementation of the algorithm.

It may appear that **Delete()** contains redundant code. Instead of calling **Search()** before invoking **DeleteByMerging()**, **Delete()** seems to forget about **Search()** and searches for the node to be deleted using its private code. But using **Search()** in function **Delete()** is a treacherous simplification. **Search()** returns a pointer to the node containing **key**. In **Delete()**, it is important to have this pointer stored specifically

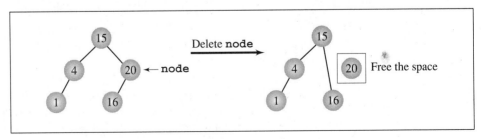

Figure 6.23: **Deleting a node with one child.**

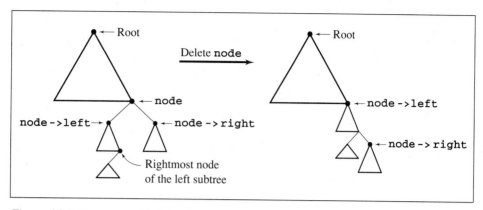

Figure 6.24: **Summary of deleting by merging.**

```
template<class genType>
void
BinarySearchTree<genType>::DeleteByMerging(TreeNode<genType>*& node)
{    TreeNode<genType> *tmp = node;

    if (node) {
        if (!node->right)        // node has no right child: its left
            node = node->left;   // child (if any) is attached to its parent;
        else if (!node->left)    // node has no left child: its right
            node = node->right;  // child is attached to its parent;
        else {                   // be ready for merging subtrees;
            tmp = node->left;    // 1. move left
            while (tmp->right)   // 2. and then right as far as possible;
                tmp = tmp->right;
            tmp->right =         // 3. establish the link between the
                node->right;     //    the rightmost node of the left
                                 //    subtree and the right subtree;
            tmp = node;          // 4.
            node = node->left;   // 5.
        }
        delete tmp;              // 6.
    }
}
```

Figure 6.25: **Implementation of algorithm for deleting by merging.**   **continued**

```
template<class genType>
void
BinarySearchTree<genType>::Delete(genType& el)
{    TreeNode<genType> *node = root, *prev = 0;

     while (node) {
          if (node->key == el)
               break;
          prev = node;
          if (node->key < el)
               node = node->right;
          else node = node->left;
     }
     if (node->key == el)
          if (node == root)
               DeleteByMerging(root);
          else if (prev->left == node)
               DeleteByMerging(prev->left);
          else DeleteByMerging(prev->right);
     else if (root)
          cout << "key " << el << " is not in the tree\n";
     else cout << "the tree is empty\n";

}
```

Figure 6.25: **Implementation of algorithm for deleting by merging.**

in one of the pointer fields of the node's parent. In other words, a caller to **Search()** is satisfied if it can access the node from any direction whereas **Delete()** wants to access it either from its parent's left or right pointer field. Otherwise, the entire branch of the tree that starts with this node is deleted instead of just the node itself. One of reasons for this is the fact that **Search()** focuses on the contents of the node of its key, and **Delete()** focuses on the node itself as an element of a larger structure, namely, a tree.

Figure 6.26 shows each step of this operation. It shows what changes are made when **Delete()** is executed. The numbers in this figure correspond to numbers put in comments in the code in Figure 6.25.

The algorithm for deletion by merging may result in increasing the height of the tree. In some cases the new tree may be highly unbalanced, as Figure 6.27a illustrates. Sometimes the height may be reduced (see Figure 6.27b). This algorithm is not necessarily inefficient, but it is certainly far from perfect. There is a need for an algorithm that does not give the tree the chance to increase its height when deleting one of its nodes.

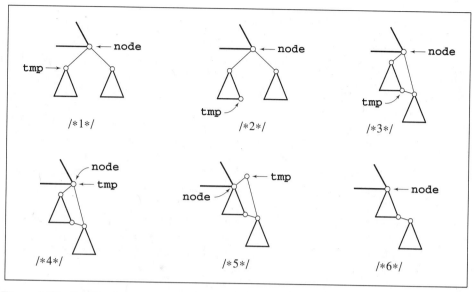

Figure 6.26: Details of deleting by merging.

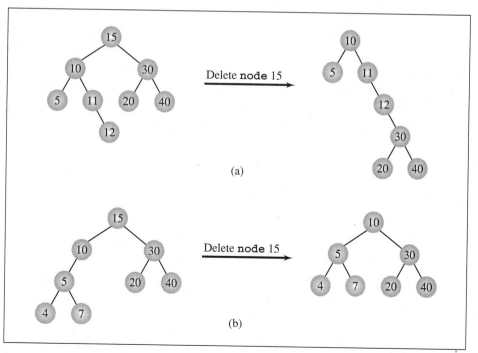

Figure 6.27: The height of a tree can be extended (a) or reduced (b) after
deleting by merging.

6.6.2   Second Solution

Another solution was proposed by Thomas Hibbard and improved by Donald Knuth. If the node has two children, the case can be reduced to one of the two simple cases: the node is a leaf or the node has only one child. This can be done by replacing the node with its immediate predecessor or successor. As already indicated in the algorithm above, a node's predecessor is the rightmost node in the left subtree; its immediate successor is the leftmost node in the right subtree. First, the predecessor has to be located. This is done, again, by moving one step to the left thereby reaching the root of the node's left subtree and then moving as far to the right as possible. Next, the value of the located node replaces the value of the node to be deleted. And that is where one of the two simple cases comes into play. If the rightmost node is a leaf, the first case applies. However, if it has one child, the second case is relevant.

To implement this algorithm, one new function, **DeleteByCopying()**, has to be written, and the procedure **Delete()** can be reused by replacing calls to **DeleteByMerging()** with calls to **DeleteByCopying()**. Figure 6.28 contains the code for the latter function.

```
template<class genType>
void
BinarySearchTree<genType>::DeleteByCopying(TreeNode<genType>*& node)
{    TreeNode<genType> *previous, *tmp = node;

     if (!node->right)                      // there is no right child
          node = node->left;                // for node;
     else if (!node->left)                  // no left child for node;
          node = node->right;
     else {
          tmp = node->left;                 // node has both children;
          previous = node;                  // 1
          while (tmp->right) {              // 2
               previous = tmp;
               tmp = tmp->right;
          }
          node->key = tmp->key;             // 3
          if (previous == node)
               previous->left  = tmp->left; // 4
          else previous->right = tmp->left; // 5
     }
     delete tmp;
}
```

Figure 6.28: **Implementation of algorithm for deleting by copying.**

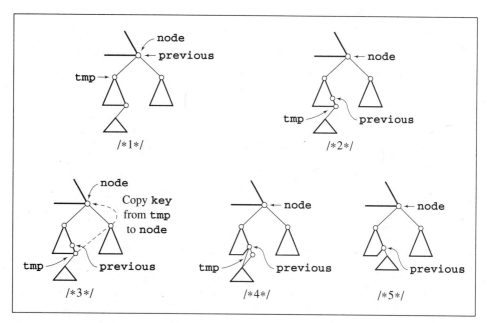

Figure 6.29: **Deleting by copying.**

A step-by-step trace is shown in Figure 6.29, and the numbers under the diagrams refer to the numbers indicated in comments included in the implementation of **DeleteByCopying()**.

This algorithm does not increase the height of the tree, but it still causes a problem if it is applied many times along with insertion. This algorithm is asymmetric; it always deletes the node of the immediate predecessor of information in **node**, reducing the height of the left subtree and leaving the right subtree unaffected. Therefore, the right subtree of **node** can grow after later insertions and if the information in **node** is again deleted, the height of the right tree remains the same. After many insertions and deletions, the entire tree becomes right-unbalanced, with right tree bushier and larger than the left subtree.

To circumvent this problem, a simple improvement can be made to the algorithm to make it symmetrical. The algorithm can alternately delete the predecessor of the information in **node** from the left subtree, and delete its successor from the right subtree. The improvement is significant. Simulations performed by Jeffrey Eppinger show that an expected internal path length for many insertions and asymmetric deletions is $\Theta(n \lg^3 n)$ for n nodes, and when symmetric deletions are used, the expected IPL becomes $\Theta(n \lg n)$. Theoretical results obtained by J. Culberson confirm these conclusions. According to Culberson, insertions and asymmetric deletions give $\Theta(n\sqrt{n})$ for the expected IPL and $\Theta(\sqrt{n})$ for the average search time, whereas symmetric deletions lead to $\Theta(\lg n)$ for the average search time, and, as before, $\Theta(n \lg n)$ for the average IPL.

These results may be of moderate importance for practical applications. Experiments show that for a 2048-node binary tree, only after 1.5 million insertions and asymmetric deletions does the IPL become worse than in a randomly generated tree.

Theoretical results are only fragmentary because of the extraordinary complexity of the problem. Arne Jonassen and Donald Knuth analyzed the problem of random insertions and deletions for a tree of only three nodes, which required using Bessel functions and bivariate integral equations, and the analysis turned out to rank among "the more difficult of all exact analyses of algorithms that have been carried out to date." Therefore, the reliance on experimental results is not surprising.

6.7 BALANCING A TREE

At the beginning of this chapter, two arguments were presented in favor of trees: they are well suited to represent the hierarchical structure of a certain domain and the search process is much faster using trees instead of linked lists. The second argument, however, does not always hold. It all depends on what the tree looks like. Figure 6.30 shows three binary search trees. All of them store the same data but obviously, the tree in Figure 6.30a is the best and Figure 6.30c is the worst. In the worst case, three tests are needed in the former and six tests are needed in the latter to locate an object. The problem with the trees in Figure 6.30b and 6.30c is that they are somewhat unsymmetrical, or lopsided; that is, objects in the tree are not distributed evenly, to the extent that the tree in the Figure 6.30c practically turned into a linked list, although, formally, it is still a tree. Such a situation does not arise in balanced trees.

A binary tree is *height-balanced* or simply *balanced* if the difference in height of both subtrees of any node in the tree is either zero or one. For example, for node K in Figure 6.30b, the difference between the heights of its subtrees being equal to one is acceptable. But for node B this difference is three, which means that the entire tree is unbalanced. For the same node B in 6.30c, the difference is the worst possible, namely five. Also, a tree is considered *perfectly balanced* if it is balanced and all leaves are to be found on one level or two levels.

Figure 6.31 shows how many nodes can be stored in binary trees of different heights. Since each node can have two children, the number of nodes on a certain level is double the number of parents residing on the previous level (except, of course, the root). For example, if 10,000 elements are stored in a perfectly balanced tree, then the tree is of height

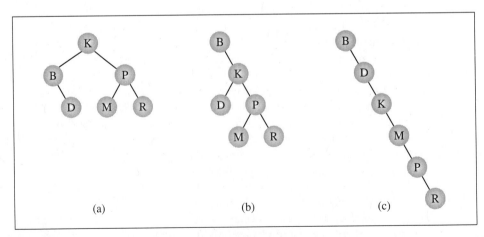

Figure 6.30: **Different binary search trees with the same information.**

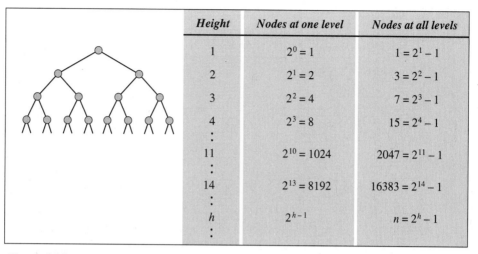

	Height	Nodes at one level	Nodes at all levels
	1	$2^0 = 1$	$1 = 2^1 - 1$
	2	$2^1 = 2$	$3 = 2^2 - 1$
	3	$2^2 = 4$	$7 = 2^3 - 1$
	4	$2^3 = 8$	$15 = 2^4 - 1$
	⋮		
	11	$2^{10} = 1024$	$2047 = 2^{11} - 1$
	⋮		
	14	$2^{13} = 8192$	$16383 = 2^{14} - 1$
	⋮		
	h	2^{h-1}	$n = 2^h - 1$
	⋮		

Figure 6.31: **Maximum number of nodes in binary trees of different heights.**

$\lceil \lg(10,001) \rceil = \lceil 13.289 \rceil = 14$. In practical terms, this means that if 10,000 elements are stored in a perfectly balanced tree, then at most fourteen nodes have to be checked to locate a particular element. This is a substantial difference compared to the 10,000 tests needed in a linked list (in the worst case). Therefore, it is worth the effort to build a balanced tree or modify an existing tree so that it is balanced.

There are a number of techniques to properly balance a binary tree. Some of them consist of constantly restructuring the tree when elements arrive and lead to an unbalanced tree. Some of them consist of reordering the data themselves and then building a tree, if an ordering of the data guarantees that the resulting tree will be balanced. This section presents a simple technique of this kind.

The linked list-like tree of Figure 6.30c is the result of a particular stream of data. Thus, if the data arrive in an ascending or descending order, then the tree resembles a linked list. The tree in Figure 6.30b is lopsided, since the first element that arrived was the letter B, which precedes almost all other letters, except A; the left subtree of B is guaranteed to have just one node. The tree in Figure 6.30a looks very good, since the root contains an element near the middle of all the possible elements, and P is more or less in the middle of K and Z. This leads us to an algorithm based on binary search technique.

When data arrive, store all of them in an array. If all possible data arrived, sort the array using one of the efficient algorithms discussed in Chapter 9. Now, designate for the root the middle element in the array. The array now consists of two subarrays: one between the beginning of the array and the element just chosen for the root, and one between the root and the end of the array. The left child of the root is taken from the middle of the first subarray, its right child an element in the middle of the second. Now, building the level containing the children of the root is finished. The next level, with children of children of the root, is constructed in the same fashion using four subarrays and the middle elements from each of them. An example of this process is shown in Figure 6.32.

The algorithm is quite simple. First, all data are stored in an array and sorted. Then the data are inserted into the tree as in the following function:

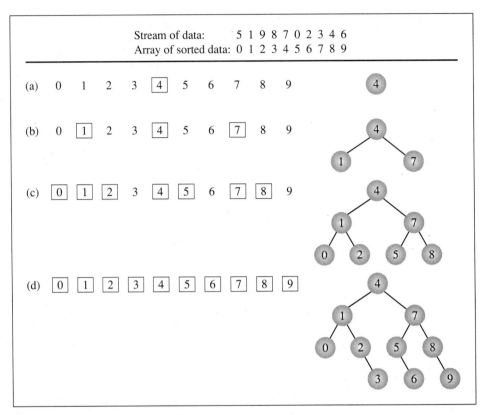

Stream of data: 5 1 9 8 7 0 2 3 4 6
Array of sorted data: 0 1 2 3 4 5 6 7 8 9

Figure 6.32: **Creating a binary search tree from an ordered array.**

```
template<class genType>
void
BinarySearchTree<genType>::Balance (genType data[], int first, int last)
{
  if (first <= last) {
     int middle = first + (last-first)/2;
     Insert(data[middle]);
     Balance (data,first,middle-1);
     Balance (data,middle+1,last);
  }
}
```

This algorithm has one serious drawback: all data must be put in an array before the tree can be created. They can be stored in the array directly from the input. In this case, the algorithm may be unsuitable when the tree has to be used while the data to be included in the tree are still coming. But the data can be transferred from an unbalanced tree to the array using inorder traversal. The tree can now be deleted and recreated using **Balance()**. This at least does not require using any sorting procedure to put data in order.

6.7.1 The DSW Algorithm

The algorithm discussed in the previous section was somewhat inefficient in that it required an additional array which needed to be sorted before the construction of a perfectly balanced tree began. To avoid sorting, it required deconstructing and then reconstructing the tree, which is inefficient except for relatively small trees. There are, however, algorithms, which require little additional storage for intermediate variables and use no sorting procedure. A very elegant algorithm, the DSW algorithm, was devised by Colin Day and later improved by Quentin F. Stout and Bette L. Warren.

The building block for tree transformations in this algorithm is the *rotation*. There are two types of rotation, left and right, which are symmetrical to one another. The right rotation of the node **Ch** about its parent **Par** is performed according to the following algorithm:

```
RotateRight (Gr, Par, Ch)
```
if **Par** *is not the root of the tree* **// i.e., if Gr is not null**
  grandparent **Gr** *of child* **Ch** *becomes* **Ch**'s *parent by replacing* **Par;**
  right subtree of **Ch** *becomes left subtree of* **Ch**'s *parent* **Par;**
  left child **Ch** *of parent* **Par** *acquires* **Par** *as its right child;*

The steps involved in this compound operation are shown in Figure 6.33. The second step is the core of the rotation, when **Par**, the parent node of child **Ch**, becomes the child of **Ch**, when the roles of a parent and its child change. However, this exchange of roles cannot affect the principal property of the tree, namely that it is a search tree. The first and the third steps of **RotateRight()** are needed to ensure that after the rotation, the tree remains a search tree.

Basically, the DSW algorithm transfigures an arbitrary binary search tree into a linked list-like tree, called a *backbone* or *vine*. Then this elongated tree is transformed in a series of passes into a perfectly balanced tree by repeatedly rotating every second node of the backbone about its parent.

In the first phase, a backbone is created using the following routine:

```
CreateBackbone(root, n)
  tmp = root;
  while (tmp != 0)
    if tmp has a left child
```

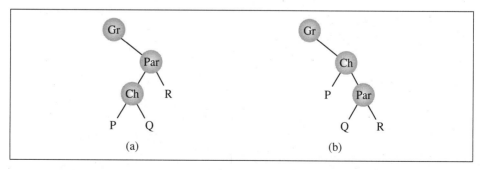

(a)   (b)

Figure 6.33: **Right rotation of child Ch about parent Par.**

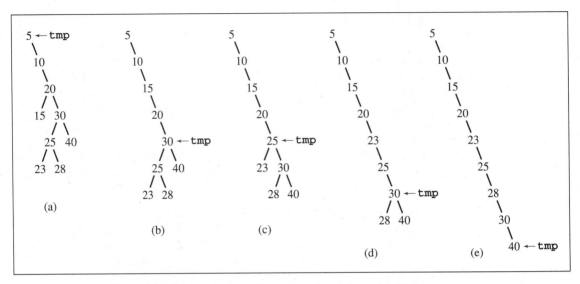

Figure 6.34: **Transforming a binary search tree into a backbone.**

> *rotate this child about* `tmp`; `// hence the left child`
> `// becomes parent of tmp;`
> set `tmp` *to the child which just became parent*;
> `else` *set* `tmp` *to its right child*;

This algorithm is illustrated in Figure 6.34. Note that a rotation requires knowledge about the parent of `tmp` so another pointer has to be maintained when implementing the algorithm.

In the worst case, the **while** loop is executed $2n - 1$ times with $n - 1$ rotations performed where n is the number of nodes in the tree; the run time of the first phase is $O(n)$.

In the second phase, the backbone is transformed into a tree but this time the tree is perfectly balanced by having leaves only on two adjacent levels. In each pass down the backbone, every second node is rotated about its parent. One such pass decreases the size of the backbone by one-half. Only the first pass may not reach the end of the backbone: it is used to account for the difference between the number n of nodes in the current tree and the number $2^{\lfloor \lg(n+1) \rfloor} - 1$ of nodes in the closest complete binary tree where $\lfloor x \rfloor$ is the closest integer less than x. That is, the overflowing nodes are treated separately.

```
CreatePerfectTree(n)
    m = 2^⌊lg (n+1)⌋-1;
    make n-m rotations starting from the top of backbone;
    while (m > 1)
        m = m/2;
        make m rotations starting from the top of backbone;
```

Figure 6.35 contains an example. The backbone in Figure 6.34e has nine nodes and is preprocessed by one pass outside the loop to be transformed into the backbone shown in Figure 6.35b. Now, two passes are executed. In each backbone, the nodes to be promoted

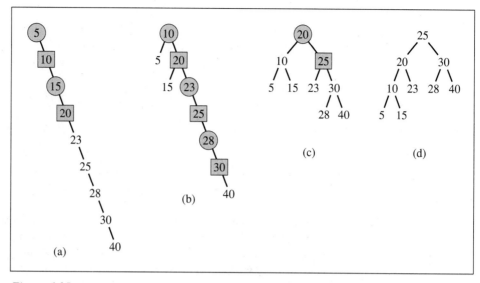

Figure 6.35: **Transforming a backbone into a perfectly balanced tree.**

by one level by left rotations are shown as squares; their parents, about which they are rotated, are marked as circles.

To compute the complexity of the tree building phase, observe that

$$m = 2^{\lfloor \lg (n+1) \rfloor} - 1 \leq 2^{\lg (n+1)} - 1 = n.$$

The number of rotations can be given now by the formula

$$n - m + \sum_{i=1}^{\lg m - 1} \frac{m}{2^i} \leq n \sum_{i=1}^{\lg m - 1} \frac{1}{2^i} \rightarrow n \text{ for large } n$$

since geometric series $\sum \frac{1}{2^i} \rightarrow 1$, that is, the number of rotations is $O(n)$. Because creating a backbone also required at most $O(n)$ rotations, the cost of global rebalancing with the DSW algorithm is optimal in terms of time and space, since it grows linearly with n, and requires a very small and fixed amount of storage.

6.7.2   AVL Trees

The previous two sections discussed algorithms which rebalanced the tree globally; each and every node could have been involved in rebalancing either by moving data from nodes or by reassigning new values to pointer fields. Tree rebalancing, however, can be performed locally if only a portion of the tree is affected when changes are required after an element is inserted into or deleted from the tree. One classical method has been proposed by Adel'son-Vel'skii and Landis which is commemorated in the name of the tree modified with this method: the AVL tree.

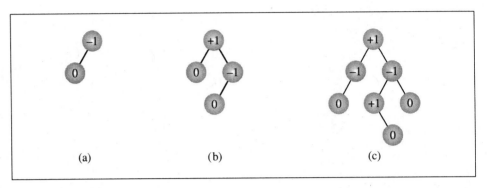

Figure 6.36: **Examples of AVL trees.**

An *AVL tree* (originally called an *admissible tree*) is a tree in which the height of left and right subtrees of every node differ by at most one. For example, all the trees in Figure 6.36 are AVL trees. Numbers in the nodes indicate the *balance factors* which are the differences between the heights of the left and right subtrees. A balance factor is the height of the right subtree minus the height of the left subtree. For an AVL tree, all balance factors should be $+1$, 0, or -1. Notice that the definition of the AVL tree is the same as the definition of the balanced tree. However, the concept of the AVL tree always implicitly includes the techniques for balancing the tree. Moreover, unlike the two methods previously discussed, the technique for balancing AVL trees does not guarantee that the resulting tree is perfectly balanced.

The definition of an AVL tree indicates that the minimum number of nodes in a tree is determined by the recurrence equation

$$AVL_h = AVL_{h-1} + AVL_{h-2} + 1$$

where $AVL_0 = 0$ and $AVL_1 = 1$ are the initial conditions[1]. As shown by Adel'son-Vel'skii and Landis, this formula leads to the following bounds on the height h of an AVL tree depending on the number of nodes n:

$$\lg(n + 1) \leq h < 1.44 \lg(n + 2) - 0.328.$$

Therefore, h is bounded by $O(\lg n)$; the worst case search requires $O(\lg n)$ comparisons. For a perfectly balanced binary tree of the same height, $h = \lceil \lg(n + 1) \rceil$. Therefore, the search time in the worst case in an AVL tree is 44% worse (it requires 44% more comparisons) than in the best case tree configuration. Empirical studies indicate that the average number of searches is much closer to the best case than to the worse and is equal to $\lg n + 0.25$ for large n (Knuth 1973). Therefore AVL trees are definitely worth studying.

If the balance factor of any node in an AVL tree becomes less than -1 or greater than 1, the tree has to be balanced. An AVL tree can become out of balance in four situations, but only two of them need to be analyzed; the remaining two are symmetrical. The first

---

[1]Numbers generated by this recurrence formula are called *Leonardo numbers*.

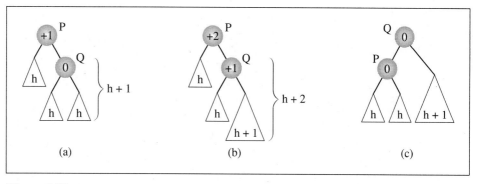

Figure 6.37: **Balancing a tree after insertion of a node in the right subtree of
node *Q*.**

case, the result of inserting a node in the right subtree of the right child, is illustrated in
Figure 6.37. The heights of the participating subtrees are indicated within these subtrees.
In the AVL tree in Figure 6.37a, a node is inserted somewhere in the right subtree of *Q*
(Figure 6.37b), which disturbs the balance of the tree *P*. In this case, the problem can be
easily rectified by rotating node *Q* about its parent *P* (Figure 6.37c) so that the balance
factor of both *P* and *Q* becomes zero, which is even better than at the outset.

The second case, resulting from inserting a node into the left subtree of the right child,
is more complex. A node is inserted into the tree in Figure 6.38a; the resulting tree is shown
in Figure 6.38b, and in more detail, in Figure 6.38c. To bring the tree back into balance, a
double rotation is performed. First, the balance of the tree *Q* is restored by rotating *R* about
node *Q* (Figure 6.38d) and then by rotating *R* again, this time about node *P* (Figure 6.38e).

In these two cases, the tree *P* is considered a stand-alone tree. However, *P* can be
part of a larger AVL tree; it can be a child of some other node in the tree. If a node is
entered into the tree and the balance of *P* is disturbed and then restored, does extra work
need to be done to the predecessor(s) of *P*? Fortunately not. Note that the heights of the
trees in Figures 6.37c and 6.38e resulting from the rotations are the same as the heights

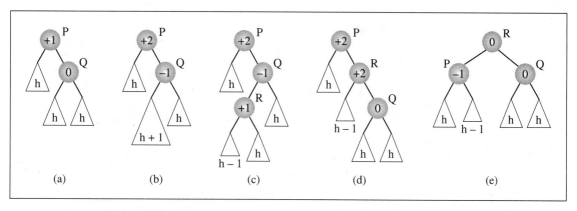

Figure 6.38: **Balancing a tree after insertion of a node in the left subtree of
node *Q*.**

of the trees before insertion (Figures 6.37a and 6.38a) and are equal to $h + 2$. This means that the balance factor of the parent of new root (Q in Figure 6.37c and R in Figure 6.38e) remains the same as it was before the insertion, and the changes made to the subtree P are sufficient to restore the balance of the entire AVL tree. The problem is in finding a node P for which the balance factor becomes unacceptable after a node has been inserted into the tree.

This node can be detected by moving up toward the root of the tree from the position in which the new node has been inserted and by updating the balance factors of the nodes encountered. Then, if a node with a ± 1 balance factor is encountered, the balance factor may be changed to ± 2 and the first node whose balance factor is changed in this way becomes the root of a subtree for which the balance has to be restored. Note that the balance factors do not have to be updated above this node since they remain the same. However, if the balance factors on the path from the newly inserted node to the root of the tree are all zero, all of them have to be updated, but no rotation is needed for any of the encountered nodes.

In Figure 6.39a, the AVL tree has a path of all zero balance factors. After a node has been appended to the end of this path (Figure 6.39b), no changes are made in the tree except for updating the balance factors of all nodes along this path.

In Figure 6.40a, a path is marked with one balance factor equal to $+1$. Insertion of a new node at the end of this path results in an unbalanced tree (Figure 6.40b), and the balance is restored by one left rotation (Figure 6.40c).

Deletion may be more time-consuming than insertion. First, we apply **DeleteByCopying()** to delete a node. This technique allows us to reduce the problem of deleting a node with two descendants to deleting a node with at most one descendant.

After a node has been deleted from the tree, balance factors are updated from the parent of the deleted node up to the root. For each node in this path whose balance factor becomes ± 2, a single or double rotation has to be performed to restore the balance of the tree. Importantly, the rebalancing does not stop after the first node P is found for which the balance factor would become ± 2 as is the case with insertion. This also means that deletion

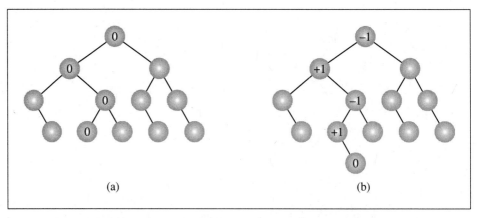

(a)   (b)

Figure 6.39: **In an AVL tree (a) a new node is inserted (b) requiring no height adjustments.**

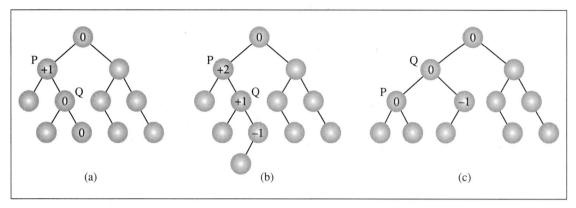

Figure 6.40: **An example of inserting a new node (b) in an AVL tree (a),
which requires one rotation (c) to restore the height balance.**

leads to at most $O(\lg n)$ rotations, since in the worst case every node on the path from the
deleted node to the root may require rebalancing.

   Deletion of a node does not have to necessitate an immediate rotation, since it may
improve the balance factor of its parent (by changing it from ± 1 to 0), but it may also
worsen the balance factor for the grandparent (by changing it from ± 1 to ± 2). We illustrate
only those cases which require immediate rotation. There are four such cases (plus four
symmetric cases). In each of these cases we assume that the left child of node P is deleted.

   In the first case, the tree in Figure 6.41a after deletion turns into the tree in Figure 6.41b. The tree is rebalanced by rotating Q about P (Figure 6.41c). The second case
requires the same rotation (Figure 6.41d–f). The third case is more complex: first R is
rotated about Q and then about P (Figure 6.41g–i). The fourth case is very similar to the
third in that it requires the same two rotations. The difference lies in the balance factor of
R, which is -1: its left subtree is higher than the right subtree. After both rotations, the
balance factor of P is -1, and Q's factor is 0.

   The previous analyses indicate that insertions and deletions require at most
$1.44 \lg(n + 2)$ searches. Also, insertion can require one single or one double rotation
and deletion can require $1.44 \lg(n + 2)$ rotations in the worst case. But as also indicated,
the average case requires $\lg(n) + .25$ searches, which reduces the number of rotations in
case of deletion to this number. To be sure, insertion in the average case may lead to one
single/double rotation. Experiments also indicate that deletions in 78% of cases require
no rebalancing at all. On the other hand, only 53% insertions do not bring the tree out of
balance (Karlton et al. 1976). Therefore the more time-consuming deletion occurs less frequently than the insertion operation, not markedly endangering the efficiency of rebalancing
AVL trees.

   AVL trees can be extended by allowing the difference in height $\Delta > 1$ (Foster 1973).
Not unexpectedly, the worst-case height increases with Δ and

$$h = \begin{cases} 1.81 \lg(n) - 0.71 & \text{if } \Delta = 2, \\ 2.15 \lg(n) - 1.13 & \text{if } \Delta = 3. \end{cases}$$

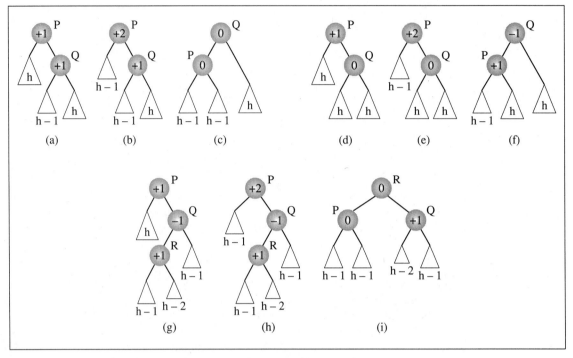

Figure 6.41: **Rebalancing an AVL tree after deleting a node.**

As experiments indicate, the average number of visited nodes increases by one-half in comparison to pure AVL trees ($\Delta = 1$), but the amount of restructuring can be decreased by a factor of 10.

■ 6.8 SELF-ADJUSTING TREES

The main concern in balancing trees is to keep them from becoming lopsided and allow leaves to occur only at one or two levels. Therefore, if a newly arriving element endangers the tree balance by creating a leaf on a level other than that at which leaves already occurred in the tree, the problem is immediately rectified by restructuring the tree locally (the AVL method) or by recreating the tree (the DSW method). However, we may question whether or not such a restructuring is always necessary. Binary search trees are used to insert, retrieve, and delete elements quickly, and the speed of performing these operations is the issue, not the shape of the tree. Performance can be improved by balancing the tree, but this is not the only method which can be used.

Another approach begins with the observation that not all elements are used with the same frequency. For example, if an element on the tenth level of the tree is used only infrequently, then the execution of the entire program is not greatly impaired by accessing this level. However, if the same element is constantly being accessed, then it makes a big difference whether it is on the tenth level or close to the root. Therefore, the strategy in self-adjusting trees is to restructure trees only by moving up the tree those elements which are used more often, creating a kind of "priority tree." The frequency of accessing nodes can be determined in a variety of ways. Each node can have a counter field which records the number of times the element has been used for any operation. Then the tree can be scanned to move the most frequently accessed elements toward the root. In a less sophisticated approach, it is assumed that an element being accessed has a good chance of being accessed again soon. Therefore it is moved up the tree. No restructuring is performed for new elements. This assumption may lead to promoting elements which are occasionally accessed, but the overall tendency is to move up elements with a high frequency of access, and for the most part, these elements will populate the first few levels of the tree.

6.8.1   Self-Restructuring Trees

A strategy proposed by Allen and Munro, and by Bitner consists of two possibilities:

1. Single rotation: Rotate a child about its parent if an element in a child is accessed unless it is the root (Figure 6.42a).
2. Moving to the root: Repeat the child-parent rotation until the element being accessed is in the root (Figure 6.42b).

Using the single rotation strategy, frequently accessed elements are eventually moved up close to the root, so that later accesses are faster than previous ones. In the move-to-the-root strategy, it is assumed that the element being accessed has a high probability to be accessed again, so it percolates right away up to the root. Even if it is not used in the next access, the element remains close to the root. These strategies, however, do not work very well in unfavorable situations, when the binary tree resembles a linked list rather than a tree as in Figure 6.43. In this case, the shape of the tree improves slowly, which may have an adverse effect on the access time of elements which are farther away from the root.

6.8.2   Splaying

A modification of the move-to-the-root strategy is called *splaying* which applies single rotations in pairs in an order depending on the links between the child, parent, and grandparent

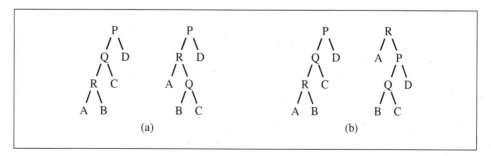

Figure 6.42: **Restructuring a tree by using (a) a single rotation or (b) moving to the root when accessing node *R*.**

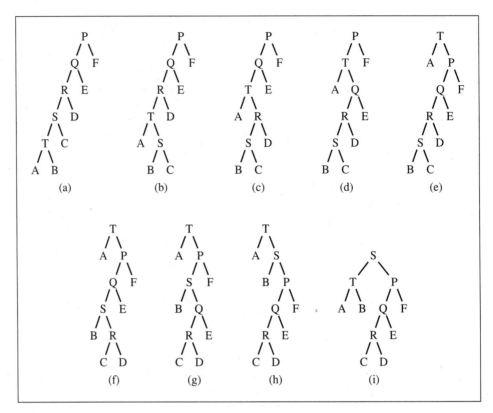

Figure 6.43: **Moving element *T* to the root (a–e) and then moving element *S* to the root (e–i).**

(Sleator, Tarjan 1985). First, three cases are distinguished, depending on the relationship between a node *R* being accessed and its parent *Q* and grandparent *P* (if any) nodes:

Case 1: Node *R*'s parent is the root.

Case 2: Homogeneous configuration: Node *R* is the left child of its parent *Q* and *Q* is the left child of its parent *P*, or *R* and *Q* are both right children.

Case 3: Heterogeneous configuration: Node *R* is the right child of its parent *Q* and *Q* is the left child of its parent *P*, or *R* is the left child of *Q* and *Q* is the right child of *P*.

The algorithm to move a node *R* being accessed to the root of the tree is as follows:

while *R is not the root*
    if *R's parent is the root*
        perform a singular splay, rotate R about its parent (Figure 6.44a);
    else if *R is in homogeneous configuration with its predecessors,*
        perform a homogeneous splay, first rotate Q about P
        and then R about Q (Figure 6.44b);

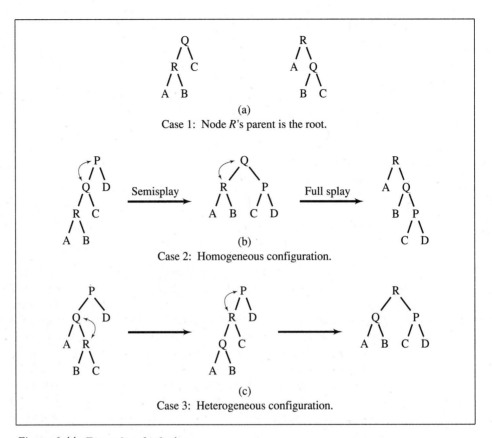

Figure 6.44: **Examples of splaying.**

```
else // if R is in heterogeneous configuration
     // with its predecessors
```
perform a heterogeneous splay, first rotate R about Q
and then about P (Figure 6.44c);

The difference in restructuring a tree is illustrated in Figure 6.45, where the tree from Figure 6.43a is used to access element T located at the fifth level. The shape of the tree is immediately improved. Then, element R is accessed (Figure 6.45c) and the shape of the tree becomes even better (Figure 6.45d).

Although splaying is a combination of two rotations except when next to the root, these rotations are not always used in the bottom-up fashion, as in the self-adjusting trees. For the homogeneous case (left-left or right-right), first the parent and the grandparent of the node being accessed are rotated, and only afterwards the node and its parent are rotated. This has the effect of moving an element to the root and flattening the tree, which has a positive impact on the accesses to be made.

The number of rotations may seem to be excessive, and it certainly would be if every time an accessed element happened to be in a leaf. In the case of a leaf, the access time is usually $O(\lg n)$, except for some initial accesses when the tree is not balanced. But

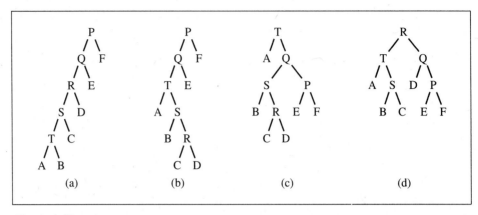

Figure 6.45: **Restructuring a tree with splaying after accessing *T* (a–c) and then *R* (c–d).**

accessing elements close to the root makes the tree unbalanced. For example, if in the tree in Figure 6.45a, the left child of the root is always accessed, then eventually the tree would also resemble a linked list, this time extending to the right. Hence, splaying is a strategy focusing upon the elements, rather than the shape of the tree. Splaying may perform well in situations in which some elements are used much more frequently than others. If elements near the root are accessed with about the same frequency as the elements on the lowest levels, then splaying may not be the best choice. In this case a strategy which stresses balancing the tree rather than frequency is better; a modification of the splaying method is a more viable option.

Semisplaying is a modification of splaying that requires only one rotation for a homogeneous splay, and continues splaying with the parent of the accessed node, not with the node itself. It is illustrated in Figure 6.44b. After *R* is accessed, its parent *Q* is rotated about *P* and splaying continues with *Q*, not with *R*. Rotation of *R* about *Q* is not performed, as it would be the case for splaying.

Figure 6.46 illustrates the advantages of semisplaying. The elongated tree from Figure 6.45a becomes more balanced with semisplaying after accessing *T* (Figures 6.46a–c), and after *T* is accessed again, the tree has basically the same number of levels. (It may have one more level if *E* or *F* was a tree higher than any of subtrees *A, B, C,* or *D*.) For implementation of this tree strategy, see the case study at the end of this chapter.

■ 6.9 HEAPS

A particular kind of binary tree, called a *heap*, has the following two properties:

1. The value of each node is not less than the values stored in each of its children

2. The tree is perfectly balanced, and the leaves in the last level are all in the leftmost positions.

To be exact, these two properties define a *max heap*. If "less" in the first property is replaced with "greater," then the definition would specify a *min heap*. This means that the

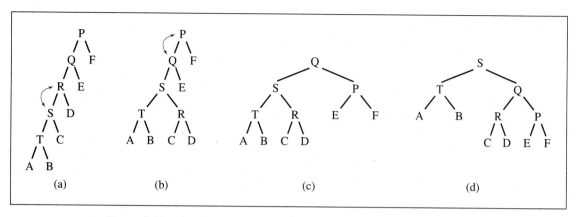

Figure 6.46: **Accessing *T* and restructuring the tree with semisplaying (a–c);**
accessing *T* again (c–d).

root of a max heap contains the largest element, whereas the root of a min heap contains the smallest. A tree has the *heap property* if each nonleaf has the first property.

The trees in Figure 6.47a are all heaps; the trees in Figure 6.47b violate the first property, and the trees in Figure 6.47c violate the second.

Interestingly, heaps can be implemented by arrays. For example, the array **data** = [2 8 6 1 10 15 3 12 11] can represent the tree in Figure 6.48 which is not a heap. The elements are placed at sequential locations representing the nodes from top to bottom and in each level from left to right. The second property reflects the fact that the array is packed, with no gaps. Now, a heap can be defined as an array **heap** of length *n* in which

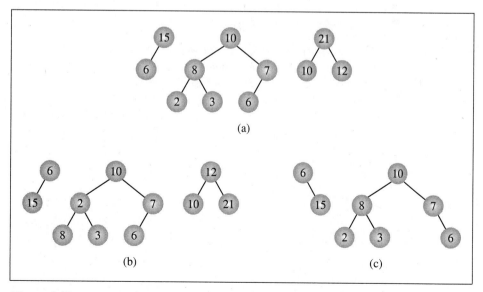

Figure 6.47: **Examples of heaps (a), and nonheaps (b, c).**

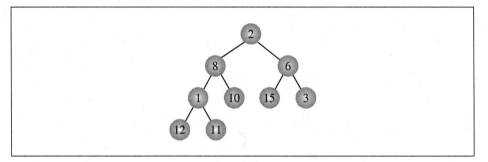

Figure 6.48: **The array [2 8 6 1 10 15 3 12 11] seen as a tree.**

$$\texttt{heap[i]} \geq \texttt{heap[2 * i + 1]}$$

and

$$\texttt{heap[i]} \geq \texttt{heap[2 * i + 2]}, \text{ for } 0 \leq i < \frac{n}{2}.$$

Due to the second condition, the number of levels in the tree is $O(\lg n)$.

Elements in a heap are not perfectly ordered. We know only that the largest element is in the root node and that for each node, all its descendants are less than or equal to that node. But the relation between sibling nodes or, to continue the kinship terminology, between uncle and nephew nodes is not determined. The order of the elements obeys a linear line of descent, disregarding lateral lines. For this reason, all the trees in Figure 6.49 are legitimate heaps, although the heap in Figure 6.49b is ordered best.

6.9.1   Heaps as Priority Queues

A heap is an excellent way to implement a priority queue. Chapter 4 used linked lists to implement priority queues, structures for which the complexity was expressed in terms of $O(n)$ or $O(\sqrt{n})$. For large n this may be too ineffective. On the other hand, a heap is a perfectly balanced tree, hence reaching a leaf requires $O(\lg n)$ searches. This efficiency is very promising. Therefore heaps can be used to implement priority queues. To this end,

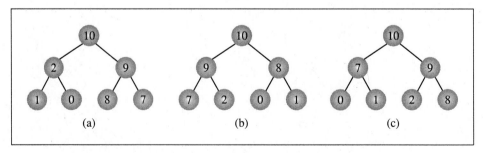

Figure 6.49: **Different heaps constructed with the same elements.**

however, two procedures have to be implemented to enqueue and dequeue elements on a priority queue.

To enqueue an element, the element is added at the end of the heap as the last leaf. For example, the number 15 is added to the heap in Figure 6.50a as the next leaf (Figure 6.50b) which destroys the heap property of the tree. To restore this property, the number 15 has to be moved up the tree until either it ends up in the root or it finds a parent which is not less than 15. In this example, the latter case occurs and 15 has to be moved only twice without reaching the root. Restoring the heap property in the case of enqueuing is achieved by moving from the last leaf toward the root.

The algorithm for enqueuing is as follows:

```
HeapEnqueue(el)
    put el at the end of queue;
    while el is not in the root and el > parent(el)
        swap el with its parent;
```

Dequeuing an element from this heap consists of removing the root element from the heap, since by the heap property it is the element with the greatest priority. Then the last leaf is put in its place and the heap property almost certainly has to be restored, this time by moving from the root down the tree. For example, 20 is dequeued from the heap in Figure 6.51a and 6 is put in its place (Figure 6.51b). To restore the heap property, 6 is swapped first with its larger child, number 15 (Figure 6.51c), and once again with the larger child, 14 (Figure 6.51d).

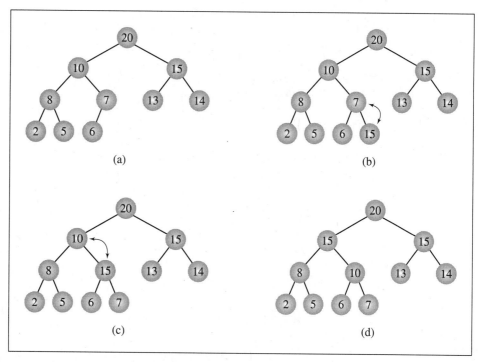

(a)

(b)

(c)

(d)

Figure 6.50: **Enqueuing an element to a heap.**

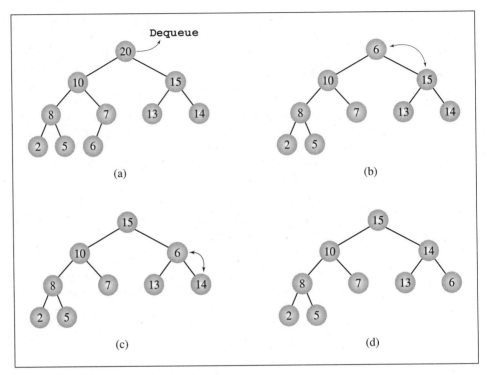

Figure 6.51: **Dequeuing an element from a heap.**

The algorithm for dequeuing is as follows:

HeapDequeue()
   extract the element from the root;
   put the element from the last leaf in its place;
   remove the last leaf;
   // both subtrees of the root are heaps;
   p = *the root;*
   while p *is not a leaf and* **p** < *any of the children*
     swap **p** *with the larger child;*

The last three lines of this algorithm can be treated as a separate algorithm which restores the heap property only if it has been violated by the root of the tree. In this case, the root element is moved down the tree until it finds a proper position. This algorithm, which is the key to the heap sort and will be discussed in detail in Chapter 9, is presented in one possible implementation in Figure 6.52.

6.9.2   Organizing Arrays as Heaps

Heaps can be implemented as arrays, and in that sense each heap is an array, but all arrays are not heaps. In some situations, however, most notably in heap sort (cf. Section 9.3.2), we need to convert an array into a heap, that is, reorganize the data in the array so that the

```
template<class genType>
void
MoveDown(genType data[],int first,int last)
{    int largest = 2*first + 1;

     while (largest <= last) {
         if (largest < last)  // first has two children (at 2*first+1 and
             if (data[largest] < data[largest+1])     //   2*first+2)
                 largest++;
     // swap values if necessary and move down
         if (data[first] < data[largest]) {
             Swap(data[first],data[largest]);
             first = largest;
             largest = 2*first+1;
         }
         else largest = last+1;   // to exit the loop: the heap property
     }                            // isn't violated by data[first]
}
```

Figure 6.52: **Implementation of algorithm to move the root element down a tree.**

resulting organization represents a heap. There are several ways to do this, but in the light of the preceding section, the simplest way is to start with an empty heap and sequentially include elements into a growing heap. This is a top-down method and it was proposed by John Williams; it extends the heap by enqueuing new elements in the heap.

Figure 6.53 contains a complete example of the top-down method. First, the number 2 is enqueued in the initially empty heap (6.53a). Next, the number 8 is enqueued, which is done by putting it at the end of the current heap (6.53b) and then swapping with its parent (6.53c). Enqueuing the third and fourth elements, the number 6 (6.53d) and then the number 1 (6.53e), necessitates no swaps. Enqueuing the fifth element, the number 10, amounts to putting it at the end of the heap (6.53f), then swapping it with its parent, the number 2 (6.53g), and then with its new parent, the number 8 (6.53h), so that eventually the number 10 percolates up to the root of the heap. All remaining steps can be traced in Figure 6.53.

To check the complexity of the algorithm, observe that in the worst case, when a newly added element has to be moved up to the root of the tree, $\lfloor \lg k \rfloor$ exchanges are made in a heap of k nodes. Therefore, if n elements are enqueued, then in the worst case

$$\sum_{k=1}^{n} \lfloor \lg k \rfloor \leq \sum_{k=1}^{n} \lg k \ = \lg 1 + \cdots + \lg n = \lg(1 * 2 * \cdots * n) = \lg(n!) = O(n \lg n),$$

exchanges are made during execution of the algorithm and the same number of comparisons. (For the last equality, $\lg(n!) = O(n \lg n)$, see Appendix A.2.) It turns out, however, that we can do better than that.

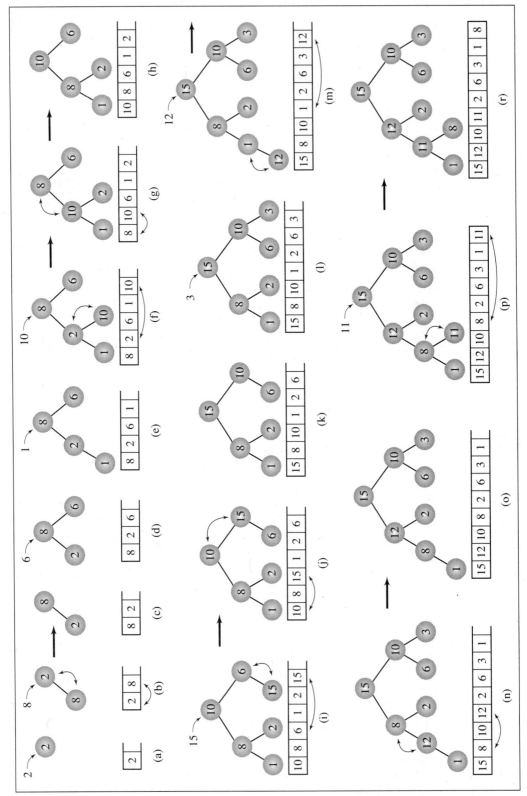

Figure 6.53: Organizing an array as a heap.

In another algorithm, developed by R. Floyd, a heap is built bottom-up. In this approach, small heaps are formed and repetitively merged into larger heaps. Figure 6.54 contains an example.

We start from the last nonleaf node, which is **data[n/2-1]**, *n* being the array size. If **data[n/2-1]** is less than one of its children, it is swapped with the larger child. In the tree in Figure 6.54a, this is the case for **data[3]** = 1 and **data[7]** = 12. After exchanging the elements a new tree is created, shown in Figure 6.54b. Next, the element **data[n/2-2]** = **data[2]** = 6 is considered. Because it is smaller than its

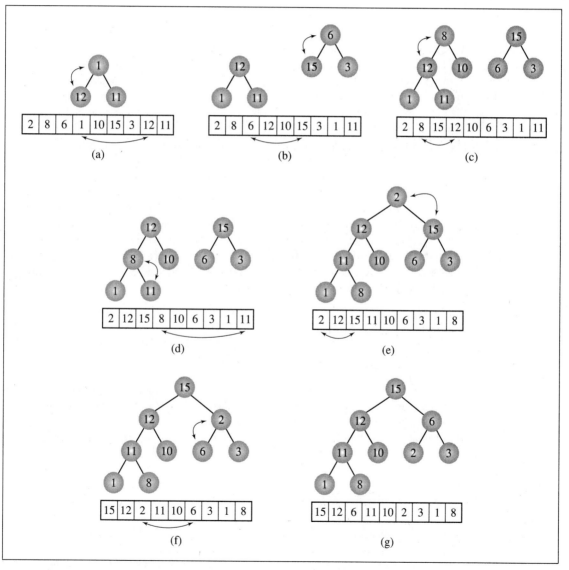

Figure 6.54: **Transforming the array [2 8 6 1 10 15 3 12 11] into a heap.**

child **data[5]** = 15, it is swapped with that child and the tree is transformed to that in Figure 6.54c. Now **data[n/2-3]** =**data[1]** = 8 is considered. Since it is smaller than one of its children, which is **data[3]** = 12, an interchange occurs, leading to the tree in Figure 6.54d. But now it can be noticed that the order established in the subtree whose root was 12 (Figure 6.54c) has been somewhat disturbed since 8 is smaller than its new child 11. This simply means that it does not suffice to compare a node's value with its children's, but a similar comparison needs to be done with grandchildren's, greatgrandchildren's, etc. until the node finds its proper position. Taking this into consideration, the next swap is made, after which the tree in Figure 6.54e is created, and only now the element **data[n/2-4]** = **data[0]** = 2 is compared with its children.

Note that the last elements (and the first three elements in the array) have to be analyzed and that both its subtrees with roots in nodes 12 and 15 are already heaps. This observation is generally true: before one element is considered, its subtrees have been already converted into heaps. Thus, a heap is created from the bottom up. If the heap property is disturbed by an interchange as in the transformation of the tree in Figure 6.54c to that in Figure 6.54d, it is immediately restored by shifting up elements that are larger than the element moved down. This is the case when 2 is exchanged with 15. The new tree is not a heap since the node 2 has still larger children (Figure 6.54f). To remedy this problem, 6 is shifted up and 2 moved down. Figure 6.54g is a heap.

To create the heap, **MoveDown()** is called $\frac{n}{2}$ times. We assume that a complete binary tree is created, that is, $n = 2^k - 1$ for some k. In the worst case, **MoveDown()** moves data from the next to the last level, consisting of $\frac{n}{4}$ nodes (truncated to the lower integer), down by one level to the level of leaves. Therefore, all nodes from this level make $1 \cdot \frac{n}{4}$ moves. Data from the second to the last level, which has $\frac{n}{8}$ nodes, are moved two levels down to reach the level of the leaves. Thus, nodes from this level perform $2 \cdot \frac{n}{8}$ moves, and so on, up to the root. The root of the tree as the tree becomes a heap is moved, again in the worst case, $\lg \frac{n}{2}$ levels down the tree to end up in one of the leaves. Since there is only one root, this contributes $\lg \frac{n}{2} \cdot 1$ moves. The total number of movements can be given by this sum

$$\sum_{i=2}^{\lg \frac{n}{2}} \frac{n}{2^i}(i - 1) = n \sum_{i=2}^{\lg \frac{n}{2}} \frac{i - 1}{2^i} < 2n = O(n),$$

since the series $\sum \frac{i}{2^i}$ converges to 2. For an array which is not a complete binary tree, the complexity is all the more bounded by $O(n)$. The worst case for comparisons is twice this value, which is also $O(n)$, since in **MoveDown()**, for each node, both children of the node are compared to each other to choose the larger, that, in turn, is compared to the node.

■ 6.10 POLISH NOTATION AND EXPRESSION TREES

One of the applications of binary trees is an unambiguous representation of arithmetical, relational, or logical expressions. In the early 1920s, a Polish logician, Jan Łukasiewicz, invented a special notation for propositional logic that allows us to eliminate all parentheses from formulas. Łukasiewicz's notation, called *Polish notation*, results, however, in less readable formulas than the parenthesized originals and it was not widely used. However, it proved useful after the emergence of computers, especially for writing compilers and interpreters.

In order to maintain readability and prevent the ambiguity of formulas, extra symbols such as parentheses, have to be used. However, if avoiding ambiguity is the only goal, then these symbols can be omitted at the cost of changing the order of symbols used in the formulas. This is exactly what the compiler does. It rejects everything that is not essential to retrieve the proper meaning of formulas, rejecting it as "syntactic sugar."

How does this notation work? Look first at the following example. What is the value of the algebraic expression

$$2 - 3 * 4 + 5?$$

The result depends on the order in which the operations are performed. If we multiply first, then subtract and add, the result is -5 as expected. If subtraction is done first, then addition and multiplication, as in

$$(2 - 3) * (4 + 5)$$

the result is -9. But if we subtract after we multiply and add, as in

$$2 - (3 * 4 + 5)$$

then the result of evaluation is -15. If we see the first expression then we know in what order to evaluate it. But the computer does not know that in such a case multiplication has a precedence over addition and subtraction. If we want to override the precedence, then parentheses are needed.

Compilers need to generate assembly code in which one operation is executed at a time and the result is retained for other operations. Therefore, all expressions have to be broken down unambiguously into separate operations and put into their proper order. That is where Polish notation is useful. It allows us to create an *expression tree*, which imposes an order on the execution of operations. For example, the first expression, $2 - 3 * 4 + 5$, which is the same as $2 - (3 * 4) + 5$, is represented by the tree in Figure 6.55a. The second and the third expressions correspond to the trees in Figures 6.55b and 6.55c. It is obvious now that in both Figures 6.55a and 6.55c we have to first multiply 3 by 4 to obtain 12. But 12 is subtracted from 2, according to the tree in Figure 6.55a, and added to 5, according to Figure 6.55c. There is no ambiguity involved in this tree representation. The final result can be computed only if intermediate results are calculated first.

Notice also that trees do not use parentheses and yet no ambiguity arises. We can maintain this parentheses-free situation if the expression tree is linearized, that is, if the tree is transformed into an expression using a tree traversal method. The three traversal methods relevant in this context are preorder, inorder, and postorder tree traversals. Using these traversals, nine outputs are generated, as shown in Figure 6.55. Interestingly, inorder traversal of all three trees results in the same output, which is the initial expression which caused all the trouble. What it means is that inorder tree traversal is not suitable for generating an unambiguous output. But the other two traversals are. They are different for

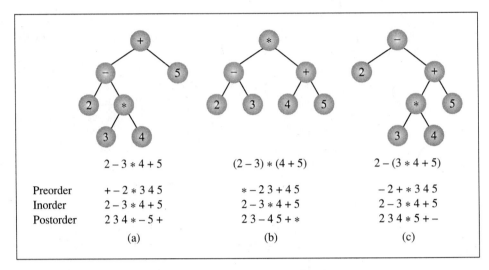

$$2 - 3 * 4 + 5 \qquad\qquad (2 - 3) * (4 + 5) \qquad\qquad 2 - (3 * 4 + 5)$$

Preorder	$+ - 2 * 3\ 4\ 5$	$* - 2\ 3 + 4\ 5$	$- 2 + * 3\ 4\ 5$
Inorder	$2 - 3 * 4 + 5$	$2 - 3 * 4 + 5$	$2 - 3 * 4 + 5$
Postorder	$2\ 3\ 4 * - 5 +$	$2\ 3 - 4\ 5 + *$	$2\ 3\ 4 * 5 + -$
	(a)	(b)	(c)

Figure 6.55: **Examples of three expression trees and results of their traversals.**

different trees, and are therefore useful for the purpose of creating unambiguous expressions and sentences.

Because of the importance of these different conventions, special terminology is used. Preorder traversal generates *prefix notation*, inorder traversal generates *infix notation*, and postorder traversal generates *postfix notation*. Note that infix notation is the notation we are accustomed to. In infix notation an operator is surrounded by its two operands. In prefix notation the operator precedes the operands, and in postfix notation the operator follows the operands. Many hand calculators operate on expressions in postfix notation. Also, some programming languages are using Polish notation. For example, Forth uses postfix notation, and Lisp and, to a large degree, Logo, use prefix notation.

6.10.1   Operations on Expression Trees

Binary trees can be created in two different ways, top-down or bottom-up. In the implementation of insertion, the first approach was used. This section applies the second approach by creating expression trees bottom-up while scanning infix expressions from left to right.

The most important part of this construction process is retaining the same precedence of operations as in the expression being scanned, as exemplified in Figure 6.55. If parentheses are not allowed, the task is simple, as parentheses allow for many levels of nesting. Therefore, an algorithm should be powerful enough to process any number of nesting levels in an expression. A natural approach is a recursive implementation. We modify the recursive descent interpreter discussed in Chapter 5's case study, and outline a recursive descent expression tree constructor.

As Figure 6.55 indicates, a node contains either an operator or an operand, the latter being either an identifier or a number. If all identifiers are one character and all numbers contain only one digit, a node can be declared in C++ as a **struct** with one key field and two pointer fields. In the more general case, when strings are allowed for identifiers

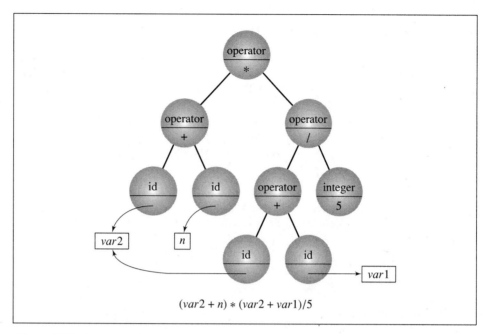

$$(var2 + n) * (var2 + var1)/5$$

Figure 6.56: **An expression tree.**

and numbers two or more digits long, a **struct** can also be used, with a type, string field, and two pointer fields, where the string field can also store a number as a string of digits, and an operator (see Figure 6.56). The declaration is

```
enum tokenType{integer, id, operatr};

struct ExprTreeNode {
      tokenType type;
      char *key;
      ExprTreeNode *left, *right;
      ExprTreeNode (tokenType t, char *k,
            ExprTreeNode *l = 0, ExprTreeNode *r = 0) { ... }
};
```

Expressions, which are converted to trees, use the same syntax as expressions in the case study in Chapter 5. Therefore, the same syntax diagrams can be used. Using these diagrams, functions for processing a factor and term have the following pseudocode (a function for processing an expression has the same structure as the function processing a term):

```
Factor(pt1, pt2)
  if (key is a number )
    return new ExprTreeNode(integer, key);
  if (key is an id)
    return new ExprTreeNode(id, key);
```

```
         if (key is '(') {
             return Expr(pt1,pt2) after discarding ')';

     Term (pt1, pt2)
       p1 = Factor(pt1,pt2);
       while (key is '/' or '*') {
         oper = key;
         p2 = Factor();
         p1 = new ExprTreeNode(operatr, oper, p1, p2);
       }
       return p1;
```

The tree structure of expressions is very suitable for code or pseudocode generation in compilers, as shown in the following pseudocode:

```
Generate(p)
   if (p->key is a number)
     return this number;
   if (p->key is an id)
     return this id;
   if (p->key is an addition operator ) {
     fout<<"add"<< Generate(p->left)<< ' << Generate(p->right);
     return NewTemporary();
   }
   if (p->key is a subtraction operator)
     ⋮
```

This structure is also very convenient for performing other symbolic operations, such as differentiation. Rules for differentiation (given in this chapter's programming assignments) are shown in the form of tree transformations in Figure 6.57 and in the pseudocode in Figure 6.58. Here **p** is a pointer to the expression to be differentiated with respect to **x**.

The rule for division is left as an exercise.

■ 6.11   CASE STUDY: COMPUTING WORD FREQUENCIES

One tool in establishing authorship of text in cases when the text is not signed, or it is attributed to someone else, is using word frequencies. If it is known that an author A wrote text T_1 and the distribution of word frequencies in a text T_2 under scrutiny is very close to the frequencies in T_1, then it is likely that T_2 was written by author A.

Regardless of how reliable this method for literary studies is, our interest lies in writing a program which scans a text file and computes the frequency of the occurrence on words in this file. For the sake of simplification, punctuation marks are disregarded and case sensitivity is disabled. Therefore, the word *man's* is counted as two words, *man* and *s*, although in fact it may be one word (for genitive), and not two words (an abbreviation for *man is* or *man has*). Some abbreviations are counted separately; for example, *s* from

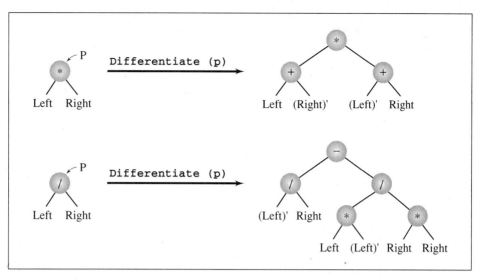

Figure 6.57: **Tree transformations for differentiation of multiplication and division.**

```
Differentiate (p,x)
  if (p is 0)
    return 0;
  if (p->key is the id x)
    return p with the key field changed to 1;
  if (p->key is another id)
    return p with the key field changed to 0;
  if (p->key is a number)
    return p with the key field changed to 0;
  if (p->key is addition or subtraction) {
    p->left = Differentiate(p->left,x);
    p->right = Differentiate(p->right,x);
    return p;
    }
  if (p->key is multiplication) {
    left = new ExpTreeNode(operatr,"*",p->left,copy(p->right));
    left->right = Differentiate(left->right,x);
    right = new ExprTreeNode(operatr,"*",copy(p->left),p->right);
    right->left = Differentiate(right->left,x);
    p->left = left;
    p->right = right;
    return p;
    }
  if (p->key is division) {
    ⋮
```

Figure 6.58: **Implementation of rules for differentiation of multiplication and division.**

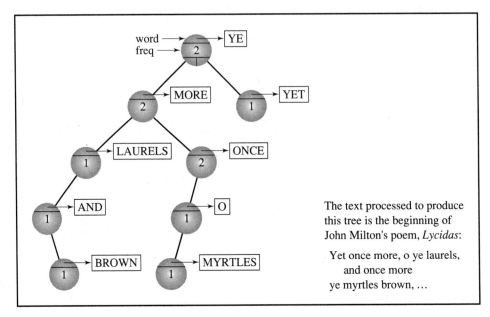

The text processed to produce this tree is the beginning of John Milton's poem, *Lycidas*:

Yet once more, o ye laurels,
and once more
ye myrtles brown, …

Figure 6.59: **Semisplay tree and array used for computing word frequencies.**

man's is considered a separate word. Similarly, separators in the middle of words such as hyphens cause portions of the same words to be considered separate words. For example, *pre-existence* is split into *pre* and *existence*. Also, by disabling case sensitivity *Good* in the phrase *Mr. Good* is considered as another occurrence of the word *good*. On the other hand, *Good* used in its normal sense at the beginning of a sentence is properly included as another occurrence of *good*.

This program focuses not so much on linguistics as on building a self-adjusting binary search tree using the semisplaying technique. If a word is encountered in the file for the first time, it is inserted in the tree. Otherwise, the semisplaying is started from the node corresponding to this word.

Another concern is storing all predecessors when scanning the tree. It is achieved by using the array **pred[]** which is used almost like a stack. We say "almost," since new predecessors (or rather pointers to these predecessors) are pushed onto **pred[]**, but elements stored in **pred[]** are not accessed only by popping them, but also by referring to elements below the topmost element. To be sure, it all can be done by popping followed by pushing, but for efficiency this way of accessing elements in **pred[]** is not followed.

Figure 6.59 shows the structure of the tree using the content of a short file and Figure 6.60 contains the complete code.

■ 6.12 EXERCISES

1. The function **Search()** given in Section 6.3 is well suited for searching binary *search* trees. Try to adopt all four traversal algorithms so that they become search procedures for any binary tree.

```
//*********************** genSplay.h ***************************
//                    generic splaying tree class

#ifndef SPLAYING
#define SPLAYING

template<class genType>
struct ElemNode {
     genType info;
     ElemNode *left, *right;
     ElemNode() { left = right = 0; }
     ElemNode(genType& el, ElemNode *l = 0, ElemNode *r = 0)
               { info = el; left = l; right = r; }
  };

template<class genType>
class SplayTree {
protected:
public:
    SplayTree()     { root = 0;        }
    void Inorder() { Inorder(root); }
    void CheckAndInsert(genType&);
private:
    ElemNode<genType> *root,
                    *pred[100];  // list of predecessors;
    int parent;      // index for the array of predecessors;

    void UpdateGrandparentOrRoot(int,ElemNode<genType>*);
    void RotateR(ElemNode<genType>*,int);
    void RotateL(ElemNode<genType>*,int);
    void Semisplay(ElemNode<genType>*);
    void Inorder(ElemNode<genType>*);
    virtual void Visit(ElemNode<genType>*) { }
    virtual void Update(genType&) { }
};
```

Figure 6.60: **Implementation of word frequency computation.**   **continued**

```
template<class genType>
void
SplayTree<genType>::UpdateGrandparentOrRoot(int i, ElemNode<genType> *p)
{
    if (i > 0)                        // if p has grandparent;
        if (pred[i-1]->right == pred[i])
            pred[i-1]->right = p;
        else pred[i-1]->left  = p;
    else root = p;
    parent--;                         // grandparent becomes parent;
}


template<class genType>
void
SplayTree<genType>::RotateR(ElemNode<genType> *p, int i)
{
    pred[i]->left = p->right;
    p->right = pred[i];
    UpdateGrandparentOrRoot(i,p);
}


template<class genType>
void
SplayTree<genType>::RotateL(ElemNode<genType> *p, int i)
{
    pred[i]->right = p->left;
    p->left = pred[i];
    UpdateGrandparentOrRoot(i,p);
}


template<class genType>
void
SplayTree<genType>::Semisplay(ElemNode<genType> *p)
{
    while (p != root) {
        if (parent == 0)              // if p's parent is the root;
            if (pred[0]->left == p)
                RotateR(p,0);
            else RotateL(p,0);
```

Figure 6.60: **Implementation of word frequency computation.**   **continued**

```
            else if (pred[parent]->left == p) // if p is left child;
                if (pred[parent-1]->left == pred[parent]) {
                    p = pred[parent];
                    RotateR(pred[parent],parent-1);
                    parent--;
                }
                else {
                    RotateR(p,parent); // rotate p and its parent;
                    RotateL(p,parent); // rotate p and its new parent;
                }
            else                            // if p is right child;
                if (pred[parent-1]->right == pred[parent]) {
                    p = pred[parent];
                    RotateL(pred[parent],parent-1);
                    parent--;
                }
                else {
                    RotateL(p,parent); // rotate p and its parent;
                    RotateR(p,parent); // rotate p and its new parent;
                }

        if (parent == -1)               // update the root of the tree;
            root = p;
    }
}


template<class genType>
void
SplayTree<genType>::CheckAndInsert(genType& key)
{   ElemNode<genType> *p = root, *prev = 0, *newNode;
    register int less;

    parent = -1;
    while (p) {
        prev = p;
        if (p->info == key) {  // if key is in the tree,
            Update(p->info);   // update its frequency field,
            Semisplay(p);      // move it upwards;
            return;            // and exit from CheckAndInsert();
        }
```

Figure 6.60: **Implementation of word frequency computation.**   continued

```
            else if (less = (key < p->info))
                   p = p->left;
            else p = p->right;
            pred[++parent] = prev; // store prev in pred[]
        }                          // the parent of p;
     if (!(newNode = new ElemNode<genType>(key))) {
         cerr << "No room for new nodes\n";
         exit(1);
     }
     if (!root)                    // if tree is empty
          root = newNode;
     else if (less)
          prev->left  = newNode;
     else prev->right = newNode;
}

template<class genType>
void
SplayTree<genType>::Inorder(ElemNode<genType> *p)
{                                 // transfer all words
     if (p) {                     // from tree to fOut
         Inorder(p->left);        // in alphabetical order;
         Visit(p);
         Inorder(p->right);
     }
}
#endif



//*********************** splay.cpp ***********************

#include <iostream.h>
#include <fstream.h>
#include <ctype.h>
#include <string.h>
#include <stdlib.h> // exit()
#include "genSplay.h"

struct InfoNode {
    char *word;
```

Figure 6.60: **Implementation of word frequency computation.**   **continued**

```
        int freq;
        InfoNode() { freq = 1; }
        int operator== (const InfoNode& ir)
            { return strcmp(word,ir.word) == 0; }
        int operator<  (const InfoNode& ir)
            { return strcmp(word,ir.word) < 0;  }
};


class WordSplay : public SplayTree<InfoNode> {
public:
    WordSplay() { differentWords = wordCnt = 0; }
    void FinalMsg(char*) const;
private:
    int differentWords, // counter of different words in text file;
        wordCnt;        // counter of all words in the same file;
    void Update(InfoNode& ir) { ir.freq++; }
    void Visit(ElemNode<InfoNode>*);
};



void
WordSplay::Visit(ElemNode<InfoNode> *p)
{
    differentWords++;
    wordCnt += p->info.freq;
}
ostream&
operator<< (ostream& out, const InfoNode& rec)
{
    out << rec.word << ": " << rec.freq << "| ";
    return out;
}


void
WordSplay::FinalMsg(char *fileName) const

    cout << "\n\nFile " << fileName
        << " contains " << wordCnt << " words among which "
        << differentWords << " are different\n";
}
```

Figure 6.60: **Implementation of word frequency computation.**   **continued**

```
void
TransferFileToTree(ifstream& fIn, WordSplay& splayTree)
{    char ch = ' ', i;
     char s[50];
     InfoNode rec;

     while (!fIn.eof()) {
         while (1)
             if (!fIn.eof() && !isalpha(ch)) // skip nonletters
                 fIn.get(ch);
             else break;
         if (fIn.eof())         // spaces at the end of fIn;
             break;
         for (i = 0; !fIn.eof() && isalpha(ch); i++) {
             s[i] = toupper(ch);
             fIn.get(ch);
         }
         s[i] = '\0';
         if (!(rec.word = new char[strlen(s)+1])) {
             cerr << "No room for new words.\n";
             exit(1);
         }
         strcpy(rec.word,s);
         splayTree.CheckAndInsert(rec);
     }
}

main(int argc, char* argv[])
{    char fileName[15];
     WordSplay splayTree;
     if (argc != 2) {
         cout << "Enter a file name: ";
         cin  >> fileName;
     }
     else strcpy(fileName,argv[1]);
     ifstream fIn(fileName);
     if (fIn.fail()) {
         cerr << "Cannot open " << fileName << endl;
         return 1;
     }
```

Figure 6.60: **Implementation of word frequency computation.**   **continued**

```
    TransferFileToTree(fIn,splayTree);
    splayTree.Inorder();
    splayTree.FinalMsg(fileName);

    fIn.close();
    fOut.close();
    return 0;
}
```

Figure 6.60: **Implementation of word frequency computation.**

2. Write functions to count the number of nodes in a binary tree, the number of leaves, the number of right children, and the height of the tree.

3. Write a function that checks whether or not a binary tree is perfectly balanced.

4. Design an algorithm to test whether a binary tree is a binary search tree.

5. Write a function to delete all leaves from a binary tree.

6. Apply `Preorder()`, `Inorder()`, and `Postorder()` to the tree in Figure 6.61, if `Visit(p)` is defined as:

(a) `if (p->left && p->key - p->left->key < 2)`
     `p->left->key += 2;`

(b) `if (!p->left)`
     `p->right = 0;`

(c) `if (!p->left) {`
     `p->left = new TreeNode<genType>;`
     `p->left->key = p->key - 1;`
   `}`

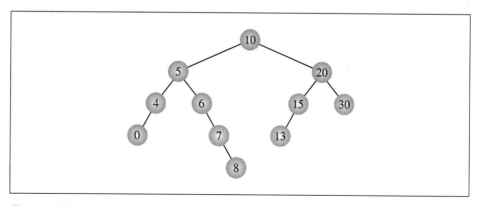

Figure 6.61: **An example of a binary search tree.**

(d) `{ tmp = p->right;`
        `p->right = p->left;`
        `p->left = tmp;`
  `}`

7. Show a tree for which the preorder and inorder traversals generate the same sequence.

8. Figure 6.55 indicates that the inorder traversal for different trees can result in the same sequence. Is this possible for the preorder or postorder traversals? If it is, show an example.

9. Draw all possible binary search trees for the three elements A, B, and C.

10. What are the minimum and maximum numbers of leaves in a balanced tree of height h?

11. Design an algorithm to create a mirror image of a tree where all the left children become right children, and vice versa, for all nodes of the tree.

12. Consider an operation R that for a given traversal method t, processes nodes in the opposite order than t, and an operation C that processes nodes of the mirror image of a given tree using traversal method t. For the three traversal methods — preorder, inorder, and postorder — determine which out of the following nine equalities are true:

$$R\,(\text{preorder}) \ = C\,(\text{preorder})$$
$$R\,(\text{preorder}) \ = C\,(\text{inorder})$$
$$R\,(\text{preorder}) \ = C\,(\text{postorder})$$
$$R\,(\text{inorder}) \ \ \ = C\,(\text{preorder})$$
$$R\,(\text{inorder}) \ \ \ = C\,(\text{inorder})$$
$$R\,(\text{inorder}) \ \ \ = C\,(\text{postorder})$$
$$R\,(\text{postorder}) = C\,(\text{preorder})$$
$$R\,(\text{postorder}) = C\,(\text{inorder})$$
$$R\,(\text{postorder}) = C\,(\text{postorder})$$

13. Using inorder, preorder, and postorder tree traversal, visit only leaves of a tree. What can you observe? How can you explain this phenomenon?

14. Define the parametrized constructor `ExprTreeNode()` so that it works in accordance with Figure 6.56; that is, it stores numbers and operators inside nodes notwithstanding the fact that `key` field is of type `char *`. Then modify the definition of `struct ExprTreeNode` so that integer is stored as integer, operator as character, and identifier as a string.

15. (a) Write a function which prints sideways each binary tree with proper indentation, as in Figure 6.62a. (b) Adopt this procedure to print a threaded tree sideways; if appropriate, print the key in the successor node, as in Figure 6.62b.

16. Outline functions for inserting and deleting a node in a threaded tree, in which threads are put only in the leaves in the way illustrated by Figure 6.63.

17. Apply the function `Balance()` to the English alphabet to create a balanced tree.

18. A sentence Dpq uses a Sheffer's alternative if it is false (only if both p and q are false). In 1925, J. Łukasiewicz simplified Nicod's axiom from which all theses of propositional logic can be derived. Transform the Nicod-Łukasiewicz axiom into an infix

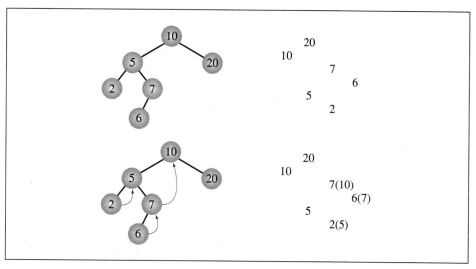

20
10
7
6
5
2

20
10
7(10)
6(7)
5
2(5)

Figure 6.62: **Printing a binary search tree (a) and a threaded tree (b)
sideways.**

parenthesized sentence and build a binary tree for it. The axiom is *DDpDqrDDsDss-DDsqDDpsDps.*

19. Write an algorithm for printing a parenthesized infix expression from an expression tree. Do not include redundant parentheses.

20. Create an algorithm that, given a pair of keys, searches a binary search tree and prints out those keys it finds which occur between the keys. For example, if the keys of the tree contain names, then the algorithm may be called to print out all names between *Doe* and *Johns.*

21. Hibbard's (1962) algorithm to delete a key from a binary search tree requires that if the node containing the key has a right child, then the key is replaced by the smallest

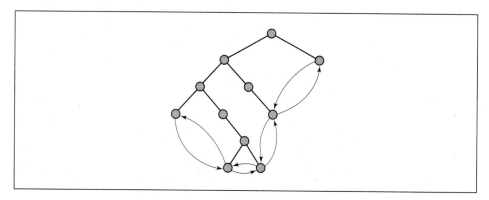

Figure 6.63: **An example of a threaded tree.**

key in the right subtree, otherwise the node with the key is removed. In what respect is Knuth's algorithm (`DeleteByCopying()`) an improvement?

22. Which tree of four nodes is the worst case for generating a backbone in DSW algorithm? Execute this procedure for this tree by hand.

23. Define a binary search tree in terms of the inorder traversal.

24. A *Fibonacci tree* can be considered the worst case AVL tree in that it has the smallest number of nodes among AVL trees of height h. Draw Fibonacci trees for $h = 1, 2, 3, 4$ and justify the name of the tree.

25. *One-sided height-balanced trees* are AVL trees in which only two balance factors are allowed: -1 and 0 or 0 and $+1$ (Zweben, McDonald 1978). What is the rationale for introducing this type of tree?

■ 6.13 PROGRAMMING ASSIGNMENTS

1. Write a program that accepts an arithmetic expression written in prefix (Polish) notation, builds an expression tree, and then traverses the tree to evaluate the expression. The evaluation should start after a complete expression has been entered.

2. A binary tree can be used to sort n elements of an array **data**. First, create a complete binary tree, a tree with all leaves at one level, whose height $h = \lceil \lg n \rceil + 1$, and store all elements of the array in the first n leaves. In each empty leaf, store an element E greater that any element in the array. Figure 6.64a shows an example for **data** = $\{8, 20, 41, 7, 2\}$, $h = \lceil \lg(5) \rceil + 1 = 4$, and $E = 42$. Then, starting from the bottom of the tree, assign to each node the minimum of its two children values, as in Figure 6.64b, so that the smallest element e_{min} in the tree is assigned to the root. Next, until the element E is assigned to the root, execute a loop that in each iteration stores E in the leaf, with the value of e_{min} and that, also starting from the bottom, assigns to each node the minimum of its two children. Figure 6.64c displays this tree after one iteration of the loop.

3. Implement a menu-driven program for managing a software store. All information about the available software is stored in a file **software**. This information includes the name, version, quantity, and price of each package. When it is invoked, the program automatically creates a binary search tree with one node corresponding to one software package, and includes as its key the name of the package and its version. Another field in this node should include the position of the record in the file **software**. The only access to the information stored in **software** should be through this tree.

   The program should allow the file and tree to be updated when new software packages arrive at the store and when some packages are sold. The tree is updated in the usual way: all packages are ordered by entry date in the file **software**; if a new package arrives, then it is put at the end of the file. If the package already has an entry in the tree (and the file), then only the quantity field is updated. If a package is sold out, the corresponding node is deleted from the tree, and the quantity field in the file will be changed to 0. For example, if the file has these entries:

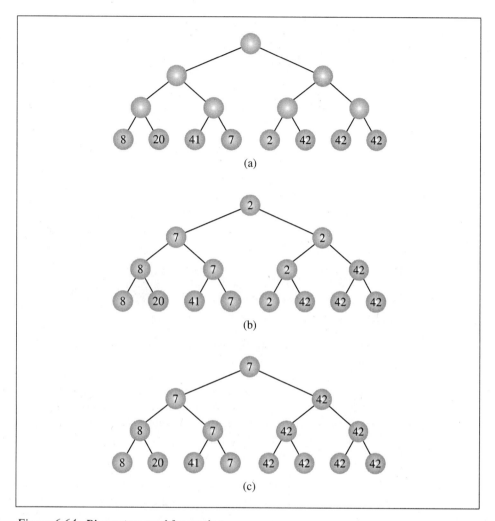

Figure 6.64: **Binary tree used for sorting.**

```
Ventura Publisher   2.0   21   795
Norton Utilities    5.0   10   145
Norton Utilities    5.5    6   195
Exp                 1.0   19   195
Exp                 2.0   27   295
```

then after selling all 6 copies of Norton Utilities 5.5, the file will be

```
Ventura Publisher   2.0   21   795
Norton Utilities    5.0   10   145
Norton Utilities    5.5    0   195
Exp                 1.0   19   195
Exp                 2.0   27   295
```

If the exit option is chosen from the menu, the program should clean up the file by moving entries from the end of the file to the positions marked with 0 quantities. For example, the file above becomes

```
Ventura Publisher  2.0   21   795
Norton Utilities   5.0   10   145
Exp                2.0   27   295
Exp                1.0   19   195
```

4. Implement algorithms for constructing expression trees and for differentiating the expressions they represent. Extend the program to simplify expression trees. For example, two nodes can be eliminated from the subtrees representing $a \pm 0, a * 1$, or $\frac{a}{1}$.

5. Write a cross-reference program which constructs a binary search tree with all words included from a text file and records the line numbers on which these words were used. These line numbers should be stored on linked lists associated with the nodes of the tree. After the input file has been processed, print in alphabetical order all words of the text file along with the corresponding list of numbers of the lines in which the words occur.

6. Perform an experiment with alternately applying insertion and deletion of random elements in a randomly created binary search tree. Apply asymmetric and symmetric deletions (discussed in this chapter) for both variants of the deletion algorithm, alternate deletions strictly with insertions, and alternate these operations randomly. This gives four different combinations. Also, use two different random number generators to ensure randomness. This leads to eight combinations. Run all of these combinations for trees of heights 500, 1000, 1500, and 2000. Plot the results and compare them with the expected IPLs indicated in this chapter.

7. Each unit in a Latin textbook contains a Latin-English vocabulary of words which have been used for the first time in a particular unit. Write a program that converts a set of such vocabularies stored in file **Latin** into a set of English-Latin vocabularies. Make the following assumptions (refer to the example shown on p. 211):

   (a) Unit names are preceded by a percent symbol.
   (b) There is only one entry per line.
   (c) A Latin word is separated by a colon from its English equivalent(s); if there is more than one equivalent, they are separated by a comma.

   To output English words in alphabetical order, create a binary search tree for each unit containing English words and linked lists of Latin equivalents. Make sure that there is only one node for each English word in the tree. For example, there is only one node for *and*, although *and* is used twice in *unit 6*: with words *ac* and *atque*. After the task has been completed for a given unit, that is, the content of the tree has been stored in an output file, delete the tree along with all linked lists from the computer memory before creating a tree for the next unit.

Here is an example of a file containing Latin-English vocabularies:

```
%Unit 5

ante : before, in front of, previously
antiquus : ancient
ardeo : burn, be on fire, desire
arma : arms, weapons
aurum : gold
aureus : golden, of gold


%Unit 6

animal : animal
Athenae : Athens
atque : and
ac : and
aurora : dawn


%Unit 7

amo : love
amor : love
annus : year
Asia : Asia
```

From these units the program should generate the following output:

```
%Unit 5

ancient : antiquus
arms : arma
be on fire : ardeo
before : ante
burn : ardeo
desire : ardeo
gold : aurum
golden : aureus
in front of : ante
of gold : aureus
previously : ante
weapons : arma
```

```
%Unit 6

Athens : Athenae
and : ac, atque
animal : animal
dawn : aurora

%Unit 7

Asia : Asia
love : amor, amo
year : annus
```

BIBLIOGRAPHY

Insertions and Deletions

[1] Culberson, Joseph, "The Effect of Updates in Binary Search Trees," in *Proceedings of the 17th Annual Symposium on Theory of Computing* (1985), 205–212.

[2] Eppinger, Jeffrey L., "An Empirical Study of Insertion and Deletion in Binary Search Trees," *Communications of the ACM* 26 (1983), 663–669.

[3] Hibbard, Thomas N., "Some Combinatorial Properties of Certain Trees with Applications to Searching and Sorting," *Journal of the ACM* 9 (1962), 13–28.

[4] Jonassen, Arne T. and Knuth, Donald E., "A Trivial Algorithm Whose Analysis Isn't," *Journal of Computer and System Sciences* 16 (1978), 301–322.

[5] Knuth, Donald E., "Deletions that Preserve Randomness," *IEEE Transactions of Software Engineering*, SE-3 (1977), 351–359.

Tree Traversals

[6] Berztiss, Alfs, "A Taxonomy of Binary Tree Traversals," *BIT* 26 (1986), 266–276.

[7] Burkhard, W.A., "Nonrecursive Tree Traversal Algorithms," *Computer Journal* 18 (1975), 227–230.

[8] Morris, Joseph M., "Traversing Binary Trees Simply and Cheaply," *Information Processing Letters* 9 (1979), 197–200.

Balancing Trees

[9] Baer, J.L. and Schwab, B., "A Comparison of Tree-Balancing Algorithms," *Communications of the ACM* 20 (1977), 322–330.

[10] Chang, Hsi and Iyengar, S. Sitharama, "Efficient Algorithms to Globally Balance a Binary Search Tree," *Communications of the ACM* 27 (1984), 695–702.

[11] Day, A. Colin, "Balancing a Binary Tree," *Computer Journal* 19 (1976), 360–361.

[12]   Martin, W.A. and Ness, D.N., "Optimizing Binary Trees Grown with a Sorting Algorithm," *Communications of the ACM* 15 (1972), 88–93.

[13]   Stout, Quentin F. and Warren, Bette L., "Tree Rebalancing in Optimal Time and Space," *Communications of the ACM* 29 (1986), 902–908.

AVL Trees

[14]   Adel'son-Vel'skii, G. M. and Landis, E. M., "An Algorithm for the Organization of Information," *Soviet Mathematics* 3 (1962), 1259–1263.

[15]   Foster, Caxton C., "A Generalization of AVL Trees," *Communications of the ACM* 16 (1973), 512–517.

[16]   Karlton, P.L., Fuller, S.H., Scroggs, R.E., and Kaehler, E.B., "Performance of Height-Balanced Trees," *Communications of the ACM* 19 (1976), 23–28.

[17]   Zweben, S.H. and McDonald, M.A., "An Optimal Method for Deletion in One-Sided Height Balanced Trees," *Communications of the ACM* 21 (1978), 441–445.

Self-Adjusting Trees

[18]   Allen, B. and Munro, I., "Self-organizing Search Trees," *Journal of the ACM* 25 (1978), 526–535.

[19]   Bitner, James R., "Heuristics that Dynamically Organize Data Structures," *SIAM Journal of Computing* 8 (1979), 82–110.

[20]   Sleator, Daniel D. and Tarjan Robert E., "Self-adjusting Binary Search Trees," *Journal of the ACM* 32 (1985), 652–686.

Heaps

[21]   Doberkat, E.E., "An Average Case Analysis of Floyd's Algorithm to Construct Heaps," *Information and Control* 61 (1984), 114–131.

[22]   Floyd, R.W., "Algorithm 245: Treesort 3," *Communications of the ACM* 7 (1964), 701.

[23]   Gonnett, Gaston H. and Munro, Ian, "Heaps on Heaps," *SIAM Journal of Computing* 15 (1986), 964–971.

[24]   McDiarmid, C.J.H. and Reed, B.A., "Building Heaps Fast," *Journal of Algorithms* 10 (1989), 351–365.

[25]   Weiss, Mark A., *Data Structures and Algorithm Analysis*, Redwood City: Benjamin/Cummings, 1992, ch. 6.

[26]   Williams, J.W.J., "Algorithm 232: Heapsort," *Communications of the ACM* 7 (1964), 347–348.

7

MULTIWAY TREES

At the beginning of the preceding chapter, a general definition of a tree was given, but the thrust of that chapter was binary trees, in particular, binary search trees. A tree was defined as either an empty structure or a structure whose children are disjoint trees $t_1, \ldots, t_k$. According to this definition, each node of this kind of tree can have more than two children. This tree is called a *multiway tree of order m*, or an *m-way tree*.

In a more useful version of a multiway tree, an order is imposed on the keys residing in each node. A *multiway search tree of order m*, or an *m-way search tree*, is a multiway tree in which

1. Each node has m children and $m - 1$ keys.

2. The keys in each node are in ascending order.

3. The keys in the first i children are smaller than the ith key.

4. The keys in the last $m - i$ children are larger than the ith key.

The m-way search trees play the same role among m-way trees that binary search trees play among binary trees, and they are used for the same purpose: fast information retrieval and update. The problems they cause are similar. The tree in Figure 7.1 is a 4-way tree in which accessing the keys can require a different number of tests for different keys: the number 35 can be found in the second node tested, the number 55 in the fifth node checked. The tree, therefore, suffers from a known malaise: it is unbalanced. This problem is of particular importance if we want to use trees to process data on secondary storage such as disks or tapes where each access is costly. Constructing such trees requires a more careful approach.

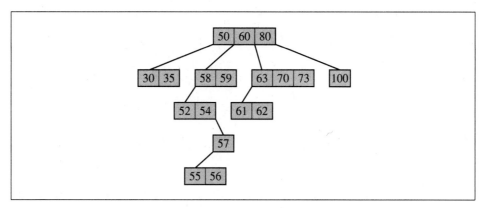

Figure 7.1: **A 4-way tree.**

■ 7.1 THE FAMILY OF B-TREES

The basic unit of I/O operations associated with a disk is a block. When information is read from a disk, the entire block containing this information is read into memory, and when information is stored on a disk, an entire block is written to the disk. Each time information is requested from a disk, this information has to be located on the disk, the head has to be positioned above the part of the disk where the information resides and the disk has to be spun so that the entire block passes underneath the head to be transferred to memory. This means that there are several time components for data access:

$$access\ time\ =\ seek\ time\ +\ rotational\ delay\ (latency)\ +\ transfer\ time.$$

This process is extremely slow compared to transferring information within memory. The first component, *seek time*, is particularly slow, since it depends on the mechanical movement of the disk head to position the head at the correct track of the disk. *Latency* is the time required to position the head above the correct block, and on the average, it is equal to the time needed to make one-half of a revolution. For example, the time to transfer 5KB (kilobytes) from a disk requiring 40 ms (milliseconds) to locate a track and making 3000 revolutions per minute and with a data transfer rate of 1000KB per second is

$$access\ time\ =\ 40\,ms + 10\,ms + 5\,ms = 55\,ms.$$

This example indicates that transferring information to and from the disk is on the order of milliseconds. On the other hand, the CPU processes data on the order of microseconds, a thousand times faster, or on the order of nanoseconds, a million times faster, or even faster. We can see that processing information on secondary storage can significantly decrease the speed of a program.

If a program constantly uses information stored in secondary storage, the characteristics of this storage have to be taken into account when designing the program. For example,

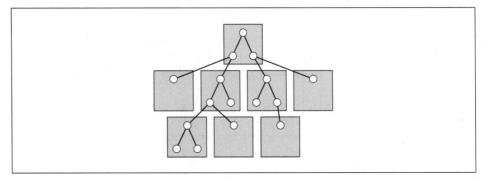

Figure 7.2: **Nodes of a binary tree can be located in different blocks on a
disk.**

a binary search tree can be spread over many different blocks on a disk, as in Figure 7.2,
so that on the average, two blocks have to be accessed. When the tree is used frequently in
a program, these accesses can significantly slow down the execution time of the program.
Also, inserting and deleting keys in this tree requires many block accesses. The binary
search tree, which is such an efficient tool when it resides entirely in memory, turns out to
be an encumbrance. In the context of secondary storage, its otherwise good performance
counts very little because the constant accessing of disk blocks that this method causes
severely hampers this performance.

It is also better to access a large amount of data at one time than to jump from one
position on the disk to another to transfer small portions of data. For example, if 10KB
have to be transferred, then using the characteristics of the disk given above, we see that

$$access\ time = 40\ ms + 10\ ms + 10\ ms = 60\ ms.$$

However, if this information is stored in two 5KB pieces then

$$access\ time = 2 * (40\ ms + 10\ ms + 5\ ms) = 110\ ms,$$

which is nearly twice as long as in the previous case. The reason is that each disk access
is very costly; if possible, the data should be organized so that the number of accesses is
minimized.

7.1.1   B-Trees

In database programs where most information is stored on disks or tapes, the time penalty
for accessing secondary storage can be significantly reduced by the proper choice of the
data structures. *B-trees* (Bayer, McCreight 1972) are one such approach.

A B-tree is a tree which operates closely with the secondary storage and can be tuned
to reduce the impediments imposed by this storage. One important property of B-trees is
the size of each node which can be made as large as the size of a block. The number of keys
in one node can vary depending on the sizes of the keys, organization of the data (are only

keys kept in the nodes or entire records?), and, of course, on the size of a block. Block size varies for each system. It can be 512 bytes, 4KB, or more; block size is the size of each node of a B-tree. The amount of information stored in one node of the B-tree can be rather large.

A *B-tree of order m* is a multiway search tree with the following properties:

1. The root has at least two subtrees unless it is a leaf.
2. Each nonroot and each nonleaf node holds $k - 1$ keys and k pointers to subtrees where $\lceil m/2 \rceil \leq k \leq m$.
3. Each leaf node holds $k - 1$ keys where $\lceil m/2 \rceil \leq k \leq m$.
4. All leaves are on the same level.[1]

According to these conditions, a B-tree is always at least half full, has few levels, and is perfectly balanced.

A node of a B-tree is usually implemented as a **struct** containing an array of $m - 1$ cells for keys, an m-cell array of pointers to other nodes, and possibly other information facilitating tree maintenance, such as the number of keys in a node and a leaf/nonleaf flag, as in

```
struct BTreeNode {
            int leaf : 1;
            int keyTally;
            keyType keys[m-1];
            BTreeNode *pointers[m];
            . . . . . . . . .
        };
```

Usually, m is large (50–500) so that information stored in one page or block of secondary storage can fit into one node. Figure 7.3a contains an example of a B-tree of order 7 which stores codes for some items. In this B-tree, the keys appear to be the only objects of interest in the tree. In most cases, however, such codes would only be fields of larger structures, possibly variant records (unions). In these cases, the array **keys** is an array of **struct**, each having a unique identifier field (such as the identifying code in Figure 7.3a). The **struct** in Figure 7.3b contains an address of the entire record on secondary storage. If the contents of one such node also reside in secondary storage, each key access would require two secondary storage accesses. In the long run, this is better than keeping the entire records in the nodes, since in this case the nodes can hold a very small number of such records. The resulting B-tree is much deeper, and search paths through the B-tree are much longer than in a B-tree with the addresses of records.

From now on, B-trees will be shown in an abbreviated form without explicitly indicating **keyTally** or the pointer fields, as in Figure 7.4.

---

[1]In this definition, the order of a B-tree specifies the *maximum* number of children. Sometimes nodes of a B-tree of order m are defined as having k keys and $k + 1$ pointers where $m \leq k \leq 2m$, which specifies the *minimum* number of children.

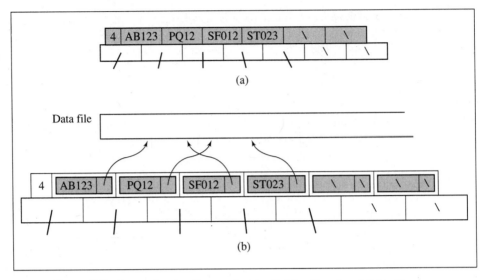

Figure 7.3: **One node of a B-tree of order 7 (a) without and (b) with an additional indirection.**

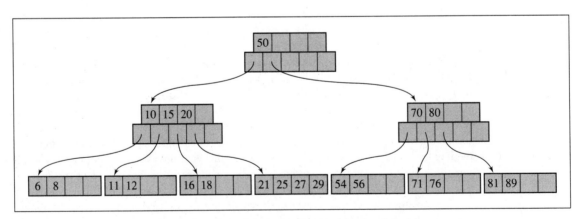

Figure 7.4: **A B-tree of order 5 shown in an abbreviated form.**

Searching in a B-Tree

The worst case of searching is when a B-tree has the smallest allowable number of pointers per nonroot node, $q = \lceil m/2 \rceil$, and the search has to reach a leaf (either for a successful or an unsuccessful search). In this case, in a B-tree of height h there are

$$1 \text{ key in the root } +$$

$$2(q - 1) \text{ keys on the second level } +$$

$$2q(q - 1) \text{ keys on the third level } +$$

$$2q^2(q - 1) \text{ keys on the fourth level } +$$

$$\vdots$$

$$2q^{h-2}(q - 1) \text{ keys in the leaves (level } h) =$$

$$1 + \left(\sum_{i=0}^{h-2} 2q^i \right) (q - 1) \text{ keys in the B-tree.}$$

With the formula for the sum of the first n elements in a geometric progression,

$$\sum_{i=0}^{n} q^i = \frac{q^{n+1} - 1}{q - 1},$$

the number of keys in the worst-case B-tree can be expressed as

$$1 + 2(q - 1) \left(\sum_{i=0}^{h-2} q^i \right) = 1 + 2(q - 1) \left(\frac{q^{h-1} - 1}{q - 1} \right) = -1 + 2q^{h-1}.$$

The relation between the number n of keys in any B-tree and the height of the B-tree is then expressed as

$$n \leq -1 + 2q^{h-1}.$$

Solving this inequality for the height h results in

$$h \leq \log_q \frac{n + 1}{2} + 1.$$

This means that for a sufficiently large order m, the height is small even for a large number of keys stored in the B-tree. For example, if $m = 200$ and $n = 2{,}000{,}000$, then $h \leq 3$; in the worst case, finding a key in this B-tree requires three seeks. If the root can be kept in memory at all times, this number can be reduced to only two seeks into secondary storage.

An algorithm for finding a key in a B-tree is simple and coded as follows:

```
BTreeNode *
BTreeSearch(keyType K, BTreeNode *node)
{    if (node != 0) {
          for (i=1; i < node->keyTally && node->keys[i-1] < K; i++);
          if (i == node->keyTally || node->keys[i-1] > K)
               return BTreeSearch(K,node->pointers[i-1]);
          else return node;
     }
     else return 0;
}
```

Inserting a Key in a B-Tree

Both the insertion and deletion operations appear to be somewhat challenging if we remember that all leaves have to be at the last level. Not even balanced binary trees require that. Implementing insertion becomes easier when the strategy of building a tree is changed. When inserting a node in a binary search tree, the tree is always built from top to bottom, resulting in unbalanced trees. If the first incoming key is the smallest, then this key is put in the root, and the root does not have a left subtree unless special provisions are made to balance the tree.

But a tree can be built from the bottom up so that the root is an entity always in flux and only at the end of all insertions can we know for sure the contents of the root. This strategy is applied to inserting keys into B-trees. In this process, given an incoming key, we go directly to a leaf and place it there, if there is room. When the leaf is full, another leaf is created, the keys are divided between these leaves, and one key is promoted to the parent. If the parent is full, the process is repeated until the root is reached and a new root created.

To approach the problem more systematically, there are three common situations encountered when inserting a key in a B-tree.

1. A key is placed in a leaf which still has some room, as in Figure 7.5. In a B-tree of order 5, a new key, 7, is placed in a leaf, preserving the order of the keys in the leaf, so that key 8 must be shifted to the right by one position.

2. The leaf in which a key should be placed is full, as in Figure 7.6. In this case, the leaf is *split*, creating a new leaf, and half of the keys are moved from the full leaf to the new leaf. But the new leaf has to be incorporated into the B-tree. The last key of the old leaf is moved to the parent, and a pointer to the new leaf is placed

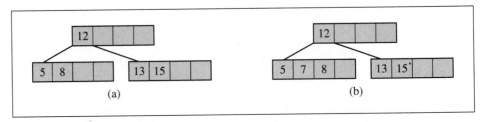

Figure 7.5: **A B-tree (a) before and (b) after insertion of the number 7 to a leaf which has available cells.**

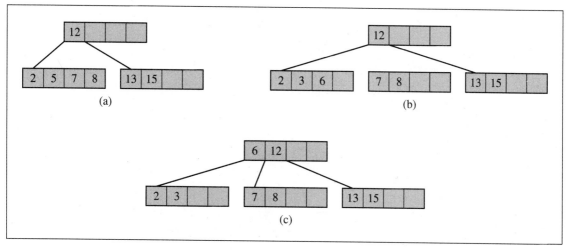

Figure 7.6: **Inserting number 6 into a full leaf.**

in the parent as well. The same procedure can be repeated for each internal node of the B-tree, so that each such split adds one more node to the B-tree. Moreover, such a split guarantees that each leaf never has less than $\lceil m/2 \rceil - 1$ keys.

3. A special case arises if the root of the B-tree is full. In this case, a new root and a new sibling of the existing root has to be created. This split results in two new nodes in the B-tree. For example, after inserting the key 13 in the third leaf in Figure 7.7a, the leaf is split (as in case 2), a new leaf is created, and the key 15 is about to be moved to the parent, but the parent has no room for it (7.7b). So the parent is split (7.7c), but now two B-trees have to be combined into one. This is achieved by creating a new root and moving the last key from the old root to it (7.7d). It should be obvious that it is the only case in which the B-tree increases in height.

An algorithm for inserting keys in B-trees follows:

```
BTreeInsert (K)
    find a leaf node to insert K;
    while (1)
        find a proper position in array keys for K;
        if node is not full
            insert K and increment KeyTally;
            return;
        else split node in node1 and node2; // node1 = node, node2 is new;
            distribute keys and pointers evenly between node1 and node2 and
            initialize properly their KeyTally's;
            K = the last key of node1;
            if node was the root
                create a new root as parent of node1 and node2;
                put K and pointers to node1 and node2 in the root, and set its keyTally to 1;
                return;
            else node = its parent; // and now process the node's parent;
```

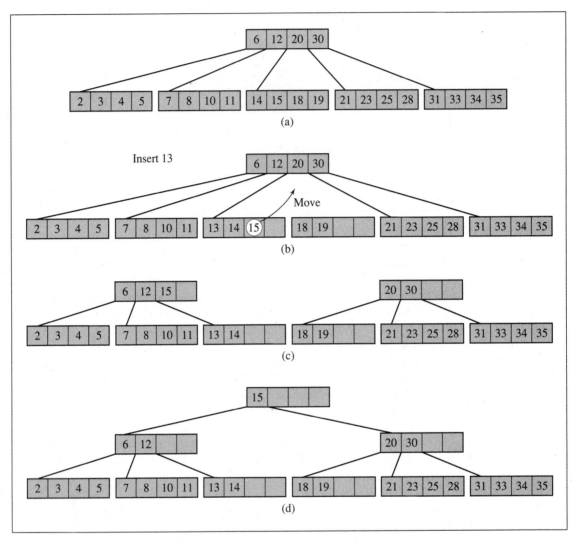

Figure 7.7: **Inserting the number 13 into a full leaf.**

Figure 7.8 shows the growth of a B-tree of order 5 in the course of inserting new keys. Note that at all times the tree is perfectly balanced.

A variation of this insertion strategy uses *presplitting*: when a search is made from the top down for a particular key, each visited node which is already full is split. In this way, no split has to be propagated upwards.

How often are node splits expected to occur? A split of the root node of a B-tree creates two new nodes. All other splits add only one more node to the B-tree. During the construction of a B-tree of p nodes, $p - h$ splits have to be performed, where h is the height of the B-tree. Also, in a B-tree of p nodes, there are at least

$$1 + (\lceil m/2 \rceil - 1)(p - 1)$$

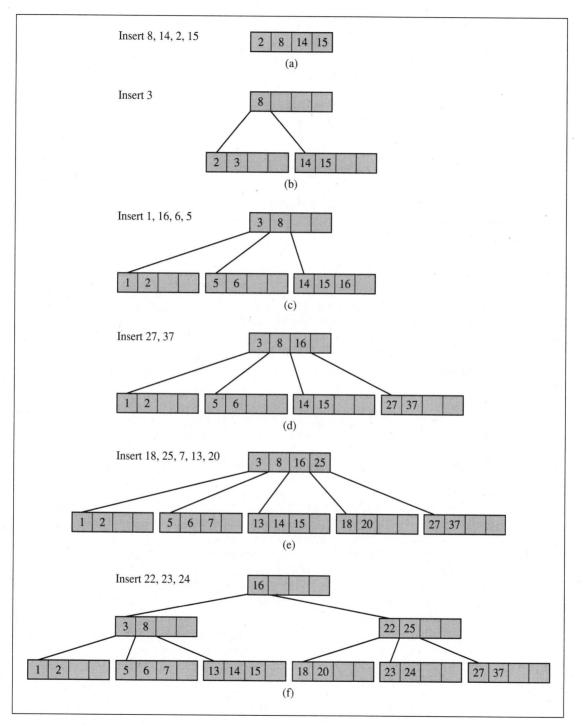

Figure 7.8: **Building a B-tree of order 5 with the BTreeInsert() algorithm.**

keys. The rate of splits with respect to the number of keys in the B-tree can be given by

$$\frac{p - h}{1 + (\lceil m/2 \rceil - 1)(p - 1)}.$$

After dividing the numerator and denominator by $p - h$ and observing that $\frac{1}{p-h} \rightarrow 0$ and $\frac{p-1}{p-h} \rightarrow 1$ with the increase of p, the average probability of a split is

$$\frac{1}{\lceil m/2 \rceil - 1}.$$

For example, for $m = 10$, this probability is equal to .25, for $m = 100$, it is .02, and for $m = 1000$, it is .002, and expectedly so: the larger the capacity of one node, the less frequently splits will occur.

Deleting a Key from a B-Tree

Deletion is to a great extent a reversal of insertion, although it has more special cases. Care has to be taken to avoid allowing any node to be less than half full after a deletion. This means that sometimes nodes have to be merged.

In deletion, there are two main cases: deleting a key from a leaf and deleting a key from a nonleaf node. In the latter case, we will use a procedure similar to **DeleteByCopying()** used for binary search trees (Section 6.6).

1. Deleting a key from a leaf.

    1.1 If after deleting a key K, the leaf is at least half full and only keys greater than K are moved to the left to fill the hole (see Figures 7.9a,b). This is the inverse of insertion's case 1.

    1.2 If after deleting K, the number of keys in the leaf is less than $\lceil m/2 \rceil - 1$, causing an *underflow*.

        1.2.1 If there is a left or right sibling with the number of keys exceeding the minimal $\lceil m/2 \rceil - 1$, then all keys from this leaf and this sibling are *redistributed* between them by moving the separator key from the parent to the leaf and moving one key from the sibling to the parent (see Figures 7.9b,c).

        1.2.2 If the leaf underflows and the number of keys in its siblings is $\lceil m/2 \rceil - 1$, then the leaf and a sibling are *merged*; the keys from the leaf, from its sibling, and the separating key from the parent are all put in the leaf, and the sibling node is discarded. The keys in the parent are moved if a hole appears (see Figures 7.9c,d). This can initiate a chain of operations if the parent underflows. The parent is now treated as though it were a leaf and either step 1.2.2 is repeated until step 1.2.1 can be executed, or the root of the tree has been reached. This is the inverse of insertion's case 2.

            1.2.2.1 A particular case results in merging a leaf or nonleaf with its sibling when its parent is the root with only one key. In this case, the keys from the node and its sibling, along with the only key of the root, are put in the node which becomes a new root and both the sibling and the old root nodes are discarded. This is the

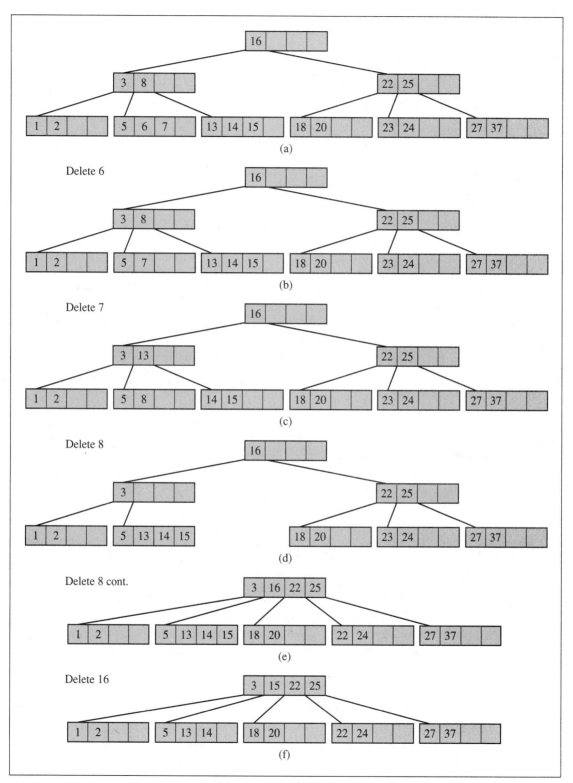

Figure 7.9: **Deleting keys from a B-tree.**

225

only case when two nodes disappear at one time. Also, the height of the tree is decreased by one (see Figures 7.9c–e). This is the inverse of insertion's case 3.

2. Deleting a key from a nonleaf. This may lead to problems with tree reorganization. Therefore, deletion from a nonleaf node is reduced to deleting a key from a leaf. The key to be deleted is replaced by its immediate successor (the predecessor could also be used) which can only be found in a leaf. This successor key is deleted from the leaf which brings us to the preceding case 1 (see Figures 7.9e,f).

Here is the deletion algorithm.

```
BTreeDelete (K)
    node = BTreeSearch(K,root);
    if (node != null)
        if node is not a leaf
            find a leaf with the closest successor S of K;
            copy S over K in node;
            node = the leaf containing S;
            delete S from node;
        else delete K from node;
        while (1)
            if node does not underflow
                return;
            else if there is a sibling of node with enough keys
                redistribute keys between node and its sibling;
                return;
            else if node's parent is the root
                if the parent has only one key
                    merge node, its sibling, and the parent to form a new root;
                else merge node and its sibling;
                return;
            else merge node and its sibling;
                node = its parent;
```

B-trees, according to their definition, are guaranteed to be at least 50% full so it may happen that 50% of space is basically wasted. How often does this happen? If it happens too often then the definition must be reconsidered or some other restrictions imposed on this B-tree. Analyses and simulations, however, indicate that after a series of numerous random insertions and deletions, the B-tree is approximately 69% full (Yao 1978), after which the changes in the percentage of occupied cells are very small. But it is very unlikely that the B-tree will ever be filled to the brim so some additional stipulations are in order.

7.1.2 B*-Trees

Since each node of a B-tree represents a block of secondary memory, accessing one node means one access of secondary memory, which is expensive compared to accessing keys in the node residing in the primary memory. Therefore, the fewer nodes that are created the better. In the worst case, nodes in a B-tree can be half full so it may be ascertained before making any split that there are no nodes with only a half of a load.

A *B*-tree* is a variant of the B-tree introduced by Donald Knuth and named by Douglas Comer. In a B*-tree, all nodes except the root are required to be at least two-thirds full, not just half full, as in a B-tree. More precisely, the number of keys in all nonroot nodes in a B-tree of order m is now k for $\lfloor \frac{2m-1}{3} \rfloor \le k \le m - 1$. The frequency of node splitting is decreased by delaying a split, and when the time comes, by splitting two nodes into three, not one into two.

A split in a B*-tree is delayed by attempting to redistribute the keys between a node and its sibling when the node overflows. Figure 7.10 contains an example of a B*-tree of order 9. The key 6 is to be inserted into the left node which is already full. Instead of splitting the node, all keys from this node and its sibling are evenly divided and the median key, key 12, is put into the parent. Notice that this not only evenly divides the keys, but also the free spaces so that the node which was full is now able to accommodate one more key.

If the sibling is also full, a split occurs: one new node is created, the keys from the node and its sibling (along with the separating key from the parent) are evenly divided among three nodes, and two separating keys are put into the parent (see Figure 7.11). All three nodes participating in the split are guaranteed to be two-thirds full.

Note that as may be expected, this increase of a *fill factor* can be done in variety of ways, and some database systems allow the user to choose a fill factor between .5 and 1. In particular, a B-tree whose nodes are required to be at least 75% is called a B**-tree (McCreight 1977). The latter suggests a tongue-in-cheek generalization: a B^n-tree is a B-tree whose nodes are required to be $\frac{n+1}{n+2}$ full.

7.1.3 B^+-Trees

Since one node of a B-tree represents one secondary memory page or block, the passage from one node to another requires a time-consuming page change. Therefore, we would like to make as few node accesses as possible. What happens if we request that all the keys in the B-tree be printed in ascending order? An inorder tree traversal can be used which is

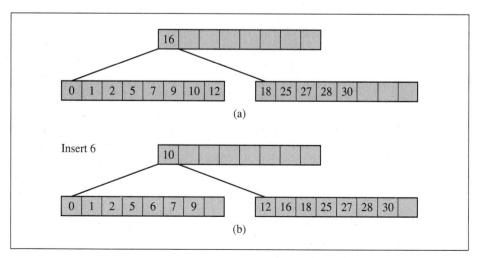

Figure 7.10: **Overflow in a B*-tree is circumvented by redistributing keys between an overflowing node and its sibling.**

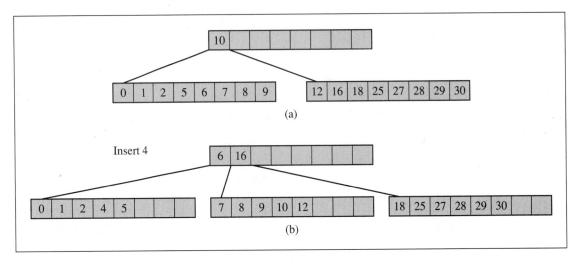

Figure 7.11: **If a node and its sibling are both full in a B*-tree, a split occurs: a new node is created and keys are distributed between three nodes.**

easy to implement but for nonterminal nodes, only one key is displayed at a time and then another page has to be accessed. Therefore, we would like to enhance B-trees to allow us to access data sequentially in a faster manner than using inorder traversal. A B^+-*tree* offers a solution (Wedekind 1974).[2]

In a B-tree references to data are made from any node of the tree, but in a B^+-tree these references are made only from the leaves. The internal nodes of a B^+-tree are indexes for fast access of data; this part of the tree is called an *index set*. The leaves have a different structure than other nodes of the B^+-tree, and usually they are linked sequentially to form a *sequence set* so that scanning this list of leaves results in sequential data. Hence a B^+-tree is truly a B plus tree: it is an index implemented as a regular B-tree plus a linked list of data. Figure 7.12 contains an example of a B^+-tree. Note that internal nodes store keys, pointers, and a key count. Leaves store keys, references to records in a data file associated with the keys, and pointers to the next leaf.

Operations on B^+-trees are not very different from operations on B-trees. Inserting a key into a leaf which still has some room requires putting the keys of this leaf in order. No changes are made in the index set. If a key is inserted into a full leaf, the leaf is split, the new leaf node is included in the sequence set, keys are distributed evenly between the old and the new leaves, and the first key from the new node is copied (not moved, as in a B-tree) to the parent. If the parent is not full, this may require a local reorganization of the keys of the parent (see Figure 7.13). A new leaf is created and included in the sequence set, keys are distributed between these two leaves, and a new separator is *copied* from the first leaf to the parent. If the parent is full, the splitting process is performed the same way as in B^+-trees. After all, the index set is a B-tree.

---

[2]The author, who considered these trees to be only "a slight variation" of B-trees, called them B*-trees.

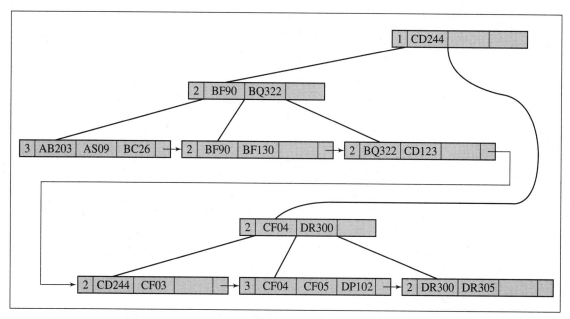

Figure 7.12: **An example of a B$^+$-tree of order 4.**

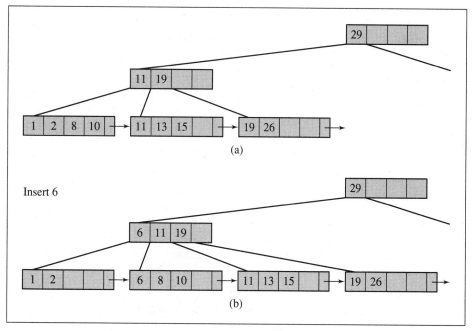

Figure 7.13: **An attempt to insert number 6 in the first leaf of a B$^+$-tree.**

Deleting a key from a leaf leading to no underflow requires putting the remaining keys in order. No changes are made to the index set. In particular, if a key which occurs only in a leaf is deleted, then it is simply deleted from the leaf but can remain in the internal node. The reason for this is that it still serves as a proper guide when navigating down the B$^+$-tree, because it still properly separates keys between two adjacent children even if the separator itself does not occur in either of the children. The deletion of key 6 from the tree in Figure 7.13b results in the tree in Figure 7.14a. Note that the number 6 is not deleted from an internal node.

When the deletion of a key from a leaf causes an underflow, then either the keys from this leaf and the keys of a sibling are redistributed between this leaf and its sibling or the leaf is deleted and the remaining keys are included in its sibling. Figure 7.14b illustrates the latter case. After deleting the number 2, an underflow occurs and two leaves are combined to form one leaf. The first key from the right sibling of the node remaining after merging is copied to the parent node and keys in the parent are put in order. Both these operations require updating the separator in the parent. Also, removing a leaf may trigger merges in the index set.

7.1.4 Prefix B$^+$-Trees

If a key occurred in a leaf and in an internal node of a B$^+$-tree, then it is enough to delete it only from the leaf since the key retained in the node is still a good guide in subsequent searches. So it really does not matter whether a key in an internal node is in any leaf or not.

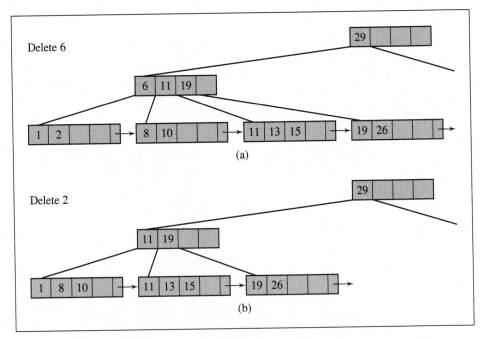

Figure 7.14: **Actions after deleting the number 6 from a B$^+$-tree in Figure 9.13b.**

What counts is that it is an acceptable separator for keys in adjacent children; for example, for two keys K_1 and K_2, the separator s must meet the condition $K_1 < s \le K_2$. This property of the separator keys is also retained if we make keys in internal nodes as small as possible by removing all redundant contents from them and still have a properly working B^+-tree.

A *simple prefix B^+-tree* (Bayer, Unterauer 1977) is a B^+-tree in which the chosen separators are the shortest prefixes that allow us to distinguish two neighboring index keys. For example, in Figure 7.12, the left child of the root has two keys, BF90 and BQ322. If a key is less than BF90, the first leaf is chosen; if it is less than BQ322, the second leaf is the right pick. But observe that we also have the same results, if instead of BF90, keys BF9 or just BF are used and instead of BQ322, one of three prefixes of this key is used: BQ32, BQ3, or just BQ. After choosing the shortest prefixes of both keys, if any key is less than BF, the search ends up in the first leaf and if the key is less than BQ, the second leaf is chosen; the result is the same as before. Reducing the size of the separators to the bare minimum does not change the result of the search. It only makes separators smaller. As a result, more separators can be placed in the same node, whereby such a node can have more children. The entire B^+-tree can have fewer levels which reduces the branching factor and makes processing the tree faster.

This reasoning does not stop at the level of parents of the leaves. It is carried over to any other level, so that the entire index set of a B^+-tree is filled with prefixes (see Figure 7.15).

The operations on simple prefix B^+-trees are much the same as the operations on B^+-trees with certain modifications to account for prefixes used as separators. In particular, after a split, the first key from the new node is neither moved nor copied to the parent, but the shortest prefix is found which differentiates it from the prefix of the last key in the old

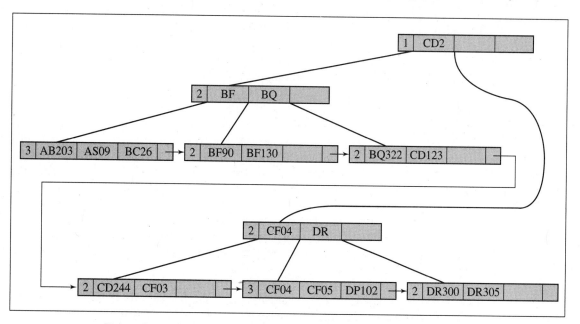

Figure 7.15: **A B^+-tree from Figure 7.12 presented as a simple prefix B-tree.**

node, the prefix is located in the parent. For deletion, however, some separators retained in the index set may turn out to be too long, but they do not have to be immediately shortened to make deletion faster.

The idea of using prefixes as separators can be carried even further if we observe that prefixes of prefixes can be omitted in lower levels of the tree, which is the idea behind a *prefix B$^+$-tree*. This method works particularly well if prefixes are long and repetitious. Figure 7.16 contains an example. Each key in the tree has a prefix AB12XY and this prefix appears in all internal nodes. This is redundant; Figure 7.16b shows the same tree with "AB12XY" stripped from prefixes in children of the root. To restore the original prefix, the key from the parent node, except for its last character, becomes the prefix of the key found in the current node. For example, the first cell of the child of the root in Figure 7.16b has the key "08." The last character of the key in the root is discarded and the obtained prefix, "AB12XY," is put in front of "08," and the new prefix, "AB12XY08," is used to determine the direction of the search.

How efficient are prefix B$^+$-trees? Experimental runs indicate that there is almost no difference in the time needed to execute algorithms in B$^+$-trees and simple prefix B$^+$-trees, but prefix B$^+$-trees need 50–100% more time. In terms of disk accesses, there is no difference between these trees in the number of times the disk is accessed for trees of 400 nodes or less. For trees of 400–800 nodes, both simple prefix B$^+$-trees and prefix B$^+$-trees require 20–25% fewer accesses (Bayer, Unterauer 1977). This indicates that simple prefix B$^+$-trees are a viable option, but prefix B$^+$-trees remain of largely theoretical interest.

7.1.5   Bit-Trees

A very interesting approach is, in a sense, taking to the extreme the prefix B$^+$-tree method. In this method, bytes are used to specify separators. In *bit-trees*, the bit level is reached (Ferguson 1992).

The bit-tree is based on the concept of a *distinction bit* (*D-bit*). A distinction bit $D(K,L)$ is the number of the most significant bit which differs in two keys K and L, and $D(K,L) = $ *key-length-in-bits* $- 1 - \lfloor \lg(K \text{ xor } L) \rfloor$. For example, the D-bit for the letters "K" and "N", whose ASCII codes are 01001011 and 01001110, is 5, the position at which the first difference between these keys has been detected; $D(\text{"K"}, \text{"N"}) = 8 - 1 - \lfloor \lg 5 \rfloor = 5$.

A bit-tree uses D-bits to separate keys in the leaves only; the remaining part of the tree is a prefix B$^+$-tree. This means that the actual keys and entire records from which these keys are extracted are stored in a data file so that the leaves can include much more information than would be the case when the keys were stored in them. Figure 7.17 contains the leaf of a bit-tree. Entries in the leaf store D-bits and pointers to data records in the data file. The leaf does not contain actual keys. The keys can be found only in the data file. The leaf entries refer to the keys indirectly by specifying distinction bits between keys corresponding to neighboring locations in the leaf. Before presenting an algorithm for processing data with bit-trees, some useful properties of D-bits need to be discussed.

All keys in the leaves are kept in ascending order. Therefore $D_i = D(K_{i-1}, K_i)$ indicates the leftmost bit that is different in these keys; this bit is always 1 since $K_{i-1} < K_i$ for $1 \le i < m$ (= order of the tree). For example, $D(\text{"N"}, \text{"O"}) = D(01001110, 01001111) = 7$, and the bit in position 7 is on, all preceding bits in both keys being the same.

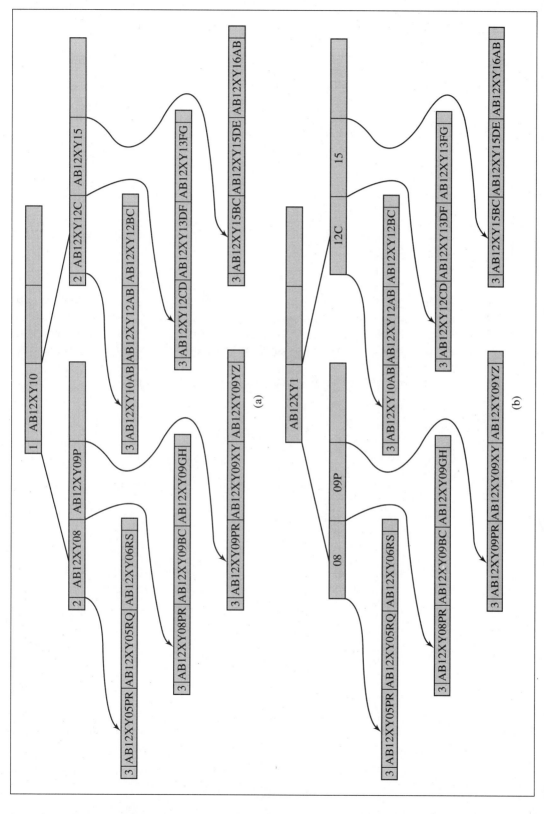

Figure 7.16: A simple prefix B[+]-tree (a) and its abbreviated version presented as a prefix B[+]-tree (b).

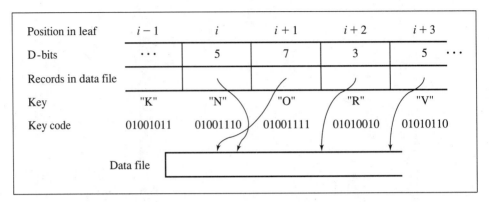

Figure 7.17: **A leaf of a bit-tree.**

Let j be the first position in a leaf for which $D_j < D_i$ and $j > i$; D_j is the first D-bit smaller than a preceding D_i. In this case, for all keys between positions i and j in this leaf, the D_i bit is 1. In the example in Figure 7.17, $j = i + 2$, since D_{i+2} is the first D-bit following position i that is smaller than D_i. Bit 5 in key "O" in position $i + 1$ is 1 as it is 1 in key "N" in position i.

The algorithm for searching a key using a bit-tree leaf is as follows:

```
BitTreeSearch(K)
    R = record R₀;
    for (i = 1; i < m; i++)
        if the Dᵢ bit in K is 1
            R = Rᵢ;
        else skip all following D-bits until a smaller D-bit is found;
    read record R from data file;
    if K == key from record R
        return R;
    else return -1;
```

Using this algorithm, we can search for "V" assuming that in Figure 7.17, $i - 1 = 0$ and $i + 3$ is the last entry in the leaf. R is initialized to R_0, and i to 1.

1. In the first iteration of the **for** loop, bit $D_1 = 5$ in key "V" $= 01010110$ is checked, and because it is 1, R is assigned R_1.

2. In the second iteration, bit $D_2 = 7$ is tested. It is 0, but nothing is skipped, as required by the **else** statement, since right away a D-bit is found which is smaller than 7.

3. The third iteration: bit $D_3 = 3$ is 1, so R becomes R_3.

4. In the fourth iteration, bit $D_4 = 5$ is checked again, and because it is 1, R is assigned R_5. This is the last entry in the leaf; the procedure is finished and R_5 is properly returned.

What happens if the desired key is not in the data file? We can try to locate "S" $=$ 01010011, using the same assumptions on $i - 1$ and $i + 3$. Bit $D_1 = 5$ is 0, so the position with D-bit 7 is skipped, and since bit $D_3 = 3$ in "S" is 1, the procedure returns record R_3. To prevent this, **BitTreeSearch()** checks whether the record it found really corresponds with the desired key. If not, a negative number is returned to indicate failure.

7.1.6   R-Trees

Spatial data are the kind of objects which are utilized frequently in many areas. Computer-assisted design, geographical data, and VLSI design are examples of domains in which spatial data are created, searched, and deleted. This type of data requires special data structures to be processed efficiently. For example, we may request that all counties in an area specified by geographical coordinates be printed, or that all buildings in walking distance from City Hall be identified. Many different data structures have been developed to accommodate this type of data. One example is an *R-tree* (Guttman 1984).

An R-tree of order m is a B-tree-like structure containing at least m entries in one node for some $m \leq$ maximum number allowable per one node (except the root). Hence, an R-tree is not required to be at least half full.

A leaf in an R-tree contains entries of the form $(rect, id)$ where $rect = ([x_0, y_0], \ldots, [x_{n-1}, y_{n-1}])$ is an n-dimensional rectangle and id is a pointer to a record in a data file. $rect$ is the smallest rectangle containing object id. For example, the entry in a leaf corresponding to an object X on a Cartesian plane as in Figure 7.18 is the pair $(([10, 100], [5, 52]), X)$.

A nonleaf node cell entry has the form $(rect, child)$ where $rect$ is the smallest rectangle encompassing all the rectangles found in *child*. The structure of an R-tree is not identical to the structure of a B-tree: the former can be viewed as a series of n keys and n pointers corresponding with these keys.

Inserting new rectangles in an R-tree is made in B-tree fashion, with splits and redistribution. A crucial operation is finding a proper leaf in which to insert a rectangle *rect*. When moving down the R-tree, the subtree chosen in the current node is the one that corresponds with the rectangle requiring the least enlargement to include *rect*. If a split occurs, new encompassing rectangles have to be created. The detailed algorithm is more involved since, among other things, it is not obvious how to divide rectangles of a node being split. The algorithm should generate rectangles which enclose rectangles of the two resulting nodes and are minimal in size.

Figure 7.19 contains an example of inserting four rectangles to an R-tree. After inserting the first three rectangles, $R_1, R_2,$ and R_3, only the root is full (Figure 7.19a). Inserting

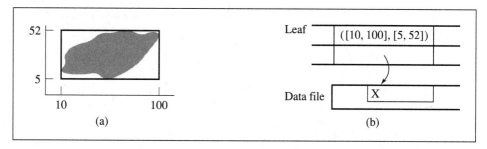

Figure 7.18: **An area X on the Cartesian plane enclosed tightly by the rectangle ([10, 100], [5, 52]). The rectangle parameters and the area identifier are stored in a leaf of an R-tree.**

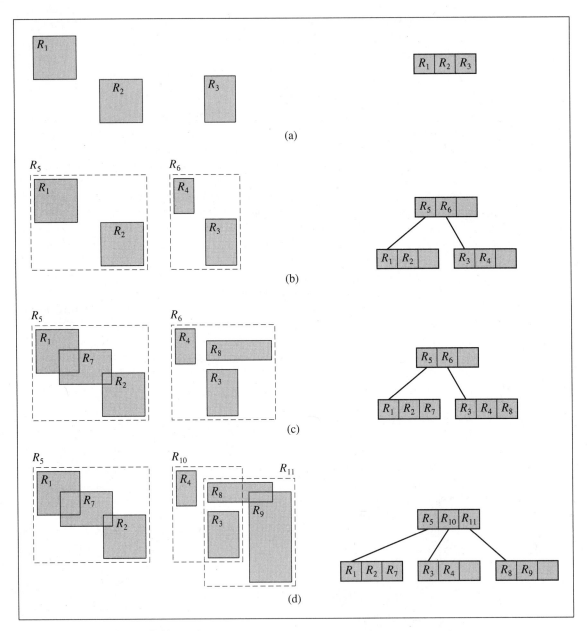

Figure 7.19: **Building an R-tree.**

R_4 causes a split, resulting in the creation of two encompassing rectangles (Figure 9.19b). Inserting R_7 changes nothing and inserting R_8 causes rectangle R_6 to be extended to accommodate R_8 (Figure 7.19c). Figure 7.19d shows another split after entering R_9 in the R-tree. R_6 is discarded and R_{10} and R_{11} are created.

A rectangle R can be contained in many other encompassing rectangles, but it can be stored only once in a leaf. Therefore, a search procedure may take a wrong path at some level h when it sees that R is enclosed by another rectangle found in a node on this level. For example, rectangle R_3 in Figure 7.19d is enclosed by both R_{10} and R_{11}. Since R_{10} is before R_{11} in the root, the search accesses the right leaf when looking for R_3. However, if R_{11} preceded R_{10} in the root, following the path corresponding with R_{11} would be unsuccessful. For large and high R-trees this overlapping becomes excessive.

A modification of R-trees, called an R^+-tree, removes this overlap (Stonebraker, Sellis, Hanson 1986; Sellis, Roussopoulos, Faloutsos 1987). The encompassing rectangles are no longer overlapping, and each encompassing rectangle is associated with all the rectangles it intersects. But now the data rectangle can be found in more than one leaf. For example, Figure 7.20 shows an R^+-tree constructed after the data rectangle R_9 was inserted into the R-tree in Figure 7.19c. Figure 7.20 replaces Figure 7.19d. Note that R_8 can be found in two leaves, since it is intersected by two encompassing rectangles, R_{10} and R_{11}. Operations on an R^+-tree make it difficult to ascertain without further manipulation that nodes are at least half full.

7.1.7   2–4 Trees

This section discusses a special case of B-tree, a B-tree of order 4. This B-tree was first discussed by Rudolf Bayer who called it a *symmetric binary B-tree* (Bayer 1972), but it is usually called a *2–3–4 tree* or just a *2–4 tree*. A 2–4 tree seems to offer no new perspectives but quite the opposite is true. In B-trees, the nodes are large to accommodate the contents of one block read from secondary storage. In 2–4 trees, on the other hand, only one, two, or at most three elements can be stored in one node. Unless the elements are very large, so large that three of them can fill up one block on a disk, there seems to be no reason for even mentioning B-trees of such a small order. Although B-trees have been introduced in the context of handling data on secondary storage, it does not mean that they have to be used only for that purpose.

We spent an entire chapter discussing binary trees, in particular, binary search trees, and developing algorithms which allow quick access to the information stored in these trees. Can B-trees offer a better solution to the problem of balancing or traversing binary trees? We would like to return now to the topics of binary trees and processing data in memory.

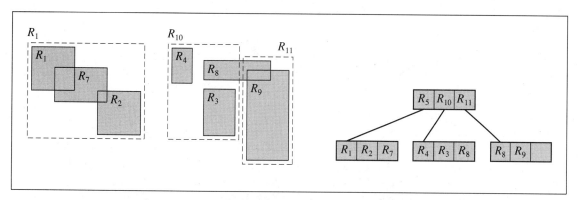

Figure 7.20: **An R^+-tree representation of the R-tree in Figure 7.19d after inserting the rectangle R_9 in the tree in Figure 7.19c.**

B-trees are well-suited to challenge the algorithms used for binary search trees, since a B-tree by its nature has to be balanced. No special treatment is needed in addition to building a tree: building a B-tree balances it at the same time. Instead of using binary search trees, we may use B-trees of small order such as 2–4 trees. However, if these trees are implemented as structures similarly to B-trees, there are three locations per node to store up to three keys and four locations per node to store up to four pointers. In the worst case, half of these cells are unused, and on the average, 69% are unused. Since space is much more at a premium in main memory than in secondary storage, we would like to avoid this wasted space. Therefore, 2–4 trees are transformed into binary tree form in which each node holds only one key. Of course, the transformation has to be done in a way that permits an unambiguous restoration of the original B-tree form.

To represent a 2–4 tree as a binary tree, two types of links between nodes are used: one type indicates links between nodes representing keys belonging to the same node of 2–4 tree, and another represents regular parent-children links. Bayer called them *horizontal* and *vertical* pointers or, more cryptically, ρ-pointers and δ-pointers; Guibas and Sedgewick in their dichromatic framework use the names *red* and *black* pointers. Not only are the names different, but the trees are also drawn a bit differently. Figure 7.21 shows nodes with two and

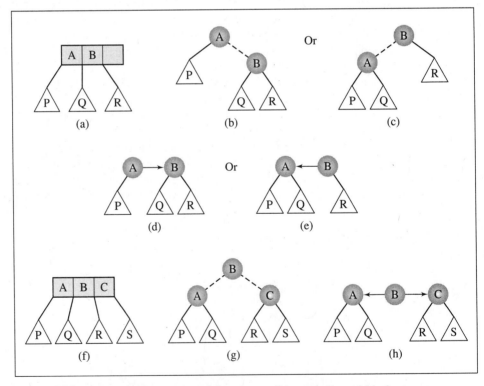

Figure 7.21: **A 3-node (a) represented in two possible ways by red-black trees (b,c) and in two possible ways by horizontal-vertical trees (d,e). A 4-node (f) represented by a red-black tree (g) and by a horizontal-vertical tree (h).**

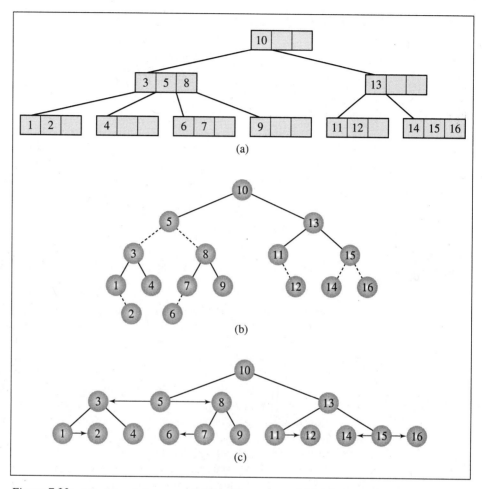

Figure 7.22: **A 2–4 tree (a) represented by a binary tree with horizontal and vertical pointers (b) and by a red-black tree (c).**

three keys, which are called *3-nodes* and *4-nodes*, and their two equivalent representations. Figure 7.22 shows a complete 2–4 tree and its binary tree equivalent. Note that the red links are drawn with dashed lines. The red-black tree better represents the exact form of a binary tree, the horizontal-vertical trees are better in retaining the shape of 2–4 trees and having leaves shown as though they were on the same level. Also, horizontal-vertical trees lend themselves easily to representing B-trees of any order, the red-black trees not so.

Both red-black trees and horizontal-vertical trees are binary trees. Each node has two pointers which can be interpreted in two ways. To make a distinction between the interpretation applied in a given context, a flag for each of the pointers is used. A node of a horizontal-vertical tree can be declared as

```
struct VHTreeNode {
              keyType key;
              VHTreeNode *left, *right;
              unsigned int LeftVert, RightVert : 1;
              . . . . . . . . . .
       };
```

The operations performed on horizontal-vertical trees should be the same as on binary trees, although their implementation is much more involved. Only searching is the same: to find a key in a horizontal-vertical tree, no distinction is made between the different types of pointers, and we can use the same searching procedure as for binary search trees: if the key is found, stop. If the key in the current node is larger than the one we are looking for, we go to the left subtree, otherwise to the right subtree.

Before discussing insertion, note that horizontal-vertical trees have the following properties:

- The path from the root to any leaf contains the same number of vertical links.
- No path from the root can have two horizontal links in a row.

Insertions restructure the tree by adding one more node and one more link to the tree. Should it be a horizontal or vertical link? Deletions restructure the tree as well by removing one node and one link but this may lead to two consecutive horizontal links. These operations are not as straightforward as for binary search trees, since some counterparts of node splitting and node merging have to be represented in horizontal-vertical trees.

A good idea when splitting 2–4 trees, as already indicated in discussion of B-trees, is to split nodes when going down the tree while inserting a key. If a 4-node is encountered, it is split before descending farther down the tree. Because this splitting is made from the top down, a 4-node can be a child of either a 2-node or a 3-node (with the usual exception: unless it is the root). Figures 7.23a and 7.23b contain an example. Splitting the node with keys B, C, and D requires creating a new node. The two nodes involved in splitting (Figure 7.23a) are 4/6 full, three nodes after splitting are 4/9 full (6/8 and 7/12, respectively, for pointer fields). Splitting nodes in 2–4 trees results in poor performance. However, if the same operations are performed on their horizontal-vertical tree equivalents, the operation is remarkably efficient. In Figures 7.23c and 7.23d the same split is performed on a horizontal-vertical tree, and the operation requires changing only two flags from horizontal to vertical and one from vertical to horizontal: only three bits are reset!

Resetting these three flags suggests the algorithm *FlagFlipping* that takes the following steps: if we visit a node n whose links are both horizontal, then reset the flag corresponding to the link from n's parent to n to "horizontal," and both flags in n to vertical.

If we have a situation as in Figure 7.24a, the split results in the 2–4 tree as in Figure 7.24b; applying *FlagFlipping* to a horizontal-vertical tree equivalent requires that only three bits are reset (Figures 7.24c and 7.24d).

Figure 7.21 indicates that the same node of a 2–4 tree can have two equivalents in a horizontal-vertical tree. Therefore, the situation in Figure 7.24a can be reflected not only by the tree in Figure 7.24c, but also by the tree in Figure 7.25a. If we proceed as before, by changing three flags as in Figure 7.24d, the tree in Figure 7.25b ends up with

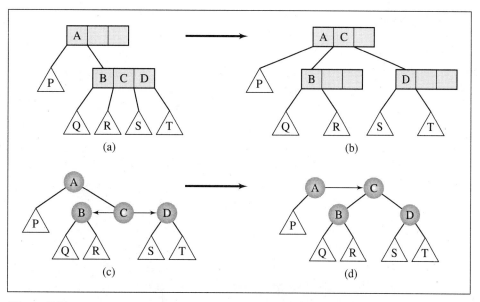

Figure 7.23: **Split of a 4-node attached to a node with one key in a 2–4 tree (a). The same split in a horizontal-vertical tree equivalent to these two nodes (c, d).**

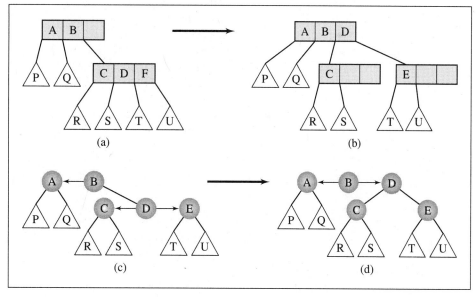

Figure 7.24: **Split of a 4-node attached to a 3-node in a 2–4 tree (a, b) and a similar operation performed on one possible horizontal-vertical tree equivalent to these two nodes (c, d).**

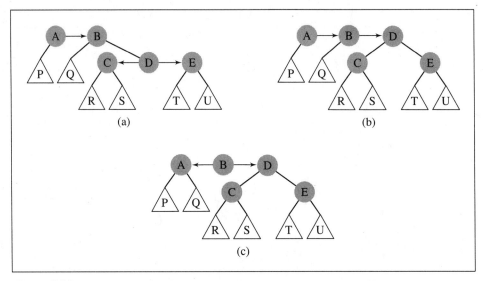

Figure 7.25: **Fixing a horizontal-vertical tree that has consecutive horizontal links.**

two consecutive horizontal links, which has no counterpart in any 2–4 tree. In this case, the three flag flips have to be followed by a rotation, namely node B is rotated about node A, two flags are flipped, and the tree in Figure 7.25c is the same as in Figure 7.24d.

Figure 7.26a contains another way in which a 4-node is attached to a 3-node in a 2–4 tree before splitting. Figure 7.26b shows the tree after splitting. Applying *FlagFlipping* to the tree in Figure 7.26c yields the tree in Figure 7.26d with two consecutive horizontal links. To restore the horizontal-vertical tree property, two rotations and two link exchanges are needed: node C is rotated about node E (Figure 7.26e) and then node C about node A, leading to the tree in Figure 7.26f.

We presented four configurations leading to a split. This number has to be doubled if the mirror images of the situations just analyzed are added. The number of special cases is rather high and this fact is reflected in the following insertion algorithm.

```
HVTreeInsert(K)
    create newNode and initialize it;
    if HVTree is empty
        root = newNode;
        return;
    for (p = root, prev = 0; p != 0;)
        if p has both flags set to 0      // horizontal
            set them to 1;                // vertical
            mark prev's link connecting it with p as 0;
        if links connecting parent of prev with prev and prev with p are both marked 0
            if both these links are left or both are right
                rotate prev about its parent;
```

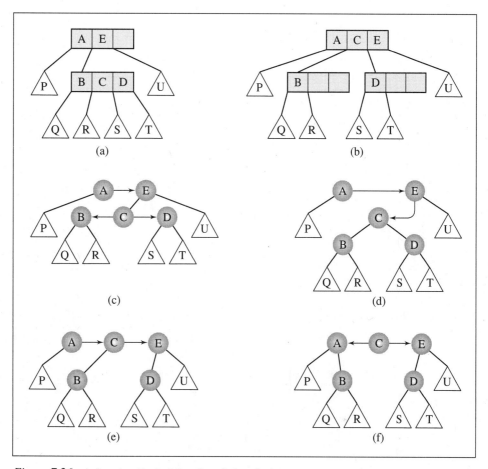

Figure 7.26: **A 4-node attached to a 3-node in a 2–4 tree.**

```
        else rotate p about prev and then p about its new parent;
     prev = p;
     if (p->key > K)
        p = p->left;
     else p = p->right;
attach newNode to prev;
mark prev's flag corresponding to its link to newNode to 0;
if link from prev's parent to prev is marked 0
     rotate prev about its parent or
     first rotate newNode about prev and then newNode about its new parent;
```

Figure 7.27 contains an example of inserting a sequence of numbers. Note that a double rotation has to be made in the tree in Figure 7.27h while 6 is being inserted. First, 9 is rotated about 5, then 9 is rotated about 11.

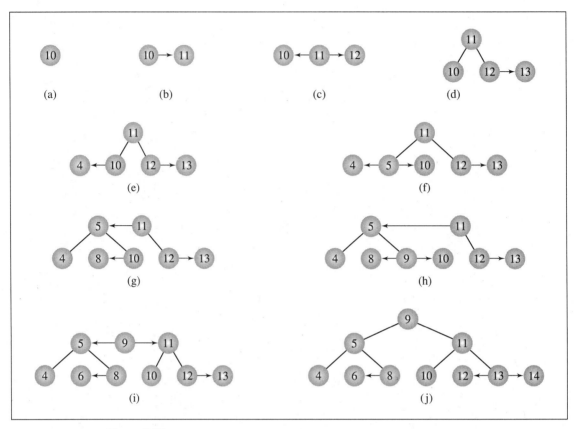

Figure 7.27: **Building a horizontal-vertical tree by inserting numbers in this sequence: 10, 11, 12, 13, 4, 5, 8, 9, 6, 14.**

How efficient is a horizontal-vertical tree in comparison with balanced trees? Since the minimum number n of nodes in a horizontal-vertical tree of height h is different for even and odd heights, the correspondence between n and h was proven to be

$$\lg(n + 1) \le h \le 2\lg(n + 2) - 2$$

The upper bound on the height of a horizontal-vertical tree is approximately $2\lg n$ which is more than the same bound for AVL trees, $1.44\lg n$. Hence, the horizontal-vertical tree may appear to be less useful than an AVL tree. However, the horizontal-vertical tree requires less tree restructuring during node insertion than the AVL tree. Moreover, this restructuring may be limited to resetting only three bits, whereas in an AVL tree, at least one rotation has to take place when rebalancing the tree. Therefore, AVL trees are preferable in programs which require little tree restructuring and use the tree primarily for information retrieval. When, on the other hand, there is a great deal of node insertion and deletion, a horizontal-vertical tree is a more prudent choice.

The horizontal-vertical trees also include AVL trees. An AVL tree can be converted into an horizontal-vertical tree by converting the links connecting the roots of subtrees of

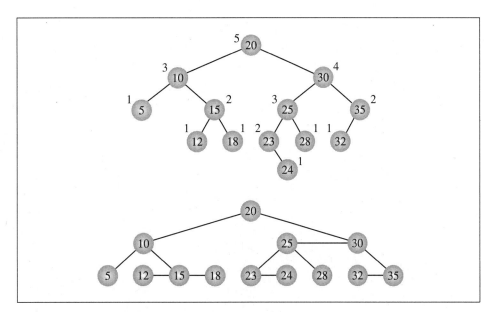

Figure 7.28: **An example of converting an AVL tree (top part) into an equivalent horizontal-vertical tree (bottom part).**

even height with children of these roots of odd height into horizontal links. Figure 7.28 illustrates this conversion.

7.2 TRIES

The preceding chapter showed that traversing a binary tree was guided by full key comparisons; each node contained a key which was compared to another key to find a proper path through the tree. The discussion of prefix B-trees indicated that this is not necessary and that only a portion of a key is required to determine the path. However, finding a proper prefix became an issue and maintaining prefixes of an acceptable form and size made the process for insertion and deletion more complicated than in standard B-trees. A tree which uses parts of the key to navigate the search is called a *trie*. The name of the tree is appropriate, as it is a portion of the word re*trie*val with convoluted pronunciation: in order to distinguish a tree from a trie in speech, trie is pronounced as "try."

Each key is a sequence of characters and a trie is organized around these characters rather than entire keys. For simplicity, assume that all the keys are made out of five capital letters: A, E, I, P, R. There are many words which can be generated out of these five letters, but our examples will use only a handful of them.

Figure 7.29 shows a trie for words which are indicated in the vertical rectangles; this form was first used by E. Fredkin. These rectangles represent the leaves of the trie, which are nodes with actual keys. The internal nodes can be viewed as arrays of pointers to subtries. At each level i, the ith letter of the key being processed is compared to the position of the array which corresponds to this letter. If the pointer in this position is null,

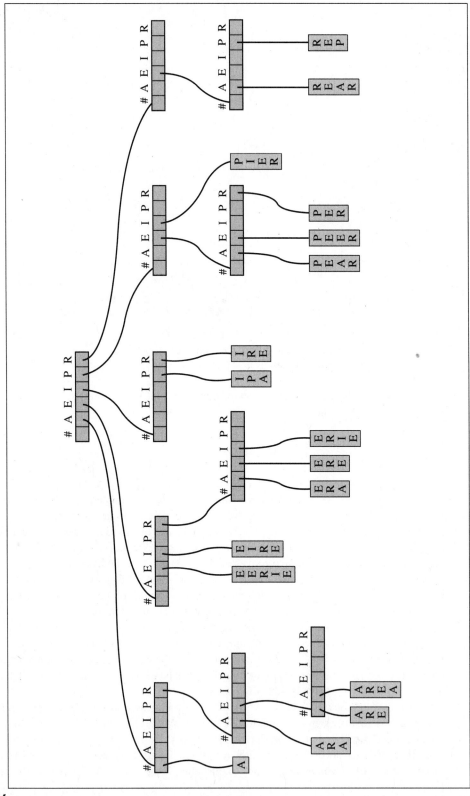

Figure 7.29: A trie of some words composed of the five letters A, E, I, R, and P. The sharp sign # indicates the end of a word which can be a prefix of another word.

the key is not in the trie which may mean a failure or a signal for key insertion. If not, we continue processing until a leaf containing this key is found. For example, we check for the word "ERIE." At the first level of the trie, the pointer corresponding to the first letter of this word, "E," is checked. The pointer is not null, so we go to the second level of the trie, to the child of the root accessible from position "E"; now the pointer in the position indicated by the second letter, "R," is tested. It is not null either, so we descend down the trie one more level. At the third level, the third letter, "I", is used to access a pointer in this node. The pointer points to a leaf containing the word "ERIE." Thus, we conclude that the search is successful. If the desired word was "ERIIE" we would fail, since we would access the same leaf as before, and obviously the two words are different. If the word were "ERPIE," we would access the same node whose one leaf contains "ERIE," but this time "P" would be used to check the corresponding pointer in the node. Since the pointer is null, we would conclude that "ERPIE" is not in the trie.

There are at least two problems. First, how do we make a distinction between two words when one is a prefix of the other? For example, "ARE" is a prefix in "AREA," so that if we are looking for "ARE" in the trie, we must not follow the path leading to "AREA." To that end, a special character is used in each node guaranteed not to be used in any word, in this case, a sharp sign, "#." Now, while searching for "ARE," then after processing "A," "R," and "E" we find ourselves at the fourth level of the trie, whose leaves are "ARE" and "AREA." Since we processed all letters of the key "ARE," we check the pointer corresponding to the end of words, "#," and since it is not empty, we conclude that the word is in the trie.

This last example points to another problem. Is it really necessary to store entire words in the trie? After we reached the fourth level when searching for "ARE" and the pointer for "#" is not null, do we have to go to the leaf to make a comparison between the key "ARE" and the contents of the leaf, also "ARE"? Not necessarily, and the example of prefix B-trees suggests the solution. The leaves may contain only the unprocessed suffixes of the words. It may even make the comparison faster in C++. If at each level of the trie the pointer w to a word is incremented, then upon reaching a leaf, we need only check `strcmp(w, leaf->key)`. This chapter's case study adopts this approach.

This example restricted the number of letters used to five but in a more realistic setting, all letters are used so that each node has 27 pointers (including "#"). The height of the trie is determined by the longest prefix, and for English words the prefix should not be a long string. For most words the matter is settled after several node visits, probably 5–7. This is true for 10,000 English words in the trie, and for 100,000. A corresponding perfectly balanced binary search tree for 10,000 words has a height $\lceil \lg 10,000 \rceil = 14$. Since most words are stored on the lowest levels of this tree, then, on the average, the search takes 13 node visits. (The average path length in a perfectly balanced tree of height h is $\lceil \lg h \rceil - 2$.) This is double the number of visits in the trie. When making a comparison in the binary search tree, the comparison is made between the key searched for and the key in the current node, whereas in the trie only one character is used in each comparison. For 100,000 words, the average number of visits in the tree increases by three since $\lceil \lg 100,000 \rceil = 17$; in the trie this number can increase by 1 or 2. Therefore, in situations where the speed of access is vital, such as in spelling checkers, a trie is a very good choice.

Due to the fact that the trie has two types of nodes, inserting a key into a trie is a bit more complicated than inserting it into a binary search tree.

```
TrieInsert(K)
    i = 0;
    p = the root;
    while not inserted
        if (K[i] == '\0')
            set the end-of-word marker in p to true;
        else if (p->ptrs[K[i]] == 0)
            create a leaf containing K and put its address in p->ptrs[K[i]];
        else if pointer p->ptrs[K[i]] is a leaf
            K_L = key in leaf p->ptrs[K[i]]
            do create a nonleaf and put its address in p->ptrs[K[i]];
                p = the new nonleaf;
            while (K[i] == K_L[i++]);
            create a leaf containing K and put its address in p->ptrs[K[i]];
            if (K_L[i] == '\0')
                set the end-of-word marker in p to true;
            else create a leaf containing K_L and put its address in p->ptrs[K_L[i]];
        else p = p->ptrs[K[i++]];
```

The inner **do** loop in this algorithm is needed when a prefix in the word **K** and in the word **K_L** is longer than the number of nodes in the path leading to the current node **p**. For example, before "REP" is inserted in the trie in Figure 7.29, the word "REAR" is stored in a leaf corresponding to the letter "R" of the root of the trie. If "REP" is now being inserted, it is not enough to replace this leaf by a nonleaf, since the second letters of both these words are the same letter "E." Hence, one more nonleaf has to be created on the third level of the trie and two leaves containing the words "REAR" and "REP" are attached to this nonleaf.

If we compare tries with binary search trees, we see that for tries, the order in which keys are inserted is irrelevant, whereas this order determines the shape of binary search trees. However, tries can be skewed by words, or rather, by the type of prefixes in words being inserted. The length of the longest identical prefix in two words determines the height of the trie. Therefore, the height of the trie is equal to the length of the longest prefix common to two words plus one (for a level to discriminate between the words with this prefix) plus one (for the level of leaves). The trie in Figure 7.29 has height five since the longest identical prefix, "ARE," is merely three letters long.

The main problem tries pose is the amount of space they require; a substantial amount of this space is basically wasted. Many nodes may have only a couple of nonnull pointers, and yet the remaining 25 pointers must reside in memory. There is a burning need to decrease the amount of required space.

One way to reduce the size of a node is by storing only those pointers which are actually in use, as in Figure 7.30 (Briandais 1959). However, the introduced flexibility concerning the size of each node somewhat complicates the implementation. Such tries can be implemented in the spirit of 2–4 tree implementation. All sibling nodes can be put on a linked list accessible from the parent node, as in Figure 7.31. One node of the previous trie corresponds now to a linked list. This means that random access of pointers stored in arrays is no longer possible, and the linked lists have to be scanned sequentially although not exhaustively, since the alphabetical order is most likely maintained. The space

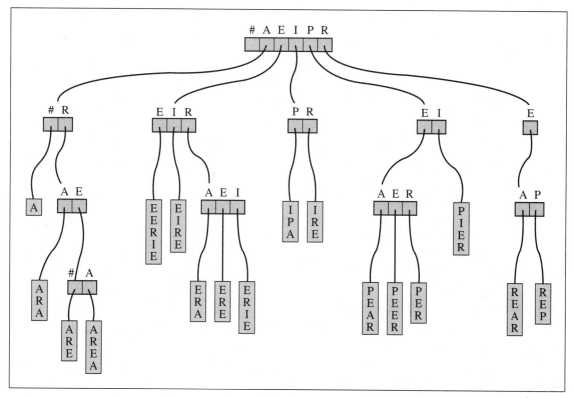

Figure 7.30: **The same trie as in Figure 7.29 with all unused pointer fields removed.**

requirements are not insignificant, either, since each node now contains two pointers which may require two or four bytes if not more, depending on the system.

Another way to reduce the space requirements is by changing the way words are tested (Rotwitt, Maine 1971). A trie *a tergo* can be built in which the reverses of words are inserted. In our example the number of nodes is about the same, but a trie *a tergo* representation for such words as "logged," "loggerhead," "loggia," and "logging" would have leaves on the third level, not on the seventh, as in a forward trie. Admittedly, for some frequently used endings, such as "tion," "ism," and "ics," the problem would reappear.

A variety of other orders can be considered, and checking every second character proved to be very useful (Bourne, Ford 1961), but solving the problem of an optimal order cannot be solved in its generality, since the problem turns out to be extremely complex (Comer, Sethi 1977).

Another way to save space is to compress the trie. One method creates a large cell-array out of all the arrays in all nonleaf nodes by interleaving these arrays so that the pointers remain intact. The starting positions of these arrays are recorded in the encompassing cell-array. For example, the three nodes shown in Figure 7.32a containing pointers p_1 through p_7 to other nodes of the trie (including leaves) are put one by one into a cell-array in a nonconflicting way as in Figure 7.32b. The problem is, how to do that efficiently time-wise

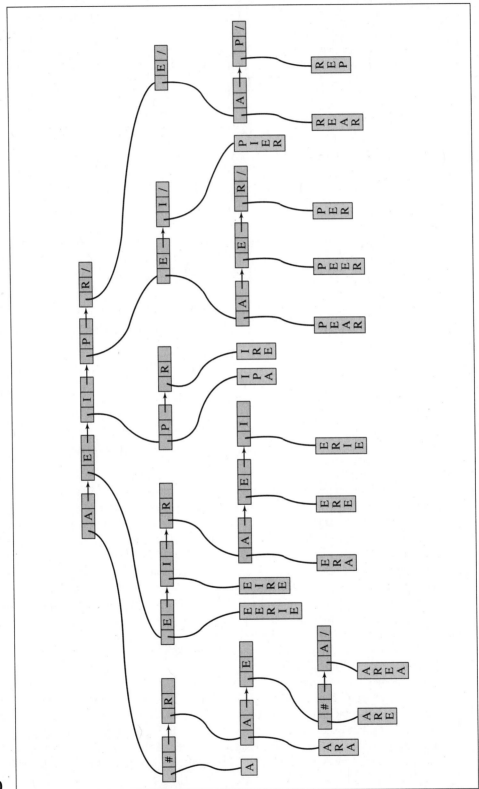

Figure 7.31: The trie from Figure 7.30 implemented as a binary tree.

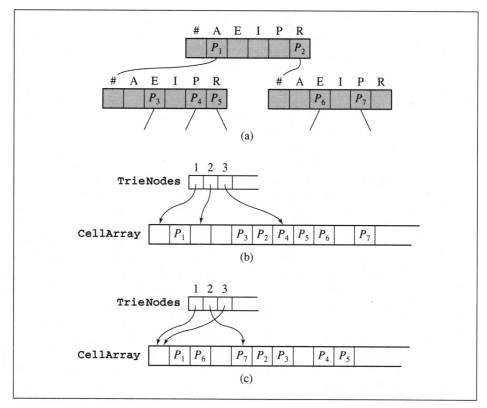

Figure 7.32: **A part of a trie before (a) and after (b) compression using the** `CompressTrie()` **algorithm and (c) after compressing it in an optimal way.**

and space-wise so that the algorithm is fast and the resulting array occupies substantially less space than all nonleaf nodes combined. In this example, all three nodes require $3 * 6 = 18$ cells, and the cell-array has 11 cells so compression rate is $(18 - 11)/18$, 39%. However, if the cells are stored as in Figure 7.32c, the compression rate is $(18 - 10)/18$, 44%.

It turns out that the algorithm which compresses the trie is exponential in the number of nodes, and inapplicable for large tries. Other algorithms may not render the optimal compression rate, but are faster (cf. Al-Suwaiyel, Horowitz 1984). One such algorithm is `CompressTree()`.

```
CompressTrie()
    set to null all nodeNum*cellNum cells of cellArray;
    for each node i
        for each position j of cellArray
            if after superimposing node on cellArray[j],...,cellArray[j+cellNum-1]
                no cell containing a pointer is superimposed on a cell with a pointer
                copy pointer cells from node to corresponding cells starting from cellArray[j];
                record j in trieNodes as the position of node in cellArray;
                break;
```

This is the algorithm that was applied to the trie in Figure 7.32a to render the arrays in Figure 7.32b. Searching such a compressed trie is similar to searching a regular trie. However, node accesses are mediated through the array **trieNodes**. If $node_1$ refers to $node_2$, the position of $node_2$ has to be found in this array and then $node_2$ can be accessed in the cell-array.

The problem with using a compressed trie is that the search can lead us astray. For instance, a search for a word starting with the letter P is immediately discontinued in the trie in Figure 7.32a, since the pointer field corresponding with this letter in the root node is null. On the other hand, in the compressed version of the same trie (Figure 7.32b), in the field corresponding with letter P, pointer P_3 can be found. But the misguided path is detected only after later encountering a null pointer field or, after reaching a leaf, after comparing the key in this leaf with the key used in searching.

One more way to compress tries is by creating a C-trie which is a bit-version of the original trie (Maly 1976). In this method, the nodes of one level of the C-trie are stored in consecutive locations of memory, and the addresses of the first nodes of each level are stored in a table of addresses. Information stored in particular nodes allows us to access the children of these nodes by computing the offsets from these nodes to their children.

Each node has four fields: a leaf/nonleaf flag, end-of-word on/off field (which functions as our sharp sign field), a K-field of *CellNum* bits corresponding to the cells with characters, and a C-field which gives the number of 1s in all the K-fields which are on the same level and precede this node. The latter integer is the number of nodes in the next level preceding the first child of this node.

The leaves store actual keys (or suffixes of keys) if they fit into the K-field+C-field. If not, the key is stored in some table and the leaf contains a reference to its position in this table. The end-of-word field is used to distinguish between these two cases. A fragment of the C-trie version of the trie from Figure 7.29 is shown in Figure 7.33. All nodes are the same size. It is assumed that the leaf can store up to three characters.

To search a key in the C-trie, the offsets have to be computed very carefully. Here is an outline of the algorithm:

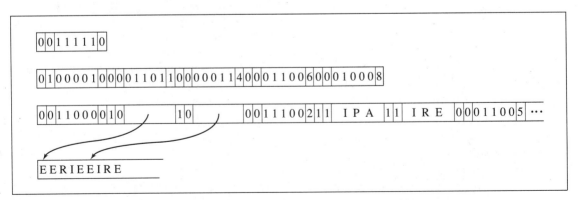

Figure 7.33: **A fragment of the C-trie representation of the trie from Figure 7.29.**

```
CTrieSearch(K)
    for (i = 1, p = the root; ; i++)
        if p is a leaf
            if K is equal to the key(p)
                return success;
            else return failure;
        else if (K[i] == '\0')
            if end-of-word field is on
                return success;
            else return failure;
        else if the bit corresponding to character K[i] is off
            return failure;
        else p = address(the first node of level i+1)
                + C-field(p)* size(one node) // to skip all children of nodes
                                             // in front of p on level i;
                + (number of 1-bits in K-field(p) to the left of the bit  // to skip
                  corresponding to K[i])* size(one node) // some children of p;
```

For example, to find "EERIE" in the C-trie in Figure 7.33, we first check in the root the bit corresponding to the first letter, "E." Since the bit is on and the root is not a leaf, we go to the second level. On the second level the address of the node to be tested is determined by adding the address of the first node on this level to the length of one node, the first, in order to skip it. The bit of this nonleaf node corresponding to the second letter of our word, also an "E," is on, so we proceed to the third level. The address of the node to be tested is determined by adding the address of the first node of the third level to the size of one node (the first node of level three). We now access a leaf node with the end-of-word field set to 0. The table of words is accessed to make a comparison between the key looked for and the key in the table.

The compression is significant. One node of the original trie of 27 pointers of two bytes each occupies 54 bytes. One node of the C-trie requires $1 + 1 + 27 + 16 = 45$ bits which can be stored in 8 bytes. But it is not without a price. This algorithm requires putting nodes of one level tightly together, but storing one node at a time in memory by using **new** does not guarantee that the nodes are put in consecutive locations, especially in a multiuser environment. Therefore, the nodes from one level have to be generated first in temporary storage and only then can a chunk of memory be requested which is large enough to accommodate all these nodes. This problem also indicates that the C-trie is ill-suited for dynamic updates. If the trie is generated only once, the C-trie is an excellent variation to be utilized. If, however, the trie needs to be frequently updated, this technique for trie compression should be abandoned.

■ 7.3 CONCLUDING REMARKS

The survey of multiway trees in this chapter is by no means exhaustive. The number of different types of multiway trees is very large. Our intention is to highlight the variety of uses to which these trees can be applied and show how the same type of tree can be applied to different areas. Of particular interest is a B-tree with all its variations. B^+-trees are commonly used in the implementation of indexes in today's relational databases. They allow very fast random access to the data, and they also allow fast sequential processing of the data.

The application of B-trees is not limited to processing information from secondary storage, although it was the original motivation in introducing these trees. A variant of B-trees, 2–4 trees, although unsuitable for processing information in secondary storage, turns out to be very useful in processing information in memory.

Also of particular use are tries, a different type of tree. With many variations, they have a vast scope of applications, and our case study illustrates one very useful application of tries.

■ 7.4   CASE STUDY: SPELLING CHECKER

An indispensable utility for any word processor is a spelling checker which allows the user to find as many spelling mistakes as possible. Depending on the sophistication of the spelling checker, the user may even see possible corrections. Spelling checkers are used mostly in an interactive environment; the user can invoke them at any time when using the word processor, make corrections on the fly, and exit even before processing the entire file. This requires writing a word processing program and in addition to it, a spelling checker module. This case study focuses on the use of tries. Therefore, the spelling checker will be a stand-alone program to be used outside a word processor. It will process a text file in batch mode not allowing word-by-word corrections after possible errors are detected.

The core of a spelling checker is a data structure allowing efficient access to words in a dictionary. Such a dictionary most likely has thousands of words so access has to be very fast to process a text file in a reasonable amount of time. Out of many possible data structures, the trie is chosen to store the dictionary words. The trie is first created after the spelling checker is invoked and afterwards the actual spelling checking takes place.

For a large number of dictionary words, the size of the trie is very important since the trie should reside in main memory without recourse to virtual memory. But as we have already observed in this chapter, tries with fixed length nodes, as in Figure 7.29, are too wasteful. In most cases only a fraction of the positions in each node is utilized, and the farther away from the root, the smaller this fraction becomes (the root may be the only node with 26 children). Creating linked lists corresponding to all utilized letters for each node reduces wasted space, as in Figure 7.31. This approach has two disadvantages: the space required for the pointer fields can be substantial and the linked lists force us to use sequential search. An improvement over the last solution is to reserve only as much space as required by the letters used by each node without resorting to the use of linked lists. An ideal solution would be a flexible array, but this data structure is lacking in C++. Therefore, we will use pseudo-flexible arrays by substituting larger arrays for existing arrays, copying the content of the old arrays to the new, and returning the old arrays to the operating system.

The key to the use of such pseudo-flexible arrays is the implementation of a node. A node is a **struct** that includes the following fields: a leaf/nonleaf flag, an end-of-word flag, a pointer to a string, and a pointer to an array of pointers to structures of the same category. Figure 7.34 contains the trie utilizing the nodes of this structure. If a string attached

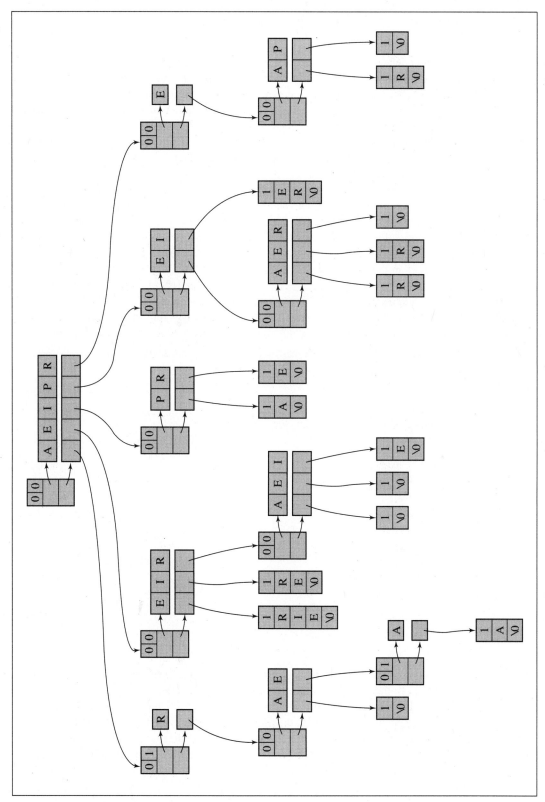

Figure 7.34: **An implementation of a trie that uses pseudo-flexible arrays. The trie has the same words as the trie in Figure 7.29.**

255

to a certain node has to be extended, a new string is created which contains the contents of the old string with a new letter inserted into the proper position, a function performed by `AddCell()`. The letters in each node are kept in alphabetical order.

The function `TrieInsert()` is an implementation of the algorithm *TrieInsert* discussed earlier in this chapter. Since the position of each letter may vary from one node to another, this position has to be determined each time, a function performed by `Position()`. Should a letter be absent in a node, `Position()` returns −1 which allows `TrieInsert()` to undertake the proper action.

Also, the discussion of tries in this chapter assumed that the leaves of the tries store full keys. This is not necessary, since the prefixes of all words are implicitly stored in the trie and can be reconstructed by garnering all the letters on the path leading to the leaf. For example, in order to access the leaf with the word "ERIE," two nonleaves have to be passed through pointers corresponding to the letters "E" and "R." Therefore, it is enough to store the suffix "IE" in the leaf instead of the entire word "ERIE." By doing this, only 13 letters of suffixes of these words have to be retained in these leaves out of the 58 letters stored in all leaves of the trie in Figure 7.29, a substantial improvement.

We also included the function `TrieSideView()` which prints the content of a trie sideways. The output generated by this function when applied to the trie in Figure 7.34 is as follows:

```
        >>REP|
        >>REA|R
    >>PI|ER
        >>PER|
        >>PEE|R
        >>PEA|R
    >>IR|E
    >>IP|A
        >>ERI|E
        >>ERE|
        >>ERA|
    >>EI|RE
    >>EE|RIE
            >>AREA|
           >>>ARE|
          >>ARA|
    >>>A|
```

Three angle brackets indicate words for which the **endOfWord** flag has been set in the corresponding node. The words with two angle brackets have leaves in the trie. Sometimes these leaves contain only the character '\0'. The vertical bar separates the prefix reconstructed when scanning the trie from the suffix which was extracted from a leaf.

Spelling checking works in a straightforward fashion by examining each word of a text file and printing out all misspelled words along with the line numbers where the misspelled words were found. Figure 7.35 contains the complete code of the spelling checker.

```
//*********************    trie.h    *********************************

const unsigned int leaf = 1u, yes = 1u;

class Trie {
public:
        Trie() : notFound(-1) { }
        Trie(char*);
        void TrieSideView()
              { *prefix = '\0'; TrieSideViewAux(0,root,prefix); }
        void TrieInsert(char*);
        WordFound(char*);
private:
        struct NonLeafNode {
                unsigned int kind      : 1;
                unsigned int endOfWord : 1;
                char *letters;
                NonLeafNode **ptrs;
                NonLeafNode() { }
                NonLeafNode(char);
        } *root;

        struct LeafNode {
                unsigned int kind : 1;
                char *word;
                LeafNode() { }
                LeafNode(unsigned int,char*);
        };

        const int notFound;
        char prefix[80];

        int  Position(NonLeafNode*,char);
        void AddCell(char,NonLeafNode*,int);
        void CreateLeaf(char,char*,NonLeafNode*);
        void TrieSideViewAux(int,NonLeafNode*,char*);
};
```

Figure 7.35: **Implementation of a spelling checker using tries.**   **continued**

```cpp
//*********************** trie.cpp ******************************

#include <iostream.h>
#include <stdlib.h>
#include <string.h>
#include "trie.h"
Trie::LeafNode::LeafNode(unsigned int k, char *suffix)
{
    word = new char[strlen(suffix)+1];
    if (word == 0) {
        cerr << "Out of memory2.\n" << endl;
        exit(1);
    }
    strcpy(word,suffix);
    kind = k;
}


Trie::NonLeafNode::NonLeafNode(char ch)
{
    ptrs = new NonLeafNode*;
    letters = new char[2];
    if (ptrs == 0 || letters == 0) {
        cerr << "Out of memory3.\n" << endl;
        exit(1);
    }
    kind = !leaf;
    endOfWord = !yes;
    *ptrs = 0;
    *letters = ch;
    *(letters+1) = '\0';
}


Trie::Trie(char* word) : notFound(-1)
{
    root = new NonLeafNode(*word); // initialize the root
    CreateLeaf(*word,word+1,root); // to avoid later tests;
}
```

Figure 7.35: **Implementation of a spelling checker using tries.**   **continued**

```
void
Trie::TrieSideViewAux (int depth, NonLeafNode *p, char *prefix)
{   register int i;                  // assumption: the root is not a leaf
                                     // and it is not null;

    if (p->kind == leaf) {
        LeafNode *lf = (LeafNode*) p;
        for (i = 1; i <= depth; i++)
            cout << "   ";
        cout << " >>" << prefix << "|" << lf->word << endl;
    }
    else {
        for (i = strlen(p->letters)-1; i >= 0; i--)
            if (*(p->ptrs + i)) {                      // add the letter
                prefix[depth] = *(p->letters + i); // corresponding to
                prefix[depth+1] = '\0';                // position i to prefix;
                TrieSideViewAux(depth+1,*(p->ptrs+i),prefix);
            }
        if (p->endOfWord == yes) {
            prefix[depth] = '\0';
            for (i = 1; i <= depth+1; i++)
                cout << "   ";
            cout << ">>>" << prefix << "|\n";
        }
    }
}


int
Trie::Position(NonLeafNode *p, char ch)
{   register int i;

    for (i = 0; i < strlen(p->letters) && *(p->letters + i) != ch; i++);
    if (i < strlen(p->letters))
        return i;
    else return notFound;
}


int
Trie::WordFound (char *word)
```

Figure 7.35: **Implementation of a spelling checker using tries.**   **continued**

```
{    NonLeafNode *p = root;
     LeafNode *lf;
     int pos;

     while (1)
         if (p->kind == leaf) {            // node p is a leaf
             lf = (LeafNode*) p;           // where the matching
             if (!strcmp(word,lf->word))   // suffix of word
                 return 1;                 // should be found;
             else return 0;
         }
         else if (*word == 0)              // the end of word has
             if (p->endOfWord == yes)      // to correspond with
                 return 1;                 // the endOfWord marker
             else return 0;                // in node p set to yes;
         else if ((pos = Position(p,*word)) != notFound &&
                  *(p->ptrs + pos)) {      // continue
             p = *(p->ptrs + pos);         // path, if possible,
             word++;
         }
         else
         return 0;                         // otherwise failure;
}


void
Trie::AddCell(char ch, NonLeafNode *p, int stop)
{    int i;
     int len = strlen(p->letters);
     char *s = p->letters;
     NonLeafNode **tmp = p->ptrs;

     p->letters = new char[len+2];
     p->ptrs    = (NonLeafNode**) new char[(len+1)*sizeof(NonLeafNode*)];
     if (p->letters == 0 || p->ptrs == 0) {
     }
     for (i = 0; i < len+1; i++)
         *(p->ptrs + i) = 0;
         cerr << "Out of memory1.\n" << endl;
         exit(1);
```

Figure 7.35: **Implementation of a spelling checker using tries.**   **continued**

```
          if (stop < len)                    // if ch does not follow all letters in p,
              for (i = len; i >= stop+1; i--) { // copy from tmp letters > ch;
                  *(p->ptrs    + i) = *(tmp + i-1);
                  *(p->letters + i) = *(s   + i-1);
              }
          *(p->letters + stop) = ch;
          for (i = stop-1; i >= 0; i--) {              // and letters < ch;
              *(p->ptrs    + i) = *(tmp + i);
              *(p->letters + i) = *(s   + i);
          }
          *(p->letters + len+1) = '\0';
          delete [] s;
      }


      void
      Trie::CreateLeaf(char ch, char *suffix, NonLeafNode *p)
      {   int pos = Position(p,ch);
          LeafNode *lf1 = new LeafNode(leaf,suffix);

          if (pos == notFound) {
              for (pos = 0; pos < strlen(p->letters) &&
                            *(p->letters + pos) < ch; pos++);
              AddCell(ch,p,pos);
          }
          *(p->ptrs + pos) = (NonLeafNode*) lf1;
      }


      void
      Trie::TrieInsert (char *word)
      {   NonLeafNode *p = root;
          LeafNode *lf2;
          int offset, pos;

          while (1) {
              pos = Position(p,*word);
              if (*word == '\0') {                 // if the end of word reached,
                  p->endOfWord = yes;              // set endOfWord to yes;
                  return;
```

Figure 7.35: **Implementation of a spelling checker using tries.** **continued**

```
        }                                   // if position in p indicated
    else if (pos == notFound) {      // by the first letter of word
        CreateLeaf(*word,word+1,p);// does not exist, create
        return;                          // a leaf and store in it the
    }                                    // unprocessed suffix of word;
    else if (pos != notFound &&      // if position *word is
    (*(p->ptrs + pos))->kind == leaf) {      // occupied by a leaf,
        lf2 = (LeafNode*) *(p->ptrs + pos); // hold this leaf;
        offset = 0;
        // create as many non-leaves as the length of identical
        // prefix of word and the string in the leaf (for cell 'R',
        // leaf 'EP' and word 'REAR', two such nodes are created;
        do {
            pos = Position(p,*(word+offset));
            *(p->ptrs + pos) = new NonLeafNode(*(word+offset+1));
            p = *(p->ptrs + pos);
            offset++;
        } while (*(word + offset) == *(lf2->word + offset-1));
        offset--;
        CreateLeaf(*(word+offset+1),word+offset+2,p);
        if (*(lf2->word+offset) == '\0') // if the end of word reached,
            p->endOfWord = yes;           // add endOfWord marker to p;
        // else, assign less space by one char to suffix of word;
        else CreateLeaf(*(lf2->word+offset),lf2->word+offset+1,p);
        delete [] lf2->word;
        delete lf2;
        return;
    }
    else {
        p = *(p->ptrs + pos);
        word++;
    }
    }
}
}


//********************* spellCheck.cpp *******************

#include <iostream.h>
#include <fstream.h>
```

Figure 7.35: **Implementation of a spelling checker using tries.** **continued**

```
#include <string.h>
#include <stdlib.h>
#include <ctype.h>
#include "trie.h"

char *
strupr(char *s)
{   char *ss = s;

    for ( ; *s = toupper(*s); s++);
    return ss;
}


main(int argc, char* argv[])
{   char fileName[15], s[80], ch;
    int i, lineNum = 1;

    ifstream dictionary("dictionary");
    if (dictionary.fail()) {
        cerr << "Cannot open 'dictionary'\n";
        return 1;
    }

    dictionary >> s;        // initialize
    Trie trie(strupr(s)); //    root;

    while (!dictionary.eof()) {  // initialize trie;
        dictionary >> s;
        if (*s)
            trie.TrieInsert(strupr(s));
    }

    cout << " SIDE VIEW:\n"; trie.TrieSideView();

    if (argc != 2) {
        cout << "Enter a file name: ";
        cin  >> fileName;
    }
    else strcpy(fileName,argv[1]);
    ifstream textFile(fileName);
```

Figure 7.35: **Implementation of a spelling checker using tries.**   **continued**

```
    if (textFile.fail()) {
        cerr << "Cannot open " << fileName << endl;
        return 1;
    }
    cout << "Misspelled words:\n";
    textFile.get(ch);
    while (!textFile.eof()) {
        if (ch == '\n')
            lineNum++;
        while (1)
            if (!textFile.eof() && !isalpha(ch)) // skip non-letters
                textFile.get(ch);
            else break;
        if (textFile.eof())          // spaces at the end of textFile;
            break;
        for (i = 0; !textFile.eof() && isalpha(ch); i++) {
            s[i] = toupper(ch);
            textFile.get(ch);
        }
        s[i] = '\0';
        if (!trie.WordFound(s))
            cout << s << " on line " << lineNum << endl;
    }
    dictionary.close();
    textFile.close();
    return 0;
}
```

Figure 7.35: **Implementation of a spelling checker using tries.**

■ 7.5 EXERCISES

1. What is the maximum number of nodes in a multiway tree of height h?

2. How many keys can a B-tree of order m and of height h hold?

3. Write a procedure which prints out the contents of a B-tree in ascending order.

4. The root of a B*-tree requires special attention since it has no sibling. A split does not render two nodes two-thirds full plus a new root with one key. Suggest some solutions to this problem.

5. Are B-trees immune to the order of the incoming data? Construct B-trees of order 3 (two keys per node) first for the sequence 1, 5, 3, 2, 4, and then for the sequence 1, 2, 3, 4, 5. Is it better to initialize B-trees with ordered data or with data in random order?

6. Draw all ten different B-trees of order 3 which can store 15 keys, and make a table that for each of these trees shows the number of nodes and the average number of visited nodes (Rosenberg, Snyder 1981). What generalization can you make about them? Would this table indicate that 1, the smaller the number of nodes, the smaller the average number of visited nodes, and 2, the smaller the average number of visited nodes, the smaller the number of nodes? What characteristics of the B-tree should we concentrate upon to make them more efficient?

7. In all our considerations concerning B-trees, we assumed that the keys are unique. However, this does not have to be the case since multiple occurrences of the same key in a B-tree do not violate the B-tree property. If these keys refer to different objects in the data file (e.g., if the key is a name, and many people can have the same name), how would you implement such data file references?

8. What is the maximum height of a B^+-tree with n keys?

9. Occasionally, in a simple prefix B^+-tree, a separator can be as large as a key in a leaf. For example, if the last key in one leaf is "Herman" and the first key in the next leaf is "Hermann," then "Hermann" must be chosen as a separator in the parent of these leaves. Suggest a procedure to enforce the shorter separator.

10. Write a function that determines the shortest separator for two keys in a simple prefix B^+-tree.

11. Would it be a good idea to use abbreviated forms of prefixes in the leaves of prefix B^+-trees?

12. If in two different positions, i and j, $i < j$ of a leaf in a bit-tree, and two D-bits are found such that $D_j = D_i$, what is the condition on at least one of the D-bits D_k for $i < k < j$?

13. If key K_i is deleted from a leaf of a bit-tree, then the D-bit between K_{i-1} and K_{i+1} has to be modified. What is the value of this D-bit if the values D_i and D_{i+1} are known? Make deletions in the leaf in Figure 7.17 to make an educated guess and then generalize this observation. In making a generalization, consider two cases: 1, $D_i < D_{i+1}$, and 2, $D_i > D_{i+1}$.

14. Write an algorithm that, for an R-tree, finds all entries in the leaves whose rectangles overlap a search rectangle R.

15. In the discussion of B-trees, which are comparable in efficiency to binary search trees, why are only B-trees of small order used, and not B-trees of large order?

16. What is the worst case of inserting a key into a 2–4 tree?

17. What is the complexity of the `CompressTrie()` algorithm in the worst case?

18. Can the leaves of the trie compressed with `CompressTrie()` still have abbreviated versions of the words, namely parts which are not included in the nonterminal nodes?

19. In the examples of tries analyzed in this chapter, we dealt only with 26 capital letters. A more realistic setting includes lowercase letters as well. However, some words require a capital letter at the beginning (names), and some require the entire word to be capitalized (acronyms). How can we solve this problem without including both lowercase and capital letters in the nodes?

20. A variant of a trie is a *digital tree* which processes information on the level of bits. Since there are only two bits, only two outcomes are possible. Digital trees are binary.

For example, to test whether the word "BOOK" is in the tree, we do not compare the first letter, "B," with the key in the root, by the first bit, 0, of the first letter (ASCII(B) = 01000010), on the second level, the second bit, and so on before we get to the second letter. Is it be a good idea to use a digital tree for a spelling checking program, as was discussed in the case study?

■ 7.6 PROGRAMMING ASSIGNMENTS

1. Extend our spelling checking program to suggest the proper spelling of a misspelled word. Consider these types of misspellings: changing the order of letters (copmuter), omitting a letter (computr), adding a letter (compueter), dittography, i.e., repeating a letter (computter), and changing a letter (compurer). For example, if the letter i is exchanged with the letter $i + 1$, then the level i of the trie should be processed before level $i + 1$.

2. A *point quadtree* is a 4-way tree used to represent points on a plane (Samet 1989). A node contains a pair of coordinates (*latitude,longitude*) and pointers to four children which represent four quadrants, NW, NE, SW, and SE. These quadrants are generated by the intersection of the vertical and horizontal lines passing through point (*lat,lon*) of the plane. Write a program which accepts the names of cities and their geographical locations (*lat,lon*) and inserts them into the quadtree. Then, the program should give the names of all cities located within distance d from a location (*Lat,Lon*), or, alternatively, within distance d from a city C.

   Figure 7.36 contains an example. Locations on the map in Figure 7.36a are inserted into the quadtree in Figure 7.36b in the order indicated by the encircled numbers shown next to the city names. For instance, when inserting Pittsburgh into the quadtree, we check in which direction it is with respect to the root. The root stores the coordinates of Louisville, and Pittsburgh is NE from it, that is, it belongs to the second child of the root. But this child already stores a city, Washington. Therefore, we ask the same question concerning Pittsburgh with respect to the current node, the second child of the root: In which direction with respect to this city is Pittsburgh? This time the answer is NW. Therefore, we go to the first child of the current node. The child is a null node, and therefore the Pittsburgh node can be inserted here.

3. Figure 7.29 indicates one source of inefficiency for tries, the path to "REAR" and "REP" leads through a node which has just one child. For longer identical prefixes, the number of such nodes can be even longer. Implement a spelling checker with a variation of the trie, called the *multiway Patricia tree* (Morrison 1968),[3] which curtails the paths in the trie by avoiding nodes with only one child. It does this by indicating for each branch how many characters should be skipped to make a test. For example, a trie from Figure 7.37a is transformed into a Patricia tree in Figure 7.37b. The paths leading to the four words with prefix "LOGG" are shortened at the cost of recording in each node the number of characters to be omitted starting from the current position in a string. Now, because certain characters are not tested along the way, the final test should be between a key searched for and the *entire* key found in a specific leaf.

---

[3]The original Patricia tree was a binary tree and the tests were made on the level of bits.

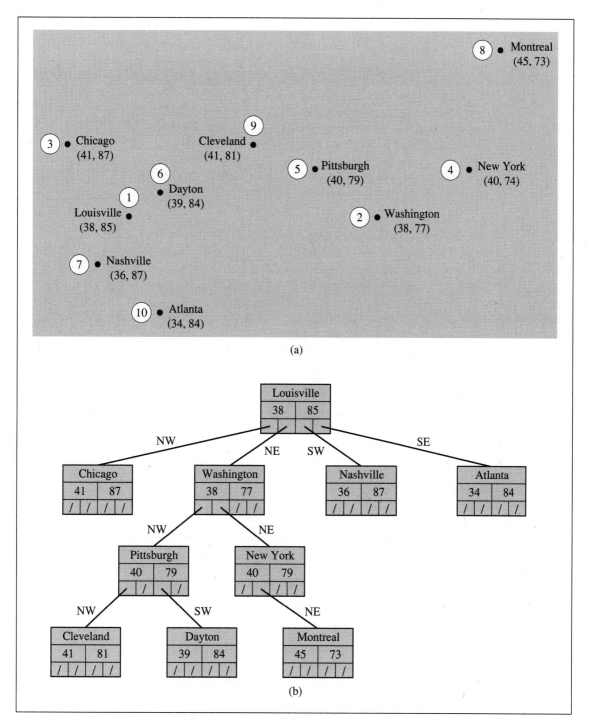

(a)

(b)

Figure 7.36: **A map indicating coordinates of some cities (a) and a quadtree containing the same (b).**

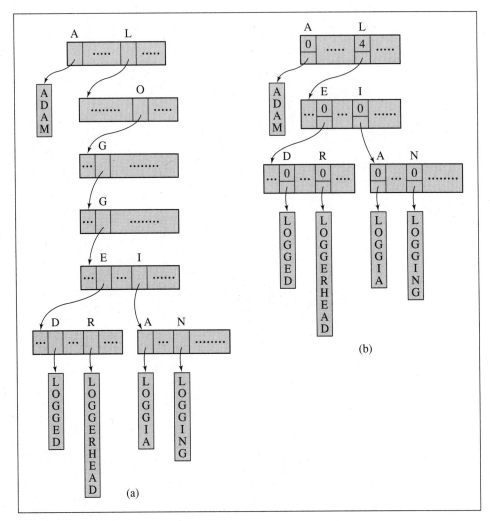

Figure 7.37: **A trie with words having long identical prefixes (a) and a Patricia tree with the same words (b).**

BIBLIOGRAPHY

B-Trees

[1]   Bayer, R., "Symmetric Binary B-trees: Data Structures and Maintenance Algorithms," *Acta Informatica* 1 (1972), 290–306.

[2]   Bayer, R. and McCreight E., "Organization and Maintenance of Large Ordered Indexes," *Acta Informatica* 1 (1972), 173–189.

[3]   Bayer, Rudolf and Unterauer, Karl, "Prefix B-trees," *ACM Transactions on Database Systems* 2 (1977), 11–26.

[4]   Comer, Douglas, "The Ubiquitous B-tree," *Computing Surveys* 11 (1979), 121–137.

[5]   Ferguson, David E., "Bit-tree: A Data Structure for Fast File Processing," *Communications of the ACM* 35 (1992), No. 6, 114–120.

[6]   Folk, Michael J. and Zoellick, Bill, *File Structure: A Conceptual Toolkit*, Reading, MA: Addison-Wesley 1987, Chs. 9, 10.

[7]   Guttman, Antonin, "R-trees: A Dynamic Index Structure for Spatial Searching," *ACM SIGMOD '84 Proc. of Annual Meeting, SIGMOD Record* 14 (1984), 47–57 [also in Stonebraker, Michael (ed.), *Readings in Database Systems*, San Mateo, CA: Kaufmann, 1988, 599–609.]

[8]   Johnson, Theodore and Shasha, Dennis, "B-trees with Inserts and Deletes: Why Free-at-Empty Is Better than Merge-at-Half," *Journal of Computer and System Sciences* 47 (1993) 45–76.

[9]   McCreight, Edward M., "Pagination of B*-trees with Variable-length Records," *Communications of the ACM* 20 (1977), 670–674.

[10] Rosenberg, Arnold L. and Snyder, Lawrence, "Time- and Space-Optimality in B-trees," *ACM Transactions on Database Systems* 6 (1981), 174–193.

[11] Sedgewick, Robert, *Algorithms*, Reading, MA: Addison-Wesley, 1988, Ch. 15.

[12] Sellis, Timos, Roussopoulos, Nick, and Faloutsos, Christos, "The R$^+$-tree: A Dynamic Index for Multi-dimensional Objects," *Proceedings of the 13th Conference on Very Large Databases* (1987), 507–518.

[13] Stonebraker, M., Sellis, T. and Hanson, E., "Analysis of Rule Indexing Implementations in Data Base Systems," *Proceedings of the First International Conference on Expert Database Systems*, Charleston, 1986, 353–364.

[14] Wedekind, H., "On the Selection of Access Paths in a Data Base System," in J. W. Klimbie, K. L. Koffeman (eds.), *Data Base Management*, Amsterdam: North-Holland 1974, 385–397.

[15] Yao, Andrew Chi-Chih, "On Random 2-3 Trees," *Acta Informatica* 9 (1978), 159–170.

Tries

[16] Al-Suwaiyel, M. and Horowitz, E., "Algorithms for Trie Compaction," *ACM Transactions on Database Systems* 9 (1984), 243–263.

[17] Bourne, Charles P. and Ford, Donald F., "A Study of Methods for Systematically Abbreviating English Words and Names," *Journal of the ACM* 8 (1961), 538–552.

[18] de la Briandais, R., "File Searching Using Variable Length Keys," *Proceedings of the Western Joint Conference*, 1959, 295–298.

[19] Comer, Douglas and Sethi, Ravi, "The Complexity of Trie Index Construction," *Journal of the ACM* 24 (1977), 428–440.

[20] Fredkin, Edward, "Trie Memory," *Communications of the ACM* 3 (1960), 490–499.

[21] Maly, Kurt, "Compressed Tries," *Communications of the ACM* 19 (1976), 409–415.

[22] Morrison, Donald R., "Patricia Trees," *Journal of the ACM* 15 (1968), 514–534.

[23] Rotwitt, T. and de Maine, P. A. D., "Storage Optimization of Tree Structured Files Representing Descriptor Sets," *Proceedings of the ACM SIGFIDET Workshop on Data Description, Access and Control*, New York, 1971, 207–217.

Quadtrees

[24] Finkel, R. A., Bentley, J. L., "Quad Trees: A Data Structure for Retrieval on Composite Keys," *Acta Informatica* 4 (1974), 1–9.

[25] Samet, Hanan, *"The Design and Analysis of Spatial Data Structures,"* Reading, MA: Addison-Wesley, 1989.

8

GRAPHS

In spite of the flexibility of trees and the many different tree applications, trees, by their nature, have one limitation, namely, they can only represent relations of hierarchical type, like relations between parent and child. Other relations are only represented indirectly, such as the relation of being a sibling. A generalization of a tree, a *graph*, is a data structure in which this limitation is lifted. Intuitively, a graph is a collection of vertices (or nodes) and the connections between them. Generally, no restriction is imposed on the number of vertices in the graph or on the number of connections one vertex can have to other vertices. Figure 8.1 contains examples of graphs. Graphs are versatile data structures that can represent a large number of different situations and events from diverse domains. Graph theory has grown into a sophisticated area of mathematics and computer science in the last 200 years since it was first studied. Many results are of theoretical interest, but in this chapter, some selected results of interest to computer scientists will be presented. Before discussing different algorithms and their applications, several definitions need to be introduced.

A *simple graph* $G = (V, E)$ consists of a nonempty set V of *vertices* and a possibly empty set E of *edges*, each edge being a set of two vertices from V. The number of vertices and edges is denoted by $|V|$ and $|E|$, respectively. A *directed graph*, or a *digraph*, $G = (V, E)$, consists of a nonempty set V of vertices and a set E of edges (also called *arcs*), where each edge is a pair of vertices from V. The difference is that one edge of a simple graph is of the form $\{v_i, v_j\}$ and for such an edge, $\{v_i, v_j\} = \{v_j, v_i\}$. In a digraph, each edge is of the form (v_i, v_j) and in this case $(v_i, v_j) \neq (v_j, v_i)$. Unless necessary, this distinction in notation will be disregarded and an edge between vertices v_i and v_j will be referred to as $edge(v_iv_j)$.

These definitions are restrictive in that they do not allow for two vertices to have more than one edge. A *multigraph* is a graph in which two vertices can be joined by multiple edges. Geometric interpretation is very simple (see Figure 8.1e). Formally, the definition is as follows: A multigraph $G = (V, E, f)$ is composed of a set of vertices V, a set of edges E, and a function $f : E \rightarrow \{\{v_i, v_j\} : v_i, v_j \in V \text{ and } v_i \neq v_j\}$. A *pseudograph* is a multigraph with the condition $v_i \neq v_j$ removed, which allows for *loops* to occur; in a pseudograph, a vertex can be joined with itself by an edge (Figure 8.1f).

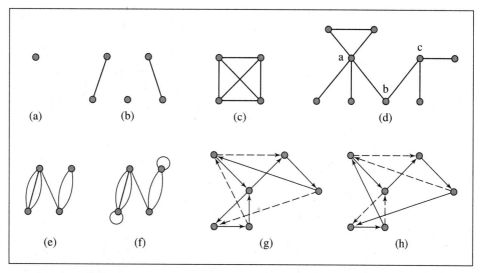

Figure 8.1: **Examples of graphs: (a)–(d) simple graphs; (c) a complete graph K_4; (e) a multigraph; (f) a pseudograph; (g) a circuit in a digraph; (h) a cycle in the digraph.**

A *path* from v_1 to v_n is a sequence of edges $edge(v_1 v_2), edge(v_2 v_3), \ldots, edge(v_{n-1} v_n)$ and is denoted as path $v_1, v_2, v_3, \ldots, v_{n-1}, v_n$. If $v_1 = v_n$ and no edge is repeated, then the path is called a *circuit* (Figure 8.1g). If all vertices in a circuit are different, then it is called a *cycle* (Figure 8.1h).

A graph is called a *weighted graph* if each edge has an assigned number. Depending on the context in which such graphs are used, the number assigned to an edge is called its weight, cost, distance, length or some other name.

A graph with n vertices is called *complete* and is denoted K_n, if for each pair of distinct vertices there is exactly one edge connecting them; that is, each vertex can be connected to any other vertex (Figure 8.1c). The number of edges in such a graph $|E| =$

$$\binom{|V|}{2} = \frac{|V|!}{2!(|V| - 2)!} = \frac{|V|(|V| - 1)}{2} = O(|V|^2).$$

A *subgraph* G' of graph $G = (V, E)$ is a graph (V', E') such that $V' \subseteq V$ and $E' \subseteq E$. A subgraph *induced* by vertices V' is a graph (V', E') such that an edge $e \in E$ iff $e \in E'$.

Two vertices v_i and v_j are called *adjacent* if the $edge(v_i v_j)$ is in E. Such an edge is called *incident with* the vertices v_i and v_j. The *degree* of a vertex v, $deg(v)$, is the number of edges incident with v. If $deg(v) = 0$ then v is called an *isolated vertex*. The definition of a graph indicating that the set of edges E can be empty allows for a graph consisting only of isolated vertices.

■ 8.1 GRAPH REPRESENTATION

There are variety of ways to represent a graph. A simple representation is given by an *adjacency list* which specifies all vertices adjacent to each vertex of the graph. This list can be implemented as a table, in which case it is called a *star representation* which can be forward or reverse, as illustrated in Figure 8.2b, or as a linked list (Figure 8.2c).

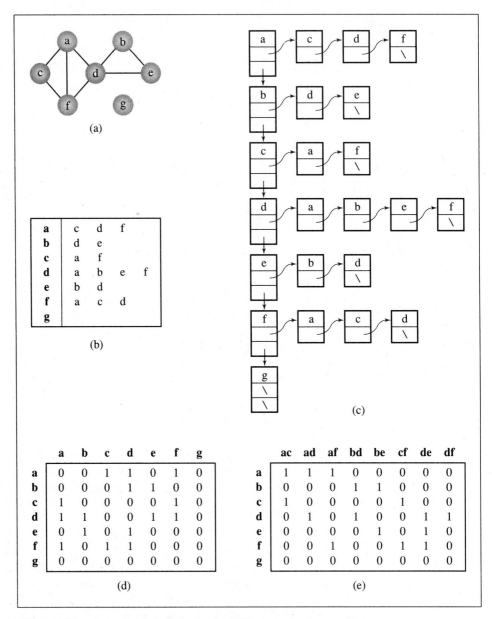

Figure 8.2: **Graph representations. A graph (a) represented as an adjacency list (b, c) and an adjacency matrix (d).**

Another representation is a matrix which comes in two forms: an adjacency matrix and an incidence matrix. An *adjacency matrix* of graph $G = (V, E)$ is a binary $|V| \times |V|$ matrix such that each entry of this matrix

$$a_{ij} = \begin{cases} 1 & \text{if there exists an } edge(v_i v_j), \\ 0 & \text{otherwise.} \end{cases}$$

An example is shown in Figure 8.2d. Note that the order of vertices $v_1, \ldots, v_{|V|}$ used for generating this matrix is arbitrary; therefore, there are $n!$ possible adjacency matrices for the same graph G. Generalization of this definition to also cover multigraphs can be easily accomplished by transforming the definition into the following form:

$$a_{ij} = \text{number of edges between } v_i \text{ and } v_j.$$

Another matrix representation of a graph is based on the incidence of vertices and edges and is called an *incidence matrix*. An incidence matrix of graph $G = (V, E)$ is a $|V| \times |E|$ matrix such that

$$a_{ij} = \begin{cases} 1 & \text{if edge } e_j \text{ is incident with vertex } v_i, \\ 0 & \text{otherwise.} \end{cases}$$

Figure 8.2e contains an example of an incidence matrix. In an incidence matrix for a multigraph, some columns are the same, and a column with only one 1 indicates a loop.

Which representation is best? It depends on the problem at hand. If our task is to process vertices adjacent to a vertex v, then the adjacency list requires only $deg(v)$ steps, whereas the adjacency matrix requires $|V|$ steps. On the other hand, inserting or deleting a vertex adjacent to v requires linked list maintenance for an adjacency list (if such an implementation is used); for a matrix it requires only changing 0 to 1 for insertion, or 1 to 0 for deletion, in one cell of the matrix.

■ 8.2 GRAPH TRAVERSALS

As in trees, traversing a graph consists of visiting each vertex only one time. The simple traversal algorithms used for trees cannot be applied here, since graphs may include cycles; hence the tree traversal algorithms would result in infinite loops. To prevent that from happening, each visited vertex can be marked to avoid revisiting it. However, graphs can have isolated vertices, which means that some parts of the graph would be left out if unmodified tree traversal methods are applied.

An algorithm for traversing a graph, known as the depth-first search algorithm, was developed by John Hopcroft and Robert Tarjan. In this algorithm, each vertex v is visited and then each unvisited vertex adjacent to v is visited. If a vertex v has no adjacent vertices or all of its adjacent vertices have been visited, we backtrack to the predecessor of v. The traversal is finished if this visiting and backtracking process leads to the first vertex where the traversal started. If there are still some unvisited vertices in the graph, the traversal continues restarting from one of the unvisited vertices.

Although it is not necessary for the proper outcome of this method, the algorithm assigns a unique number to each accessed vertex so that vertices are now renumbered. This will prove useful in later applications of this algorithm.

```
DFS(v)
    num(v) = i++;
    for all vertices u adjacent to v
```

```
        if num(u) is 0
            attach edge(uv) to edges;
            DFS(u);

DepthFirstSearch()
    for all vertices v
        num(v) = 0;
    edges = null;
    i = 1;
    while there is a vertex v such that num(v) is 0
        DFS(v);
    output edges;
```

Figure 8.3 contains an example with the numbers $num(v)$ assigned to each vertex v shown in parentheses. Having made all necessary initializations, **DepthFirstSearch()** calls **DFS(a)**. **DFS()** is first invoked for vertex a; $num(a)$ is assigned number 1. a has four adjacent vertices and vertex e is chosen for the next invocation, **DFS(e)**, which assigns number 2 to this vertex, i.e., $num(e) = 2$, and puts the $edge(ae)$ in **edges**. Vertex e has two unvisited adjacent vertices, and **DFS()** is called for the first of them, the vertex f. The call **DFS(f)** leads to the assignment $num(f) = 3$, and puts the $edge(ef)$ in **edges**. Vertex f has only one unvisited adjacent vertex, i; thus the fourth call, **DFS(i)**, leads to the assignment $num(i) = 4$ and to the attaching of $edge(fi)$ to **edges**. Vertex i has only visited adjacent vertices; hence, we return to call **DFS(f)** and then to **DFS(e)** in which vertex i is accessed only to learn that $num(i)$ is not 0, whereby the $edge(ei)$ is not included in **edges**. The rest of the execution can be seen easily in Figure 8.3b. Solid lines indicate edges included in the set **edges**.

Note that this algorithm guarantees generating a tree (or a forest, a set of trees) which includes or spans over all vertices of the original graph. A tree which meets this condition is called a *spanning tree*. The fact that a tree is generated is ascertained by the fact that the algorithm does not include in the resulting tree any edge which leads from the currently analyzed vertex to a vertex already analyzed. An edge is added to **edges** only if the condition in "**if** $num(u)$ *is* 0" is true, that is, if vertex u reachable from vertex v has

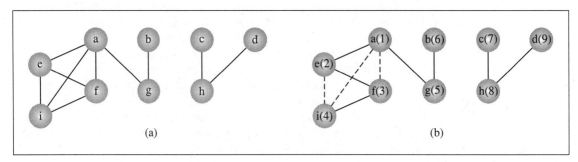

(a) (b)

Figure 8.3: **An example of application of DepthFirstSearch()
algorithm to a graph.**

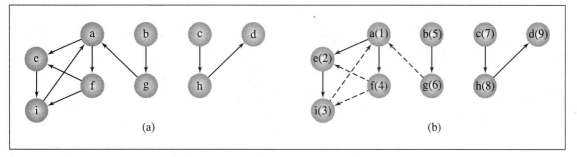

Figure 8.4: **DepthFirstSearch()** algorithm applied to a digraph.

not been processed. As a result, certain edges in the original graph do not appear in the resulting tree. The edges included in this tree are called *forward edges* (or *tree edges*), and the edges not included in this tree are called *back edges* and are shown as dashed lines.

Figure 8.4 illustrates the execution of this algorithm for a digraph. Notice that the original graph results in three spanning trees, although we started with only two isolated subgraphs.

The complexity of **DepthFirstSearch()** is $O(|V| + |E|)$, since: 1, initializing *num(v)* for each vertex *v* requires $|V|$ steps. 2, **DFS(v)** is called *deg(v)* times for each *v*, i.e., once for each edge of *v* (to spawn into more calls or to finish the chain of recursive calls), hence the total number of calls is $2|E|$. 3, searching for vertices as required by the statement

while *there is a vertex* **v** *such that num(***v***) is* **0**

can be assumed to require $|V|$ steps. For a graph with no isolated parts, the loop makes only one iteration, and an initial vertex can be found in one step, although it may take $|V|$ steps. For a graph with all isolated vertices, the loop iterates $|V|$ times and each time a vertex can be chosen also in one step, although in an unfavorable implementation, the *i*th iteration may require *i* steps, whereby the loop would require $O(|V|^2)$ steps in total. For example, if an adjacency list is used, then for each *v*, the condition in the loop,

for *all vertices* **u** *adjacent to* **v**

is checked *deg(v)* times. However, if an adjacency matrix is used, then the same condition is used $|V|$ times, whereby the algorithm's complexity becomes $O(|V|^2)$.

As we shall see, many different algorithms are based on **DFS()**; however, some algorithms are more efficient if the underlying graph traversal is not depth first but breadth first. We have already encountered these two types of traversals in Chapter 6; recall that the depth-first algorithms rely on the use of a stack (explicitly, or implicitly, in recursion), and breadth-first traversal uses a queue as the basic data structure. Not surprisingly, this idea can also be extended to graphs, as shown in the following pseudocode:

```
BreadthFirstSearch()
    for all vertices u
        num(u) = 0;
```

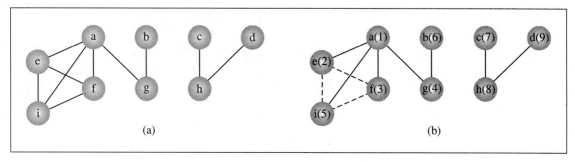

Figure 8.5: **An example of application of `BreadthFirstSearch()` algorithm to a graph.**

```
edges = null;
i = 1;
while there is a vertex v such that num(v) == 0
    num(v)=i++;
    Enqueue(v);
    while queue is not empty
        v = Dequeue();
        for all vertices u adjacent to v
            if num(u) is 0
                num(u) = i++;
                Enqueue(u);
                attach edge(vu) to edges;
    output edges;
```

Examples of processing a simple graph and a digraph are shown in Figures 8.5 and 8.6. `BreadthFirstSearch()` first tries to mark all neighbors of a vertex *v* before proceeding to other vertices, whereas `DFS()` picks one neighbor of a *v* and then proceeds to a neighbor of this neighbor before processing any other neighbors of *v*.

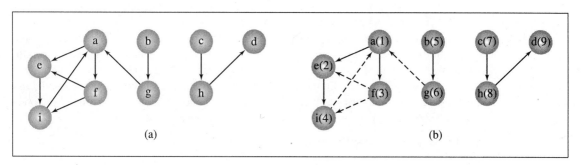

Figure 8.6: `DepthFirstSearch()` **algorithm applied to a digraph.**

■ 8.3 SHORTEST PATHS

Finding the shortest path is a classical problem in graph theory and a large number of different solutions have been proposed. Edges are assigned certain weights representing, for example, distances between cities, times separating execution of certain tasks, costs of transmitting information between locations, amounts of some substance transported from one place to another, etc. When determining the shortest path from vertex *v* to vertex *u*, information about distances between intermediate vertices *w* has to be recorded. This information can be recorded as a label associated with these vertices, where the label is only the distance from *v* to *w*, or the distance along with the predecessor of *w* in this path. The methods of finding the shortest path rely on these labels. Depending on how many times these labels are updated, the methods solving the shortest path problem are divided in two classes: label-setting methods and label-correcting methods.

For *label-setting methods*, in each pass through the vertices still to be processed, one vertex is set to a value which remains unchanged to the end of the execution. This, however, limits such methods to processing graphs with only positive weights. The second category includes *label-correcting methods* which allow for the changing of *any* label during application of the method. These two methods can be applied to graphs with negative weights and with no *negative cycle*—a cycle composed of edges with weights adding up to a negative number—but it guarantees that for all vertices, the current distances indicate the shortest path only after the processing of the graph is finished. Most of the label-setting and label-correcting methods, however, can be subsumed to the same form which allows finding the shortest paths from one vertex to all other vertices (Gallo, Pallottino 1986):

```
GenericShortestPathAlgorithm(weighted simple digraph, vertex first)
    for all vertices v
        currDist(v) = ∞;
    currDist(first) = 0;
    initialize toBeChecked;
    while toBeChecked is not empty
        v = a vertex in toBeChecked;
        remove v from toBeChecked;
        for all vertices u adjacent to v
            if currDist(u) > currDist(v) + weight(edge(vu))
                currDist(u) = currDist(v) + weight(edge(vu));
                predecessor(u) = v;
                add u to toBeChecked if it is not there;
```

In this generic algorithm, a label consists of two elements:

$$label(v) = (currDist(v), predecessor(v)).$$

This algorithm leaves two things open: the organization of the set **toBeChecked** and the order of assigning new values to *v* in the assignment statement

$$\mathbf{v} = a\ vertex\ in\ \mathbf{toBeChecked};$$

It should be clear that the organization of **toBeChecked** can determine the order of choosing new values for *v*, but it also determines the efficiency of the algorithm.

What distinguishes label-setting methods from label-correcting methods is the method of choosing the value for *v*, which is always a vertex in **toBeChecked** with the smallest current distance. One of the first label-setting algorithms was developed by Dijkstra.

In Dijkstra's algorithm, a number of paths $p_1, \ldots, p_n$ from a vertex *v* are tried, and each time the shortest path is chosen among them, which may mean that the same path p_i can be continued by adding one more edge to it. But if p_i turns out to be longer than any other path that can be tried, p_i is abandoned and this other path is tried by resuming from where it was left and by adding one more edge to it. Since paths can lead to vertices with more that one outgoing edge, new paths for possible exploration are added for each outgoing edge. Each vertex is tried once, all paths leading from it are opened, and the vertex itself is put away and not used any more. After all vertices are visited, the algorithm is finished. Dijkstra's algorithm is as follows:

DijkstraAlgorithm(*weighted simple* **digraph**, *vertex* **first**)
    for *all vertices* **v**
        currDist(**v**) = ∞;
    currDist(**first**) = 0;
    toBeChecked = *all vertices*;
    while toBeChecked *not empty*
        v = *a vertex in* **toBeChecked** *with minimal currDist*(**v**);
        remove **v** *from* **toBeChecked**;
        for *all vertices* **u** *adjacent to* **v** *and in* **toBeChecked**
            if *currDist*(**u**) > *currDist*(**v**)+ *weight*(*edge*(**vu**))
                currDist(**u**) = *currDist*(**v**)+ *weight*(*edge*(**vu**));
                predecessor(**u**) = **v**;

Dijkstra's algorithm is obtained from the generic method by being more specific about which vertex is to be taken from **toBeChecked**, so that the line

    v = *a vertex in* **toBeChecked**;

is replaced by line

    v = *a vertex in* **toBeChecked** *with minimal currDist*(**v**);

and by extending the condition in the **if** statement whereby the current distance of vertices eliminated from **toBeChecked** is set permanently.[1] Note that the structure of **toBeChecked** is not specified, and the efficiency of the algorithms depends of the data type of **toBeChecked**, which determines how quickly a vertex with minimal distance can be retrieved.

Figure 8.7 contains an example. The table in this figure shows all iterations of the **while** loop. There are ten iterations, since there are ten vertices. The table indicates the current distances determined up until the current iteration with the members of **toBeChecked** shown in each line.

---

[1]Dijkstra used six sets to ascertain this condition, three for vertices, three for edges.

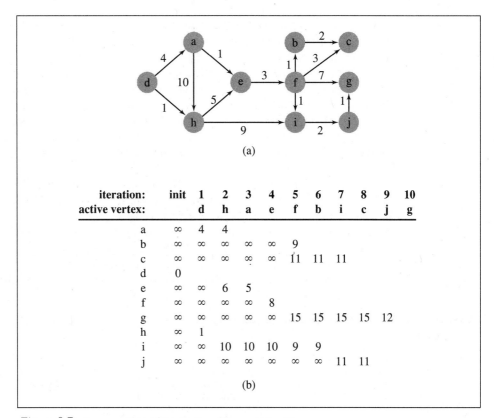

(a)

iteration:	init	1	2	3	4	5	6	7	8	9	10
active vertex:		d	h	a	e	f	b	i	c	j	g
a	∞	4	4								
b	∞	∞	∞	∞	∞	9					
c	∞	∞	∞	∞	∞	11	11	11			
d	0										
e	∞	∞	6	5							
f	∞	∞	∞	∞	8						
g	∞	∞	∞	∞	∞	15	15	15	15	12	
h	∞	1									
i	∞	∞	10	10	10	9	9				
j	∞	∞	∞	∞	∞	∞	∞	11	11		

(b)

Figure 8.7: **An execution of DijkstraAlgorithm().**

The list **toBeChecked** is initialized to $\{d\}$, the current distances of all vertices are initialized to a very large value, marked here as ∞, and in the first iteration, the current distances of d's neighbors are set to numbers equal to the weights of the edges from d. Now, there are two candidates for the next try, a and h, since d was excluded from **toBeChecked**. In the second iteration, h is chosen, since its current distance is minimal, and then the two vertices accessible from h, namely e and i, acquire the current distances 6 and 10. Now, there are three candidates in **toBeChecked** for the next try, a, e, and i. Since a has the smallest current distance, it is chosen in the third iteration. Eventually, in the tenth iteration, **toBeChecked** becomes empty and the execution of the algorithm completes.

The complexity of Dijkstra's algorithm is $O(|V|^2)$. The first **for** loop and the **while** loop are executed $|V|$ times. For each iteration of the **while** loop, (a) a vertex v in **toBeChecked** with minimal current distance has to be found, which requires $O(|V|)$ steps, and (b) the **for** loop iterates $deg(v)$ times, which is also $O(|V|)$. The efficiency can be improved by using a heap to store and order vertices and adjacency lists (Johnson 1977). Using a heap turns the complexity of this algorithm into $O((|E| + |V|) \lg |V|)$; each time through the **while** loop, the cost of restoring the heap after adding a new vertex is proportional to $O(\lg |V|)$. Also, in each iteration, only adjacent vertices are updated on an adjacency list, so that the total updates for all vertices considered in all iterations is proportional to $|E|$, and each list update corresponds to the cost of $\lg |V|$ of the heap update.

Dijkstra's algorithm is not general enough in that it fails when negative weights are used in graphs. To see why, change the weight of *edge(ah)* from 10 to −10. Note that the path *d, a, h, e* is now −1, whereas the path *d, a, e* as determined by the algorithm is 5. The reason for overlooking this less costly path is that the vertices with the current distance set from ∞ to a value are not checked any more: first, successors of vertex *d* are scrutinized and *d* is removed from **toBeChecked**, then the vertex *h* is removed from **toBeChecked**, and only afterwards the vertex *a* is considered as a candidate to be included in the path from *d* to other vertices. But now, the *edge(ah)* is not taken into consideration, since the condition in the **for** loop prevents the algorithm from doing this. To overcome this limitation, a label-correcting method is needed.

One of the first label-correcting algorithms was devised by Lester Ford. Like Dijkstra's algorithm, it uses the same method of setting current distances, but Ford's method does not permanently determine the shortest distance for any vertex until it processes the entire graph. It is more powerful than Dijkstra's method in that it can process graphs with negative weights (but not graphs with negative cycles).

As required by the original form of the algorithm, all edges are monitored to find a possibility for an improvement of the current distance of vertices, so that the algorithm can be presented in this pseudocode:

FordAlgorithm(*weighted simple* **digraph**, *vertex* **first**)
    for *all vertices* **v**
        currDist(**v**) = ∞;
    currDist(**first**) = 0;
    while *there is an edge*(**vu**) *such that currDist*(**u**) > *currDist*(**v**)+ *weight*(*edge*(**vu**))
        currDist(**u**) = *currDist*(**v**)+ *weight*(*edge*(**vu**));

To impose a certain order on monitoring the edges, an alphabetically ordered sequence of edges can be used so that the algorithm can repeatedly go through the entire sequence and adjust the current distance of any vertex if needed. Figure 8.8 contains an example. The graph includes edges with negative weights. The table indicates iterations of the **while** loop and current distances updated in each iteration, where one iteration is defined as one pass through the edges. Note that a vertex can change its current distance during the same iteration. However, at the end, each vertex of the graph can be reached through the shortest path from the starting vertex (vertex *c* in the example in Figure 8.8).

The computational complexity of this algorithm is $O(|V||E|)$. There will be at most $|V| - 1$ passes through the sequence of $|E|$ edges, since $|V| - 1$ is the longest possible path. In the first pass, at least all one-edge paths are determined, in the second pass, all two-edge paths are determined, and so on. However, for graphs with irrational weights, this complexity is $O(2^{|V|})$ (Gallo, Pallottino 1986).

We have seen in the case of Dijkstra's algorithm that the efficiency of an algorithm can be improved by scanning edges and vertices in a certain order, which, in turn, depends on the data structure used to store them. The same holds true for label-correcting methods. In particular, **FordAlgorithm()** does not specify the order of checking edges. In the example illustrated in Figure 8.8, a simple solution is used in that all adjacency lists of all vertices were visited in each iteration. However, in this approach all the edges are checked every time, which is not necessary and more judicious organization of the list of vertices can limit the number of visits per vertex. Such an improvement is based on the

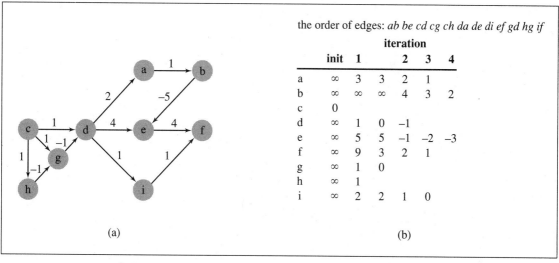

the order of edges: *ab be cd cg ch da de di ef gd hg if*

	init	1	2	3	4
			iteration		
a	∞	3	3	2	1
b	∞	∞	∞	4	3	2
c	0				
d	∞	1	0	−1	
e	∞	5	5	−1	−2	−3
f	∞	9	3	2	1
g	∞	1	0		
h	∞	1			
i	∞	2	2	1	0

(a)   (b)

Figure 8.8: `FordAlgorithm()` **applied to a digraph with negative weights.**

`GenericShortestPathAlgorithm()` by explicitly referring to the `toBeChecked` list which in `FordAlgorithm()` is used only implicitly: it simply is the set of all vertices *V* and remains such for the entire run of the algorithm. This leads us to a general form of a label-correcting algorithm as expressed in this pseudocode:

`LabelCorrectingAlgorithm(`*weighted simple* `digraph`*, vertex* `first)`
  for *all vertices* **v**
    currDist(**v**) = ∞;
  currDist(`first`) = 0;
  `toBeChecked` = {`first`};
  while `toBeChecked` *not empty*
    v = *a vertex in* `toBeChecked`;
    remove **v** *from* `toBeChecked`;
    for *all vertices* **u** *adjacent to* **v**
      if *currDist*(**u**) > *currDist*(**v**)+ *weight*(*edge*(**vu**))
        currDist(**u**) = *currDist*(**v**)+ *weight*(*edge*(**vu**));
        predecessor(**u**) = **v**;
        add **u** *to* `toBeChecked` *if it is not there*;

The efficiency of particular instantiations of this algorithm hinges on the data structure used for the `toBeChecked` list and on operations for extracting elements from this list and including them into it.

One possible organization of this list is a queue: vertex *v* is dequeued from `toBe-Checked` and if the current distance of any of its neighbors, *u*, is updated, *u* is enqueued onto `toBeChecked`. It seems like a natural choice, and, in fact, it was one of the earliest, used in 1968 by C. Witzgall (Deo, Pang 1984). However, it is not without flaws, since it sometimes reevaluates the same labels more times than necessary. Figure 8.9 contains

active vertex

	c	d	g	h	a	e	i	d	g	b	f	a	e	i	d	b	f	a	i	e	b	f	e
queue		d	g	h	a	e	i	d	g	b	f	a	e	i	d	b	f	a	i	e	b	f	e
			g	h	a	e	i	d	g	b	f	a	e	i	d	b	f	a	i	e	b	f	e
				h	a	e	i	d	g	b	f	a	e	i	d	b	f	a	i	e	b	f	
						e	i	d	g	b	f	a	e	i	d	b			i	e			
							i	d	g	b	f		e	i	d								
														i	d								
a	∞	∞	3	3	3	3	3	3	2	2	2	2	2	2	2	1							
b	∞	∞	∞	∞	∞	4	4	4	4	4	4	4	3	,3	3	3	3	3	2				
c	0																						
d	∞	1	1	0	0	0	0	0	0	−1													
e	∞	∞	5	5	5	5	5	5	4	4	−1	−1	−1	−1	−1	−1	−2	−2	−2	−2	−2	−3	
f	∞	∞	∞	∞	∞	∞	9	3	3	3	3	3	3	3	2	2	2	2	2	1			
g	∞	1	1	1	0																		
h	∞	1																					
i	∞	∞	2	2	2	2	2	2	1	1	1	1	1	1	1	0							

Figure 8.9: **An execution of `LabelCorrectingAlgorithm()`, which uses a queue.**

an example of an excessive reevaluation. The table in this figure shows all changes on **toBeChecked** implemented as a queue when **LabelCorrectingAlgorithm()** is applied to the graph in Figure 8.8a. The vertex d is updated three times. These updates cause three changes to its successors, a and i, and two changes to another successor, e. The change of a translates into two changes to b and these into two more changes to e. To avoid such repetitious updates, a doubly ended queue, or deque, can be used.

The choice of a deque as a solution to this problem is attributed to D. D'Esopo (Pollack, Wiebenson 1960) and was implemented by Pape. In this method, the vertices included in **toBeChecked** for the first time are put at the end of the list; otherwise they are added at the front. The rationale for this procedure is that if a vertex v is included for the first time, then there is a good chance that the vertices accessible from v have not been processed yet, so that they will be processed after processing v. On the other hand, if v has been processed at least once, then it is likely that the vertices reachable from v are still on the list waiting for processing; by putting v at the end of the list, these vertices may very likely be reprocessed due to the update of *currDist(v)*. Therefore, it is better to put v in front of their successors to avoid an unnecessary round of updates. Figure 8.10 shows changes in the deque during the execution of **LabelCorrectingAlgorithm()** applied to the same graph as before, the graph in Figure 8.8a. This time the number of iterations is dramatically reduced. Although d is again evaluated three times, these evaluations are performed before processing its successors, so that a and i are processed once and e twice. However, this algorithm has a problem of its own, because in the worst case its performance is an exponential function of the number of vertices. (See Exercise 13 at the end of this chapter.) But in the average case, as Pape's experimental runs indicate, this implementation fares at least 60% better than the previous, queue solution.

						active vertices							
		c	d	g	d	h	g	d	a	e	i	b	e	f
deque		d	g	d	h	g	d	a	e	i	b	e	f
		g	h	h	a	a	a	e	i	b	f	f
		h	a	a	e	e	e	i	b	f
			e	e	i	i	i
			i	i
a	∞	∞	3	3	2	2	2	1
b	∞	∞	∞	∞	∞	∞	∞	∞	2
c	0
d	∞	1	2	0	0	0	−1
e	∞	∞	5	5	4	4	4	3	3	3	3	−3
f	∞	∞	∞	∞	∞	∞	∞	∞	∞	7	1
g	∞	1	1	1	1	0
h	∞	1
i	∞	∞	2	2	1	1	1	0

Figure 8.10: **An execution of `LabelCorrectingAlgorithm()` which applies a dequeue.**

Instead of using a deque, which combines two queues, the two queues can be used separately. In this version of the algorithm, vertices stored for the first time are enqueued on $queue_1$, otherwise on $queue_2$. Vertices are dequeued from $queue_1$ if it is not empty, otherwise from $queue_2$ (Gallo, Pallottino 1988).

Another version of the label-correcting method is the *threshold algorithm* which also uses two lists. Vertices are taken for processing from $list_1$. A vertex is added to the end of $list_1$ if its label is below the current threshold level and to $list_2$ otherwise. If $list_1$ is empty, then the threshold level is changed to a value greater than a minimum label among the labels of the vertices in $list_2$ and then the vertices with the label values below the threshold are moved to $list_1$ (Glover, Glover, Klingman 1986).

Still another algorithm is a *small label first* method. In this method, a vertex is included at the front of a deque if its label is smaller than the label at the top of the deque, otherwise it is put at the end of the deque (Bertsekas 1993). To some extent, this method includes the main criterion of label-setting methods. The latter methods always retrieve the minimal element from the list; the small label first method puts a vertex with the label smaller than the label of the front vertex at the top. The approach can be carried to its logical conclusion by requiring each vertex to be included in the list according to its rank, so that the deque would turn into a priority queue and the resulting method would become a label-correcting version of Dijkstra's algorithm.

8.3.1 All-to-all Shortest Path Problem

Although the task of finding all shortest paths from any vertex to any other vertex seems to be more complicated that the task of dealing with one source only, a method designed by Stephen Warshall and implemented by Robert W. Floyd and P.Z. Ingerman does it in a surprisingly simple way providing that an adjacency matrix is given that indicates all the edge weights of the graph (or digraph). The graph can include negative weights. The algorithm is as follows:

```
WFIalgorithm(matrix weight)
    for i = 1 to |V|
        for j = 1 to |V|
            for k = 1 to |V|
                if weight[j,k] > weight[j,i] + weight[i,k]
                    weight[j,k] = weight[j,i] + weight[i,k];
```

The outermost loop refers to vertices which may be on a path between the vertex with index j and the vertex with index k. For example, in the first iteration, when $i = 1$, all paths $v_j v_1 v_k$ are considered and if there is currently no path from v_j to v_k and v_k is reachable from v_j, it is established, with its weight equal to $weight(edge(v_j v_1)) + weight(edge(v_1 v_k))$, or the current weight of this path, $weight(edge(v_j v_k))$, is changed to this value, if it is less than $weight(edge(v_j v_k))$. As an example, consider the graph and the corresponding adjacency matrix in Figure 8.11. This figure also contains tables which show changes in the matrix for each value of j and the changes in paths as established by the algorithm. After the first iteration, the matrix and the graph remain the same, since a has no incoming edges (Figure 8.11a). They also remain the same in the last iteration, when $j = 5$; no change is introduced to the matrix because vertex e has no outgoing edges. A better path, one with lower combined weight, is always chosen, if possible. For example, the direct, one-edge path from b to e in Figure 8.11c is abandoned after a two-edge path from b to e is found with a lower weight, as in Figure 8.11d.

This algorithm also allows us to detect cycles if the diagonal is initialized to ∞ and not to zero. If any of the diagonal values is changed, then the graph contains a cycle. Also, if an initial value of ∞ between two vertices in the matrix is not changed to a finite value, it is an indication that one vertex cannot be reached from another.

The simplicity of the algorithm is reflected in the ease with which its complexity can be computed: since all three **for** loops are executed $|V|$ times, its complexity is $|V|^3$. This is a good efficiency for dense, nearly complete graphs, but in sparse graphs there is no need to check for all possible connections between vertices. For sparse graphs, it may be more beneficial to use a one-to-all method $|V|$ times, that is, apply it to each vertex separately. This should be a label-setting algorithm, which as a rule has better complexity than a label-correcting algorithm. However, a label-setting algorithm cannot work with graphs with negative weights. To solve this problem, we have to modify the graph so that it does not have negative weights and it guarantees to have the same shortest paths as the original graph. Fortunately, such a modification is possible (Edmonds, Karp 1972).

Observe first, that for any vertex v, the length of the shortest path to v is never greater than the length of the shortest path to any of its predecessors w plus the length of edge from w to v, or

$$dist(v) \leq dist(w) + weight(edge(wv))$$

for any vertices v and w. This inequality is equivalent to the inequality

$$0 \leq weight'(edge(wv)) = weight(edge(vw)) + dist(w) - dist(v).$$

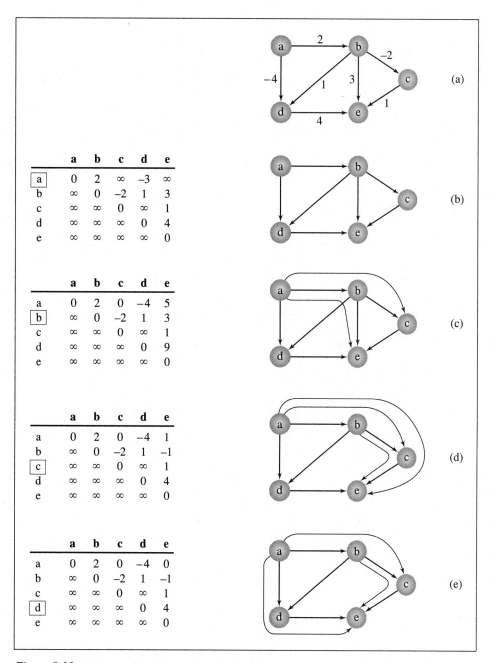

	a	b	c	d	e
a	0	2	∞	−3	∞
b	∞	0	−2	1	3
c	∞	∞	0	∞	1
d	∞	∞	∞	0	4
e	∞	∞	∞	∞	0

	a	b	c	d	e
a	0	2	0	−4	5
b	∞	0	−2	1	3
c	∞	∞	0	∞	1
d	∞	∞	∞	0	9
e	∞	∞	∞	∞	0

	a	b	c	d	e
a	0	2	0	−4	1
b	∞	0	−2	1	−1
c	∞	∞	0	∞	1
d	∞	∞	∞	0	4
e	∞	∞	∞	∞	0

	a	b	c	d	e
a	0	2	0	−4	0
b	∞	0	−2	1	−1
c	∞	∞	0	∞	1
d	∞	∞	∞	0	4
e	∞	∞	∞	∞	0

Figure 8.11: **An execution of WFIalgorithm().**

Hence, changing *weight*(*e*) to *weight'*(*e*) for all edges *e* renders a graph with nonnegative edge weights. Now note that the shortest path $v_1, v_2, \ldots, v_k$ is

$$\sum_{i=1}^{k-1} weight'(edge(v_i v_{i+1})) = \left(\sum_{i=1}^{k-1} weight(edge(v_i v_{i+1})) \right) + dist(v_1) - dist(v_k).$$

Therefore, if the length L' of the path from v_1 to v_k is found in terms of nonnegative weights, then the length L of the same path in the same graph using the original weights, some possibly negative, is $L = L' - dist(v_1) + dist(v_k)$.

But because the shortest paths have to be known to make such a transformation, the graph has to be preprocessed by one application of a label-correcting method. Only afterwards are the weights modified and then a label-setting method is applied $|V|$ times.

■ 8.4 CYCLE DETECTION

Many algorithms rely on detecting cycles in graphs. We have just seen that as a side effect, **WFIalgorithm()** allows for detecting cycles in graphs. However it is a cubic algorithm, which in many situations is too inefficient. Therefore other cycle detection methods have to be explored.

One such algorithm is obtained directly from **DepthFirstSearch()**. For undirected graphs it is enough to add only one line in **DFS(v)** to detect cycles, which is an **else** statement as in

```
CycleDetectionDFS(v)
    num(v) = i++;
    for all vertices u adjacent to v
        if num(u) is 0
            attach edge(uv) to edges;
            CycleDetectionDFS(u);
        else cycle detected;
```

For digraphs, the situation is a bit more complicated, since there may be edges between different spanning subtrees, called *side edges* (see *edge*(*ga*) in Figure 8.4b). An edge (a back edge) indicates a cycle if it joins two vertices already included in the same spanning subtree. To consider only this case, a number higher than any number generated in subsequent searches is assigned to a vertex being currently visited after all its descendants have also been visited. In this way, if a vertex is about to be joined by an edge with a vertex with a lower number, we declare a cycle detection. The algorithm is now

```
DigraphCycleDetectionDFS(v)
    num(v) = i++;
    for all vertices u adjacent to v
        if num(u) is 0
            attach edge(uv) to edges;
            DigraphCycleDetectionDFS(u);
        else if num(u) is not ∞
            cycle detected;
    num(v) = ∞;
```

8.4.1 Union-Find Problem

Let us recall from a preceding section that depth-first search guaranteed generating a spanning tree in which no element of edges used by `DepthFirstSearch()` led to a cycle with other elements of **edges**. This was due to the fact that if vertices *v* and *u* belonged to **edges** then the *edge(vu)* was disregarded by `DepthFirstSearch()`. A problem arises when `DepthFirstSearch()` is modified so that it can detect whether a specific *edge(vu)* is part of a cycle (see Exercise 20). Should such a modified depth-first search be applied to each edge separately, then the total run would be $O(|E|(|E| + |V|))$, which could turn into $O(|V|^4)$ for dense graphs. Hence, a better method needs to be found.

The task is to determine if two vertices are in the same set. Two operations are needed to implement this task: finding the set to which a vertex *v* belongs and uniting two sets into one if vertex *v* belongs to one of them and *w* to another. This is known as the *union-find* problem.

The sets used to solve the union-find problem are implemented with circular linked lists; each list is identified by a vertex which is the root of the tree to which the vertices in the list belong. But first, all vertices are numbered with integers $0, \dots, |V| - 1$ which are used as indices in three arrays: **root[]** to store a vertex index identifying a set of vertices, **next[]** to indicate the next vertex on a list, and **length[]** to indicate the number of vertices in a list.

We use circular lists to be able to combine two lists right away, as illustrated in Figure 8.12. Lists L1 and L2 (Figure 8.12a) are merged into one by interchanging **next** pointers in both lists (Figure 8.12b or, the same list, Figure 8.12c). However, the vertices in L2 have to "know" to which list they belong; therefore, their root indicators have to be changed to the new root. Since it has to be done for all vertices of list L2, then L2 should be the shorter of the two lists. To determine the length of lists, the third array is used, **length[]**, but only lengths for the identifying nodes (roots) have to be updated. Therefore, the lengths indicated for other vertices which were roots (and at the beginning each of them was) are disregarded.

The union operation performs all the necessary tasks, so the find operation becomes trivial. By constantly updating the array **root[]**, the set, to which a vertex *j* belongs, can be immediately identified, since it is a set whose identifying vertex is **root[j]**. Now, after the necessary initializations,

```
Initialize()
    for i = 0 to |V| - 1
        root[i] = next[i] = i;
        length[i] = 1;
```

Figure 8.12: **Concatenating two circular linked lists.**

`Union()` can be defined as follows:

```
Union(edge(vu))
    if (root[u] == root[v])                         // disregard this edge,
        return;                                      // since v and u are in
    else if (length[root[v]] < length[root[u]])// the same set; combine
        rt = root[v];                               // two sets into one;
        length[root[u]] += length[rt];
        root[rt] = root[u];                         // update root of root and
        for (j = next[rt]; j != rt; j = next[j])// then other vertices
            root[j] = root[u];                      // in circular list;
        Swap( next[rt],next[root[u]]);              // merge two lists;
        add edge(vu) to spanningTree;
    else  // if length[root[v]] >= length[root[u]]
        // proceed as before, with v and u reversed;
```

An example of the application of `Union()` to merge lists is shown in Figure 8.13. After initialization, there are $|V|$ unary sets or one-node linked lists, as in Figure 8.13a. After executing `Union()` several times, smaller linked lists are merged into larger ones and each time the new situation is reflected in the three arrays as shown in Figure 8.13b-c.

The complexity of `Union()` lists depends on the number of vertices that have to be updated when merging two lists, specifically, on the number of vertices on the shorter list, since this number determines how many times the **for** loop in `Union()` iterates. Since this number can be between 1 and $|V|/2$, the complexity of `Union()` is given by $O(|V|)$.

■ 8.5 SPANNING TREES

Consider the graph representing the airline connections between seven cities maintained by one company (Figure 8.14a). If the economic situation forces the company to shut down as many connections as possible, which of them should be retained to make sure that it is still possible to reach any city from any other city, if only indirectly? One possibility is the graph 8.14b. City a can be reached from the city d using the path d, c, a, but it is also possible to use the path d, e, b, a. Since the number of retained connections is the issue, there is still the possibility we can reduce this number. It should be clear that the minimum number of such connections form a tree, because alternate paths arise as the result of cycles in the graph. Hence, to create the minimum number of connections, a spanning tree should be created, and such a spanning tree would be the byproduct of `DepthFirstSearch()`. Clearly, we can create different spanning trees (Figure 8.14c–d), i.e., decide to retain different sets of connections, but all these trees have six edges and we cannot get any better than that.

The solution to this problem is not optimal in that the distances between cities have not been taken into account. Since there are alternative six-edge connections between cities, the company uses the cost of these connections to choose the best, guaranteeing the optimum cost. This can be achieved by having maximally short distances for the six connections. This problem can now be phrased as finding a *minimum spanning tree* which is a spanning tree in which the sum of the weights of its edges is minimal. The previous problem of

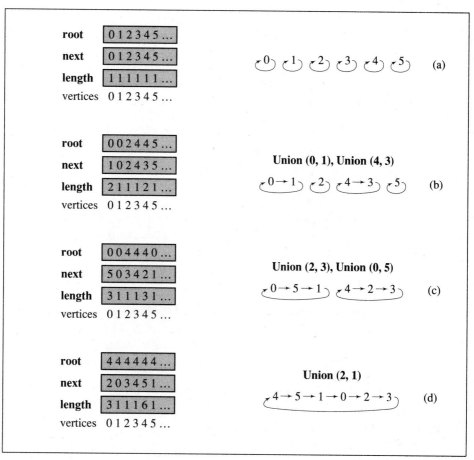

Figure 8.13: An example of application of Union() to merge lists.

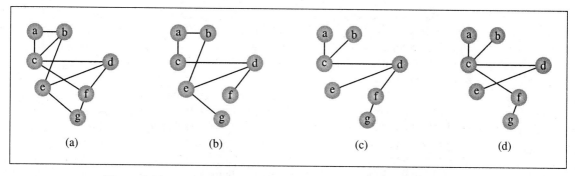

Figure 8.14: A graph representing the airline connections between seven cities (a) and three possible sets of connections (b–d).

finding a spanning tree in a simple graph is a case of the minimum spanning tree problem in that the weights for each edge are assumed to be equal to one. Therefore, each spanning tree is a minimum tree in a simple graph.

The minimum spanning tree problem has many solutions and only a handful of them are presented here. (For a review of these methods, see Graham, Hell 1985.) These algorithms can be divided in the following categories:

1. Creating and expanding at the same time many trees to be merged into larger trees (Boruvka's algorithm).
2. Expanding a set of trees to form one spanning tree (Kruskal's algorithm).
3. Creating and expanding only one tree by adding new branches to it (Jarnik-Prim's algorithm).
4. Creating and expanding only one tree by adding new branches to it and possibly removing branches from it (Dijkstra's method).

8.5.1   Boruvka's Algorithm

Probably the first algorithm for finding the minimum spanning tree was devised in 1926 by Otakar Boruvka. In this method, we start with $|V|$ one-vertex trees and for each vertex v, we look for an *edge*(vw) of minimum weight among all edges outgoing from v, and create small trees by including these edges. Then, we look for edges of minimal weight that can connect the resulting trees into larger trees. The process is finished when one tree is created. Here is a pseudocode for this algorithm:

BoruvkaAlgorithm *(weighted connected undirected* **graph)**
    make each vertex the root of a one-node tree;
  while *there is more than one tree*
     for *each tree* **t**
       e *= minimum weight edge (***vu***) where* **v** *is included in* **t** *and* **u** *is not;*
      create a tree by combining **t** *and the tree that includes* **u**
       if such a tree does not exist yet;

For example, for the graph in Figure 8.15a, out of seven one-vertex trees, two trees are created, since for vertices a and c, *edge*(ac) is chosen, for vertex b, *edge*(ab) is chosen, for vertex d, *edge*(df) is chosen, for vertex e, *edge* (eg) is chosen, and for vertices f and g, *edge*(fg) is chosen (Figure 8.15b). Afterwards, for the tree(abc) and the tree($defg$), *edge*(cf) is selected, since it is the shortest edge that connects these two trees, resulting in one spanning tree.

How many iterations are required? In each iteration of the **while** loop, each of the existing r trees is joined with an edge to at least one tree. In the worst case, $r/2$ trees are generated; in the best case, one tree is generated. In the subsequent iteration there would be $r/4$ trees, etc. In the worst case, $\lg |V|$ iterations are needed, where $|V|$ is the initial number of one-vertex trees.

Boruvka's method lends itself very nicely to parallel processing, since for each tree, a minimal edge has to be found independently.

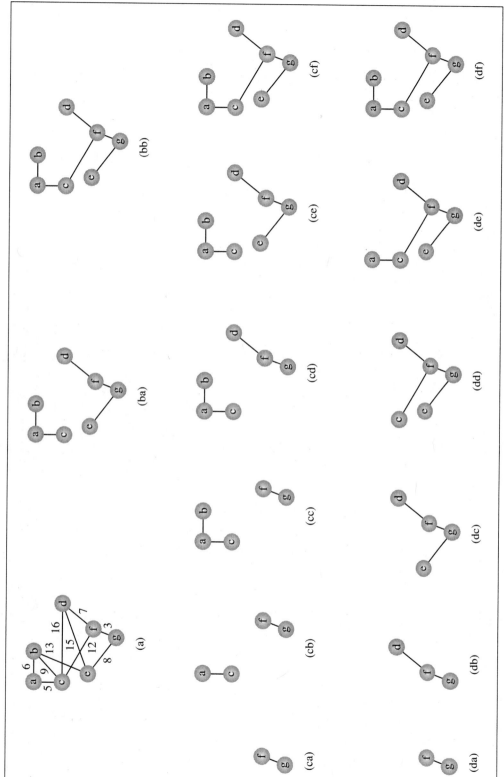

Figure 8.15: A spanning tree of graph (a) found with Boruvka's algorithm (ba,bb), with Kruskal's algorithm (ca–cf), with Jarnik-Prim's algorithm (da–df), and with Dijkstra's method (ea–el).

continued

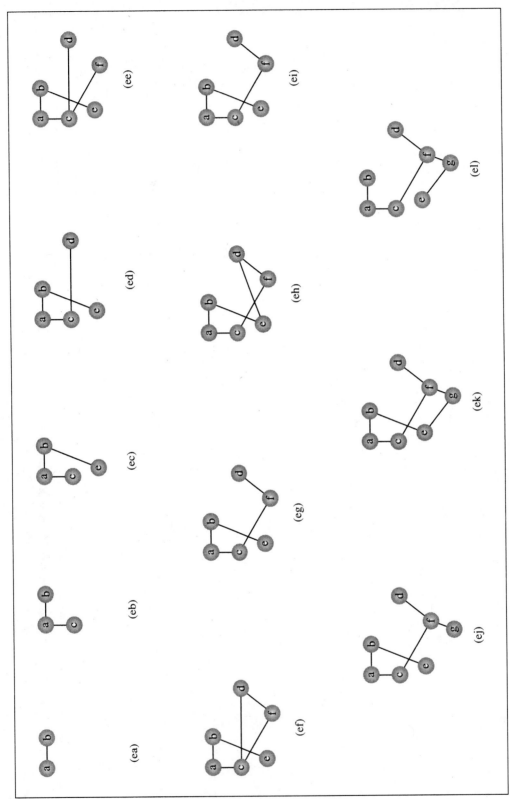

Figure 8.15: A spanning tree of graph (a) found with Boruvka's algorithm (ba,bb), with Kruskal's algorithm (ca–cf), with Jarnik-Prim's algorithm (da–df), and with Dijkstra's method (ea–el).

8.5.2   Kruskal's Algorithm

One popular algorithm was devised by Joseph Kruskal. In this method, all edges are ordered by weight and then each edge in this ordered sequence is checked to see whether it can be considered part of the tree under construction. It is added to the tree if no cycle arises after its inclusion. This simple algorithm can be summarized as follows:

```
KruskalAlgorithm(weighted connected undirected graph)
    tree = null;
    edges = sequence of all edges of graph sorted by weight;
    for (i = 1; i ≤ |E| and |tree| < |V| − 1; i++)
        if eᵢ from edges does not form a cycle with edges in tree
            add eᵢ to tree;
```

Figure 8.15ca–cf contains a step-by-step example of Kruskal's algorithm.

The complexity of this algorithm is determined by the complexity of the sorting method applied, which for an efficient sorting is $O(|E| \lg |E|)$. It also depends on the complexity of the method used for cycle detection. If we use `Union()` to implement Kruskal's algorithm, then the `for` loop of `KruskalAlgorithm()` becomes

```
for (i = 1; i ≤ |E| and |tree| < |V| − 1; i++)
    Union(eᵢ = edge(vu));
```

Although `Union()` can be called up to $|E|$ times, it is exited after one (the first) test if a cycle is detected and it performs a union, which is of complexity $O(|V|)$, only for $|V| - 1$ edges added to `tree`. Hence, the complexity of `KruskalAlgorithm()`'s `for` loop is $O(|E| + (|V| - 1)|V|)$ which is $O(|V|^2)$. Therefore, the complexity of `KruskalAlgorithm()` is determined by the complexity of a sorting algorithm which is $O(|E| \lg |E|)$, that is, $O(|E| \lg |V|)$.

8.5.3   Jarnik-Prim's Algorithm

Another algorithm was discovered by Vojtech Jarnik in 1936 and later rediscovered by Robert Prim. In this method, all of the edges are also initially ordered, but a candidate for inclusion in the spanning tree is an edge which not only does not lead to cycles in the tree, but also is incident to a vertex already in the tree:

```
JarnikPrimAlgorithm(weighted connected undirected graph)
    tree = null;
    edges = sequence of all edges of graph sorted by weight;
    for i = 1 to |V| − 1
        for j = 1 to |edges|
            if eⱼ from edges does not form a cycle with edges in tree and
                is incident to a vertex in tree
                    add eⱼ to tree;
                    break;
```

Figure 8.15 da–df contains a step-by-step example of Jarnik-Prim's algorithm. The spanning tree resulting from this algorithm is the same as given by the Kruskal algorithm; however, the order in which edges have been added to the tree is different. The inner loop of `JarnikPrimAlgorithm()` can be $O(E)$ in the worst case, and since the outer loop iterates $|V| - 1$ times, the inner loop may iterate $O(|V||E|)$ times in total. However, this complexity can be substantially improved by a careful implementation of **edges**.

The difference between the Kruskal algorithm and the Jarnik-Prim algorithm is that the latter always keeps the tree being constructed in one piece, so that it is a tree at all stages of application of this algorithm. The Kruskal algorithm is more concerned about the outcome, so it considers it irrelevant that in the middle of its execution the spanning tree may not be a tree at all, but at best a collection of trees. But the Kruskal algorithm guarantees that at the end, there is only one spanning tree. Therefore, the Jarnik-Prim algorithm may be considered more elegant, as we see a tree being expanded at all times. The price for this elegance is that the only edges that can be added to the tree are the ones which are not isolated from the tree built so far, so that certain edges may need to be reconsidered several times. In the Kruskal algorithm each edge needs to be considered only once, since if it leads to a cycle at one stage, it all the more would lead to a cycle at a later stage and hence it does not have to be reconsidered any more. Hence, the Kruskal algorithm is faster.

8.5.4   Dijkstra's Method

Kruskal's and Jarnik-Prim's algorithms required that all the edges be ordered before beginning to build the spanning tree. This, however, is not necessary; it is possible to build a spanning tree by using any order of edges. A method was proposed by Dijkstra (1960), and independently by Robert Kalaba and since no particular order of edges is required here, their method is more general than the other two.

```
DijkstraMethod(weighted connected undirected graph)
    tree = null;
    edges = an unsorted sequence of all edges of graph;
    for j = 1 to |E|
        add eⱼ to tree;
        if there is a cycle in tree
            remove an edge with maximum weight from this only cycle;
```

In this algorithm, the tree is being expended by adding to it edges one by one, and if a cycle is detected, then an edge in this cycle with maximum weight is discarded. An example of building the minimum spanning tree with this method is shown in Figure 8.15ea-el.

■ 8.6   CONNECTIVITY

In many problems we are interested in finding a path in the graph from one vertex to any another vertex. For undirected graphs this means that there are no separate pieces, or subgraphs, of the graph; for a digraph it means that there are some places in the graph to which we can get from some directions but are not necessarily able to return to the starting points.

8.6.1   Connectivity in Undirected Graphs

An undirected graph is called *connected* when there is a path between any two vertices of the graph. The depth-first search algorithm can be used for recognizing whether a graph is connected provided that the loop heading

while *there is a vertex* **v** *such that num(*v*) ==* 0

is removed. Then after the algorithm is finished, we have to check whether the list **edges** includes all vertices of the graph, or simply check if **i** is equal to the number of vertices.

Connectivity comes in degrees: a graph can be more or less connected and it depends on the number of different paths between its vertices. A graph is called *n-connected* if there are at least *n* different paths between any two vertices, that is, there are *n* paths between any two vertices that have no vertices in common. A special type of graph is a *2-connected*, or *biconnected*, graph for which there are at least two different paths between any two vertices. A graph is not biconnected if a vertex can be found which always has to be included in the path between at least two vertices *a* and *b*. In other words, if this vertex is removed from the graph (along with incident edges) then there is no way to find a path from *a* to *b*, which means that the graph is split into two separate subgraphs. Such vertices are called *articulation points* or *cut vertices* and vertices *a* and *b* in Figure 8.1d are examples of articulation points. If an edge causes a graph to be split into two subgraphs, it is called a *bridge*, as for example, the *edge(bc)* in Figure 8.1d. The subgraphs that result from removing an articulation point or a bridge are called *blocks* or *biconnected components*. It is important to know how to decompose a graph into biconnected components.

Articulation points can be detected by extending the depth-first search algorithm. This algorithm creates a tree with forward edges (the graph edges included in the tree) and back edges (the edges not included). A vertex *v* in this tree is an articulation point if it has at least one subtree unconnected with any of its predecessors by a back edge; because it is a tree, certainly none of *v*'s predecessors is reachable from any of its successors by a forward link. For example, the graph in Figure 8.16a is transformed into a depth-first search tree (Figure 8.16c), and this tree has four articulation points, *b, d, h,* and *i* since there is no back edge from any node below *d* to any node above it in the tree, and no back edge from any vertex in the right subtree of *h* to any vertex above *h*. But vertex *g* cannot be an articulation point, because its only subtree is connected to a vertex above it. The four vertices divide the graph into the five blocks indicated in Figure 8.16c by dotted lines.

A special case for an articulation point is when a vertex is a root with more than one descendant. In Figure 8.16a the vertex chosen for the root, *a*, has three incident edges, but only one of them becomes a forward edge in Figures 8.16b and 8.16c, since the other two are processed by depth-first search. Therefore, if this algorithm again recursively reaches *a*, there is no untried edge. If *a* were an articulation point, there would be at least one such untried edge and this would indicate that *a* is a cut vertex. So *a* is not an articulation point. To sum it up, we say that a vertex *v* is an articulation point

1. if *v* is the root of the depth-first search tree and *v* has more than one descendant in this tree, or

2. if at least one of *v*'s subtrees includes no vertex connected by a back edge with any of *v*'s predecessors.

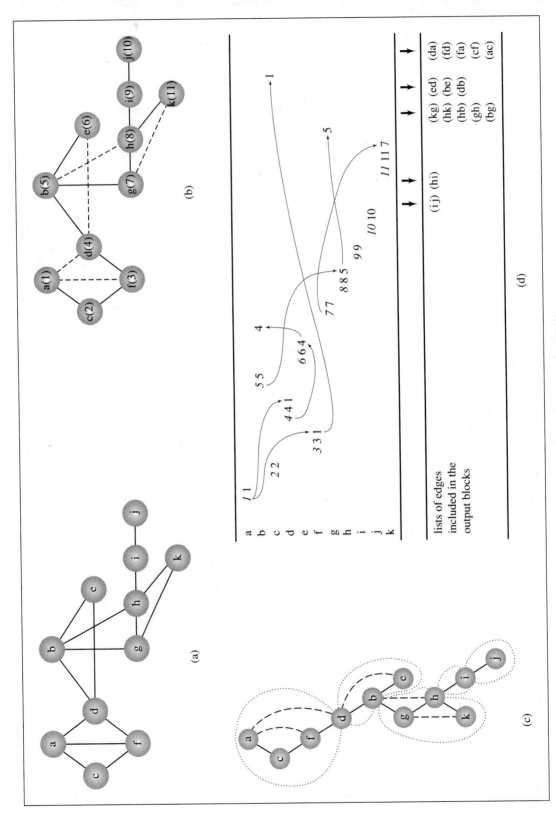

Figure 8.16: **Finding blocks and articulation point using `BlockDFS()` algorithm.**

To find articulation points, a parameter $pred(v)$ is used, defined as $\min(num(v), num(u_1), \ldots, num(u_k))$ where $u_1, \ldots, u_k$ are vertices connected by a back edge with a descendant of v or with v itself. Because the higher a predecessor of v is, the lower its number is, choosing a minimum number means choosing the highest predecessor. For the tree in Figure 8.16c, $pred(c) = pred(d) = 1$, $pred(b) = 4$, and $pred(k) = 7$.

The algorithm uses a stack to store all currently processed edges. After an articulation point is identified, the edges corresponding to a block of the graph are output. The algorithm is given as follows.

```
BlockDFS(v)
    pred(v) = num(v) = i++;
    for all vertices u adjacent to v
        if edge(uv) is not on stack
            Push(edge(uv));
        if num(u) is 0
            BlockDFS(u);
            if pred(u) ≥ num(v)            // if there is no edge from u to a
                e = Pop();                  // vertex above v, output a block
                while e != edge(vu)         // by popping all edges off the
                    output e;               // stack until edge(vu) is
                    e = Pop();              // popped off;
                output e;                   // e == edge(vu);
            else pred(v) = min(pred(v),pred(u));  // take a predecessor higher up in
        else if v is not the parent of u    // tree;
            pred(v) = min(pred(v),num(u));   // update when back edge from v is
                                             // found;
BlockSearch()
    for all vertices v
        num(v) = 0;
    i = 1;
    while there is a vertex v such that num(v) == 0
        BlockDFS(v);
```

An example of the execution of this algorithm is shown in Figure 8.16d as applied to the graph in Figure 8.16a. The table lists all changes in $pred(v)$ for vertices v processed by the algorithm and the arrows show the source of the new values of $pred(v)$. For each vertex v, **BlockDFS(v)** first assigns two numbers: $num(v)$, shown in italic; and $pred(v)$, which may change during the execution of **BlockDFS(v)**. For example, a is processed first with $num(a)$ and $pred(a)$ set to 1. The $edge(ac)$ is pushed onto the stack, and since $num(c)$ is 0, the algorithm is invoked for c. At this point, $num(c)$ and $pred(c)$ are set to 2. Next, the algorithm is invoked for f, a descendant of c, so that $num(f)$ and $pred(f)$ are set to 3, and then it is invoked for a, a descendant of f. Since $num(a)$ is not 0 and a is not f's parent, $pred(f)$ is set to $1 = \min(pred(f),num(a)) = \min(3, 1)$.

This algorithm also outputs the edges in detected blocks, and these edges are shown in Figure 8.16d at the moment when they were output after popping them off the stack.

8.6.2   Connectivity in Directed Graphs

For directed graphs, connectedness can be defined in two ways, depending on whether or not the direction of the edges is taken into account. A directed graph is *weakly connected* if the undirected graph with the same vertices and the same edges is connected. A directed graph is called *strongly connected* if for each pair of vertices there is a path between them in both directions. The entire digraph is not always strongly connected, but it may be composed of *strongly connected components* (SCC) which are defined as subsets of vertices of the graph such that each of these subsets induces a strongly connected digraph.

To determine SCCs, we also refer to depth-first search. Let vertex v be the first vertex of an SCC for which depth-first search is applied. Such a vertex is called the *root of the SCC*. Since each vertex u in this SCC is reachable from v, $num(v) < num(u)$, and only after all such vertices u have been visited, the depth-first search backtracks to v. In this case, which is recognized by the fact that $pred(v) = num(v)$, the SCC accessible from the root can be output.

The problem now is how to find all such roots of the digraph, which is analogous to finding articulation points in an undirected graph. To that end the parameter $pred(v)$ is also used, but this time $pred(v)$ is the lowest number chosen among $num(v)$, and $pred(u)$, where u is a vertex reachable from v and belonging to the same SCC as v. How can we determine whether two vertices belong to the same SCC before SCC has been determined? The apparent circularity is solved by using a stack that stores all vertices belonging to the SCCs under construction. The topmost vertices on the stack belong to the currently analyzed SCC. Although construction is not finished, we at least know which vertices are already included in the SCC. The algorithm attributed to Tarjan is as follows:

```
StrongDFS(v)
  pred(v) = num(v) = i++;
  Push(v);
  for all vertices u adjacent to v
    if num(u) is 0
      StrongDFS(u);
      pred(v) = min(pred(v),pred(u));        // take a predecessor higher up in
                                             // tree; update if back edge found
    else if num(u) < num(v) and u is on stack  // to vertex u in the same SCC;
      pred(v) = min(pred(v),num(u));
  if pred(v) == num(v)                        // if the root of a SCC is found,
    w = Pop();                                // output this SCC, i.e.,
    while w != v                              // pop all vertices off the stack
      output w;                               // until v is popped off;
      e = Pop();
    output w;                                 // w == v;


StronglyConnectedComponentSearch()
  for all vertices v
    (v) = 0;
  i = 1;
  while there is a vertex v such that num(v) == 0
    StrongDFS(v);
```

Figure 8.17 contains an example of execution of Tarjan's algorithm. The digraph in Figure 8.17a is processed by series of calls to **StrongDFS()** which assigns to vertices *a* though *k* the numbers shown in parentheses in Figure 8.17b. During this process, five SCCs are detected: $\{a, c, f\}, \{b, d, e, g, h\}, \{i\}, \{j\}$, and $\{k\}$. Figure 8.17c contains the depth-first search tree created by this process. Note that two trees are created, so that the number of trees does not have to correspond to the number of SCCs, as the number of trees did not correspond to the number of blocks in the case for undirected graphs. Figure 8.17d indicates, in italics, numbers assigned to *num(v)* and all changes of parameter *pred(v)* for all vertices *v* in the graph, and shows the SCCs output during the processing of the graph.

■ 8.7 TOPOLOGICAL SORT

In many situations there is a set of tasks to be performed. For some pairs of tasks it matters which task is performed first whereas for other pairs the order of execution is unimportant. For example, students need to take into consideration which courses are prerequisites or corequisites for other courses when making a schedule for the upcoming semester, so that Computer Programming II cannot be taken before Computer Programming I, but the former can be taken along with, say, Ethics or Introduction to Sociology.

The dependencies between tasks can be shown in the form of a digraph. A *topological sort* linearizes a digraph, that is, it labels all its vertices with numbers $1, \ldots, |V|$ so that $i < j$ only if there is a path from vertex v_i to vertex v_j. The digraph must not include a cycle, otherwise a topological sort is impossible.

The algorithm for a topological sort is rather simple. We have to find a vertex *v* with no outgoing edges, called a *sink* or a *minimal vertex*, and then disregard all edges leading from any vertex to *v*. The summary of the topological sort algorithm is as follows:

```
TopologicalSort(digraph)
    for i = 1 to |V|
        find a minimal vertex v;
        num(v) = i;
        remove from digraph vertex v and all edges incident with v;
```

Figure 8.18 contains an example of an application of this algorithm. The graph in Figure 8.18a undergoes a sequence of deletions (Figure 8.18b–f) and results in the sequence g, e, b, f, d, c, a.

Actually, it is not necessary to remove the vertices and edges from the digraph while it is processed if it can be ascertained that all successors of the vertex being processed have already been processed, so they can be considered as deleted. And once again depth-first search comes to the rescue. By the nature of this method, if the search backtracks to a vertex *v*, then all successors of *v* can be assumed to have already been searched, so they can be output and deleted from the digraph. Here is how depth-first search can be adapted to topological sort:

```
TS(v)
    num(v) = i++;
    for all vertices u adjacent to v
```

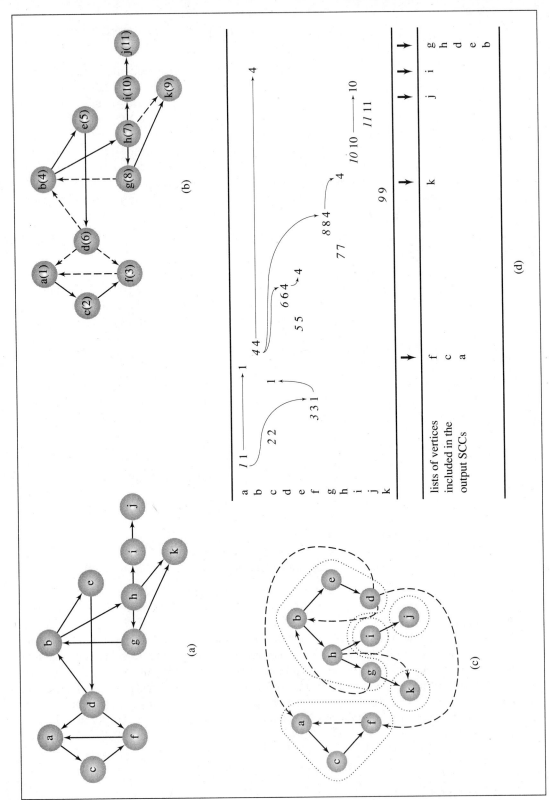

Figure 8.17: **Finding strongly connected components with** StrongDFS ( ) **algorithm.**

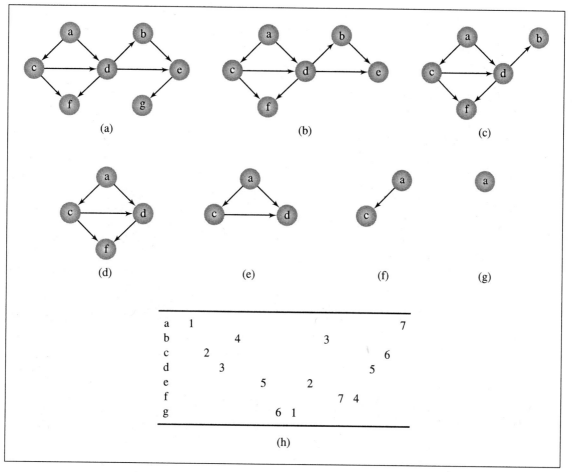

Figure 8.18: **Executing topological sort.**

```
      if num(u) == 0
          TS(u);
      else if TSNum(u) == 0
          error;              // a cycle detected;
  TSNum(v) = j++;             // after processing all successors of v,
                              // assign to v a number larger than
                              // assigned to any of its successors;

TopologicalSorting(digraph)
    for all vertices v
        num(v) = TSNum(v) = 0;
    i = j = 1;
    while there is a vertex v such that num(v) == 0
        TS(v);
    output vertices according to their TSNum's;
```

The table in Figure 8.18h indicates the order in which this algorithm assigns *num(v)*, the first number in each row, and *TSNum(v)*, the second number, for each vertex *v* of the graph in Figure 8.18a.

■ 8.8 NETWORKS

8.8.1 Maximum Flows

An important type of graph is a network. A network can be exemplified by a pipeline used to deliver water from one source to one destination. However, water is not simply pumped through one pipe, but through many pipes with many pumping stations in between. The pipes are of different diameter and the stations are of different power, so that the amount of water that can be pumped may differ from one pipeline to another. For example, the pipeline in Figure 8.19 has eight pipes and six pumping stations. The numbers shown in this figure are the maximum capacities of each pipeline. For example, the pipe going northeast from the source *s*, the pipe *sa*, has a capacity of 5 units (say, 5 thousand gallons per hour). The problem is to maximize the capacity of the entire network so that it can transfer the maximum amount of water. It may not be obvious how to accomplish this goal. Notice that the pipe *sa* coming from the source goes to a station which has only one outgoing pipe, *ab*, of capacity 4. This means that we cannot put 5 units through pipe *sa*, since pipe *ab* cannot transfer it. Also, the amount of water coming to station *b* has to be controlled as well, since if both incoming pipes, *ab* and *cb*, are used to full capacity, then the outgoing pipe, *bt*, cannot process it either. It is far from obvious, especially for large networks, what the amounts of water put through each pipe should be to utilize the network maximally. Computational analysis of this particular network problem was initiated by Lester R. Ford and D. Ray Fulkerson. Since their work, scores of algorithms have been published to solve this problem.

Before the problem is stated more formally, we would like to give some definitions. A *network* is a digraph with one vertex *s*, called the *source*, with no incoming edges, and one vertex *t*, called the *sink*, with no outgoing edges. (These definitions are chosen for their intuitiveness; however, in a more general case, both source and sink can be any two vertices.) With each edge *e* we associate a number *cap(e)* called the *capacity* of the edge. A *flow* is a real function $f : E \rightarrow R$ which assigns a number to each edge of the network and which meets these two conditions:

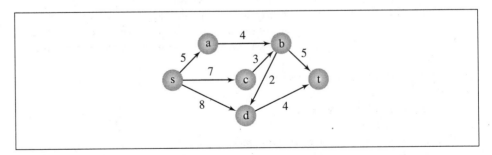

Figure 8.19: **A pipeline with eight pipes and six pumping stations.**

1. The flow through an edge e cannot be greater than its capacity, or $0 \le f(e) \le cap(e)$ (capacity constraint).

2. Except for the source and the sink, the total flow coming to a vertex v is the same as the total flow coming from it, or $\sum_u f(edge(uv)) = \sum_w f(edge(vw))$, where v is neither the source nor the sink (flow conservation).

The problem now is to maximize the flow f so that the sum $\sum_u f(edge(ut))$ has a maximum value for any possible function f. This problem is called a *maximum-flow* (or *max-flow*) *problem*.

An important concept used in the Ford-Fulkerson algorithm is the concept of cut. A *cut separating s and t* is a set of edges between vertices of set X and vertices of set $\bar{X}$; any vertex of the graph belongs to one of these sets and source s is in X and sink t is in $\bar{X}$. For example, in Figure 8.19, if $X = \{s, a\}$ then $\bar{X} = \{b, c, d, t\}$ and the cut is the set of edges $\{(a, b), (s, c), (s, d)\}$. This means that if all edges belonging to this set are cut, then there is no way to get from s to t. Let us define the capacity of the cut as the sum of capacities of all its edges leading from a vertex in X to a vertex in $\bar{X}$; thus, $cap\{(a, b), (s, c), (s, d)\} = cap(a, b) + cap(s, c) + cap(s, d) = 19$. Now, it should be clear that the flow through the network cannot be greater than the capacity of any cut. This observation leads to the *max-flow min-cut theorem* (Ford, Fulkerson 1956):

Theorem. In any network, the maximal flow from s to t is equal to the minimal capacity of any cut.

This theorem states what is expressed in the metaphor of a chain being as strong as its weakest link. Although there may be cuts with great capacity, the cut with the smallest capacity determines the flow of network. For example, although the capacity $cap\{(a, b), (s, c), (s, d)\} = 19$, two edges coming to t cannot transfer more than 9 units. Now we have to find a cut which has the smallest capacity among all possible cuts and transfer through each edge of this cut as many units as the capacity allows. To that end, a new concept is used.

A *flow-augmenting path* from s to t is a sequence of edges from s to t such that for each edge in this path, the flow $f(e) < cap(e)$ on forward edges and $f(e) > 0$ on backward edges. It means that such a path is not optimally used yet and it can transfer more units than it is currently transferring. If the flow for at least one edge of the path reaches its capacity, then obviously the flow cannot be augmented. Note that the path does not have to consist only of forward edges, so that examples of paths in Figure 8.19 are s, a, b, t, and s, d, b, t. Backward edges are what they are, backward; they push back some units of flow, decreasing the flow of the network. If they can be eliminated, then the overall flow in the network can be increased. Hence, the process of augmenting flows of paths is not finished until the flow for such edges is zero. Our task now is to find an augmenting path if it exists. Since there may be a very large number of paths from s to t, finding an augmenting path is a nontrivial problem and Ford and Fulkerson (1957) devised the first algorithm to accomplish it in a systematic manner.

The *labeling* phase of the algorithm consists of assigning to each vertex v a label which is the pair

$$label(v) = (parent(v), slack(v))$$

where *parent*(*v*) is the vertex from which *v* is being accessed and *slack*(*v*) is the amount of flow which can be transferred from *s* to *v*. The forward and backward edges are treated differently. If a vertex *u* is accessed from *v* through a forward edge, then

$$label(u) = (v^+, \min(slack(v), slack(edge(vu)))),$$

where

$$slack(edge(vu)) = cap(edge(vu)) - f(edge(vu)),$$

which is the difference between the capacity of *edge*(*vu*) and the amount of flow currently carried by this edge. If the edge from *v* to *u* is backward (i.e., forward from *u* to *v*), then

$$label(u) = (v^-, \min(slack(v), f(edge(uv)))).$$

After a vertex is labeled, it is stored for later processing. In this process, only this *edge*(*vu*) is labeled which allows for some more flow to be added, which for forward edges is possible, when *slack*(*edge*(*vu*)) > 0 and for backward edges, when *f*(*edge*(*uv*)) > 0. However, finding one such path may not finish the entire process. The process is finished if we are stuck in the middle of the network unable to label any more edges. If we reach the sink *t*, the flows of the edges on the augmenting path that was just found are updated by increasing flows of forward edges and decreasing flows of backward edges and the process restarts in the quest for another augmenting path. Here is a summary of the algorithm.

```
AugmentPath(network with source s and sink t)
    for each edge e in the path from s to t
        if forward(e)
            f(e) += slack(t);
        else f(e) -= slack(t);


FordFulkersonAlgorithm(network with source s and sink t)
    set flow of all edges and vertices to 0;
    label(s) = (null,∞);
    labeled = {s};
    while labeled is not empty // while not stuck;
        detach a vertex v from labeled;
        for all unlabeled vertices u adjacent to v
            if forward(edge(vu)) and slack(edge(vu)) > 0
                label(u) = (v⁺, min(slack(v), slack(edge(vu))))
            else if backward(edge(vu)) and f(edge(uv)) > 0
                label(u) = (v⁻, min(slack(v), f(edge(uv))));
            if u got labeled
                if u == t
                    AugmentPath(network);
                    labeled = {s};    // look for another path;
                else include u in labeled;
```

Notice that this algorithm is noncommittal with respect to the way the network should be scanned. In exactly what order should vertices be included in `labeled` and detached from it? This question is left open and we choose push and pop as implementations of these two operations, thereby processing the network in a depth-first fashion.

Figure 8.20 illustrates an example. Each edge has two numbers associated with it, the capacity and the current flow, and initially the flow is set to zero for each edge (8.20a). We begin by putting the vertex s in `labeled`. In the first iteration of the `while` loop, s is detached from `labeled`, and in the `for` loop, label $(s,2)$ is assigned to the first adjacent vertex, a, label $(s,4)$ to vertex c, and label $(s,1)$ to vertex e (Figure 8.20b), and all three vertices are pushed onto `labeled`. The `for` loop is exited and since `labeled` is not empty, the `while` loop begins its second iteration. In this iteration, a vertex is popped off from `labeled`, which is e, both unlabeled vertices incident to e, vertices d and f, are labeled and pushed onto `labeled`. Now, the third iteration of the `while` loop begins by popping f from `labeled` and labeling its only unlabeled neighbor, vertex t. Because t

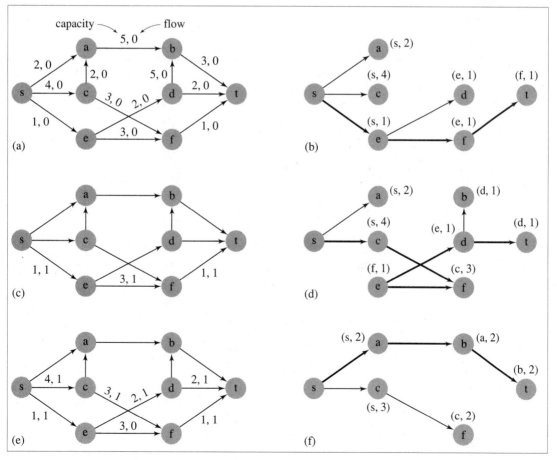

Figure 8.20: **An execution of `FordFulkersonAlgorithm()` using depth-first search.**   continued

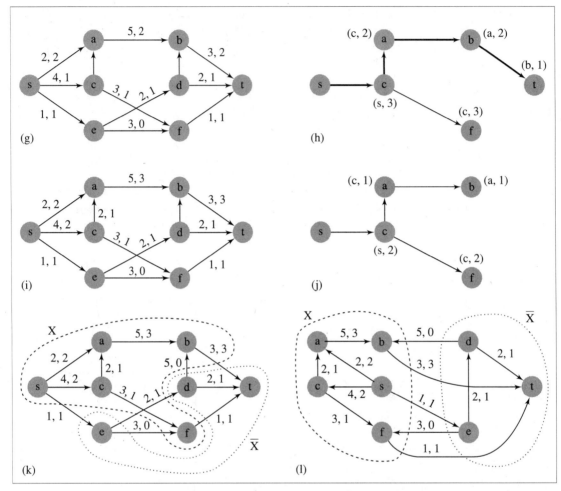

Figure 8.20: **An execution of FordFulkersonAlgorithm() using depth-first search.**

is the sink, the flows of all edges on the augmenting path s, e, f, t are updated in the inner **for** loop (Figure 8.20c), **labeled** is reinitialized to $\{s\}$, and the next round begins to find another augmenting path.

The next round starts with the fourth iteration of the **while** loop. In its eighth iteration the sink is reached (Figure 8.20d) and flows of edges on the new augmenting path are updated (Figure 8.20e). Note that this time one edge, *edge(fe)*, is a backward edge. Therefore, its flow is decremented, not incremented as is the case for forward edges. Afterwards, two more augmenting paths are found and corresponding edges are updated. In the last round, we are unable to reach the sink (Figure 8.20j), which means that all augmenting edges have been found and the maximum flow has been determined.

If after finishing execution of the algorithm all vertices labeled in the last round, including the source, are put in the set X and the unlabeled vertices in the set $\bar{X}$, then we have a min-cut (Figure 8.20k). For clarity, both sets are also shown in Figure 8.20l. Note that all the edges from X to $\bar{X}$ are used in full capacity, and all the edges from $\bar{X}$ to X do not transfer any flow at all.

The complexity of this algorithm is not necessarily a function of the number of vertices and edges in the network. Consider the network in Figure 8.21. Using a depth-first implementation, we could choose the augmenting path s, a, b, t with flows of all three edges set to 1. The next augmenting path could be s, b, a, t with flows of two forward edges set to 1 and the flow of one backward $edge(ba)$ reset to 0. Next time, the augmenting path could be the same as the first, with flows of two edges set to 2 and with the vertical edge set to 1. It is clear that an augmenting path could be chosen $2 * 10$ times, although there are only four vertices in the network.

The problem with `FordFulkersonAlgorithm()` is that it uses the depth-first approach when searching for an augmenting path. But as already mentioned, this choice does not stem from the nature of this algorithm. The depth-first approach attempts to reach the sink as soon as possible. However, trying to find the shortest augmenting path gives better results. This leads to a breadth-first approach (Edmonds, Karp 1972). The breadth-first processing uses the same procedure as `FordFulkersonAlgorithm()` except that this time `labeled` is a queue. Figure 8.22 illustrates an example.

To determine one single augmenting path, the algorithm requires at most $2|E|$, or $O(|E|)$ steps, to check both sides of each edge. The shortest augmenting path in the network can have only one edge and the longest path can have at most $|V| - 1$ edges. Therefore, there can be augmenting paths of lengths $1, 2, \ldots, |V| - 1$. The number of augmenting paths of a certain length is at most $|E|$. Therefore, to find all augmenting paths of all possible lengths, the algorithm needs to perform $O(|V||E|)$ steps. And since finding one such path is of order $O(|E|)$, the algorithm is of order $O(|V||E|^2)$.

Although the pure breadth-first search approach is better than the pure depth-first search implementation, it still is far from ideal. We will not fall into a loop of tiny increments

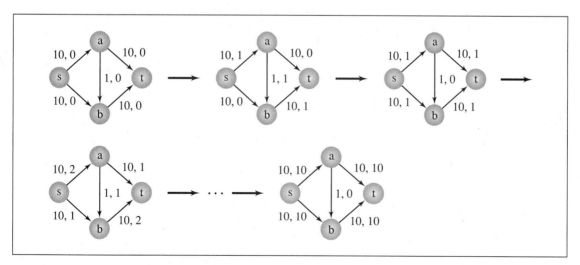

Figure 8.21: **An example of an inefficiency of**
`FordFulkersonAlgorithm()`.

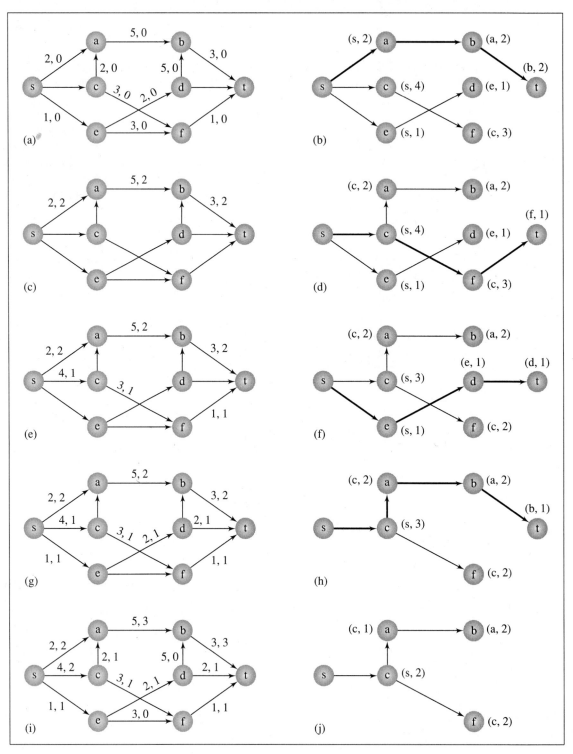

Figure 8.22: An execution of `FordFulkersonAlgorithm()` using breadth-first search.

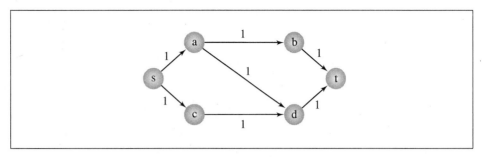

Figure 8.23: **An example of blocking (maximal) flow.**

of augmenting steps any more, but there still seems to be a great deal of wasted effort. In breadth-first search, a large number of vertices are labeled to find the shortest path (shortest in a given iteration). Then all these labels are discarded to recreate them when looking for another augmenting path (*edge*(*sc*), *edge*(*se*), and *edge*(*cf*) in Figure 8.22b,d). Therefore, it is desirable to reduce this redundancy. Also, there is some merit to using the depth-first approach in that it attempts to aim at the goal, the sink, without expanding a number of paths at the same time and finally choosing only one and discarding the rest. Hence, the Solomonic solution appears to use both approaches, depth-first and breadth-first. Breadth-first prepares the ground to prevent loops of small increments from happening (as in Figure 8.21) and to guarantee that depth-first search takes the shortest route. Only afterwards the depth-first search is launched to find the sink by aiming right at it. An algorithm based upon this principle was devised first by Efim A. Dinic[2].

In Dinic's algorithm, up to $|V| - 1$ passes (or phases) through the network are performed and in each pass, all augmenting paths of the same length from the source to the sink are determined. Then among these paths, only some or all these augmenting paths are augmented. Consider the network in Figure 8.23 with all edges of capacity one. It has three augmenting paths, s, a, b, t, then s, a, d, t and finally s, c, d, t. However, if the second path, s, a, d, t, is augmented, then the remaining two paths cannot push any flow to the sink. Out of three augmenting paths only one is actually augmented. In situations like this, the flow which has been determined is called a *blocking* or *maximal flow*.

All augmenting paths form a *layered network* (also called a *level network*). Extracting layered networks from the underlying network starts from the lowest values. First, a layered network of a path of length one is found, if such a network exists. After the network is processed, a layered network of paths of length two is determined, if it exists, and so on. For example, the layered network with the shortest paths corresponding with the network in Figure 8.24a is shown in Figure 8.24b. In this network, all augmenting paths are of length three. Layered networks with a single path of length one and two do not exist. The layered network is created using breadth-first processing and only forward edges which can carry more flow and backward edges which already carry some flow are included. Otherwise, even if an edge may lay on a short path from the source to the sink, it is not included. Note that the layered network is determined by breadth-first search that begins in the sink and ends in the source.

---

[2]Pronounced: Dinits.

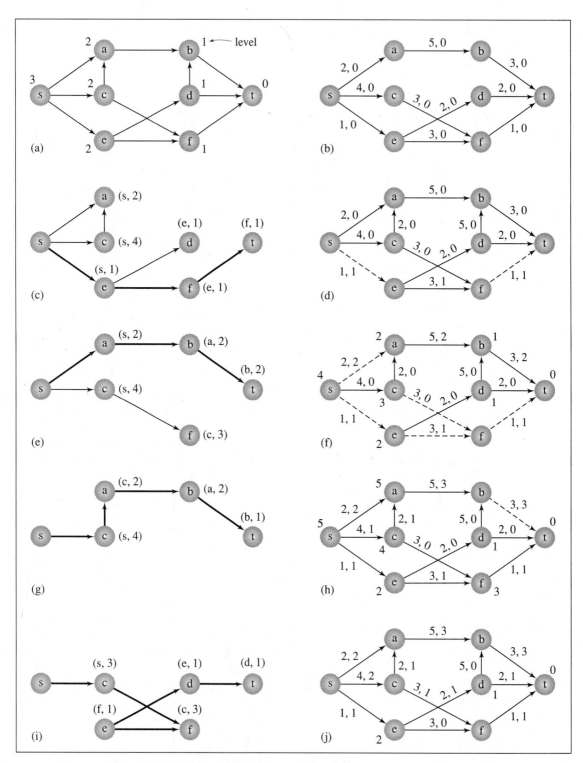

Figure 8.24: **An execution of DinicAlgorithm().**

Now, since all the paths in a layered network are of the same length, it is possible to avoid redundant tests of edges that are a part of augmenting paths. If in a current layered network there is no way to go from a vertex v to any of its neighbors, then in later tests in the same layered network there will be the same situation, hence checking again all neighbors of v is not needed. Therefore, if such a dead end vertex v is detected, all edges incident with v are marked as blocked, so that there will be no possibility to get to v from any direction. Also, all saturated edges are considered blocked. All blocked edges are shown in dashed lines in Figure 8.24.

After a layered network is determined, the depth-first process finds as many augmenting paths as possible. Since all paths are of the same length, depth-first search does not go to the sink through some longer sequence of edges. After one such path is found, it is augmented and another augmenting path of the same length is looked for. For each such path, at least one edge becomes saturated, so that eventually no augmenting path can be found. For example, in the layered network in Figure 8.24b that includes only augmenting paths three edges long path, s, e, f, t is found (Figure 8.24c), and all its edges are augmented (Figure 8.24d). Then only one more three-edge path is found, the path s, a, b, t (8.24e), since, for example, previous augmentation saturated $edge(ft)$ so that the partial path s, c, f ends with a dead end. Also, since no other vertex can be reached from f, all edges incident with f are blocked (Figure 8.24f), so that an attempt to find the third three-edge augmenting path will only test vertex c, but not vertex f, since $edge(cf)$ is blocked.

If no more augmenting paths can be found, a higher level layered network is found and augmenting paths for this network are searched for. The process stops when no layered network can be formed. For example, out of the network in Figure 8.24f, the layered network in Figure 8.24g is formed, which has only one four-edge path. To be sure, this is the only augmenting path for this network. After augmenting this path, the situation in the network is as in Figure 8.24h, and the last layered network is formed which also has only one path, this time a path of five edges. The path is augmented (Figure 8.24j) and then no other layered network can be found. This algorithm can be summarized in the following pseudocode:

```
LayerNetwork(network with source s and sink t)
    for all vertices u
        level(t) = -1;
    level(t) = 0;
    Enqueue(t);
    while queue is not empty
        v = Dequeue();
        for all vertices u adjacent to v such that level(u) == -1
            if forward(edge(uv)) and slack(edge(uv)) > 0 or
                backward(edge(uv)) and f(edge(vu)) > 0
                    level(u) = level (v)+1;
                    Enqueue(u);
            if u == s
                return success;
    return failure;
```

```
ProcessAugmentingPaths(network with source s and sink t)
    unblock all edges;
    labeled = {s};
    while labeled not empty // while not stuck;
        pop v from labeled;
        for all unlabeled vertices u adjacent to v such that
                edge (vu) is not blocked and level(v) == level(u) -1
            if forward(edge(vu)) and slack(edge(vu)) > 0
                label(u) = (v⁺, min(slack(v), slack(edge(vu))))
            else if backward(edge(vu)) and f(edge(uv)) > 0
                label(u) = (v⁻, min(slack(v), f(edge(uv))));
            if u got labeled
                if u == t
                    AugmentPath();
                    block saturated edges;
                    labeled = {s};      // look for another path;
                else push u onto labeled;
        if no neighbor of v has been labeled
            block all edges incident with v;


DinicAlgorithm(network with source s and sink t)
    set flows of all edges and vertices to 0;
    label(s) = (null,∞);
    while LayerNetwork(network) is successful
        ProcessAugmentingPaths(network);
```

What is the complexity of this algorithm? There are maximum $|V| - 1$ layerings (phases) and up to $O(|E|)$ steps to layer the network. Hence, finding all the layered networks requires $O(|V||E|)$ steps. Moreover, there are $O(|E|)$ paths per phase (per one layered network) and, due to blocking, $O(|V|)$ steps to find one path, and since there are $O(|V|)$ layered networks, in the worst case, $O(|V|^2|E|)$ steps are required to find the augmenting paths. This estimation determines the efficiency of the algorithm, which is better than $O(|V||E|^2)$ for breadth-first **FordFulkersonAlgorithm()**. The improvement is in the number of steps to find one augmenting path, which is now $O(|V|)$, not $O(|E|)$, as before. The price for this improvement is the need to prepare the network by creating layered networks, which, as established, requires an additional $O(|V||E|)$ steps.

The difference in pseudocode for **FordFulkersonAlgorithm()** and **Process AugmentingPaths()** is not large. The most important difference is in the amplified condition for expanding a path from a certain vertex v: only the edges to adjacent vertices u which do not extend augmenting paths beyond the length of paths in the layered network are considered.

8.8.2 Maximum Flows of Minimum Cost

In the previous discussion, edges had two parameters, capacity and flow: how much flow they can carry and how much flow they are actually carrying. But although many different maximum flows through the network are possible, we choose the one dictated by the

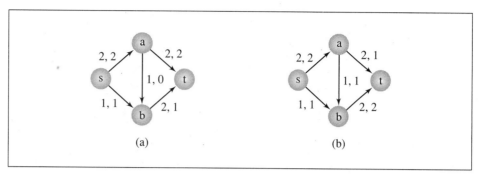

Figure 8.25: **Two possible maximum flows for the same network.**

algorithm currently in use. For example, Figure 8.25 illustrates two possible maximum flows for the same network. Note that in the first case, the *edge(ab)* is not used at all; only in the second case are all the edges transferring some flow. The breadth-first algorithm leads to the first maximum flow and finishes our quest for maximum flow after identifying it. However, in many situations this is not a good decision. If there are many possible maximum flows, it does not mean that any one of them is equally good.

Consider the following example. If edges are roads between some locations then it is not enough to know that a road has one or two lanes to properly choose a route. If the *distance(a, t)* is very long and *distance(a, b)* and *distance(b, t)* are relatively short, then it is better to consider the second maximum flow (Figure 8.25b) as a viable option rather than the first (Figure 8.25a). However, this may not be enough. The shorter way can have no pavement: it can be muddy, hilly, close to the avalanche areas, sometimes blocked by boulders, among other disadvantages. Hence, using the distance as the sole criterion for choosing a road is insufficient. Taking the roundabout way may bring us to the destination faster and cheaper (to mention only time and gasoline burned).

We clearly need a third parameter for an edge, the *cost* of transferring one unit of flow through this edge. The problem now is how to find a maximum flow at minimum cost. More formally, if for each edge *e*, the *cost(e)* of sending one unit of flow is determined so that it costs $n \cdot cost(e)$ to transmit n units of flow over edge *e*, then we need to find a maximum flow f of minimum cost, or a flow such that

$$cost(f) = \min\{\textstyle\sum_{e \in E} f(e) \cdot cost(e) : f \text{ is a maximum flow}\}.$$

Finding all possible maximum flows and comparing their costs is not a feasible solution because the amount of work to find all such flows can be prohibitive. Algorithms are needed that find not only a maximum flow but the maximum flow at minimum cost.

One strategy is based on the following theorem, proven first by W.S. Jewell, R.G. Busacker, and P.J. Gowen, and implicitly used by M. Iri (Ford, Fulkerson 1962):

Theorem. If f is a minimal-cost flow with the flow value v and p is the minimum cost augmenting path sending a flow of value 1 from the source to the sink, then the flow $f + p$ is minimal and its flow value is $v + 1$.

The theorem should be intuitively clear. If we determined the cheapest way to send v units of flow through the network and afterwards found a path for sending 1 unit of flow from the source to the sink, then we found the cheapest way to send $v + 1$ units using the route which is a combination of the route already determined and the path just found. If this augmenting path allows for sending 1 unit for minimum cost, then it also allows for sending two units at minimum cost, and also three units, up to n units, where n is the maximum amount of units that can be sent through this path; that is,

$$n = \min\{capacity(e) - f(e) : e \text{ is an edge in minimum cost augmenting path}\}.$$

This also suggests how we can proceed systematically to find the cheapest maximum route. We start with all flows set to zero. In the first pass we find the cheapest way to send one unit and then send as many units through this path as possible. After the second iteration, we find a path to send one unit at least cost and we send through this path as many units as this path can hold, and so on until no further dispatch from the source can be made or the sink cannot accept any more flow.

Note that the problem of finding maximum flow of minimum cost bears some resemblance to the problem of finding the shortest path, since the shortest path can be understood as the path with minimum cost. Hence, a procedure is needed to find the shortest path in the network so that as much flow as possible can be sent through this path. Therefore, a reference to an algorithm which solves the shortest path problem should not be surprising. We modify Dijkstra's algorithm used for solving the one-to-one shortest path problem (see Exercise 7 at the end of this chapter). Here is the algorithm:

```
ModifiedDijkstraAlgorithm(network, s, t)
    for all vertices u
        f(u) = 0;
        cost(u) = ∞;
    set flows of all edges to 0;
    label(s) = (null,∞,0);
    labeled = null;
    while (1)
        v = a vertex not in labeled with minimal cost(v);
        if v == t
            if cost(t) == ∞ // no path from s to t can be found;
                return failure;
            else return success;
        add v to labeled;
        for all vertices u not in labeled and adjacent to v
            if forward(edge(vu)) and slack(edge(vu)) > 0 and cost(v)+ cost(vu) < cost(u)
                label(u) = (v⁺,min(slack(v), slack(edge(vu)), cost(v)+ cost(vu))
            else if backward(edge(vu)) and f(edge(uv)) > 0 and cost(v)− cost(uv) < cost(u)
                label(u) = (v⁻,min(slack(v), f(edge(uv)), cost(v)− cost(uv));

MaxFlowMinCostAlgorithm(network with source s and sink t)
    while ModifiedDijkstraAlgorithm(network,s,t) is successful
        AugmentPath(network,s,t);
```

`ModifiedDijkstraAlgorithm()` keeps track of three things at a time, so that the label for each vertex is the triple

$$label(u) = (parent(u), flow(u), cost(u)).$$

First, for each vertex u it records the predecessor v, the vertex through which u is accessible from the source s. Second, it records the maximum amount of flow that can be pushed through the path from s to u and eventually to t. Third, it stores the cost of passing all the edges from the source to u. For forward $edge(vu)$, $cost(u)$ is the sum of the costs already accumulated in v plus the cost of pushing one unit of flow through $edge(vu)$. For backward $edge(vu)$, the unit cost of passing through this edge is subtracted from the $cost(v)$ and stored in $cost(u)$. Also, flows of edges included in augmanted paths are updated; this task is performed by `AugmentPath()` (see p. 304).

Figure 8.26 illustrates an example. In the first iteration of the `while` loop, `labeled` becomes $\{s\}$ and the three vertices adjacent to s are labeled, $label(a) = (s, 2, 6)$, $label(c) = (s, 4, 2)$, and $label(e) = (s, 1, 1)$. Then the vertex with the smallest cost is chosen, namely vertex e. Now, `labeled` $= \{s, e\}$ and two vertices acquire new labels, $label(d) = (e, 1, 3)$ and $label(f) = (e, 1, 2)$. In the third iteration, vertex c is chosen, since its cost, 2, is minimal. Vertex a receives a new label, $(c, 2, 3)$, since the cost of accessing it from s through c is smaller than accessing it directly from s. Vertex f which is adjacent to c does not get a new label, since the cost of sending one unit of flow from s to f through c, 5, exceeds the cost of sending this unit through e, which is 2. In the fourth iteration, f is chosen, `labeled` becomes $\{s, e, c, f\}$, and $label(t) = (f, 1, 5)$. After the seventh iteration, the situation in the graph is as pictured in Figure 8.26b. The eighth iteration is exited right after the sink t is chosen, after which the path s, e, f, t is augmented (Figure 8.26c). The execution continues, `ModifiedDijkstraAlgorithm()` is invoked four more times, and in the last invocation no other path can be found from s to t. Note that the same paths were found here as in Figure 8.20 although in a different order, which was due to the cost of these paths: the cost of the first detected path is 5 (Figure 8.26b), 6 is the cost of the second path (Figure 8.26d), 8 is the cost of the third (Figure 8.26f), and 9 is the cost of the fourth (Figure 8.26h).

■ 8.9 CASE STUDY: DISTINCT REPRESENTATIVES

Let there be a set of committees, $C = \{C_1, ..., C_n\}$, each committee having at least one person. The problem is to determine, if possible, representatives from each committee so that each committee is represented by one person and each person can represent only one committee. For example, if there are three committees, $C_1 = \{M_5, M_1\}, C_2 = \{M_2, M_4, M_3\}$, and $C_3 = \{M_3, M_5\}$, then one possible representation is: member M_1 represent committee C_1, M_2 represents C_2, and M_5 represents C_3. However, if we have these three committees: $C_4 = C_5 = \{M_6, M_7\}$, and $C_6 = \{M_7\}$, then no distinct representation can be created, since there are only two members in all three committees combined. The latter observation has been proven by P. Hall in the *system of distinct representatives* theorem which can be phrased in the following way:

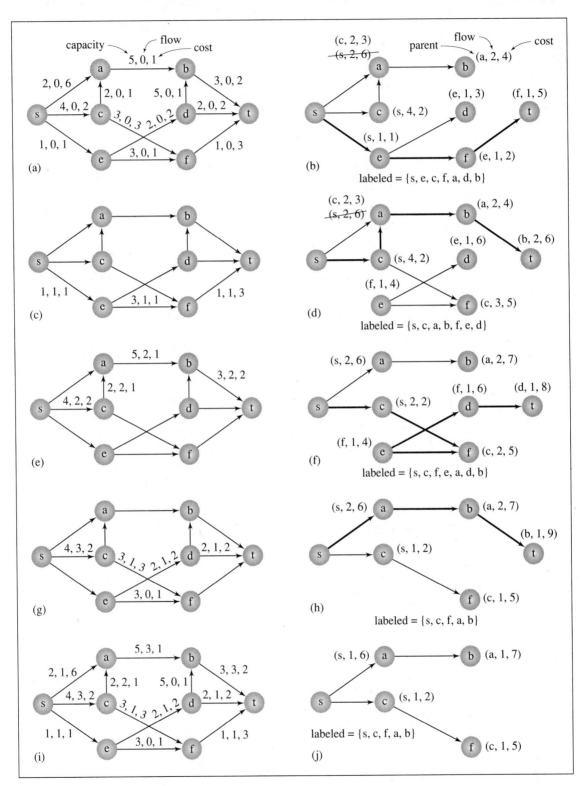

Figure 8.26: **Finding a maximum flow of minimum cost.**

Theorem. A nonempty collection of finite nonempty sets $C_1, \ldots, C_n$ has a system of distinct representatives iff for any $i \leq n$, the union $C_{k_1} \cup, \ldots, \cup C_{k_i}$ has at least n elements.

The problem can be solved by creating a network and trying to find a maximum flow in this network. For example, the network in Figure 8.27a can represent the membership of the three committees C_1, C_2, and C_3. There is a dummy sink vertex connected to nodes representing committees, the committee vertices are connected to vertices representing their members, and the member vertices are all connected to a dummy sink vertex. We assume that each edge e's capacity $cap(e) = 1$. A system of distinct representatives is found if the maximum flow in the network equals the number of committees. The paths determined by a particular maximum flow algorithm determine the representatives. For example, member M_1 represents the committee C_1 if a path s, C_1, M_1, t is determined.

The implementation has two main stages. First, a network is created using a set of committees and members stored in a file. Then, the network is processed to find augmenting paths corresponding to members representing committees. The first stage is specific to the system of distinct representatives. The second stage can be used for finding the maximum flow of any network since it assumes that the network has been created before it begins.

When reading committees and members from a file, we assume that the name of a committee is always followed by a semicolon, then by a list of members separated by commas and ended with a semicolon. An example is the following file **committees**:

```
C2: M2, M4, M3;
C1: M5, M1;
C3: M3, M5;
```

In preparation for creating a network, two trees are generated, a **committeeTree** and **memberTree**. The information stored in each node includes the name of committee or member, an **idNum** assigned by the program using a running counter **numOfVertices**,

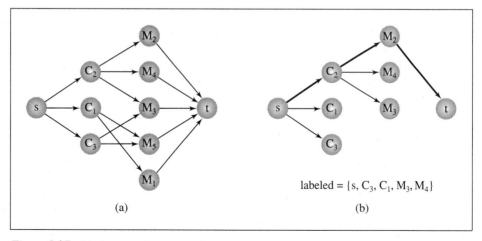

Figure 8.27: **(a) A network representing membership of three committees, C_1, C_2, and C_3 and (b) the first augmenting path found in this network.**

and an adjacency list to be included later in network. Figure 8.28a shows `committeeTree` corresponding to the committees of the example file. The adjacency lists are shown in simplified form, with member `idNum` only (for their full form, see Figure 8.28b); the names of the members are shown above the nodes of these adjacency lists. A separate adjacency list, `sourceList`, is built for the source vertex.

After the file is processed and all committees and members are included in the trees, the generation of the network begins. The network is represented by the array `vertices`. The index of each cell corresponds to the `idNum` assigned to each node of the two trees. Each cell `i` includes information necessary for proper processing of the vertex `i`: the name of the vertex, vertex slack, labeled/nonlabeled flag, adjacency list, parent in the current augmenting path, and pointer to a node `i` in the parent's adjacency list. Note that the fields pointing to lists used in creating the trees have to be set to null, since otherwise these lists would be deleted by destructors at the end of execution of `ReadCommittees()`.

An adjacency list of a vertex `i` represents edges incident with `i`. The information in each node of such a list includes `idNum`, the capacity of the edge, its flow, the forward/backward flag, and a pointer to the twin. If there is an edge from vertex `i` to vertex `j`, then the adjacency list for `i` includes a node representing a forward edge from `i` to `j`, and the adjacency list for `j` has a node corresponding to a backward edge from `j` to `i`. Hence, each edge is represented twice in the network. If a path is augmented, then augmenting an edge means updating two nodes on two adjacency lists. To make this possible, each node on such a list points to its twin, or rather, points to a node representing the same edge taken in the opposite direction.

In this algorithm, the source node is always processed first, since it is always pushed first onto `labeled`. Because the algorithm requires processing only unlabeled vertices, there is no need to include the source vertex in any adjacency list, since the edge from any vertex to the source has no chance to be included in any augmenting path. Also, after the sink is reached, the process of finding an augmenting path is discontinued, whereby no edge incident with the sink is processed, so there is no need to keep an adjacency list for the sink.

The structure created by `ReadCommittees()` using the file `committees` is shown in Figure 8.28b; this structure represents the network also shown in Figure 8.27a.

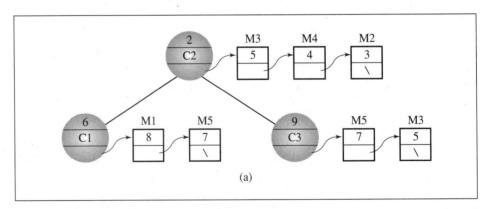

(a)

Figure 8.28: (a) The committeeTree created by `ReadCommittees()` using the contents of the file committees. **continued**

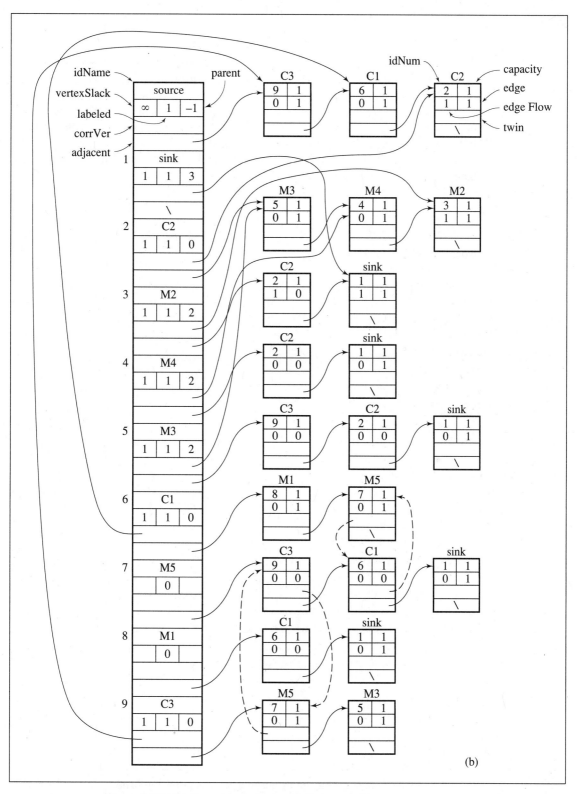

Figure 8.28: **(b) the network representation created by**
FordFulkersonMaxFlow().

319

The numbers in the nodes and array cells are put by **FordFulkersonMaxFlow()** right after finding the first augmenting path, 0, 2, 3, 1, that is, the path *source, C_2, M_2, sink* (Figure 8.27b). Nodes in the adjacency list of a vertex **i** do not include the names of vertices accessible from **i**, only their **idNum**; therefore, these names are shown above each node. The dashed lines show twin edges. In order not to clutter Figure 8.28 with too many links, only the links for two pairs of twin nodes are shown.

The representation determined by this program is as follows: member M_2 represents committee C_2, M_5 represents C_1, and M_3 represent C_3.

Figure 8.29 contains the code for this program.

```
template<class genType>
#include <iostream.h>
#include <fstream.h>
#include <ctype.h>
#include <stdlib.h>
#include <string.h>
#include <values.h>
#include "genLstSt.h"
#include "genSLLst.h"
#include "genBSTre.h"


class LocalTree;


class Network {
public:
    Network() : yes(1), forward(1), sink(1), source(0), none(-1),
                numOfVertices(2) {
        sourceVer.idNum = source;
        sinkVer.idNum = sink;
        sourceVer.edge = !forward;
        sinkVer.edge = forward;
        sourceVer.capacity = sinkVer.capacity = 1;
        sourceVer.edgeFlow = sinkVer.edgeFlow = 0;
    }
    void ReadCommittees(char *committees);
    void AugmentPath();
    void FordFulkersonMaxFlow();
    void Print();
private:
    friend LocalTree;
```

Figure 8.29: **An implementation of the distinct representatives problem.**   **continued**

```
      const int sink, source, none;
      const unsigned int yes, forward : 1;
      int numOfVertices;
      struct Vertex {
            int idNum, capacity, edgeFlow;
            unsigned int edge : 1;            // direction;
            Vertex *twin; // edge in opposite direction;
            Vertex() { }
            Vertex(int id, int c, int ef, int e, Vertex *t = 0)
               { idNum = id; capacity = c; edgeFlow = ef; edge = e; twin = t; }
            int operator== (Vertex v) { return idNum == v.idNum; }
      } sourceVer, sinkVer;
      struct VertexArrayRec {
            char *idName;
            int vertexSlack;
            unsigned int labeled : 1;
            int parent;
            SinglyLinkedList<Vertex> adjacent;
            Vertex *corrVer;      // corresponding vertex: vertex on parent's
            VertexArrayRec() { } // list of adjacent vertices with the same
      } *vertices;                // idNum and the cell's index;
      struct NetTreeNode {
            int idNum;
            char *idName;
            SinglyLinkedList<Vertex> adjacent;
            NetTreeNode() { }
            int operator<  (NetTreeNode& tr)
                { return strcmp(idName,tr.idName) < 0;   }
            int operator== (NetTreeNode& tr)
                { return strcmp(idName,tr.idName) == 0; }
      };
      friend ostream& operator<< (ostream&, Network::NetTreeNode&);
      friend ostream& operator<< (ostream&, Network::Vertex&);
      SLLStack<int> labeled;
      int EdgeSlack(Vertex *u) { return u->capacity - u->edgeFlow; }
      int min(int n, int m) { return n < m ? n : m; }
      int Labeled(Vertex *p)
            { return vertices[p->idNum].labeled == yes; }
      void Label(Vertex*,int);
} net;
```

Figure 8.29: **An implementation of the distinct representatives problem.**   **continued**

```
ostream&
operator<< (ostream& out, Network::NetTreeNode& tr)
{
    out << tr.idNum << ' ' << tr.idName << ' ';
    return out;
}


// define new Visit() to be used by Inorder() from genBSTre.h;

class LocalTree : public BinarySearchTree<Network::NetTreeNode> {
    void Visit(TreeNode<Network::NetTreeNode>* p)
        { net.vertices[p->key.idNum].idName   = p->key.idName;
          net.vertices[p->key.idNum].adjacent = p->key.adjacent;
          p->key.adjacent.SetToNull();
        }
};


ostream& operator<< (ostream& out, Network::Vertex& vr)
{
    out << vr.idNum  << ' ' << vr.capacity << ' ' << vr.edgeFlow << ' '
        << vr.edge   << ' ';
    return out;
}


void
Network::Print()
{   register int i;

    for (i = 0; i < numOfVertices; i++) {
        cout << i << ": "
             << vertices[i].idName    << ' '
             << vertices[i].vertexSlack << ' '
             << vertices[i].labeled   << ' '
             << vertices[i].parent    << ' '
             << vertices[i].corrVer   << "-> ";
        vertices[i].adjacent.PrintAll(cout);
        cout << endl;
    }
}
```

Figure 8.29: **An implementation of the distinct representatives problem.**   **continued**

```
void
Network::ReadCommittees(char *fileName)
{   char i, name[80], *s;
    int lastMember;
    LocalTree committeeTree, memberTree;
    Vertex memberVer(0,1,0,!forward), *memberVerAddr;
    Vertex commVer(0,1,0,forward), *commVerAddr;
    NetTreeNode committeeTreeNode, memberTreeNode, *member;
    SinglyLinkedList<Vertex> sourceList;

    ifstream fIn(fileName);
    if (fIn.fail()) {
        cerr << "Cannot open " << fileName << endl;
        exit(1);
    }
    while (!fIn.eof()) {
        fIn >> name[0]; // skip leading spaces;
        if (fIn.eof())  // spaces at the end of file;
            break;
        for (i = 0; name[i] != ':'; )
            name[++i] = fIn.get();
        for (i--; isspace(name[i]); i--); // discard trailing spaces;
        name[i+1] = '\0';
        s = new char[strlen(name)+1];
        strcpy(s,name);
        committeeTreeNode.idNum  = commVer.idNum = numOfVertices++;
        committeeTreeNode.idName = s;
        for (lastMember = !yes; lastMember != yes; ) {
            fIn >> name[0]; // skip leading spaces;
            for (i = 0; name[i] != ',' && name[i] != ';'; )
                name[++i] = fIn.get();
            if (name[i] == ';')
                lastMember = yes;
            for (i--; isspace(name[i]); i--); // discard trailing spaces;
            name[i+1] = '\0';
            s = new char[strlen(name)+1];
            strcpy(s,name);
            memberTreeNode.idName = s;
            commVer.edge = !forward;
```

Figure 8.29: **An implementation of the distinct representatives problem.** **continued**

```
            if ((member = memberTree.IsInTree(memberTreeNode)) == 0) {
                memberVer.idNum = memberTreeNode.idNum = numOfVertices++;
                memberTreeNode.adjacent.Add(sinkVer);
                memberTreeNode.adjacent.Add(commVer);
                commVerAddr = memberTreeNode.adjacent.Find(commVer);
                memberTree.Insert(memberTreeNode);
                memberTreeNode.adjacent.SetToNull();
            }
            else {
                memberVer.idNum = member->idNum;
                member->adjacent.Add(commVer);
                commVerAddr = member->adjacent.Find(commVer);
            }
            memberVer.edge = forward;
            committeeTreeNode.adjacent.Add(memberVer);
            memberVerAddr = committeeTreeNode.adjacent.Find(memberVer);
            memberVerAddr->twin = commVerAddr;
            commVerAddr->twin = memberVerAddr;
        }
        commVer.edge = forward;
        sourceList.Add(commVer);
        committeeTree.Insert(committeeTreeNode);
        committeeTreeNode.adjacent.SetToNull();
    }
    fIn.close();
    vertices = new VertexArrayRec[numOfVertices];
    vertices[source].idName = "source";
    vertices[sink].idName   = "sink";
    vertices[source].adjacent = sourceList;
    vertices[source].parent = none;
    sourceList.SetToNull();  // prevent the lists from wiping them
                             // out by destructor ~singlyLinkedList();
    committeeTree.Inorder(); // transfer data from both trees
    memberTree.Inorder();    // to array vertices[];
    Print();
}
```

Figure 8.29: **An implementation of the distinct representatives problem.**   **continued**

```
void
Network::Label(Vertex *u, int v)
{
    vertices[u->idNum].labeled = yes;
    if (u->edge == forward)
        vertices[u->idNum].vertexSlack =
            min(vertices[v].vertexSlack,EdgeSlack(u));
    else vertices[u->idNum].vertexSlack =
            min(vertices[v].vertexSlack,u->edgeFlow);
    vertices[u->idNum].parent  = v;
    vertices[u->idNum].corrVer = u;
}


void
Network::AugmentPath()
{   register int i, sinkSlack = vertices[sink].vertexSlack;
    Vertex *u;

    cout << " Augmenting path: ";
    for (i = sink; i != source; i = vertices[i].parent) {
        cout << vertices[i].idName << " <= ";
        if (vertices[i].corrVer->edge == forward)
            vertices[i].corrVer->edgeFlow += sinkSlack;
        else vertices[i].corrVer->edgeFlow -= sinkSlack;
        if (vertices[i].parent != source && i != sink)
            vertices[i].corrVer->twin->edgeFlow =
                vertices[i].corrVer->edgeFlow;
    }
    cout << "source;" << endl;
    for (i = 0; i < numOfVertices; i++)
        vertices[i].labeled = !yes;
}


void
Network::FordFulkersonMaxFlow()
{   register int i, v;
    Vertex *u;
    SinglyLinkedList<Vertex>::Node *er;
```

Figure 8.29: **An implementation of the distinct representatives problem.**   **continued**

```
    for (i = 0; i < numOfVertices; i++) {
        vertices[i].labeled = !yes;
        vertices[i].vertexSlack = 0;
        vertices[i].parent = none;
    }
    vertices[source].vertexSlack = MAXINT;
    labeled.Clear();
    labeled.Push(source);
    while (!labeled.IsEmpty()) {    // while not stuck;
        v = labeled.Pop();
        for (er = vertices[v].adjacent.Head(), u = &er->info;
             er; er = er->next, u = &er->info)
            if (!Labeled(u)) {
                if (u->edge == forward && EdgeSlack(u) > 0)
                    Label(u,v);
                else if (u->edge != forward && u->edgeFlow > 0)
                    Label(u,v);
                if (Labeled(u))
                    if (u->idNum == sink) {
                        AugmentPath();
                        labeled.Clear();
                        labeled.Push(source);// look for another path;
                    }
                    else {
                        labeled.Push(u->idNum);
                        vertices[u->idNum].labeled = yes;
                    }
            }
    }
}


main(int argc, char* argv[])
{   char fileName[30];

    if (argc != 2) {
        cout << "Enter a file name: ";
        cin.getline(fileName,30);
    }
```

Figure 8.29: **An implementation of the distinct representatives problem.**   **continued**

```
    else strcpy(fileName,argv[1]);
    net.ReadCommittees(fileName);
    net.FordFulkersonMaxFlow();
    return 0;
}
```

Figure 8.29: **An implementation of the distinct representatives problem.**

■ 8.10 EXERCISES

1. Look carefully at the definition of a graph. In one respect, graphs are more specific than trees. What is it?

2. What is the relation between the sum of the degrees of all vertices and the number of edges of graph $G = (V,E)$?

3. What is the complexity of **BreadthFirstSearch()**?

4. Show that a simple graph is connected iff it has a spanning tree.

5. Show that a tree with n vertices has $n - 1$ nodes.

6. How can **DijkstraAlgorithm()** be applied to undirected graphs?

7. How can **DijkstraAlgorithm()** be modified to become an algorithm for finding the shortest path from vertex a to b?

8. The last clause from **GenericShortestPathAlgorithm()**

    add u *to* **toBeChecked** *if it is not there;*

    is not included in **DijkstraAlgorithm()**. Can this action cause any trouble?

9. Modify **FordAlgorithm()** so that it does not fall into an infinite loop if applied to a graph with negative cycles.

10. For what digraph does the **while** loop of **FordAlgorithm()** iterate only one time? Two times?

11. Can **FordAlgorithm()** be applied to undirected graphs?

12. Make necessary changes in **FordAlgorithm()** to adapt it to solving the all-to-one shortest path problem and apply the new algorithm to vertex f in the graph in Figure 8.8. Using the same order of edges, produce a table similar to the table shown in this figure.

13. The D'Esopo-Pape algorithm is exponential in the worst case. Consider the following method to construct pathological graphs of n vertices (Kershenbaum 1981), each vertex identified by a number $1, \ldots, n$:

    ```
    KershenbaumAlgorithm()
        construct a two-vertex graph with vertices 1 and 2, and edge(1,2) = 1;
        for (k = 3; k <= n; k++)
            add vertex k;
            for (i = 2; i < k; i++)
    ```

$$add\ edge(\mathbf{k},\mathbf{i})\ with\ weight(edge(\mathbf{k},\mathbf{i})) = weight(edge(\mathbf{1},\mathbf{i}));$$
$$weight(edge(\mathbf{1},\mathbf{i})) = weight(\mathbf{1},\mathbf{i}) + 2^{\mathbf{k}-3} + 1;$$
$$add\ edge(\mathbf{1},\mathbf{k})\ with\ weight(edge(\mathbf{1},\mathbf{k})) = 1;$$

The vertices adjacent to vertex 1 are put in ascending order and the remaining adjacency lists are in descending order. Using this algorithm, construct a five-vertex graph and execute the D'Esopo-Pape algorithm showing all changes in the deque and all edge updates. What generalization can you make about applying Pape's method to such graphs?

14. What do you need to change in **GenericShortestPathAlgorithm()** in order to covert it to Dijkstra's one-to-all algorithm?

15. Enhance **WFIalgorithm()** to indicate the shortest paths, in addition to their lengths.

16. **WFIalgorithm()** finishes execution gracefully even in the presence of a negative cycle. How do we know that the graph contains such a cycle?

17. The original implementation of **WFIalgorithm()** given by Floyd is as follows:

```
WFIalgorithm2 (matrix weight)
    for i = 1 to |V|
        for j = 1 to |V|
            if weight[j,i] < ∞
                for k = 1 to |V|
                    if weight[i,k] < ∞
                        if (weight[j,k] > weight[j,i] + weight[i,k])
                            weight[j,k] = weight[j,i] + weight[i,k];
```

Is there any advantage to this longer implementation?

18. One method of finding shortest paths from all vertices to all other vertices requires us to transform the graph so that it does not include negative weights. We may be tempted to do it by simply finding the smallest negative weight k and adding $-k$ to the weights of all edges. Why is this method inapplicable?

19. For which edges does $\leq$ in the inequality

$$dist(v) \leq dist(w) + weight(edge(wv))\ \text{for any vertex } w.$$

become $<$?

20. Modify **CycleDetectionDFS()** so that it could determine whether a particular edge is part of a cycle in an undirected graph.

21. When would **KruskalAlgorithm()** require $|E|$ iterations?

22. Our implementation of **Union()** requires three arrays. Is it possible to use only two of them and still have the same information concerning roots, next vertices, and lengths? Consider using negative numbers.

23. How can the second minimum spanning tree be found?

24. Is the minimum spanning tree unique?

25. How can the algorithms for finding the minimum spanning tree be used to find the maximum spanning tree?

26. The algorithm `BlockSearch()`, when used for undirected graphs, relies on the following observation: In a depth-first search tree created for an undirected graph, each back edge connects a successor to a predecessor (and not, for instance, a sibling to a sibling). Show the validity of this observation.

27. What is the complexity of `BlockSearch()`?

28. Blocks in undirected graphs are defined in terms of edges and the algorithm `Block DFS()` stores edges on the stack to output blocks. On the other hand, SCCs in digraphs are defined in terms of vertices and the algorithm `StrongDFS()` stores vertices on the stack to output SCC. Why?

29. Consider a possible implementation of `TopologicalSort()` in the following routine:

```
MinimalVertex(digraph)
    v = a vertex of digraph;
    while v has a successor
        v = successor(v);
    return v;
```

What is the disadvantage of using this implementation?

30. A *tournament* is a digraph in which there is exactly one edge between every two vertices.

   (a) How many edges does a tournament have?

   (b) How many different tournaments of n edges can be created?

   (c) Can each tournament be topologically sorted?

   (d) How many minimal vertices can a tournament have?

   (e) A *transitive tournament* is a tournament which has *edge(vw)* if it has *edge(vu)* and *edge(uw)*. Can such a tournament have a cycle?

31. Does considering loops and parallel edges complicate the analysis of networks? How about multiple sources and sinks?

32. `FordFulkersonAlgorithm()` assumes that it terminates. Do you think such an assumption is safe?

33. `FordFulkersonAlgorithm()` executed in a depth-first fashion has some redundancy. First, all outgoing edges are pushed onto the stack and then the last is popped off to be followed by the algorithm. For example, in the network in Figure 8.20a, first, all three edges coming out of vertex s are pushed, and only afterwards is the last of them, *edge(se)*, followed. Modify `FordFulkersonAlgorithm()` so that the first edge coming out of a certain vertex is immediately followed, and the second is followed only if the first does not lead to the sink. Consider using recursion.

34. Find the capacity of the cut determined by the set $X = \{s, d\}$ in the graph in Figure 8.19.

35. What is the complexity of Dinic's algorithm in a network where all edges have a capacity of one?

36. Why does `DinicAlgorithm()` start from the sink to determine a layered network?

37. The member function `ReadCommittees()` in the case study uses two trees, `committeeTree` and `memberTree`, to generate adjacency lists and then initialize the array `vertices`. However, one tree would be sufficient. What do you think is the reason for using two trees, not one?

■ 8.11   PROGRAMMING ASSIGNMENTS

1. All algorithms discussed in this chapter for determining the minimum spanning tree have one thing in common: they start building the tree from the beginning and they add new edges to the structure which eventually becomes such a tree. However, we can go in the opposite direction and build this tree by successively removing edges to break cycles in the graph until no circuit is left. In this way, the graph turns into the tree. The edges chosen for removal should be the edges of maximum weight among those which can break any cycle in the tree (for example, Dijkstra's method). This algorithm somewhat resembles the Kruskal method, but since it works in the opposite direction, it can be called a Kruskal method *à rebours*. Use this approach to find the minimum spanning tree for the graph of distances between at least a dozen cities.

2. Write a graphics demonstration program to show the difference between Kruskal's method and Jarnik-Prim's algorithm. Randomly generate 50 vertices and display them in the left half of the screen. Then, randomly generate 200 edges and display them. Make sure that the graph is connected. After the graph is ready, create the minimum spanning tree using Kruskal's method and display each edge included in the tree. (Use a different color than the one used during graph generation.) Then, display the same graph in the right half of the screen and create the minimum spanning tree using Jarnik-Prim's algorithm and display all edges being included in the tree.

3. A multigraph is called Eulerian if, during its traversal, each edge is traversed only once. In such a graph, each vertex has an even degree since such traversal requires returning to a starting vertex v; if a vertex is entered using one edge, it should be exited using another edge. Fleury is attributed with the oldest algorithm which allows us to find an Eulerian path, a path which includes each edge of the graph only one time. The algorithm takes great care to not traverse a bridge. A bridge is an edge whose removal disconnects the graphs G_1 and G_2, since if traversal of G_1 is not completed before traversing such an edge to pass to G_2, it is not possible to return to G_1. Only after the entire subgraph G_1 has been traversed can the path lead through such an edge. Fleury's algorithm is as follows:

```
FleuryAlgorithm(undirected simple graph)
    v = a starting vertex; // any vertex;
    path = v;
    untraversed = all edges of graph;
    while v has untraversed edges
```

```
if edge(vu) is the only one untraversed edge
    e = edge(vu);
else e = edge(vu) in v which is not a bridge;
path = path + u;
remove e from untraversed;
    v = u;
if untraversed is null
    success;
else failure;
```

Write a program to determine an Eulerian path in an Eulerian multigraph. Note that for cases when a vertex has more than one untraversed edge, a connectivity checking algorithm should be applied.

4. An important problem in database management is preventing deadlocks between transactions. A transaction is a sequence of operations on records in the database. In large databases many transactions can be executed at the same time. This can lead to inconsistencies if the order of executing operations is not monitored. However, this monitoring may cause transactions to block each other, thereby causing a deadlock. To detect a deadlock, a wait-for graph is constructed to show which transaction waits for which. Use a binary locking mechanism to implement a wait-for graph. In this mechanism, if a record R is accessed by a transaction T then T puts a lock on R and this record cannot be processed by any other transaction before T is finished. Release all locks put on by a transaction T when T finishes. The input is composed of the following commands: $read(T, A)$, $write(T, A)$, $end(T)$. For example, if input is

$$read(T_1, A_1), read(T_2, A_2), read(T_1, A_2), write(T_1, A_2), end(T_1) \ldots,$$

then T_1 is suspended when attempting to execute the step $read(T_1, A_2)$, and $edge(T_1, T_2)$ is created, since T_1 waits for T_2 to finish. If T_1 does not have to wait, resume its execution. After each graph update, check for a cycle in the graph. If a cycle is detected, interrupt execution of the youngest transaction T and put its steps at the end of the input.

   Note that some records might have been modified by such a transaction, so they should be restored to their state before T started. But such a modification could have been used by another transaction which should also be interrupted. In this program, do not address the problem of restoring the values of records (the problem of rolling back transactions and of cascading this rolling back). Concentrate on updating and monitoring the wait-for graph. Note that if a transaction is finished, its vertex should be removed from the graph, which may be what other transactions are waiting for.

5. Write a rudimentary spreadsheet program. Display a grid of cells with columns A through H and rows 1 through 20. Accept input in the first row of the screen. The commands are of the form *column row entry*, where *entry* is a number, a cell address preceded by a plus (e.g., +A5), a string, or a function preceded by an at sign, @. The functions are: *max, min, avg,* and *sum.* During the execution of your

program, build and modify the graph reflecting the situation in the spreadsheet. Show the proper values in proper cells. If a value in a cell is updated then the values in all cells depending on it should also be modified. For example, after the following sequence of entries:

```
A1 10
B1 20
A2 30
D1 +A1
C1 @sum(A1..B2)
D1 +C1
```

both cells C1 and D1 should display number the 60.

Consider using a modification of the interpreter from Chapter 5 as an enhancement of this spreadsheet so that arithmetic expressions could also be used to enter values, such as

```
C3 2*A1
C4 @max(A1..B2) - (A2 + B2)
```

BIBLIOGRAPHY

[1]   Ahuja, Ravindra K., Magnanti, Thomas L., and Orlin, James B., *Network Flows: Theory, Algorithms, and Applications*, Englewood Cliffs: Prentice-Hall, 1993.

[2]   Bertsekas, Dimitri P., "A Simple and Fast Label Correcting Algorithm for Shortest Paths," *Networks* 23 (1993), 703–709.

[3]   Deo, Narsingh, and Pang, Chi-yin, "Shortest Path Algorithms: Taxonomy and Annotation," *Networks* 14 (1984), 275–323.

[4]   Dijkstra, E.W., "A Note On Two Problems in Connection with Graphs," *Numerische Mathematik* 1 (1959), 269–271.

[5]   Dijkstra, E.W., "Some Theorems on Spanning Subtrees of a Graph," *Indagationes Mathematicae* 28 (1960), 196–199.

[6]   Dinic, E.A., "Algorithm for Solution of a Problem of Maximum Flow in a Network with Power Estimation [Mistranslation of: with Polynomial Bound]," *Soviet Mathematics Doklady* 11 (1970), 1277–1280.

[7]   Edmonds, J., and Karp, Richard M., "Theoretical Improvement in Algorithmic Efficiency for Network Flow Problems," *Journal of the ACM* 19 (1972), 248–264.

[8]   Floyd, Robert W., "Algorithm 97: Shortest Path," *Communications of the ACM* 5 (1962), 345.

[9]   Ford, L.R., and Fulkerson D.R., "Maximal Flow Through a Network," *Canadian Journal of Mathematics* 8 (1956), 399–404.

[10] Ford, L.R., and Fulkerson, D.R., "A Simple Algorithm for Finding Maximal Network Flows and an Application to the Hitchcock Problem," *Canadian Journal of Mathematics* 9 (1957), 210–218.

[11] Ford, L.R., and Fulkerson, D.R., *Flows in Networks*, Princeton: Princeton University Press, 1962.

[12] Gallo, G., and Pallottino, S., "Shortest Path Methods: A Unified Approach," *Mathematical Programming Study* 26 (1986), 38–64.

[13] Gallo, G., and Pallottino, S., "Shortest Path Methods," *Annals of Operations Research* 7 (1988), 3–79.

[14] Gibbons, Alan, *Algorithmic Graph Theory*, Cambridge University Press, 1985.

[15] Glover, F., Glover, R., and Klingman, D., "The Treshhold Shortest Path Algorithm," *Networks* 14 (1986).

[16] Gould, Ronald, *Graph Theory*, Menlo Park: Benjamin/Cummings, 1988.

[17] Graham, R.L. and Hell, Pavol, "On the History of the Minimum Spanning Tree Problem," *Annals of the History of Computing* 7 (1985), 43–57.

[18] Hall, P., "On Representatives of Subsets," *Journal of the London Mathematical Society* 10 (1935), 26–30.

[19] Ingerman, P.Z., "Algorithm 141: Path Matrix," *Communications of the ACM* 5 (1962), 556.

[20] Johnson, Donald B., "Efficient Algorithms for Shortest Paths in Sparse Networks," *Journal ACM* 24 (1977), 1–13.

[21] Kalaba, Robert, "On Some Communication Network Problems," *Combinatorial Analysis*, Providence: American Mathematical Society (1960), 261–280.

[22] Kershenbaum, Aaron, "A Note on Finding Shortest Path Trees," *Networks* 11 (1981), 399–400.

[23] Kruskal, Joseph B., "On the Shortest Spanning Tree of a Graph and the Traveling Salesman Problem," *Proceedings of the American Mathematical Society* 7 (1956), 48–50.

[24] Papadimitriou, Christos H., and Steiglitz, Kenneth, *Combinatorial Optimization: Algorithms and Complexity*, Englewood Cliffs: Prentice-Hall, 1982.

[25] Pape, U., "Implementation and Efficiency of Moore-Algorithms for the Shortest Route Problem," *Mathematical Programming* 7 (1974), 212–222.

[26] Pollack, M., and Wiebenson, W., "Solution of the Shortest-Route Problem—A Review," *Operations Research* 8 (1960), 224–230.

[27] Prim, Robert C., "Shortest Connection Networks and Some Generalizations," *Bell System Technical Journal* 36 (1957), 1389–1401.

[28] Tarjan, Robert E., *Data Structures and Network Algorithms*, Philadelphia: Society for Industrial and Applied Mathematics, 1983.

[29] Warshall, Stephen, "A Theorem on Boolean Matrices," *Journal of the ACM* 9 (1962), 11–12.

SORTING

The efficiency of data handling can often be substantially increased if the data are sorted according to some criteria of order. For example, it would be practically impossible to find a name in the telephone directory if the names were not alphabetically ordered. The same can be said about dictionaries, book indexes, payrolls, bank accounts, student lists, and other alphabetically organized materials. The convenience of using sorted data is unquestionable and must be addressed in computer science as well. Although a computer can grapple with an unordered telephone book more easily and quickly than a human, it would be extremely inefficient to have the computer process such an unordered data set. It is often necessary to sort data before processing.

The first step is to choose the criteria which will be used to order data. This choice will vary from application to application and must be defined by the user. Very often, the sorting criteria are natural, as in the case of numbers. A set of numbers can be sorted in ascending or descending order. The set of five positive integers (5, 8, 1, 2, 20) can be sorted in ascending order resulting in the set (1, 2, 5, 8, 20), or in descending order, resulting in the set (20, 8, 5, 2, 1). Names in the phone book are ordered alphabetically by last name, which is the natural order. For alphabetic and nonalphabetic characters the ASCII code is commonly used, although other choices such as EBCDIC are possible. Once a criterion is selected, the second step is how to put a set of data in order using that criterion.

The final ordering of data can be obtained in a variety of ways and only some of them can be considered meaningful and efficient. To decide which method is better, certain criteria of efficiency have to be established and a method for quantitatively comparing different algorithms must be chosen.

To make the comparison machine-independent, certain critical properties of sorting algorithms should be defined when comparing alternative methods. Two such properties are the number of comparisons and the number of data movements. The choice of these two properties should not be surprising. To sort a set of data, the data have to be compared and moved as necessary; the efficiency of these two operations depends on the size of the data set.

Since determining the precise number of comparisons is not always necessary or possible, an approximate value can be computed. For this reason the number of comparisons and movements is approximated with big-O notation by giving the order of magnitude of these numbers. But the order of magnitude can vary depending on the initial ordering of data. How much time, for example, does the machine spend on data ordering if the data are already ordered? Does it recognize this initial ordering immediately or is it completely unaware of that fact? Hence, the efficiency measure also indicates the "intelligence" of the algorithm. For this reason, the number of comparisons and movements is computed (if possible) for the following three cases: best case (often, data already in order), worst case (usually, data in reverse order), and average case (random ordering). Some sorting methods perform the same operations regardless of the initial ordering of data. It is easy to measure the performance of such algorithms, but the performance itself is usually not very good. Many other methods are more flexible and their performance measures for all three cases differ.

The number of comparisons and the number of movements do not have to coincide. An algorithm can be very efficient on the former and perform poorly on the latter, or vice versa. Therefore, practical reasons must aid in the choice of which algorithm to use. For example, if only simple keys are compared, such as integers or characters, then the comparisons are relatively fast and inexpensive. If strings or arrays of numbers are compared, then the cost of comparisons goes up substantially, and the weight of the comparison measure becomes more important. If, on the other hand, the data items moved are large, such as structures, then the movement measure may stand out as the determining factor in efficiency considerations. All theoretically established measures have to be used with discretion, and theoretical considerations should be balanced with practical applications. After all, the practical applications serve as a rubber stamp for theory decisions.

Sorting algorithms, whose number can be counted in the hundreds, are of different levels of complexity. A simple method can be only 20% less efficient than a more elaborate one. If sorting is used in the program once in a while and only for small sets of data, then using a sophisticated and slightly more efficient algorithm may not be desirable; the same operation can be performed using a simpler method and simpler code. But if thousands of items are to be sorted, then a gain of 20% must not be neglected. Simple algorithms often perform better with a small amount of data than their more complex counterparts whose effectiveness may only become obvious when data samples become very large.

■ 9.1   ELEMENTARY SORTING ALGORITHMS

9.1.1   Insertion Sort

An *insertion sort* starts by considering the two first elements of the array `data`, which are `data[0]` and `data[1]`. If they are out of order, an interchange takes place. Then, the third element, `data[2]`, is considered and inserted into its proper place. If `data[2]` is less than `data[0]` and `data[1]`, these two elements are shifted by one position to the right; `data[0]` is placed at position 1, `data[1]` at position 2, and `data[2]` at position

0. If `data[2]` is less than `data[1]` and not greater than `data[0]`, then only `data[1]` is moved to the position 2 and its place is taken by `data[2]`. If, finally, `data[2]` is greater than both its predecessors, it stays in its current position. Each element `data[i]` is inserted into its proper location j such that $0 \le j < i$, and all elements greater than `data[i]` are moved to the right by one position.

An outline of the insertion sort algorithm is as follows:

```
for(i = 1; i < n; i++)
```
       place `data[i]` *in its proper position;*
       move all elements `data[j]` *greater than* `data[i]` *by one position;*

Note that sorting is restricted only to a fraction of the array in each iteration, and only in the last pass is the whole array considered.

Figure 9.1 contains an implementation of the insertion sort.

Since an array having only one element is already ordered, the program starts sorting from the second position, position 1. Figure 9.2 shows what changes are made to the array [5 2 3 8 1] when `Insertion()` executes.

An advantage of using the insertion sort is that it sorts the array only when it is really necessary. If the array is already in order, no substantial moves are performed; only the variable `tmp` is initialized and the value stored in it is moved back to the same position. The algorithm recognizes that part of the array is already sorted and stops execution accordingly. But, it recognizes only this, and the fact that elements may already be in their proper positions is overlooked. Therefore, they can be moved from these positions and then later moved back. This happens to numbers 2 and 3 in the example in Figure 9.2. Another disadvantage is that if an item is being inserted, all elements greater than the one being inserted have to be moved. Insertion is not localized and may require moving a significant

```
template<class genType>
void
Insertion (genType data[], int n)
{   register int i,j;
    genType tmp;

    for (i = 1; i < n; i++) {
        tmp = data[i];
        j = i;
        while (j > 0 && tmp < data[j-1]) {
            data[j] = data[j-1];
            j--;
        }
        data[j] = tmp;
    }
}
```

Figure 9.1: **Implementation of the insertion sort.**

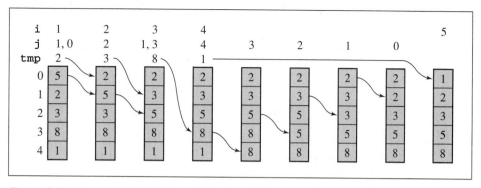

Figure 9.2: **The array [5 2 3 8 1] sorted by insertion sort.**

number of elements. Considering that an element can be moved from its final position only to be placed there again later, the number of redundant moves can slow down execution substantially.

The program for the insertion sort uses a **for** loop, a **while** loop, and an **if** statement nested within each other. The number of iterations of the **for** loop is determined by the value of n and is always $n - 1$. The number of iterations of the **while** loop is yet to be computed. However, this number is needed to find the number of key comparisons and the number of assignments.

The best case is when the data are already in order. Only one comparison is made for each position i, so there are $n - 1$ comparisons, which is $O(n)$, and $2(n - 1)$ moves, all of them redundant.

The worst case is when the data are in reverse order. In this case, for each i, the item **data[i]** is less than every item **data[0],...,data[i-1]**, and it is swapped with each of them. For each iteration i of the **for** loop, there are i comparisons and, the total number of comparisons for all iterations of this loop is

$$\sum_{i=1}^{n-1} i = 1 + 2 + \cdots + (n - 1) = \frac{n(n - 1)}{2} = O(n^2).$$

The number of times the assignment in the **while** loop is executed can be computed using the same formula. The number of times **tmp** is loaded and unloaded in the **for** loop is added to that, resulting in the total number of moves:

$$\frac{n(n - 1)}{2} + 2(n - 1) = \frac{n^2 + 3n - 4}{2} = O(n^2).$$

Only extreme cases have been taken into consideration. What happens if the data are in random order? Is the sorting time closer to the time of the best case, $O(n)$, or to the worst case, $O(n^2)$? Or is it something in between? The answer is not immediately evident and requires certain introductory computations. The **for** loop always executes $n - 1$ times, but it is also necessary to determine the number of iterations of the **while** loop. For every iteration i of the **for** loop, the **while** loop compares data either $1, 2, \ldots,$ or i times depending on how far away the item **data[i]** (stored in **tmp**) is from its proper position in the currently sorted subarray **data**$_{0\ldots i-1}$. If it is already in this position, the loop condition is executed only one time to test that everything is in order and exits immediately. If it is one position away from its proper place, the program goes around the loop only once, but checks the loop condition two times. If it is j positions away from its final location, the condition in the **while** loop is tested $j + 1$ times and the body of the loop is executed j times.

Under the assumption of equal probability of occupying array cells, the average number of times the **while** loop compares data during one iteration i of the **for** loop can be computed by adding all the possible numbers of times such tests are performed and dividing that by the number of such possibilities. The result is

$$\frac{1 + 2 + \cdots + i}{i} = \frac{\frac{1}{2}i(i + 1)}{i} = \frac{i + 1}{2}.$$

To compute the average number of comparisons and assignments, the probability that a given item is in its proper position needs to be determined first. It is obvious that there is only one such proper position. In an i-cell array (assuming random distribution of items in the array) the probability that an item is in its right place is $\frac{1}{i}$, and the probability that it is out of place is $1 - \frac{1}{i} = \frac{i-1}{i}$. If an item is in its proper place, only one comparison is made to establish this fact, and the item is moved only to and from **tmp**. On the other hand, when the item is out of place, on the average, $\frac{i+1}{2} + 1$ moves must be performed (two to move the item itself to **tmp** and from **tmp**, and $\frac{i+1}{2} - 1$ moves of elements greater than the item) and $\frac{i+1}{2}$ comparisons. Putting this all together results in an average number of comparisons (P = probability) equal to

P(item is in the right place) $*$ *Number (operations per item in the right place)* $+$

P(item out of place) $*$ *Number (operations per item out of place)* $=$

$$\frac{1}{i} * 1 + \frac{i - 1}{i} * \frac{i + 1}{2} = \frac{i^2 + 1}{2i}$$

and the average number of moves is

$$\frac{1}{i} * 2 + \frac{i - 1}{i} * \left(\frac{i + 1}{2} + 1\right) = \frac{i^2 + 2i + 1}{2i}.$$

But these two numbers refer only to one single item and one single iteration of the **for** loop, and the array contains n such items. To obtain the average number of all comparisons and all moves, the computed figures for all i's (for all iterations of the **for** loop) from 1 to $n - 1$ have to be added. The result for the number of comparisons is

$$\sum_{i=1}^{n-1} \frac{i^2 + 1}{2i} = \frac{1}{2}\sum_{i=1}^{n-1} i + \frac{1}{2}\sum_{i=1}^{n-1} \frac{1}{i} = \frac{\frac{1}{2}n(n - 1)}{2} + \frac{1}{2}H_{n-1}$$

$$= \frac{n(n - 1)}{4} + \frac{1}{2}H_{n-1} = O(n^2) + O(\ln n) = O(n^2).$$

(See Appendix A.1 for the definition of H.) The number of assignments is

$$\sum_{i=1}^{n-1} \frac{i^2 + 2i + 1}{2i} = \frac{n^2 + 3n - 4}{4} + \frac{1}{2}H_{n-1} = O(n^2).$$

This answers the question: Is the number of assignments and comparisons for a randomly ordered array closer to the best or to the worst case? Unfortunately, it is closer to the latter, which means that on the average, when the size of array is doubled, the sorting time has to be multiplied by 4.

9.1.2   Selection Sort

The selection sort is an attempt to localize the exchanges of array elements by finding a misplaced element first and putting it in its final place. The element with the lowest value is selected and exchanged with the element in the first position. Then, the smallest value among the remaining elements `data[1],...,data[n-1]` is found and put in the second position. This selection and placement by finding, in each pass `i`, the lowest value among the elements `data[i],...,data[n-1]` and swapping it with `data[i]` is continued until all elements are in their proper positions. The following pseudocode reflects the simplicity of the algorithm:

```
for(i = 0; i < n-1; i++)
    select the smallest element among data[i],...,data[n-1];
    swap it with data[i];
```

It is rather obvious that `n-2` should be the last value for `i` since if all elements but the last have been already considered and placed in their proper position, then the nth element (occupying position `n-1`) has to be the largest. Figure 9.3 contains the complete C++ implementation of the selection sort.

```
template<class genType>
void
Selection(genType data[], int n)
{    register int i,j,least;

    for (i = 0; i < n-1; i++) {
        for (j = i+1, least = i; j < n; j++)
            if (data[j] < data[least])
                least = j;
        Swap(data[least],data[i]);
    }
}
```

Figure 9.3: **Implementation of the selection sort.**

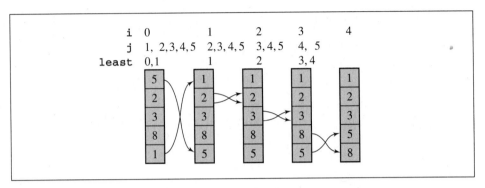

Figure 9.4: **The array [5 2 3 8 1] sorted by selection sort.**

Figure 9.4 illustrates how the array [5 2 3 8 1] is sorted by selection sort.

The analysis of the performance of the function **Selection()** is simplified by the presence of two **for** loops with lower and upper bounds. The number of times the loops execute can be computed in advance. The outer loop executes **n** − 1 times and for each **i** between 0 and **n**−2 the inner loop iterates **j** = (**n** − 1) − **i** times. Because comparisons of keys are done in the inner loop, there are

$$\sum_{i=0}^{n-2}(n-1-i) = (n-1) + \cdots + 1 = \frac{n(n-1)}{2} = O(n^2)$$

comparisons. This number stays the same for all cases. There can be some savings only in the number of swaps. Note that if the assignment in the **if** statement is executed, only the index **j** is moved, not the item located currently at position **j**. Array elements are swapped unconditionally in the outer loop as many times as this loop executes, which is **n** − 1. Thus, in all cases items are moved the same number of times, 3 ∗ (**n** − 1).

The best thing about this sort is the required number of assignments, which can hardly be beaten by any other algorithm. However, it might seem somewhat unsatisfactory that the total number of exchanges, 3 ∗ (**n** − 1), is the same for all cases. Obviously, no exchange is needed if an item is in its final position. The algorithm disregards that and swaps such an item with itself making three redundant moves. The problem can be alleviated by making **Swap()** a conditional operation. The condition preceding the **Swap()** should indicate that no item less than **data[least]** has been found among elements **data[i+1],...,data[n-1]**. The last line of **Selection()** might be replaced by the lines:

```
if (data[i] != data[least])
    Swap (data[least], data[i]);
```

This increases the number of array element comparisons by **n** − 1, but this increase can be avoided by noting that there is no need to compare items. We proceed as we did in the case of the **if** statement of **Selection()** by comparing the indexes and not the items. The last line of **Selection()** can be replaced by:

```
if (i != least)
    Swap (data[least], data[i]);
```

Is such an improvement worth the price of introducing a new condition in the procedure, and adding $n - 1$ index comparisons as a consequence? It depends on what types of elements are being sorted. If the elements are numbers or characters, then interposing a new condition to avoid execution of redundant swaps gains little in efficiency. But if the elements in **data** are large compound entities such as arrays or structures, then one swap (which requires three assignments) may take the same amount of time as, say, 100 index comparisons, and using a conditional **Swap()** is recommended.

9.1.3   Bubble Sort

A bubble sort can be best understood if the array to be sorted is envisaged as a vertical column whose smallest elements are at the top and whose largest elements are at the bottom. The array is scanned from the bottom up and two adjacent elements are interchanged if they are found to be out of order with respect to each other. First, items **data[n-1]** and **data[n-2]** are compared and swapped if they are out of order. Next, **data[n-2]** and **data[n-3]** are compared and their order is changed if necessary, and so on up to **data[1]** and **data[0]**. In this way the smallest element is bubbled up to the top of the array.

However, this is only the first pass through the array. The array is scanned again comparing consecutive items and interchanging them when needed, but this time the last comparison is done for **data[2]** and **data[1]** since the smallest element is already in its proper position, namely position 0. The second pass bubbles the second smallest element of the array up to the second position, position 1. The procedure continues until the last pass when only one comparison, **data[n-1]** with **data[n-2]**, and possibly one interchange is performed. The simplest declaration of the function **BubbleSort()** can be given in the form shown in Figure 9.5.

Figure 9.6 illustrates the changes performed in the array [5 2 3 8 1] during the execution of **BubbleSort()**.

Using two **for** loops simplifies the implementation. It is straightforward to determine the number of comparisons and assignments. In each case (best, average, and worst) the

```
template<class genType>
void
BubbleSort (genType data[], int n)
{    register int i,j;

    for (i = 0; i < n-1; i++)
        for (j = n-1; j > i; --j)
            if (data[j] < data[j-1])
                Swap(data[j],data[j-1]);

}
```

Figure 9.5: **Implementation of the bubble sort.**

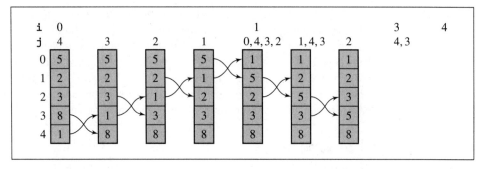

Figure 9.6: **The array [5 2 3 8 1] sorted by bubble sort.**

function makes

$$\sum_{i=0}^{n-2}(n-1-i) = \frac{n(n-1)}{2} = O(n^2)$$

comparisons. This formula also computes the number of swaps in the worst case when the array is in reverse order. In this case, $\frac{3n(n-1)}{2}$ moves have to be made.

The best case, when all elements are already ordered, requires no swaps. If an i-cell array is in random order, then there is only one chance in i that an item is in its proper position and that this item will not be moved. When executing the ith iteration of the outer loop, the inner loop scans only part of the array **data**, from $n-1$ to $i+1$. In this restricted subarray **data[i+1],...,data[n-1]**, there is only one chance out of $(n-1) - i$ to make no swap. It follows from the fact that the subarray is randomly ordered. The probability that an item occupies its proper position is $\frac{1}{(n-1)-i}$. Since this probability is the same for every item **data[i+1],...,data[n-1]**, only one $\left(\frac{1}{n-i-1} * (n-i-1)\right)$ item will be in its proper location. In other words, there is only one chance out of $n-i-1$ for the inner loop to execute no move.

On the other hand, if an item is out of place, it is swapped $\frac{n-i-1}{2}$ times on the average. It can be swapped either one time, or two times, or ... $(n-1) - (i+1)$ times. After averaging the sum of all these possible numbers of swaps by the number of these possibilities, $(n-1) - (i+1)$, the average number of swaps is obtained. Furthermore, the probability of interchanging elements for the subarray **data[i+1],...,data[n-1]** is $1 - \frac{1}{n-i-1} = \frac{n-i-2}{n-i-1}$. Therefore, an item randomly picked from among **data[i+1],...,data[n-1]** is swapped on the average

$$\frac{1}{n-i-1} * 0 + \frac{n-i-2}{n-i-1} * \frac{n-i-1}{2} = \frac{n-i-2}{2}$$

times. If such figures are summed over all iterations i of the outer **for** loop, the result is

$$\sum_{i=0}^{n-2}\frac{n-i-2}{2} = \frac{1}{2}\sum_{i=0}^{n-2}n - \frac{1}{2}\sum_{i=0}^{n-2}i - \sum_{i=0}^{n-2}1$$

$$= \frac{n(n-1)}{2} - \frac{(n-1)(n-2)}{4} - (n-1) = \frac{n^2 - 3n + 2}{4}$$

swaps, which is equal to $\frac{3}{4}(n^2 - 3n + 2)$ moves.

Implementing a bubble sort using two **for** loops is extremely inefficient because it performs comparisons even if the array is already ordered. Therefore, the number of comparisons in the best and worst cases is the same. The procedure can be optimized by making a provision for the case of a sorted array. If the array is sorted, the procedure terminates. To do that, a flag must be added to the outer **for** loop indicating whether or not it is necessary to make the next pass. Such a flag, denoted as **again**, is set to true (anything but zero) every time an interchange occurs that indicates there is a need to scan the array again. Figure 9.7 contains an implementation of the bubble sort that uses this flag.

The best case is when the array is already sorted; this will be known right after the first pass through the outer **for** loop. In this case $n-1$ comparisons are made and no swaps are necessary. It is already an improvement because the number of comparisons comes down from $O(n^2)$ to $O(n)$. The worst case is the same as in the previous implementation: $\frac{n(n-1)}{2}$ comparisons and the same number of swaps $\left(\frac{3n(n-1)}{2} \text{ moves}\right)$ are made. What happens in the average case?

The number of comparisons in iteration i of the outer **for** loop is $n-i-1$. This is the number of times the inner **for** loop is executed. If after pass i through the outer loop the array is ordered, then the total number of comparisons is

$$(n-1)+(n-2)+\cdots+(n-i-1) = (i+1)n - (1+\cdots+(i+1))$$

$$= (i+1)n - \frac{(i+2)(i+1)}{2}$$

$$= \frac{2in+2n-3i-i^2-2}{2}.$$

In the worst case when $i=n-2$ (last pass), the figure equals $\frac{n(n-1)}{2}$, the efficiency of the original algorithm. But usually, $i<n-2$, and the number of comparisons of the improved algorithm is less than $\frac{n(n-1)}{2}$.

```
template<class genType>
void
NewBubbleSort (genType data[], int n)
{   register int i,j,again;

    for (i = 0, again = 1; i < n-1 && again; i++)
        for (j = n-1, again = 0; j > i; --j)
            if (data[j] < data[j-1]) {
                Swap(data[j],data[j-1]);
                again = 1;
            }
}
```

Figure 9.7: **Implementation of the bubble sort using a flag indicating a sorted array.**

The order of magnitude of the number that has just been computed is still not known. First, the average number of iterations i needs to be determined. The probability that an item is in its proper position is $\frac{1}{n}$. But how many items can be expected to be in their proper positions? Just $n * \frac{1}{n} = 1$ so $n - 1$ items are out of place. On the average, the array is sorted after $i = n - 1$ passes. Since $i < n$, $2in = O(n^2)$ by the rule of product, and $\frac{2in - 2n - 3i - i^2 - 2}{2} = O(n^2)$. Consequently, the improved version of the bubble sort is only as efficient as the original version in the average case.

The number of moves can be computed in a similar fashion. The average number of moves in one single iteration is $\frac{n-i-2}{2} = \frac{n-i}{2} - 1$. Again, assuming that after iteration i of the outer **for** loop the sorting is finished, there are

$$\frac{n}{2} + \frac{n-1}{2} + \frac{n-2}{2} + \cdots + \frac{n-i}{2} - (i+1) = \frac{2n(i+1) - i(i+1)}{4} - (i+1)$$

swaps with three moves per swap. Note that for $i = n - 2$ the formula turns into $\frac{n^2 - 3n + 2}{4}$, which is **BubbleSort()**'s average case. The same reasoning used in the analysis of comparisons shows that this number is of the order of n^2.

NewBubbleSort() is certainly an improvement over **BubbleSort()** because redundant comparisons are excluded, but the algorithm remains basically what it was: the bubble sort. It still painstakingly bubbles items step by step up toward the top of the array. It looks at two adjacent array elements at a time and swaps them if they are not in order. If an element has to be moved from the bottom to the top, it is exchanged with every element in the array. It does not skip them as the selection sort did. In addition, the algorithm concentrates only on the item that is being bubbled up. Therefore, all elements that distort the order are moved, even those that are already in their final positions (see numbers 2 and 3 in Figure 9.6, the situation analogous to that in the insertion sort).

What is the bubble sort's performance in comparison with the insertion and selection sorts? In the average case, the bubble sort makes approximately twice as many comparisons and moves as the insertion sort, as many comparisons as the selection sort, and n times more moves than the selection sort.

It could be said that insertion sort is twice as fast as bubble sort. In fact it is, but this fact does not immediately follow from the performance estimates. The point is that when determining a formula for the number of comparisons, only comparisons of data items have been included. The actual code for each algorithm involves more than just that. In **BubbleSort()**, for example, there are two loops, both of which compare indexes: **i** and **n-1** in the first loop, **j** and **i** in the second. All in all, there are $\frac{n(n-1)}{2}$ such comparisons and this number should not be treated too lightly. It becomes less and less negligible if the data items are large structures. But, if **data** consists of integers, then comparing the data takes a similar amount of time as comparing indexes. A more thorough treatment of the problem of efficiency should focus on more than just data comparison and exchange but should also include the overhead necessary for the implementation of the algorithm.

■ 9.2 DECISION TREES

The three sorting methods analyzed in previous sections were not very efficient. This leads to several questions: Can any better level of efficiency for a sorting algorithm be expected? Can algorithms, at least theoretically, be more efficient by executing faster? If so, when can we be satisfied with an algorithm and be sure that the sorting speed is unlikely to be increased? We need a quantitative measurement to estimate a *lower bound* of sorting speed.

This section focuses on the comparisons of two elements and not the element interchange. The questions are: On the average, how many comparisons have to be made to sort n elements? Or, what is the best estimate of the number of item comparisons if an array is assumed to be ordered randomly?

Every sorting algorithm can be expressed in terms of a binary tree in which the arcs carry the labels Y(es) or N(o). Nonterminal nodes on the tree contain conditions or queries for labels, and the leaves have all possible orderings of the array to which the algorithm is applied. This type of tree is called a *decision tree*. Since the initial ordering cannot be predicted, all possibilities have to be listed in the tree in order for the sorting procedure to grapple with any array and any possible initial order of data. This initial order determines which path is taken by the algorithm, and what sequence of comparisons is actually chosen. Note that different trees have to be drawn for arrays of different length.

Figure 9.8 illustrates decision trees for the insertion and bubble sorts for an array [a b c]. The tree for insertion sort has six leaves, and the tree for bubble sort has eight leaves. How many leaves does a tree for an n-element array have? Such an array can be ordered in $n!$ different ways, as many ways as the possible permutations of the array elements, and all of these orderings have to be stored in the leaves of the decision tree. Thus, the tree for insertion sort has six leaves since $n = 3$, and $3! = 6$.

But as the example of the decision tree for bubble sort indicates, the number of leaves does not have to equal $n!$. In fact, it is never less than $n!$ which means that it can be greater than $n!$. This is a consequence of the fact that a decision tree can have leaves corresponding

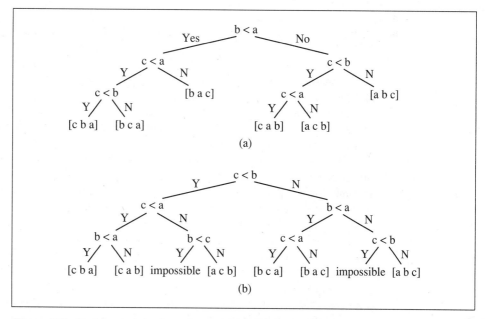

Figure 9.8: **Decision trees for insertion sort (a) and bubble sort (b) as applied to the array [a b c].**

to failures, not only to possible orderings. The failure nodes are reached by an inconsistent sequence of operations. Also, the total number of leaves can be greater than $n!$ since some orderings (permutations) can occur in more than one leaf, since the comparisons may be repeated.

One of the interesting properties of decision trees is the average number of arcs traversed from the root to reach a leaf. Because one arc represents one comparison, the average number of arcs reflects the average number of key comparisons when executing a sorting algorithm.

As already established in Chapter 6, an i-level complete decision tree has 2^{i-1} leaves, and $2^{i-1} - 1$ nonterminal nodes (for $i \geq 1$), and $2^i - 1$ total nodes. Because all noncomplete trees with the same number of i levels have fewer nodes than that, $k + m \leq 2^i - 1$, where m is the number of leaves and k the number of nonleaves. Also, $k \leq 2^{i-1} - 1$ and $m \leq 2^{i-1}$. The latter inequality is used as an approximation for m. Hence, in an i-level decision tree, there are at most 2^{i-1} leaves.

Now, a question arises: What is a relationship between the number of leaves of a decision tree and the number of all possible orderings of an n-element array? There are $n!$ possible orderings and each one of them is represented by a leaf in a decision tree. But, the tree has also some extra nodes due to repetitions and failures. Therefore, $n! \leq m \leq 2^{i-1}$, or $2^{i-1} \geq n!$. This inequality answers the following question: How many comparisons are performed when using a certain sorting algorithm for an n-element array in the worst case. Or rather, what is the lowest or the best figure expected in the worst case? Note that this analysis pertains to the worst case. We assume that i is a level of a tree, regardless of whether or not it is complete; i always refers to the longest path leading from the root of the tree to the lowest tree level which is also the largest number of comparisons needed to reach an ordered configuration of array stored in the root. First, the inequality $2^{i-1} \geq n!$ is transformed into $i - 1 \geq \lg(n!)$ which means that the path length in a decision tree with at least $n!$ leaves must be at least $\lg(n!)$, or rather, it must be $\lceil \lg(n!) \rceil$, where $\lceil x \rceil$ is an integer not less than x. See the example in Figure 9.9.

It can be proven that for a randomly chosen leaf of an m-leaf decision tree, the length of the path from the root to the leaf is not less than $\lg m$, and that both in the average case and the worst case, the required number of comparisons, $\lg(n!)$, is big-O of $n \lg n$ (see Appendix A.2). That is, $O(n \lg n)$ is the best that can be expected also in average cases.

It is interesting to compare this approximation to some of the numbers computed for sorting methods, especially for the average and worst cases. For example, an insertion sort requires only $n - 1$ comparisons in the best case, but in the average and the worst cases, this sort turns into an n^2 algorithm since the functions relating the number of comparisons to the number of elements are, for these cases, the big-Os of n^2. This is much greater than $n \lg n$, especially for large numbers. Consequently, an insertion sort is not an ideal algorithm. The quest for better methods can be continued with at least the expectation that the number of comparisons should be approximated by $n \lg n$ rather than n^2.

The difference between these two functions is best seen in Figure 9.10 if the performance of the algorithms analyzed so far is compared with the expected performance $n \lg n$ in the average case.

The numbers in the table in Figure 9.10 show that if 100 items are sorted, the desired algorithm is four times faster than the insertion sort and eight times faster than the selection and bubble sorts. For 1000 items it would be 25 and 50 times faster. For 10,000 the

These are some possible decision trees for an array of three elements. These trees must have at least 3! = 6 leaves. For the sake of example it is assumed that each tree has one extra leaf (a repetition or a failure). In the worst and average cases, the number of comparisons is $i - 1 \geq \lceil \lg(n!) \rceil$. In this example, $n = 3$, so $i - 1 \geq \lceil \lg 3! \rceil = \lceil \lg 6 \rceil \approx \lceil 2.59 \rceil = 3$. And, in fact, only for the "best looking," that is, best balanced tree (a), the non-rounded length of average path is less than three.

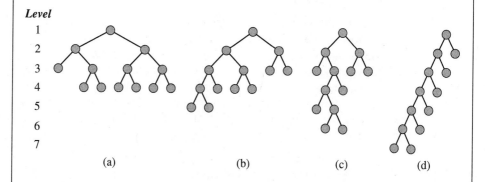

These are the sums of the paths from the root to all leaves in trees (a)–(d) and the average path lengths:

(a) $2 + 3 + 3 + 3 + 3 + 3 + 3 = 20$; average $= \dfrac{20}{7} \approx 2.86$;

(b) $4 + 4 + 3 + 3 + 3 + 2 + 2 = 21$; average $= \dfrac{21}{7} = 3$;

(c) $2 + 4 + 5 + 5 + 3 + 2 + 2 = 23$; average $= \dfrac{23}{7} \approx 3.29$;

(d) $6 + 6 + 5 + 4 + 3 + 2 + 1 = 27$; average $= \dfrac{27}{7} \approx 3.86$.

Figure 9.9: **Examples of decision trees for an array of three elements.**

Sort Type	n	100	1,000	10,000
Insertion	$\dfrac{n(n-1)}{4}$	2,475	249,750	24,997,500
Selection, bubble	$\dfrac{n(n-1)}{2}$	4,950	499,500	49,995,000
Expected	$n \lg n$	664	9,967	132,890

Figure 9.10: **Number of comparisons performed by the simple sorting methods and by an algortihm whose efficiency is estimated by the function $n \lg n$.**

difference in performance differs by factors of 188 and 376, respectively. This can only serve to encourage the search for an algorithm embodying the performance of the function $n \lg n$.

■ 9.3 EFFICIENT SORTING ALGORITHMS

9.3.1 Shell Sort

The $O(n^2)$ limit for a sorting method is much too large and must be broken in order to improve efficiency and decrease run time. How can this be done? The problem is that the time required for ordering an array by the three sorting algorithms usually grows faster than the size of the array. In fact, it is customarily a quadratic function of that size. It may turn out to be more efficient to sort parts of the original array first, and then, if they are at least partially ordered, sort the entire array. If the subarrays are already sorted, we are that much closer to the best case of an ordered array than initially. A general outline of such a procedure is as follows:

> *divide* **data** *into* **h** *subarrays;*
> for (i = 1; i <= h; i++)
>   *sort subarray* **data**$_i$;
> *sort array* **data**;

If h is too small, then the subarrays **data**$_i$ of array **data** could be too large, and sorting algorithms might prove inefficient as well. On the other hand, if h is too large, then too many small subarrays are created, and although they are sorted, it does not substantially change the overall order of **data**. Lastly, if only one such partition of **data** is done, the gain on the execution time may be rather modest. To solve that problem, several different subdivisions are used and for every subdivision, the same procedure is applied separately, as in:

> *determine numbers* **h**$_t$ . . . **h**$_1$ *of ways of dividing array* **data** *into subarrays;*
> for (h=h$_t$; t > 1; t--, h=h$_t$)
>   *divide* **data** *into* **h** *subarrays;*
>   for (i = 1; i <= h; i++)
>   *sort subarray* **data**$_i$;
> *sort array* **data**;

This idea is the basis of the *diminishing decrement sort*, also known as the *Shell sort* named after Donald L. Shell who designed this technique. Note that this pseudocode does not identify a specific sorting method for ordering the subarrays; it can be any simple method. Usually, however, the Shell sort uses the insertion sort.

The heart of the Shell sort is an ingenious division of the array **data** into several subarrays. The trick is that elements spaced farther apart are compared first, then the elements closer to each other are compared, and so on, until adjacent elements are compared on the last pass. The original array is logically subdivided into subarrays by picking every h_tth element as part of one subarray. Therefore, there are h_t subarrays, and for every $h = 1, \ldots, h_t$,

$$\text{data}_{h,h}[i] = \text{data}\,[h_t * i + (h - 1)].$$

For example, if $h_t = 3$, the array **data** is subdivided into three subarrays $\text{data}_1, \text{data}_2$, and data_3 so that

$$\text{data}_{31}[0] = \text{data}[0], \text{data}_{31}[1] = \text{data}[3], \ldots, \text{data}_{31}[i] = \text{data}[3i], \ldots$$
$$\text{data}_{32}[0] = \text{data}[1], \text{data}_{32}[1] = \text{data}[4], \ldots, \text{data}_{32}[i] = \text{data}[3i+1], \ldots$$
$$\text{data}_{33}[0] = \text{data}[2], \text{data}_{33}[1] = \text{data}[5], \ldots, \text{data}_{33}[i] = \text{data}[3i+2], \ldots$$

and these subarrays are sorted separately. After that, new subarrays are created with an $h_{t-1} < h_t$, and the insertion sort is applied to them. The process is repeated until no subdivisions can be made. If $h_t = 5$, the process of extracting subarrays and sorting them is called a 5-sort.

Figure 9.11 shows the elements of the array **data** that are five positions apart and are logically inserted into a separate array, "logically" since physically they still occupy the same positions in **data**. For each value of increment h_t, there are h_t subarrays and each of them is sorted separately. As the value of the increment decreases, the number of subarrays decreases accordingly, and their sizes grow. Since much of **data**'s disorder has been removed in the earlier iterations, on the last pass the array is much closer to its final form than before all the intermediate h-sorts.

There is still one problem that has to be addressed, namely choosing the optimal value of the increment. In the example in Figure 9.11, the value of 5 is chosen to begin with, then 3, and 1 is used for the final sort. But why these values? Unfortunately, no convincing answer can be given. In fact, any decreasing sequence of increments can be used as long

data before 5-sort	10	8	6	20	4	3	22	1	0	15	16
Five subarrays before sorting	10	—	—	—	—	3	—	—	—	—	16
		8	—	—	—	—	22				
			6	—	—	—	—	1			
				20	—	—	—	—	0		
					4	—	—	—	—	15	
The five subarrays after sorting	3	—	—	—	—	10	—	—	—	—	16
		8	—	—	—	—	22				
			1	—	—	—	—	6			
				0	—	—	—	—	20		
					4	—	—	—	—	15	
data after 5-sort and before 3-sort	3	8	1	0	4	10	22	6	20	15	16
Three subarrays before sorting	3	—	—	0	—	—	22	—	—	15	
		8	—	—	4	—	—	6	—	—	16
			1	—	—	10	—	—	20		
Three subarrays after sorting	0	—	—	3	—	—	15	—	—	22	
		4	—	—	6	—	—	8	—	—	16
			1	—	—	10	—	—	20		
data after 3-sort and before 1-sort	0	4	1	3	6	10	15	8	20	22	16
data after 1-sort	0	1	3	4	6	8	10	15	16	20	22

Figure 9.11: **The array [10 8 6 20 4 3 22 1 0 15 16] sorted by Shell sort.**

as the last one, h_1, is equal to 1. Donald Knuth has shown that even if there are only two increments, $\left(\frac{16n}{\pi}\right)^{\frac{1}{3}}$ and 1, the Shell sort is more efficient than the insertion sort since it takes $O(n^{\frac{5}{3}})$ time instead of $O(n^2)$. But the efficiency of the Shell sort can be improved by using a larger number of increments. It is imprudent, however, to use sequences of increments like 1, 2, 4, 8, ... or 1, 3, 6, 9, ... since the mixing effect of data is lost.

For example, when using 4-sort and 2-sort, a subarray data, $\text{data}_{2,i}$, for $i = 1, 2$, consists of elements of two arrays $\text{data}_{4,i}$ and $\text{data}_{4,j}$, where $j = i + 2$, and only those. It is much better if elements of $\text{data}_{4,i}$ do not meet together again in the same array since a faster reduction in the number of exchange inversions is achieved if they are sent to different arrays when performing the 2-sort. Using only powers of two for the increments, as in Shell's original algorithm, the items in the even and odd positions of the array do not interact until the last pass when the increment equals 1. This is where the mixing effect (or lack thereof) comes into play. But there is no formal proof indicating which sequence of increments is optimal. Extensive empirical studies along with some theoretical considerations suggest that it is a good idea to choose increments satisfying the conditions

$$h_1 = 1$$

$$h_{i+1} = 3h_i + 1$$

and stop with h_t for which $h_{t+2} \geq n$. For $n = 10,000$, this gives the sequence

$$1, 4, 13, 40, 121, 364, 1093, 3280.$$

Experimental data have been approximated by the exponential function, the estimate, $1.21n^{\frac{5}{4}}$, and the logarithmic function $.39n \ln^2 n - 2.33n \ln n = O(n \ln^2 n)$. The first form fits the results of the tests better. $1.21n^{1.25} = O(n^{1.25})$ is much better than $O(n^2)$ for the insertion sort, but it is still much greater than the expected $O(n \lg n)$ performance.

Figure 9.12 contains a function to sort the array **data** using the Shell sort. Note that before sorting starts, increments are computed and stored in the array **increments**.

The core of the Shell sort is to divide an array into subarrays by taking elements h positions apart. There are three features of this algorithm that vary from one implementation to another:

1. The sequence of increments
2. A simple sorting algorithm applied in all passes except the last
3. A simple sorting algorithm applied only in the last pass, for 1-sort

In our implementation as in Shell's, the insertion sort is applied in all h-sorts, but other sorting algorithms can be used. For example, Dobosiewicz uses the bubble sort for the last pass and the insertion sort for other passes. Incerpi and Sedgewick use two iterations of the cocktail shaker sort and a version of bubble sort in each h-sort and finish with the insertion sort obtaining what they call a *shakersort*. All these versions perform better than simple sorting methods, although there are some differences in performance between these versions. Analytical results concerning the complexity of these sorts are not available. All the results regarding complexity are of an empirical nature.

```
template<class genType>
void
ShellSort (genType data[], int arrSize)
{   register int i, j, hCnt, h;
    int increments[20], k;
    genType tmp;

//  create an appropriate number of increments h
    for (h = 1, i = 0; h < arrSize; i++) {
        increments[i] = h;
        h = 3*h + 1;
    }
 // loop on the number of different increments h
    for ( i--; i >= 0; i--) {
        h = increments[i];
     // loop on the number of subarrays h-sorted in ith pass
        for (hCnt = h; hCnt<2*h; hCnt++) {
         // insertion sort for subarray containing every hth element
         // of array data
            for (j = hCnt; j < arrSize; ) {
                tmp = data[j];
                k = j;
                while (k-h >= 0 && tmp < data[k-h]) {
                    data[k] = data[k-h];
                    k -= h;
                }
                data[k] = tmp;
                j += h;
            }
        }
    }
}
```

Figure 9.12: **Implementation of the Shell sort.**

9.3.2 Heap Sort

The selection sort makes $O(n^2)$ comparisons and is very inefficient, especially for large n. But it performs relatively few moves. If the comparison part of the algorithm is improved, the end result can be promising.

The *heap sort* was invented by John Williams and uses the approach inherent to the selection sort. It finds among the n elements the one that precedes all other $n - 1$ elements, then the least element among those $n - 1$ items, etc., until the array is sorted. To have the array sorted in ascending order, the heap sort puts the largest element at the end of the array, then the second largest in the front of it, and so on. The heap sort starts from the end of the array by finding the largest elements, whereas the selection sort starts from the beginning using the smallest elements. The final order in both cases is indeed the same.

The heap sort uses a heap as described in Chapter 6. A heap is a binary tree with the following two properties:

1. The value of each node is not less than the values stored in each of its children.
2. The tree is perfectly balanced and the leaves in the last level are all in the leftmost positions.

A node has the *heap property* if it satisfies condition 1.

The first condition can be used in sorting, but the rationale behind the second might not be immediately apparent. The goal is to use only the array being sorted without using any additional storage for the array elements. Although so far in this book, trees have been implemented as linked structures, it is inefficient to continue along these lines since some more storage is necessary for the tree or at least for pointer fields. For the implementation of the heap sort, at least in the context of sorting arrays, using an array is more effective in terms of space. A heap can be defined as an array **heap** of length n in which

heap[i] $\geq$ **heap[2*i + 1]**

and

heap[i] $\geq$ **heap[2*i + 2]**, for $0 \leq i < \frac{n}{2}$.

According to the second property of heaps, the number of levels in the tree is $O(\lg n)$.

Elements in a heap are not perfectly ordered. It is only known that the largest element is in the root node and that for each node, all its descendants are not greater than that node.

As Figure 9.13 shows, the tree representation of the array **data** = [2 8 6 1 10 15 3 12 11] is not a heap. If the array represented a heap then the root would contain the largest element. Suppose we make it a heap. To sort the array, it is necessary to move the root to the end of the array. To avoid losing data, we swap the root with the last element of the array, and can now exclude the last element from any further consideration. But what about the rest of the array, **data[0]**, **data[1]**, ..., **data[n-2]**? Since we swapped the root with the last element, the root is not necessarily still the largest element of the remaining ones, so the array is no longer a heap. If we then create a heap out of the remaining nodes, we can exchange the root with **data[n-2]** putting the second largest element in its proper place. The process can be repeated for **data[0]**, **data[1]**, ..., **data[n-3]** until only one element, **data[0]**, is left and it must be in its proper place.

First, a heap has to be created out of the array that represents a binary tree. In this example we use a bottom-up method devised by Floyd and described in Section 6.9.2. All steps leading to transformation of the array into a heap are shown in Figure 9.13 (cf. Figure 6.54).

Writing the function **HeapSort()** is simple if the function **MoveDown()** from Section 6.9 is used. First, the tree has to be transformed to a heap by starting to build it

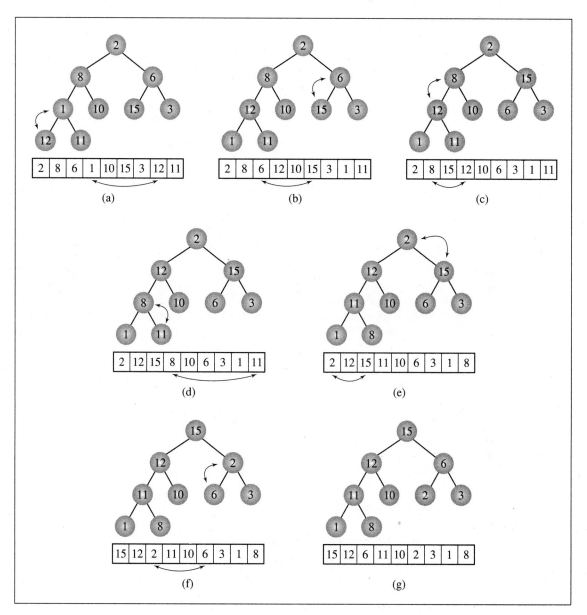

Figure 9.13: **Transforming the array [2 8 6 1 10 15 3 12 11] into a heap.**

from the last nonleaf node (since leaves are trivially heaps), and adding one more node in each iteration to form partial heaps. After that transformation is finished, the heap is sorted by exchanging the root element, that is, the first element of the array, with the last unsorted element and then transforming such a tree again to a heap, until all data are sorted.

The outline for the heap sort algorithm is

```
HeapSort(data, n)
    transform data into a heap;
    i = n - 1;
    while(i > 1)
        swap the root with the last element;
        i--;
        restore the heap property for the tree data[0]..data[i];
```

Figure 9.14 contains an implementation of the heap sort algorithm.

How does the second part of the algorithm work? After the heap has been built (Figures 9.13g and 9.15a), the largest element can be moved to the end of the array. Its place is taken by 8, violating the heap property. The heap property has to be restored, but this time it is done for the tree excluding the largest element, 15. Since it is already in its proper position, it does not need to be considered any more and is removed (pruned) from the tree as indicated by dashed lines in Figure 9.15. Now the largest element among `data[0],data[1],...,data[n-2]` is looked for. `MoveDown()` is called to construct a heap out of all elements of **data** except the last one, `data[n-1]`, which results in the heap in Figure 9.15c. Number 12 is sifted up and swapped with 1 resulting in the tree in Figure 9.15d. `MoveDown()` is called again to select 11 (Figure 9.15e), and the element

```
template<class genType>
void
HeapSort(genType data[], int size)
{   register int i,j;

  // create a heap
    for (i = size/2 - 1; i >= 0; --i)
        MoveDown (data,i,size-1);

  // move the root item to the end of the array data
  // and restore the heap property to the tree
  // data[0],...,data[i-2] by selecting the largest item

    for (i = size-1; i > 1; --i) {
        Swap(data[0],data[i]);
        MoveDown(data,0,i-1);
    }
    if (data[0] > data[1])
        Swap(data[0],data[1]);
}
```

Figure 9.14: **Implementation of the heap sort.**

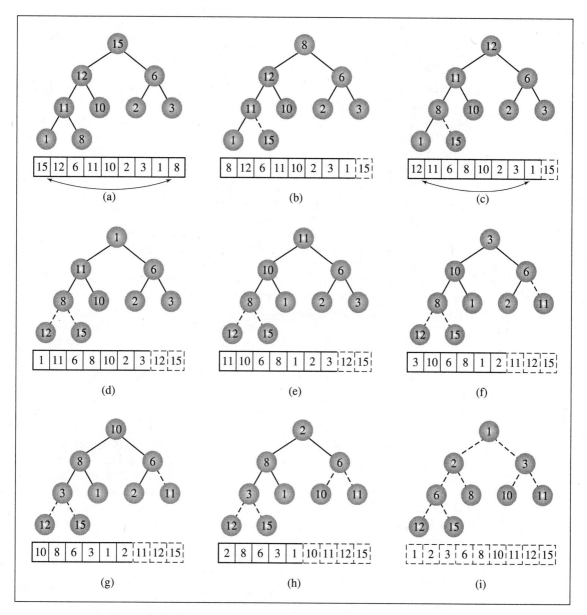

Figure 9.15: **Execution of the heap sort on the array [15 12 6 11 10 2 3 1 8] which is the heap constructed in Figure 9.13.**

is swapped with the last element of the current subarray, which is 3 (Figure 9.15f). Now, the number 10 is selected (Figure 9.15g) and exchanged with 2 (Figure 9.15h). The reader can easily construct trees and heaps for the next passes through the second **for** loop of the function **HeapSort()**. After the last pass, the array is in ascending order and the tree is ordered accordingly.

This procedure might be considered inefficient because the movement of data seems to be extensive. All effort is applied to moving the largest element to the leftmost side of the array in order to move it to the farthest right position. But therein lies its efficiency. To create the heap in the first **for** loop of **HeapSort()**, **MoveDown()** performs $O(n)$ steps (see Section 6.9.2).

The second loop of **HeapSort()**, the selection loop, is executed $n - 2$ times, each time replacing the root by node i. In the worst case, this causes **MoveDown()** to execute its **while** loop $\lg i$ times to bring this node down to the level of the leaves. Thus, the total number of moves in all the executions of **MoveDown()** in this part of **HeapSort()** is $\sum_{i=2}^{n-1} \lg i$, which is bounded by $(n - 1)\lg(n - 1) = O(n \lg n)$ from above and by $\frac{n}{2}\lg n = O(n \lg n)$ from below. The $n - 2$ swaps in the second **for** loop of **HeapSort()** and the one possible swap after the loop have to be added, resulting in $O(n) + O(n \lg n) + (n - 1) = O(n \lg n)$ exchanges for the whole procedure in the worst case.

For the best case, when the array is in reverse order, **MoveDown()** is called $\frac{n}{2}$ times in the creation phase but no moves are performed. The second loop of **HeapSort()** makes one swap to eliminate the largest element by moving it to the end of array, resulting in only $n - 1$ moves. In the best case, only two comparisons are made for each node: $2\left(\frac{n}{2} - 1\right)$ comparisons in the first **for** loop of **HeapSort()** and $2(n - 2)$ in the second. Thus, the total number of comparisons in the best case is $O(n)$.

Considering that the number of comparisons is $O(n)$ in the best case and $O(n \lg n)$ in the worst case, big-O of this number in the average case is expected to fall between n and $n \lg n$. However, it can be proved that the best we can expect in the average case is $O(n \lg n)$, which narrows down the choice for the number of comparisons to $O(n \lg n)$.

9.3.3   Quicksort

The Shell sort approached the problem of sorting by dividing the original array into subarrays, sorting them separately, and then dividing them again to sort the new subarrays until the whole array is sorted. The goal was to reduce the original problem to subproblems that can be solved more easily and quickly. The same reasoning was a guiding principle for C. A. R. Hoare, who invented an algorithm, appropriately called a *quicksort*.

The original array is divided into two subarrays, the first of which contains all elements less than a chosen key called the *bound* or *pivot*. The second array includes elements equal to or greater than the bound. The two subarrays can be sorted separately, but before this is done, the partition process is repeated for both subarrays. As a result, two new bounds are chosen, one for each subarray. The four subarrays are created because each subarray obtained in the first phase is now divided into two segments. This process of partitioning is carried down until there are only one-cell arrays that do not need to be sorted at all. By dividing the task of sorting a large array into two simpler tasks and then dividing those tasks into simpler tasks, it turns out that in the process of getting prepared to sort, the data have been already sorted. Since the sorting has been somewhat dissipated in the preparation process, this preparation process is the core of quicksort.

Quicksort is recursive in nature because it is applied to both subarrays of an array at each level of partitioning. This technique is summarized in the following pseudocode:

```
QuickSort(array)
    if length(array) > 1
```

```
// partition array into subarray₁ and subarray₂
while there are elements left in array
    if element < bound
        include element in subarray₁;
    else include element in subarray₂;
QuickSort(subarray₁);
QuickSort(subarray₂);
```

To partition an array, two operations have to be performed: a bound has to be found and the array has to be scanned to place the elements in the proper subarrays. Elements are placed in the first subarray if they are less than the bound, and in the second otherwise. However, choosing a good bound is not a trivial task. The problem is that the subarrays should be approximately the same length. If an array contains the numbers 1 through 100 (in any order) and the number 2 is chosen as a bound, then an imbalance results because the first subarray contains only one number after partitioning, whereas the second has 99 numbers.

A number of different strategies for selecting a bound have been developed. One of the simplest consists of taking the first element of an array as a bound. That approach can suffice for some applications. However, since many arrays to be sorted already have many elements in their proper positions, a more cautious approach is to choose the element located in the middle of the array. This approach is incorporated in the implementation of quicksort contained in Figure 9.16.

The next step is to scan the array, referring all the time to the chosen bound. To this end, two indexes, `upper` and `lower`, are used; they are initialized to the first and the last positions of the array. Suppose that initially the array has the following elements:

```
┌─────────────────┬───┬────────────────────┐
│ 1  5  4  7  8   │ 6 │ 6  3  8  12  10     │
└─────────────────┴───┴────────────────────┘
  ↑                 ↑                    ↑
 lower             bound               upper
```

Now `lower` is moved right until an element not smaller than the `bound` is encountered, as in

```
┌─────────────────┬───┬────────────────────┐
│ 1  5  4  7  8   │ 6 │ 6  3  8  12  10     │
└─────────────────┴───┴────────────────────┘
        ↑                             ↑
      lower                         upper
```

after which `upper` takes over by moving to the left until it finds an element not greater than the `bound`, which is 3:

```
┌─────────────────┬───┬────────────────────┐
│ 1  5  4  7  8   │ 6 │ 6  3  8  12  10     │
└─────────────────┴───┴────────────────────┘
        ↑                 ↑
      lower             upper
```

Now the elements `data[lower]` and `data[upper]` are exchanged:

```
┌─────────────────┬───┬────────────────────┐
│ 1  5  4  3  8   │ 6 │ 6  7  8  12  10     │
└─────────────────┴───┴────────────────────┘
        ↑                 ↑
      lower             upper
```

```
template<class genType>
void
QuickSort (genType data[], int first, int last)
{   int lower = first, upper = last;
    genType bound = data[(first + last) / 2];

    // partition

    while (lower <= upper) {
        while (data[lower] < bound)
            lower++;
        while (bound < data[upper])
            upper--;
        if (lower < upper)
            Swap(data[lower++],data[upper--]);
        else lower++;
    }

    // call QuickSort recursively for both subarrays

    if (first < upper)
        QuickSort (data,first,upper);
    if (upper+1 < last)
        QuickSort (data,upper+1,last);
}
```

Figure 9.16: **Implementation of quicksort.**

After which **lower** is incremented and **upper** decremented:

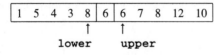

In the second iteration of the outer **while** loop the elements **data[lower]** and **data[upper]** are swapped:

| 1 | 5 | 4 | 3 | 6 | 6 | 8 | 7 | 8 | 12 | 10 |

↑   ↑

lower   upper

followed by moving both `lower` and `upper` so that they become equal:

$$\boxed{1 \quad 5 \quad 4 \quad 3 \quad 6 \;\Big|\; 6 \;\Big|\; 8 \quad 7 \quad 8 \quad 12 \quad 10}$$

⇈

`lower upper`

Now the other `while` loop is executed for the third time only to increment `lower`:

$$\boxed{1 \quad 5 \quad 4 \quad 3 \quad 6 \;\Big|\; 6 \;\Big|\; 8 \quad 7 \quad 8 \quad 12 \quad 10}$$

↑ ↑

`upper   lower`

Since the pointers `upper` and `lower` have crossed, no more iterations of the outer `while` loop are performed, and the partitioning of this array is complete. The sorting process, however, is not finished even though the array looks more ordered than initially. Only the partitioning process for the entire array is finished, and now `QuickSort()` calls itself on the two subarrays of the array produced by this partition, [1 5 4 3 6 6] and [8 7 8 12 10]. The process is executed for all other partitions. The arrays under consideration become smaller until nothing is left to partition. Figure 9.17 summarizes the whole sorting process and all the partitions.

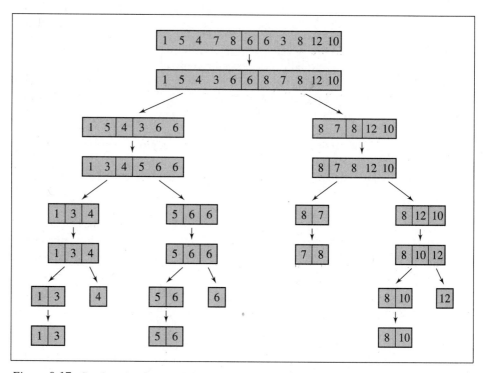

Figure 9.17: **Sorting the array [1 5 4 7 8 6 6 3 8 12 10] with quicksort implemented by** `QuickSort()`**.**

In this implementation, the main property of the bound, that it is a boundary item, is used only to start the process of division of the array **data** into two sections. In that process itself, the bound is treated on a par with other array elements. As a result, it can end up in either the first or the second subarray. In Figure 9.17, the bound is always inserted into the first subarray. On the other hand, if the array [1 2 8 3 4 10] is partitioned, then the bound is put in the second subarray, [8 10]. The process of sorting can be arranged so that the bound does not end up in either subarray but is placed on the borderline between the two subarrays. In this way, the bound is located in its final position and can be excluded from further processing. To ensure that the bound is not moved around, it is stashed in the first position and after partitioning is done, it is moved to its proper position.

To that end, before the outer loop is entered, the bound is located in the first position by the statements

```
Swap(data[first], data[(first + last) / 2]);
bound = data[first];
```

If the condition of the first inner loop stays the same, i.e., if it still is

```
while (data[lower] < bound)
```

the range can be crossed if the bound is the largest element of the currently partitioned array. For example, in the array [12 10 5 2], for which the bound is 12, the pointer **lower** does not stop on the last element of array, 2; it exceeds the array range in search of an element that is greater than or equal to the bound, 12. There is a temptation to add one more test to this condition, **lower < last**, to prevent this. The resulting condition is

```
while (data[lower] < bound && lower < last).
```

The second test is necessary only in extreme cases, but is executed almost all the time. Therefore, it is desirable to combine both tests to speed up execution of the loop. This can be accomplished by using only the first test, **data[lower] < bound**, if an element guaranteed to be greater than any item in the array is added to the end of the original array. In that case, if the bound happens to be the largest item, then the test **data[lower] < bound** fails on this additional element (or on a proper element of the array if the segment under scrutiny is not the rightmost). At the cost of introducing one element to the array, the **while** loop condition contains one test instead of two. Needless to say, some knowledge about the sorted data is necessary to ascertain that the added element is really the largest.

Figure 9.18 contains the new implementation of the quicksort.

Now, the same array can be sorted, this time with a large number appended to the end and by putting the bound in the first cell of the array. After these two steps, the array is

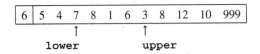

Both pointers are processed which after the first round leads to

```
template<class genType>
void
QSort (genType data[], int first, int last)
{   int lower = first+1, upper = last;
    genType bound;

    Swap(data[first],data[(first+last)/2]);
    bound = data[first];

    // partition

    while (lower <= upper) {
        while (data[lower] < bound)
            lower++;
        while (bound < data[upper])
            upper--;
        if (lower < upper)
            Swap(data[lower++],data[upper--]);
        else lower++;
    }
    Swap(data[upper],data[first]);

    // call QSort() recursively for both subarrays

    if (first < upper-1)
        QSort (data,first,upper-1);
    if (upper+1 < last)
        QSort (data,upper+1,last);
}
```

Figure 9.18: **Modified implementation of quicksort.**

The numbers 3 and 7 are exchanged as in

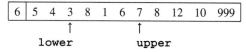

and the pointers are moved again. After the second round the array is

```
6  5  4  3  8  1  6  7  8  12  10  999
            ↑     ↑
         lower  upper
```

This time 6 and 8 are interchanged as in

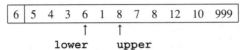

```
6 | 5   4   3   6   1   8   7   8   12   10   999 |
            ↑       ↑
          lower   upper
```

and the pointers are moved again which leads eventually to their crossing as

```
6 | 5   4   3   6   1   8   7   8   12   10   999 |
              ↑   ↑
          upper  lower
```

Now the bound 6 can take its final position, currently occupied by 1, and be left there for good as in

```
1 | 5   4   3   6   6   8   7   8   12   10   999 |
              ↑  ↑
          lower  upper
```

From now on one less element is considered because only the arrays [1 5 4 3 6] and [8 7 8 12 10] are passed for further processing. Figure 9.19 summarizes this process.

A simple comparison of Figure 9.17 and Figure 9.19 shows that in the second algorithm, partitioning is performed seven times, whereas in the first it is executed ten times — 30% worse. The second algorithm is a substantial improvement.

The worst case occurs if in each invocation of **QSort()**, the smallest (or largest) element of the array is chosen for the bound. In the second example this is the case if we try to sort the array [3 5 1 2 4 6]. The first bound is the number 1 and the array is broken into an empty array and the array [5 3 2 4 6]. The new bound is the number 2 and again only one

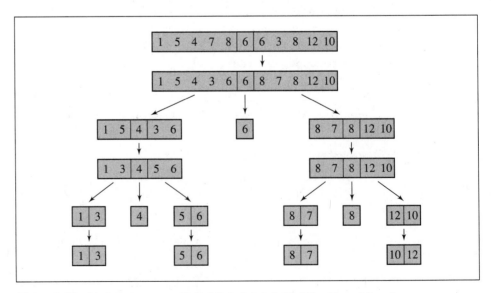

Figure 9.19: **Sorting the array [1 5 4 7 8 6 6 3 8 12 10] with quicksort implemented by QSort().**

nonempty array, [5 3 4 6], is obtained as the result of partitioning. The next bound and arrays returned by partition are 3 and [5 4 6], and lastly, 4 and [5 6]. The algorithm then operates on arrays of size $n, n - 1, n - 2, \ldots, 2$. The partitions require $n - 2 + n - 3 + \cdots + 1$ comparisons and for each partition, only the bound is placed in the proper position. This results in a run time equal to $O(n^2)$, which is hardly a desirable result, especially for large arrays or files.

The best case is when the bound divides an array into two even parts. The array of length n is divided into two arrays both of approximately length $\frac{n}{2}$; to be more precise, one of them has $\lfloor \frac{n-1}{2} \rfloor$ elements and the other may have one element more, $\lceil \frac{n-1}{2} \rceil$. If the bounds for both subarrays are well chosen, the partitions produce four new subarrays, each of them with approximately $\frac{n}{4}$ cells. If again the bounds for all four subarrays divide them evenly, the partitions result in eight subarrays, each with at most $\frac{n}{8}$ elements. There are then

$$n + 2\frac{n}{2} + 4\frac{n}{4} + 8\frac{n}{8} + \cdots + x\frac{n}{x}$$

comparisons performed for all partitions. This number can be computed if the value of x is known. This value equals the number of times partitioning has been performed during the run of **QSort()**. Because it is assumed that the bound always divides the array into two even (or almost even) parts, then $x = \lceil \lg n \rceil \approx \lg n$. Thus, the above sum is approximated by $n \lg n$.

To answer the question asked before: is the average case, when the array is ordered randomly, closer to the best case, $n \lg n$, or to the worst, $O(n^2)$? Some calculations show that the average case requires only $O(n \lg n)$ comparisons (see Appendix 3), which is the desired result. The validity of this figure can be strengthened by referring to the tree in Figure 9.19. This tree indicates how important it is to keep the tree balanced, for the smaller number of levels, the quicker the sorting process. In the extreme case the binary tree can be turned into a linked list in which every nonleaf node has only one child. That rather rare phenomenon is possible and prevents us from calling the quicksort the ideal sort. But, the quicksort seems to be closest to such an ideal because, as analytic studies indicate, the quicksort outperforms other efficient sorting methods by a factor of two.

How can the worst case be avoided? The partition procedure should produce arrays of approximately the same size, which can be achieved if a good bound is chosen. This is the crux of the matter: How can the best bound be found? Only two methods will be mentioned. The first method randomly generates a number between **first** and **last**. This number is used as an index of the bound which is then interchanged with the first element of the array. In this method, the partition process proceeds as before. Good random number generators may slow down the execution time as they themselves often use sophisticated and time-consuming techniques. Thus, this method is not highly recommended.

The second method chooses a median of three elements: the first, middle, and last. For the original array [1 5 4 7 8 6 6 3 8 12 10], the number 6 is chosen from the set [1 6 10], and for the first generated subarray the bound 4 is chosen from the set [1 4 6]. Obviously, there is the possibility that all three elements are always the smallest (or the largest) in the array, but it does not seem very likely.

Is quicksort the ideal sorting algorithm? It is certainly the best — usually. It is not bulletproof, however, and some problems have already been addressed in this section. First, everything hinges on which element of the file or array is chosen for the bound. Ideally, it should be the median element of the array. An algorithm to choose a bound should be flexible enough to handle all possible orderings of the data to be sorted. Because some cases always slip by these algorithms, from time to time the quicksort can be expected to be anything but quick.

Second, it is inappropriate to use the quicksort for small arrays. For arrays with fewer than ten items, the insertion sort is more efficient than the quicksort. In this case, the initial pseudocode can be changed to

```
QuickSort(array)
    if length(array) > 10
        partition array into subarray₁ and subarray₂;
        QuickSort(subarray₁);
        QuickSort(subarray₂);
    else Insertion(array);
```

and the implementations changed accordingly.

9.3.4   Mergesort

The problem with quicksort is that its complexity in the worst case is big-O of n^2 because it is difficult to control the partitioning process. Different methods of choosing a bound attempt to make the behavior of this process fairly regular. However, there is no guarantee that partitioning will result in arrays of approximately the same size. Another strategy is to make partitioning as simple as possible and concentrate on merging the two sorted arrays. This strategy is characteristic of *mergesort*. It was one of the first sorting algorithms used on a computer and was developed by John von Neumann.

Mergesort belongs to the category of divide-and-conquer algorithms by merging its sorted halves into one sorted array. However, these halves have to be sorted first which is accomplished by merging the already sorted halves of these halves. This process of dividing arrays into two halves stops when the array has fewer than two elements. The algorithm is recursive in nature and can be summarized in the following pseudocode:

```
MergeSort(data)
    if data has at least two elements
        MergeSort(left half of data);
        MergeSort(right half of data);
        Merge(both halves into a sorted list);
```

The core of this algorithm is to merge two subarrays into one, which is a relatively simple task, as indicated in this pseudocode:

```
Merge(array1, array2, array3)
    i1, i2, i3 are properly initialized;
    while both array2 and array3 contain elements
        if array2[i2] < array3[i3]
            array1[i1++] = array2[i2++];
        else array1[i1++] = array3[i3++];
    load into array1 the remaining elements of either array2 or array3;
```

For example, if **array2** $=[1\ 4\ 6\ 8\ 10]$ and **array3** $= [2\ 3\ 5\ 22]$ then the resulting **array1** $= [1\ 2\ 3\ 4\ 5\ 6\ 8\ 10\ 22]$.

The pseudocode for **Merge()** suggests that **array1**, **array2**, and **array3** are physically separate entities. However, for the proper execution of **MergeSort()**, **array1** is a concatenation of **array2** and **array3**, so that **array1** before the execution of **Merge()** is [1 4 6 8 10 2 3 5 22]. In this situation, **Merge()** leads to erroneous results, since after the second iteration of the **while** loop, **array2** is [1 2 6 8 10] and **array1** is [1 2 6 8 3 5 10 22]. Therefore, a temporary array has to be used during the merging process. At the end of the merging process the contents of this temporary array are transferred to **array1**. Because **array2** and **array3** are subarrays of **array1**, they do not need to be passed as parameters to **Merge()**. Instead, indexes for the beginning and the end of **array1** are passed, since **array1** can be a part of another array. The new pseudocode is

```
Merge (array1, first, last)
    mid = (first + last) / 2;
    i1 = 0;
    i2 = first;
    i3 = mid + 1;
    while both left and right subarrays of array1 contain elements
        if array1[i2] < array1[i3]
                temp[i1++] = array1[i2++];
        else temp[i1++] = array1[i3++];
    load into temp the remaining elements of array1;
    load to array1 the content of temp;
```

Since the entire **array1** is copied to **temp** and then **temp** is copied back to **array1**, the number of movements in each execution of **Merge()** is always the same and is equal to $2 * (\texttt{last} - \texttt{first} + 1)$. The number of comparisons depends on the ordering in **array1**. If **array1** is in order or if the elements in the right half precede the elements in the left half, the number of comparisons is $(\texttt{first} + \texttt{last})/2$. The worst case is when the last element of one half precedes only the last element of the other half, as in [1 6 10 12] and [5 9 11 13]. In this case, the number of comparisons is $\texttt{last} - \texttt{first}$. For an n-element array the number of comparisons is $n - 1$.

The pseudocode for **MergeSort()** is now

```
MergeSort (data, first, last)
    if first < last
        mid = (first + last) / 2;
        MergeSort(data, first, mid);
        MergeSort(data, mid+1, last);
        Merge(data, first, last);
```

Figure 9.20 illustrates an example using this sorting algorithm.

This pseudocode can be used to analyze the computing time for mergesort.

For an n-element array the number of movements is computed by the following recurrence relation:

$$M(1) = 0,$$

$$M(n) = 2M\left(\frac{n}{2}\right) + 2n$$

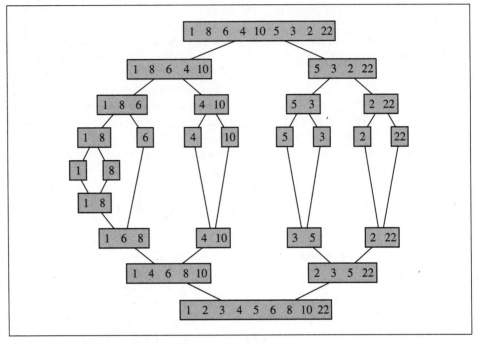

Figure 9.20: **The array [1 8 6 4 10 5 3 2 22] sorted by mergesort.**

$M(n)$ can be computed in the following way:

$$M(n) = 2\left(2M\left(\frac{n}{4}\right) + 2\left(\frac{n}{2}\right)\right) + 2n = 4M\left(\frac{n}{4}\right) + 4n$$

$$= 4\left(2M\left(\frac{n}{8}\right) + 2\left(\frac{n}{4}\right)\right) + 4n = 8M\left(\frac{n}{8}\right) + 6n$$

$$\vdots$$

$$= 2^i M\left(\frac{n}{2^i}\right) + 2in.$$

Choosing $i = \lg n$, so that $n = 2^i$, allows us to infer

$$M(n) = 2^i M\left(\frac{n}{2^i}\right) + 2in = nM(1) + 2n\lg n = 2n\lg n = O(n\lg n).$$

The number of comparisons in the worst case is given by a similar relation:

$$C(1) = 0,$$

$$C(n) = 2C\left(\frac{n}{2}\right) + n - 1$$

which also results in $C(n)$ being $O(n\lg n)$.

The speed of mergesort falls between the speed of quicksort and heapsort. It can be made more efficient by replacing recursion with iteration (see the exercises at the end of this chapter), or by applying insertion sort to small portions of an array, a technique that was suggested for quicksort. However, mergesort has one serious drawback: the need for additional storage for merging arrays, which for large amounts of data could be an insurmountable obstacle. One solution to this drawback uses a linked list; analysis of this method is left as an exercise.

9.3.5 Radix Sort

Radix sort is a popular way of sorting used in everyday life. To sort library cards, we may create as many piles of cards as letters in the alphabet, each pile containing authors whose names start with the same letter. Then, each pile is sorted separately using the same method; namely, piles are created according to the second letter of the authors' names. This process continues until the number of times the piles are divided into smaller piles equals the number of letters of the longest name. This method is actually used when sorting mail in the post office and it was used to sort 80 column cards of coding information in the early days of computers.

When sorting library cards, we proceed from left to right. This method can also be used for sorting mail since all zip codes have the same length. However, it may be inconvenient for sorting lists of integers, because they may have an unequal number of digits. If applied, this method would sort the list [123 23 234 3 567] into the list [123 23 234 3 567]. To get around this problem, zeros can be added in front of each number to make them of equal length, so that the list [123 023 234 003 567] is sorted into the list [003 023 123 234 567]. Another technique looks at each number as a string of bits so that all integers are of equal length. This approach will be discussed shortly. Still another way to sort integers is by proceeding right to left, and this method is discussed now.

When sorting integers, ten piles numbered 0 through 9 are created and, initially, integers are put in a given pile according to their rightmost digit, so that 93 is put in pile 3. Then, piles are combined and the process is repeated, this time with the second leftmost digit; in this case, 93 ends up on pile 9. The process ends after the leftmost digit of the longest number is processed. The algorithm can be summarized in the following pseudocode:

```
RadixSort()
    for (d = 1; d <= the position of the rightmost digit; d++)
        distribute all numbers among piles 0 through 9 according to the dth digit;
        put all integers on one list;
```

The key to obtaining a proper outcome is the way the ten piles are implemented and then combined together. For example, if these piles are implemented as stacks, then the integers 93, 63, 64, 94 are put on piles 3 and 4 (other piles being empty):

```
pile 3:   63   93
pile 4:   94   64
```

These piles are then combined into the list 63, 93, 94, 64. When sorting them according to the second rightmost digit, the piles are as follows:

```
pile 6:   64   63
pile 9:   94   93
```

and the resulting list is 64, 63, 94, 93. The processing is finished, but the result is an improperly sorted list.

However, if piles are organized as queues, the relative order of elements on the list is retained. When integers are sorted according to digit d, then within each pile, integers are sorted with regard to the part of integer extending from digit 1 to $d - 1$. For example, if after the third pass, pile 5 contains the integers 12534, 554, 3590, then this pile is ordered with respect to the last two digits of each number. This property is called the *stability* of a sorting algorithm; stability is a key attribute of radix sort.

Figure 9.21 illustrates another example of radix sort.

list: 10, 1234, 9, 7234, 67, 9181, 733, 197, 7, 3									
							7		
			3	7234			197		
10	9181		733	1234			67		9
piles: 0	1	2	3	4	5	6	7	8	9

pass 1

list: 10, 9181, 733, 3, 1234, 7234, 67, 197, 7, 9									
9			7234						
7			1234						
3	10		733			67		9181	197
piles: 0	1	2	3	4	5	6	7	8	9

pass 2

list: 3, 7, 9, 10, 733, 1234, 7234, 67, 9181, 197									
67									
10									
9									
7	197	7234							
3	9181	1234					773		
piles: 0	1	2	3	4	5	6	7	8	9

pass 3

list: 3, 7, 9, 10, 67, 9181, 197, 1234, 7234, 773									
773									
197									
67									
10									
9									
7									
3	1234						7234		9181
piles: 0	1	2	3	4	5	6	7	8	9

pass 4

list: 3, 7, 9, 10, 67, 197, 773, 1234, 7234, 9181

Figure 9.21: **Sorting the list 10, 1234, 9, 7234, 67, 9181, 733, 197, 7, 3 with radix sort.**

```
const int radix = 10;
const int digits = 5;

template<class genType>
void
RadixSort(genType data[], const int n)
{   register int i, j, k, factor;
    Queue<genType> queues[radix];

    for (i = 0, factor = 1; i < digits; factor *= radix, i++) {
        for (j = 0; j < n; j++)
            queues[(data[j] / factor) % radix].Enqueue(data[j]);
        for (j = k = 0; j < radix; j++)
            while (!queues[j].IsEmpty())
                data[k++] = queues[j].Dequeue();
    }
}
```

Figure 9.22: **Implementation of radix sort.**

Figure 9.22 contains an implementation of radix sort. This program assumes that all queue processing functions have been implemented. In fact, they are implemented as inline functions, to avoid the overhead incurred by function calls. In this program, **queues** is an array of ten queue classes.

This algorithm does not rely on data comparison as did the previous sorting methods. For each integer from **data**, two operations are performed: division by a **factor** to disregard digits preceding digit d being processed in the current pass, and division modulo **radix** (equal to 10) to disregard all digits following d for a total of $2nd = O(n)$ operations. The operation **div** can be used which combines both **/** and **%**. In each pass all integers are moved to piles and then back to **data** for a total of $2nd = O(n)$ moves. The algorithm requires additional space for piles, which if implemented as linked lists, is equal to $2n$ or $3n$ words, depending on the size of pointer fields. Our implementation uses only **for** loops with counters; therefore it requires the same amount of passes for each case: best, average, and worst. The body of the only **while** loop is always executed n times to dequeue integers from all queues.

The foregoing discussion treated integers as combinations of digits. But, as already mentioned, they can be regarded as combinations of bits, usually 16 bits. This time, division and division modulo is not appropriate since for each pass, one bit for each number has to be extracted. In this case, only two queues are required. Figure 9.23 contains the code for this implementation.

Division is replaced here by the bitwise and-operation **&**. The variable **mask** has one bit set to 1 and the rest of them are set to 0. After each iteration this 1 is shifted to the left. If **data[j] & mask** has a nonzero value, then **data[j]** is put in **queues[1]**; otherwise it is put in **queues[0]**. Bitwise and is much faster than integer division, but in

```
template<class genType>
void
BitRadixSort(genType data[], const int n)
{   register int i, j, k, factor, mask = 1;
    const int bits = sizeof(genType)*8;
    Queue<eltype> queues[2];

    for (i = 0; i < bits; i++) {
        for (j = 0; j < n; j++)
            queues[data[j] & mask ? 1 : 0].Enqueue(data[j]);
        mask <<= 1;
        k = 0;
        while (!queues[0].IsEmpty())
            data[k++] = queues[0].Dequeue();
        while (!queues[1].IsEmpty())
            data[k++] = queues[1].Dequeue();
    }
}
```

Figure 9.23: **Modified implementation of radix sort.**

this example, 16 passes are needed, instead of 5 when the largest integer is 5 digits long. This means $32n$ data movements as opposed to $10n$.

Quicker operations cannot outweigh a larger number of moves: **BitRadixSort()** is much slower than **RadixSort()** because the queues are implemented as linked lists and for each item included in a particular queue, a new record has to be created and attached to the queue. For each item copied back to the original array, the record has to be detached from the queue and disposed of using **delete**. Although theoretically obtained performance $O(n)$ is truly impressive, it does not include operations on queues, and it hinges upon the efficiency of the queue implementation.

A better implementation is an array of size n for each queue, which requires creating these queues only once. The efficiency of the algorithm depends only on the number of exchanges (copying to and from queues). However, if radix r is a large number and a large amount of data has to be sorted, then this solution requires r queues of size n and the number $(r + 1) * n$ (original array included) may be unrealistically large.

A better solution uses one integer array **allQueues** of size n representing linked lists of indexes of numbers belonging to particular queues. Cell i of the array **queueHeads** contains an index of the first number in **data** which belongs to this queue, whose j^{th} digit is i. **queueTails** contains a position in **data** of the last number whose j^{th} digit is i. Figure 9.24 illustrates the situation after the first pass, for $j = 1$. **queueHeads[4]** is 1 which means that the number in position 1 in **data**, 1234, is the first number found in **data** with 4 as the last digit. Cell **allQueues[1]** contains the number 3, which is an index of the next number in **data** with 4 as the last digit, number 7234. Finally, **allQueues[3]** is -1 to indicate the end of the numbers meeting this condition.

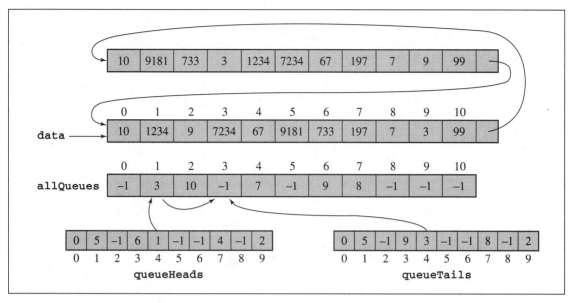

Figure 9.24: **An implementation of radix sort.**

The next stage orders data according to information gathered in **allQueues**. It copies all the data from the original array to some temporary storage and then back to this array. To avoid the second copy, two arrays can be used, constituting a two-element circular linked list. After copying, the pointer to the list is moved to the next record, and the array in this record is treated as storage of numbers to be sorted. Therefore, **data** in Figure 9.24 is not an array, but a pointer to a structure, whose info field is an array of data.

The improvement is remarkable. Whereas **RadixSort()** and **BitRadixSort()** have the worst performance among nonelementary sorts (and sometimes they fare even worse than the elementary sorts), their improvements (let them be called **RadixSort2()** and **BitRadixSort2()**) outperform **RadixSort()** and **BitRadixSort()** dramatically. The performance of **RadixSort2()** and **BitRadixSort2()** is comparable to the performance of other nonelementary sorting techniques.

■ 9.4 CONCLUDING REMARKS

Figure 9.25 compares the run times for different sorting algorithms and different numbers of integers being sorted. They were all run on a Sun IPX. At each stage, the number of integers has been doubled to see the factors by which the run times raise. These factors are included in each column except for the first three columns and shown along with the run times. The factors are rounded to one decimal place, whereas run times (in seconds) are rounded to two decimal places. For example, selection sort required 1.42 seconds to sort an array of 2000 integers in ascending order and 5.68 seconds to sort 4000 integers also in ascending order. Doubling the number of data is associated with the increase of run time by a factor of $5.68/1.42 \approx 4.0$; the latter number follows number 5.68 in the fourth column.

	2,000			4,000					
	Ascending	**Random**	**Descending**	**Ascending**		**Random**		**Descending**	
Insertion	0.00	0.97	2.07	0.02	—	3.88	4.0	8.12	4.1
Selection	1.42	1.42	1.43	5.68	4.0	5.52	3.9	5.80	4.0
BubbleSort	1.38	2.62	4.00	5.32	3.8	10.33	3.9	15.88	4.0
NewBubbleSort	0.00	2.58	3.98	0.00	—	10.45	4.0	16.15	4.0
ShellSort	0.02	0.05	0.03	0.03	2.0	0.12	2.3	0.07	2.0
HeapSort	0.08	0.07	0.07	0.17	2.0	0.17	2.5	0.15	2.3
MergeSort	0.03	0.03	0.05	0.08	2.5	0.10	3.0	0.10	2.0
QuickSort	0.02	0.03	0.03	0.03	2.0	0.07	2.0	0.05	1.5
QSort	0.02	0.07	0.03	0.05	3.0	0.07	1.0	0.05	1.5
RadixSort	1.55	1.07	1.23	4.45	2.9	2.15	2.0	3.07	2.5
BitRadixSort	5.30	3.35	4.30	20.37	3.8	8.98	2.7	15.41	3.6
RadixSort2	0.08	0.18	0.10	0.20	2.4	0.40	2.2	0.25	2.5
BitRadixSort2	0.18	0.18	0.17	0.40	2.2	0.38	2.1	0.40	2.4
	8,000			**16,000**					
	Ascending	**Random**	**Descending**	**Ascending**		**Random**		**Descending**	
Insertion	0.02 1.0	15.48 4.0	31.78 3.9	0.02	1.0	1 m 3.63	4.1	2 m 4.36	3.9
Selection	22.15 3.9	21.88 4.0	22.72 3.9	1 m 28.98	4.0	1 m 33.38	4.3	1 m 30.81	4.0
Bubblesort	21.40 4.0	41.47 4.0	1 m 2.53 3.9	1 m 25.61	4.0	2 m 52.28	4.2	4 m 14.52	4.1
NewBubbleSort	0.00 —	41.83 4.0	1 m 2.36 3.9	0.02	—	2 m 49.16	4.0	4 m 18.52	4.1
ShellSort	0.10 3.0	0.27 2.3	0.18 2.7	0.20	2.0	0.67	2.4	0.33	1.8
HeapSort	0.38 2.3	0.35 2.1	0.33 2.2	0.85	2.2	0.77	2.2	0.73	2.2
MergeSort	0.18 2.2	0.22 2.2	0.18 1.8	0.41	2.3	0.47	2.2	0.40	2.2
QuickSort	0.10 3.0	0.17 2.5	0.10 2.0	0.22	2.2	0.35	2.1	0.22	2.2
QSort	0.10 2.0	0.17 2.5	0.17 2.3	0.20	2.0	0.37	2.2	0.25	2.1
RadixSort	11.92 2.7	4.61 2.1	9.72 3.2	1 m 18.63	6.5	9.98	2.2	1 m 6.25	5.8
BitRadixSort	46.15 2.3	30.33 3.4	1 m 7.45 4.4	4 m 44.87	6.2	2 m 4.63	4.1	4 m 43.55	4.4
RadixSort2	0.42 2.1	0.80 2.0	0.45 1.8	0.88	2.1	1.62	2.0	0.93	2.1
BitRadixSort2	0.75 1.9	0.77 2.0	0.80 2.0	1.53	2.0	1.60	2.1	1.55	1.9

Figure 9.25: **Comparison of run times for different sorting algorithms and different numbers of integers to be sorted.**

Note that the run time for elementary sorting methods grows by approximately a factor of four after the number of integers is doubled, whereas the same factor for nonelementary methods is approximately two (except for `RadixSort()` and `BitRadixSort()`).

Several observations can be made about these experimental measures.

1. Among the simple sorting algorithms — insertion, selection, and the two bubble sorts — the insertion sort is the fastest in the average case, `NewBubbleSort()` is the faster when data are already in order, and the selection sort is the best for the reverse order. Because the average case is expected most of the time, the insertion sort is preferable to all other elementary sorting algorithms.

2. `NewBubbleSort()` is excellent, as expected, for ordered data, but in the average and worst cases, it behaves almost exactly the way the regular bubble sort does. Therefore it is not much of an improvement over `BubbleSort()`.

3. The quicksort is the best algorithm among all the sorting procedures. However, although `QSort()` is supposed to be an improvement of `QuickSort()`, it is not. The reason is that although `QSort()` is called a fewer number of times than `QuickSort()`, it involves one unconditional swap, which is three moves per call. Because integers are swapped in virtually no time, the time gained on the reduction of the number of calls is reflected in the final run time of `QSort()` when integers are being sorted. On the other hand, moving larger items (arrays, structures, etc.) can be significantly slower than moving integers. The time spent on additional swaps outweighs the time gained on the reduction of calls.

4. The Shell sort turns out to be an excellent sorting procedure in spite of its run time of the order of $n^{1.25}$.

5. The heap sort gives somewhat disappointing results despite its promising $n \lg n$ function. Remember, however, that $n \lg n$ is just an approximation. In the long run, this algorithm is better than the Shell sort with its unimpressive $n^{1.25}$. The former approximation discards all small terms and constants that can be very large and that, in the short run, can make the algorithm execute poorly. But, what "in the long run" means is not reflected in the approximation. It can be 1000, 100,000, 10,000,000, or even some larger number, so that for practical reasons, the theoretically obtained results may not be of much value.

6. The best examples of how theoretically obtained results can sometimes be misleading are the run times of `RadixSort()` and `BitRadixSort()`. Such results should usually be qualified by a discussion of how the algorithms are implemented. These two functions use the linked list implementation of queues, which leads to time-consuming memory allocation and deallocation. Using arrays to implement queues leads to a dramatic improvement.

■ 9.5 CASE STUDY: ADDING POLYNOMIALS

Adding polynomials is a common algebraic operation and is usually a simple calculation. It is a known rule that to add two terms, they must contain the same variables raised to the same powers, and the resulting term retains these variables and powers, except that its coefficient is computed by simply adding coefficients of both terms. For example,

$$3x^2y^3 + 5x^2y^3 = 8x^2y^3,$$

but $3x^2y^3$ and $5x^2z^3$, or $3x^2y^3$ and $5x^2y^2$ cannot be conveniently added, since the first pair of terms has different variables, and the variables in the second pair are raised to different powers. We would like to write a program that computes the sum of two polynomials entered by the user. For example, if

$$3x^2y^3 + 5x^2w^3 - 8x^2w^3z^4 + 3$$

and

$$-2x^2w^3 + 9y - 4xw - x^2y^3 + 8x^2w^3z^4 - 4$$

are entered, the program should output

$$-4wx + 3w^3x^2 + 2x^2y^3 + 9y - 1.$$

The order of variables in a term is irrelevant; for example, x^2y^3 and y^3x^2 represent exactly the same term. Before any additional operation is performed, the program must order all the variables in each term to make them homogeneous, and then add them. But before we embark on the problem of implementing the algorithms, we have to decide how to represent the polynomials in C++. Out of many possibilities, a linked list representation is chosen, with each record on the list representing one term. A term is composed of three types of elements: a coefficient, variables, and exponents. A polynomial is simply a linked list of such records. For example,

$$-x^2y + y - 4x^2y^3 + 8x^2w^3z^4$$

is represented by the linked list in Figure 9.26.

This figure shows that the variables and exponents are stored in two arrays, separately from the coefficient. The program assumes that a term can have at most five different variables. Another simplification in this program is to use only one-digit numbers and one-letter variable names.

The first operation to perform on these polynomials is to order their variables. After a polynomial is entered, a linked list is created and submitted to a sorting routine. Because the arrays to be sorted are very small, a simple bubble sort is chosen. Care has to be taken to sort only the part of each array that stores variable names and not the entire array. Otherwise the null characters stored in the cells following the variables will be moved to the front of the array. This problem does not arise if these unused cells contain a character with a high ASCII code, such as tilde, "~." It is more efficient to sort only the part of the array that stores the actual variables, thereby speeding up the sorting process.

The second task is to add the polynomials. In the case of addition, there is no great need to differentiate between these polynomials. It is easier to create one polynomial immediately by putting the two linked lists together and then apply an addition procedure. Of course, one linked list can be created at the outset but because the program is to be extended by the student, this path is not followed.

Now addition is reduced to simplification. In the linked list, all identical terms (identical except for the coefficients) have to be collapsed together and any redundant records eliminated. For example, if the list being processed is as in Figure 9.27a, then the list in Figure 9.27b results from the simplification operation.

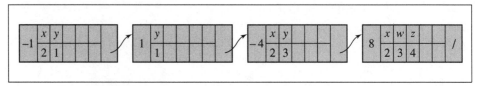

Figure 9.26: **A linked list representation of the expression** $-x^2y + y - 4x^2y^3 + 8x^2w^3z^4$**.**

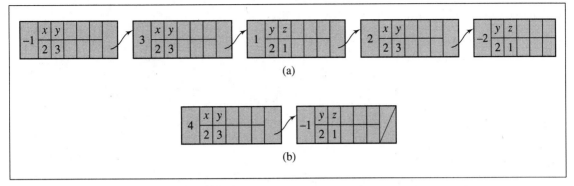

Figure 9.27: **Transforming a list representing the expression $-x^2y^3 +$ $3x^2y^3 + y^2z + 2x^2y^3 - 2y^2z$ (a) into a list which represents a simplified version of this expression, $4x^2y^3 - y^2z$ (b).**

An algorithm for such a simplification is as follows:

set **p1** *to the beginning of the list;*
while (p1 != 0)
    for(p2 = p1 -> next; p2 != 0;)
        if *terms pointed by* **p1** *and* **p2** *are the same (except coefficients)*
           add coefficient from **p2** *to coefficient from* **p1***;*
           eliminate term **p2** *from the linked list ;*
        move **p2** *to the next record ;*
    move **p1** *to the next record ;*

When printing the result, remember that not everything should be printed. If the coefficient is zero, a term is omitted. If it is one or minus one, the term is printed, but the coefficient is not included (except for the sign), unless the term has just a coefficient. If an exponent is one, it is also omitted.

Another printing challenge is ordering terms in a polynomial, that is, converting a somewhat disorganized polynomial

$$-z^2 - 2w^2x^3 + 5 + 9y - 5z - 4wx - x^2y^3 + 3w^2x^3z^4 + 10yz$$

into the tidier form

$$-4wx - 2w^2x^3 + 3w^2x^3z^4 - x^2y^3 + 9y + 10yz - 5z - z^2 + 5.$$

To accomplish this, the linked list representing a polynomial has to be sorted. But this chapter only discussed sorting arrays. Arrays have one undeniable advantage over linked lists: they allow random access to the elements stored in them, which is frequently required by sorting algorithms. To allow random access to the elements in a linked list, an array of pointers to records should be used. The strategy we choose in our program is to adapt a sorting algorithm in which random access does not affect efficiency to linked lists, thereby eliminating the need for an array of pointers. Our choice is the selection sort. Since the linked lists representing polynomials should not be excessively long, the efficiency of selection sort is acceptable.

Figure 9.28 contains the complete code for the program to add polynomials.

```
#include <iostream.h>
#include <ctype.h>
#include <stdlib.h>
#include "sorts1.h"

const int size = 5;

struct Variable {
        char id;
        int exp;
        Variable() {}
        int operator< (const Variable v) // overloaded < is used
            {return id < v.id; }         // by BubbleSort() to
                                         // compare two Variables;
};

struct Term {
        int coeff;
        Variable vars[size];
        Term *next;
        Term() {}
        int operator== (const Term&);
};

class Polynomial {
public:
    Polynomial() {}
    Term GetPolyn();
private:
    Variable var;
    int coef, i, tmp;

    void SelectionListSort(Term*);
    void TermSwap(Term*,Term*);
    void Order(Term*);
    void Error(char *s) { cerr << s << endl; exit(1); }
    friend Term operator+ (Term&,Term&);
};

void
```

Figure 9.28: **Implementation of program to add polynomials.**   **continued**

```
Bubblesort (Variable v[])      //              yzxw -> xywz
{   register int i, j, n;      // compare two variable structs
    Variable tmp;              // using id fields only but swap entire
                              // structs (with Swap() in BubbleSort());
    for (n = size-1; !v[n].id; n--); // move to the last variable
    BubbleSort(v,n+1);              // in the array v of variables;
}


int
operator< (const Term& term1, const Term& term2)
{   int i;

    if (!term1.vars[0].id)
        return 0;                 // term1 is just a coefficient
    else if (!term2.vars[0].id)
        return 1;                 // term2 is just a coefficient
    for (i = 0; i < size; i++)
        if (term1.vars[i].id < term2.vars[i].id)
            return 1;             // term1 precedes term2
        else if (term2.vars[i].id < term1.vars[i].id)
            return 0;             // term2 precedes term1
        else if (term1.vars[i].exp < term2.vars[i].exp)
            return 1;             // term1 precedes term2
        else if (term2.vars[i].exp < term1.vars[i].exp)
            return 0;             // term2 precedes term1
}


void
Polynomial::TermSwap(Term *term1, Term *term2)
{
    Swap(term1->coeff,term2->coeff); // generic Swap() from
    for (i = 0; i < size; i++)       // sorts1.h is used;
        Swap(term1->vars[i],term2->vars[i]);
}


void
Polynomial::SelectionListSort (Term *pol)
{   Term *tmp1, *tmp2, *least;

    if (pol)
```

Figure 9.28: **Implementation of program to add polynomials.**   **continued**

```
                for (tmp1 = pol; tmp1->next; tmp1 = tmp1->next) {
                    for (tmp2 = tmp1->next, least = tmp1; tmp2; tmp2 = tmp2->next)
                        if (*tmp2 < *least)
                            least = tmp2;
                    if (tmp1 != least)
                        TermSwap(least,tmp1);
                }
    }


    void
    Polynomial::Order(Term *p)
    {                               // order alphabetically variables in
        for ( ; p; p = p->next)     // each term separately by calling
            Bubblesort(p->vars);    // Bubblesort;
    }


    Term
    Polynomial::GetPolyn()
    {   char ch, sign, coeffUsed;
        Term *pol, *tmp;
        int i;

        cin >> ch;
        pol = tmp = new Term;
        while (1) {
            coeffUsed = 0;
            if (!isalnum(ch) && ch != ';' && ch != '-' && ch != '+')
                Error("Wrong character entered2");
            tmp->next = 0;
            tmp->coeff = 0;
            for(i = 0; i < size; i++) {
                tmp->vars[i].id = '\0';
                tmp->vars[i].exp = 0;
            }
            sign = 1;
            while (ch == '-' || ch == '+') { // first get sign(s) of Term
                if (ch == '-')
                        sign *= -1;
                cin >> ch;
            }
```

Figure 9.28: **Implementation of program to add polynomials.**   **continued**

```
            if (isdigit(ch)) {                // and then its coefficient;
                cin.putback(ch);
                cin >> tmp->coeff >> ch;
                tmp->coeff *= sign;
                coeffUsed = 1;
            }
            else tmp->coeff = sign;
            for (i = 0; isalnum(ch) && i < size+1; i++) { // process this term:
                tmp->vars[i].id = ch;         // get a variable name
                cin >> ch;
                if (isdigit(ch)) {            // and an exponent (if any);
                    cin.putback(ch);
                    cin >> tmp->vars[i].exp >> ch;
                }
                else tmp->vars[i].exp = 1;
            }
            if (i > size)
                Error("Too many Variables in a Term"); // e.g., 2abcdef + 5r;
            else if (ch == ';')     // finish if a semicolon is entered;
                if (coeffUsed || i > 0)
                    break;
                else Error("Term is missing");  // e.g., 2x - ; or just ';'
            else if (ch != '-' && ch != '+') {   // e.g., 2x  4y;
                cout << "wrong character after term " << ch << endl;
                exit(1);
            }
            else {                  // create a new record for a new term
                tmp->next = new Term;
                tmp = tmp->next;   // and include it in the linked list;
            }
        }
    }
    Order(pol);
    return *pol;
}


// two terms are equal if all varibles are the same and
// corresponding variables are raised to the same power;
// the first cell of the record containing a term is excluded
// from comparison, since it stores coefficient of the term;

int
```

Figure 9.28: **Implementation of program to add polynomials.**   **continued**

```
Term::operator== (const Term& term)
{    register int i;

     for (i = 0; vars[i].id  == term.vars[i].id  &&
                 vars[i].exp == term.vars[i].exp && i < size; i++);
     return i == size;
}


Term
operator+ (Term& polyn1, Term& polyn2)
{    Term *prev1, *prev2, *p1, *p2, *p3;
     Polynomial pol;

     for (p1 = &polyn1; p1->next; p1 = p1->next); // make one polynomial
     p1->next = &polyn2;                          // out of two;
     for (p1 = &polyn1; p1; p1 = p1->next)        // add equal terms;
         for (prev2 = p1, p2 = p1->next; p2; p2 = p2->next)
             if (*p1 == *p2) {
                  p1->coeff += p2->coeff;
                  prev2->next = p2->next;
             }
             else prev2 = p2;
     prev1 = new Term;                            // create a dummy record
     prev1->next = &polyn1;                       // to precede polyn1;
     for (p1 = p3 = &polyn1; p1; p1 = p1->next)
         if (p1->coeff == 0)              // remove all terms with
             if (p1 == p3) {              // coefficient equal to zero;
                  prev1 = p3;
                  p3 = p3->next;          // if they are at the beginning
             }
             else prev1->next = p1->next;// of the list, change the value
         else prev1 = prev1->next;
     pol.SelectionListSort(p3);
     return *p3;                          // of polyn1;
}


ostream&
operator<< (ostream& out, const Term& polyn)
{    int afterFirstTerm = 0, i;
     Term *pol = (Term*) &polyn;
```

Figure 9.28: **Implementation of program to add polynomials.**   **continued**

```
        out << "The result is:\n";
        for ( ; pol; pol = pol->next) {
            out.put(' ');
            if (pol->coeff < 0)                  // put '-' before polynomial
                out.put('-');                     // and between terms (if needed);
            else if (afterFirstTerm)              // don't put '+' in front of
                cout.put('+');                    // polynomial;
            afterFirstTerm++;
            if (pol->coeff != 1 && pol->coeff != -1)
                out << ' ' << abs(pol->coeff);    // print a coefficient
            else if (!pol->vars[0].id)            // if it is not 1 nor -1, or
                out << " 1";                      // the term has only a coefficient
            else out.put(' ');
            for (i = 0; pol->vars[i].id && i < size; i++) {
                out << pol->vars[i].id;           // print a varable name
                if (pol->vars[i].exp != 1)        // and an exponent, only
                    out << pol->vars[i].exp;      // if it is not 1.
            }
        }
        out << endl;
        return out;
}


main()
{   Polynomial polyn;

    cout << "Enter two polynomials ended with a semicolon:\n";
    cout << polyn.GetPolyn() + polyn.GetPolyn();
    return 0;
}
```

Figure 9.28: **Implementation of program to add polynomials.**

■ 9.6 EXERCISES

1. How would you check whether one word is an anagram of another word, e.g., *plum* and *lump*?

2. In our implementation of bubble sort, a sorted array was scanned bottom-up in order to bubble up the smallest element. What modifications are needed to make it work top-down to bubble down the largest element?

3. A *cocktail shaker sort* designed by Donald Knuth is a modification of bubble sort in which the direction of bubbling changes in each iteration: in one iteration the smallest element is bubbled up, in the next the largest is bubbled down, in the next the second smallest is bubbled up, and so forth. Implement this new algorithm and explore its complexity.

4. Apply **Insertion()**, **Selection()**, **BubbleSort()**, and **NewBubbleSort()** to these three arrays of numbers:

(a) [1 2 3 4 5 6]

(b) [6 5 4 3 2 1]

(c) [6 1 4 3 2 5]

and draw diagrams as in Figures 9.2, 9.4, and 9.6.

5. Insertion sort goes sequentially through the array when making comparisons to find a proper place for an element currently processed. Consider using binary search instead and give a complexity of the resulting insertion sort.

6. Draw decision trees for all the sorting algorithms from the previous problem as applied to the array [a b c d].

7. Trace all changes in the following arrays:

(a) [0 1 2 3 4 5 6 7 8 9]

(b) [9 8 7 6 5 4 3 2 1 0]

(c) [6 1 4 3 2 7 5 0 8 9]

sorted using **ShellSort()**, **HeapSort()**, **QuickSort()**, and **QSort()** and draw diagrams such as in Figures 9.11, 9.17, 9.19, and 9.20.

8. Which of the algorithms discussed in this chapter would be easily adaptable to singly linked lists? To doubly linked lists?

9. What exactly are the smallest and largest numbers of movements and comparisons to sort four elements using **HeapSort()**, **QuickSort()**, and **MergeSort()**?

10. The main **while** loop of **QuickSort()** is **while (lower <= upper);** why can it not be replaced by **while (lower < upper)**? Apply **QuickSort()** with the first and then with the second condition to array [8 5 9 4 3 6 7].

11. Implement and test **MergeSort()**.

12. Show that for mergesort the number of comparisons $C(n) = n \lg n - 2^{\lg n} + 1$.

13. The proof of the complexity of the number of movements for mergesort used an assumption that n is a power of two. Show that the same result can be obtained if n is not a power of two. Try to reduce this problem to the one already solved by adding, for the sake of proof, some elements to the array being sorted.

14. Implement and analyze the complexity of the following nonrecursive version of mergesort. First, merge subarrays of length 1 into $\frac{n}{2}$ two-cell subarrays, possibly using a one one-cell array. The resulting arrays are then merged into $\frac{n}{4}$ four-cell subarrays possibly, with one smaller array, having 1, 2, or 3 cells, etc., until the entire array is ordered. Note that this is a bottom-up approach to the mergesort implementation as opposed to the top-down approach discussed in this chapter.

15. **MergeSort()** merges the subarrays of an array which is already in order. Another top-down version of mergesort alleviates this problem by merging only *runs*, subarrays

with ordered elements. Merging is applied only after two runs are determined. For example, in the array [6 7 8 3 4 10 11 12 13 2], first, runs [6 7 8] and [3 4] are merged to become [3 4 6 7 8], then runs [10 11 12 13] and [2] are merged to become [2 10 11 12 13], and finally, runs [3 4 6 7 8] and [2 10 11 12 13] are merged to become [2 3 4 6 7 8 10 11 12 13]. Implement this algorithm and investigate its complexity. A mergesort that takes advantage of a partial ordering of data, that is, uses the runs, is called a *natural sort*. A version that disregards the runs by always dividing arrays into (almost) even sections is referred to as *straight merging*.

16. To avoid doubling the work space needed when arrays are sorted with mergesort, it may be better to use a linked list of data instead of an array. In what situations is this approach better? Implement this technique and discuss its complexity.

17. A sorting algorithm is said to be *stable* if equal keys remain in the same relative order in the output as they are in the initial array; if $a[i]$ equals $a[j]$ and $i < j$ then ith element ends up in kth position, and jth element in mth position then $k < m$. Which sorting algorithms are stable?

18. Consider a *slow sorting* algorithm, which applies selection sort to every ith element of an n-element array, where i takes on values $n/2, n/3, \ldots, n/n$ (Julstrom 1992). First, selection sort is applied to two elements of the array, the first and the middle element, then to three elements, separated by the distance $n/3$, etc., and finally to every element. Compute the complexity of this algorithm.

■ 9.7 PROGRAMMING ASSIGNMENTS

1. At the end of the section discussing a quicksort, two techniques for choosing the bound were mentioned: using a randomly chosen element from the file, and using a median element of the first, middle, and the last elements of the array. Implement these two versions of quicksort, apply them to large arrays, and compare their run times.

2. The Board of Education maintains a database of substitute teachers in the area. If a temporary replacement is necessary for a certain subject, an available teacher is sent to the school that requests him or her. Write a menu-driven program maintaining this database.

The file **substitutes** lists the first and last names of the substitute teachers, an indication of whether or not they are currently available (Y(es) or N(o)), and a list of numbers which represents the subjects they can teach. An example of **substitutes** is:

```
Hilliard Roy        Y   0 4 5
Ennis John          N   2 3
Nelson William      Y   1 2 4 5
Baird Lyle          Y   1 3 4 5
Geiger Melissa      N   3 5
Kessel Warren       Y   3 4 5
Scherer Vincent     Y   4 5
```

```
Hester Gary       N  0 1 2 4
Linke Jerome      Y  0 1
Thornton Richard  N  2 3 5
```

Create a **struct teacher**, with three fields: index, left child, and right child. Declare an array **subjects** with the same number of cells as the number of subjects, each cell storing a pointer to **struct teacher**, which is really a pointer to the root of a binary search tree of teachers teaching a given subject. Also, declare an array **names** with each cell holding one entry from the file.

First, prepare the array **names** to create binary search trees. In order to do that, load all entries from **substitutes** to **names**, and sort **names** using one of the algorithms discussed in this chapter. Afterwards, create a binary tree using the function **Balance()** from Section 6.1: go through the array **names**, and for each subject associated with each name, create a node in the tree corresponding to this subject. The index field of such a node indicates a location in **names** of a teacher teaching this subject. (Note that **Insert()** in **Balance()** should be able to go to a proper tree). Figure 9.29 shows the ordered array **names** and trees accessible from **subjects** as created by **Balance()** for our sample file.

Allow the user to reserve teachers if so requested. If the program is finished and an exit option is chosen, load all entries from **names** back to **substitutes**, this time with updated availability information.

3. Implement different versions of Shell sort by mixing simple sorts used in h-sorts, 1-sort, and different sequences of increments. Run each version with (at least) any of the following sequences:

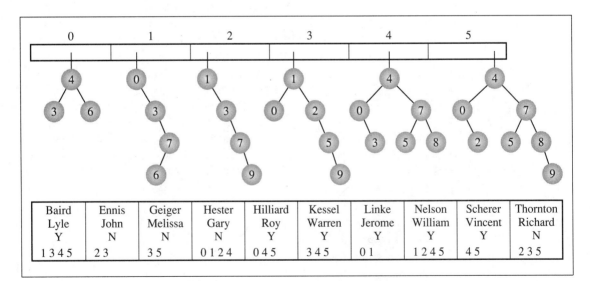

Baird	Ennis	Geiger	Hester	Hilliard	Kessel	Linke	Nelson	Scherer	Thornton
Lyle	John	Melissa	Gary	Roy	Warren	Jerome	William	Vincent	Richard
Y	N	N	N	Y	Y	Y	Y	Y	N
1 3 4 5	2 3	3 5	0 1 2 4	0 4 5	3 4 5	0 1	1 2 4 5	4 5	2 3 5

Figure 9.29: **Data structures used by the Board of Education for substitute teachers.**

(a) $h_1 = 1, h_{i+1} = 3h_i + 1$ and stop with h_t for which $h_{t+2} \geq n$ (Knuth)

(b) $2^k - 1$ (Hibbard)

(c) $2^k + 1$ (Papernov and Stasevich)

(d) Fibonacci numbers

(e) $\frac{n}{2}$ is the first increment and then $h_i = .75h_{i+1}$ (Dobosiewicz)

Run all these versions for at least five sets of data of sizes 1000, 5000, 10,000, 50,000, and 100,000. Tabulate and plot the results and try to approximate them with some formula expressing the complexity of these versions.

4. Extend the program from the case study to include polynomial multiplication.

5. Extend the program from the case study to include polynomial differentiation. For the rules, see the exercises in Chapter 5.

BIBLIOGRAPHY

Sorting Algorithms

[1] Flores, Ivan, *Computer Sorting*, Englewood Cliffs, NJ: Prentice-Hall, 1969.

[2] Knuth, Donald E., *The Art of Computer Programming, Vol. 3: Sorting and Searching*, Reading, MA: Addison-Wesley, 1975.

[3] Lorin, H., *Sorting and Sort Systems*, Reading, MA: Addison-Wesley, 1975.

[4] Mehlhorn, Kurt, *Data Structures and Algorithms, Vol. 1: Sorting and Searching*, Berlin: Springer, 1984.

[5] Rich, R., *Internal Sorting Methods Illustrated with PL/1 Programs*, Englewood Cliffs, NJ: Prentice-Hall, 1972.

Shell Sort

[6] Dobosiewicz, W., "An Efficient Variation of Bubble Sort," *Information Processing Letters* 11 (1980), 5–6.

[7] Gale, David and Karp, Richard M., "A Phenomenon in the Theory of Sorting," *Journal of Computer and System Sciences* 6 (1972), 103–115.

[8] Incerpi, Janet and Sedgewick, Robert, "Practical Variations of Shellsort," *Information Processing Letters* 26 (1987/88), 37–43.

[9] Shell, Donald L., "A High-Speed Sorting Procedure," *Communications of the ACM* 2 (1959), 30–32.

[10] Weiss, Mark A. and Sedgewick, Robert, "Tight Lower Bounds for Shellsort," *Journal of Algorithms* 11 (1990), 242–251.

Heap Sort

[11] Williams, John W. J., "Algorithm 232: Heapsort," *Communications of the ACM* 7 (1964), 347–348.

Quicksort

[12] Dromey, R. G., "Exploiting Partial Order with Quicksort," *Software Practice and Experience* 14 (1984), 509–518.

[13] Frazer, William D. and McKellar, Archie C., "Samplesort: A Sampling Approach to Minimal Storage Tree Sorting," *Journal of the ACM* 17 (1970), 496–507.

[14] Hoare, Charles A. R., "Algorithm 63: Quicksort," *Communications of the ACM* 4 (1961), 321.

[15] Hoare, Charles A. R., "Quicksort," *Computer Journal* 2 (1962), 10–15.

[16] Huang, B. C. and Knuth, Donald, "A One-Way, Stackless Quicksort Algorithm," *BIT* 26 (1986), 127–130.

[17] Motzkin, D., "Meansort," *Communications of the ACM* 26 (1983), 250–251.

[18] Sedgewick, Robert, *Quicksort*, New York: Garland, 1980.

Mergesort

[19] Dvorak, S. and Durian, B., "Unstable Linear Time $O(1)$ Space Merging," *The Computer Journal* 31 (1988), 279–283.

[20] Huang, B. C. and Langston, M. A., "Practical In-Place Merging," *Communications of the ACM* 31 (1988), 348–352.

[21] Knuth, Donald, "Von Neumann's First Computer Program," *Computing Surveys* 2 (1970), 247–260.

Slow Sorting

[22] Julstrom, A., "Slow Sorting: A Whimsical Inquiry," *SIGCSE Bulletin* 24 (1992), no. 3, 11–13.

Decision Trees

[23] Moret, B.M.E., "Decision Trees and Algorithms," *Computing Surveys* 14 (1982), 593–623.

10

HASHING

The main operation used by the searching methods described in the preceding chapters was comparison of keys. In a sequential search, the table that stores the elements is searched successively to determine which cell of the table to check, and the key comparison determines whether or not an element has been found. In a binary search, the table that stores the elements is divided successively into halves to determine which cell of the table to check and again, the key comparison determines whether or not an element has been found. Similarly, the decision to continue the search in a binary search tree in a particular direction is accomplished by comparing keys.

A different approach to searching calculates the position of the key in the table based on the value of the key. The value of the key is the only indication of the position. When the key is known, the position in the table can be accessed directly, without making any other preliminary tests, as required in a binary search or when searching a tree. This means that the search time is reduced from $O(n)$, as in a sequential search, or from $O(\lg n)$, as in a binary search, to 1 or at least $O(1)$; regardless of the number of elements being searched, the run time is always the same. But this is just an ideal, and in real applications, this ideal can only be approximated.

We need to find a function h which can transform a particular key K, be it a string, number, record, etc., into an index into the table used for storing items of the same type as K. The function h is called a *hash function*. If h transforms different keys into different numbers, it is called a *perfect hash function*. To create a perfect hash function, which is always the goal, the table has to contain at least the same number of positions as the number of elements being hashed. But the number of elements is not always known ahead of time. For example, a compiler keeps all variables used in a program in a symbol table. C variable names can be up to 31 characters long[1] and can contain any combination of 63 characters

---

[1] Only internal names can be 31 characters long; for external names only the first 8 characters are significant because some linkers impose this limitation.

(upper and lower cases, digits, and an underscore). There are $53 * \sum_{i=0}^{30} 63^i$ possible variable names (a variable name cannot start with a digit), far too many to be stored in a table which has a position associated with each variable name. Real programs use only a fraction of the vast number of possible variable names, so a table size of 1000 cells is usually adequate.

But even if this table can accommodate all the variables in the program, how can we design a function h which allows the compiler to immediately access the position associated with each variable? All the letters of the variable name can be added together and the sum can be used as an index. In this case, the table needs 3782 cells (for a variable K made out of 31 letters "z," $h(K) = 31 * 122 = 3782$). But even with this size, the function h does not return unique values. For example, $h(\text{"abc"}) = h(\text{"acb"})$. This problem is called *collision* and will be discussed later. The worth of a hash function depends on how well it avoids collisions. Avoiding collisions can be achieved by making the function more sophisticated, but this sophistication should not go too far, since the computational cost in determining $h(K)$ can be prohibitive, and less sophisticated methods may be faster.

■ 10.1 HASH FUNCTIONS

The number of hash functions that can be used to assign positions to n items in a table of m positions (for $n \leq m$) is equal to m^n. The number of perfect hash functions is the same as the number of different placements of these items in the table and is equal to $\frac{m!}{(m-n)!}$. For example, for 50 elements and a 100-cell array there are $100^{50} = 10^{100}$ hash functions out of which "only" 10^{94} (one in a million) are perfect. Most of these functions are too unwieldy for practical applications and cannot be represented by a concise formula. However, even among functions which can be expressed with a formula, the number of possibilities is vast. This section discusses some specific types of hash functions.

10.1.1 Division

A hash function must guarantee that the number it returns is a valid index to one of the table cells. The simplest way to accomplish this is to use division modulo $TSize = sizeof(table)$, as in $h(K) = K \bmod TSize$, if K is a number. It is best if $TSize$ is a prime number. Otherwise, $h(K) = (K \bmod p) \bmod TSize$ for some prime $p > TSize$ can be used. However, nonprime divisors may work equally well as prime divisors providing that they do not have prime factors less than 20 (Lum et al., 1971). The division method is usually the preferred choice for the hash function if very little is known about the keys.

10.1.2 Folding

In this method the key is divided into several parts (which conveys the true meaning of the word *hash*). These parts are combined or folded together and are often transformed in a certain way to create the target address. There are two types of folding: *shift folding* and *boundary folding*.

The key is divided into several parts and these parts are then processed using a simple operation such as addition, to combine these parts in a certain way. In shift folding, they are put one underneath another and then processed. For example, a Social Security Number

(SSN) 123–45–6789 can be divided into three parts, 123, 456, and 789, and then these parts can be added up. The resulting number, 1368, can be divided modulo *TSize* or, if the size of the table is 1000, the first three digits can be used for the address. To be sure, the division can be done in many different ways. Another possibility is to divide the same number 123-45-6789 into five parts, say, 12, 34, 56, 78, and 9, add them up, and divide the result modulo *TSize*.

With boundary folding, the key is seen as being written on a piece of paper which is folded on the borders between different parts of the key. In this way, every other part will be put in the reverse order. Consider the same three parts of the SSN: 123, 456, and 789. The first part, 123, is taken in the same order, then the piece of paper with the second part is folded underneath it so that 123 is aligned with 654, which is the second part, 456, in reverse order. When the folding continues, 789 is aligned with the two previous parts. The result is $123+654+789=1566$.

In both versions, the key is usually divided into even parts of some fixed size plus some remainder and then added up. This process is simple and fast, especially when bit patterns are used instead of numerical values. A bit-oriented version of shift folding is obtained by applying the exclusive or operation, ^.

In the case of strings, one approach processes all characters of the string by "xor'ing" them together and using result for the address. For example, for the string "abcd," h("abcd") = "a"^"b"^"c"^"d". However, this simple method results in addresses between the numbers 0 and 127. For better results, chunks of strings are "xor'ed" together rather than single characters. These chunks are composed of the number of characters equal to the number of bytes in an integer. Since an integer in a C++ implementation for the IBM PC computer is two bytes long, h("abcd") = "ab" xor "cd" (most likely divided modulo *TSize*). Such a function is used in the case study in this chapter.

10.1.3 Mid-Square Function

In the mid-square method, the key is *squared* and the middle or *mid* part of the result is used as the address. If the key is a string, it has to be preprocessed to produce a number by using, for instance, folding. In a mid-square hash function, the entire key participates in generating the address so that there is a better chance that different addresses are generated for different keys. For example, if the key is 3121, then $3121^2 = 9740641$, and for the 1000-cell table, h(3121) = 406 which is the middle part of 3121^2. In practice, it is more efficient to choose a power of two for the size of the table and extract the middle part of the bit representation of the square of a key. If we assume that the size of the table is 1024, then, in this example, the binary representation of 3121^2 is the bit string 1001010*0101000010*1100001 with the middle part shown in italics. This middle part, the binary number 0101000010, is equal to 322. This part can easily be extracted by using a mask and a shift operation.

10.1.4 Extraction

In the extraction method, only a part of the key is used to compute the address. For the Social Security Number 123–45–6789, this method might use the first four digits, 1234, the last four, 6789, the first two combined with the last two, 1289, or some other combination. Each time, only a portion of the key is used. If this portion is carefully chosen, it can be sufficient for hashing provided that the omitted portion distinguishes the keys only in an insignificant way. For example, in some university settings, all international students' ID numbers start with 999. Therefore, the first three digits can be safely omitted in a hash function which uses student IDs for computing table positions. Similarly, the starting digits of the ISBN code are the same for all books published by the same publisher, e.g., 0534 for PWS Publishing Company. Therefore, they should be excluded from the computation of addresses if a data table contains only books from one publisher.

10.1.5   Radix Transformation

Using the radix transformation, the key K is transformed into another number base; K is expressed in a numerical system using a different radix. If K is the decimal number 345, then its value in base 9 (nonal) is 423. This value is then divided modulo *TSize* and the resulting number is used as the address of the location to which K should be hashed. Collisions, however, cannot be avoided. If *TSize* = 100, then although 345 and 245 (decimal) is not hashed to the same location, 345 and 264 are, since 264 decimal is 323 in the nonal system, and both 423 and 323 return the number 23 when divided modulo 100.

■ 10.2   COLLISION RESOLUTION

Note that straightforward hashing is not without its problems, since for almost all hash functions, more than one key can be assigned to the same position. For example, if the hash function h_1 applied to names returns the ASCII value of the first letter of each name, i.e., $h_1(name) = name[0]$, then all names starting with the same letter are hashed to the same position. This problem can be solved by finding a function which distributes names more uniformly in the table. For example, the function h_2 could add the first two letters, i.e., $h_2(name) = name[0] + name[1]$, which is better than h_1. But even if all the letters are considered, i.e., $h_3(name) = name[0] + \cdots + name[\mathbf{strlen}(name) - 1]$, the possibility of hashing different names to the same location still exists. The function h_3 is the best of the three because it distributes the names most uniformly for the three defined functions, but it also tacitly assumes that the size of the table has been increased. If the table had only 26 positions, which is the number of different values returned by h_1, there is no improvement using h_3 instead of h_1. Therefore, one more factor can contribute to avoiding conflicts between hashed keys, namely the size of the table. Increasing this size may lead to better hashing, but it does not always! These two factors — hash function and table size — may minimize the number of collisions, but they cannot completely eliminate them. The problem of collision has to be dealt with in a way that always guarantees a solution.

There are scores of strategies which attempt to avoid hashing multiple keys to the same location. Only a handful of these methods will be discussed in this chapter.

10.2.1   Open Addressing

In the open addressing method, when a key collides with another key, the collision is resolved by finding an available table entry other than the position (address) to which the colliding key is originally hashed. If position $h(K)$ is occupied, then the positions in the probing sequence

$$norm(h(K) + p(1)), norm(h(K) + p(2)), \ldots, norm(h(K) + p(i)), \ldots$$

are tried, until either an available cell is found, the same positions are tried repeatedly, or the table is full. Function p is a *probing function*, i is a *probe*, and *norm* is a *normalization function*, most likely, division modulo the size of the table.

The simplest method is *linear probing*, for which $p(i) = i$, and for the ith probe, the position to be tried is $(h(K) + i)$ mod *TSize*. In linear probing, the position in which a key can be stored is found by sequentially searching all positions starting from the position calculated by the hash function, until an empty cell is found. If the end of the table is reached and no empty cell has been found, the search is continued from the beginning of the table and stops — in the extreme case — in the cell preceding the one from which the search started. Linear probing, however, has a tendency to create clusters in the table. Figure 10.1 contains an example where a key K_i is hashed to the position i. In Figure 10.1a, three keys, $A_5, A_2,$ and A_3 have been hashed to their home positions. Then B_5 arrives (Figure 10.1b) whose home position is occupied by A_5. Since the next position is available, B_5 is stored there. Next, A_9 is stored with no problem, but B_2 is stored in position 4, two positions from its home address. A large cluster has already been formed. Next, B_9 arrives. Position 9 is not available and since it is the last cell of the table, the search starts from the beginning of the table, whose first slot can now host B_9. The next key, C_2, ends up in position 7, five positions from its home address.

In this example, the empty cells following clusters have a much greater chance to be filled than other positions. This probability is equal to $(sizeof(cluster) + 1)/TSize$. Other empty cells have only $1/TSize$ chance of being filled. If a cluster is created, it has a tendency

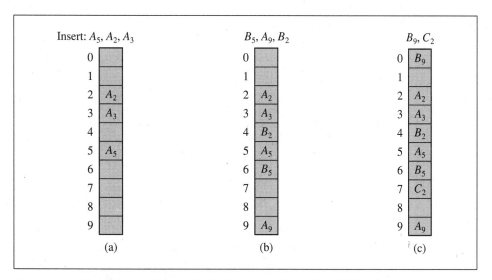

Figure 10.1: **Resolving collisions with the linear probing method. Subscripts indicate the home positions of the keys being hashed.**

to grow and the larger a cluster becomes, the larger the likelihood is that it will become even larger. This fact undermines the performance of the hash table for storing and retrieving data. The problem at hand is how to avoid cluster build-up. An answer can be found in a more careful choice of the probing function p.

One such choice is a quadratic function, so that the resulting formula is

$$p(i) = h(K) + (-1)^{i-1}((i+1)/2)^2 \text{ for } i = 1, 2, \ldots, TSize - 1.$$

This rather cumbersome formula can be expressed in a simpler form as a sequence of probes:

$$h(K) + i^2, h(K) - i^2 \text{ for } i = 1, 2, \ldots, (TSize - 1)/2.$$

Including the first attempt to hash K, this results in the sequence:

$$h(K), h(K) + 1, h(K) - 1, h(K) + 4, h(K) - 4, \ldots, h(K) + (TSize - 1)^2/4,$$
$$h(K) - (TSize - 1)^2/4$$

all divided modulo $TSize$. The size of the table should not be an even number, since only the even positions or only the odd positions would be tried, depending on the value of $h(K)$. Ideally, the table size should be a prime $4K + 3$ for an integer K, which guarantees the inclusion of all positions in the probing sequence (Radke 1970). For example, if $K = 4$, then $TSize = 19$, and assuming that $h(K) = 9$ for some K, the resulting sequence of probes is[2]

$$9, 10, 8, 13, 5, 18, 0, 6, 12, 15, 3, 7, 11, 1, 17, 16, 2, 14, 4$$

The table from Figure 10.1 would have the same keys in a different configuration, as in Figure 10.2. It still takes two probes to locate B_2 in some location, but for C_2 only four probes are required, not five.

Note that the formula determining the sequence of probes chosen for quadratic probing is not $h(K) + i^2$, for $i = 1, 2, \ldots, TSize - 1$, because the first half of the sequence

$$h(K) + 1, h(K) + 4, h(K) + 9, \ldots, h(K) + (TSize - 1)^2$$

covers only half of the table and the second half of the sequence repeats the first half in the reverse order. For example, if $TSize = 19$, and $h(K) = 9$, then the sequence is

$$9, 10, 13, 18, 6, 15, 7, 1, 16, 14, 14, 16, 1, 7, 15, 6, 18, 13, 10.$$

---

[2]Special care should be taken for negative numbers. When implementing these formulas, the operator % means division modulo a modulus. However, this operator is usually implemented as the *remainder* of division. For example, $-6 \% 23$ would be equal to -6, and not to 17, as expected. Therefore, when using the operator % for the implementation of division modulo, the modulus (the right operand of %) should be added to the result when the result is negative. Therefore, $(-6 \% 23) + 23$ returns 17.

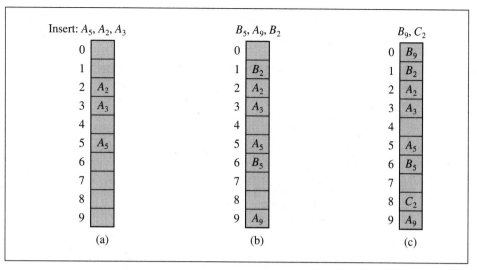

Figure 10.2: **Using quadratic probing for collision resolution.**

This is not an accident. The probes which render the same address are of the form

$$i = TSize/2 + 1 \text{ and } j = TSize/2 - 1,$$

and they are probes for which

$$i^2 \bmod TSize = j^2 \bmod TSize,$$

that is,

$$(i^2 - j^2) \bmod TSize.$$

In this case,

$$(i^2 - j^2) = (TSize/2 + 1)^2 - (TSize/2 - 1)^2$$
$$= (TSize^2/4 + TSize + 1 - TSize^2/4 + TSize - 1)$$
$$= 2TSize$$

and, to be sure, $2TSize \bmod TSize = 0$.

Although using quadratic search gives much better results than linear probing, the problem of cluster buildup is not avoided altogether, since for keys hashed to the same location, the same probe sequence is used. Such clusters are called *secondary clusters*. These secondary clusters, however, are less harmful than primary clusters.

Another possibility is to have p be a random number generator (Morris 1968), which eliminates the need to take special care about the table size. This approach prevents the formation of secondary clusters but it causes a problem with repeating the same probing sequence for the same keys. If the random number generator is initialized at the first invocation, then different probing sequences are generated for the same key K. Consequently, K is hashed more than once to the table and even then it might not be found when searched. Therefore, the random number generator should be initialized to the same seed for the same key before beginning the generation of the probing sequence. This can be achieved in C++ by using the **srand()** function with a parameter which depends on the key, for example $p(i) = $ **srand**$(sizeof(K)) * i$ or **srand**$(K[0]) + i$ or such. To avoid relying on **srand()**, a random number generator can be written which ascertains that each invocation generates a unique number between 0 and $TSize - 1$. The following algorithm was developed by Robert Morris for tables with $TSize = 2^n$ for some integer n:

```
GenerateNumber()
    static int r = 1;
    r = 5*r;
    r = mask out n + 2 low-order bits of r;
    return r/4;
```

The problem of secondary clustering is best addressed with *double hashing* (also called *rehashing* or *linear quotient hashing*). This method utilizes two hash functions, one for accessing the primary position of a key, h, and a second function, h_p, for resolving conflicts. The probing sequence becomes

$$h(K), h(K) + h_p(K), \ldots, h(K) + i * h_p(K), \ldots$$

(all divided modulo $TSize$). The table size should be a prime number so that each position in the table can be included in the sequence. Experiments indicate that secondary clustering is generally eliminated, because the sequence depends on the values of h_p which, in turn, depend on the key. Therefore, if the key K_1 is hashed to the position j, the probing sequence is

$$j, j + h_p(K_1), j + 2 * h_p(K_1), \ldots$$

(all divided modulo $TSize$). If another key K_2 is hashed to $j + h_p(K_1)$, then the next position tried is $j + h_p(K_1) + h_p(K_2)$, not $j + 2 * h_p(K_1)$, which avoids secondary clustering if h_p is carefully chosen. Also, even if K_1 and K_2 are hashed primarily to the same position j, the probing sequences can be different for each. This, however, depends on the choice of the second hash function, h_p, which may render the same sequences for both keys. This is the case for function $h_p(K) = $ **strlen**(K), when both keys are of the same length.

Using two hash functions can be time-consuming, especially for sophisticated functions. Therefore, the second hash function can be defined in terms of the first, as in $h_p(K) = i * h(K) + 1$. The probing sequence for K_1 is

$$j, 2j + 1, 3j + 1, \ldots$$

(modulo $TSize$). If K_2 is hashed to $2j + 1$ then the probing sequence for K_2 is

$$2j + 1, 4j + 3, 6j + 4, \ldots$$

which does not conflict with the former sequence. Thus it does not lead to cluster buildup.

How efficient are all these methods? Obviously, it depends on the size of table and on the number of elements which are already in the table. The inefficiency of these methods is especially evident for *unsuccessful searches*, searching for elements which are not in the table. The more elements that are in the table, the more likely it is that clusters will form (primary or secondary) and the more likely it is that these clusters are large.

Consider the case when linear probing is used for collision resolution. If K is not in the table, then starting from the position $h(K)$, all consecutively occupied cells are checked; the longer the cluster, the longer it takes to determine that K, in fact, is not in the table. In the extreme case, when the table is full, we have to check all the cells starting from $h(K)$ and ending with $(h(K) - 1)$ mod *TSize*. Therefore, the search time increases with the number of elements in the table.

There are formulas which approximate the number of times for successful and unsuccessful searches for different hashing methods. These formulas were developed by Donald Knuth and are considered by Thomas Standish to be "among the prettiest in computer science." Figure 10.3 contains these formulas. Figure 10.4 contains a table showing the number of searches for different percentages of occupied cells. This table indicates that the formulas from Figure 10.3 provide only approximations of the number of searches. This is particularly evident for the higher percentages. For example, if 90% of the cells are occupied, then linear probing requires 50 trials to determine that the key being searched for is not in the table. However, for the full table of 10 cells, this number is 10, not 50.

For the lower percentages, the approximations computed by these formulas are closer to the real values. The table in Figure 10.4 indicates that if the table is 65% full, then linear probing requires, on average, fewer than two trials to find an element in the table. Since this number is usually an acceptable limit for a hash function, linear probing requires 35% of the spaces in the table to be unoccupied to keep performance at an acceptable level. This may be considered too wasteful, especially for very large tables or files. This percentage is lower for a quadratic search (25%) and for double hashing (20%), but it may still be considered large. Double hashing requires one cell out of five to be empty, which is a relatively high fraction. But all these problems can be solved by allowing more than one item to be stored in a given position or in an area associated with one position.

	Linear Probing	Quadratic Probing[1]	Double Hashing
Successful search	$\dfrac{1}{2}\left(1 + \dfrac{1}{1 - LF}\right)$	$1 - \ln(1 - LF) - \dfrac{LF}{2}$	$\dfrac{1}{LF} \ln \dfrac{1}{1 - LF}$
Unsuccessful search	$\dfrac{1}{2}\left(1 + \dfrac{1}{(1 - LF)^2}\right)$	$\dfrac{1}{1 - LF} - LF - \ln(1 - LF)$	$\dfrac{1}{1 - LF}$
	Load Factor $\quad LF = \dfrac{\text{number of elements in the table}}{\text{table size}}$		

[1]The formulas given in this column approximate any open addressing method which causes secondary clusters to arise, and quadratic probing is only one of them.

Figure 10.3: **Formulas approximating, for different hashing methods, the average numbers of trials for successful and unsuccessful searches (Knuth 1973).**

	Linear Probing		Quadratic Probing		Double Hashing	
LF	Successful	Unsuccessful	Successful	Unsuccessful	Successful	Unsuccessful
0.05	1.0	1.1	1.0	1.1	1.0	1.1
0.10	1.1	1.1	1.1	1.1	1.1	1.1
0.15	1.1	1.2	1.1	1.2	1.1	1.2
0.20	1.1	1.3	1.1	1.3	1.1	1.2
0.25	1.2	1.4	1.2	1.4	1.2	1.3
0.30	1.2	1.5	1.2	1.5	1.2	1.4
0.35	1.3	1.7	1.3	1.6	1.2	1.5
0.40	1.3	1.9	1.3	1.8	1.3	1.7
0.45	1.4	2.2	1.4	2.0	1.3	1.8
0.50	1.5	2.5	1.4	2.2	1.4	2.0
0.55	1.6	3.0	1.5	2.5	1.5	2.2
0.60	1.8	3.6	1.6	2.8	1.5	2.5
0.65	1.9	4.6	1.7	3.3	1.6	2.9
0.70	2.2	6.1	1.9	3.8	1.7	3.3
0.75	2.5	8.5	2.0	4.6	1.8	4.0
0.80	3.0	13.0	2.2	5.8	2.0	5.0
0.85	3.8	22.7	2.5	7.7	2.2	6.7
0.90	5.5	50.5	2.9	11.4	2.6	10.0
0.95	10.5	200.5	3.5	22.0	3.2	20.0

Figure 10.4: **A table presenting the average numbers of successful searches and unsuccessful searches for different collision resolution methods.**

10.2.2   Chaining

Keys do not have to be stored in the table itself. In *chaining*, each position of the table is associated with a linked list or *chain* of structures whose `info` fields store keys or references to keys. This method is called *separate chaining* and a table of references (pointers) is called a *scatter table*. In this method, the table can never overflow, since the linked lists are only extended upon the arrival of new keys, as illustrated in Figure 10.5. For short linked lists, this is a very fast method but increasing the length of these lists can significantly degrade retrieval performance. Performance can be improved by maintaining an order on all these lists so that for unsuccessful searches, an exhaustive search is not required in most cases.

This method requires additional space for maintaining pointers. The table stores only pointers and each record requires one pointer field. Therefore, for n keys, $n + TSize$ pointers are needed, which for large n, can be a very demanding requirement.

A version of chaining called *coalesced hashing* (or *coalesced chaining*) combines linear probing with chaining. In this method, the first available position is found for a key colliding with another key, and this position and its index are stored with the key already in the table. In this way, a sequential search down the table can be avoided by directly accessing the next element on the linked list. Each position *pos* of the table stores a `struct` of two fields: an `info` field for a key and the `next` field with the index of the next key which is hashed to *pos*. Available positions can be marked by, say, −2 in the next field; −1 can be used to indicate the end of a chain. This method requires $TSize * sizeof(index)$ more space

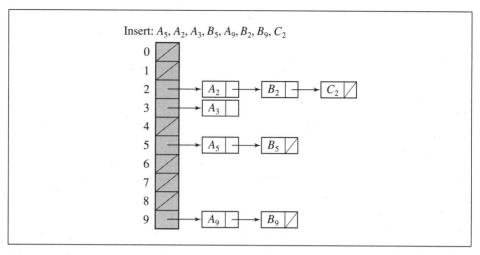

Figure 10.5: **In chaining, colliding keys are put on the same linked list.**

for the table, in addition to the space required for the keys. This is less than for chaining, but the table size limits the number of keys which can be hashed into the table.

An overflow area known as a *cellar* can be allocated to store keys for which there is no room in the table. This area should be allocated dynamically if the algorithm is implemented using a list of arrays.

Figure 10.6 illustrates an example where coalesced hashing puts a colliding key in the last position of the table. In Figure 10.6a, no collision occurs. In Figure 10.6b, B_5 is put in the last cell of the table, which is found occupied by A_9 when it arrives. Hence, A_9 is attached to the list accessible from position 9. In Figure 10.6c, two new colliding keys are added to the corresponding lists.

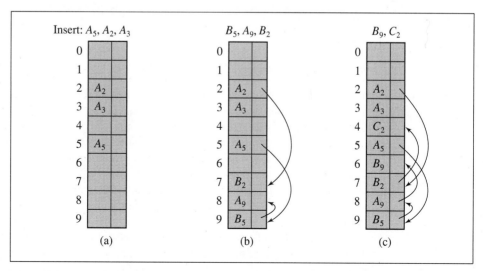

Figure 10.6: **Coalesced hashing puts a colliding key in the last available position of the table.**

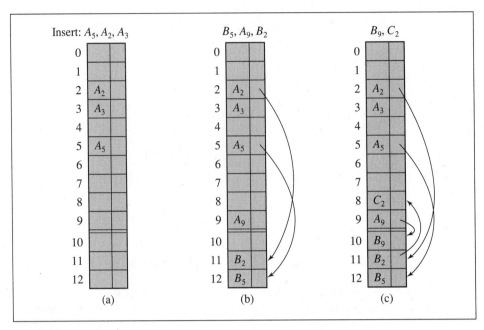

Figure 10.7: **Coalesced hashing which uses a cellar.**

Figure 10.7 illustrates coalesced hashing which uses a cellar. Noncolliding keys are stored in their home positions, as in Figure 10.7a. Colliding keys are put in the last available slot of the cellar and added to the list starting from its home position, as in Figure 10.7b. In Figure 10.7c, the cellar is full so an available cell is taken from the table when C_2 arrives.

10.2.3   Bucket Addressing

Another solution to the collision problem is to store colliding elements in the same position in the table. This can be achieved by associating a *bucket* with each address. A bucket is a block of space large enough to store multiple items.

By using buckets, the problem of collisions is not totally avoided. If a bucket is already full, then an item hashed to it has to be stored somewhere else. By incorporating the open addressing approach, the colliding item can be stored in the next bucket if it has an available slot when using linear probing, as illustrated in Figure 10.8, or it can be stored in some other bucket when, say, quadratic probing is used.

The colliding items can also be stored in an overflow area. In this case, each bucket includes a field that indicates whether the search should be continued in this area or not. It can be simply a yes/no marker. In conjunction with chaining, this marker can be the number indicating the position in which the beginning of the linked list associated with this bucket can be found in the overflow area (see Figure 10.9).

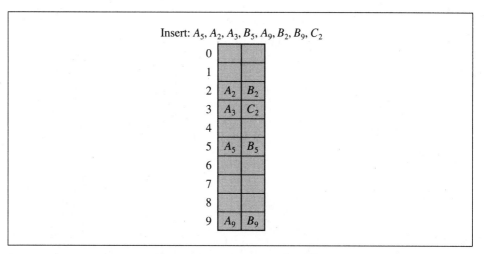

Figure 10.8: **Collision resolution with buckets and linear probing method.**

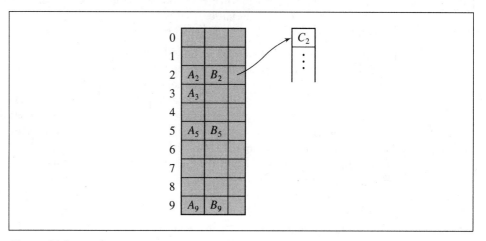

Figure 10.9: **Collision resolution with buckets and overflow area.**

■ 10.3 DELETION

How can we remove data from a hash table? With a chaining method, deleting an element leads to the deletion of a node from a linked list holding the element. For other methods, a deletion operation may require a more careful treatment of collision resolution, except for the rare occurrence when a perfect hash function is used.

Consider the table in Figure 10.10a in which the keys are stored using linear probing. The keys have been entered in the following order: A_1, A_4, A_2, B_4, B_1. After A_4 is deleted and position 4 is freed (Figure 10.10b), we try to find B_4 by first checking position 4. But this position is now empty so we may conclude that B_4 is not in the table. The same result

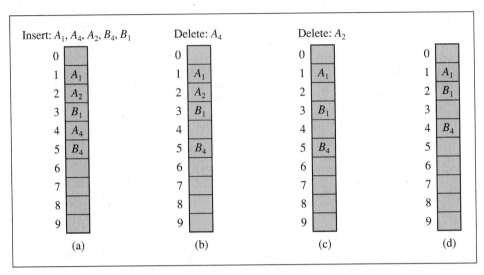

Figure 10.10: **Linear search in the situation where both insertion and deletion**
of keys is permitted.

occurs after deleting A_2 and marking cell 2 as empty (Figure 10.10c). Then, the search for B_1 is unsuccessful, since if we are using linear probing, the search terminates at position 2. The situation is the same for the other open addressing methods.

    If we leave deleted keys in the table with markers indicating that they are not valid elements of the table, any subsequent search for an element does not terminate prematurely. When a new key is inserted, it overwrites a key which is only a space filler. However, for a large number of deletions and a small number of additional insertions, the table becomes overloaded with deleted records, which increases the search time since the open addressing methods require testing the deleted elements. Therefore, the table should be purged after a certain number of deletions by moving undeleted elements to the cells occupied by deleted elements. Cells with deleted elements which are not overwritten by this procedure are marked as free. Figure 10.10d illustrates this situation.

■ 10.4 PERFECT HASH FUNCTIONS

All the cases discussed so far assumed that the body of data is not precisely known. Therefore, the hash function only rarely turned out to be an ideal hash function in the sense that it immediately hashed a key to its proper position and avoided any collisions. In most cases, some collision resolution technique had to be included, since sooner or later, a key would arrive which conflicted with another key in the table. Also, the number of keys is rarely known in advance, so the table had to be large enough to accommodate all the arriving data. Moreover, the table size contributed to the number of collisions: the larger the table, the smaller number of collisions (providing that the hash function took table size into consideration). All this was caused by the fact that the body of data to be hashed in the table was not precisely known ahead of time. Therefore, first a hash function was devised and then the data were processed.

In many situations, however, the body of data is fixed so a hash function can be devised after the data are known. Such a function may really be a perfect hash function if it hashes items on the first attempt. In addition, if such a function requires only as many cells in the table as the number of data, so that no empty cell remains after hashing is completed, it is called a *minimal perfect hash function*. Wasting time for collision resolution and wasting space for unused table cells is avoided in a minimal perfect hash function.

Processing a fixed body of data is not an uncommon situation. Consider the following examples: a table of reserved words used by assemblers or compilers, files on unerasable optical disks, dictionaries, and lexical databases.

Algorithms for choosing a perfect hash function usually require tedious work, due to the fact that perfect hash functions are rare. As already indicated for 50 elements and a 100-cell array, only one in one million is perfect. Other functions lead to collisions.

10.4.1   Cichelli's Method

One algorithm to construct a minimal perfect hash function was developed by Richard J. Cichelli. It is used to hash a relatively small number of reserved words. The function is of the form

$$h(word) = (length(word) + g(firstletter(word)) + g(lastletter(word))) \bmod TSize,$$

where g is the function to be constructed. The function g assigns values to letters so that the resulting function h returns unique hash values for all words in a predefined set of words. The values assigned by g to particular letters do not have to be unique. The algorithm has three parts: computation of the letter occurrences, ordering the words, and searching. The last step is the heart of this algorithm and uses an auxiliary function `Try()`. Cichelli's algorithm for constructing g and h is as follows:

```
choose a value for Max;
compute the number of occurrences of each first and last letter in the set of all words;
order all words in accordance to the frequency of occurrence of the first and the last letters;
Search(wordList)
    if wordList is empty
        halt;
    word = first word from wordList;
    word_list = wordList with the first word detached;
    if the first and the last letters of word are assigned values
        if word is processed for the first time
            Try(word,-1,-1); // -1 signifies 'value already assigned'
            if success
                Search (wordList);
            put word at the beginning of wordList and detach its hash value;
    else for each n,m in {0,...,Max}
            Try(word,n,m);
            if success
                Search (wordList);
        put word at the beginning of wordList and detach its hash value;
    else if either the first or the last letter has a value
        for each n in {0,...,Max}
```

continued

```
        Try(word,-1,n) or Try(word,n,-1);
    if success
        Search (wordList);
    put word at the beginning of wordList and detach its hash value;

Try(word,firstLetterValue,lastLetterValue)
    if h(word) has not been claimed
        reserve h(word);
        reserve firstLetterValue, and/or lastLetterValue
        if not −1 (i.e., not reserved);
        return success;
    return failure;
```

We can use this algorithm to build a hash function for the names of nine Muses: Calliope, Clio, Erato, Euterpe, Melpomene, Polyhymnia, Terpsichore, Thalia, and Urania. A simple count of the letters renders the number of times a given letter occurs as a first and last letter (case sensitivity is disregarded): E (6), A (3), C (2), O (2), T (2), M (1), P (1), and U (1). According to these frequencies, the words can be put in the following order: Euterpe (E occurs 6 times as the first and the last letter), Calliope, Erato, Terpsichore, Melpomene, Thalia, Clio, Polyhymnia, and Urania.

Now the procedure **Search()** is applied. Figure 10.11 contains a summary of its execution, in which Max = 4. First, the word Euterpe is tried. E is assigned the value of

		reserved hash values
Euterpe	E = 0 h = 7	{7}
Calliope	C = 0 h = 8	{7 8}
Erato	O = 0 h = 5	{5 7 8}
Terpsichore	T = 0 h = 2	{2 5 7 8}
Melpomene	M = 0 h = 0	{0 2 5 7 8}
Thalia	A = 0 h = 6	{0 2 5 6 7 8}
Clio	h = 4	{0 2 4 5 6 7 8}
Polyhymnia	P = 0 h = 1	{0 1 2 4 5 6 7 8}
Urania	U = 0 h = 6 *	{0 1 2 4 5 6 7 8}
Urania	U = 1 h = 7 *	{0 1 2 4 5 6 7 8}
Urania	U = 2 h = 8 *	{0 1 2 4 5 6 7 8}
Urania	U = 3 h = 0 *	{0 1 2 4 5 6 7 8}
Urania	U = 4 h = 1 *	{0 1 2 4 5 6 7 8}
Polyhymnia	P = 1 h = 2 *	{0 2 4 5 6 7 8}
Polyhymnia	P = 2 h = 3	{0 2 3 4 5 6 7 8}
Urania	U = 0 h = 6 *	{0 2 3 4 5 6 7 8}
Urania	U = 1 h = 7 *	{0 2 3 4 5 6 7 8}
Urania	U = 2 h = 8 *	{0 2 3 4 5 6 7 8}
Urania	U = 3 h = 0 *	{0 2 3 4 5 6 7 8}
Urania	U = 4 h = 1	{0 1 2 3 4 5 6 7 8}

Figure 10.11: **Subsequent invocations of the searching procedure with *Max* = 4 in Cichelli's algorithm assign the indicated values to letters and to the list of reserved hash values. The star indicates a failure.**

0, whereby h(Euterpe) = 7 which is put on the list of reserved hash values. Everything goes well until Urania is tried. All five possible values for U result in an already reserved hash value. The procedure backtracks to the preceding step, when Polyhymnia was tried. Its current hash value is detached from the list, and the value of 1 is tried for the letter P, which causes a failure, but 2 for P gives 3 for the hash value, so the algorithm can continue. Urania is tried again five times, and the fifth attempt is successful. All the names have been assigned unique hash values and the search process is finished. If the values for each letter are A = C = E = O = M = T = 0, P = 2, and U = 4, then h is the minimal perfect hash function for the nine Muses.

The searching process in Cichelli's algorithm is exponential since it uses an exhaustive search, and as such, it is inapplicable to a large number of words. Also, it does not guarantee that a perfect hash function can be found. For a small number of words, however, it usually gives good results. This program often needs to be run only once and the resulting hash function can be incorporated into another program. Cichelli applied his method to the Pascal reserved words. The result was a hash function which reduced the run time of a Pascal cross reference program by 10% after it replaced the binary search used previously.

There have been many successful attempts to extend Cichelli's technique and overcome its shortcomings. One technique modified the terms involved in the definition of the hash function. For example, another term, the alphabetic position of the second to last letter in the word, is added to the function definition (Sebesta, Taylor 1986), or the following definition is used (Haggard, Karplus 1986):

$$h(word) = length(word) + g_1(firstletter(word)) + \cdots + g_{length(word)}(lastletter(word)).$$

Cichelli's method can also be modified by partitioning the body of data into separate buckets for which minimal perfect hash functions are found. The partitioning is performed by a grouping function, gr, which for each word indicates the bucket to which it belongs. Then a general hash function is generated whose form is

$$h(word) = bucket_{gr(word)} + h_{gr(word)}(word)$$

(e.g., Lewis, Cook 1986). The problem with this approach is that it is difficult to find a generally applicable grouping function tuned to finding minimal perfect hash functions.

Both these ways — modifying hash function and partitioning — are not entirely successful if the same Cichelli's algorithm is used. Although Cichelli ends his paper with the adage: "When all else fails, try brute force," the attempts to modify his approach included devising a more efficient searching algorithm to circumvent the need for brute force. One such approach is incorporated in the FHCD algorithm.

10.4.2   The FHCD Algorithm

The FHCD algorithm (Fox et al. 1992) searches for a minimal perfect hash function of the form

$$h(word) = h_0(word) + g(h_1(word)) + g(h_2(word))$$

(modulo *TSize*), where g is the function to be determined by the algorithm. To define the functions h_i, three tables T_0, T_1, and T_2, of random numbers are defined, one for each function h_i. Each word is equal to a string of characters $c_1 c_2 \ldots c_m$ corresponding to a triple $(h_0(word), h_1(word), h_2(word))$ whose elements are calculated according to the formulas

$$h_0 = (T_0(c_1) + \cdots + T_0(c_m)) \bmod n$$

$$h_1 = (T_1(c_1) + \cdots + T_1(c_m)) \bmod r$$

$$h_2 = ((T_2(c_1) + \cdots + T_2(c_m)) \bmod r) + r$$

where n is the number of all words in the body of data, r is a parameter usually equal to $n/2$ or less, and $T_i(c_j)$ is the number generated in table T_i for c_j. The function g is found in three steps: *mapping*, *ordering*, and *searching*.

In the mapping step, n triples $(h_0(word), h_1(word), h_2(word))$ are created. The randomness of functions h_i usually ascertains the uniqueness of these triples; should they not be unique, new tables T_i are generated. Next, a *dependency graph* is built. It is a bipartite graph with half of its vertices corresponding to the h_1 values and labeled 0 through $r - 1$ and the other half to the h_2 values and labeled r through $2r - 1$. Each word corresponds to an edge of the graph between the vertices $h_1(word)$ and $h_2(word)$. The mapping step is expected to take $O(n)$ time.

As an example, we again use the set of names of the nine Muses. To generate three tables T_i, the standard function **rand()** is used and with these tables, a set of nine triples is computed, as shown in Figure 10.12a. Figure 10.12b contains a corresponding dependency graph with $r = 3$. Note that some vertices cannot be connected to any other vertices, and some pairs of vertices can be connected with more than one arc.

The ordering step rearranges all the vertices so that they can be partitioned into a series of levels. When a sequence $v_1, \ldots, v_t$ of vertices is established, then a level $K(v_i)$ of keys is defined as a set of all the edges which connect v_i with those v_js for which $j \leq i$. The sequence is initiated with a vertex of maximum degree. Then, for each successive position i of the sequence, a vertex v_i is selected from among the vertices having at least one connection to the vertices $v_1, \ldots, v_{i-1}$ which has maximal degree. When no such vertex can be found, any vertex of maximal degree is chosen from among the unselected vertices. Figure 10.12c contains an example.

In the last step, searching, hash values are assigned to keys, level by level. The g-value for the first vertex is chosen randomly among the numbers $0, \ldots, n - 1$. For the other vertices, because of their construction and ordering, we have the following relation: if $v_i < r$ then $v_i = h_1$. Thus, each word in $K(v_i)$ has the same value $g(h_1(word)) = g(v_i)$. Also, $g(h_2(word))$ has already been defined, since it is equal to some v_j which has already been processed. Analogical reasoning can be applied to the case when $v_i > r$ and then $v_i = h_2$. For each word, either $g(h_1(word))$ or $g(h_2(word))$ is known. The second g-value is found randomly for each level so that the values obtained from the formula of the minimal perfect hash function h indicate the positions in the hash table which are available. Because the first choice of a random number will not always fit all words on a given level to the hash table, other random numbers may need to be tried.

The searching step for the nine Muses starts with randomly choosing $g(v_1)$. Let $g(2) = 2$, where $v_1 = 2$. The next vertex is $v_2 = 5$, so that $K(v_2) = \{Erato\}$. According to Figure 10.12a, $h_0(Erato) = 3$, and because the edge *Erato* connects v_1 and v_2, either

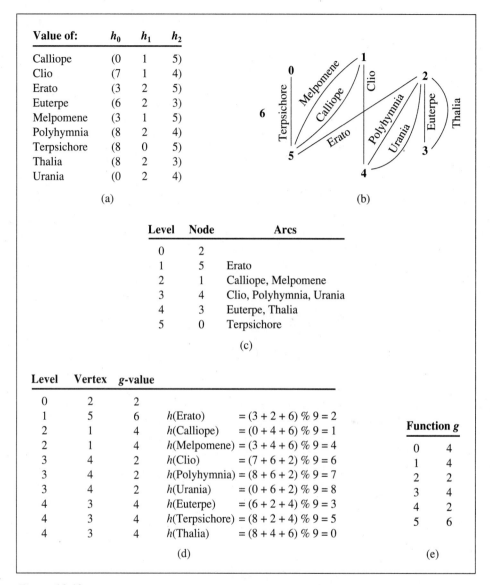

Value of:	h_0	h_1	h_2
Calliope	(0	1	5)
Clio	(7	1	4)
Erato	(3	2	5)
Euterpe	(6	2	3)
Melpomene	(3	1	5)
Polyhymnia	(8	2	4)
Terpsichore	(8	0	5)
Thalia	(8	2	3)
Urania	(0	2	4)

(a)

(b)

Level	Node	Arcs
0	2	
1	5	Erato
2	1	Calliope, Melpomene
3	4	Clio, Polyhymnia, Urania
4	3	Euterpe, Thalia
5	0	Terpsichore

(c)

Level	Vertex	g-value	
0	2	2	
1	5	6	$h(\text{Erato}) = (3 + 2 + 6) \% 9 = 2$
2	1	4	$h(\text{Calliope}) = (0 + 4 + 6) \% 9 = 1$
2	1	4	$h(\text{Melpomene}) = (3 + 4 + 6) \% 9 = 4$
3	4	2	$h(\text{Clio}) = (7 + 6 + 2) \% 9 = 6$
3	4	2	$h(\text{Polyhymnia}) = (8 + 6 + 2) \% 9 = 7$
3	4	2	$h(\text{Urania}) = (0 + 6 + 2) \% 9 = 8$
4	3	4	$h(\text{Euterpe}) = (6 + 2 + 4) \% 9 = 3$
4	3	4	$h(\text{Terpsichore}) = (8 + 2 + 4) \% 9 = 5$
4	3	4	$h(\text{Thalia}) = (8 + 4 + 6) \% 9 = 0$

Function g

0	4
1	4
2	2
3	4
4	2
5	6

(d)

(e)

Figure 10.12: **Applying the FHCD algorithm to the names of nine Muses.**

$h_1(\text{Erato})$ or $h_2(\text{Erato})$ must be equal to v_1. We can see that $h_1(\text{Erato}) = 2 = v_1$, and so $g(h_1(\text{Erato})) = g(v_1) = 2$. A value for $g(v_2) = g(h_2(\text{Erato})) = 6$ is chosen randomly. From this, $h(\text{Erato}) = (h_0(\text{Erato}) + g(h_1(\text{Erato})) + g(h_2(\text{Erato}))) \bmod TSize = (3 + 2 + 6) \bmod 9 = 2$. This means that position 2 of the hash table is no longer available. The new g-value, $g(5) = 6$, is retained for later use.

Now, $v_3 = 1$ is tried, with $K(v_3) = \{\text{Calliope, Melpomene}\}$. The h_0-values for both words are retrieved from the table of triples and the $g(h_2)$-values are equal to 6 for both words, since $h_2 = v_2$ for both of them. Now we must find a random $g(h_1)$-value such that the hash function h computed for both words renders two numbers different from 2, since position two is already occupied. Assume that this number is 4. As a result, h(Calliope) $= 1$ and h(Melpomene) $= 4$. Figure 10.12d contains a summary of all the steps. Figure 10.12e shows the values of the function g. Through these values of g, the function h becomes a minimal perfect hash function. However, since g is given in a tabular form and not with a neat formula, it has to be stored as a table to be used every time function h is needed, which may not be a trivial task. The function $g : \{0, \ldots, 2r - 1\} \rightarrow \{0, \ldots, n - 1\}$, and the size of g's domain increases with r. The parameter r is approximately $n/2$, which for large databases means that the table storing all values for g is not of a negligible size. This table has to be kept in main memory to make computations of the hash function efficient.

■ 10.5   HASH FUNCTIONS FOR EXTENDIBLE FILES

All the methods discussed so far work on tables of fixed sizes. This is a reasonable assumption for arrays, but for files this may be too restrictive. After all, file sizes change dynamically by adding new elements or deleting old ones. Some hashing techniques can be used in this situation such as coalesced hashing or hashing with chaining, but some of them may be inadequate. New techniques have been developed which specifically take into account the variable size of the table or file. We can distinguish two classes of such techniques: directory and directoryless.

In the directory schemes, key access is mediated by the access to a directory or an index of keys in the structure. There are several techniques and modifications to those techniques in the category of the directory schemes. We mention only a few: *expandable hashing* (Knott 1971), *dynamic hashing* (Larson 1978), and *extendible hashing* (Fagin et al. 1979). All three methods distribute keys among buckets in a similar fashion. The main difference is the structure of the index (directory). In expandable hashing and dynamic hashing, a binary tree is used as an index of buckets. On the other hand, in extendible hashing, a directory of records is kept in a table.

One directoryless technique is *virtual hashing* which is defined as "any hashing which may dynamically change its hashing function" (Litwin 1978). This change of hashing function compensates for the lack of a directory. An example of this approach is linear hashing (Litwin 1980). In the following pages, one method from each category will be discussed.

10.5.1   Extendible Hashing

Assume that a hashing technique is applied to a dynamically changing file composed of buckets, and each bucket can hold only a fixed number of items. Extendible hashing accesses the data stored in buckets indirectly through an index which is dynamically adjusted to reflect changes in the file. The characteristic feature of extendible hashing is the organization of the index, which is an expandable table.

A hash function applied to a certain key indicates a position in the index, and not in the file (or table of keys). Values returned by such a hash function are called *pseudokeys*. In this way, the file requires no reorganization when data are added to it or deleted from it, since these changes are indicated in the index. Only one hash function h can be used, but depending on the size of the index, only a portion of the address $h(K)$ is utilized. A simple

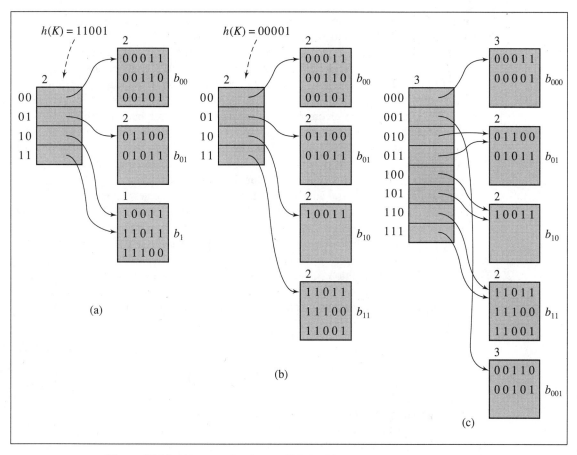

Figure 10.13: **An example of extendible hashing.**

way to achieve this effect is by looking at the address $h(K)$ as a string of bits from which only the i leftmost bits can be used. The number i is called the *depth* of the directory. In Figure 10.13a, the depth is equal to two.

As an example, assume that the hash function h generates patterns of five bits. If this pattern is the string 01011 and depth is two, then the two leftmost bits, 01, are considered to be the position in the directory containing the pointer to a bucket in which the key can be found or into which it is to be inserted. In Figure 10.13, the values of h are shown in the buckets, but these values only represent the keys which are actually stored in these buckets.

Each bucket has a *local depth* associated with it that indicates the number of leftmost bits in $h(K)$. The leftmost bits are the same for all keys in the bucket. In Figure 10.13, the local depths are shown on top of each bucket. For example, the bucket b_{00} holds all keys for which $h(K)$ starts with 00. More importantly, the local depth indicates whether the bucket can be accessed from only one location in the directory, or from at least two. In the first case, when the local depth is equal to the depth of directory, it is necessary to change the size of the directory after the bucket is split in the case of an overflow. When the local depth is smaller than the directory depth, splitting the bucket only requires changing half of the pointers pointing to this bucket so that they point to the newly created one.

Figure 10.13b illustrates this case. After a key with h-value 11001 arrives, its two first bits (since depth = 2) direct it to the fourth position of the directory, from which it is sent to the bucket b_1 which contains keys whose h-value starts with 1. An overflow occurs, b_1 is split into b_{10} (the new name for the old bucket) and b_{11}. The local depths of these two buckets are set to two. The pointer from position 11 points now to b_{11}, and the keys from b_1 are redistributed between b_{10} and b_{11}.

The situation is more complex if an overflow occurs in a bucket with a local depth equal to the depth of the directory. For example, consider the case when a key with h-value 00001 arrives at the table in Figure 10.13b and is hashed through position 00 (its first two bits) to bucket b_{00}. A split occurs, but the directory has no room for the pointer to the new bucket. As a result, the directory is doubled in size so that its depth is now equal to three, b_{00} becomes b_{000} with an increased local depth, and the new bucket is b_{001}. All the keys from b_{00} are divided between the new bucket: those whose h-value start with 000 become elements of b_{000}; the remaining keys, those with prefix 001, are put in b_{001}, as in Figure 10.13c. Also, all the slots of the new directory have to be set to their proper values by having *newdirectory*[2 * i] = *olddirectory*[i] and *newdirectory*[2 * i + 1] = *olddirectory*[i] for *i*'s ranging over positions of the *olddirectory*, except for the position referring to the bucket which just has been split.

The following algorithm inserts a record into a file using extendible hashing.

```
ExtendibleHashingInsert(K)
    bitPattern = h(K);
    p = directory[depth(directory) leftmost bits of bitPattern];
    if space is available in bucket b_d pointed to by p
        place K in the bucket;
    else split bucket b_d into b_d0 and b_d1;
        set local depth of b_d0 and b_d1 to depth(b_d)+1;
        distribute records from b_d between b_d0 and b_d1;
        if depth(b_d) < depth(directory)
            update the half of the pointers which pointed to b_d to point to b_d1;
        else double the directory and increment its depth;
            set directory entries to proper pointers;
```

An important advantage of using extendible hashing is that it avoids a reorganization of the file if the directory overflows. Only the directory is affected. Because the directory in most cases is kept in the main memory, the cost of expanding and updating it is very small. However, for large files of small buckets, the size of the directory can become so large that it may be put in virtual memory or explicitly in a file, which may slow down the process of using the directory. Also, the size of the directory does not grow uniformly, since it is doubled if a bucket with a local depth equal to the depth of the directory is split. This means that for large directories there will be many redundant entries in the directory. To rectify the problem of an overgrown directory, Lomet proposed using extendible hashing until the directory becomes too large to fit into the main memory. Afterwards, the pages are doubled instead of the directory and the bit(s) in the bit pattern $h(K)$ that come after the first *depth* bits are used to distinguish between different parts of the bucket. For example, if *depth* = 3 and a bucket b_{10} has been quadrupled, its parts are distinguished with bit strings 00, 01, 10, and 11. Now, if $h(K) = 101\textit{01}101$, the key K is searched for in the second portion, 01, of b_{101}.

10.5.2   Linear Hashing

Extendible hashing allows the file to expand without reorganizing it, but it requires storage place for an index. In the method developed by Witold Litwin, no index is necessary because new buckets generated by splitting existing buckets are always added in the same, linear way, so there is no need to retain indexes. To this end, a pointer *split* indicates which bucket is to be split next. After the bucket pointed to by *split* is divided, the keys in this bucket are distributed between this bucket and the newly created bucket which is added to the end of the table. Figure 10.14 contains a sequence of initial splits in which *TSize* = 3. Initially, the pointer *split* is zero. If the loading factor exceeds a certain level, a new bucket is created, keys from bucket zero are distributed between bucket zero and bucket three, and *split* is incremented. How is this distribution performed? If only one hash function is used then it hashes keys from bucket zero to bucket zero before and after splitting. This means that one function is not sufficient.

At each level of splitting, linear hashing maintains two hash functions, h_{level} and $h_{level+1}$, such that $h_{level}(K) = K$ mod $(TSize * 2^{level})$. The first hash function, h_{level}, hashes keys to buckets which have not yet been split on the current level. The second function, $h_{level+1}$, is used for hashing keys to already split buckets. The algorithm for linear hashing is as follows:

initialize: `split = 0; level = 0;`

```
LinerHashingInsert(K)
  if hlevel(K) < split         // bucket hlevel(K) has been split
    hashAddress = hlevel+1(K);
  else hashAddress = hlevel(K);
```
insert `K` *in a corresponding bucket or an overflow area;*
`if` *the loading factor is high*
  create a new bucket with index `split + TSize * 2`*level*`;`
  redistribute keys from bucket `split` *between buckets* `split` *and* `split + TSize * 2`*level*`;`

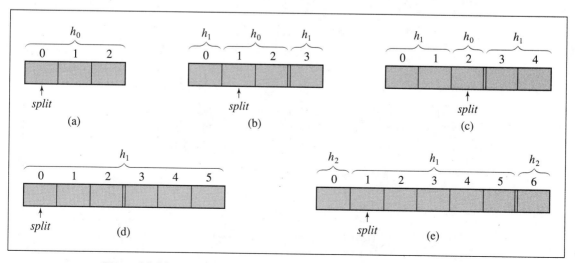

Figure 10.14: **Splitting buckets in the linear hashing technique.**

```
split++;
if split == TSize * 2^{level} // all buckets on the current
                              // level have been split;
    level++;                  // proceed to the next level
    split = 0;
```

It may still be unclear when to split a bucket. Most likely, as the algorithm assumes, a threshold value of the loading factor is used to decide whether or not to split a bucket. This threshold has to be known in advance and its magnitude is chosen by the program designer. To illustrate, assume that keys can be hashed to buckets in a file. If a bucket is full, the overflowing keys can be put on a linked list in an overflow area. Consider the situation in Figure 10.15a. In this figure, $TSize = 3$, $h_0(K) = K \bmod TSize$, $h_1(K) = K \bmod 2 * TSize$. Let the size of the overflow area $OSize = 3$, and let the highest acceptable loading factor which equals the number of elements divided by the number of slots in the file and in the overflow area be 80%. The current loading factor in Figure 10.15a is 75%. If the key 10 arrives, it is hashed to location 1, but the loading factor increases to 83%. The first bucket is split and the keys are redistributed using function h_1, as in Figure 10.15b. Note that the first bucket had the lowest load out of all three buckets and yet it was the bucket that was split.

Assume that 21 and 36 have been hashed to the table (Figure 10.15c), and now 25 arrives. This causes the loading factor to increase to 87%, resulting in another split, this time the split of the second bucket, which results in the configuration shown in Figure 10.15d. After hashing 27 and 37, another split occurs and Figure 10.15e illustrates the new situation. Because *split* reached the last value allowed on this level, it is assigned the value of zero, and the hash function to be used in subsequent hashing is h_1, the same as before, and a new function, h_2, is defined as $K \bmod 4 * TSize$.

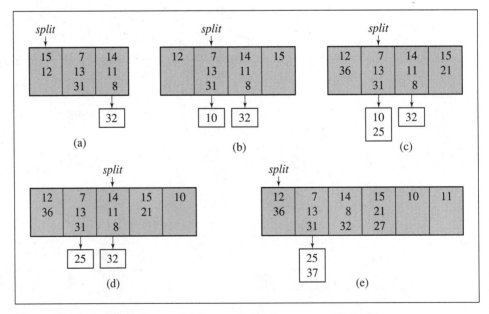

Figure 10.15: **Inserting keys to buckets and overflow area with the linear hashing technique.**

Note that linear hashing requires the use of some overflow area since the order of splitting is predetermined. In the case of files this may mean more than one file access. This area can be explicit and different from buckets, but it can be introduced somewhat in the spirit of coalesced hashing by utilizing empty space in the buckets (Mullin 1981). In a directory scheme, on the other hand, an overflow area is not necessary although it can be used.

As in a directory scheme, linear hashing increases the address space by splitting a bucket. It also redistributes the keys of the split bucket between the buckets that result from the split. Because no indexes are maintained in linear hashing, this method is faster and requires less space than previous methods. The increase in efficiency is particularly noticeable for large files.

■ 10.6   CASE STUDY: HASHING WITH BUCKETS

The most serious problem to be solved in programs which rely on a hash function to insert and retrieve items from an undetermined body of data is resolving collision. Depending on the technique, allowing deletion of items from the table can significantly increase the complexity of the program. In this case study, a program will be developed which allows the user to insert to and delete elements from the file **names** interactively. This file contains names and phone numbers, and is initially ordered alphabetically. At the end of the session the file will be ordered with all updates included. To that end, the **outfile** is used throughout the execution of the program. **outfile** is the file of buckets initialized as empty. Elements which cannot be hashed to the corresponding bucket in this file are stored in the file **overflow**. At the end of the session, both files are combined and sorted to replace the contents of the original file **names**.

The **outfile** is used here as the hash table. First, this file is prepared by filling it with **tableSize * bucketSize** empty records (one record is simply a certain number of bytes). Next, all entries of **names** are transferred to **outfile** to buckets indicated by the hash function. This transfer is performed by the function **Insertion()** which includes the hashed item in the bucket indicated by the hash function, or in **overflow** if the bucket is full. In the latter case, **overflow** is searched from the beginning and if a position occupied by a deleted record is found, the overflow item replaces it. If the end of **overflow** is reached, the item is put at the end of this file.

After initializing **outfile**, a menu is displayed and the user chooses to insert a new record, delete an old one, or exit. For insertion, the same function is used as before. No duplicates are allowed. When the user wants to delete an item, the hash function is used to access the corresponding bucket, and the linear search of positions in the bucket is performed until the item is found, in which case the deletion marker "#" is written over the first character of the item in the bucket. During this search an empty entry can be found, which indicates that the item is not in the file, or that the end of the bucket can be reached. In this case the search continues sequentially in **overflow** until either the item is found or the end of the file is encountered.

If the user chooses to exit, the undeleted entries of **overflow** are transferred to **outfile**, and all undeleted entries of **outfile** are sorted using an external sort. To that end, the quicksort is applied both to **outfile** and to an array **pointers[]** which contains the addresses of entries in `outfile`. For comparison, the entries in `outfile` can be accessed but the elements in `pointers[]` are moved, not the elements of `outfile`.

After this indirect sorting is accomplished, the data in `outfile` have to be put in alphabetical order, which is accomplished by transferring entries from `outfile` to `name` using the order indicated in `pointers[]`, that is, by going down the array and retrieving the entry in `outfile` through the address stored in the currently accessed cell.

Here is an example. If the contents of the original file are

```
Adam 123-4567        Brenda 345-5352      Brendon 983-7373
Charles 987-1122     Jeremiah 789-4563    Katherine 823-1573
Patrick 757-4532     Raymond 090-9383     Thorsten 929-6632
```

the hashing generates the `outfile`:

```
Katherine 823-1573   |*                   ||
Adam 123-4567        |Brenda 345-5352      ||
Raymond 090-9383     |Thorsten 929-6632    ||
```

and the file `overflow`:

```
Brendon 983-7373     |Charles 987-1122     ||
Jeremiah 789-4563    |Patrick 757-4532     ||
```

(The vertical bars are *not* included in the file; one bar divides the records in the same bucket, two bars separate different buckets.)

After inserting `Carol 654-6543` and deleting `Brenda 345-5352` and `Jeremiah 789-4563`, the files' contents are:
`outfile`:

```
Katherine 823-1573   |Carol 654-6543       ||
Adam 123-4567        |#renda 345-5352      ||
Raymond 090-9383     |Thorsten 929-6632    ||
```

and `overflow`:

```
Brendon 983-7373     |Charles 987-1122     ||
#eremiah 789-4563    |Patrick 757-4532     ||
```

A subsequent deletion of `Brendon 983-7373` and insertion of `Maggie 733-0983` changes only `overflow`:

```
#rendon 983-7373     |Charles 987-1122     ||
Maggie 733-0983      |Patrick 757-4532     ||
```

After the user chooses to exit, undeleted records from `overflow` are transferred to `outfile` which now includes:

```
Katherine 823-1573   |Carol 654-6543       ||
Adam 123-4567        |#renda 345-5352      ||
Raymond 090-9383     |Thorsten 929-6632    ||
Charles 987-1122     |Maggie 733-0983      ||
Patrick 757-4532     |
```

This file is sorted and the outcome is:

```
Adam 123-4567        |Carol 654-6543     ||
Charles 987-1122     |Katherine 823-1573 ||
Maggie 733-0983      |Patrick 757-4532   ||
Raymond 090-9383     |Thorsten 929-6632  ||
```

Figure 10.16 contains the code for this program.

```cpp
#include <iostream.h>
#include <fstream.h>
#include <string.h>
#include <ctype.h>
#include <iomanip.h>


const int bucketSize = 2, tableSize = 3, strLen = 20;
const int recordLen = strLen, arrSize = 3*bucketSize*tableSize;

class File {
public:
    File() : empty('*'), delMarker('#'), true(1), false(0),
                unit(sizeof(int)/sizeof(char))
             { *command = '\0'; }
    void ProcessFile(ifstream&);
private:
    const char empty, delMarker;
    const int true, false, unit;
    int pointers[arrSize], tmp, arrCnt;
    char line[recordLen+1], command[strLen];
    char name[recordLen+1], name2[recordLen+1], rec[recordLen+1];
    int inserted, address, counter, done, deleted, i;
    unsigned xor, remainder;
    fstream outfile, overflow, sorted, outf;

    int  Hash(char*);
    void Swap(int& i, int& j) { tmp = i; i = j; j = tmp; }
    void GetName();
    void Insert() { GetName(); Insertion(); }
    void Insertion();
    void Delete();
    void Partition(int,int,int&);
    void QSort(int,int);
```

Figure 10.16: **Implementation of hashing using buckets.**   **continued**

```
      void SortFile();
      void CombineFiles();
};


int
File::Hash(char *s)
{
    for (xor = 0; strlen(s) >= unit; s += unit) // xor at once the number
        xor ^= *(unsigned *) s;          // of bytes (chars) equal to the
                                         // number of bytes in an integer;
    if (strlen(s)) {                     // include also remaining
        strcpy ((char *)&remainder,s);   // characters (whose number is
        xor ^= remainder;                // less than the value of unit);
    }
    return (xor % tableSize) * bucketSize * recordLen;
}


void
File::GetName()
{
    cout << "Enter name: ";
    cin.getline(line,recordLen+1);
    for (i = strlen(line); i < recordLen; i++)
        line[i] = ' ';
    line[recordLen] = '\0';
}


void
File::Insertion()
{
    address = Hash(line);
    outfile.seekg(address,ios::beg);
    name[recordLen] = '\0';
    done = inserted = false;
    counter = 0;
    while (!done && outfile.getline(name,recordLen+1)) {
        if (name[0] == empty) {
            outfile.seekg(address+counter*recordLen,ios::beg);
            outfile << line << setw(strlen(line)-recordLen);
```

Figure 10.16: **Implementation of hashing using buckets.**   **continued**

```
                    done = inserted = true;
            }
            else if (!strcmp(name,line)) {
                cout << line << " is already in the file\n";
                return;
            }
            else counter++;
            if (counter == bucketSize)
                done = true;
            else outfile.seekg(address+counter*recordLen,ios::beg);
        }
        if (!inserted) {
            done = false;
            counter = 0;
            overflow.clear();
            overflow.seekg(0,ios::beg);
            while (!done && overflow.getline(name,recordLen+1)) {
                if (name[0] == delMarker)
                    done = true;
                else if (!strcmp(name,line)) {
                    cout << line << " is already in the file\n";
                    return;
                }
                else counter++;
            }
            overflow.clear();
            if (done)
                 overflow.seekg(counter*recordLen,ios::beg);
            else overflow.seekg(0,ios::end);
            overflow << line << setw(strlen(line)-recordLen);
        }
}

void
File::Delete()
{
    GetName();
    address = Hash(line);
    outfile.clear();
    outfile.seekg(address,ios::beg);
```

Figure 10.16: **Implementation of hashing using buckets.**   **continued**

```
        counter = 0;
        done = deleted = false;
        name2[recordLen] = '\0';
        while (!done && outfile.getline(name2,recordLen+1)) {
            if (!strcmp(line,name2)) {
                outfile.seekg(address+counter*recordLen,ios::beg);
                outfile.put(delMarker);
                done = deleted = true;
            }
            else counter++;
            if (counter == bucketSize)
                done = true;
            else outfile.seekg(address+counter*recordLen,ios::beg);
        }
        if (!deleted) {
            done = false;
            counter = 0;
            overflow.clear();
            overflow.seekg(0,ios::beg);
            while (!done && overflow.getline(name2,recordLen+1)) {
                if (!strcmp(line,name2)) {
                    overflow.clear();
                    overflow.seekg(counter*recordLen,ios::beg);
                    overflow.put(delMarker);
                    done = deleted = true;
                }
                else counter++;
                overflow.seekg(counter*recordLen,ios::beg);
            }
        }
        if (!deleted)
            cout << line << " is not in database\n";
}


void
File::Partition (int low, int high, int& pivotLoc)
{   char rec[recordLen+1], pivot[recordLen+1];
    register int i, lastSmall;
```

Figure 10.16: **Implementation of hashing using buckets.**   **continued**

```
        Swap(pointers[low],pointers[(low+high)/2]);
        outfile.seekg(pointers[low]*recordLen,ios::beg);
        rec[recordLen] = pivot[recordLen] = '\0';
        outfile.getline(pivot,recordLen+1);
        for (lastSmall = low, i = low+1; i <= high; i++) {
            outfile.seekg(pointers[i]*recordLen,ios::beg);
            outfile.getline(rec,recordLen+1);
            if (strcmp(rec,pivot) < 0) {
                lastSmall++;
                Swap(pointers[lastSmall],pointers[i]);
            }
        }
        Swap(pointers[low],pointers[lastSmall]);
        pivotLoc = lastSmall;
}


void
File::QSort(int low, int high)
{   int pivotLoc;

    if (low < high) {
        Partition(low, high, pivotLoc);
        QSort(low, pivotLoc-1);
        QSort(pivotLoc+1, high);
    }
}


void
File::SortFile()
{
    QSort(1,pointers[0]);    // pointers[0] contains the # of elements;
    rec[recordLen] = '\0';   // put data from outfile in sorted order
    for (i = 1; i <= pointers[0]; i++) {              // in file sorted;
        outfile.seekg(pointers[i]*recordLen,ios::beg);
        outfile.getline(rec,recordLen+1);
        sorted << rec << setw(strlen(rec)-recordLen);
    }
}
```

Figure 10.16: **Implementation of hashing using buckets.**   **continued**

```
// data from overflow file and outfile are all stored in outfile and
// prepared for external sort by loading positions of the data to an array;

void
File::CombineFiles()
{
    counter = bucketSize*tableSize;
    outfile.seekg(0,ios::end);
    overflow.seekg(0,ios::beg);
    rec[recordLen] = '\0';
    while (overflow.getline(rec,recordLen+1)) { // transfer from
        if (rec[0] != delMarker) {         // overflow to outfile only
            counter++;                     // valid (not deleted) items;
            outfile << rec << setw(strlen(rec)-recordLen);
        }
    }
    outfile.seekg(0,ios::beg);             // load to array pointers positions
    arrCnt = 1;                            // of valid data stored in output file;
    for (i = 0; i < counter; i++) {
        outfile.seekg(i*recordLen,ios::beg);
        outfile.getline(rec,recordLen+1);
        if (rec[0] != empty && rec[0] != delMarker)
            pointers[arrCnt++] = i;
    }
    pointers[0] = --arrCnt; // store the number of data in position 0;
}

void
File::ProcessFile(ifstream& fIn)
{
    outfile.open("outfile",ios::in|ios::out);
    sorted.open("sorted",ios::in|ios::out);
    overflow.open("overflow",ios::in|ios::out);
    for (i = 1; i <= tableSize*bucketSize*recordLen; i++) // initialize
        outfile << empty;                                 // outfile;
    line[recordLen] = '\0';
    while (fIn.getline(line,recordLen+1)) // load infile to outfile;
        Insertion();
    while (strcmp(command,"exit")) {
```

Figure 10.16: **Implementation of hashing using buckets.** **continued**

```
            cout << "Enter command (insert, delete, or exit): ";
            cin.getline(command,strLen+1);
            if (!strcmp(command,"insert"))
                Insert();
            else if (!strcmp(command,"delete"))
                Delete();
            else if (strcmp(command,"exit"))
                cout << "Wrong command entered, please retry.\n";
        }
        CombineFiles();
        SortFile();
        outfile.close();
        sorted.close();
        overflow.close();
}

main(int argc, char* argv[])
{   char fileName[30];
    File fClass;

    if (argc != 2) {
        cout << "Enter a file name: ";
        cin.getline(fileName,30);
    }
    else strcpy(fileName,argv[1]);
    ifstream fIn(fileName);
    if (fIn.fail()) {
        cerr << "Cannot open " << fileName << endl;
        return 1;
    }
    fClass.ProcessFile(fIn);
    fIn.close();
    return 0;
}
```

Figure 10.16: **Implementation of hashing using buckets.**

■ 10.7 EXERCISES

1. What is the minimum number of keys which are hashed to their home positions using the linear probing technique? Show an example using a 5-cell array.

2. Consider the following hashing algorithm (Bell, Kaman 1970). Let Q and R be the quotient and remainder obtained by dividing K by $TSize$, and the probing sequence be created by the following recurrence formula:

$$h_i(K) = \begin{cases} R & \text{if } i = 0, \\ h_{i-1}(K) + Q \bmod Tsize & \text{otherwise.} \end{cases}$$

What is the desirable value of $TSize$? What condition should be imposed on Q?

3. Is there any advantage to using binary search trees instead of linked lists in the separate chaining method?

4. In Cichelli's method for constructing the minimal hash function, why are all words first ordered according to the occurrence of the first and the last letters? The subsequent searching algorithm does not make any reference to this order.

5. Trace the execution of the searching algorithm used in Cichelli's technique with $Max = 3$. (See the illustration of such a trace for $Max = 4$ in Figure 10.11.)

6. In which case does Cichelli's method not guarantee to generate a minimal perfect hash function?

7. Apply the FHCD algorithm to the nine Muses with $r = n/2 = 4$ and then with $r = 2$. What is the impact of the value of r on the execution of this algorithm?

8. Strictly speaking, the hash function used in extendible hashing also dynamically changes. In what sense is this true?

9. Consider an implementation of extendible hashing that allows buckets to be pointed to by only one pointer. The directory contains null pointers so that all pointers in the directory are unique except the null pointers. What keys are stored in the buckets? What are the advantages and disadvantages of this implementation?

10. How would the directory used in extendible hashing be updated after splitting if the last $depth$ bits of $h(K)$ are considered an index to the directory, not the first $depth$ bits?

11. List the similarities and differences between extendible hashing and B^+-trees.

12. What is the impact of the uniform distribution of a hash function over the buckets in extendible hashing on the frequency of splitting?

13. What impact does a decision that an overflow area not be used have on the performance of linear hashing? Indicate possible changes in the algorithm and in the time/space performance.

14. Outline an algorithm to delete a key from a table when the linear hashing method is used for inserting keys.

15. The function `Hash()` applied in the case study uses the exclusive or (xor) operation to fold all the characters into a string. Would it be a good idea to replace it by bitwise and or bitwise or?

■ 10.8 PROGRAMMING ASSIGNMENTS

1. As discussed in this chapter, the linear probing technique used for collision resolution has a rapidly deteriorating performance if a relatively small percentage of the cells are available. This problem can be solved using another technique for resolving collisions, but also by finding a better hash function, ideally, a perfect hash function. Write a program that evaluates the efficiency of various hashing functions combined with the linear probing method. Have your program write a table similar to the one in Figure 10.4 which gives the averages for successful and unsuccessful trials of locating items in the table. Use functions for operating on strings and a large text file whose words will be hashed to the table. Here are some examples of such functions (all values are divided modulo *TSize*):

   (a) FirstLetter(s) + SecondLetter(s) + · · · + LastLetter(s)

   (b) FirstLetter(s) + LastLetter(s) + length(s) (R. Cichelli);

   (c) `for (i = 1, index = 0; i < strlen(s); i++)`
   `    index = (26 * index + s[i] - ' ');` (M.V. Ramakrishna)

2. Write a program which inserts records into a file, and retrieves and deletes them using either extendible hashing or the linear hashing technique.

3. Extend the program presented in the case study by creating a linked list of overflowing records associated with each bucket of the intermediate file **unsorted**. Note that if a bucket has no empty cells, the search continues in the overflow area. In the extreme case, it may mean that the bucket holds only deleted items and new items are inserted in the overflow area. Therefore, it may be advantageous to have a purging function that, after a certain number of deletions, is automatically invoked. This function would transfer items from the overflow area to the main file which are hashed to buckets with deleted items. Write such a function.

BIBLIOGRAPHY

[1] Bell, James R. and Kaman, Charles H., "The Linear Quotient Hash Code," *Communications of the ACM* 13 (1970), 675–677.

[2] Cichelli, Richard J., "Minimal Perfect Hash Function Made Simple," *Communications of the ACM* 23 (1980), 17–19.

[3] Enbody, R.J. and Dy, H.C., "Dynamic Hashing Schemes," *Computing Surveys* 20 (1988), 85–113.

[4] Fagin, Ronald, Nievergelt, Jurg, Pippenger, Nicholas, and Strong, H. Raymond, "Extendible Hashing — A Fast Access Method for Dynamic Files," *ACM Transactions on Database Systems* 4 (1979), 315–344.

[5] Fox, Edward A., Heath, Lenwood S., Chen, Qi F., and Daoud, Amjad M., "Practical Minimal Perfect Hash Functions for Large Databases," *Communications of the ACM* 35 (1992), 105–121.

[6] Haggard, G. and Karplus, K., "Finding Minimal Perfect Hash Functions," *SIGCSE Bulletin* 18 (1986), no. 1, 191–193.

[7] Knott, G.D., "Expandable Open Addressing Hash Table Storage and Retrieval," *Proceedings of the ACM SIGFIDET Workshop on Data Description, Access, and Control*, 1971, 186–206.

[8] Knuth, Donald, *The Art of Computer Programming*, Vol. 3, Reading, MA: Addison-Wesley, 1973.

[9] Larson, Per A., "Dynamic Hashing," *BIT* 18 (1978), 184–201.

[10] Larson, Per A., "Dynamic Hash Tables," *Communications of the ACM* 31 (1988), 446–457.

[11] Lewis, Ted G. and Cook, Curtis R.," Hashing for Dynamic and Static Internal Tables," *IEEE Computer*, October 1986, 45–56.

[12] Litwin, Witold, "Virtual Hashing: A Dynamically Changing Hashing," *Proceedings of the Fourth Conference of Very Large Databases*, 1978, 517–523.

[13] Litwin, Witold, "Linear Hashing: A New Tool for File and Table Addressing," *Proceedings of the Sixth Conference of Very Large Databases*, 1980, 212–223.

[14] Lomet, David B., "Bounded Index Exponential Hashing," *ACM Transactions on Database Systems* 8 (1983), 136–165.

[15] Lum, V.Y., Yuen, P.S.T., and Dood, M., "Key-to-Address Transformation Techniques: A Fundamental Performance Study on Large Existing Formatted Files," *Communications of the ACM* 14 (1971), 228–239.

[16] Morris, Robert, "Scatter Storage Techniques," *Communications of the ACM* 11 (1968), 38–44.

[17] Mullin, James K., "Tightly Controlled Linear Hashing Without Separate Overflow Storage," *BIT* 21 (1981), 390–400.

[18] Radke, Charles E., "The Use of the Quadratic Search Residue," *Communications of the ACM* 13 (1970), 103–105.

[19] Sebesta, Robert W. and Taylor, Mark A., "Fast Identification of Ada and Modula-2 Reserved Words," *Journal of Pascal, Ada, and Modula-2*, March/April 1986, 36–39.

[20] Tharp, Alan L., *File Organization and Processing*, New York: Wiley, 1988.

[21] Vitter, Jeffrey S. and Chen, Wen C., *Design and Analysis of Coalesced Hashing*, New York: Oxford University Press, 1987.

11

DATA COMPRESSION

Transfer of information is essential for the proper functioning of any structure on any level and any type of organization. The faster an exchange of information occurs, the smoother the structure functions. Improvement of the rate of transfer can be achieved by improving the medium through which data are transferred, or by changing the data themselves so that the same information can be transmitted within a shorter time interval.

Information can be represented in a form which exhibits some redundancy. For example, in a database, it is enough to say about a person that he is "M" or she is "F," instead of spelling out the whole words, "male" and "female," or to use 1 and 2 to represent the same information. The number one hundred twenty eight can be stored as 80 (hexadecimal), 128, 1000000 (binary), CXXVIII, $\rho\kappa\eta$ (the Greek language used letters as digits), or | | | ... | (128 bars). If numbers are stored as the sequences of digits representing them, then 80 is the shortest form. Numbers are represented in binary form in computers.

■ 11.1 CONDITIONS FOR DATA COMPRESSION

When transferring information, the choice of the data representation determines how fast the transfer will be performed. A judicious choice can improve the throughput of a transmission channel without changing the channel itself. There are many different methods of *data compression* (or *compaction*) that reduce the size of the representation without affecting the information itself.

Assume that there are n different symbols used to code messages. For a binary code, $n = 2$; for Morse code, $n = 3$: the dot, the dash, and the blank separating the sequences of dots and dashes that represent letters. Assume also that all symbols m_i forming a set M have been independently chosen and are known to have probabilities of occurrence $P(m_i)$, and the symbols are coded with strings of 0s and 1s. Then $P(m_1) + \cdots + P(m_n) = 1$. The information content of the set M, called the *entropy* of the source M, is defined by

$$L_{ave} = P(m_1)L(m_1) + \cdots + P(m_n)L(m_n) \tag{11.1}$$

where $L(m_i) = -\lg(P(m_i))$, which is the minimum length of code for symbol m_i. Claude E. Shannon established in 1948 that Equation 11.1 gives the best possible average length of a code when the symbols constituting the codes and the frequencies of their use are known. No data compression algorithm can be better than L_{ave}, and the closer it is to this number, the better is its compression rate.

For example, if there are three symbols $m_1, m_2,$ and m_3 with the probabilities .25, .25, and .5, respectively, then the lengths of the codes assigned to them are:

$$-\lg(P(m_1)) = -\lg(P(m_2)) = -\lg(.25) = \lg\left(\frac{1}{.25}\right) = \lg(4) = 2, \text{ and}$$

$$-\lg(P(m_3)) = \lg(2) = 1,$$

and the average length of a code is

$$L_{ave} = P(m_1) * 2 + P(m_2) * 2 + P(m_3) * 1 = 1.5.$$

Various data compression techniques attempt to minimize the average code length by devising an optimal code that depends on the probability P with which a symbol is being used. If a symbol is issued infrequently, it can be assigned a code of many symbols. For frequently issued symbols, very short encodings are more to the point.

Some restrictions need to be imposed on the prospective codes:

1. Each code corresponds to exactly one symbol.
2. Decoding should not require any lookahead; after reading each symbol, it should be possible to determine whether the end of a string encoding a symbol of the original message has been reached. A code meeting this requirement is called a code with the *prefix property*, and it means that no code is a prefix of another code. Therefore, no special punctuation is required to separate two codes in a coded message.

The second requirement can be illustrated by three different encodings of three symbols as given in the following table:

Symbol	Code₁	Code₂	Code₃
A	1	1	11
B	2	22	12
C	12	12	21

The first code does not allow us to make a distinction between AB and C, since both are coded as 12. The second code does not have this ambiguity, but it requires performing a lookahead, as in 1222: the first 1 can be decoded as A. The following 2 may indicate that A was improperly chosen, and 12 should have been decoded as C. It may be that A is a proper choice, if the third symbol is 2. Since 2 is found, AC is chosen as the tentatively decoded string, but the fourth symbol is another 2. Hence the first turn was wrong, and A has been ill-chosen. The proper decoding is CB. All these problems arise, since both $code_1$ and $code_2$ violate the prefix property. Only $code_3$ can be unambiguously decoded as read.

For an optimal code, two more stipulations are specified.

3. The length of the code for a given symbol should not exceed the length of the code of a less probable symbol, that is, if $P(m_i) \leq P(m_j)$ then $L(m_i) \geq L(m_j)$ for $1 \leq i, j \leq n$.

4. In an optimal encoding system, there should not be any unused codes either as stand-alone encodings or as prefixes for longer codes, since this would mean that longer codes were created unnecessarily. For example, the sequence of codes 01, 000, 001, 100, 101 for a certain set of five symbols is not optimal, since the code 11 is not used anywhere; this encoding can be turned into an optimal sequence 01, 10, 11, 000, 001.

In the following sections, several data compression methods will be presented. To compare the efficiency of these methods when applied to the same data, the same measure will be used. This measure is the *compression rate* (also called the *fraction of data reduction*) and it is defined as the ratio

$$\frac{\text{length(input)} - \text{length(output)}}{\text{length(input)}} \tag{11.2}$$

and is expressed as a percentage, indicating the amount of redundancy removed from the input.

■ 11.2 HUFFMAN CODING

The construction of an optimal code was developed by David Huffman, who utilized a tree structure in this construction: a binary tree for a binary code. The algorithm is surprisingly simple and can be summarized as follows:

```
Huffman()
        for each symbol create a tree with a single root node and order all trees
            according to the probability of symbol occurrence;
        while more than one tree is left
            take the two trees t₁, t₂ with the lowest frequencies f₁, f₂ (f₁ ≤ f₂)
                and create a tree with t₁ and t₂ as its children and with
                the frequency in the new root equal to f₁ + f₂;
        associate 0 with each left branch and 1 with each right branch;
        create a unique code for each symbol by traversing the tree from the root
            to the leaf containing the frequency corresponding to this
            symbol and by putting all encountered 0s and 1s together;
```

The resulting tree has a probability of 1 in its root.

Huffman himself saw the structure resulting from the application of his algorithm as a net of tributary rivers eventually flowing into a large river. He thought associating 1s and 0s with branches was analogous to "the placing of signs by a water-borne insect at each of these junctions as he journeys downstream" with right turn posts (marked with a 1) and left turn posts (marked with a 0), which allow this insect to return back to the starting point.

It should be noted that the algorithm is not deterministic in the sense of producing a unique tree because for trees with equal frequencies in the roots, the algorithm does not prescribe their positions with respect to each other either at the beginning or during execution. If t_1 with frequency f_1 is in the sequence of trees and the new tree t_2 is created with $f_2 = f_1$, should t_2 be positioned to the left of t_1, or to the right? Also, if there are three trees t_1, t_2, and t_3 with the same lowest frequency in the entire sequence, which two trees should be chosen to create a new tree? There are three possibilities for choosing two trees. As a result, different trees can be obtained depending on where the trees with equal frequencies are placed in the sequence with respect to each other. Regardless of the shape of the tree, the average length of code remains the same.

To assess the compression efficiency of the Huffman algorithm, a definition of the *weighted path length* will be used, which is the same as Equation 11.1 except that $L(m_i)$ is interpreted as the number of 0s and 1s in the code assigned to symbol m_i by this algorithm.

Figure 11.1 contains an example for the five letters A, B, C, D, and E with frequencies .39, .21, .19, .12, and .09, respectively. The trees in Figures 11.1a and 11.1b are different in the way in which the two nodes containing a frequency of .21 have been chosen to be combined with tree .19 to create a tree of .40. Regardless of the choice, the lengths of the codes associated with the five letters A through E are the same, namely, 2, 2, 2, 3, and 3, respectively. However, the codes assigned to them are slightly different, as shown in Figures 11.1c and 11.1d, which present abbreviated (and more commonly used) versions of the way the trees in Figures 11.1a and 11.1b were created. The average length for the latter two trees is

$$L_{\text{Huf}} = .39 * 2 + .21 * 2 + .19 * 2 + .12 * 3 + .09 * 3 = 2.21,$$

which is very close to 2.09 (only 5% off), the average length computed according to the formula (11.1):

$$L_{\text{ave}} = .39 * 1.238 + .21 * 2.252 + .19 * 2.396 + .12 * 3.059 + .09 * 3.474 = 2.09.$$

Corresponding letters in Figures 11.1a and 11.1b have been assigned codes of the same length. Obviously, the average length for both trees is the same. But each way of building a Huffman tree, starting from the same data, should result in the same average length, regardless of the shape of the tree. Figure 11.2 shows two Huffman trees for the letters P, Q, R, S, and T with the frequencies .1, .1, .1, .2, and .5, respectively. Depending on how the lowest frequencies are chosen, different codes are assigned to these letters with different lengths, at least for some of them. However, the average length remains the same and is equal to 2.0.

The Huffman algorithm can be implemented in a variety of ways, at least as many as the number of ways a priority queue can be implemented. The priority queue is the natural data structure in the context of the Huffman algorithm since it requires removing the two smallest frequencies, and inserting the new frequency in the proper position.

One way to implement this algorithm is to use a singly-linked list of pointers to trees, which reflects closely what Figure 11.1a illustrates. The linked list is initially ordered

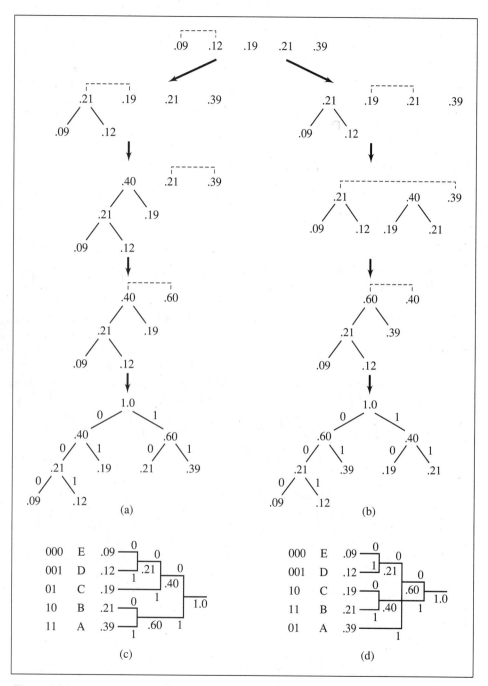

Figure 11.1: **Two Huffman trees created for five letters A, B, C, D, and E with frequencies .39, .21, .19, .12, and .09.**

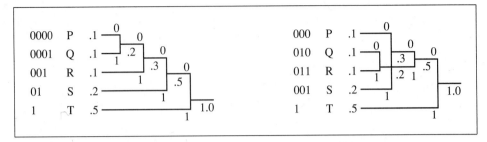

Figure 11.2: **Two Huffman trees generated for letters P, Q, R, S, and T with frequencies .1, .1, .1, .2, and .5.**

according to the frequencies stored in the trees, all of them consisting of just a root. Then, repeatedly, the two trees with the smallest frequencies are chosen; the tree with the smaller frequency is replaced by a newly created tree, and the node with the pointer to the tree with higher frequency is removed from the linked list. From trees having the same frequency in their roots, the first tree encountered is chosen.

In another implementation, all frequency nodes are first ordered, and that order is maintained throughout the operation. From such an ordered list, the first two trees are always removed to create a new tree from them, which is inserted close to the end of the list. To that end, a doubly linked list of pointers to trees with an immediate access to the beginning and to the end of this list can be used. Figure 11.3 contains a trace of the execution of this algorithm for the letters A, B, C, D, and E with the same frequencies as in Figure 11.1. Codes assigned to these letters are also indicated in Figure 11.3. Note that they are different from the codes in Figure 11.1, although their lengths are the same. Unlike the previous algorithm, this implementation creates a binary search tree.

The two preceding algorithms built Huffman trees bottom-up by starting with a sequence of trees and collapsing them together to a gradually smaller number of trees and eventually, to one tree. However, this tree can be built top-down, starting from the highest frequency. But only the frequencies to be placed in the leaves are known. The highest frequency, to be put in the root, is known if lower frequencies, in root's children, have been determined; the latter are known if still lower frequencies have been computed, and so on. Therefore, creating nonterminal nodes has to be deferred until the frequencies to be stored in them are found. It is very convenient to use the following recursive algorithm to implement a Huffman tree:

```
CreateHuffmanTree(freq)
```
declare the frequencies $f_1, f_2,$ *and the Huffman tree* **Htree;**
if *only two frequencies are left in* **freq**
    return *a tree with* f_1, f_2 *in the leaves and* $f_1 + f_2$ *in the root;*
else *remove the two smallest frequencies from* **Freq** *and assign them to* f_1 *and* f_2;
    insert $f_1 + f_2$ *to* **freq;**
    Htree = CreateHuffmanTree(freq);
    in **Htree** *make the leaf with* $f_1 + f_2$ *the parent of two leaves with* f_1 *and* f_2;
    return Htree;

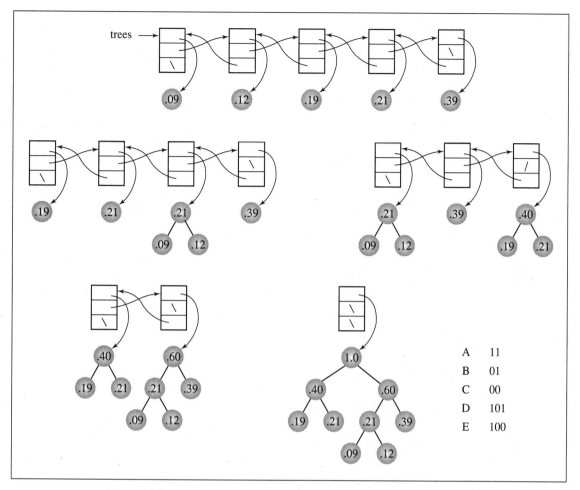

Figure 11.3: **Using a doubly linked list to create the Huffman tree for the letters from Figure 11.1.**

Figure 11.4 contains a summary of the trace of the execution of this algorithm for the letters A, B, C, D, and E with the frequencies as shown in Figure 11.1. Indentation indicates consecutive calls to **CreateHuffmanTree()**.

One implementation of a priority queue is a min heap which can also be used to implement this algorithm. In this heap, each nonterminal node has a smaller frequency than the frequencies in its children, and because the smallest frequency is in the root, that one is simple to remove. But after it is removed, the root is empty. Therefore, the largest element is put in the root and the heap property is restored. Then the second element can be removed from the root, and replaced with a new element which represents the sum of frequency of the root and the frequency just removed.

Afterwards, the heap property has to be restored again. After one such sequence of operations, the heap has one less node: two frequencies from the previous heap have been removed and a new one has been added. But it is not enough to create the Huffman tree: the new frequency is a parent of the frequencies just removed, and this information must

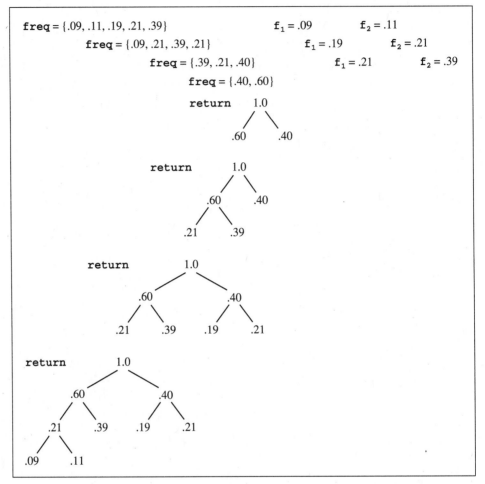

Figure 11.4: **Top-down construction of a Huffman tree using recursive implementation.**

be retained. To that end, three arrays can be used: *indexes* containing the indexes of the original frequencies and the frequencies created during the process of creating the Huffman tree; *frequencies*, an array of the original and newly created frequencies; and *parents*, an array of indexes indicating the positions of the parents of the elements stored in *frequencies*. A positive number in *parents* indicates the left child and a negative number indicates the right child. Codes are created by accumulating 0s and 1s when going from leaves to the root using the array *parents*, which functions as an array of pointers. It is important to note that in this particular implementation frequencies are sorted indirectly: the heap is actually made up of indexes to frequencies, and all exchanges take place in *indexes*.

Figure 11.5 illustrates an example of using a heap to implement the Huffman algorithm. The heaps in steps (a), (e), (i), and (m) in Figure 11.5 are ready for processing. First, the highest frequency is put in the root, as in steps (b), (f), (j), and (n) of Figure 11.5. Next, the heap is restored (steps (c), (g), (k), and (o) in the figure) and the root frequency is set to the sum of the two smallest frequencies (steps (d), (h), (l), and (p) in Figure 11.5). Processing is complete when there is only one node in the heap.

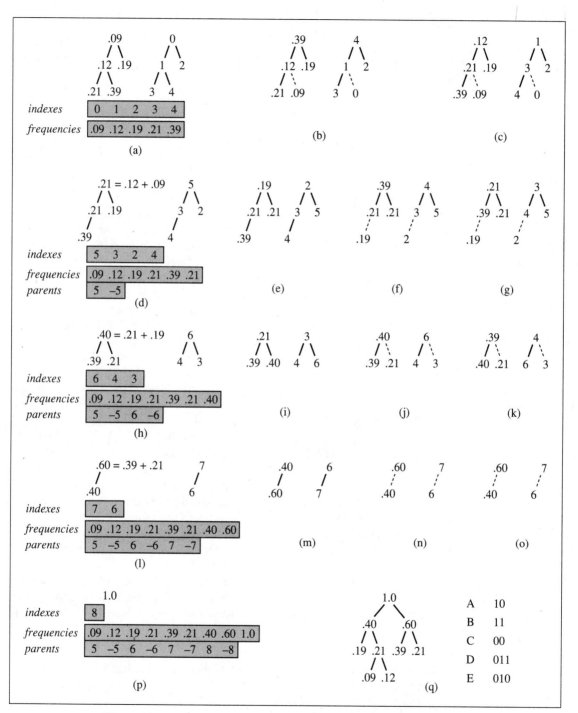

Figure 11.5: **Huffman algorithm implemented with a heap.**

Using the Huffman tree, a table can be constructed which gives the equivalents for each symbol in terms of 1s and 0s encountered along the path leading to each of the leaves of the tree. For our example, the tree from Figure 11.3 will be used, and the resulting table is:

A	11
B	01
C	00
D	101
E	100

The coding process transmits coded equivalents of the symbols to be sent. For example, instead of sending ABAAD, the sequence 11011111101 is dispatched with the average number of bits per one letter equal to $11/5 = 2.2$, almost the same as 2.09, the value specified by the formula for L_{ave}. To decode this message, the conversion table has to be known to the message receiver. Using this table, a Huffman tree can be constructed with the same paths as the tree used for coding, but its leaves would (for the sake of efficiency) store the symbols instead of their frequencies. In this way, upon reaching a leaf, the symbol can be retrieved directly from it. Using this tree, each symbol can be decoded uniquely. For example, if 1001101 is received, then we try to reach a leaf of the tree using the path indicated by leading 1s and 0s. 1 takes us to the right, 0 to the left and another 0 again to the left, whereby we end up in a leaf containing E. After reaching this leaf, decoding continues by starting from the root of the tree and trying to reach a leaf using the remaining 0s and 1s. Since 100 has been processed, 1101 has to be decoded. Now, 1 takes us to the right and another 1 again to the right, which is a leaf with A. We start again from the root, and the sequence 01 is decoded as B. The entire message is now decoded as EAB.

At this point, a question can be asked: Why send 11011111101 instead of ABAAD? This is supposed to be data compression, but the coded message is twice as long as the original. Where is the advantage? Note precisely the way in which messages are sent. A, B, C, D, and E are single letters, and letters, being characters, require one byte (eight bits) to be sent, using the extended ASCII code. Therefore, the message ABAAD requires five bytes (40 bits). On the other hand, 0s and 1s in the coded version can be sent as single bits. Therefore, if 11011111101 is regarded not as a sequence of the characters "0" and "1," but as a sequence of bits, then only 11 bits are needed to send the message, one-fourth of what is required to send the message in its original form, ABAAD.

This example raises one problem: both the encoder and the decoder have to use the same coding, the same Huffman tree. Otherwise, the decoding will be unsuccessful. How can the encoder let the decoder know which particular code has been used? There are at least two possibilities:

1. Both the encoder and decoder agree beforehand on a particular Huffman tree and both use it for sending any message.
2. The encoder constructs the Huffman tree afresh every time a new message is sent and sends the conversion table along with the message. The decoder either uses the table to decode the message or reconstructs the corresponding Huffman tree and then performs the translation.

The second strategy is more versatile, but its advantages are visible only when large files are encoded and decoded. For our simple example, ABAAD, sending both the table of codes and the coded message 11011111101, is hardly perceived as data compression. However, if a file contains a message of 10,000 characters using the characters A through E, then the space saved is significant. Using the probabilities indicated above for these letters, we project that there are approximately 3900 As, 2100 Bs, 1900 Cs, 1200 Ds, and 900 Es. Hence, the number of bits needed to code this file is

$$3900 * 2 + 2100 * 2 + 1900 * 2 + 1200 * 3 + 900 * 3 = 22,100 \text{ bits} = 2,762.5 \text{ bytes},$$

which is approximately one-fourth of the 10,000 bytes required for sending the original file. Even if the conversion table is added to the file, this proportion is only minimally affected.

However, even with this approach there may be some room for improvement. As indicated, an ideal compression algorithm should give the same average code length as computed from Equation 11.1. The symbols from Figure 11.1 have been assigned codes whose average length is 2.21, approximately 5% worse than the ideal 2.09. Sometimes, however, the difference is larger. Consider, for example, three symbols X, Y, and Z with frequencies .1, .1, and .8. Figure 11.6a shows a Huffman tree for these symbols, with codes

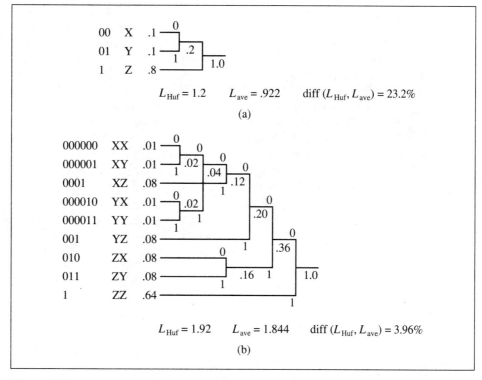

Figure 11.6: **Improving the average length of the code by applying the Huffman algorithm to pairs of letters (b) instead of single letters (a).**

assigned to them. The average length, according to this tree, is

$$L_{\text{Huf}} = 2 * .1 + 2 * .1 + 1 * .8 = 1.2,$$

and the best expected average, L_{ave}, is .922. Therefore, there is a possibility we can improve the Huffman coding by approximately 23.2%, ignoring the fact that at this point, a full 23.2% improvement is not possible because the average is below 1. How is this possible? As already stated, all Huffman trees result in the same average weighted path length. Therefore, no improvement can be expected if only the symbols X, Y, and Z are used to construct this tree.

On the other hand, if all possible pairs of symbols are used for building a Huffman tree, the data rate can be reduced. Figure 11.6b illustrates this procedure. Out of three symbols X, Y, and Z, nine pairs are created whose frequencies are computed by multiplying the frequencies of both symbols. For example, since the frequency for both X and Y is .1, the frequency of pair XY is .01 = .1 * .1. The average L_{Huf} is 1.92 and the expected average L_{ave} is 1.84 (twice the previous L_{ave}), with the difference between these averages being 4%. This represents a 19.2% improvement at the cost of including a larger conversion table (nine entries instead of three) as part of the message to be sent. If the message is large and the number of symbols used in the message is relatively small, then the increase in the size of the table is insignificant. However, for a large number of symbols, the size of the table may be much too large to notice any improvement. For 26 English letters the number of pairs is 676 which is considered relatively small. But if all printable characters have to be distinguished in an English text, from the blank character (ASCII code 32), to the tilde (ASCII code 126), plus the carriage return character, then there are $(126 - 32 + 1) + 1 = 96$ characters and 9216 pairs of characters. Many of these pairs are not likely to occur at all (e.g., XQ, or KZ), but even if 50% of them are found, the resulting table containing these pairs along with codes associated with them may be too large to be useful.

Using pairs of symbols is still a good idea, even if the number of symbols is large. For example, a Huffman tree can be constructed for all symbols and for all pairs of symbols that occur at least five times. The efficiency of the variations of Huffman encoding can be measured by comparing the size of compressed files. Experiments were performed on an English text, PL/1 program file, and a digitized photographic image (Rubin 1976). When only single characters were used, the compression rates were approximately 40%, 60%, and 50%, respectively. When single characters were used along with the 100 most frequent groups (not only two characters long), the compression rates were 49%, 73%, and 52%. When the 512 most frequent groups were used, the compression rates were around 55%, 71%, and 62%.

11.2.1 Adaptive Huffman Coding

The foregoing discussion assumed that the frequencies of messages are known in advance. A natural question is: How do we know them? Our answer is: From experience. There are a number of approaches for gaining this experience.

One solution computes the number of occurrences of each symbol expected in messages in some fairly large sample of texts of, say, 10 million characters. For messages in natural languages such as English, such samples may include some literary works, newspaper articles, and a portion of an encyclopedia. After each character's frequency has been determined, a conversion table can be constructed for use by both the sending and receiving ends of the data transfer. This eliminates the need to include such a table every time a file is transmitted.

However, this method may not be useful for sending some specialized files, even if written in English. A computer science paper includes a much higher percentage of digits and parentheses, especially if it includes extensive illustrations in Lisp or C++ code, than a paper on the prose of Jane Austen. In such circumstances, it is more judicious to use the text to be sent to determine the needed frequencies, which also requires enclosing the table as overhead in the file being sent. A preliminary pass through this file is required before an actual conversion table can be constructed. However, the file to be preprocessed may be very large, and the preprocessing slows down the entire transmission process. Secondly, the file to be sent may not be known in its entirety when it is being sent, and yet compression is necessary: for example, when a text is being typed and sent line by line, then there is no way to know the contents of the whole file at the time of sending. In such a situation, an adaptive compression is a viable solution.

One approach in adaptive coding uses a preliminary set of frequencies based on a fragment of text to be transmitted or on an educated guess. Then, a conversion table is built which contains an additional counter field, and the table is adjusted during data transmission. Figure 11.7 contains an example.

1. At the beginning, the letters A through E are assigned the bit strings indicated in the top row of the table. If the first letter encountered in the text to be encoded is B, then the corresponding bit string, 01, is transmitted, and the counter for B is

11	01	00	101	100	Encountered	Transmitted
A	B	C	D	E		
0	0	0	0	0		
					B	01
B	A	C	D	E		
1	0	0	0	0		
					B	11
B	A	C	D	E		
2	0	0	0	0		
					D	101
B	D	A	C	E		
2	1	0	0	0		
					A	00
B	D	A	C	E		
2	1	1	0	0		
					A	00
B	A	D	C	E		
2	2	1	0	0		
					E	100
B	A	D	E	C		
2	2	1	1	0		
					B	11

Figure 11.7: **Execution of an adaptive algorithm.**

incremented. Then the letter B along with its counter is placed at the beginning of the table. Letter A is slid to the right, where it acquires a new code, 01. The new code for B is 11.

2. The second encountered character is also B, so bit string 11 is issued, the new code for B. The counter for B is incremented and because it has again the highest value among all counters, the position of B remains unchanged.

3. The third letter is D so 101 is sent. Then the counter for D is incremented, which gives D the second rank among all the letters in the table, and D is moved to the second position, with A and C moved to the right.

4. Now A is encountered so 00 is transmitted, but after incrementing A's counter, A stays in the same position.

5. The letter A is found again, 00 is issued, but the increment of the counter causes the movement of A to the second position, where its new code is 01. Letter D is slid to A's place, and inherits the previous code of A, 00.

6. The sixth letter found is E, its code 100 is sent, and its counter becomes 1. E moves higher to the fourth position and C acquires the lowest rank.

In this approach, a table of frequencies is used at the beginning. However, adaptive Huffman coding does not have to use any frequencies. It can be truly adaptive by assuming nothing about the initial distribution of the symbols used in a given message. Such an adaptive Huffman coding was devised first by Robert G. Gallager and then improved by Donald Knuth and by Jeffrey S. Vitter.

In their approach, counters in the Huffman tree of symbols are used for each symbol and updated every time an input symbol is being coded. This leads to a restructuring of the tree so that the following *sibling property* is retained: if nodes are listed top-down and right-to-left, then the frequencies (counters) in this list are nonincreasing. This breadth-first, right-to-left traversal ascertains that the Huffman tree remains a Huffman tree after each update. All unused symbols are kept in one node with a frequency of zero, and each symbol encountered in the input has its own node in the tree. Initially the tree has just one 0-node with all the symbols. If an input symbol did not yet appear in the input, the 0-node is split in two, with the new 0-node containing all the elements except the newly encountered one and the node referring to this new element whose counter is set to one. Both nodes become children of the one parent whose counter is also set to one. If a symbol already has a node in the tree, its counter is incremented. However, such an increment may endanger the sibling property, so this property must be restored by exchanging the node N, which is violating this property, with the last node with the smaller frequency, if it is not N's parent. This node is found by going from N upward and from left to right. Then the counter increment is done for N's (possibly new) parent, which may also lead to tree transformation to restore the sibling property. This process is continued until the root is reached. In this way, the counters are updated on the *new* path from N to the root.

For each symbol the code that is issued is obtained by scanning the Huffman tree from the root to the node corresponding to this symbol *before* any transformation in the tree takes place.

There are two different types of codes transmitted during this process. If a symbol being coded has already appeared before, then the normal coding procedure is applied: the Huffman tree is scanned from the root to the node holding this symbol to determine its code. If a symbol appears for the first time, just sending the Huffman code of the 0-node does not suffice, since this node holds all the unused symbols. Therefore, along with the code which indicates the path to the 0-node, the code which indicates the position of the encountered symbol is sent. For the sake of simplicity, assume that it is simply the number of ones corresponding to this position followed by a zero. For example, when the character "c" is coded for the first time, its code, 001110, is a combination of the code for the 0-node, 00, and the code 1110 indicating that "c" can be found in the third position in the list of unused symbols associated with the 0-node. After a symbol is removed from the list in the 0-node, its place is taken by the last symbol of this list. This also indicates that the encoder and receiver have to agree on the alphabet being used and its ordering. A step-by-step example for the string "aafcccbd" is shown in Figure 11.8. Note in the figure that some

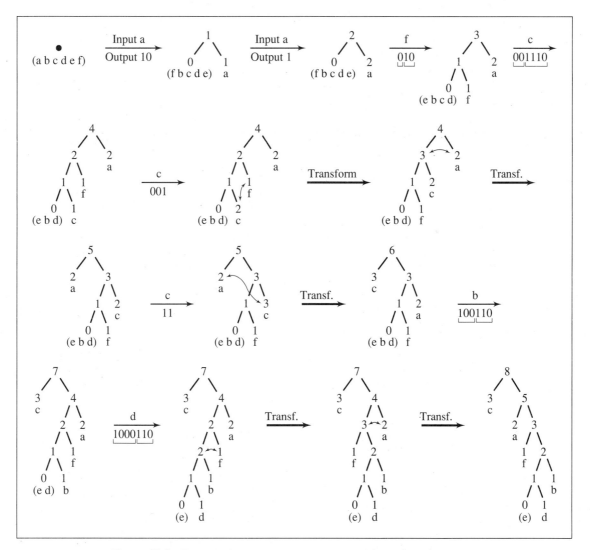

Figure 11.8: **Transmitting the message "aafcccbd" using an adaptive Huffman algorithm.**

codes have two parts underlined: one part is a position of the symbol being transmitted and the other part is the code of the 0-node.

Adaptive Huffman coding surpasses simple Huffman coding in two respects: it requires only one pass through the input, and it adds only an alphabet to the output. Both versions are relatively fast, and, more importantly, they can be applied to any kind of file, not only to text files. They can compress object or executable files equally well by using bytes as letters to be coded, although such files are already compressed: each byte represents two hexadecimal digits. Therefore, units of these files are half-bytes, not whole bytes. For the execution of the Huffman encoding it makes no difference, since processing the bytes of an executable file is comparable to processing pairs of characters, instead of single characters, in text files. The problem with executable files, however, is that they generally use larger character sets than source code files, and the distribution of these characters is more uniform than found in text files. Therefore, the Huffman trees are large, the codes are of similar length, and the output file is not much smaller than the original; it is compressed merely by 10–20%.

■ 11.3   SHANNON-FANO CODE

Another efficient method that generates an optimal code as n approaches infinity was developed by C. E. Shannon and R. M. Fano. The algorithm is as follows:

> *Order the set of symbols according to the frequency of occurrence;*
> `ShannonFano` (*sequence S*)
>   `if S` *has two elements*
>   *attach 0 to the code of one element and 1 to the code of another;*
>   `else if S` *has more than one element*
>   *divide S into two subsequences S$_1$, and S$_2$, with the minimal*
>   *difference between probabilities of each subsequence;*
>   *extend the code for each symbol in S$_1$ by attaching 0, and attaching*
>   *1 to each code for symbols in S$_2$;*
>   `ShannonFano (S`$_1$`);`
>   `ShannonFano (S`$_2$`);`

Figure 11.9 contains the same symbols as Figure 11.1. First, the sequence $S = (A, B, C, D, E)$ is divided into subsequences $S_1 = (C, D, E)$, and $S_2 = (A, B)$ since the dif-

E	.09	000
D	.12	001
C	.19	01
B	.21	10
A	.39	11

Figure 11.9: **Execution of Shannon-Fano algorithm applied to five letters A, B, C, D, and E with frequencies .39, .21, .19, .12, and .09.**

ference between $P(S_1) = P(C) + P(D) + P(E)$ and $P(S_2) = P(A) + P(B)$ is the smallest among all subsequences of S obtained by dividing S into two sequences. The next closest candidate is subsequences (A) and (B, C, D, E) with probabilities .39 and .61, but these subsequences are rejected since the difference, $.61 - .39$, is greater than $.6 - .4$. The code for each letter from S_1 starts with a zero, and the code for S_2 starts with a one. Next, the sequence S_1 is divided into $S_{11} = (D, E)$ and $S_{12} = (C)$ with probabilities .21 and .19. The codes for D and E are extended by attaching a zero to them, and the code for C by attaching one, so that the latter becomes 01. Since the sequence S_{11} has two elements, the code for one of them, E, is extended by adding another zero and the code for D is extended by adding a one. Sequence S_2 has also two elements and their codes are also appropriately extended. Figure 11.9 summarizes these steps.

The average length of codes generated by the Shannon-Fano method for the five letters A, B, C, D, and E with frequencies .39, .21, .19, .12, and .09 is

$$L_{SF} = .39 * 2 + .21 * 2 + .19 * 2 + .12 * 3 + .09 * 3 = 2.21,$$

which is the same as the average code length generated by the Huffman algorithm. Generally, however, this is not the case. The closer the probabilities are to negative powers of two, the more efficient the Shannon-Fano algorithm becomes; it can only give as good results as the Huffman algorithm, but will not surpass it.

Both the Huffman and Shannon-Fano algorithms are concerned with redundancy. Therefore, symbols with different probabilities are represented by variable-length codes as they assign shorter codes to more frequently used characters. This reduces the storage required for a coded message and reduces the time needed to transmit the message. A serious drawback of both algorithms is the requirement to know the frequencies before the coding begins, although adaptive Huffman code alleviates this problem. Also, the codes resulting from the application of both algorithms are very sensitive and require a flawless transmission of data, since the change of only one bit changes the message being transferred. An area of active research is the construction and analysis of self-correcting codes that accounts for possible distortion during transmission.

■ 11.4 RUN-LENGTH ENCODING

A *run* is defined as a sequence of identical characters. For example, the string $s = $ "aaabba" has three runs: a run of three "a"s, followed by a run of two "b"s and of one "a." The run-length encoding technique takes advantage of the presence of runs and represents them in an abbreviated, compressed form.

If runs are of the same characters, as in the string $s = $ "nnnn***r%%%%%%", then instead of transmitting this string, information about runs can be transferred. Each run is coded by the pair (n, ch), where ch is a character, and n the integer representing the number of consecutive characters ch in the run. The string s is coded as 4n3*1r7%. However, a problem arises if one of the characters being transferred is a digit, as in 11111111111544444 which is represented as 1111554 (for 11 1s, 1 5, and 5 4s). Therefore, for each run, instead of the number n, a character can be used whose ASCII value is n. For example, the run of 43 consecutive letters "c" is represented as +c ("+" has ASCII code 43), and the run of 49 1s would be coded as 11 ("1" has ASCII code 49).

This technique is only efficient when at least two-character runs are transmitted, because for one-character runs, the code is twice as long as the character. Therefore, the technique should be applied only to runs of at least two characters. This requires using a marker indicating that what is being transmitted is either run in an abbreviated form or a literal character. Three characters are needed to represent a run: a compression marker cm, a literal character ch, and a counter n, which make up a triple $\langle cm, ch, n \rangle$. The problem of choosing the compression marker is especially delicate, since it should not be confused with a literal character being transmitted. If a regular text file is transmitted, then the character '~'+1 can be chosen. If there is no restriction on the characters transmitted, then whenever the compression marker itself occurs in the input file, we transmit the compression markers twice. The decoder discards one such marker upon receiving two of them in a row retaining just one as a part of the data being received. For example, %% in a `printf` statement in C indicates to print just one percent sign, or \\ in a Common Lisp file indicates to print just one backslash. Since for each literal marker two of them must be sent, an infrequently used marker should be chosen. In addition, runs of markers are not sent in a compressed form.

Since compressing runs results in a sequence of three characters, this technique should be applied to runs of at least four characters. The maximum length of a run that can be represented by the triple $\langle cm, ch, n \rangle$ is 255 for 8-bit ASCII if the number n represents the number of characters in the run. But because only runs of four or more characters are encoded, n can represent the number of actual characters in the run minus 4. For example, if $n = 1$ then there are five characters in the run. In this case, the longest run representable by one triple has 259 characters.

The run-length encoding is only modestly efficient for text files in which only the blank character has a tendency to be repeated. In this case, a predecessor of this technique can be applied, *null suppression*, which compresses only runs of blanks, which eliminates the need to identify the character being compressed. As a result, pairs $\langle cm, n \rangle$ are used for runs of three or more blanks. This simple technique is used in the IBM 3780 BISYNC transmission protocol where throughput gain is between 30 and 50 percent.

Run-length encoding is very useful when applied to files which are almost guaranteed to have many runs of at least four characters. One example is relational databases. All records in the same relational database file have to be of equal length. Records (rows, tuples) are collections of fields, which may be — and most often are — longer than the information stored in them. Therefore, they have to be padded with some character. In dBaseIII+, padding is done with blanks; in Paradox, padding is done with zeros (nulls), thereby creating a large collection of runs whose only purpose is to fill up free space in each field of every record. A similar method of creating equal-length file records is applied in Quickbasic's random files.

Another candidate for compression using run-length encoding is facsimile images, which are composed of combinations of black and white pixels. For low resolution there are about 1.5 million pixels per page. Thus transmission of one page at 4800 bps requires 5 minutes. Clearly, some compression method is necessary.

A serious drawback of run-length encoding is that it relies entirely on the occurrences of runs. In particular, this method taken by itself is unable to recognize the high frequency of the occurrence of certain symbols which call for short codes. For example, AAAABBBB can be compressed, since it is composed of two runs, and ABABABAB cannot, although both messages are made up of the same letters. On the other hand, ABABABAB is compressed by Huffman encoding into the same number of codes as AAAABBBB, without taking into consideration the presence of runs. Therefore, it seems appropriate to combine both methods as this chapter's case study will.

■ 11.5 ZIV-LEMPEL CODE

The problem with some of the methods discussed thus far is that they require some knowledge about the data before encoding takes place. A "pure form" of the Huffman encoder has to know the frequencies of symbol occurrences before codes are assigned to the symbols. Some versions of the adaptive Huffman encoding can circumvent this limitation, not by relying on previous knowledge of the source characteristics, but by building this knowledge in the course of data transmission. Such a method is called a *universal coding scheme*, and Ziv-Lempel code is an example of a universal data compression code.

In Ziv-Lempel code, a buffer of symbols is maintained. The first l_1 positions hold the l_1 most recently encoded symbols from the input, and the remaining l_2 positions contain the l_2 symbols about to be encoded. In each iteration, starting from one of the first l_1 positions, the buffer is searched for a substring matching a prefix of a string located in the second portion of the buffer. If such a match is found, a code is transmitted; the code is a triple composed of the position in which the match was found, the length of match, and the first mismatching symbol. Then, the entire content of the buffer is shifted to the left by the length of match plus one. Some symbols are shifted out. Some new symbols from the input are shifted in. To initiate this process, the first l_1 positions are filled up with l_1 copies of the first symbol of the input.

As an example, consider the case when $l_1 = l_2 = 4$, and the input is the string "aababacbaacbaadaaa..." Positions in the buffer are indexed with the numbers 0–7. The initial situation is shown at the top of Figure 11.10. The first symbol of the input is "a," and positions 0 through 3 are filled up with "a"s. The first four symbols of the input, "aaba", are placed in the remaining positions. The longest prefix matching any substring which begins

Input	Buffer	Code Transmitted
aababacbaacbaadaa ...	aaaa	a
	↓	
aababacbaacbaadaa ...	aaaaaaba	22b
	↓	
abacbaacbaadaaa ...	aaababac	23c
	↓	
baacbaadaaa ...	abacbaac	12a
	↓	
cbaadaaa ...	cbaacbaa	03a
	↓	
daaa ...	cbaadaaa	30d
aaa ...	...	

Figure 11.10: **Encoding the string "aababacbaacbaadaaa ..."**
with Ziv-Lempel algorithm.

in any position between 0 and 3 is "aa." Therefore, the generated code is a triple $\langle 2, 2, b \rangle$, or simply 22b: the match starts in position two, it is two symbols long, and the symbol following this match is "b." Next, a left shift occurs, three "a"s are shifted out, and the string "bac" is shifted in. The longest match also starts in position two and is three symbols long, namely "aba," with "c" following it. The issued code is 23c. Figure 11.10 illustrates a few more steps; the arrows point to the beginning of matches.

The numbers l_1 and l_2 are chosen in this example so that only two bits are needed for each. Because each symbol requires one byte (eight bits), one code can be stored in 12 bits. Therefore, l_1 and l_2 should be powers of two, so that no binary number is unused. If l_1 is 5, then three bits are needed to code all possible positions 0 through 4, and the three bit combinations corresponding to the numbers 5, 6, and 7 are not used.

A more frequently applied version of Ziv-Lempel algorithm uses a table of codes created during data transmission. A simple algorithm for encoding can be presented as follows (Welch 1984):

```
ZLWcompress()
    enter all letters to the table;
    initialize string s to the first letter from input;
    while any input left
        read character c
        if s+c is in the table
            s = s+c;
        else output code(s);
            enter s+c to the table;
            s = c;
    output code(s);
```

String **s** is always at least one-character long. After reading a new character, the concatenation of string **s** and character **c** is checked in the table. A new character is read if the concatenation **s+c** is in the table. If it is not, the code for **s** is output, the concatenation **s+c** is stored in the table, and **s** is initialized to **c**. Figure 11.11 shows a trace of the execution of this procedure applied to the input "aababacbaacbaadaaa..." Figure 11.11a contains the generated output. The portions of the string for which codes already exist in the table are underlined. Figure 11.11b contains the table with the strings in full form and Figure 11.11c contains the strings in abbreviated form, represented by a number and a character.

A crucial component of the efficiency is the organization of the table. Clearly, for more realistic examples, hundreds and thousands of entries can be expected in this table, so that an efficient searching method has to be used. A second concern is the size of the table, which grows particularly when new long strings are entered in it. The problem of size is addressed by storing in the table codes for the prefix and the last characters of strings. For example, if "ba" is assigned the code number 7, then "baa" can be stored in the table as a number of its prefix, "ba," and the last character, "a," that is, as 7a (see Figure 11.11c). In this way, all table entries have the same length. The problem of searching is addressed by using a hash function.

For decoding, the same table is created by updating it for each incoming code except the first. For each code, a corresponding prefix and a character is retrieved from the table. Since the prefix is also a code (except for single characters), it requires another table

String:	a	a	b	a b	a	c	b a	a c	b a a	d	a a	a	...
Output Codes:	1	1	2	6	1	3	7	9	11	4	5		

(a)

Iteration	String	Code		Iteration	String	Code
	a	1			a	1
	b	2			b	2
	c	3			c	3
	d	4			d	4
1	aa	5		1	1a	5
2	ab	6		2	1b	6
3	ba	7		3	2a	7
4	aba	8		4	6a	8
5	ac	9		5	1c	9
6	cb	10		6	3b	10
7	baa	11		7	7a	11
8	acb	12		8	9b	12
9	baad	13		9	11d	13
10	da	14		10	4a	14
11	aaa	15		11	5a	15

(b)　　　　　　　　　　(c)

Figure 11.11: **Modified Ziv-Lempel algorithm applied to the string aababacbaacbaadaaa...**

lookup, as the entire string is decoded. This is clearly a recursive procedure which may be implemented with an explicit stack. This is necessary since the decoding process applied to prefixes yields a string in the reverse order. The decoding procedure can be summarized as follows:

```
ZLWdecompress()
```
enter all letters to the table;
read `priorcode` *and output one character corresponding to it;*
`while` *codes still left*
  read `code;`
  `if code` *not in the table* `//special case: c+s+c+s+c, also if s is null;`
    enter in table string(`priorcode`*) +* *firstchar(string(*`priorcode`*));*
    output string(`priorcode`*) +* *firstchar(string(*`priorcode`*));*
  `else` *enter in table string(*`priorcode`*) +* *firstchar(string(*`code`*));*
    output string(`code`*);*
  `priorcode = code;`

This relatively simple algorithm has to consider a special case, when a code being processed has no corresponding entry in the table. This situation arises when the string being decoded contains a substring "cScSc," where "c" is a single character, and "cS" is already in the table.

All of the discussed compression algorithms are widely used. UNIX has three compression programs: *pack* uses the Huffman algorithm, *compact* is based on the adaptive Huffman method, and *compress* uses the adaptive Ziv-Lempel coding (implemented by

Welch). According to the system manuals, *pack* compresses text files by 25–40%, *compact* by 40%, and *compress* by 40–50%. The rate of compression is better for Ziv-Lempel coding. It is also faster.

11.6 CASE STUDY: HUFFMAN METHOD WITH RUN-LENGTH ENCODING

As indicated in the discussion of run-length encoding, this method is suitable for files which are almost guaranteed to have many runs of at least four symbols; otherwise no compression is achieved. The Huffman algorithm, on the other hand, can be applied to files with only runs that are one to three symbols long. This method can be applied to single symbols, such as letters, but also to pairs of symbols, to triples, and to a collection of variable length sequences of symbols. Incorporating run-length encoding in the Huffman method works exceedingly well for files with many long runs and moderately well for files with a small number of runs and a large number of different symbols.

For files with no runs, this method is reduced to plain Huffman encoding. In this approach, a file to be compressed is scanned first to determine all runs, including one-, two- and three-symbols long. Runs composed of the same symbols but of different length would be treated as different "super-symbols" which are used to create a Huffman tree. For example, if the message to be compressed is AAABAACCAABA, then the super-symbols included in the Huffman tree are AAA, B, AA, CC, and A, and not symbols A, B, and C. In this way, the number of codes to be created grows from three for the symbols to five for the super-symbols. The conversion table becomes larger, but the codes assigned to the runs are much shorter than in straight run-length encoding. In the run-length encoding, this code is always three bytes long (24 bits). In the Huffman code it may be even one bit long.

First, an input file is scanned and all super-symbols are collected in the array **data[]** by the function **GarnerData()**, and sorted according to the frequency of occurrence. Figure 11.12a illustrates the positions of the data in the array. Next, the sorted data are stored in the output file to be used by the decoder to create the same Huffman tree that the encoder is about to create. **CreateHuffmanTree()** generates the tree of Huffman codes using information collected in **data[]**. To that end, a doubly linked list of single node trees is created first, similar to the list in Figure 11.3. Then, repeatedly, the two trees with the lowest frequencies are combined to create one tree, which eventually results in one Huffman tree, as in Figure 11.12b.

After the tree has been created, the positions of all nodes, in particular the leaves, can be determined whereby the codes of all symbols in the leaves can be generated. Each node in this tree has seven fields but only five of them are shown, just for leaves. The codes are stored as numbers which are represented as binary sequences of 0s and 1s. For example, the code for CC is 7, 111 in binary. However, these numbers are always the same length, and 7 is stored as three bits set to 1 preceded by 29 bits set to 0, $0 \dots 0111$. It is, therefore, unclear how many bits out of 32 are included in the sequence representing the code for a certain symbol. Is it 111, 0111, 00111, or some other sequence? The code field for single As is 0; is code for A 0, 00, 000, or some more 0s? To avoid ambiguity, the **codeLen** field stores the number of bits included in the code for a given symbol. Since **codeLen** for A is 2, and **code** is 0, then the code sequence representing A is 00.

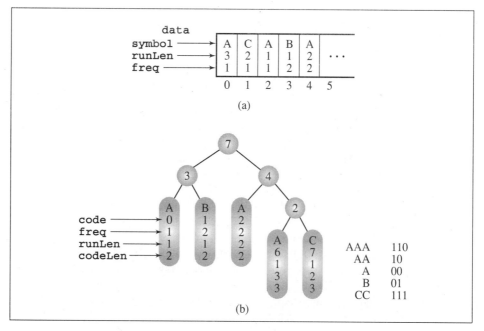

Figure 11.12: **(a) Contents of the array data after the message AAABAACCAABA has been processed. (b) Huffman tree generated from these data.**

After the Huffman tree is generated and the leaves are filled with relevant information, the process of coding information in the input file can be initiated. Because searching for particular symbols directly in the tree is too time-consuming, an array **chars[]** of linked lists corresponding to each ASCII symbol is created. The nodes of the linked lists are simply leaves of the tree linked through right pointers, and each list has as many nodes as the number of different run lengths of a given symbol in the input file. It gives immediate access to a particular linked list, but some linked lists may be long if there are many run lengths of a given symbol.

Next, the file is scanned for the second time to find for each super-symbol and its corresponding code in the Huffman tree, and to transmit it to the output file. As the sequences are retrieved from the tree, they are tightly packed into a four-byte numerical variable **pack**. The first encountered super-symbol in the input file is AAA with code 110 which is stored in **pack** so **pack** contains the sequence 0...0110. After B is retrieved from the file, its code, 01, is attached to the end of **pack**. As a result, the contents of **pack** have to be shifted to the left by two positions to make room for 01, and then 01 is stored in it using the bit-wise operation |. Now, **pack** contains the string 0..011001. After **pack** is filled up with codes, it is output as a sequence of four bytes to the output file.

Particular care has to be taken to put exactly 32 bytes in **pack**. When there are fewer available positions in **pack** than the number of bits in a code, only a portion of the code is put in **pack**. Then **pack** is output and the remaining portion of code is put in **pack** before any other symbol is decoded. For example, if **pack** currently contains 001 ... 10011, **pack** can take only two more bits. Since the code 1101 is four bits long, the contents of **pack** are shifted to the left by two positions, 1...1001100, and the first two bits of the code, 11, are put at the end of **pack** after which **pack**'s contents are 1...1001111. Next, **pack** is output as four bytes (characters), and the remaining two bits of the code, 01, are put into **pack**, which now contains 0...001.

Another problem is with the last codes. The encoder fills the output file with bytes (in this case, with chunks of four bytes), each containing eight bits. What happens if there are no symbols left, but there is still room in **pack**? The decoder has to know that some bits at the end of file should not be decoded. If they are, some spurious characters will be added to the decoded file. In this implementation, the problem is solved by transmitting the number of characters to be decoded at the beginning of the encoded file. The decoder decodes only this number of codes. Even if some bits are left in the coded file, they are not included in the decoding process. This is a problem which arises in our example. The message AAABAACCAABA is encoded as the sequence of codes 110,01,10,111,10,01,00, and the contents of **pack** are 000000000000000011001101111100100. If the encoding process is finished, the contents are shifted to the left by the number of unused bits, whereby **pack** becomes 11001101111001000000000000000000 and is output as a sequence of four bytes, 11001101, 11100100, 00000000, and 00000000, or in a more readable, decimal notation, as 205, 228, 0, and 0. The last sixteen bits do not represent any codes, and if it is not indicated, they are decoded as eight pairs of As, whose code is 00. To prevent this, the output file includes the number of coded characters, namely twelve: A, A, A, B, A, A, C, C, A, A, B, and A. The output file also includes the number of all symbols in the Huffman tree. For this example it is the number five, since five different super-symbols can be found in the input file, and in the Huffman tree: AAA, B, AA, CC, and A. Therefore, the structure of the output file is as follows: the number of super-symbols, **dataIndex**, number of characters, contents of **data[]** (symbols, run-lengths, and frequencies), and codes of all super-symbols found in the input file.

As expected, this implementation gives particularly good results for database files, giving a compression rate of 60%. The compression rate for Lisp files is 50% (runs of parentheses), for text files, 40%, and for executable files, merely 13%.

Figure 11.13 contains the complete code for the encoder.

```
//*************************  Huffman.h  **************************

const int maxSymbols = 1000,
          codeTypeBytes = 4,
          byte = 8,
          ASCII = 256,
          intSize = sizeof(int);

#if (intSize == 4)                    // make sure that storage place
typedef unsigned int codeType;  // for code is four bytes long;
#else
```

Figure 11.13: **Implementation of Huffman method with run-length encoding.**   **continued**

```
typedef unsigned long codeType;
#endif

class HuffmanClass {
    const codeType mask;
    int dataIndex;
    fstream fOut;

public:
    HuffmanClass() : mask(0xff) { dataIndex = 0; }
    void CompressFile(char*, ifstream&);
private:
    struct HuffmanNode {
        char symbol;
        codeType code;
        codeType freq;
        int runLen;
        int codeLen;
        HuffmanNode *left, *right;
        HuffmanNode() { left = right = 0; }
        HuffmanNode(char s, codeType f, int r,
                HuffmanNode *lt = 0, HuffmanNode *rt = 0)
            { symbol = s; freq = f; runLen = r; left = lt; right = rt; }
    } *HuffmanTree, *chars[ASCII + 1];

    struct listNode {
        HuffmanNode *tree;
        listNode *next, *prev;
        listNode() { next = prev = 0; }
        listNode(listNode *p, listNode *n) { prev = p; next = n; }
    };

    struct dataRec {
        char symbol;
        int runLen;
        codeType freq;
    } data[maxSymbols];

    void Error(char *s) { cerr << s << endl; exit(1); }
    void Insert(char ch, int runLen);
```

Figure 11.13: **Implementation of Huffman method with run-length encoding.**   **continued**

```
    void Output(codeType pack);
    void GarnerData(ifstream&);
    void OutputFrequencies(ifstream&);
    void SortData();
    void CreateHuffmanTree();
    void CreateCodes(HuffmanNode *p, codeType code, int level);
    void TransformTreeToArrayOfLists (HuffmanNode *p);
    void TransmitCode(ifstream&);
};


void
HuffmanClass::Output(codeType pack)
{   register int i;
    char s[codeTypeBytes];

    for (i = codeTypeBytes - 1; i >= 0; i--) {
        s[i] = pack & mask;
        pack >>= byte;
    }
    for (i = 0; i < codeTypeBytes; i++)
        fOut.put(s[i]);
}


void
HuffmanClass::Insert(char ch, int runLen)
{   register int i;

    if (dataIndex < maxSymbols) {
        for (i = 0; i < dataIndex; i++)
            if (data[i].symbol == ch && data[i].runLen == runLen) {
                data[i].freq++;
                break;
            }
        if (i == dataIndex) {
            data[dataIndex].symbol = ch;
            data[dataIndex].runLen = runLen;
            data[dataIndex++].freq = 1;
        }
    }
}
```

Figure 11.13: **Implementation of Huffman method with run-length encoding.**   **continued**

```
        else Error("Too many symbols");
}


void
HuffmanClass::GarnerData(ifstream& fIn)
{   char ch, ch2;
    register int runLen;

    for (fIn.get(ch); !fIn.eof(); ch = ch2) {
        for (runLen = 1, fIn.get(ch2); !fIn.eof() && ch2 == ch; runLen++)
            fIn.get(ch2);
        Insert(ch,runLen);
    }
}


void
HuffmanClass::OutputFrequencies(ifstream& fIn)
{   char ch;
    register int i, j, temp2;
    codeType temp4;

    ch = temp2 = dataIndex;
    temp2 >>= byte;
    fOut.put(temp2).put(ch);
    temp4 = fIn.tellg();
    Output(temp4);
    for (j = 0; j < dataIndex; j++) {
        fOut.put(data[j].symbol);
        ch = temp2 = data[j].runLen;
        temp2 >>= byte;
        fOut.put(temp2).put(ch);
        temp4 = data[j].freq;
        Output(temp4);
    }
}


void
HuffmanClass::SortData()        // selection sort: it makes relatively few
{   register int j,i,smallest;  // movements of data, and comparison
    dataRec tmp;                // involves only one field of structure;
```

Figure 11.13: **Implementation of Huffman method with run-length encoding.**   **continued**

```
    for (i = 0; i < dataIndex; i++) {
        for (j = i+1, smallest = i; j < dataIndex; j++)
            if (data[j].freq < data[smallest].freq)
                smallest = j;
        tmp = data[smallest];
        data[smallest] = data[i];
        data[i] = tmp;
    }
}


void
HuffmanClass::CreateHuffmanTree()
{   listNode *p, *newNode, *head, *tail;
    codeType newFreq;
    register int i;

    // initialize list pointers;
    head = tail = new listNode;
    head->tree = new HuffmanNode(data[0].symbol,data[0].freq,data[0].runLen);
    for (i = 1; i < dataIndex; i++) { // create the rest of the list;
        tail->next = new listNode(tail,0);
        tail = tail->next;
        tail->tree =
            new HuffmanNode(data[i].symbol,data[i].freq,data[i].runLen);
    }
    while (head != tail) {                    // create one Huffman tree;
        newFreq = head->tree->freq + head->next->tree->freq;
        for (p = tail; p && p->tree->freq > newFreq; p = p->prev);
        newNode = new listNode(p,p->next);
        p->next = newNode;
        if (p == tail)
            tail = newNode;
        else newNode->next->prev = newNode;
        newNode->tree =
            new HuffmanNode('\0',newFreq,0,head->tree,head->next->tree);
        head = head->next->next;
        delete head->prev->prev;
        delete head->prev;
        head->prev = 0;
    }
```

Figure 11.13: **Implementation of Huffman method with run-length encoding.**   **continued**

```
        HuffmanTree = head->tree;
        delete head;
}


void
HuffmanClass::CreateCodes(HuffmanNode *p, codeType code, int level)
{
        if (p->left == 0 && p->right == 0) {         // if p is a leaf,
                p->code    = code;                   // store code
                p->codeLen = level;                  // and its length,
        }
        else {                                       // otherwise add 0
                CreateCodes(p->left,  code<<1,    level+1); // for left branch
                CreateCodes(p->right,(code<<1)+1,level+1); // and 1 for right;
        }
}


void
HuffmanClass::TransformTreeToArrayOfLists (HuffmanNode *p)
{
        if (p->left == 0 && p->right == 0) {         // if p is a leaf,
                p->right = chars[(unsigned char)p->symbol]; // include it in
                chars[(unsigned char)p->symbol] = p;  // a list associated
        }                                             // with symbol found in p;
        else {
                TransformTreeToArrayOfLists(p->left);
                TransformTreeToArrayOfLists(p->right);
        }
}


void
HuffmanClass::TransmitCode(ifstream& fIn)
{   codeType packCnt = 0, hold, maxPack = sizeof(codeType)*byte;
        register codeType pack = 0;
        char s[codeTypeBytes];
        char ch, ch2;
        int bitsLeft, i, runLength;
        HuffmanNode *p;
```

Figure 11.13: **Implementation of Huffman method with run-length encoding.   continued**

```
    for (fIn.get(ch); !fIn.eof(); ) {
        for (runLength = 1, fIn.get(ch2); ch2 == ch; runLength++)
            fIn.get(ch2);
        for (p = chars[(unsigned char) ch]; p && runLength != p->runLen;
            p = p->right);
        if (!p)
            Error("A problem in TransmitCode()");
        if (p->codeLen < maxPack - packCnt) {       // if enough room in
            pack = (pack << p->codeLen) | p->code;  // pack to store new
            packCnt += p->codeLen;                  // code, shift its
        }                                           // content to the left
                                                    // and attach new code;

        else {                                      // otherwise move
            bitsLeft = maxPack - packCnt;           // pack's content to
            pack <<= bitsLeft;                      // the left by the
            if (bitsLeft != p->codeLen) {           // number of left
                hold = p->code;                     // spaces and if new
                hold >>= p->codeLen - bitsLeft;     // code is longer than
                pack |= hold;                       // room left, transfer
            }                                       // only as many bits as
                                                    // can be fitted in pack;
            else pack |= p->code;                   // if new code
                                                    // exactly fits in
                                                    // pack, transfer it;

            Output(pack);                           // output pack as
                                                    // four chars;

            if (bitsLeft != p->codeLen) {           // transfer
                pack = p->code;                     // unprocessed bits
                packCnt = maxPack - (p->codeLen - bitsLeft); // of new
                packCnt = p->codeLen - bitsLeft;    // code to pack;
            }
            else packCnt = 0;
        }
        ch = ch2;
    }
    if (packCnt != 0) {
        pack <<= maxPack - packCnt; // transfer left over codes and some 0's
        Output(pack);
    }
}
```

Figure 11.13: **Implementation of Huffman method with run-length encoding.**   **continued**

```
void
HuffmanClass::CompressFile(char *inFileName, ifstream& fIn)
{   int i;
    char outFileName[30];

    strcpy(outFileName,inFileName);
    if (strchr(outFileName,'.'))                    // if there is an extension
        strcpy(strchr(outFileName,'.')+1,"z"); // overwrite it with 'z'
    else strcat(outFileName,".z");                  // else add extension '.z';
    fOut.open(outFileName,ios::out|ios::binary);

    GarnerData(fIn);
    SortData();
    OutputFrequencies(fIn);
    CreateHuffmanTree();
    CreateCodes(HuffmanTree,0,0);
    for (i = 0; i <= ASCII; i++)
        chars[i] = 0;
    TransformTreeToArrayOfLists(HuffmanTree);

    fIn.clear();        // clear especially the eof flag;
    fIn.seekg(0,ios::beg);
    TransmitCode(fIn);

    cout.precision(2);
    cout << "Compression rate = " <<
            100.0*(fIn.tellg()-fOut.tellg())/fIn.tellg() << "%\n"
        << "Compression rate without table = " <<
            100.0*(fIn.tellg()-fOut.tellg()+dataIndex*(2+4))/fIn.tellg();
}


//*********************** encoder.cpp ************************
#include <iostream.h>
#include <fstream.h>
#include <time.h>
#include <string.h>
#include <stdlib.h>
#include "Huffman.h"
```

Figure 11.13: **Implementation of Huffman method with run-length encoding.**   **continued**

```
main(int argc, char* argv[])
{   char fileName[30];
    HuffmanClass Huffman;

    if (argc != 2) {
        cout << "Enter a file name: ";
        cin  >> fileName;
    }
    else strcpy(fileName,argv[1]);
    ifstream fIn(fileName,ios::binary);
    if (fIn.fail()) {
        cerr << "Cannot open " << fileName << endl;
        return 1;
    }
    Huffman.CompressFile(fileName,fIn);
    fIn.close();
    return 0;
}
```

Figure 11.13: **Implementation of the Huffman method with run-length encoding.**

■ 11.7 EXERCISES

1. For which frequencies $P(m_i)$ of n symbols is the average length maximal? When is it minimal?

2. Software engineering uses *decision tree analysis* to decide, among other things, whether to use previously written procedures or modules, to buy them from an outside vendor, or to create a system from scratch. A decision tree used in such analysis has branches marked with the probabilities of occurrences, as in Figure 11.14. According to this figure, $100,000 will be spent if the system is created from the beginning and the development effort is estimated as simple, and $70,000 will be spent if many simple changes need to be made to the modules already available in-house. Calculate the expected cost for each of the three possibilities: to create, reuse, or buy, using Equation 11.1. Note that the decision tree in Figure 11.14 is a set of three weighted trees.

3. Find L_{ave} for the letters X, Y, and Z and their frequencies .05, .05, and .9 and compare it to L_{Huf} computed for single letters and pairs of letters, as in Figure 11.6. Does L_{Huf} satisfactorily approximate L_{ave}? How can we remedy the problem?

4. Assess the complexity of all the implementations of the Huffman algorithm suggested in this chapter.

5. What are the lengths of the Huffman codes of the least probable messages with respect to each other?

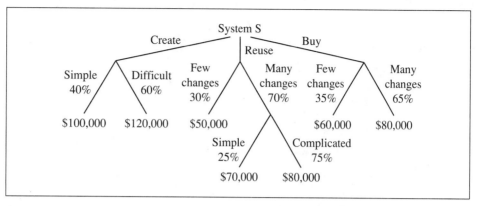

Figure 11.14: **Decision tree.**

6. In the adaptive Huffman algorithm, first the code for an encountered symbol is issued and then the conversion table is updated. Could the table be updated first and then the new code for this symbol issued? Why or why not?

7. What problem arises if in run-length encoding, triples of the form $\langle cm, n, ch \rangle$ are used instead of triples of the form $\langle cm, ch, n \rangle$?

8. Explain the significance of putting all probabilities in order before starting the Shannon-Fano method.

9. In Figure 11.10, $l_1 = l_2 = 4 = 2^2$. In what respect does the choice of $l_1 = l_2 = 16 = 2^4$ simplify the implementation of the Ziv-Lempel algorithm?

10. In which situation does the Ziv-Lempel algorithm perform best? Worst?

11. Describe the process of decoding using the Ziv-Lempel method. What string is coded by this sequence of codes: b,31a,23b,30c,21a,32a?

12. Using the modified Ziv-Lempel method with the table initialized with the letters a, b, c, decode the string coded as 1 2 4 3 1 4 9 5 8 12 2.

■ 11.8 PROGRAMMING ASSIGNMENTS

1. A large number of messages with very low probabilities in a long series of messages require a large number of very long codes (Hankamer 1979). Instead, one code can be assigned to all these messages and if needed, this code is sent along with the message. Write a program for coding and decoding this approach by adapting the Huffman algorithm.

2. Write an encoder and decoder that uses the run-length encoding technique.

3. Write an encoder and a decoder using run-length encoding to transmit voice, with the voice simulated by a certain function f. Voice is generated continuously, but it is measured at $t_0, t_1, t_2, \ldots$, where $t_i - t_{i-1} = \delta$, for some time interval δ. If $f(t_i) - f(t_{i-1}) < \epsilon$ for some tolerance ϵ, then the numbers $f(t_i)$ and $f(t_{i-1})$ are treated as equal. Therefore, for runs of such equal values, a compressed version can be transmitted in the

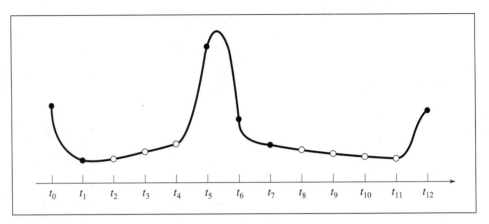

Figure 11.15: **A function representing voice frequency.**

form of a triple $\langle cm, f(t_i), n \rangle$ with cm being a negative number. In Figure 11.15, circles represent the numbers included in a run indicated by the first preceding bullet; in this example, two runs are sent. What is a potential danger of this technique, known also as the *zero-order predictor*? How can this be solved? Try your program on the functions $\frac{\sin n}{n}$ and $\ln n$.

4. Modify the case study for adaptive compression. Use the first byte of the transmitted file as an indicator of whether or not adaptive compression is meant to be used.

BIBLIOGRAPHY

Data Compression Methods

[1]   Bell, Timothy C., Cleary, J.G., and Witten, Ian H., *Text Compression*, Englewood Cliffs: Prentice-Hall, 1990.

[2]   Davisson, Lee D. and Gray, Robert M. (eds.), *Data Compression*, Stroudsburg: Dowden, Hutchinson & Ross, 1976.

[3]   Lelever, Debra A. and Hirschberg, Daniel S., "Data Compression," *ACM Computing Surveys* 19 (1987), 261–296.

[4]   Lynch, Thomas J., *Data Compression: Techniques and Applications*, New York: Van Nostrand Reinhold, 1985.

[5]   Rubin, Frank, "Experiments in Text File Compression," *Communications of the ACM* 19 (1976), 617–623.

[6]   Smith, Peter D., *An Introduction to Text Processing*, Cambridge: The MIT Press, 1990, Ch. 4.

[7]   Storer, James A., *Data Compression: Methods and Theory*, Rockville, MD: Computer Science Press, 1988.

[8]   Storer, James A., "Data Compression Bibliography," in Storer, J.A. (ed.), *Image and Text Compression*, Boston: Kluwer, 1992, 279–349.

[9]   Williams, Ross N., *Adaptive Data Compression*, Boston: Kluwer, 1989.

Huffman Coding

[10] Gallager, Robert G., "Variations on a Theme of Huffman," *IEEE Transactions on Information Theory* IT-24 (1978), 668–674.

[11] Hankamer, M., "A Modified Huffman Procedure with Reduced Memory Requirement," *IEEE Transactions on Communication* COM-27 (1979), 930–932.

[12] Huffman, David A., "A Method for the Construction of Minimum-Redundancy Codes," *Proceedings of the Institute of Radio Engineers* 40 (1952), 1098–1101 (also in Davisson & Gray).

[13] Knuth, Donald E., "Dynamic Huffman Coding," *Journal of Algorithms* 6 (1985), 163–180.

[14] Vitter, Jeffrey S., "Design and Analysis of Dynamic Huffman Coding," *Journal of the ACM* 34 (1987), 825–845.

[15] Vitter, Jeffrey S., "Algorithm 673: Dynamic Huffman Coding," *ACM Transactions on Mathematical Software* 15 (1989), 158–167.

Run-Length Encoding

[16] Pountain, Dick, "Run-Length Encoding," *Byte* 12 (1987), No. 6, 317–320.

Ziv-Lempel Code

[17] Miller, Victor S. and Wegman, Mark N., "Variations on a Theme by Ziv and Lempel," in Apostolico A. and Galil, Z. (eds.), *Combinatorial Algorithms on Words*, Berlin: Springer, 1985, 131–140.

[18] Welch, Terry A., "A Technique for High-Performance Data Compression," *Computer* 17 (1984), 6, 8–19.

[19] Ziv, Jacob and Lempel, Abraham, "A Universal Algorithm for Sequential Data Compression," *IEEE Transactions on Information Theory* IT-23 (1977), 337–343.

MEMORY MANAGEMENT

The preceding chapters rarely looked behind the scenes to see how programs are actually executed and how variables of different types are stored. The reason is that this book emphasizes data structures rather than the inner workings of the computer. The latter belongs more to a book about operating systems or assembly language programming than to a discussion of data structures.

But at least in one case such a reference was inescapable, namely when discussing recursion in Chapter 5. Using recursion was explained in terms of the run-time stack, in terms of the way the computer actually works. We also alluded to this level when discussing dynamic memory allocation. It is hard to discuss dynamic memory allocation without a keen awareness of the structure of computer memory and the realization that without **new**, pointers may point to unallocated memory locations. In addition, **delete** should be used to avoid exhausting the computer's memory resources. Managing memory in C++ is the responsibility of the programmer and memory may become clogged with unreachable locations which were not deallocated with **delete** if the programmer is not sufficiently careful. The most efficient and elegant program structure may be disempowered if too much memory is allocated.

The *heap* is the region of main memory from which portions of memory are dynamically allocated upon request of a program. (This heap has nothing to do with the special tree structure called a heap in Section 6.9.) In languages such as Fortran, Cobol, or Pascal, the compiler determines how much memory is needed to run programs. In languages which allow dynamic memory allocation, the amount of memory required cannot always be determined prior to the program run. To that end, the heap is used. If a C++ program requests memory by issuing a call to **new**, a certain number of bytes is allocated from the heap and the address to the first byte of this portion is returned.

As was already mentioned, in C++, memory management is the programmer's responsibility. A different policy in memory management is to shift the responsibility for memory allocation and deallocation from the programmer to the operating system, or to a part of the operating system called the *memory manager*. The memory manager accounts for the pool of free memory blocks, assigns memory blocks to the user programs, and cleans up memory by returning unneeded blocks to the memory pool.[1] Importantly, these functions are performed automatically without the user's intervention. The user may become aware of this process by being forced to wait until the memory cleaning process is finished, but the memory manager decides when it should be done.

Automatic storage reclamation is a luxury which is not a part of every language environment. It emerged with Lisp and most research on storage reclamation was done in the Lisp environment. But automatic storage reclamation is also done in connection with Smalltalk, Prolog, C++, Modula-3, and other languages. Automatic memory cleanup relieves the programmer of the task of keeping track of when to allocate and release memory.

One problem which a well-designed memory manager has to solve is that of the configuration of available memory. When returning memory with **delete**, the programmer has no control over this configuration. In particular, after many allocations and deallocations, the heap is divided into small pieces of available memory sandwiched between chunks of memory in use. If a request comes to allocate *n* bytes of memory, the request may not be met if there is not enough contiguous memory in the heap, although the total of available memory may far surpass *n*. This phenomenon is called *external fragmentation*. Changing memory configuration and in particular, putting available memory in one part of the heap and allocated memory in another solves this problem. Another problem is *internal fragmentation*, when allocated memory chunks are larger than requested. It is an inherent drawback of some memory management techniques. A handful of the many storage reclamation techniques will be discussed in this chapter.

■ 12.1   THE SEQUENTIAL-FIT METHODS

A simple organization of memory could require a linked list of all memory blocks which is updated after a block is either requested or returned. The blocks on such linked lists can be organized in a variety of ways, according to the block sizes or the block addresses. Whenever a block is requested, a decision has to be made concerning which block to allocate and how to treat the portion of the block exceeding the requested size.

For reasons of efficiency, doubly linked lists of blocks are maintained with links residing in the blocks. Each available block of memory uses a portion of itself for two links. Also, both available and reserved blocks have two fields to indicate their status (available or reserved) and their size.

In the sequential-fit methods, all available memory blocks are linked together and the list is searched to find a block whose size is larger than or the same as the requested size. A simple policy for handling returned blocks of memory is to coalesce them with neighboring blocks and reflect this fact by properly adjusting the links in the linked list.

The order of searching the list for such a block determines the division of these methods into several categories. The *first-fit* algorithm allocates the first block of memory large enough to meet the request. The *best-fit* algorithm allocates a block which is closest

---

[1]The memory manager also performs other functions, such as scheduling access to shared data, moving code and data between the main and secondary memory, and keeping one process away from another.

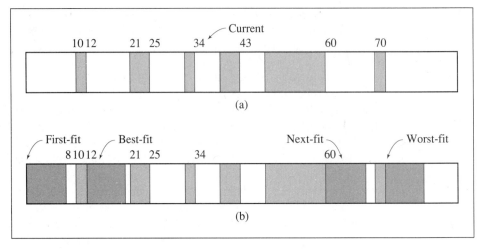

Figure 12.1: **Memory allocation using sequential-fit methods.**

in size to the request. The *worst-fit* method finds the largest block on the list so that after returning its portion equal to the requested size, the remaining part is large enough to be used in later requests. The *next-fit* method allocates the next available block which is sufficiently large.

Figure 12.1a contains a memory configuration after several requests and returns of memory blocks. Figure 12.1b illustrates which portion of memory would be allocated by which sequential-fit method to satisfy a request for 8KB of memory.

The most efficient method is the first-fit procedure. The next-fit method is of comparable speed, but causes more extensive external fragmentation because it scans the list of blocks starting from the current position and reaches the end of the list much earlier than the first-fit method. But the best-fit algorithm is even worse in that respect since it searches for the closest match with respect to size. The parts of blocks remaining after returning the required size are small and practically unusable. The worst-fit algorithm attempts to prevent this type of fragmentation by avoiding, or at least delaying, the creation of small blocks.

The way the blocks are organized on the list determines how fast the search for an available block succeeds or fails. For example, to optimize the best-fit and the worst-fit methods, the blocks should be arranged by size. For other methods, the address ordering is adequate.

■ 12.2 THE NONSEQUENTIAL-FIT METHODS

The sequential-fit methods being what they are, sequential methods may become inefficient for large memory. In the case of large memory, a nonsequential search would be desirable. One strategy divides the heap into an arbitrary number of lists, each list holding blocks of the same size (Ross 1967). Larger blocks are split into smaller blocks to satisfy requests and new lists may be created. Since the number of such lists can become large, they can be organized as a tree.

Another approach is based on the observation that the number of sizes requested by a program is limited, although the sizes may differ from one program to another. Therefore, the list of blocks of different sizes can be kept short if it can be determined which sizes are the most popular. This leads to an *adaptive exact-fit* technique which dynamically creates and adjusts storage block lists which fit the requests exactly (Oldehoeft, Allan 1985).

In adaptive exact-fit, a size-list of block lists of a particular size returned to memory pool during the last T allocations is maintained. A block b is added to a particular block list if this block list holds blocks of b's size and b has been returned by the program. When a request comes for a block of b's size, a block from its block list is detached to meet the request. Otherwise a more time-consuming search for a block in the heap is triggered using one of the sequential-fit methods.

The exact-fit method disposes of entire block lists if no request comes for a block from this list in the last T allocations. In this way, lists of infrequently used block sizes are not maintained and the list of block lists is kept small to allow a sequential search of this list. Because it is not a sequential search of the memory, the exact-fit method is not considered a sequential-fit method.

Figure 12.2 contains an example of a size-list and a heap created using the adaptive exact-fit method. The memory is fragmented, but if a request comes for a block of size 7, the allocation can be done immediately, since the size-list has an entry for size 7, so that memory does not have to be searched. A simple algorithm for allocating blocks is as follows:

```
t = 0;

Allocate (reqSize)
    t++;
    if a block list bl with reqSize blocks is on sizeList
        lastref (bl) = t;
        b = head of blocks(bl);
        if b was the only block accessible from bl
            detach bl from sizeList;
    else b = search-the-heap-for-a-block-of(reqSize);
    dispose of all block lists on sizeList for which t - lastref(bl) < T;
    return b;
```

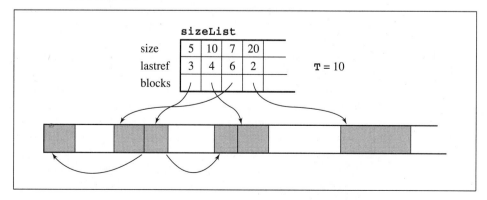

Figure 12.2: **An example configuration of size-list and the heap created by the adaptive exact-fit method.**

A procedure for returning blocks is even simpler.

This algorithm highlights the problem of memory fragmentation. The algorithm must be expanded to deal with this problem successfully. One solution is to write a function to compact the heap after a certain number of allocations and deallocations. A noncompacting approach may consist in liquidating the size-list and building it anew after some predetermined period. The authors of this method claim that fragmentation problem "failed to materialize," but that can be attributed to the configurations of their tests. It certainly materializes in sequential-fit methods, and in another nonsequential-fit strategy to be discussed in the next section.

12.2.1 Buddy Systems

Nonsequential memory management methods known as *buddy systems* do not just assign memory in sequential slices, but divide it into two buddies which are merged whenever possible. In the buddy system two buddies are never free. A block can have either a buddy used by the program or none.

The classic buddy system is the *binary buddy system* (Knowlton 1965). The binary buddy system assumes that storage consists of 2^m locations for some integer m, with addresses $0, \ldots, 2^m - 1$, and that these locations can be organized into blocks whose lengths can only be powers of 2. There is also an array **avail[]** such that for each $i = 0, \ldots, m$, **avail[i]** is the head of a doubly linked list of blocks of the same size, 2^i.

The name of this method is derived from the fact that each block of memory (except the entire memory) is coupled with a buddy *of the same size* which participates with the block in reserving and returning chunks of memory. The buddy of a block of length 2^i is determined by complementing bit $i + 1$ in the address of this block. This is strictly related to the lengths of blocks which can only be powers of 2. In particular, all blocks of size 2^i have 0s in the i rightmost positions and differ only in the remaining bits. For example, if memory has only eight locations, then the possible addresses of blocks of size one are {000, 001, 010, 011, 100, 101, 110, 111}, addresses of blocks of size two are {000, 010, 100, 110}, of size four {000, 100}, and of size eight {000}. Note that in the second set of addresses, the last bit is 0, and the addresses refer to blocks of size 2^1. The third set of addresses has two ending 0s, since the size of the blocks is 2^2. Now, for the second set, there are two pairs of blocks and their buddies: {(000, 010), (100, 110)}; for the third set there is only one pair, (000, 100). Hence, the difference between a block of size 2^i and its buddy is only in bit $i + 1$.

If a request arrives to allocate a memory block of size s, then the buddy system returns a memory block whose size is greater than or equal to s. Since there are many candidates for such blocks, the list of such blocks is checked in **avail[]** whose size k is the smallest among all $k \geq s$. This list of blocks can be found in location **avail[k]**. If the list is empty, then the next list of blocks is checked in position $k + 1$, then in position $k + 2$, and so on. The search continues until a nonempty list is found (or the end of **avail[]** is reached), and then a block is detached from it.

The algorithm for memory allocation in binary buddy system is as follows:

size of memory $= 2^m$ *for some* **m;**
avail[i] = **-1** *for* **i** = **0,...,m-1;**
avail[m] = *address(heap)***;**

```
Reserve(reqSize)
    roundedSize = ⌈lg(reqSize)⌉;
    availSize = min(roundedSize,...,m) for which avail[availSize] > -1;
    if no such availSize exists
        failure;
    block = avail[availSize];
    detach block from list avail[availSize];
    while (roundedSize < availSize)      // while an available block
        availSize--;                     // is too large - split it;
        block = left half of block;
        insert buddy of block in list avail[availSize];
    return block;
```

Each free block of the buddy system should include four fields indicating its status, its size, and its two neighbors in the list. On the other hand, reserved blocks include only a status field. Figure 12.3a illustrates the structure of a free block in the buddy system. The block is marked as free with the status field set to 0. The size is specified as 2^5 locations. No predecessor is specified so this block is pointed to by `avail[5]`. The size of its successor is also 2^5 locations. Figure 12.3b illustrates a reserved block whose status field is set to 1.

Figure 12.4 contains an example of reserving three blocks, assuming that the memory in use is of size $2^7 = 128$ locations. First, the entire memory is free (Figure 12.4a). Then, 18 locations are requested, so `roundedSize` = ⌈lg(18)⌉ = 5. But `availSize` = 7, so the memory is split into two buddies, each of size 2^6. The second buddy is marked as available by setting the status field and including it into the list `avail[6]` (Figure 12.4b). `availSize` is still greater than `roundedSize`, so another iteration of the `while` loop of `Reserve()` is executed. The first block is split into two and the second buddy is included in the list `avail[5]` (Figure 12.4c). The first buddy is marked as reserved and returned to the caller of `Reserve()` for use. Note that only a portion of the returned block is really needed. However the entire block is marked as reserved.

Next, a block of 14 locations is requested; now, `roundedSize` = ⌈lg(14)⌉ = 4, `availSize` = 5, and the block pointed to by `avail[5]` is claimed (Figure 12.4d). This block is too large since `roundedSize` < `availSize`, so the block is divided into two buddies. The first buddy is marked as reserved and returned and the second is included in a list (Figure 12.4e). Finally, a block of 16 locations is requested. After two iterations of the `while` loop of `Reserve()`, the configuration pictured in Figure 12.4g

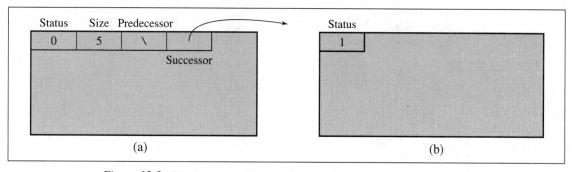

Figure 12.3: **Block structure in the binary buddy system.**

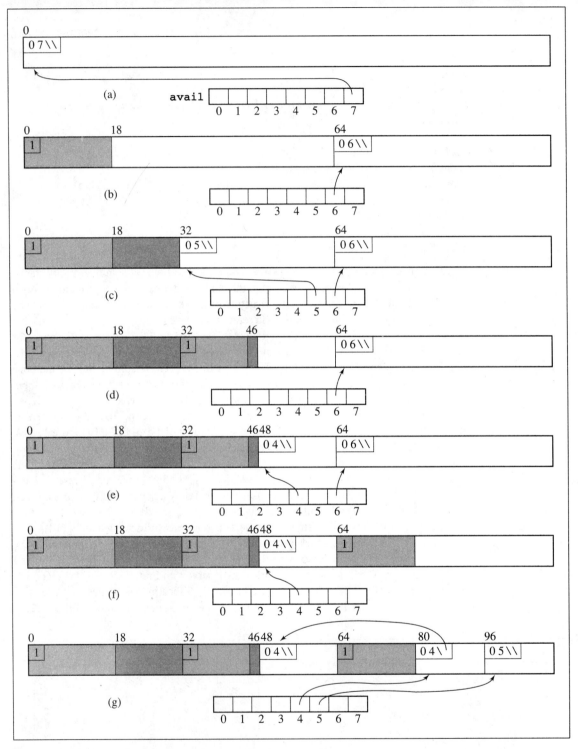

Figure 12.4: **Reserving three blocks of memory using the binary buddy system.**

emerges; there are two available blocks of 16 locations and both are linked up together in list **avail[4]**.

To be sure, blocks of memory are not only claimed, but they are returned, and so they have to be included in the pool of available blocks. Before they are included, the status of each block's buddy is checked. If the buddy is available, the block is combined with its buddy to create a block twice as large as before the combination. If the buddy of the new block is available, it is also combined with its buddy, resulting in a still larger block of memory. This process continues until the entire memory is combined into one block or a buddy is not available. This coalescing creates blocks of available memory as large as possible. The algorithm for including a block in the pool of available blocks is as follows:

```
Include(block)
   blockSize = size(block);
   buddy = address(block) with bit blockSize+1 set to its complement;
   while status(buddy) is 0                    // buddy has not
         and size(buddy) == blockSize          // been claimed;
         and blockSize != lg(size of memory)   // buddy exists;
      detach buddy from list avail[blockSize];
      block = block plus buddy;   // coalesce block and its buddy;
      set status(block) to 0;
      blockSize++;
      buddy = address(now extended block) with bit blockSize+1 set to its complement;
   include block in list avail[blockSize];
```

Figure 12.5 illustrates this process. A block previously claimed is now released (Figure 12.5a), and because the buddy of this block is free, it is combined with the block resulting in a double-sized block, which is included in the list **avail[5]** (Figure 12.5b). Releasing another block allows the memory manager to combine this block with its buddy and the resulting block with its buddy (Figure 12.5c). Note that the free portion of the leftmost block (marked with the darker screen) did not participate in this coalescing process and is still considered occupied. Also, the two rightmost blocks in Figure 12.5a, although adjacent, were not combined because they are not buddies. Buddies in the binary buddy method have to be of the same size.

The binary buddy system, although relatively efficient in terms of speed, may be inefficient in terms of space. Figure 12.4a shows that the two leftmost blocks amount to a size of 48 locations, but that only 32 of them are in use, since the user really needs $18+14$ locations. This means that one-third of these two blocks is wasted. This can get even worse if the number of locations requested is always slightly more than a power of two. In this case, approximately 50% of memory is not in actual use. This is a problem with internal fragmentation which results from the need to round all requests to the nearest larger power of two.

Also, there may be a problem with external fragmentation; a request may be refused although the amount of available space is sufficient to meet it. For example, for the configuration of memory in Figure 12.4g, a request for 50 locations is refused because there is no block available of a size of 64 locations or more. A request for 33 locations is treated similarly and for the same reason, although there are 33 available consecutive locations. But one of these locations belongs to another block which puts it out of reach.

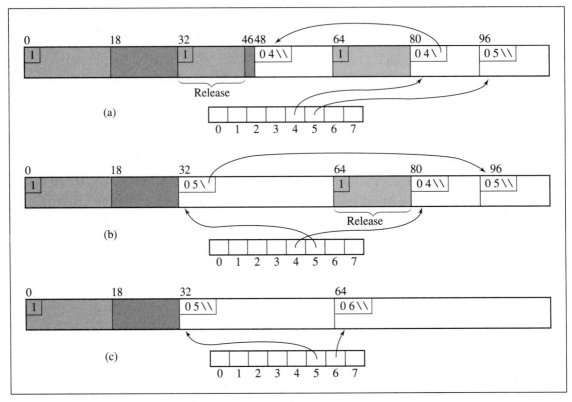

Figure 12.5: **Returning a block to the pool of blocks (a), resulting in coalescing one block with its buddy (b). Returning another block leads to two coalescings (c).**

These problems are brought about by the fact that the binary buddy system uses a simple division of blocks into two even parts, which results in the division of memory not sufficiently tuned to incoming requests. The sequence of block sizes possible in this system is $1, 2, 4, 8, 16, \ldots, 2^m$. An improvement of the binary buddy system can be obtained if this sequence is rendered by the recurrence equation

$$s_i = \begin{cases} 1 & \text{if } i = 0, \\ s_{i-1} + s_{i-1} & \text{otherwise,} \end{cases}$$

which can be considered a particular case of a more general equation:

$$s_i = \begin{cases} c_1 & \text{if } i = 0, \\ \vdots & \vdots \\ c_k & \text{if } i = k - 1, \\ s_{i-1} + s_{i-k} & \text{otherwise.} \end{cases}$$

If $k = 1$ then this equation renders the equation for the binary buddy system. If $k = 2$ then the obtained formula is a very familiar equation for a Fibonacci sequence:

$$s_i = \begin{cases} 1 & \text{if } i = 0, 1, \\ s_{i-1} + s_{i-2} & \text{otherwise.} \end{cases}$$

This leads to the *Fibonacci buddy system* developed by Daniel S. Hirschberg. He chose 3 and 5 as the values for s_0 and s_1. If $k > 2$ then we enter the realm of the *generalized Fibonacci systems* (Hinds 1975).

The problem with the Fibonacci buddy system is that finding a buddy of a block is not always simple. In the binary buddy system, the information stored in the size field of the block is sufficient to compute the address of the buddy. If the size holds the number k, then the address of the buddy is found by complementing the bit $k + 1$ in the address of the block. This works regardless of whether the block has a right buddy or a left buddy. The reason for this simplicity is that only powers of two for the sizes of all blocks are used and each block and its buddy are of the same size.

In the Fibonacci system this approach is inapplicable, yet it is necessary to know whether a returned block has a right or a left buddy in order to combine the two. Not surprisingly, finding the buddy of a block may be rather demanding in terms of time or space. To this end, Hirschberg used a table which could have nearly a thousand entries if buffers of up to 17,717 locations are allowed. His method can be simplified if a proper flag is included in each block but a binary Left/Right flag may be insufficient. If block b_1 marked as Left is coalesced with its buddy, block b_2, then the question is, how to find the buddy of the resulting block, b_3? An elegant solution uses two binary flags instead of one: a buddy-bit and a memory-bit (Cranston, Thomas 1975). If a block b_1 is split into blocks b_{left} and b_{right}, then buddy-bit(b_{left}) = 0; buddy-bit(b_{right}) = 1; memory-bit(b_{left}) = buddy-bit(b_1), and finally, memory-bit(b_{right}) = memory-bit(b_1) (see Figure 12.6a). The last two

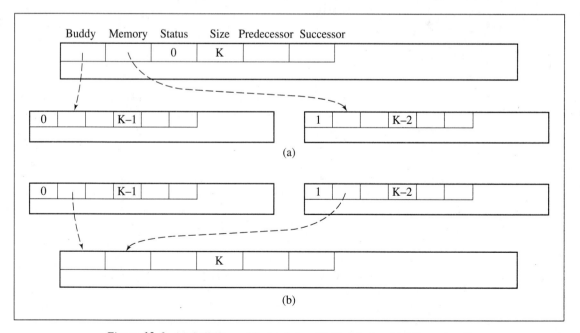

Figure 12.6: (a) **Splitting a block of size *Fib(k)* into two buddies using the buddy-bit and the memory-bit. (b) Coalescing two buddies utilizing information stored in buddy- and memory-bits.**

assignments preserve some information about predecessors: memory-bit(b_{left}) indicates whether its parent is a left or right buddy and memory-bit(b_{right}) is a bit of information to indicate the same status for one of the predecessors of its parent. Note that the coalescing process is an exact reversal of splitting (see Figure 12.6b).

The algorithms for reserving blocks and for returning them are in many respects similar to the algorithms used for the binary buddy system. An algorithm for reserving blocks is as follows:

```
avail[i]  =  -1 for i = 0,...,m-1;
avail[m]  =  address(heap);
```

```
ReserveFib(reqSize)
    availSize = the position of the first Fibonacci number greater than reqSize
                  for which avail[availSize] > -1;
    if no such availSize exists
        failure;
    block = avail[availSize];
    detach block from list avail[availSize];
    while Fib(availSize-1) > reqSize   // while an available block is
                                        // too large - split it;  choose
        if reqSize > Fib(availSize-2) // smaller of the buddies if it's
            insert block's larger part in avail[availSize-1]; // large enough;
            block = block's smaller part;
        else insert block's smaller part in avail[availSize-2];
            block = block's larger part;
        availSize = size(block);
        set_flags(block);
        set_flags(block's buddy);
    return block;
```

Another extension of the binary buddy system is a *weighted buddy system* (Shen, Peterson 1974). Its goal, as in the case of Fibonacci systems, is to decrease the amount of internal fragmentation by allowing more block sizes than in the binary system. Block sizes in the weighted buddy system in memory of 2^m of unary blocks are 2^k for $0 \leq k \leq m$, and $3 * 2^k$, for $0 \leq k \leq m - 2$; the sizes are $1, 2, 3, 4, 6, 8, 12, 16, 24, 32, \ldots$, which is nearly twice as many different sizes than in the binary method. If necessary, blocks of size 2^k are split into blocks $3 * 2^{k-2}$ and 2^{k-2}, and the blocks of size $3 * 2^k$ are split into blocks 2^{k+1} and 2^k. Note that the buddy of a 2^k block cannot be uniquely determined since it can have a right buddy of size either 2^{k+1} or $3 * 2^k$, or it can have a left buddy of size 2^{k-1}. To distinguish between these three cases, a two-bit flag *type* is added to each block. However, simulations indicate that the weighted buddy system is three times slower and generates larger external fragmentation than the binary buddy system. As mentioned, the weighted buddy system requires two additional bits per block, and the algorithm is more complex than in the binary buddy system, since it requires considering more cases when coalescing blocks.

A buddy system which takes a middle course between the binary system and the weighted system is a *dual buddy system* (Page, Hagins 1986). This method maintains two separate memory areas, one with block sizes 1, 2, 4, 8, 16, $\ldots$, 2^i, $\ldots$ and another with block sizes 3, 6, 9, 18, 36,..., $3 * 2^j$,.... In this way, the binary buddy method is applied in two areas. Internal fragmentation of the dual method is more or less halfway between that of the binary and weighted methods. External fragmentation in the dual buddy system is almost the same as that of the binary buddy system.

To conclude this discussion, observe that many times, internal fragmentation is inversely proportional to external fragmentation because internal fragmentation is avoided if allocated blocks are as close in size to the requested blocks as possible. But this means that some small splinter blocks are generated which are of little use. These small blocks can be compacted together to form a large block with sequential-fit methods, but compaction does not square very well with the buddy system approach. In fact, the variant buddy system, which is an elaboration of the weighted buddy method, attempts to compact memory but the complexity of the algorithm undermines its usefulness (Bromley 1980).

■ 12.3   GARBAGE COLLECTION

In the preceding sections the main concern in evaluating algorithms was how they fragment the available memory. The reason for this problem is that block sizes vary from request to request during the run of the program. In many circumstances, however, the sizes are fixed, and the dynamic allocation methods do not have to be concerned with memory fragmentation; they can focus on other issues such as memory compaction or the perennial size/speed trade-off. Such algorithms are known as *garbage collectors* which clean up a memory of fixed size blocks, although many times they are extended to handle variable size blocks.

A garbage collection method is usually a part of the environment of list processing languages, in particular, Lisp. A garbage collector is automatically invoked when very little memory is available; the execution of the program is suspended and it resumes after garbage collection is finished. Since garbage collectors have been developed in particular in the context of list processing languages, a discussion of how these languages use memory is in order.

The world of Lisp is rather uniform: its variables refer either to *atoms* (numbers or characters) or to linked lists. Each node in a list has two pointers, *head* and *tail*, or in Lisp terminology, *car* and *cdr*. Lisp operations process such lists, which many times result in very complex linked structures such as binary trees or graphs (cycles are permitted). Pointers to all linked structures currently utilized by the program are stored in a *root set* which contains all *root pointers*. The garbage collector's task is to determine those parts of memory which are accessible from any of these pointers and parts which are not currently in use and can be returned to the free memory pool.

The garbage collection methods usually include two phases, which may be implemented as distinct passes or can be integrated:

1. The *marking* phase — to identify all currently used blocks.
2. The *reclamation* phase — when all unmarked blocks are returned to the memory pool; this phase can also include memory compaction.

12.3.1   Mark-and-Sweep

A classical method of collecting garbage is the *mark-and-sweep* technique which clearly distinguishes the two phases. First, memory cells currently in use are marked by traversing each linked structure, and then the memory is swept to glean unused (garbage) cells and put them together in a memory pool.

Marking

A simple marking procedure looks very much like preorder tree traversal. If a node is not marked then it is marked and if it is not an atomic node, marking continues for its *head* and for its *tail*:

```
Marking (node)
   if node is not marked
      mark node;
      if node is not an atom
         Marking(head(node));
         Marking(tail(node));
```

This procedure is called for each element of the root set. The problem with this succinct and elegant algorithm is that it may cause the run-time stack to overflow, which is a very real prospect considering the fact that the list being marked can be very long. Therefore, an explicit stack can be used, so that there is no need to store on the run-time stack the data necessary to properly resume execution after returning from recursive calls. Here is an example of an algorithm which uses an explicit stack:

```
MarkingWithStack (node)
   Push(node);
   while stack is not empty
      node = Pop();
      while node is an unmarked nonatom
         mark node;
         Push(tail(node));
         node = head(node);
      if node is an unmarked atom
         mark node;
```

The problem of an overflow is not avoided altogether. If the stack **st** is implemented as an array, the array may turn out to be too small. If it is implemented as a linked list, it may be impossible to use, since the stack requires memory resources which have just been used up, and in the restoration of which the stack was supposed to participate. There are two ways to avoid this predicament: using a stack of limited size and invoking some operations in case of stack overflow, or trying not to use any stack at all.

A useful algorithm which requires no explicit stack was developed by Schorr and Waite. The basic idea is to, in a sense, incorporate the stack in the list being processed. This technique belongs in the same category as the stackless tree traversal techniques discussed in Section 6.4.3. In the Schorr and Waite marking method, some links are temporarily reversed when traversing the list to "remember" the path back and their original setting is restored after marking all cells accessible from a position in which the reversal has been performed. When a marked node or an atom is encountered, the algorithm returns to the preceding node. However, it can return to a node through the *head* field or through the *tail* field. In the former case, the *tail* path has to be explored, and the algorithm has to use a marker to indicate whether both *head* and *tail* paths have been checked, or only the *head* path has been checked. To that end, the algorithm uses one additional bit called a *tag* bit. If the *head* of a cell is accessed, then the tag bit remains zero, so that upon return to this cell, the path accessible from *tail* will be followed, in which case the tag bit is set to one and reset to zero upon return. The summary of the algorithms is as follows:

```
InvertLink (p1, p2, p3)
    tmp = p3;
    p3 = p1;
    p1 = p2;
    p2 = tmp;


SWmarking (curr)
    prev = null;
    while (1)
        mark curr;
        if head(curr) is marked or atom
            if head(curr) is an unmarked atom
                mark head(curr);
            while tail(curr) is marked or atom
                if tail(curr) is an unmarked atom
                    mark tail(curr);
                while prev not null and tag(prev) is 1// go back
                    tag(prev) = 0;
                    InvertLink(curr,prev,tail(prev));
                if prev not null
                    InvertLink(curr,prev,head(prev));
                else finished;
            tag(curr) = 1;
            InvertLink(prev,curr,tail(curr));
        else   InvertLink(prev,curr,head(curr));
```

Figure 12.7 illustrates an example. Each part of this figure shows changes in the list after the indicated operations have been performed. Note that atom nodes do not require a tag bit. Figure 12.7a contains the list before marking. Each nonatomic node has four parts: a marking bit, a tag bit, and *head* and *tail* fields. The marking and tag bits are initialized to 0. There is one more bit not shown in this figure, an atom/nonatom flag.

Here is a description of each iteration of the **while** loop and the figure number which contains the structure of the list after that iteration.

Iteration 1: Execute **InvertLink(prev,curr,**head(curr)) (Figure 12.7b).

Iteration 2: Execute another **InvertLink(prev,curr,**head(curr)) (Figure 12.7c).

Iteration 3: Execute still another **InvertLink(prev,curr,**head(curr)) (Figure 12.7d).

Iteration 4: Mark *tail*(curr) and execute **InvertLink(curr,prev,**head(prev)) (Figure 12.7e), execute another **InvertLink(curr,prev,**head(prev)) (Figure 12.7f), set *tag*(curr) to 1, and execute **InvertLink(prev,curr,** *tail*(curr)) (Figure 12.7g).

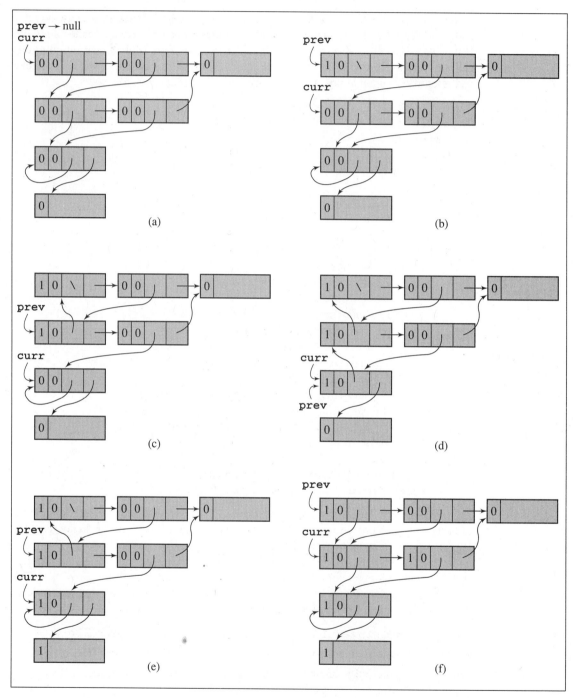

Figure 12.7: **An example of execution of the Schorr and Waite algorithm for** **continued**
marking used memory cells.

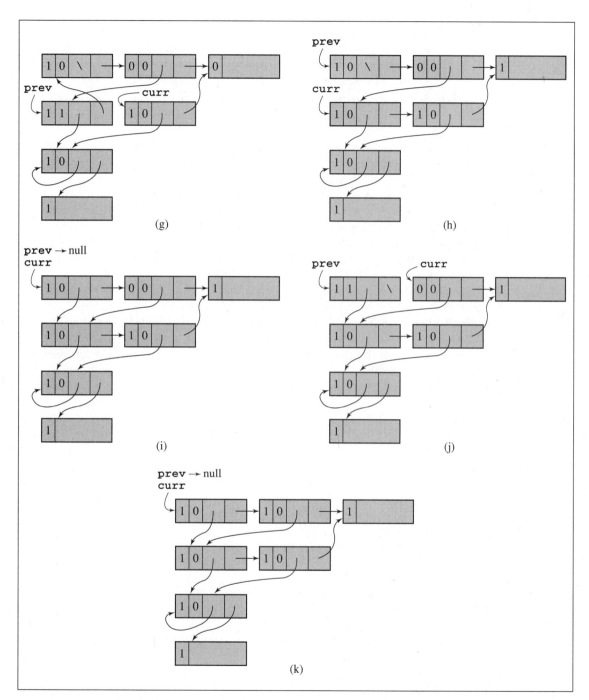

Figure 12.7: **An example of execution of the Schorr and Waite algorithm for marking used memory cells.**

Iteration 5: Mark *tail*(**curr**) to 1, set *tag*(**prev**) to 0, and execute **InvertLink(curr, prev,** *tail*(**prev**)) (Figure 12.7h). Execute **InvertLink(curr,prev,** *head*(**prev**)) (Figure 12.7i), set *tag*(**curr**) to 1, and execute **InvertLink(prev,curr,** *tail*(**curr**)) (Figure 12.7j).

Iteration 6: Set *tag*(**prev**) to 0 and execute **InvertLink(curr,prev,** *tail*(**prev**)) (Figure 12.7k). The algorithm completes and **prev** becomes *null*.

Note that the algorithm has no problem with cycles in lists. **SWmarking()** is slower than **MarkingWithStack()**, since it requires two visits per cell: pointer maintenance and an additional bit. Hence, disposing of a stack does not seem to be the best solution. Other approaches attempt to combine a stack with some form of overflow handling. Schorr and Waite proposed such a solution by resorting to their link inversion technique if a fixed-length stack becomes full. Other techniques are more discriminating about what information should be stored on the stack. For example, **MarkingWithStack()** unnecessarily pushes onto the stack the nodes which have empty *tail* fields, nodes whose processing is finished after the *head* path is finished.

The method devised by Wegbreit requires no tag bit and uses a bit stack instead of a pointer stack to store one bit for each node on the trace path whose *head* and *tail* fields both reference nonatoms. The trace path is the path from the current node to the root pointer. But as in the SW algorithm, link inversion is still in use. An improvement of this method is the Fastmark algorithm (Kurokawa 1981). As in Wegbreit's method, the Fastmark algorithm retains information about nodes which refer to nonatoms on the stack. But the stack stores pointers to nodes, not bits, so link inversion is necessary.

```
Fastmark(node)
    if node is not an atom
        mark node;
    while (1)
        if both head(node) and tail(node) are marked or atoms
            if stack is empty
                finished;
            else node = Pop();
        else if only tail(node) is not marked nor is it atom
            mark tail(node);
            node = tail(node);
        else if only head(node) is not marked nor is it atom
            mark head(node);
            node = head(node);
        else if both head(node) and tail(node) are not marked nor are they atoms
            mark both head(node) and tail(node);
            Push(tail(node));
            node = head(node);
```

The reader is encouraged to apply this algorithm to the list in Figure 12.7a. However, the vexing problem of stack overflow is still not completely resolved. Although the Fastmark algorithm claims to require approximately 30 locations in most situations, some degenerate cases may occur which require thousands of locations in the stack. Therefore, Fastmark has to be extended to be robust. The basic idea of the resulting *stacked-node-checking algorithm* is to delete from the stack nodes that are already marked or nodes whose *head* or *tail* path have already been traced. However, even this improved algorithm will run out of space occasionally, in which situation "it gives up and advises a fatal stack overflow error" (Kurokawa 1981). Hence, the Schorr and Waite approach with its two techniques, stacking and list reversal, is more reliable although slower.

Space Reclamation

After all the cells currently in use have been marked, the reclamation process returns all unmarked locations in memory to the memory pool by going sequentially through memory, cell by cell, starting from highest address and inserting all unmarked locations in the *avail-list*. Upon completion of this process, all locations on the *avail-list* are in ascending order. During this process, all mark bits are reset to 0 so that at the end the mark bits of all used and unused locations are 0. This simple algorithm is as follows:

```
Sweep()
    for each location from the last to the first
        if mark(location) is 1
            insert location in front of avail-list;
            set mark(location) to 0;
```

The `Sweep()` algorithm makes a pass through the entire memory. If we add a pass required for marking and the subsequent maintenance of the *avail-list* containing locations sparsely scattered throughout memory, this rather undesirable situation calls for improvement.

Compaction

After the reclamation process is complete, the available locations are interspersed with the cells being used by the program. This requires *compaction*. If all available cells are in contiguous order, then there is no need to maintain the *avail-list*. Also, if garbage collection is used for reclaiming cells of variable cells, then having all available cells in sequence is highly desirable. Compaction is also necessary when garbage collection processes virtual memory. In this way, responses to memory requests can be performed with a minimal number of accesses. Another situation in which compacting is beneficial is when the run-time stack and a heap are used at the same time. C++ is an example of a language implemented in this way. The heap and the stack are in opposite sides of memory and they grow toward one another. If occupied memory cells on the heap can be kept away from the stack, then the stack has more room for expansion.

A simple *two-pointer algorithm* for memory compaction uses an approach similar to the one utilized in partitioning in quicksort: two pointers scan memory starting from the opposite sides of memory. After the first pointer finds an unmarked cell and the second finds a marked cell, the contents of the marked cell are moved to the unmarked cell and its new location is recorded in the old location. This process continues after the pointers cross. Then, the compacted part is scanned to readjust the *head* and *tail* pointers. If the pointers of the copied cells refer to locations beyond the compacted area, the old locations are accessed to retrieve the new address. Here is the algorithm:

```
Compact()
    lo = the bottom of memory;
    hi = the top of memory;
    while (lo < hi)   // scan the entire memory;
        while *lo (the cell pointed to by lo) is marked
            lo++;
        while *hi is not marked
            hi--;
        unmark cell *hi;
        *lo = *hi;
        tail(*hi--) = lo++;  // leave forwarding address;
    lo = the bottom of memory;
    while (lo <= hi)   // scan only the compacted area;
        if *lo is not atom and head(*lo) > hi
            head(*lo) = tail(head(*lo));
        if *lo is not atom and tail(*lo) > hi
            tail(*lo) = tail(tail(*lo));
        lo++;
```

Figure 12.8 illustrates this process in the case where there are two available spots in front of cell *A*, to which cells *B* and *C* can be moved. Figure 12.8a illustrates the situation in memory before compaction. In Figure 12.8b, cells B and C have been moved into these spots with the *tail* fields of the old cells indicating the new positions. Figure 12.8c illustrates the compacted part of memory after checking the *head* and *tail* fields of all cells and updating them in case they referred to positions beyond the compacted area.

This simple algorithm is inefficient in that it requires one pass through memory to mark cells, one pass to move marked cells into contiguous locations, and one pass through the compacted area to update pointers; two and a half memory passes are required. One way to reduce the number of passes is to integrate marking and sweeping, which opens up a new category of methods.

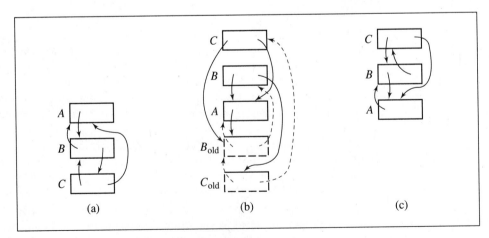

Figure 12.8: **An example of memory compaction.**

12.3.2   Copying Methods

Copying algorithms are cleaner than the previous methods in that they do not touch garbage. They process only the cells accessible from the root pointers and put them together; the unprocessed cells are available. An example of a copying method is the *stop-and-copy algorithm* which divides memory in two *semispaces* one of which is only used for allocating memory (Fenichel, Yochelson 1969). After the allocation pointer reaches the end of the semispace, all the cells being used are copied to the second semispace which becomes an active space, and the program resumes execution (see Figure 12.9).

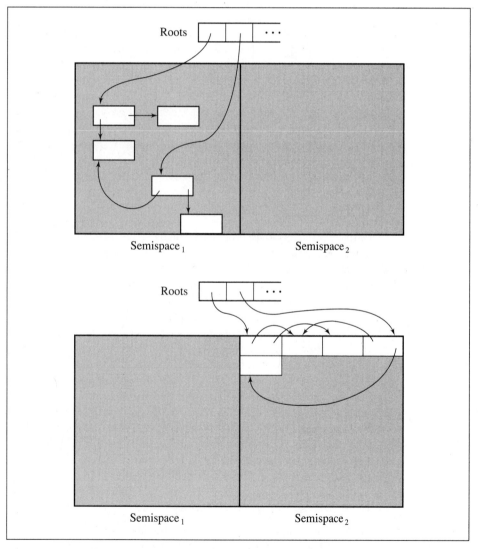

Figure 12.9:   **A situation in memory before copying the contents of cells in use from semispace₁ to semispace₂ (a) and the situation right after copying (b). All used cells are packed contiguously.**

Lists can be copied using breadth-first traversal (Cheney 1970). If lists were just binary trees with no cross references, the algorithm would be the same as the breadth-first tree traversal discussed in Section 6.4.1. However, lists can have cycles and cells on one list can point to cells on another. In the latter case this algorithm produces multiple copies of the same cell. In the former case it falls into an infinite loop. The problem can be easily solved, as in `Compact()`, by retaining a forward address in the cell being copied. This allows the copying procedure to refer to a cell after it has already been copied. This algorithm requires no marking phase and no stack. The breadth-first traversal also allows it to combine two additional tasks: copying lists and updating pointers. The algorithm deals with garbage only indirectly, since it does not really access unneeded cells. The more garbage that is in memory, the faster the algorithm.

Note that the cost of garbage collection decreases with the increase of the size of memory (semispaces). Actually, not only does the number of collections drop with the increase of memory, but the time per one collection decreases, which is a more unexpected result. For example, a program run in 4MB memory requires 34 collections with the average of 6.8 seconds per collection. The same program run in 16MB memory requires only 3 collections with 2.7 seconds per collection — a very significant improvement. To be sure, if memory is really large (64MB in this example), no garbage collection is needed (Appel 1987). This also indicates that shifting the responsibility for free locations from the programmer (as in C++ or Pascal) to the garbage collector does not have to lead to slower programs. All this is true under the assumption that a large memory is available.

12.3.3   Incremental Garbage Collection

Garbage collectors in list processing languages are invoked automatically when the available memory resources become scanty. If this happens during the execution of a program, the garbage collector suspends program execution until the garbage collector finishes its task. Garbage collection may take several seconds, which may turn into minutes in time-sharing systems. This situation may not be acceptable in real-time systems in which the fast response of a program is vital. Therefore, it is oftentimes desirable to create *incremental garbage collectors* whose execution is interleaved with the execution of the program. Program execution is suspended only for a brief moment, allowing the collector to clean memory to some extent, leaving some unprocessed portion of memory to be cleaned later. Therein lies the problem. After the collector partially processes some lists, the program can change or mutate those lists. For this reason, a program used in connection with an incremental garbage collection is called a *mutator*. Such changes have to be taken into consideration after the collector resumes execution, possibly to reprocess some cells or entire lists. This additional burden indicates that incremental collectors require more effort than regular collectors. In fact, it has been shown that incremental collectors require twice the processing power of regular collectors (Wadler 1976).

Copying Methods in Incremental Garbage Collection

An incremental algorithm based on the stop-and-copy technique has been devised by Henry Baker (1978). As in stop-and-copy, the Baker algorithm also uses two semispaces, called *fromspace* and *tospace*, which are both active to ensure proper cooperation between the mutator and the collector. The basic idea is to allocate cells in tospace starting from its top and always copy the same number, k, of cells from fromspace to tospace upon request.

In this way, the collector can perform its task without incurring any undue interruption of the mutator's work. After all reachable cells have been copied to tospace, the roles of the semispaces are interchanged.

The collector maintains two pointers. The first pointer is *scan* which points to a cell whose *head* and *tail* lists should be copied to tospace if they still are in fromspace. Since these lists may be larger than k, they may not be processed at one time. Up to k cells accessible by breadth-first traversal are copied from fromspace and the copies are put at the end of the queue. This queue is simply accessible by the second pointer, *bottom*, which points to the beginning of the free space in tospace. The collector can process *tail* of the current cell during the same time slice, but it may wait until the next turn. Figure 12.10 contains an example. If a request comes to allocate a cell whose *head* points to P and *tail* to Q (as in Lisp's $cons(P,Q)$), with both P and Q residing in tospace, then a new cell is allocated in the upper part of tospace with both its pointer fields properly initialized. Assuming that $k = 2$, two cells are copied from the *head* list of the cell pointed to by *scan*, and the *tail* is processed when the next request comes. As in stop-and-copy, Baker's algorithm retains a forwarding address in the original cell in fromspace to its copy in tospace just in case later allocations refer to this original.

Special care must be taken when the *head* and/or *tail* of a cell being allocated refer to a cell in fromspace, either already copied or still in fromspace. Because the cells at the top of tospace are not processed by the collector, retaining a pointer in any of them to fromspace cells leads to fatal consequences after fromspace becomes tospace since the latter cells are now considered available and filled with new contents. The mutator could at one point use the pointer to the original, and at a later point could use a copy, leading to inconsistencies. Hence, the mutator is preceded by a *read barrier* which precludes utilizing references to cells in fromspace. In the case of a reference to fromspace, we have to check whether this cell has a forwarding address, an address in its *tail* to a location in tospace. If the answer is yes, the forwarding address is used in the allocation. Otherwise, the cell referred to in the current allocation has to be copied *before* the actual allocation takes place. For example, if the *head* of a cell to be allocated is to point to P, a cell in fromspace which has already been copied, as illustrated in Figure 12.11a, P's new address is stored in *head* (see Figure 12.11b). If the *tail* of the new cell is to point to Q which is still untouched in fromspace, Q is copied to tospace (along with one descendant, since $k = 2$) and only afterwards is the *tail* of the new cell initialized to copy of Q.

Baker's algorithm lends itself to various modifications and improvements. For example, to avoid constant condition tests when allocating new cells, an indirection field is included in every cell. If a cell is in tospace, the indirection field points to itself, otherwise it points to its copy in tospace (Brooks 1984). Tests are avoided, but indirection pointers have to be maintained for every cell instead. Another way to solve this problem is by utilizing hardware facilities, if available. For example, memory protection facilities can prevent the mutator's access to cells not processed by collector: all pages of the heap with unprocessed cells are read-protected (Ellis, Li, Appel 1988). If the mutator attempts to access such a page, the access is trapped and an exception raised, forcing the collector to process this page so that mutator can resume execution. But this method can undermine the incremental collection since after the semispaces change roles, traps are invoked frequently and each trap requires that an entire page of the heap be processed. Some additional provisions may be needed such as not requiring a scan of the entire page in case of a trap. On the other hand, if the heap is not accessed too frequently, this is not a problem.

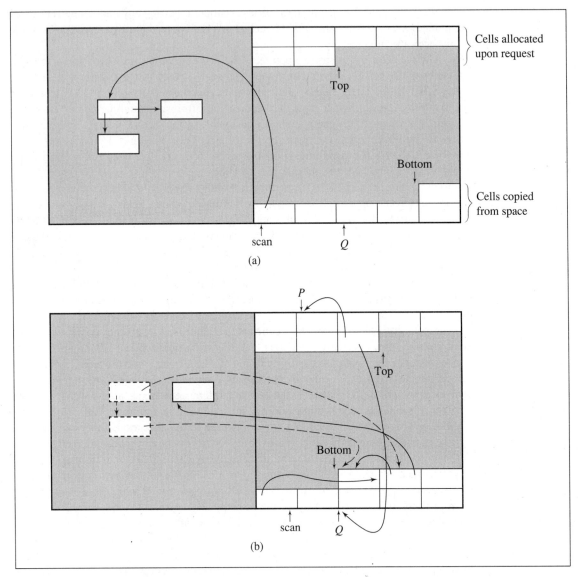

Figure 12.10: **A situation in memory before (a) and after (b) allocating a cell with *head* and *tail* pointers referring to cells P and Q in tospace according to the Baker algorithm.**

An interesting modification to Baker's algorithm is a technique based on the observation that most allocated cells are needed for a very short time; only some of them are used for longer timespans. This leads to a *generational garbage collection* technique which divides all allocated cells into at least two generations and focuses its attention on the youngest generation which generates most of the garbage. Such cells do not need to be copied, saving the garbage collector some work. Moreover, the constant checking and

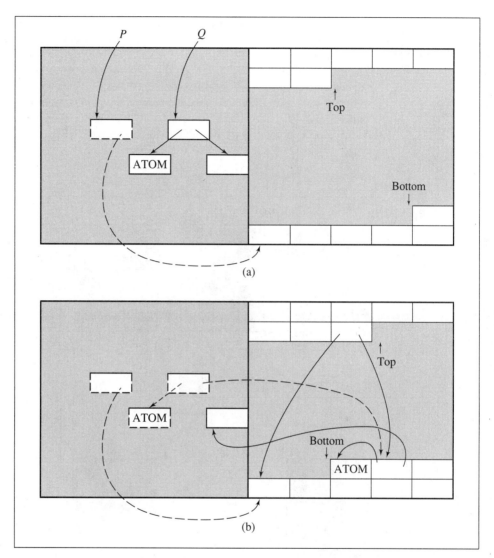

Figure 12.11: **Changes performed by the Baker algorithm when addresses *P* and *Q* refer to cells in fromspace, *P* to an already copied cell, *Q* to a cell still in fromspace.**

copying of long-lived cells is unnecessarily wasteful, so testing garbage production among such cells is performed only infrequently.

In a classic version of a generational garbage collector, the address space is divided into several regions, $r_1, \ldots, r_n$, not just into tospace and fromspace; each of these regions holds cells of the same generation (Lieberman, Hewitt 1983). Most pointers point to cells of an older generation. Some of them, however, can point forward in time (e.g., when Lisp's *rplaca* is used). In this method, such forward references are made indirectly through an *entry table* associated with each region. A pointer from a region r_i does not point to a cell c in a region r_{i+j} but to a cell c' in the entry table associated with r_{i+j}; c' contains a pointer to c. If a region r_i becomes full, all reachable cells are copied to another region r_i' and all regions with generations younger than r_i are visited to update pointers referring to cells which just have been transferred to the new region. Regions with generations older than r_i do not have to be visited. Presumably only a few references in the entry table of r_i are updated (see Figure 12.12). The problem of cleaning the entry tables can be solved by storing in each table, along with each pointer, a unique identifier for a region to which the pointer refers. The identifier is updated along with the pointer. Some pointers may be abandoned, as the pointer in the entry table for region r_{i+1} in Figure 12.12b, and they are ready to be cleaned up after the region itself is abandoned.

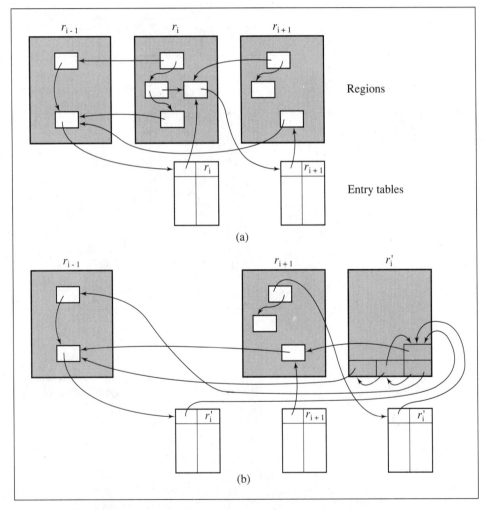

Figure 12.12: **A situation in three regions before (a) and after (b) copying reachable cells from region r_i to region r_i' in Lieberman-Hewitt technique of generational garbage collection.**

Noncopying Methods

In incremental methods based on copying, the problem is not so much with the content of the original cell and its copy, but with their positions or addresses in memory, which by necessity have to be different. The mutator must not treat these addresses on a par, otherwise the program crashes. Therefore, some mechanisms are needed to maintain the integrity of addressing, and the read barrier serves this purpose. But we may need to avoid copying altogether; after all, the first garbage collection method, mark-and-sweep, did not use copies. However, because of the exhaustive and uninterrupted passes, the mark-and-sweep method was too costly, and in real-time systems it is simply unacceptable. Yet, the simplicity of this method is very appealing and an attempt was made by Taiichi Yuasa to adapt it to real-time constraints, with satisfactory results.

Yuasa's algorithm also has two phases: one for marking reachable (used) cells, and one for sweeping memory by including in *avail-list* all unused (unmarked) cells. The marking phase is similar to that used in the mark-and-sweep method except that it is incremental; each time the marking procedure is invoked, it marks only k_1 cells for some small constant k_1. After k_1 cells have been marked, the mutator resumes execution. The constant k_2 is used during the sweeping phase to decide how many cells have to be processed before execution is turned over to the mutator. The garbage collector remembers whether it is in the middle of marking or sweeping. The procedure for marking or sweeping is always invoked after one cell is requested from memory by a procedure which creates one new root pointer and initializes its *head* and *tail* fields, as in the following pseudocode:

```
CreateRootPtr(p,q,r)  // Lisp's cons
    if collector is in the marking phase
        mark up to k₁ cells;
    else if collector is in the sweeping phase
        sweep up to k₂ cells;
    else if the number of cells on availList is low
        push all root pointers onto collector's stack st;
    p = first cell on availList;
    head(p) = q;
    tail(p) = r;
    mark p if it is in the unswept portion of heap;
```

Remember that the mutator can scramble some graphs accessible from root pointers, which is particularly important if it happens during the marking phase, since it may cause certain cells to remain unmarked even though they are accessible. Figure 12.13 contains an example. After all of the roots have been pushed onto stack **st** (Figure 12.13a), and roots r_3 and r_2 have been processed and root r_1 is being processed (Figure 12.13b), the mutator executes two assignments: *head*(r_3) is changed to *tail*(r_1), and *tail*(r_1) is assigned r_2 (Figure 12.13c). If the marking process is now restarted, it has no chance to mark *head*$(r_3) = c_5$, since the entire graph r_3 is assumed to have been processed. This leads to including the cell *head*(r_3) in the *avail-list* during the sweeping phase. To prevent that, the function which updates either *head* or *tail* of any cell pushes the old value of the field being updated onto the stack used by garbage collector. For example,

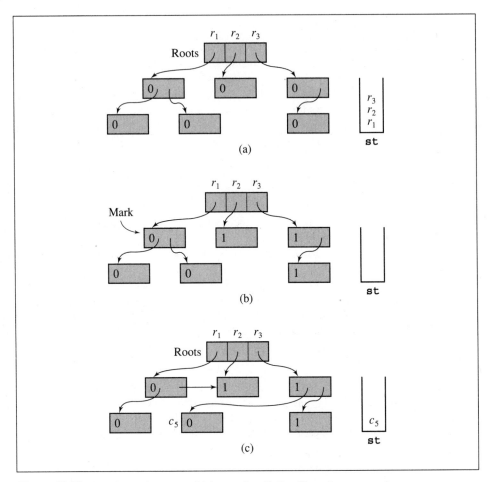

Figure 12.13: **An inconsistency which results if, in Yuasa's noncopying incremental garbage collector, a stack is not used to record cells possibly unprocessed during the marking phase.**

```
UpdateTail(p,q)   // Lisp's rplacd
    if collector is in the marking phase
        mark tail(p);
        st.Push(tail(p));
    tail(p) = q;
```

In the marking phase, the stack **st** is popped up k_1 times and for each pointer **p** popped off, its *head* and *tail* are marked.

The sweeping phase incrementally goes through memory, includes in *avail-list* all unmarked cells, and unmarks all marked cells. For the sake of consistency, if a new cell is allocated, it remains unmarked if a certain part of memory has been already swept. Otherwise, the next round of marking could lead to distorted results. Figure 12.14 illustrates

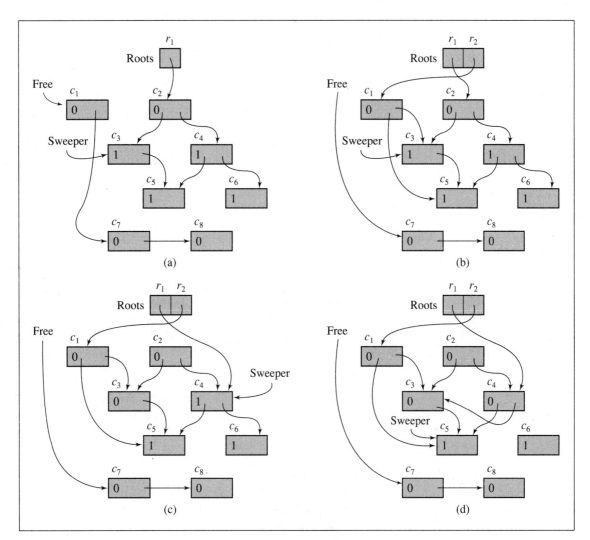

Figure 12.14: **Memory changes during the sweeping phase using Yuasa's method.**

an example. The pointer *sweeper* has already reached cell c_3, and now the mutator requests a new cell by executing **CreateRootPtr**(r_2, c_5, c_3), whereby the first cell is detached from *avail-list* and made a new root (Figure 12.14b). But the newly allocated cell is not marked, since it precedes *sweeper* in memory.

   If some cell is released in the swept area, it becomes garbage but it is not swept up until sweeping restarts from the beginning of memory. For example, after assigning *tail*(r_1) to r_1, cell c_2 becomes unreachable, and yet it is not reclaimed now by adding it to *avail-list* (Figure 12.14c). The same thing happens to cells having higher addresses than the current value of *sweeper* as it is the case with cell c_6 after assigning *tail*(r_2) to *tail*(r_1) (Figure 12.14d). This is called *floating garbage*; floating garbage is collected in the next cycle.

■ 12.4 CONCLUDING REMARKS

When assessing the efficiency of memory management algorithms, and especially garbage collectors, we have to be careful to avoid Paul Wilson's castigation that standard textbooks overstress the asymptotic complexity of algorithms missing the key point: "the constant factors associated with various costs" (Wilson 1992). This is especially apparent in the case of nonincremental algorithms whose cost is usually proportional either to the size n of the heap (mark-and-sweep) or to the number m of reachable cells (stop-and-copy). This is an immediate indication of the superiority of the latter techniques, especially when the number of surviving cells is small compared to the heap size. However, when we take into consideration that the cost of sweeping is minuscule compared to the cost of copying, the difference in efficiency is not so obvious. In fact, as it has been shown, real-time performances of the mark-and-sweep and the stop-and-copy techniques are very similar (Zorn 1990).

This example indicates that there are two main sources affecting the efficiency of algorithms: the behavior of the program and the characteristics of the underlying hardware. If a program allocates memory for a long time, then m approaches n; scanning only reachable cells is close to scanning the entire heap (or its region). This is especially important for generational garbage collectors, whose efficiency relies on the assumption that most allocated cells are used for a very brief interval. On the other hand, if sweeping a cell is not much faster than copying it, then copying techniques have an edge.

Asymptotic complexity is too imprecise and the published research on memory management indicates little preoccupation with computing this characteristic of algorithms. "The constant factors associated with various costs" are much more relevant. Also, fine-grained measures of efficiency are proposed but not all of them are easy to measure, such as the amount of work per memory cell reclaimed, rate of object creation, average lifetime of objects, or the density of accessible objects (Lieberman, Hewitt 1983).

Memory management algorithms are usually closely tied to the hardware which may determine which algorithm is chosen. For example, garbage collection can be substantially sped up if some dedicated hardware is used. In Lisp machines, the read barrier is implemented in hardware and microcode, which points to those incremental garbage collectors which rely on this barrier. Without hardware support, processing time in such collectors takes approximately 50% of program run time. If this hardware support is lacking, non-copying algorithms are a better choice. In real-time systems, where the responsiveness of the computer is the issue, additional overhead of the garbage collector is added. It may be less noticeable than in the case of nonincremental collectors, since at no time does a program have to wait in a visible way for the collector to finish its task. However, the tuning of incremental methods should be proportional to real-time constraints.

■ 12.5 CASE STUDY: AN IN-PLACE GARBAGE COLLECTOR

Copying algorithms for garbage collectors are efficient in that they do not require processing unused cells. Cells which are not processed are considered garbage at the end of collection. However, these algorithms are inefficient in copying reachable cells from one semispace to another. An in-place garbage collector attempts to retain the advantages of copying algorithms without producing copies of the reachable cells (Baker 1992).

The in-place algorithm constantly maintains two doubly linked lists, `freeList` and `nonFreeList`. `freeList` initially contains all cells of **heap**, and a cell is moved from `freeList` to the other list if a request comes to construct a list or construct a new atom. After `freeList` becomes empty, the function `Collect()` is invoked. This function first transfers all root pointers from `nonFreeList` to an intermediate `toBeMarkedList`. Then, `Collect()` detaches cells from `toBeMarkedList` one at a time and transfers each cell to another temporary list, `markedList`, after setting its **mark** field to **marked**. Also, for each nonatom cell, `Collect()` attaches the unmarked **head** and **tail** pointers to `toBeMarkedList`. In the case study, they are attached to the beginning of `toBeMarkedList`, leading to a depth-first traversal of list structures. For breadth-first traversal (as in Cheney's algorithm), they have to be attached to the end of `toBeMarkedList`, which requires another pointer to the end of the list. Note that although a cell is transferred to `markedList`, it is also marked to prevent infinite loops of cyclic structures and redundant processing of interconnected noncycling structures.

After `toBeMarkedList` becomes empty, all reachable cells of **heap** have been processed and `Collect()` is almost done. Before returning from `Collect()`, all cells left in `nonFreeList` become members of `freeList`, and all marked cells are put on `nonFreeList` after changing their **mark** fields to **!marked**. `Program()` can now resume.

To be sure, the garbage collector is part of a program's environment and is executed in the background almost unbeknown to the user. To exemplify the working of a garbage collector, some elements of the program background are simulated in the case study, in particular the heap and the symbol table.

The heap is implemented as an array of **struct** with two flag fields, atom/nonatom and marked/nonmarked, and two pointer fields which are really integer fields indicating positions in **heap** of the previous and next cells (if any). In accordance with this implementation, both permanent lists, `freeList` and `nonFreeList`, and both temporary lists, `toBeMarkedList` and `markedList`, are simply integers indicating the index in **heap** of the first cell on a given list (if any).

The symbol table is implemented as an array **roots** of root pointers. No explicit variable names are used, only indexes to **heap** cells. For example, if **roots** is [3 2 4 0], then only four variables are currently in use by `Program()`, `roots[0]` through `roots[3]`, and these variables are pointing to cells 3, 2, 4, and 0 in **heap**. The numbers 0–3 are subscripts to more palpable variable names, such as var_0, var_1, var_2, and var_3.

The user `Program()` is just a coarse simulator which does nothing but require allocations and reallocations on **heap**. These requirements are generated randomly and classified by the type of requirement: 30% are atom (re)allocations, 60% are list (re)allocations, 5% are **head** updates, and the remaining 5% are **tail** updates. The percentages can be assigned differently and the distribution of assignments can be tuned to the number of previously made assignments by introducing changes to `Program()`. The size of **heap** and the size of array of pointers can also be modified.

`Program()` generates a random number **rn** between 0 and 99 to indicate the operation to be performed. Then, variables are randomly chosen from **roots**. For example, if **rn** is 11, **roots** is [3 2 4 0], and **p** is 2, then the cell **roots[p]** = 4 of **heap** indicated by variable 2 becomes an atom by storing the value of **val** in its **value** field and **atom** in its **kind** flag. If **p** is 4, this indicates that a new variable (variable 4 or var_4) has to be created in position 4 of **roots**, and position **roots[4]** is assigned the first value from **freeList**.

To see that this program does something, a simple **PrintList()** function is supplied which prints elements on a given list.

Figure 12.15 contains the code for the in-place garbage collector.

```
//*********************   heap.h    *****************************

#ifndef HEAP_CLASS
#define HEAP_CLASS


const int maxHeap =  10;
const int maxRoot = 100;


#define Head(p)    heap[p].info.links[head]
#define Tail(p)    heap[p].info.links[tail]
#define Value(p)   heap[p].info.value
#define Prev(p)    heap[p].prev
#define Next(p)    heap[p].next
#define Kind(p)    heap[p].kind
#define Mark(p)    heap[p].mark


class Heap {
public:
      int rootCnt;
      Heap();
      int  RootIsNotAtom(int p)
          { return Kind(roots[p]) != atom; }
      void UpdateHead(int p, int q)              // Lisp's rplaca;
          { Head(roots[p]) = roots[q]; }
      void UpdateTail(int p, int q)              // Lisp's rplacd;
          { Tail(roots[p]) = roots[q]; }
      void AllocateAtom(int,int);
      void AllocateList(int,int,int);
      void PrintList(int,char*);
      void PrintHeap();
private:
      const int empty, OK, head, tail;
```

Figure 12.15: **Implementation of an in-place garbge collector.**   **continued**

```cpp
        const unsigned int atom, marked;
        struct Cell {
                unsigned int kind : 1;
                unsigned int mark : 1;
                int prev, next;
                union {
                        int value;      // value for atom,
                        int links[2];   // head and tail for nonatom;
                        } info;
                } heap[maxHeap];
        int roots[maxRoot], freeList, nonFreeList;

        void Insert(int,int&);
        void Detach(int,int&);
        void Transfer(int cell, int& list1, int& list2)
            { Detach(cell,list1); Insert(cell,list2); }
        void Collect();
        AllocateAux(int);
};


#endif


//*************************   heap.cpp   *****************************

#include <iostream.h>
#include "heap.h"


Heap::Heap() : empty(-1), OK(1), head(0),
              tail(1), atom(1), marked(1)
{   register int i;

    freeList = nonFreeList = empty;
    rootCnt = 0;
    for (i = maxHeap-1; i >= 0; i--) {
        Insert(i,freeList);
        Mark(i) = !marked;
    }
}
```

Figure 12.15: **Implementation of an in-place garbge collector.**   **continued**

```
void
Heap::Detach (int cell, int& list)
{
    if (Next(cell) != empty)
        Prev(Next(cell)) = Prev(cell);
    if (Prev(cell) != empty)
        Next(Prev(cell)) = Next(cell);
    if (cell == list)                      // head of the list;
        list = Next(cell);
}


void
Heap::Insert (int cell, int& list)
{
    Prev(cell) = empty;
    Next(cell) = list;
    if (list != empty)
        Prev(list) = cell;
    list = cell;
}


void
Heap::Collect()
{   register int p, hold;
    int toBeMarkedList = empty, markedList  = empty;

    for (p = 0; p < rootCnt; p++)
        Transfer(roots[p],nonFreeList,toBeMarkedList);
    for (p = toBeMarkedList; p != empty; p = hold) {
        hold = Next(p);              // needed, since transfer changes
        Transfer(p,toBeMarkedList,markedList);  // the next field;
        Mark(p) = marked;
        if (Kind(p) != atom && Mark(p) != marked) {
            Transfer(Head(p),nonFreeList,toBeMarkedList);
            Transfer(Tail(p),nonFreeList,toBeMarkedList);
        }
    }
    for (p = markedList; p != empty; p = Next(p))
        Mark(p) = !marked;
```

Figure 12.15: **Implementation of an in-place garbge collector.**   **continued**

```
        freeList = nonFreeList;
        nonFreeList = markedList;
}


Heap::AllocateAux(int p)
{
    if (p == maxRoot) {
        cout << "No room for new roots\n";
        return !OK;
    }
    if (freeList == empty)
        Collect();
    if (freeList == empty) {
        cout << "No room in heap for new cells\n";
        return !OK;
    }
    if (p == rootCnt)
        roots[rootCnt++] = p;
    roots[p] = freeList;
    Transfer(freeList,freeList,nonFreeList);
    return OK;
}


void
Heap::AllocateAtom (int p, int val)     // an instance of Lisp's setf;
{
    if (AllocateAux(p) == OK) {
        Kind(roots[p]) = atom;
        Value(roots[p]) = val;
    }
}


void
Heap::AllocateList(int p, int q, int r) // Lisp's cons;
{
    if (AllocateAux(p) == OK) {
        Kind(roots[p]) = !atom;
        Head(roots[p]) = roots[q];
```

Figure 12.15: **Implementation of an in-place garbge collector.**   **continued**

```
          Tail(roots[p]) = roots[r];
      }
}

void
Heap::PrintList(int list, char *name)
{   int i;

    cout << name;
    for (i = list; i != empty; i = Next(i))
        cout << "(" << i << " " << Head(i) << " " << Tail(i) << ")";
    cout << endl;
}

void
Heap::PrintHeap()
{   register int i;

    cout << "roots: ";
    for (i = 0; i < rootCnt; i++)
        cout << roots[i] << " ";
    cout << endl;
    for (i = 0; i < maxHeap; i++)
        cout << "(" << i << " " << Kind(i) << " " << Mark(i) << " "
             << Prev(i) << " " << Next(i) << " " << Head(i) << " "
             << Tail(i) << ") ";
    cout << endl;
    PrintList(freeList,"FreeList");
    PrintList(nonFreeList,"NonFreeList");
}

//************************  collector.cpp  **************************

#include <iostream.h>
#include <stdlib.h>
#include "heap.h"

Heap heap;

void
Program()
```

Figure 12.15: **Implementation of an in-place garbge collector.**   **continued**

```
{    static int val = 123;
     int rn = rand()%100 + 1;
     int p = rand() % (heap.rootCnt+1) + 1; // possibly new root;
     int q = rand() % heap.rootCnt + 1;
     int r = rand() % heap.rootCnt + 1;

     if (rn < 20)
          heap.AllocateAtom(p,val++);
     else if (rn < 90)
          heap.AllocateList(p,q,r);
     else if (rn < 95 && heap.RootIsNotAtom(q))
          heap.UpdateHead(q,r);
     else if (heap.RootIsNotAtom(q))
          heap.UpdateTail(q,r);
     heap.PrintHeap();
}


main()
{    int i;

     heap.AllocateAtom(0,13);      // to start off:
     heap.AllocateAtom(1,14);      //    create two atoms
     heap.AllocateList(2,0,1);     //    and one nonatom;
     for (i = 0; i < 10; i++)
          Program();
     return 0;
}
```

Figure 12.15: **Implementation of an in-place garbage collector.**

■ 12.6 EXERCISES

1. What happens to the first-fit method if it is applied to a list ordered by block sizes?

2. How does the effort leading to coalescing blocks in sequential-fit methods depend on the order of blocks on the list? How can possible problems caused by these orders be solved?

3. The *optimal-fit* method determines which block to allocate after examining a sample of blocks to find the closest match to the request and the first block exceeding this match (Campbell 1971). What does the efficiency of this method depend on? How does this algorithm compare to the efficiency of other sequential-fit methods?

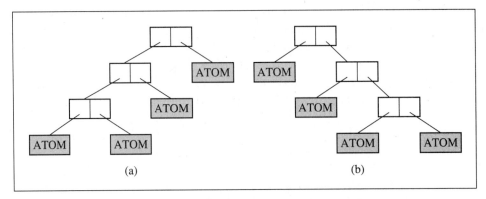

Figure 12.16: **Left degenerate (a) and right degenerate (b) list structures.**

4. In what circumstances can the size-list in the adaptive exact-fit method be empty (except at the beginning)? What is its maximal size and when can it be this size?

5. Why in the buddy system are doubly linked, not singly linked, lists of blocks used?

6. Give an algorithm for returning blocks to the memory pool using the Fibonacci buddy system.

7. Apply `MarkingWithStack()` to the left degenerate and right degenerate list structures in Figure 12.16. How many calls to `Pop()` and `Push()` are executed for each case? Are all of them necessary? How would you optimize the code to avoid unnecessary operations?

8. In a *reference count method* of garbage collection, each cell c has a counter field whose value indicates how many other cells refer (point) to it. The counter is incremented every time another cell refers to c, and decremented if a reference is deleted. The garbage collector uses this counter when sweeping memory: if a cell's count is zero, the cell can be reclaimed since it is not pointed to by any other cell. Discuss the advantages and disadvantages of this garbage collection method.

9. In Baker's algorithm, the scanning performed by the collector should be finished before *bottom* reaches *top* in tospace to flip spaces. What should the value of k be to ascertain this? Assume that n is the maximum number of cells required by a program, and $2m$ is the number of cells in fromspace and in tospace. What is the impact of doubling the value of k when it is an integer and when it is a fraction (for example, if it is .5 then one copy is made per two requests)?

10. In a modification of Baker's algorithm which requires updating heap pages in the case when the mutator's access is trapped (Ellis, Li, Appel 1988), there is a problem with objects which may cross the page boundary. Suggest a solution to this problem.

■ 12.7 PROGRAMMING ASSIGNMENTS

1. Implement the following memory allocation method developed by W. A. Wulf, C. B. Weinstock, and C. B. Johnsson (Standish 1980) called the *quick-fit* method. For an experimentally found number n of the most frequently requested sizes of blocks, this

method uses an array *avail* of $n + 1$ cells, each cell i pointing to a linked list of blocks of size i. The last cell $(n + 1)$ refers to a block of other, less frequently needed sizes. It may also be a pointer to a linked list, but because of possibly a large number of such blocks, another organization is recommended, such as a binary search tree. Write functions to allocate and deallocate blocks. If a block is returned, coalesce it with its neighbors. To test your program, randomly generate sizes of blocks to be allocated from memory simulated by an array whose size is a power of two.

2. In the dual buddy system, two parts of memory are managed by the binary buddy method. But the number of such areas can be larger (Page, Hagins 1986). Write a program to operate on three such areas, with block sizes of the form $2^i, 3 * 2^j$, and $5 * 2^k$. For a requested block size s, round s to the nearest block size which can be generated by this method. For example, size 11 is rounded up to 12, which is the number from the second area. If this request cannot be accommodated in this area, 12 is rounded up to the next possibly available number, which is 15, a number from the third area. If there is no available block of this or greater size in this area either, the first area is tried. In case of failure, keep requests on a list and process them as soon as a block of a sufficient size is coalesced. Run your program changing three parameters: the intervals for which blocks are reserved, the number of incoming requests, and the overall size of memory.

3. Implement a simple version of a generational garbage collector which uses only two regions (Appel 1989). The heap is divided into two even parts. The upper part holds cells which have been copied from the lower part as cells reachable from the root pointers. The lower part is used for memory allocation and holds only newer cells (see Figure 12.17a). After this part becomes full, the garbage collector cleans it by copying all reachable cells to the upper part (Figure 12.17b), after which allocations are made starting from the beginning of the lower part. After several turns, the upper part becomes full too, and the cells being copied from the lower part are in reality copied to the lower part (Figure 12.17c). In this case, the cleanup process of the upper part is begun by copying all reachable cells from the upper part to the lower part (Figure 12.17d), and then all reachable cells are copied to the beginning of the upper part (Figure 12.17e).

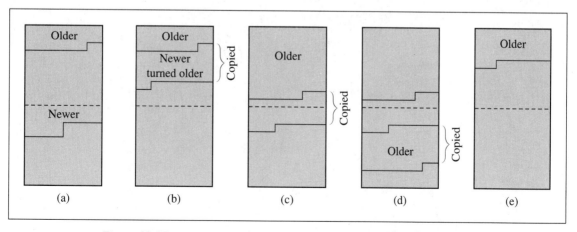

Figure 12.17: **A heap with two regions for Appel's generational garbage collection.**

4. The case study presents an in-place nonincremental garbage collector. Modify and extend it to become an incremental collector. In this case, **Program()** becomes **Mutator()** which allows **Collector()** to process **k** cells, for some value of **k**. To prevent **Mutator()** from introducing inconsistencies in structures possibly not completely processed by **Collector()**, **Mutator()** should transfer any unmarked cell from **freeList** to **toBeMarkedList**.

Another very elegant modification is obtained by grouping all four lists in a circular list, creating what Henry Baker (1992) called a *treadmill* (Figure 12.18a).

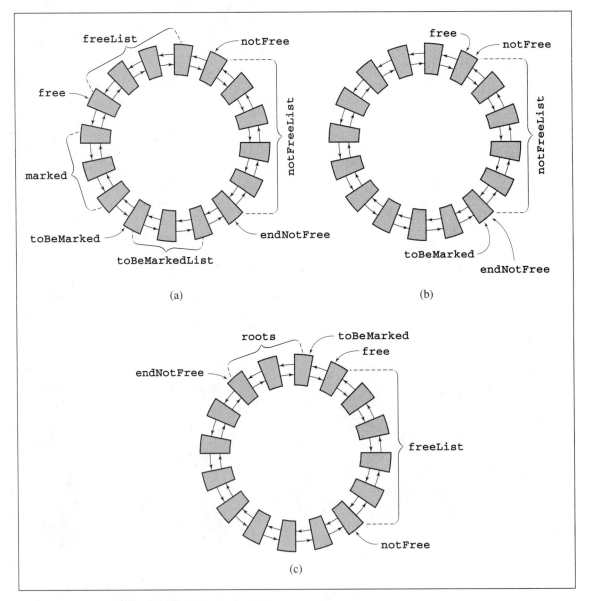

Figure 12.18: **Baker's treadmill.**

Pointer `free` is moved in a clockwise direction if a new cell is requested, pointer `toBeMarked` is moved **k** times when allowed by the mutator. For each nonatom cell currently scanned by `toBeMarked`, its *head* and *tail* are transferred in front of `toBeMarked` if they are not marked. After `toBeMarked` meets `endNotFree`, there are no cells to be marked, and after `free` meets `notFree`, there are no free cells on the list of free cells (Figure 12.18b). In this case, what remains between `notFree` and `endNotFree` (former `nonFreeList`) is garbage, and hence can be utilized by the mutator. Therefore, the roles of `notFree` and `endNotFree` are exchanged; it is as though `notFreeList` became `freeList` (Figure 12.18c). All root pointers are transferred to a part of the treadmill between `toBeMarked` and `endFree` (to create a seed of the former `toBeMarkedList`) and the mutator can resume execution.

BIBLIOGRAPHY

Memory Management

[1] Smith, Harry F., *Data Structures: Form and Function*, San Diego, CA: Harcourt-Brace-Jovanovich, 1987, Ch. 11.

[2] Standish, Thomas A., *Data Structure Techniques*, Reading, MA: Addison-Wesley, 1980, Chs. 5, 6.

Sequential-fit Methods

[3] Campbell, J. A., "A Note on an Optimal-Fit Method for Dynamic Allocation of Storage," *Computer Journal* 14 (1971), 7–9.

Nonsequential-fit Methods

[4] Oldehoeft, Rodney R. and Allan, Stephen J., "Adaptive Exact-Fit Storage Management," *Communications of the ACM* 28 (1985), 506–511.

[5] Ross, Douglas T., "The AED Free Storage Package," *Communications of the ACM* 10 (1967), 481–492.

Buddy Systems

[6] Bromley, Allan G., "Memory Fragmentation in Buddy Methods for Dynamic Storage Allocation," *Acta Informatica* 14 (1980), 107–117.

[7] Cranston, Ben and Thomas, Rick, "A Simplified Recombination Scheme for the Fibonacci Buddy System," *Communications of the ACM* 18 (1975), 331–332.

[8] Hinds, James A., "An Algorithm for Locating Adjacent Storage Blocks in the Buddy System," *Communications of the ACM* 18 (1975), 221–222.

[9] Hirschberg, Daniel S., "A Class of Dynamic Memory Allocation Algorithms," *Communications of the ACM* 16 (1973), 615–618.

[10] Knowlton, Kenneth C., "A Fast Storage Allocator," *Communications of the ACM* 8 (1965), 623–625.

[11] Page, Ivor P. and Hagins, Jeff, "Improving Performance of Buddy Systems," *IEEE Transactions on Computers* C-35 (1986), 441–447.

[12] Shen, Kenneth K. and Peterson, James L., "A Weighted Buddy Method for Dynamic Storage Allocation," *Communications of the ACM* 17 (1974), 558–562.

Garbage Collection

[13] Appel, Andrew W., "Garbage Collection Can Be Faster than Stack Allocation," *Information Processing Letters* 25 (1987), 275–279.

[14] Appel, Andrew W., "Simple Generational Garbage Collection and Fast Allocation," *Software — Practice and Experience* 19 (1989), 171–183.

[15] Baker, Henry G., "List Processing in Real Time on a Serial Computer," *Communications of the ACM* 21 (1978), 280–294.

[16] Baker, Henry G., "The Treadmill: Real-Time Garbage Collection Without Motion Sickness," *ACM SIGPLAN Notices* 27 (1992), No. 3, 66–70.

[17] Brooks, Rodney A., "Trading Data Space for Reduced Time and Code Space in Real-Time Collection on Stock Hardware," *SIGPLAN Symposium on Lisp and Functional Programming*, Austin, 1984, 108–113.

[18] Cheney, C.J., "A Nonrecursive List Compacting Algorithm," *Communications of the ACM* 13 (1970), 677–678.

[19] Cohen, Jacques, "Garbage Collection of Linked Data Structures," *Computing Surveys* 13 (1981), 341–367.

[20] Ellis, John R., Li, Kai, and Appel, Andrew W., "Real-Time Concurrent Collection on Stock Multiprocessors," *SIGPLAN Notices* 23 (1988), No. 7, 11–20.

[21] Fenichel, Robert R. and Yochelson, Jerome C., "A Lisp Garbage-Collector for Virtual-Memory Computer Systems," *Communications of the ACM* 12 (1969), 611–612.

[22] Kurokawa, Toshiaki, "A New Fast and Safe Marking Algorithm," *Software — Practice and Experience* 11 (1981), 671–682.

[23] Layer, D. Kevin and Richardson, Chris, "Lisp Systems in the 1990s," *Communications of the ACM* 34 (1991), No. 9, 49–57.

[24] Lieberman, Henry and Hewitt, Carl, "A Real-Time Garbage Collector Based on the Lifetimes of Objects," *Communications of the ACM* 26 (1983), 419–429.

[25] Schorr, H. and Waite, W. M., "An Efficient Machine-Independent Procedure for Garbage Collection in Various List Structures," *Communications of the ACM* 10 (1967), 501–506.

[26] Wadler, Philip L., "Analysis of Algorithm for Real-Time Garbage Collection," *Communications of the ACM* 19 (1976), 491–500, 20 (1977), 120.

[27] Wegbreit, Ben, "A Space-Efficient List Structure Tracing Algorithm," *IEEE Transactions on Computers* C-21 (1972), 1009–1010.

[28] Wilson, Paul R., "Uniprocessor Garbage Collection Techniques," in Bekkers, Yves, Cohen, Jacques (eds.), *Memory Management*, Berlin: Springer, 1992, 1–42.

[29] Yuasa, Taiichi, "Real-Time Garbage Collection on General-Purpose Machine," *Journal of Systems and Software* 11 (1990), 181–198.

[30] Zorn, Benjamin, "Comparing Mark-and-Sweep and Stop-and-Copy Garbage Collection," *Proceedings of the 1990 ACM Conference on Lisp and Functional Programming*, Nice, 1990, 87–98.

A

COMPUTING BIG-O

■ A.1 HARMONIC SERIES

In some computations in this book, the convention H_n is used for harmonic numbers. The *harmonic numbers H_n* are defined as the sums of the *harmonic series*, a series of the form $\sum_{i=1}^{n} \frac{1}{i}$. This is a very important series for the analysis of searching and sorting algorithms. It is proved that

$$H_n = \ln n + \gamma + \frac{1}{2n} - \frac{1}{12n^2} + \frac{1}{120n^4} - \epsilon,$$

where $n \geq 1, 0 < \epsilon < \frac{1}{256n^6}$, and *Euler's constant* $\gamma \approx 0.5772$. This approximation, how-ever, is very unwieldy, and in the context of our analyses, not necessary in this form. H_n's largest term is almost always $\ln n$, the only increasing term in H_n. Thus, H_n can be referred to as big-O of $\ln n$.

■ A.2 APPROXIMATION OF THE FUNCTION lg(n!)

The roughest approximation of $\lg(n!)$ can be obtained by observing that each number in the product $n! = 1 * 2 * \cdots * (n-1) * n$ is less than or equal to n. Thus, $n! \leq n^n$ (only for $n = 1$, $n = n^n$), which implies that $\lg(n!) < \lg(n^n) = n\lg n$ and that $\lg(n!)$ is $O(n\lg n)$.

It has just been established that $\lg(n!)$ is a big-O of $n\lg n$. But, remember from the discussion of the big-O notation that a given function can be a big-O of more than just one function. Can $\lg(n!)$ be approximated by a function smaller than $n\lg n$ such as cn or $\lg^2 n$? Theoretically, it is possible since the approximation has been computed using only an upper bound on $\lg(n!)$. First, $n!$ is approximated using a lower bound which has to be computed first.

If the elements of the product $n!$ are grouped appropriately, as in

$$P_{n!} = (1 * n)(2 * (n - 1))(3 * (n - 2)) \cdots (i * (n - i + 1)) \dots, \text{ for } 1 \le i \le \frac{n}{2},$$

then it can be noted that there are $\frac{n}{2}$ such terms and $n! = P_{n!}$ for even ns or $\frac{n+1}{2}$ terms and $n! = P_{n!}\frac{n+1}{2}$ for odd ns. We claim that each term of $P_{n!}$ is not less than n, or

$$1 \le i \le \frac{n}{2} \Rightarrow i(n - i + 1) \ge n.$$

In fact, this holds because

$$\frac{n}{2} \ge i = \frac{i(i - 1)}{i - 1} \Rightarrow i(n - 2i + 2) \ge n$$

and, as can easily be checked,

$$i \ge 1 \Rightarrow (n - 2i + 2) \le (n - i + 1).$$

A lower bound $n^{\frac{n}{2}}$ can then be computed since $n! = P_{n!} \ge n^{\frac{n}{2}}$, or $\lg(n!) \ge \frac{n}{2} \lg n = O(n \lg n)$. This assumes that n is even. If n is odd, it has to be raised to the power of $\frac{n+1}{2}$, which introduces no substantial change.

The number $\lg(n!)$ has been estimated using the lower and upper bounds of this function, and the result is $n^{\frac{n}{2}} \le n! \le n^n$, or $\frac{n}{2} \lg n \le \lg(n!) \le n \lg n$. To approximate $\lg(n!)$, lower and upper bounds have been used that both grow at the rate of $n \lg n$. This implies that $\lg(n!)$ grows at the same rate, or that $\lg(n!)$ is $O(n \lg n)$. In other words, any sorting algorithm using comparisons on an array of size n must make at least $O(n \lg n)$ comparisons in the worst case. Thus, the function $n \lg n$ approximates the optimal number of comparisons in the worst case.

However, this result seems unsatisfactory because it refers only to the worst case and such a case only occurs occasionally. Most of the time, average cases with random orderings of data occur. Is the number of comparisons really better in such cases, and is it a reasonable assumption that the number of comparisons in the average case can be better than $O(n \lg n)$? Unfortunately, this conjecture has to be rejected and the following computations will prove it false.

Our conjecture is that in any binary tree with m leaves, the average number of arcs leading from the root to a leaf is greater than or equal to $\lg m$.

For $m = 2, \lg m = 1$, if there is just a root with two leaves, then there is only one arc to every one of them. Assume that the proposition holds for a certain $m \ge 2$, and that

$$\text{Ave}_m = \frac{p_1 + \cdots + p_m}{m} \ge \lg m,$$

where each p_i is a path (the number of arcs) from the root to node i. Now consider a randomly chosen leaf with two children about to be attached. This leaf converted to a nonterminal node has an index m (this index is chosen to simplify the notation) and a path from the root to the node m is p_m. After adding two new leaves, the total number of leaves is incremented by one and the path for both these appended leaves is $p_{m+1} = p_m + 1$. Is it true now that

$$\text{Ave}_{m+1} = \frac{p_1 + \cdots + p_{m-1} + 2p_m + 2}{m + 1} \geq \lg(m + 1)?$$

From the definition of Ave_m and Ave_{m+1} and from the fact that $p_m = \text{Ave}_m$ (since leaf m was chosen randomly),

$$(m + 1)\text{Ave}_{m+1} = m\text{Ave}_m + p_m + 2 = (m + 1)\text{Ave}_m + 2.$$

Is it true now that

$$(m + 1)\text{Ave}_{m+1} \geq (m + 1)\lg(m + 1),$$

or

$$(m + 1)\text{Ave}_{m+1} = (m + 1)\text{Ave}_m + 2 \geq (m + 1)\lg m + 2 \geq (m + 1)\lg(m + 1)?$$

This is transformed into

$$2 \geq \lg\left(\frac{m + 1}{m}\right)^{m+1} = \lg\left(1 + \frac{1}{m}\right) + \lg\left(1 + \frac{1}{m}\right)^{m} \rightarrow \lg 1 + \lg e = \lg e \approx 1.44$$

which is true for any $m \geq 1$. This completes the proof of the conjecture.

This proves that for a randomly chosen leaf of a m-leaf decision tree, the reasonable expectation is that the path from the root to the leaf is no longer than $\lg m$. The number of leaves in such a tree is not less than $n!$, which is the number of all possible orderings of an n-element array. If $m \geq n!$, then $\lg m \geq \lg(n!)$. That is the unfortunate result indicating that an average case requires also, like the worst case, $\lg(n!)$ comparisons (length of path = number of comparisons), and as already estimated, $\lg(n!)$ is big-O of $n \lg n$. This is also the best that can be expected in average cases.

■ A.3   BIG-O FOR AVERAGE CASE OF QUICKSORT

Let $C(n)$ be the number of comparisons required to sort an array of n cells. Because the arrays of size 1 and 0 are not partitioned, $C(0) = C(1) = 0$. Assuming a random ordering of an n-element array, any element can be chosen as the bound; the probability that any element will become the bound is the same for all of them. With $C(i - 1)$ and $C(n - i)$ denoting the numbers of the comparisons required to sort the two subarrays, there are

$$C(n) = n - 1 + \frac{1}{n}\sum_{i=1}^{n}(C(i - 1) + C(n - i)), \text{ for } n \geq 2$$

comparisons, where $n - 1$ is the number of comparisons in the partition of the array of size n. First, some simplification can be done:

$$C(n) = n - 1 + \frac{1}{n}\left(\sum_{i=1}^{n} C(i-1) + \sum_{i=1}^{n} C(n-i)\right)$$

$$= n - 1 + \frac{1}{n}\left(\sum_{i=1}^{n} C(i-1) + \sum_{j=1}^{n} C(j-1)\right)$$

$$= n - 1 + \frac{2}{n}\sum_{i=0}^{n-1} C(i)$$

or

$$nC(n) = n(n-1) + 2\sum_{i=0}^{n-1} C(i)$$

To solve the equation, the summation operator is removed first. To that end, the last equation is subtracted from an equation obtained from it,

$$(n+1)C(n+1) = (n+1)n + 2\sum_{i=0}^{n} C(i)$$

resulting in

$$(n+1)C(n+1) - nC(n) = (n+1)n - n(n-1) + 2\left(\sum_{i=0}^{n} C(i) - \sum_{i=0}^{n-1} C(i)\right) = 2C(n) + 2n$$

from which

$$\frac{C(n+1)}{n+2} = \frac{C(n)}{n+1} + \frac{2n}{(n+1)(n+2)} = \frac{C(n)}{n+1} + \frac{4}{n+2} - \frac{2}{n+1}.$$

This equation can be expanded, which gives

$$\frac{C(2)}{3} = \frac{C(1)}{2} + \frac{4}{3} - \frac{2}{2} = \frac{4}{3} - \frac{2}{2}$$

$$\frac{C(3)}{4} = \frac{C(2)}{3} + \frac{4}{4} - \frac{2}{3}$$

$$\frac{C(4)}{5} = \frac{C(3)}{4} + \frac{4}{5} - \frac{2}{4}$$

$$\vdots$$

$$\frac{C(n)}{n+1} = \frac{C(n-1)}{n} + \frac{4}{n+1} - \frac{2}{n}$$

$$\frac{C(n+1)}{n+2} = \frac{C(n)}{n+1} + \frac{4}{n+2} - \frac{2}{n+1}$$

from which

$$\frac{C(n+1)}{n+2} = \left(\frac{4}{3} - \frac{2}{2}\right) + \left(\frac{4}{4} - \frac{2}{3}\right) + \left(\frac{4}{5} - \frac{2}{4}\right) + \cdots + \left(\frac{4}{n+1} - \frac{2}{n}\right)$$

$$+ \left(\frac{4}{n+2} - \frac{2}{n+1}\right)$$

$$= \frac{2}{2} + \frac{2}{3} + \frac{2}{4} + \frac{2}{5} + \cdots + \frac{2}{n} + \frac{2}{n+1} + \frac{4}{n+2}$$

$$= -4 + 2H_{n+2} + \frac{2}{n+2}.$$

Note that H_{n+2} is a harmonic number. Using an approximation for this number (cf. Appendix A.1)

$$C(n) = (n+1)\left(-4 + 2H_{n+1} + \frac{2}{n+1}\right)$$

$$= (n+1)\left(-4 + 2O(\ln n) + \frac{2}{n+1}\right)$$

$$= O(n \lg n).$$

■ A.4   AVERAGE PATH LENGTH IN RANDOM BINARY TREE

In Chapter 6, an approximation is used for the average path length in a randomly created binary search tree. Assuming that

$$P_n(i) = \frac{((i-1)(P_{i-1} + 1) + (n-i)(P_{n-i} + 1))}{n},$$

this approximation is given by this recurrence relation

$$P_1 = 0,$$

$$P_n = \frac{1}{n}\sum_{i=1}^{n} P_n(i) = \frac{1}{n^2}\sum_{i=1}^{n}((i-1)P_{i-1} + 1) + (n-i)(P_{n-i} + 1)),$$

$$P_n = \frac{2}{n^2}\sum_{i=1}^{n-1} i(P_i + 1). \tag{1}$$

From this we also have

$$P_{n-1} = \frac{2}{(n-1)^2}\sum_{i=1}^{n-2} i(P_{i-1} + 1). \tag{2}$$

After multiplying this equation by $\frac{(n-1)^2}{n^2}$ and subtracting the resulting equation from (1) we have

$$P_n = P_{n-1} - \frac{n^2 - 1}{n^2} + \frac{2(n-1)}{n^2} = \frac{(n-1)}{n^2}(P_{n-1}(n+1) + 2)$$

After successive applications of this formula to each P_{n-1}, we have

$$P_n = \frac{n-1}{n^2}\left((n+1)\frac{(n-2)}{(n-1)^2}\left(n\frac{(n-3)}{(n-2)^2}\left((n-1)\frac{(n-4)}{(n-3)^2}\right.\right.\right.$$
$$\left.\left.\left.\left(\cdots\frac{1}{2^2}(P_13 + 2)\cdots\right) + 2\right) + 2\right) + 2\right)$$

$$P_n = 2\left(\frac{n-1}{n} + \frac{(n+1)(n-2)}{(n-1)n^2} + \frac{(n+1)(n-3)}{n(n-1)(n-2)} + \frac{(n+1)(n-4)}{n(n-2)(n-3)} + \cdots + \frac{1}{2 \cdot 3}\right)$$

$$P_n = 2\left(\frac{n+1}{n}\right)\sum_{i=1}^{n-1}\frac{n-i}{(n-i+1)(n-i+2)} = 2\left(\frac{n+1}{n}\right)\sum_{i=1}^{n-1}\left(\frac{2}{n-i+2} - \frac{1}{n-i+1}\right)$$

$$P_n = 2\left(\frac{n+1}{n}\right)\frac{2}{n+1} + 2\left(\frac{n+1}{n}\right)\left(\sum_{i=1}^{n}\frac{1}{n} - 2\right) = 2\left(\frac{n+1}{n}\right)H_n - 4.$$

So P_n is $O(2 \ln n)$.

NAME INDEX

Ackermann, W., 111
Adel'son-Vel'skii, G. M., 175–176, 213
Ahuja, R. K., 332
Allan, S. J., 461, 497
Allen, B., 181, 213
Al-Suwaiyel, M., 251, 269
Appel, A. W., 478, 479, 494, 495, 498
Auslander, M. A., 137

Bachmann, P., 15
Baer, J. L., 212
Baker, H., 479–480, 487, 494, 496, 498
Barron, D. W., 136
Bayer, R., 216, 231–232, 237–238, 268
Bell, J. R., 420–421
Bell, T. C., 456
Bentley, J. L., 74, 269
Berlioux, P., 136
Bertsekas, D. P., 283, 332
Berztiss, A., 212
Bird, R. S., 137
Bitner, J. R., 181, 213
Bizard, P., 136
Blackstone, J. H., 86, 94
Boruvka, O., 290
Bourne, C. P., 249, 269
Brassard, G., 26
Briandais, R. de la, 248, 269
Bromley, A. G., 469, 497
Brooks, R. A., 479, 498
Burge, W. H., 137
Burkhard, W. A., 212
Busacker, R. G., 313

Campbell, J. A., 493, 497
Cardelli, L., 12
Chang, H., 212

Chen, Q. F., 421
Chen, W. C., 422
Cheney, C. J., 478, 487, 498
Cichelli, R. J., 401–403, 421
Cleary, J. G., 456
Cohen, J., 498
Comer, D., 227, 249, 268
Cook, C. R., 403, 422
Copes, W., 94
Cranston, B., 467, 497
Culberson, J., 169, 212

Daoud, A. M., 421
Davisson, L. D., 456
Day, C., 173, 212
Deo, N., 281, 332
D'Esopo, D., 282
Dijkstra, E. W., 98, 137, 278, 294, 332
Dinic, E. A., 309, 332
Doberkat, E. E., 213
Dobosiewicz, W., 350, 385
Dood, M., 422
Dromey, R. G., 386
Dvorak, S., 386
Durian, B., 386
Dy, H. C., 421

Edmonds, J., 284, 307, 332
Ege, R. K., 13
Ellis, J. R., 479, 494, 498
Enbody, R. J., 421
Eppinger, J., 169, 212

Fagin, R., 406, 421
Faloustos, C., 237, 269
Fano, R. M., 438
Fenichel, R. R., 477, 498

Ferguson, D. E., 232, 269
Finkel, R. A., 269
Fleming, B., 13
Fleury, 330
Flores, I., 385
Floyd, R. W., 189, 213, 283, 332, 352
Folk, M. J., 269
Ford, D. F., 249, 269
Ford, L. R., 280, 302–303, 313, 332
Foster, C. C., 179, 213
Foster, J. M., 74
Fox, E. A., 403, 421
Frazer, W. D., 386
Fredkin, E., 245, 269
Fulkerson, D. R., 302–303, 313, 332
Fuller, S. H., 213

Gale, D., 385
Gallager, R. G., 436, 457
Gallo, G., 277, 280, 283, 333
Gibbons, A., 333
Glover, F., 283, 333
Glover, R., 283, 333
Gonnett, G. H., 213
Gowen, P. J., 313
Graham, R. L., 290
Gray, R. M., 456
Guibas, L., 238
Guttman, A., 235, 269

Haggard, G., 403, 422
Hagins, J., 468, 495, 497
Hall, P., 315, 333
Hamilton, W., 12
Hankamer, M., 455, 457
Hansen, W. J., 74
Hanson, E., 237, 269

SUBJECT INDEX